Artificial Intelligence
Foundations of Computational Agents

Artificial intelligence, including machine learning, has emerged as a transformational science and engineering discipline. *Artificial Intelligence: Foundations of Computational Agents* presents AI using a coherent framework to study the design of intelligent computational agents. By showing how the basic approaches fit into a multidimensional design space, readers learn the fundamentals without losing sight of the bigger picture. The new edition also features expanded coverage on machine learning material, as well as on the social and ethical consequences of AI and ML. The book balances theory and experiment, showing how to link them together, and develops the science of AI together with its engineering applications. Although structured as an undergraduate and graduate textbook, the book's straightforward, self-contained style will also appeal to an audience of professionals, researchers, and independent learners. The second edition is well-supported by strong pedagogical features and online resources to enhance student comprehension.

David Poole is a Professor of Computer Science at the University of British Columbia. He is a co-author of three artificial intelligence books including *Statistical Relational Artificial Intelligence: Logic, Probability, and Computation*. He is a former Chair of the Association for Uncertainty in Artificial Intelligence, the winner of the Canadian AI Association (CAIAC) 2013 Lifetime Achievement Award, and a Fellow of the Association for the Advancement Artificial Intelligence (AAAI) and CAIAC.

Alan Mackworth is a Professor of Computer Science at the University of British Columbia. He has authored over 130 papers and co-authored two books: *Computational Intelligence: A Logical Approach* and *Artificial Intelligence: Foundations of Computational Agents*. His awards include the AIJ Classic Paper Award and the ACP Award for Research Excellence. He has served as President of IJCAI, AAAI and CAIAC. He is a Fellow of AAAI, CAIAC and the Royal Society of Canada.

Artificial Intelligence

Foundations of Computational Agents

David L. Poole
University of British Columbia, Canada

Alan K. Mackworth
University of British Columbia, Canada

CAMBRIDGE
UNIVERSITY PRESS

University Printing House, Cambridge CB2 8BS, United Kingdom

One Liberty Plaza, 20th Floor, New York, NY 10006, USA

477 Williamstown Road, Port Melbourne, VIC 3207, Australia

4843/24, 2nd Floor, Ansari Road, Daryaganj, Delhi - 110002, India

79 Anson Road, #06-04/06, Singapore 079906

Cambridge University Press is part of the University of Cambridge.

It furthers the University's mission by disseminating knowledge in the pursuit of education, learning and research at the highest international levels of excellence.

www.cambridge.org
Information on this title: www.cambridge.org/9781107195394
DOI: 10.1017/9781108164085

First edition published 2010
Second edition published 2017

Printed in United States of America by Sheridan Books, Inc

A catalogue record for this publication is available from the British Library

ISBN 978-1-107-19539-4 Hardback

Contents

2 Agent Architectures and Hierarchical Control

Figures

Preface

Artificial Intelligence: Foundations of Computational Agents is a book about the science of artificial intelligence (AI). AI is the study of the design of intelligent computational agents. The book is structured as a textbook but it is designed to be accessible to a wide audience.

We wrote this book because we are excited about the emergence of AI as an integrated science. As with any science being developed, AI has a coherent, formal theory and a rambunctious experimental wing. Here we balance theory and experiment and show how to link them together intimately. We develop the science of AI together with its engineering applications. We believe the adage, "There is nothing so practical as a good theory." The spirit of our approach is captured by the dictum, "Everything should be made as simple as possible, but not simpler." We must build the science on solid foundations; we present the foundations, but only sketch, and give some examples of, the complexity required to build useful intelligent systems. Although the resulting systems will be complex, the foundations and the building blocks should be simple.

This second edition results from extensive revision throughout the text. We have restructured the material based on feedback from instructors who have used the book in classes. We have brought it up to date to reflect the current state of the art, made parts that were difficult for students more straightforward, added more intuitive explanations, and coordinated the pseudocode algorithms with new open-source implementations of the algorithms in Python and Prolog. We have resisted the temptation to just keep adding more material. AI research is expanding so rapidly now that the volume of potential new text material is vast. However, research teaches us not only what works but also what does not work so well, allowing us to be highly selective. We have included more material on machine learning techniques that have proven successful. However, research also has trends and fashions. We have removed techniques that have been shown to be less promising, but we distinguish them from the techniques that are merely out of fashion. We include some currently unfashionable material if the problems attacked still remain and the techniques have the potential to form the basis for future research and development. We have further developed the concept of a single design space for intelligent agents, showing how many bewilderingly diverse techniques can be seen in a simple, uniform framework. This allows us to emphasize the principles underlying the foundations of computational agents, making those ideas more accessible to students.

The book can be used as an introductory text on artificial intelligence for advanced undergraduate or graduate students in computer science or related disciplines such as computer engineering, philosophy, cognitive science, or psychology. It will appeal more to the technically minded; parts are technically challenging, focusing on learning by doing: designing, building, and implementing systems. Any curious scientifically oriented reader will benefit from studying the book. Previous experience with computational systems is desirable, but prior study of the foundations upon which we build, including logic, probability, calculus, and control theory, is not necessary, because we develop the concepts as required.

The serious student will gain valuable skills at several levels ranging from expertise in the specification and design of intelligent agents to skills for implementing, testing, and improving real software systems for several challenging application domains. The thrill of participating in the emergence of a new science of intelligent agents is one of the attractions of this approach. The practical skills of dealing with a world of ubiquitous, intelligent, embedded agents are now in great demand in the marketplace.

The focus is on an intelligent agent acting in an environment. We start with simple agents acting in simple, static environments and gradually increase the power of the agents to cope with more challenging worlds. We explore ten dimensions of complexity that allow us to introduce, gradually and with modularity, what makes building intelligent agents challenging. We have tried to structure the book so that the reader can understand each of the dimensions separately and we make this concrete by repeatedly illustrating the ideas with four different agent tasks: a delivery robot, a diagnostic assistant, a tutoring system, and a trading agent.

The agent we want the student to envision is a hierarchically designed agent that acts intelligently in a stochastic environment that it can only partially observe – one that reasons online about individuals and relationships among them, has complex preferences, learns while acting, takes into account other agents, and acts appropriately given its own computational limitations. Of course, we cannot start with such an agent; it is still a research question to build such agents. So we introduce the simplest agents and then show how to add each of these complexities in a modular way.

We have made a number of design choices which distinguish this book from competing books, including our earlier book.

- We have tried to give a coherent framework in which to understand AI. We have chosen not to present disconnected topics that do not fit together. For example, we do not present disconnected logical and probabilistic views of AI, but we have presented a multidimensional design space in which the students can understand the big picture, in which probabilistic and logical reasoning coexist.

- We decided that it is better to clearly explain the foundations upon which more sophisticated techniques can be built, rather than present these more sophisticated techniques. This means that a larger gap may exist between what is covered in this book and the frontier of science. But it also means that the student will have a better foundation to understand current and future research.

- One of the more difficult decisions we made was how to linearize the design space. Our previous book [Poole et al., 1998] presented a relational language early and built the foundations in terms of this language. This approach made it difficult for the students to appreciate work that was not relational, for example, in reinforcement learning that is developed in terms of states. In this book, we have chosen a relations-late approach. This approach probably reflects better the research over the past few decades where there has been much progress in reasoning and learning for feature-based representations. It also allows the student to understand that probabilistic and logical reasoning are complementary. The book, however, is structured so that an instructor could present relations earlier.

We provide open-source Python implementations of the algorithms (http://www.aipython.org); these are designed to be useful and to highlight the main ideas without extra frills to interfere with the main ideas. This book uses examples from AIspace.org (http://www.aispace.org), a collection of pedagogical applets that we have been involved in designing. To gain further experience in building intelligent systems, a student should also experiment with a high-level symbol-manipulation language, such as Haskell, Lisp or Prolog. We also provide implementations in AILog, a clean logic programming language related to Prolog, designed to demonstrate many of the issues in this book. These tools are intended to be helpful, but not essential to an understanding or use of the ideas in this book.

Our approach, through the development of the power of the agent's capabilities and representation language, is both simpler and more powerful than the traditional approach of surveying and cataloging various applications of AI. However, as a consequence, some applications such as the details of computational vision or computational linguistics are not covered in this book.

We have chosen not to present an encyclopedic view of AI. Not every major idea that has been investigated is presented here. We have chosen some basic ideas upon which other, more sophisticated, techniques are based and have tried to explain the basic ideas in detail, sketching how these can be expanded.

Figure 1 (page xxvii) shows the topics covered in the book. The solid lines depict prerequisites. Often the prerequisite structure does not include all subtopics. Given the medium of a book, we have had to linearize the topics. However, the book is designed so the topics are teachable in any order satisfying the prerequisite structure.

The references given at the end of each chapter are not meant to be comprehensive; we have referenced works that we have directly used and works that we think provide good overviews of the literature, by referencing both classic works and more recent surveys. We hope that no researchers feel slighted by their omission, and we are happy to have feedback where someone feels that an idea has been misattributed. Remember that this book is *not* a survey of AI research.

We invite you to join us in an intellectual adventure: building a science of intelligent agents.

David Poole
Alan Mackworth

Acknowledgments

Thanks to Randy Goebel for valuable input on this book. We also gratefully acknowledge the helpful comments on the first edition and earlier drafts of the second edition received from Guy van den Broeck, David Buchman, Giuseppe Carenini, Cristina Conati, Mark Crowley, Matthew Dirks, Bahare Fatemi, Pooyan Fazli, Robert Holte, Holger Hoos, Manfred Jaeger, Mehran Kazemi, Mohammad Reza Khojasteh, Jacek Kisyński, Richard Korf, Bob Kowalski, Kevin Leyton-Brown, Josje Lodder, Marian Mackworth, Gabriel Murray, Sriraam Natarajan, Alex Poole, Alessandro Provetti, Mark Schmidt, Marco Valtorta, and the anonymous reviewers. Thanks to the students who pointed out many errors in the earlier drafts. Thanks to Jen Fernquist for the website design. David would like to thank Thomas Lukasiewicz and The Leverhulme Trust for sponsoring

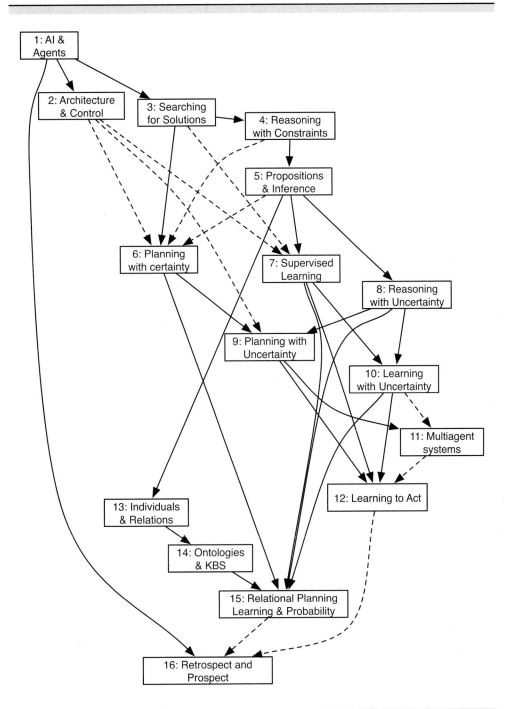

Figure 1: Overview of chapters and dependencies

his sabbatical in Oxford, where much of this second edition was written. We are grateful to James Falen for permission to quote his poem on constraints.

The quote at the beginning of Chapter 9 is reprinted with permission of Simon & Schuster, Inc. from THE CREATIVE HABIT: Learn it and Use It by Twyla Tharp with Mark Reiter. Copyright 2003 by W.A.T. Ltd. All Rights Reserved.

Thanks to our editor Lauren Cowles and the staff at Cambridge University Press for all their support, encouragement and help. All the mistakes remaining are ours.

Part I

Agents in the World: What are Agents and How Can They be Built?

Chapter 1

Artificial Intelligence and Agents

The history of AI is a history of fantasies, possibilities, demonstrations, and promise. Ever since Homer wrote of mechanical "tripods" waiting on the gods at dinner, imagined mechanical assistants have been a part of our culture. However, only in the last half century have we, the AI community, been able to build experimental machines that test hypotheses about the mechanisms of thought and intelligent behavior and thereby demonstrate mechanisms that formerly existed only as theoretical possibilities.

– Bruce Buchanan [2005]

This book is about artificial intelligence, a field built on centuries of thought, which has been a recognized discipline for over 60 years. As Buchanan points out in the quote above, we now have the tools to test hypotheses about the nature of thought itself, as well as to solve practical tasks. Deep scientific and engineering problems have already been solved and many more are waiting to be solved. Many practical applications are currently deployed and the potential exists for an almost unlimited number of future applications. In this book, we present the principles that underlie intelligent computational agents. These principles can help you understand current and future work in AI and equip you to contribute to the discipline yourself.

1.1 What is Artificial Intelligence?

Artificial intelligence, or **AI**, is the field that studies *the synthesis and analysis of computational agents that act intelligently*. Let us examine each part of this definition.

An **agent** is something that acts in an environment; it does something. Agents include worms, dogs, thermostats, airplanes, robots, humans, companies, and countries.

We are interested in what an agent does; that is, how it **acts**. We judge an agent by its actions.

An agent acts **intelligently** when

- what it does is appropriate for its circumstances and its goals, taking into account the short-term and long-term consequences of its actions
- it is flexible to changing environments and changing goals
- it learns from experience
- it makes appropriate choices given its perceptual and computational limitations

A **computational agent** is an agent whose decisions about its actions can be explained in terms of computation. That is, the decision can be broken down into primitive operations that can be implemented in a physical device. This computation can take many forms. In humans this computation is carried out in "wetware"; in computers it is carried out in "hardware." Although there are some agents that are arguably not computational, such as the wind and rain eroding a landscape, it is an open question whether all intelligent agents are computational.

All agents are limited. No agents are omniscient or omnipotent. Agents can only observe everything about the world in very specialized domains, where "the world" is very constrained. Agents have finite memory. Agents in the real world do not have unlimited time to act.

The central **scientific goal** of AI is to understand the principles that make intelligent behavior possible in natural or artificial systems. This is done by

- the **analysis** of natural and artificial agents
- formulating and testing hypotheses about what it takes to construct intelligent agents and
- designing, building, and experimenting with computational systems that perform tasks commonly viewed as requiring intelligence.

As part of science, researchers build **empirical systems** to test hypotheses or to explore the space of possible designs. These are quite distinct from **applications** that are built to be useful for an application domain.

The definition is not for intelligent **thought** alone. We are only interested in **thinking** intelligently insofar as it leads to more intelligent **behavior**. The role of thought is to affect action.

The central **engineering goal** of AI is the **design** and **synthesis** of useful, intelligent artifacts. We actually want to build agents that act intelligently. Such agents are useful in many applications.

1.1.1 Artificial and Natural Intelligence

Artificial intelligence (AI) is the established name for the field, but the term "artificial intelligence" is a source of much confusion because artificial intelligence may be interpreted as the opposite of real intelligence.

For any phenomenon, you can distinguish real versus fake, where the fake is non-real. You can also distinguish natural versus artificial. Natural means occurring in nature and artificial means made by people.

Example 1.1 A tsunami is a large wave in an ocean. Natural tsunamis occur from time to time and are caused by earthquakes or landslides. You could imagine an artificial tsunami that was made by people, for example, by exploding a bomb in the ocean, yet which is still a real tsunami. One could also imagine fake tsunamis: either artificial, using computer graphics, or natural, for example, a mirage that looks like a tsunami but is not one.

It is arguable that intelligence is different: you cannot have *fake* intelligence. If an agent behaves intelligently, it is intelligent. It is only the external behavior that defines intelligence; acting intelligently is being intelligent. Thus, artificial intelligence, if and when it is achieved, will be real intelligence created artificially.

This idea of intelligence being defined by external behavior was the motivation for a test for intelligence designed by Turing [1950], which has become known as the **Turing test**. The Turing test consists of an imitation game where an interrogator can ask a witness, via a text interface, any question. If the interrogator cannot distinguish the witness from a human, the witness must be intelligent. Figure 1.1 (on the next page) shows a possible dialog that Turing suggested. An agent that is not really intelligent could not fake intelligence for arbitrary topics.

There has been much debate about the usefulness of Turing test. Unfortunately, although it may provide a test for how to recognize intelligence, it does not provide a way to realize intelligence.

Recently Levesque [2014] suggested a new form of question, which he called a **Winograd schema** after the following example of Winograd [1972]:

- The city councilmen refused the demonstrators a permit because they feared violence. Who feared violence?

- The city councilmen refused the demonstrators a permit because they advocated violence. Who advocated violence?

These two sentences only differ in one word feared/advocated, but have the opposite answer. Answering such a question does not depend on trickery or lying, but depends on knowing something about the world that humans understand, but computers currently do not.

Interrogator: In the first line of your sonnet which reads "Shall I compare thee to a summer's day," would not "a spring day" do as well or better?

Witness: It wouldn't scan.

Interrogator: How about "a winter's day," That would scan all right.

Witness: Yes, but nobody wants to be compared to a winter's day.

Interrogator: Would you say Mr. Pickwick reminded you of Christmas?

Witness: In a way.

Interrogator: Yet Christmas is a winter's day, and I do not think Mr. Pickwick would mind the comparison.

Witness: I don't think you're serious. By a winter's day one means a typical winter's day, rather than a special one like Christmas.

Figure 1.1: Part of Turing's possible dialog for the Turing test

Winograd schemas have the property that (a) humans can easily disambiguate them and (b) there is no simple grammatical or statistical test that could disambiguate them. For example, the sentences above would not qualify if "demonstrators feared violence" was much less or more likely than "councilmen feared violence" (or similarly with advocating).

Example 1.2 The following examples are due to Davis [2015]:

- Steve follows Fred's example in everything. He [admires/influences] him hugely. Who [admires/influences] whom?

- The table won't fit through the doorway because it is too [wide/narrow]. What is too [wide/narrow]?

- Grace was happy to trade me her sweater for my jacket. She thinks it looks [great/dowdy] on her. What looks [great/dowdy] on Grace?

- Bill thinks that calling attention to himself was rude [to/of] Bert. Who called attention to himself?

Each of these have their own reasons why one answer is preferred to the other. A computer that can reliably answer these questions needs to know about all of these reasons, and require the ability to do **commonsense reasoning**.

The obvious naturally intelligent agent is the human being. Some people might say that worms, insects, or bacteria are intelligent, but more people would say that dogs, whales, or monkeys are intelligent (see Exercise 1.1 (page 47)). One class of intelligent agents that may be more intelligent than humans is the class of **organizations**. Ant colonies are a prototypical example of organizations. Each individual ant may not be very intelligent, but an ant colony can act more intelligently than any individual ant. The colony can discover food and exploit it very effectively as well as adapt to changing circumstances. Corporations can be more intelligent than individual people. Companies develop, manufacture, and distribute products where the sum of the skills required is much more than any individual could master. Modern computers, from low-level hardware to high-level software, are more complicated than any human can understand, yet they are manufactured daily by organizations of humans. Human **society** viewed as an agent is arguably the most intelligent agent known.

It is instructive to consider where human intelligence comes from. There are three main sources:

Biology Humans have evolved into adaptable animals that can survive in various habitats.

Culture Culture provides not only language, but also useful tools, useful concepts, and the wisdom that is passed from parents and teachers to children.

Lifelong learning Humans learn throughout their life and accumulate knowledge and skills.

These sources interact in complex ways. Biological evolution has provided stages of growth that allow for different learning at different stages of life. Biology and culture have evolved together; humans can be helpless at birth presumably because of our culture of looking after infants. Culture interacts strongly with learning. A major part of lifelong learning is what people are taught by parents and teachers. Language, which is part of culture, provides distinctions in the world that are useful for learning.

When building an intelligent system, the designers have to decide which of these sources of intelligence need to be programmed in, and which can be learned. It is very unlikely we will be able to build an agent that starts with a clean slate and learns everything. Similarly, most interesting and useful intelligent agents learn to improve their behavior

1.2　A Brief History of Artificial Intelligence

Throughout human history, people have used technology to model themselves. There is evidence of this from ancient China, Egypt, and Greece bearing witness to the universality of this activity. Each new technology has, in its turn, been exploited to build intelligent agents or models of mind. Clockwork, hydraulics, telephone switching systems, holograms, analog computers, and digital computers have all been proposed both as technological metaphors for intelligence and as mechanisms for modeling mind.

About 400 years ago people started to write about the nature of thought and reason. Hobbes (1588–1679), who has been described by Haugeland [1985, p. 85] as the "Grandfather of AI," espoused the position that thinking was symbolic reasoning like talking out loud or working out an answer with pen and paper. The idea of symbolic reasoning was further developed by Descartes (1596–1650), Pascal (1623–1662), Spinoza (1632–1677), Leibniz (1646–1716), and others who were pioneers in the philosophy of mind.

The idea of symbolic operations became more concrete with the development of computers. Babbage (1792–1871) designed the first general-purpose computer, the **Analytical Engine**, but it was not built until 1991 at the Science Museum of London. In the early part of the twentieth century, there was much work done on understanding computation. Several models of computation were proposed, including the Turing machine by Alan Turing (1912–1954), a theoretical machine that writes symbols on an infinitely long tape, and the lambda calculus of Church (1903–1995), which is a mathematical formalism for rewriting formulas. It can be shown that these very different formalisms are equivalent in that any function computable by one is computable by the others. This leads to the **Church–Turing thesis**:

> Any effectively computable function can be carried out on a Turing machine (and so also in the lambda calculus or any of the other equivalent formalisms).

Here **effectively computable** means following well-defined operations; "computers" in Turing's day were people who followed well-defined steps and computers as we know them today did not exist. This thesis says that all computation can be carried out on a Turing machine or one of the other equivalent computational machines. The Church–Turing thesis cannot be proved but it is a hypothesis that has stood the test of time. No one has built a machine that has carried out computation that cannot be computed by a Turing machine. There is no evidence that people can compute functions that are not Turing computable. An agent's actions are a function of its abilities, its history, and its goals or preferences. This provides an argument that computation is more than just a metaphor for intelligence; reasoning *is* computation and computation can be carried out by a computer.

Once real computers were built, some of the first applications of computers were AI programs. For example, Samuel [1959] built a checkers program in 1952 and implemented a program that learns to play checkers in the late 1950s. His program beat the Connecticut state checkers champion in 1961. Wang [1960] implemented a program that proved every logic theorem (nearly 400) in *Principia Mathematica* [Whitehead and Russell, 1910, 1912, 1913]. Newell and Simon [1956] built a program, Logic Theorist, that discovers proofs in propositional logic.

In addition to work on high-level symbolic reasoning, there was also much work on low-level learning inspired by how **neurons** work. McCulloch and Pitts [1943] showed how a simple thresholding "formal neuron" could be the basis for a Turing-complete machine. The first learning for these neural networks was described by Minsky [1952]. One of the early significant works was the **perceptron** of Rosenblatt [1958]. The work on neural networks went into decline for a number of years after the 1968 book by Minsky and Papert [1988], which argued that the representations learned were inadequate for intelligent action.

The early programs concentrated on learning and search as the foundations of the field. It became apparent early that one of the main tasks was how to represent the knowledge required for intelligent action. Before learning, an agent must have an appropriate target language for the learned knowledge. There have been many proposals for representations from simple features to neural networks to the complex logical representations of McCarthy and Hayes [1969] and many in between, such as the frames of Minsky [1975].

During the 1960s and 1970s, natural language understanding systems were developed for limited domains. For example, the STUDENT program of Daniel Bobrow [1967] could solve high school algebra tasks expressed in natural language. Winograd's [1972] SHRDLU system could, using restricted natural language, discuss and carry out tasks in a simulated blocks world. CHAT-80 [Warren and Pereira, 1982] could answer geographical questions placed to it in natural language. Figure 1.2 (on the next page) shows some questions that CHAT-80 answered based on a database of facts about countries, rivers, and so on. All of these systems could only reason in very limited domains using restricted vocabulary and sentence structure. Interestingly, IBM's **Watson**, which beat the world champion in the TV game show Jeopardy!, used a similar technique to CHAT-80 [Lally et al., 2012]; see Section 13.6 (page 612).

During the 1970s and 1980s, there was a large body of work on **expert systems**, where the aim was to capture the knowledge of an expert in some domain so that a computer could carry out expert tasks. For example, **DENDRAL** [Buchanan and Feigenbaum, 1978], developed from 1965 to 1983 in the field of organic chemistry, proposed plausible structures for new organic compounds. **MYCIN** [Buchanan and Shortliffe, 1984], developed from 1972 to 1980, diagnosed infectious diseases of the blood, prescribed antimicrobial therapy, and explained its reasoning. The 1970s and 1980s were also a period when AI reasoning became widespread in languages such as **Prolog** [Colmerauer and Roussel, 1996; Kowalski, 1988].

During the 1990s and the 2000s there was great growth in the subdisciplines of AI such as perception, probabilistic and decision-theoretic reasoning, planning, embodied systems, machine learning, and many other fields. There has also been much progress on the foundations of the field; these form the frame-

Does Afghanistan border China?

What is the capital of Upper_Volta?

Which country's capital is London?

Which is the largest African country?

How large is the smallest American country?

What is the ocean that borders African countries and that borders Asian countries?

What are the capitals of the countries bordering the Baltic?

How many countries does the Danube flow through?

What is the total area of countries south of the Equator and not in Australasia?

What is the average area of the countries in each continent?

Is there more than one country in each continent?

What are the countries from which a river flows into the Black_Sea?

What are the continents no country in which contains more than two cities whose population exceeds 1 million?

Which country bordering the Mediterranean borders a country that is bordered by a country whose population exceeds the population of India?

Which countries with a population exceeding 10 million border the Atlantic?

Figure 1.2: Some questions CHAT-80 could answer

work of this book.

1.2.1   Relationship to Other Disciplines

AI is a very young discipline. Other disciplines as diverse as philosophy, neurobiology, evolutionary biology, psychology, economics, political science, sociology, anthropology, control engineering, statistics, and many more have been studying aspects of intelligence much longer.

The science of AI could be described as "synthetic psychology," "experimental philosophy," or "computational epistemology"– **epistemology** is the study of knowledge. AI can be seen as a way to study the nature of knowledge and intelligence, but with a more powerful experimental tool than was previously available. Instead of being able to observe only the external behavior of intelligent systems, as philosophy, psychology, economics, and sociology have traditionally been able to do, AI researchers experiment with executable models of intelligent behavior. Most important, such models are open to inspection, redesign, and experiment in a complete and rigorous way. Modern computers provide a way to construct the models about which philosophers have only been able to theorize. AI researchers can experiment with these models as opposed to just discussing their abstract properties. AI theories can be empirically grounded in implementations. Moreover, we are often surprised when simple agents exhibit complex behavior. We would not have known this without implementing the agents.

It is instructive to consider an analogy between the development of **flying machines** over the past few centuries and the development of thinking machines over the past few decades. There are several ways to understand flying. One is to dissect known flying animals and hypothesize their common structural features as necessary fundamental characteristics of any flying agent. With this method, an examination of birds, bats, and insects would suggest that flying involves the flapping of wings made of some structure covered with feathers or a membrane. Furthermore, the hypothesis could be tested by strapping feathers to one's arms, flapping, and jumping into the air, as Icarus did. An alternative methodology is to try to understand the principles of flying without restricting oneself to the natural occurrences of flying. This typically involves the construction of artifacts that embody the hypothesized principles, even if they do not behave like flying animals in any way except flying. This second method has provided both useful tools – airplanes – and a better understanding of the principles underlying flying, namely **aerodynamics**.

AI takes an approach analogous to that of aerodynamics. AI researchers are interested in testing general hypotheses about the nature of intelligence by building machines that are intelligent and that do not necessarily mimic humans or organizations. This also offers an approach to the question, "Can computers really think?" by considering the analogous question, "Can airplanes really fly?"

AI is intimately linked with the discipline of computer science because the study of computation is central to AI. It is essential to understand algorithms, data structures, and combinatorial complexity to build intelligent machines. It is also surprising how much of computer science started as a spinoff from AI, from timesharing to computer algebra systems.

Finally, AI can be seen as coming under the umbrella of **cognitive science**. Cognitive science links various disciplines that study cognition and reasoning, from psychology to linguistics to anthropology to neuroscience. AI distinguishes itself within cognitive science by providing tools to build intelligence rather than just studying the external behavior of intelligent agents or dissecting the inner workings of intelligent systems.

1.3 Agents Situated in Environments

AI is about practical reasoning: reasoning in order to do something. A coupling of perception, reasoning, and acting comprises an **agent**. An agent acts in an

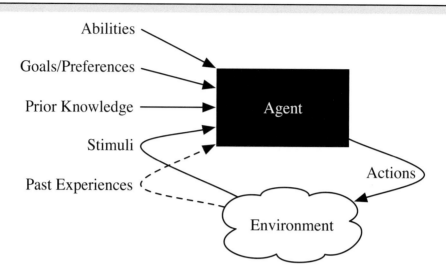

Figure 1.3: An agent interacting with an environment

environment. An agent's environment may well include other agents. An agent together with its environment is called a **world**.

An agent could be, for example, a coupling of a computational engine with physical sensors and actuators, called a **robot**, where the environment is a physical setting. It could be the coupling of an advice-giving computer, an **expert system**, with a human who provides perceptual information and carries out the task. An agent could be a program that acts in a purely computational environment, a **software agent**.

Figure 1.3 shows a black box view of an agent in terms of its inputs and outputs. At any time, what an agent does depends on:

- **prior knowledge** about the agent and the environment
- **history** of interaction with the environment, which is composed of
    - **stimuli** received from the current environment, which can include **observations** about the environment, as well as actions that the environment imposes on the agent and
    - **past experiences** of previous actions and stimuli, or other data, from which it can learn
- **goals** that it must try to achieve or **preferences** over states of the world
- **abilities**, the primitive actions the agent is capable of carrying out.

Inside the black box, an agent has some internal **belief state** that can encode beliefs about its environment, what it has learned, what it is trying to do, and what it intends to do. An agent updates this internal state based on stimuli. It uses the belief state and stimuli to decide on its actions. Much of this book is about what is inside this black box.

This is an all-encompassing view of intelligent agents varying in complexity from a simple thermostat, to a diagnostic advising system whose perceptions and actions are mediated by human beings, to a team of mobile robots, to society itself.

Purposive agents have preferences or goals. They prefer some states of the world to other states, and they act to try to achieve the states they prefer most. The non-purposive agents are grouped together and called **nature**. Whether or not an agent is purposive is a modeling assumption that may, or may not, be appropriate. For example, for some applications it may be appropriate to model a dog as purposive, and for others it may suffice to model a dog as non-purposive.

If an agent does not have preferences, by definition it does not care what world state it ends up in, and so it does not matter to it what it does. The reason to design an agent is to instill preferences in it – to make it prefer some world states and try to achieve them. An agent does not have to know its preferences explicitly. For example, a thermostat is an agent that senses the world and turns a heater either on or off. There are preferences embedded in the thermostat, such as to keep the occupants of a room at a pleasant temperature, even though the thermostat arguably does not know these are its preferences. The preferences of an agent are often the preferences of the designer of the agent, but sometimes an agent can acquire goals and preferences at run time.

1.4 Designing Agents

Artificial agents are designed for particular tasks. Researchers have not yet got to the stage of designing an agent for the task of surviving and reproducing in a natural environment.

1.4.1 Design Time, Offline and Online Computation

In deciding what an agent will do, there are three aspects of computation that must be distinguished: (1) the computation that goes into the design of the agent, (2) the computation that the agent can do before it observes the world and needs to act, and (3) the computation that is done by the agent as it is acting.

- **Design time computation** is the computation that is carried out to design the agent. It is carried out by the designer of the agent, not the agent itself.
- **Offline computation** is the computation done by the agent before it has to act. It can include compilation and learning. Offline, an agent can take background knowledge and data and compile them into a usable form called a **knowledge base**. **Background knowledge** can be given either at design time or offline.

- **Online computation** is the computation done by the agent between observing the environment and acting in the environment. A piece of information obtained online is called an **observation**. An agent typically must use its knowledge base, its beliefs and its observations to determine what to do next.

It is important to distinguish between the knowledge in the mind of the designer and the knowledge in the mind of the agent. Consider the extreme cases:

- At one extreme is a highly specialized agent that works well in the environment for which it was designed, but is helpless outside of this niche. The designer may have done considerable work in building the agent, but the agent may not need to do very much to operate well. An example is a thermostat. It may be difficult to design a thermostat so that it turns on and off at exactly the right temperatures, but the thermostat itself does not have to do much computation. Another example is a car painting robot that always paints the same parts in an automobile factory. There may be much design time or offline computation to get it to work perfectly, but the painting robot can paint parts with little online computation; it senses that there is a part in position, but then it carries out its predefined actions. These very specialized agents do not adapt well to different environments or to changing goals. The painting robot would not notice if a different sort of part were present and, even if it did, it would not know what to do with it. It would have to be redesigned or reprogrammed to paint different parts or to change into a sanding machine or a dog washing machine.

- At the other extreme is a very flexible agent that can survive in arbitrary environments and accept new tasks at run time. Simple biological agents such as insects can adapt to complex changing environments, but they cannot carry out arbitrary tasks. Designing an agent that can adapt to complex environments and changing goals is a major challenge. The agent will know much more about the particulars of a situation than the designer. Even biology has not produced many such agents. Humans may be the only extant example, but even humans need time to adapt to new environments.

Even if the flexible agent is our ultimate dream, researchers have to reach this goal via more mundane goals. Rather than building a universal agent, which can adapt to any environment and solve any task, they have built particular agents for particular environmental niches. The designer can exploit the structure of the particular niche and the agent does not have to reason about other possibilities.

Two broad strategies have been pursued in building agents:

- The first is to simplify environments and build complex reasoning systems for these simple environments. For example, factory robots can do sophisticated tasks in the engineered environment of a factory, but they may be hopeless in a natural environment. Much of the complexity of the task can be reduced by simplifying the environment. This is also important for building practical systems because many environments can be engineered to make them simpler for agents.

- The second strategy is to build simple agents in natural environments. This is inspired by seeing how **insects** can survive in complex environments even though they have very limited reasoning abilities. Researchers then make the agents have more reasoning abilities as their tasks become more complicated.

One of the advantages of simplifying environments is that it may enable us to prove properties of agents or to optimize agents for particular situations. Proving properties or optimization typically requires a model of the agent and its environment. The agent may do a little or a lot of reasoning, but an observer or designer of the agent may be able to reason about the agent and the environment. For example, the designer may be able to prove whether the agent can achieve a goal, whether it can avoid getting into situations that may be bad for the agent (**safety**), whether it will get stuck somewhere (**liveness**), or whether it will eventually get around to each of the things it should do (**fairness**). Of course, the proof is only as good as the model.

The advantage of building agents for complex environments is that these are the types of environments in which humans live and where we want our agents to be.

Even natural environments can be abstracted into simpler environments. For example, for an autonomous car driving on public roads the environment can be conceptually simplified so that everything is either a road, another car or something to be avoided. Although autonomous cars have sophisticated sensors, they only have limited actions available, namely steering, accelerating and braking.

Fortunately, research along both lines, and between these extremes, is being carried out. In the first case, researchers start with simple environments and make the environments more complex. In the second case, researchers increase the complexity of the behaviors that the agents can carry out.

1.4.2   Tasks

One way that AI representations differ from computer programs in traditional languages is that an AI representation typically specifies *what* needs to be computed, not *how* it is to be computed. We might specify that the agent should find the most likely disease a patient has, or specify that a robot should get

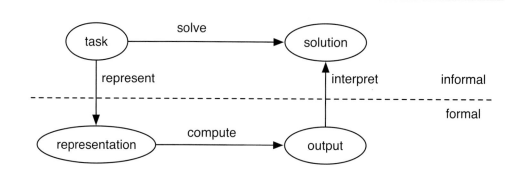

Figure 1.4: The role of representations in solving tasks

coffee, but not give detailed instructions on how to do these things. Much AI reasoning involves searching through the space of possibilities to determine how to complete a task.

Typically, a task is only given informally, such as "deliver parcels promptly when they arrive" or "fix whatever is wrong with the electrical system of the house."

The general framework for solving tasks by computer is given in Figure 1.4. To solve a task, the designer of a system must:

- determine what constitutes a solution
- represent the task in a way a computer can reason about
- use the computer to compute an output, which is answers presented to a user or actions to be carried out in the environment, and
- interpret the output as a solution to the task.

Knowledge is the information about a domain that can be used to solve tasks in that domain. To solve many tasks requires much knowledge, and this knowledge must be represented in the computer. As part of designing a program to solve tasks, we must define how the knowledge will be represented. A **representation language** is used to express the knowledge that is used in an agent. A **representation** of some piece of knowledge is the particular data structures used to encode the knowledge so it can be reasoned with. A **knowledge base** is the representation of all of the knowledge that is stored by an agent.

A good representation language is a compromise among many competing objectives. A representation should be:

- rich enough to express the knowledge needed to solve the task.
- as close to a natural specification of the task as possible; it should be compact, natural, and maintainable. It should be easy to see the relationship between the representation and the domain being represented, so that it

is easy to determine whether the knowledge represented is correct. A small change in the task should result in a small change in the representation of the task.

- amenable to efficient computation, or **tractable**, which means that the agent can act quickly enough. To ensure this, representations exploit features of the task for computational gain and trade off accuracy and computation time.

- able to be acquired from people, data and past experiences.

Many different representation languages have been designed. Many of these start with some of these objectives and are then expanded to include the other objectives. For example, some are designed for learning, perhaps inspired by neurons, and then expanded to allow richer task solving and inference abilities. Some representation languages are designed with expressiveness in mind, and then inference and learning are added on. Some language designers focus on tractability and enhance richness, naturalness and the ability to be acquired.

1.4.3   Defining a Solution

Given an informal description of a task, before even considering a computer, an agent designer should determine what would constitute a solution. This question arises not only in AI but in any software design. Much of **software engineering** involves refining the specification of the task.

Tasks are typically not well specified. Not only is there usually much left unspecified, but also the unspecified parts cannot be filled in arbitrarily. For example, if a user asks a trading agent to find out all the information about resorts that may have unsanitary food practices, they do not want the agent to return all the information about all resorts, even though all of the information requested is in the result. However, if the trading agent does not have complete knowledge about the resorts, returning all of the information may be the only way for it to guarantee that all of the requested information is there. Similarly, one does not want a delivery robot, when asked to take all of the trash to the garbage can, to take everything to the garbage can, even though this may be the only way to guarantee that all of the trash has been taken. Much work in AI is motivated by **commonsense reasoning**; we want the computer to be able to reach commonsense conclusions about the unstated assumptions.

Given a well-defined task, the next issue is whether it matters if the answer returned is incorrect or incomplete. For example, if the specification asks for all instances, does it matter if some are missing? Does it matter if there are some extra instances? Often a person does not want just any solution but the best solution according to some criteria. There are four common classes of solutions:

Optimal solution   An **optimal solution** to a task is one that is the best solution according to some measure of solution quality. For example, a robot may need to take out as much trash as possible; the more trash it can take out, the better. In a more complex example, you may want the delivery robot to take as much of the trash as possible to the garbage can, minimizing the distance traveled, and explicitly specify a trade-off between the effort required and the proportion of the trash taken out. There are also costs associated with making mistakes and throwing out items that are not trash. It may be better to miss some trash than to waste too much time. One general measure of desirability, known as **utility**, is used in decision theory (page 426).

Satisficing solution   Often an agent does not need the best solution to a task but just needs some solution. A **satisficing solution** is one that is good enough according to some description of which solutions are adequate. For example, a person may tell a robot that it must take all of trash out, or tell it to take out three items of trash.

Approximately optimal solution   One of the advantages of a cardinal measure of success is that it allows for approximations. An **approximately optimal solution** is one whose measure of quality is close to the best that could theoretically be obtained. Typically, agents do not need optimal solutions to tasks; they only need to get close enough. For example, the robot may not need to travel the optimal distance to take out the trash but may only need to be within, say, 10% of the optimal distance. Some approximation algorithms guarantee that a solution is within some range of optimal, but for some algorithms no guarantees are available.

For some tasks, it is much easier computationally to get an approximately optimal solution than to get an optimal solution. However, for other tasks, it is just as difficult to find an approximately optimal solution that is guaranteed to be within some bounds of optimal as it is to find an optimal solution.

Probable solution   A **probable solution** is one that, even though it may not actually be a solution to the task, is likely to be a solution. This is one way to approximate, in a precise manner, a satisficing solution. For example, in the case where the delivery robot could drop the trash or fail to pick it up when it attempts to, you may need the robot to be 80% sure that it has picked up three items of trash. Often you want to distinguish the **false-positive error** rate (the proportion of the answers given by the computer that are not correct) from the **false-negative error** rate (the proportion of those answers not given by the computer that are indeed correct). Some applications are much more tolerant of one of these types of errors than the other.

These categories are not exclusive. A form of learning known as probably approximately correct (PAC) learning considers probably learning an approximately correct concept (page 328).

1.4.4   Representations

Once you have some requirements on the nature of a solution, you must represent the task so a computer can solve it.

Computers and human minds are examples of **physical symbol systems**. A **symbol** is a meaningful pattern that can be manipulated. Examples of symbols are written words, sentences, gestures, marks on paper, or sequences of bits. A **symbol system** creates, copies, modifies, and destroys symbols. Essentially, a symbol is one of the patterns manipulated as a unit by a symbol system. The term physical is used, because symbols in a physical symbol system are physical objects that are part of the real world, even though they may be internal to computers and brains. They may also need to physically affect action or motor control.

Much of AI rests on the **physical symbol system hypothesis** of Newell and Simon [1976]:

> A physical symbol system has the necessary and sufficient means for general intelligent action.

This is a strong hypothesis. It means that any intelligent agent is necessarily a physical symbol system. It also means that a physical symbol system is all that is needed for intelligent action; there is no magic or an as-yet-to-be-discovered quantum phenomenon required. It does not imply that a physical symbol system does not need a body to sense and act in the world. There is some debate as to whether hidden variables, that have not been assigned a meaning, but are useful, can be considered as symbols. The physical symbol system hypothesis is an empirical hypothesis that, like other scientific hypotheses, is to be judged by how well it fits the evidence, and by what alternative hypotheses exist. Indeed, it could be false.

An intelligent agent can be seen as manipulating symbols to produce action. Many of these symbols are used to refer to things in the world. Other symbols may be useful concepts that may or may not have external meaning. Yet other symbols may refer to internal states of the agent.

An agent can use a physical symbol system to model the world. A **model** of a world is a representation of an agent's beliefs about what is true in the world or how the world changes. The world does not have to be modeled at the most detailed level to be useful. All models are **abstractions**; they represent only part of the world and leave out many of the details. An agent can have a very simplistic model of the world, or it can have a very detailed model of the world. The **level of abstraction** provides a partial ordering of abstraction. A lower-level abstraction includes more details than a higher-level abstraction. An agent can have multiple, even contradictory, models of the world. Models are judged not by whether they are correct, but by whether they are useful.

Example 1.3 A delivery robot can model the environment at a high level of abstraction in terms of rooms, corridors, doors, and obstacles, ignoring distances, its size, the steering angles needed, the slippage of the wheels, the weight of parcels, the details of obstacles, the political situation in Canada, and virtually everything else. The robot could model the environment at lower levels of abstraction by taking some of these details into account. Some of these details may be irrelevant for the successful implementation of the robot, but some may be crucial for the robot to succeed. For example, in some situations the size of the robot and the steering angles may be crucial for not getting stuck around a particular corner. In other situations, if the robot stays close to the center of the corridor, it may not need to model its width or the steering angles.

Choosing an appropriate level of abstraction is difficult for the following reasons:

- A high-level description is easier for a human to specify and understand.

- A low-level description can be more accurate and more predictive. Often high-level descriptions abstract away details that may be important for actually solving the task.

- The lower the level, the more difficult it is to reason with. This is because a solution at a lower level of detail involves more steps and many more possible courses of action exist from which to choose.

- An agent may not know the information needed for a low-level description. For example, the delivery robot may not know what obstacles it will encounter or how slippery the floor will be at the time that it must decide what to do.

It is often a good idea to model an environment at multiple levels of abstraction. This issue is further discussed in Section 2.3 (page 56).

Biological systems, and computers, can be described at multiple levels of abstraction. At successively lower levels of animals are the neuronal level, the biochemical level (what chemicals and what electrical potentials are being transmitted), the chemical level (what chemical reactions are being carried out), and the level of physics (in terms of forces on atoms and quantum phenomena). What levels above the neuronal level are needed to account for intelligence is still an open question. These levels of description are echoed in the hierarchical structure of science itself, where scientists are divided into physicists, chemists, biologists, psychologists, anthropologists, and so on. Although no level of description is more important than any other, we conjecture that you do not have to emulate every level of a human to build an AI agent but rather you can emulate the higher levels and build them on the foundation of modern computers. This conjecture is part of what AI studies.

The following are two levels that seem to be common to both biological and computational entities:

- The **knowledge level** is the level of abstraction that considers what an agent knows and believes and what its goals are. The knowledge level considers what an agent knows, but not how it reasons. For example, the delivery agent's behavior can be described in terms of whether it knows that a parcel has arrived or not and whether it knows where a particular person is or not. Both human and robotic agents are describable at the knowledge level. At this level, you do not specify how the solution will be computed or even which of the many possible strategies available to the agent will be used.

- The **symbol level** is a level of description of an agent in terms of the reasoning it does. To implement the knowledge level, an agent manipulates symbols to produce answers. Many cognitive science experiments are designed to determine what symbol manipulation occurs during reasoning. Whereas the knowledge level is about what the agent believes about the external world and what its goals are in terms of the outside world, the symbol level is about what goes on inside an agent to reason about the external world.

1.5 Agent Design Space

Agents acting in environments range in complexity from thermostats to companies with multiple goals acting in competitive environments. Here we describe ten dimensions of complexity in the design of intelligent agents. These dimensions may be be considered separately but must be combined to build an intelligent agent. These dimensions define a **design space** for AI; different points in this space are obtained by varying the values on each dimension.

These dimensions give a coarse division of the design space for intelligent agents. There are many other design choices that must also be made to build an intelligent agent.

1.5.1 Modularity

The first dimension is the level of modularity.

Modularity is the extent to which a system can be decomposed into interacting modules that can be understood separately.

Modularity is important for reducing complexity. It is apparent in the structure of the brain, serves as a foundation of computer science, and is an important aspect of any large organization.

Modularity is typically expressed in terms of a hierarchical decomposition. In the **modularity dimension**, an agent's structure is one of the following:

- **flat** – there is no organizational structure
- **modular** – the system is decomposed into interacting modules that can be understood on their own
- **hierarchical** – the system is modular, and the modules themselves are decomposed into simpler modules, each of which are hierarchical systems or simple components.

In a flat or modular structure the agent typically reasons at a single level of abstraction. In a hierarchical structure the agent reasons at multiple levels of abstraction. The lower levels of the hierarchy involve reasoning at a lower level of abstraction.

Example 1.4   In taking a trip from home to a holiday location overseas, an agent, such as yourself, must get from home to an airport, fly to an airport near the destination, then get from the airport to the destination. It also must make a sequence of specific leg or wheel movements to actually move. In a flat representation, the agent chooses one level of abstraction and reasons at that level. A modular representation would divide the task into a number of subtasks that can be solved separately (e.g., booking tickets, getting to the departure airport, getting to the destination airport, and getting to the holiday location). In a hierarchical representation, the agent will solve these subtasks in a hierarchical way, until the task is reduced to simple tasks such a sending an http request or taking a particular step.

A hierarchical decomposition is important for reducing the complexity of building an intelligent agent that acts in a complex environment. Large organizations have a hierarchical organization so that the top-level decision makers are not overwhelmed by details and do not have to micromanage all activities of the organization. Procedural abstraction and object-oriented programming in computer science are designed to enable simplification of a system by exploiting modularity and abstraction. There is much evidence that biological systems are also hierarchical.

To explore the other dimensions, we initially ignore the hierarchical structure and assume a flat representation. Ignoring hierarchical decomposition is often fine for small or moderately sized tasks, as it is for simple animals, small organizations, or small to moderately sized computer programs. When tasks or systems become complex, some hierarchical organization is required.

How to build hierarchically organized agents is discussed in Section 2.3 (page 56).

1.5.2   Planning Horizon

The planning horizon dimension is how far ahead in time the agent plans. For example, consider a dog as an agent. When a dog is called to come, it should turn around to start running in order to get a reward in the future. It does not act only to get an immediate reward. Plausibly, a dog does not act for goals arbitrarily far in the future (e.g., in a few months), whereas people do (e.g., working hard now to get a holiday next year).

How far the agent "looks into the future" when deciding what to do is called the **planning horizon**. For completeness, we include the non-planning case where the agent is not reasoning in time. The time points considered by an agent when planning are called **stages**.

In the **planning horizon dimension**, an agent is one of the following:

- A **non-planning agent** is an agent that does not consider the future when it decides what to do or when time is not involved.

- A **finite horizon** planner is an agent that looks for a fixed finite number of stages. For example, a doctor may have to treat a patient but may have time for a test and so there may be two stages to plan for: a testing stage and a treatment stage. In the degenerate case where an agent only looks one time step ahead, it is said to be **greedy** or **myopic**.

- An **indefinite horizon** planner is an agent that looks ahead some finite, but not predetermined, number of stages. For example, an agent that must get to some location may not know a priori how many steps it will take to get there, but, when planning, it does not consider what it will do after it gets to the location.

- An **infinite horizon** planner is an agent that plans on going on forever. This is often called a **process**. For example, the stabilization module of a legged robot should go on forever; it cannot stop when it has achieved stability, because the robot has to keep from falling over.

1.5.3   Representation

The **representation dimension** concerns how the world is described.

The different ways the world could be are called **states**. A state of the world specifies the agent's internal state (its belief state) and the environment state.

At the simplest level, an agent can reason explicitly in terms of individually identified states.

Example 1.5   A thermostat for a heater may have two belief states: *off* and *heating*. The environment may have three states: *cold*, *comfortable*, and *hot*. There are thus six states corresponding to the different combinations of belief and environment states. These states may not fully describe the world, but they are adequate to describe what a thermostat should do. The thermostat should move to, or stay in, *heating* if the environment is *cold* and move to, or stay in, *off* if the environment is *hot*. If the environment is *comfortable*, the thermostat should stay in its current state. The thermostat agent keeps the heater on in the *heating* state and keeps the heater off in the *off* state.

Instead of enumerating states, it is often easier to reason in terms of features of the state or propositions that are true or false of the state. A state may be described in terms of **features**, where a feature has a value in each state (see Section 4.1, (page 125)).

Example 1.6   An agent that has to look after a house may have to reason about whether light bulbs are broken. It may have features for the position of each switch, the status of each switch (whether it is working okay, whether it is shorted, or whether it is broken), and whether each light works. The feature *position_s_2* may be a feature that has value *up* when switch s_2 is up and has value *down* when the switch is down. The state of the house's lighting may be described in terms of values for each of these features. These features depend on each other, but not in arbitrarily complex ways; for example, whether a light is on may just depend on whether it is okay, whether the switch is turned on, and whether there is electricity.

A **proposition** is a Boolean feature, which means that its value is either *true* or *false*. Thirty propositions can encode $2^{30} = 1,073,741,824$ states. It may be easier to specify and reason with the thirty propositions than with more than a billion states. Moreover, having a compact representation of the states indicates understanding, because it means that an agent has captured some regularities in the domain.

Example 1.7   Consider an agent that has to recognize letters of the alphabet. Suppose the agent observes a binary image, a 30×30 grid of pixels, where each of the 900 grid points is either black or white. The action is to determine which of the letters $\{a, \ldots, z\}$ is drawn in the image. There are 2^{900} different possible states of the image, and so $26^{2^{900}}$ different functions from the image state into the characters $\{a, \ldots, z\}$. We cannot even represent such functions in terms of the state space. Instead, handwriting recognition systems define features of the image, such as line segments, and define the function from images to characters in terms of these features. Modern implementations learn the features that are useful.

When describing a complex world, the features can depend on **relations** and **individuals**. What we call an *individual* could also be called a **thing**, an **object** or an **entity**. A relation on a single individual is a **property**. There is a feature for each possible relationship among the individuals.

Example 1.8   The agent that looks after a house in Example 1.6 could have the lights and switches as individuals, and relations *position* and *connected_to*.

Instead of the feature *position_s2* $= up$, it could use the relation *position*(s_2, up). This relation enables the agent to reason about all switches or for an agent to have general knowledge about switches that can be used when the agent encounters a switch.

Example 1.9 If an agent is enrolling students in courses, there could be a feature that gives the grade of a student in a course, for every student–course pair where the student took the course. There would be a *passed* feature for every student–course pair, which depends on the *grade* feature for that pair. It may be easier to reason in terms of individual students, courses and grades, and the relations *grade* and *passed*. By defining how *passed* depends on *grade* once, the agent can apply the definition for each student and course. Moreover, this can be done before the agent knows of any of the individuals and so before it knows any of the features.

The two-argument relation *passed*, with 1000 students and 100 courses can represent $1000 * 100 = 100000$ propositions and so 2^{100000} states.

By reasoning in terms of relations and individuals, an agent can reason about whole classes of individuals without ever enumerating the features or propositions, let alone the states. An agent may have to reason about infinite sets of individuals, such as the set of all numbers or the set of all sentences. To reason about an unbounded or infinite number of individuals, an agent cannot reason in terms of states or features; it must reason at the relational level.

In the **representation dimension**, the agent reasons in terms of

- states
- features, or
- individuals and relations (often called **relational representations**).

Some of the frameworks will be developed in terms of states, some in terms of features and some in terms of individuals and relations.

Reasoning in terms of states is introduced in Chapter 3. Reasoning in terms of features is introduced in Chapter 4. We consider relational reasoning starting in Chapter 13.

1.5.4 Computational Limits

Sometimes an agent can decide on its best action quickly enough for it to act. Often there are computational resource limits that prevent an agent from carrying out the best action. That is, the agent may not be able to find the best action quickly enough within its memory limitations to act while that action is still the best thing to do. For example, it may not be much use to take 10 minutes to derive what was the best thing to do 10 minutes ago, when the agent has to act *now*. Often, instead, an agent must trade off how long it takes to get

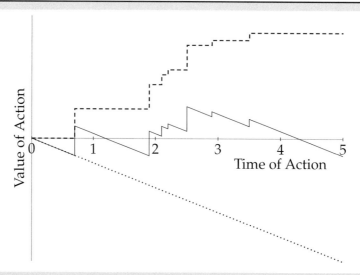

Figure 1.5: Solution quality as a function of time for an anytime algorithm. The agent starts at time 0 and has to choose an action. As time progresses, the agent can determine better actions. The value to the agent of the best action found so far, if it had been carried out at time 0, is given by the dashed line. The reduction in value to the agent by waiting to act is given by the dotted line. The difference between these, the net value to the agent, is given by the solid line.

a solution with how good the solution is; it may be better to find a reasonable solution quickly than to find a better solution later because the world will have changed during the computation.

The **computational limits dimension** determines whether an agent has

- **perfect rationality**, where an agent reasons about the best action without taking into account its limited computational resources, or

- **bounded rationality**, where an agent decides on the best action that it can find given its computational limitations.

Computational resource limits include computation time, memory, and numerical accuracy caused by computers not representing real numbers exactly.

An **anytime algorithm** is an algorithm where the solution quality improves with time. In particular, it is one that can produce its current best solution at any time, but given more time it could produce even better solutions. We can ensure that the quality does not decrease by allowing the agent to store the best solution found so far and return that when asked for a solution. Although the solution quality may increase with time, waiting to act has a cost; it may be better for an agent to act before it has found what would be the best solution.

Example 1.10   Figure 1.5 shows how the computation time of an anytime algorithm can affect the solution quality. The agent has to carry out an action but

can do some computation to decide what to do. The absolute solution quality, had the action been carried out at time zero, shown as the dashed line at
the top, is improving as the agent takes time to reason. However, there is a
penalty associated with taking time to act. In this figure, the penalty, shown
as the dotted line at the bottom, is proportional to the time taken before the
agent acts. These two values can be added to get the discounted quality, the
time-dependent value of computation; this is the solid line in the middle of
the graph. For the example of Figure 1.5, an agent should compute for about
2.5 time units, and then act, at which point the discounted quality achieves its
maximum value. If the computation lasts for longer than 4.3 time units, the
resulting discounted solution quality is worse than if the algorithm outputs the
initial guess it can produce with virtually no computation. It is typical that the
solution quality improves in jumps; when the current best solution changes,
there is a jump in the quality. The penalty associated with waiting is rarely a
straight line; it is typically a function of deadlines, which may not be known by
the agent.

To take into account bounded rationality, an agent must decide whether it
should act or reason for longer. This is challenging because an agent typically
does not know how much better off it would be if it only spent a little bit more
time reasoning. Moreover, the time spent thinking about whether it should
reason may detract from actually reasoning about the domain.

1.5.5   Learning

In some cases, a designer of an agent may have a good model of the agent and
its environment. But often a designer does not have a good model, and so an
agent should use data from its past experiences and other sources to help it
decide what to do.

The **learning dimension** determines whether

- **knowledge is given**, or

- **knowledge is learned** (from data or past experience).

Learning typically means finding the best model that fits the data. Sometimes this is as simple as tuning a fixed set of parameters, but it can also mean
choosing the best representation out of a class of representations. Learning is
a huge field in itself but does not stand in isolation from the rest of AI. There
are many issues beyond fitting data, including how to incorporate background
knowledge, what data to collect, how to represent the data and the resulting
representations, what learning biases are appropriate, and how the learned
knowledge can be used to affect how the agent acts.

Learning is considered in Chapters 7, 10, 12, and 15.

1.5.6   Uncertainty

An agent could assume there is no uncertainty, or it could take uncertainty in the domain into consideration. Uncertainty is divided into two dimensions: one for uncertainty from sensing and one for uncertainty about the effects of actions.

Sensing Uncertainty

In some cases, an agent can observe the state of the world directly. For example, in some board games or on a factory floor, an agent may know exactly the state of the world. In many other cases, it may only have some noisy perception of the state and the best it can do is to have a probability distribution over the set of possible states based on what it perceives. For example, given a patient's symptoms, a medical doctor may not actually know which disease a patient has and may have only a probability distribution over the diseases the patient may have.

The **sensing uncertainty dimension** concerns whether the agent can determine the state from the stimuli:

- **Fully observable** means the agent knows the state of the world from the stimuli.

- **Partially observable** means the agent does not directly observe the state of the world. This occurs when many possible states can result in the same stimuli or when stimuli are misleading.

Assuming the world is fully observable is a common simplifying assumption to keep reasoning tractable.

Effect Uncertainty

A model of the **dynamics** of the world is a model of how the world changes as a result of actions, or how it changes even if there is no action. In some cases an agent knows the effects of its action. That is, given a state and an action, the agent can accurately predict the state resulting from carrying out that action in that state. For example, a software agent interacting with the file system of a computer may be able to predict the effects of deleting a file given the state of the file system. However, in many cases, it is difficult to predict the effects of an action, and the best an agent can do is to have a probability distribution over the effects. For example, a teacher not know the effects explaining a concept, even if the state of the students is known. At the other extreme, if the teacher has no inkling of the effect of its actions, there would be no reason to choose one action over another.

The dynamics in the **effect uncertainty dimension** can be

- **deterministic** when the state resulting from an action is determined by an action and the prior state, or

- **stochastic** when there is only a probability distribution over the resulting states.

This dimension only makes sense when the world is fully observable. If the world is partially observable, a stochastic system can be modeled as a deterministic system where the effect of an action depends on some unobserved feature. It is a separate dimension because many of the frameworks developed are for the fully observable, stochastic action case.

Planning with deterministic actions is considered in Chapter 6. Planning with stochastic actions is considered in Chapter 9.

1.5.7   Preference

Agents normally act to have better outcomes. The only reason to choose one action over another is because the preferred action leads to more desirable outcomes.

An agent may have a simple goal, which is a proposition the agent wants to be true in a final state. For example, the goal of getting Sam coffee means the agent wants to reach a state where Sam has coffee. Other agents may have more complex preferences. For example, a medical doctor may be expected to take into account suffering, life expectancy, quality of life, monetary costs (for the patient, the doctor, and society), the ability to justify decisions in case of a lawsuit, and many other desiderata. The doctor must trade these considerations off when they conflict, as they invariably do.

The **preference dimension** considers whether the agent has goals or richer preferences:

- A **goal** is either an **achievement goal**, which is a proposition to be true in some final state, or a **maintenance goal**, a proposition that must be true in all visited states. For example, the goals for a robot may be to deliver a cup of coffee and a banana to Sam, and not to make a mess or hurt anyone.

- **Complex preferences** involve trade-offs among the desirability of various outcomes, perhaps at different times. An **ordinal preference** is where only the ordering of the preferences is important. A **cardinal preference** is where the magnitude of the values matters. For example, an ordinal preference may be that Sam prefers cappuccino over black coffee and prefers black coffee over tea. A cardinal preference may give a trade-off between the wait time and the type of beverage, and a mess versus taste trade-off, where Sam is prepared to put up with more mess in the preparation of the coffee if the taste of the coffee is exceptionally good.

Goals are considered in Chapter 6. Complex preferences are considered in Chapter 9.

1.5.8   Number of Agents

An agent reasoning about what it should do in an environment where it is the only agent is hard enough. However, reasoning about what to do when there are other agents who are also reasoning is much more difficult. An agent in a multiagent setting should reason strategically about other agents; the other agents may act to trick or manipulate the agent or may be available to cooperate with the agent. With multiple agents, it is often optimal to act randomly because other agents can exploit deterministic strategies. Even when the agents are cooperating and have a common goal, the task of coordination and communication makes multiagent reasoning more challenging. However, many domains contain multiple agents and ignoring other agents' strategic reasoning is not always the best way for an agent to reason.

Taking the point of view of a single agent, the **number of agents dimension** considers whether the agent explicitly considers other agents:

- **Single agent** reasoning means the agent assumes that there are no other agents in the environment or that all other agents are part of **nature**, and so are non-purposive. This is a reasonable assumption if there are no other agents or if the other agents are not going to change what they do based on the agent's action.

- **Multiple agent** reasoning (or **multiagent reasoning**) means the agent takes the reasoning of other agents into account. This occurs when there are other intelligent agents whose goals or preferences depend, in part, on what the agent does or if the agent must communicate with other agents.

Reasoning in the presence of other agents is much more difficult if the agents can act simultaneously or if the environment is only partially observable. Multiagent systems are considered in Chapter 11.

1.5.9   Interaction

An agent living in an environment usually does not have the luxury of offline thinking while the world waits for it to consider the best option. However, offline reasoning, where the agent can reason about the best thing to do before having to act, is often a simplifying assumption.

The **interaction dimension** considers whether the agent does

- **offline reasoning** where the agent determines what to do before interacting with the environment, or

Dimension	Values
Modularity	flat, modular, hierarchical
Planning horizon	non-planning, finite stage, indefinite stage, infinite stage
Representation	states, features, relations
Computational limits	perfect rationality, bounded rationality
Learning	knowledge is given, knowledge is learned
Sensing uncertainty	fully observable, partially observable
Effect uncertainty	deterministic, stochastic
Preference	goals, complex preferences
Number of agents	single agent, multiple agents
Interaction	offline, online

Figure 1.6: Dimensions of complexity

- **online reasoning** where the agent must determine what action to do while interacting in the environment, and needs to make timely decisions.

Some of the algorithms are simplified to do what could be called pure thought, without interaction with the environment. More sophisticated agents reason while acting; this includes long-range strategic reasoning as well as reasoning for reacting in a timely manner to the environment.

1.5.10   Interaction of the Dimensions

Figure 1.6 summarizes the dimensions of complexity. Unfortunately, we cannot study these dimensions entirely independently because they interact in complex ways. Here we give some examples of the interactions.

The representation dimension interacts with the modularity dimension in that some modules in a hierarchy may be simple enough to reason in terms of a finite set of states, whereas other levels of abstraction may require reasoning about individuals and relations. For example, in a delivery robot, a module that maintains balance may only have a few states. A module that must prioritize the delivery of multiple parcels to multiple people may have to reason about multiple individuals (e.g., people, packages, and rooms) and the relations between them. At a higher level, a module that reasons about the activity over the day may only require a few states to cover the different phases of the day (e.g., there might be three states of the robot: busy, available for requests, and recharging).

The planning horizon interacts with the modularity dimension. For example, at a high level, a dog may be getting an immediate reward when it comes and gets a treat. At the level of deciding where to place its paws, there may be a long time until it gets the reward, and so at this level it may have to plan for an indefinite stage.

Sensing uncertainty probably has the greatest impact on the complexity of reasoning. It is much easier for an agent to reason when it knows the state of the world than when it does not. Although sensing uncertainty with states is well understood, sensing uncertainty with individuals and relations is an active area of current research.

The uncertainty dimensions interact with the modularity dimension: at one level in a hierarchy, an action may be deterministic, whereas at another level, it may be stochastic. As an example, consider the result of flying to Paris with a companion you are trying to impress. At one level you may know where you are (in Paris); at a lower level, you may be quite lost and not know where you are on a map of the airport. At an even lower level responsible for maintaining balance, you may know where you are: you are standing on the ground. At the highest level, you may be very unsure whether you have impressed your companion.

Preference models interact with uncertainty because an agent needs to trade off between satisfying a major goal with some probability or a less desirable goal with a higher probability. This issue is explored in Section 9.1 (page 426).

Multiple agents can also be used for modularity; one way to design a single agent is to build multiple interacting agents that share a common goal of making the higher-level agent act intelligently. Some researchers, such as Minsky [1986], argue that intelligence is an emergent feature from a "society" of unintelligent agents.

Learning is often cast in terms of learning with features – determining which feature values best predict the value of another feature. However, learning can also be carried out with individuals and relations. Learning with hierarchies, sometimes called **deep learning**, has enabled the learning of more complex concepts. Much work has been done on learning in partially observable domains, and learning with multiple agents. Each of these is challenging in its own right without considering interactions with multiple dimensions.

The interaction dimension interacts with the planning horizon dimension in that when the agent is reasoning and acting online, it also needs to reason about the long-term horizon. The interaction dimension also interacts with the computational limits; even if an agent is reasoning offline, it cannot take hundreds of years to compute an answer. However, when it has to reason about what to do in, say 1/10 of a second, it needs to be concerned about the time taken to reason, and the trade-off between thinking and acting.

Two of these dimensions, modularity and bounded rationality, promise to make reasoning more efficient. Although they make the formalism more complicated, breaking the system into smaller components, and making the approximations needed to act in a timely fashion and within memory limitations, should help build more complex systems.

1.6 Prototypical Applications

AI applications are widespread and diverse and include medical diagnosis, scheduling factory processes, robots for hazardous environments, game playing, autonomous cars, natural language translation systems, personal assistants and tutoring systems. Rather than treating each application separately, we abstract the essential features of such applications to allow us to study the principles behind intelligent reasoning and action.

Four application domains are developed in examples throughout the book. Although the particular examples presented are simple – otherwise they would not fit into the book – the application domains are representative of the range of domains in which AI techniques can be, and are being, used.

The four application domains are as follows:

- An **autonomous delivery robot** roams around a building delivering packages and coffee to people in the building. This delivery agent should be able to find paths, allocate resources, receive requests from people, make decisions about priorities, and deliver packages without injuring people or itself.

- A **diagnostic assistant** helps a human troubleshoot tasks and suggests repairs or treatments to rectify the tasks. One example is an electrician's assistant that suggests what may be wrong in a house, such as a fuse blown, a light switch broken, or a light burned out, given some symptoms of electrical problems. Another example is a medical diagnostician that finds potential diseases, useful tests, and appropriate treatments based on knowledge of a particular medical domain and a patient's electronic health record, which records the patient's history of symptoms, tests, test results, treatments, etc. A diagnostic assistant should be able to explain its reasoning to the person who is acting in the world. That person is responsible for their actions. It is possible that some people will be sued in the future for not using a diagnostic assistant, which may be able to point out options that the person did not take into account.

- A **tutoring system** interacts with a student, presenting information about some domain and giving tests of the student's knowledge or performance. This entails more than presenting information to students. Doing what a good teacher does, namely tailoring the information presented to each student based on his or her knowledge, learning preferences, and misunderstandings, is more challenging. The system must understand the subject matter, the student and how students learn.

- A **trading agent** knows what a person wants and can buy goods and services on the person's behalf. It should know the person's requirements and preferences and how to trade off competing objectives. For example, for a family holiday, a travel agent must book hotels, airline flights, rental cars, and entertainment, all of which must fit together. It should determine the customer's trade-offs. If the most suitable hotel cannot accommodate the family for all of the days, it should determine whether they prefer to stay in that hotel for only part of the stay and move in the middle or they prefer to not move hotels. It may even be able to shop around for specials or to wait until good deals come up.

A **smart house** can be seen as a mix of these, taking aspects of each of the other application domains. These domains will be used for the motivation for the examples in the book. In the next sections, we discuss each application domain in detail.

1.6.1   An Autonomous Delivery Robot

Imagine a robot with wheels and the ability to pick up and put down objects. It has sensing capabilities allowing it to recognize objects and to avoid obstacles. It can be given orders in natural language and obey them, making reasonable choices about what to do when its goals conflict. Such a robot could be used in an office environment to deliver packages, mail, and/or coffee, or it could be embedded in a wheelchair to help disabled people. It should be useful as well as safe.

In terms of the black box characterization of an agent in Figure 1.3 (page 12), the autonomous delivery robot has as inputs

- prior knowledge, provided by the agent designer, about the agent's capabilities, what objects it may encounter and have to differentiate, what requests mean, and perhaps about its environment, such as a map

- past experience obtained while acting, for instance, about the effects of its actions, what objects are common in the world, and what requests to expect at different times of the day

- goals in terms of what it should deliver and when, as well as preferences specifying trade-offs, such as when it must forgo one goal to pursue another, or the trade-off between acting quickly and acting safely, and

- stimuli about its environment from observations from input devices such as cameras, sonar, touch, sound, laser range finders, or keyboards as well as stimuli such as the agent being forcibly moved or crashing.

The robot's outputs are motor controls specifying how its wheels should turn, where its limbs should move, and what it should do with its grippers. Other outputs may include speech and a video display.

In terms of the dimensions of complexity, the simplest case for the robot is a flat system, represented in terms of states, with no uncertainty, with achievement goals, with no other agents, with given knowledge, and with perfect rationality. In this case, with an indefinite stage planning horizon, the problem of deciding what to do is reduced to the problem of finding a path in a graph of states. This is explored in Chapter 3.

Each dimension can add conceptual complexity to the task of reasoning:

- A hierarchical decomposition can allow the complexity of the overall system to be increased while allowing each module to be simple and able to be understood by itself. This is explored in Chapter 2.

- Robots in simple environments can be modeled in terms of explicit states, but the state space soon explodes when more detail is considered. Modeling and reasoning in terms of features allows for a much more compact and comprehensible system. For example, there may be features for the robot's location, the amount of fuel it has, what it is carrying, and so forth. Reasoning in terms of features can be exploited for computational gain, because some actions may only affect a few of the features. Planning in terms of features is discussed in Chapter 6. When dealing with multiple individuals (e.g., multiple items to deliver), it may need to reason in terms of individuals and relations. Planning in terms of individuals and relations is explored in Section 15.1 (page 692).

- The planning horizon can be finite if the agent only looks ahead a few steps. The planning horizon can be indefinite if there is a fixed set of goals to achieve. It can be infinite if the agent has to survive for the long term, with ongoing requests and actions, such as delivering mail whenever it arrives and recharging its battery when its battery is low.

- There could be goals, such as "deliver coffee to Chris and make sure you always have power." A more complex goal may be to "clean up the lab, and put everything where it belongs." There can be complex preferences, such as "deliver mail when it arrives and service coffee requests as soon as possible, but it is more important to deliver messages marked as urgent, and Chris really needs her coffee quickly when she asks for it."

- There can be sensing uncertainty because the robot does not know exactly what is in the world, or where it is, based on its limited sensors.

- There can be uncertainty about the effects of an action, both at the low level, say due to slippage of the wheels, or at the high level because the agent might not know whether putting the coffee on Chris's desk succeeded in delivering coffee to her.

- There can be multiple robots, which can coordinate to deliver coffee and parcels and compete for power outlets. There may also be children out to trick the robot, or pets that get in the way.

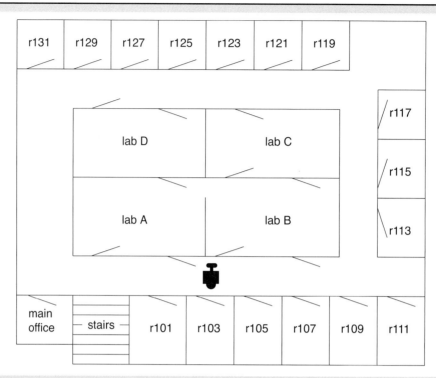

Figure 1.7: A typical laboratory environment for the delivery robot. This shows the locations of the doors and which way they open.

- A robot has a great deal to learn, such as how slippery floors are as a function of their shininess, where Chris hangs out at different parts of the day and when she will ask for coffee, and which actions result in the highest rewards.

Figure 1.7 depicts a typical laboratory environment for a delivery robot. This environment consists of four laboratories and many offices. In our examples, the robot can only push doors, and the directions of the doors in the diagram reflect the directions in which the robot can travel. Rooms require keys and those keys can be obtained from various sources. The robot must deliver parcels, beverages, and dishes from room to room. The environment also contains a stairway that is potentially hazardous to the robot.

1.6.2 A Diagnostic Assistant

A **diagnostic assistant** is intended to advise a human about some particular system such as a medical patient, the electrical system in a house, or an automobile. The diagnostic assistant should advise about potential underlying faults or diseases, what tests to carry out, and what treatment to prescribe. To give such advice, the assistant requires a model of the system, including knowledge of potential causes, available tests, and available treatments, and observations of the system (which are often called **symptoms**).

To be useful, the diagnostic assistant must provide added value, be easy for a human to use, and not be more trouble than it is worth. A diagnostic assistant connected to the Internet can draw on expertise from throughout the world, and its actions can be based on the most up-to-date research. However, it must be able to justify why the suggested diagnoses or actions are appropriate. Humans are, and should be, suspicious of computer systems that are opaque and impenetrable. When humans are responsible for what they do, even if their actions are based on a computer system's advice, the system needs to convince the human that the suggested actions are defensible.

In terms of the black box definition of an agent in Figure 1.3 (page 12), the diagnostic assistant has as inputs

- prior knowledge, such as how switches and lights normally work, how diseases or malfunctions manifest themselves, what information tests provide, the effects of repairs or treatments, and how to find out information.

- past experience, in terms of data of previous cases that include the effects of repairs or treatments, the prevalence of faults or diseases, the prevalence of symptoms for these faults or diseases, and the accuracy of tests. These data can also be about about similar artifacts or patients, as well as the actual one being diagnosed.

- goals of fixing the device or preferences between repairing or replacing components, or a patient's preferences between living longer or reducing pain.

- stimuli that are observations of symptoms of a device or patient.

The output of the diagnostic assistant is in terms of recommendations of treatments and tests, along with a rationale for its recommendations.

> **Example 1.11** Figure 1.8 (on the next page) shows an electrical distribution system in a house. In this house, power comes into the house through circuit breakers and then it goes to power outlets or to lights through light switches. For example, light l_1 is on if there is power coming into the house, if circuit breaker cb_1 is *on*, and if switches s_1 and s_2 are either both up or both down. This is the sort of model that normal householders have of the electrical power in the house, which they could use to determine what is wrong given evidence about the position of the switches and which lights are on and which are off. The diagnostic assistant is there to help a householder or an electrician troubleshoot electrical problems.

Each dimension is relevant to the diagnostic assistant:

- Hierarchical decomposition allows for very-high-level goals to be maintained while treating the lower-level causes and allows for detailed monitoring of the system. For example, in a medical domain, one module

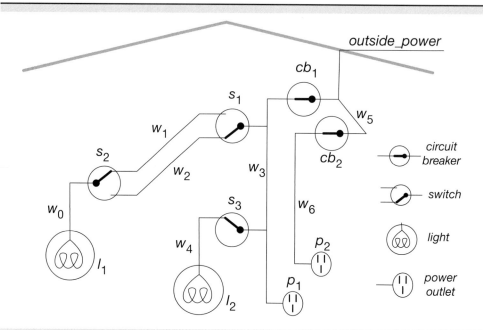

Figure 1.8: An electrical environment for the diagnostic assistant

could take the output of a heart monitor and give higher-level observations such as notifying when there has been a change in the heart rate. Another module could take in this observation and other high-level observations and notice what other symptoms happen at the same time as a change in heart rate. In the electrical domain, Figure 1.8 is at one level of abstraction; a lower level could specify the voltages, how wires are spliced together, and the internals of switches.

- Most systems are too complicated to reason about in terms of the states, and so they are usually described in terms of the features or individual components and relations among them. For example, a human body may be described in terms of the values for the state of different body parts. If we want to reason in terms of tests and outcomes, where there can be an unbounded number of tests, these need to treated as individuals. A system for skin cancer may need to deal with an unbounded number of blemishes on the skin; each blemish can be represented as an individual.

- It is possible to reason about a static system, such as reasoning about what could be wrong when a light is off given the position of switches. It is also possible to reason about a sequence of tests and treatments, where the agents keep testing and treating until the problem is fixed, or where the agent carries out ongoing monitoring of a system, continuously fixing whatever gets broken.

- Sensing uncertainty is the fundamental problem that faces diagnosis. Diagnosis is required if an agent cannot directly observe the internal state of the system.

- Effect uncertainty also exists in that an agent may not know the outcome of a treatment and, often treatments have unanticipated outcomes.

- The goal may be as simple as "fix what is wrong," but often there are complex trade-offs involving costs, pain, life expectancy, the probability that the diagnosis is correct, and the uncertainty as to efficacy and side effects of the treatment.

- Although it is often a single-agent task, diagnosis becomes more complicated when multiple experts are involved who perhaps have competing experience and models. There may be other patients with whom an agent must compete for resources (e.g., doctor's time, operating rooms).

- Learning is fundamental to diagnosis. It is through learning that we understand the progression of diseases and how well treatments work or do not work. Diagnosis is a challenging domain for learning, because all patients are different, and each individual doctor's experience is only with a few patients with any particular set of symptoms. Doctors also see a biased sample of the population; those who come to see them usually have unusual or painful symptoms.

- Diagnosis often requires a quick response, which may not allow for the time to carry out exhaustive reasoning or perfect rationality.

1.6.3   An Intelligent Tutoring System

An **intelligent tutoring system** is a computer system that tutors students in some domain of study.

For example, in a tutoring system to teach elementary physics, such as mechanics, the system may present the theory and worked-out examples. The system can ask the student questions and it must be able to understand the student's answers, as well as determine the student's knowledge based on what answers were given. This should then affect what is presented and what other questions are asked of the student. The student can ask questions of the system, and so the system should be able to solve problems in the physics domain.

In terms of the black box definition of an agent in Figure 1.3 (page 12), an intelligent tutoring system has the following as inputs:

- prior knowledge, provided by the agent designer, about the subject matter being taught, teaching strategies, possible errors, and misconceptions of the students.

- past experience, which the tutoring system has acquired by interacting with students, about what errors students make, about how many examples it takes various students to learn various topics, and about what students forget. This can be information about students in general or about a particular student.

- preferences about the importance of each topic, the level of achievement of the student that is desired, and the frustration that the student will put up with. There are often complex trade-offs among these.

- stimuli include observations of a student's test results and observations of the student's interaction (or non-interaction) with the system. Students can also ask questions or request help on new examples.

The output of the tutoring system is the information presented to the student, tests the students should take, answers to questions, and reports to parents and teachers.

Each dimension is relevant to the tutoring system:

- There should be both a hierarchical decomposition of the agent and a decomposition of the task of teaching. Students should be taught the basic skills before they can be taught higher-level concepts. The tutoring system has high-level teaching strategies, but, at a much lower level, it must design the details of concrete examples and specific questions for a test.

- A tutoring system may be able to reason in terms of the state of the student. However, it is more realistic to have multiple features for the student and the subject domain. A physics tutor may be able to reason in terms of features that are known at design time if the examples are fixed and it is only reasoning about one student. For more complicated cases, the tutoring system should refer to individuals and relations. If the tutoring system or the student can create examples with multiple individuals, the system may not know the features at design time and will have to reason in terms of individual problems and features of these problems.

- In terms of planning horizon, for the duration of a test, it may be reasonable to assume that the domain is static and that the student does not learn while taking a test. For some subtasks, a finite horizon may be appropriate. For example, there may be a teach, test, re-teach sequence. For other cases, there may be an indefinite horizon where the system may not know at design time how many steps it will take until the student has mastered some concept. It may also be possible to model teaching as an ongoing process of learning and testing with appropriate breaks, with no expectation of the system finishing.

- Uncertainty will play a large role. The system cannot directly observe the knowledge of the student. All it has is some sensing input, based on questions the student asks or does not ask, and test results. The system will not know for certain the effects of a particular teaching episode.

- Although it may be possible to have a simple goal such as to teach some particular concept, it is more likely that complex preferences must be taken into account. One reason is that, with uncertainty, there may be no way to guarantee that the student knows the concept being taught; any method that tries to maximize the probability that the student knows a concept will be very annoying, because it will repeatedly teach and test if there is a slight chance that the student's errors are due to misunderstanding as opposed to fatigue or boredom. More complex preferences would enable a trade-off among fully teaching a concept, boring the student, the time taken, and the amount of retesting. The user may also have a preference for a teaching style that should be taken into account.

- It may be appropriate to treat this as a single-agent task. However, the teacher, the student, and the parent may all have different preferences that must be taken into account. Each of these agents may act strategically by not telling the truth.

- We would expect the system to be able to learn about what teaching strategies work, how well some questions work at testing concepts, and what common mistakes students make. It could learn general knowledge, or knowledge particular to a topic (e.g., learning about what strategies work for teaching mechanics) or knowledge about a particular student, such as learning what works for Sam.

- One could imagine that choosing the most appropriate material to present may take a lot of computation time. However, the student must be responded to in a timely fashion. Bounded rationality would play a part in ensuring that the system does not compute for a long time while the student is waiting.

1.6.4 A Trading Agent

A **trading agent** is like a robot, but instead of interacting with a physical environment, it interacts with an information environment. Its task is to procure goods and services for a user. It must be able to be told the needs of a user, and it must interact with sellers (e.g., on the Web). The simplest trading agent involves proxy bidding for a user on an auction site, where the system will keep bidding until the user's price limit is reached. A more complicated trading agent will buy multiple complementary items, like booking a flight, a hotel, and a rental car that fit together, in addition to trading off competing preferences of the user. **Web services** provide tools on the Web that provide individual components that need to be combined to give users what they want. Another example of a trading agent is one that monitors how much food and groceries are in a household, monitors the prices, and orders goods before they are needed, while trying to keep costs to a minimum.

In terms of the black box definition of an agent in Figure 1.3 (page 12), the trading agent has as inputs

- prior knowledge about types of goods and services, selling practices, and how auctions work

- past experience about where is the best place to look for specials, how prices vary with time in an auction, and when specials tend to turn up

- preferences in terms of what the user wants and how to trade off competing goals

- stimuli including observations about what items are available, their price, and, perhaps, how long they are available.

The output of the trading agent is either a recommendation the user can accept or reject, or an actual purchase.

The trading agent should take all of the dimensions into account:

- Hierarchical decomposition is essential because of the complexity of domains. Consider the task of making all of the arrangements and purchases for a custom holiday for a traveler. It is simpler to have a module that can purchase a ticket and optimize connections and wait times, rather than doing this at the same time as determining the quickest route to get to the taxi stand at the airport.

- The state space of the trading agent is too large to reason in terms of explicit states or even features. The trading agent will have to reason in terms of individual customers, days, hotels, flights, and so on.

- A trading agent typically does not make just one purchase, but must make a sequence of purchases, often a large number of sequential decisions (e.g., purchasing one hotel room may require booking ground transportation, which may in turn require baggage storage), and often plans for ongoing purchasing, such as for an agent that makes sure a household has enough food on hand at all times.

- There is often sensing uncertainty in that a trading agent does not know all of the available options and their availability, but must find out information that can become old quickly (e.g., if a hotel becomes booked up). A travel agent does not know whether a flight will be canceled or delayed or whether the passenger's luggage will be lost. This uncertainty means that the agent must plan for the unanticipated.

- There is also effect uncertainty in that the agent does not know whether an attempted purchase will succeed.

- Complex preferences are at the core of the trading agent. The main problem is in allowing users to specify what they want. The preferences of users are typically in terms of functionality, not components. For example, typical computer buyers have no idea of what hardware to buy, but they know what functionality they want and they also want the flexibility to be able to use new software features that might not even exist yet. Similarly, in a travel domain, what activities a user may want may depend on the location. Users also may want the ability to participate in a local custom at their destination, even though they may not know what those customs are.

- A trading agent has to reason about other agents. In commerce, prices are governed by supply and demand; this means that it is important to reason about the other competing agents. This happens particularly in a world where many items are sold by auction. Such reasoning becomes particularly difficult when there are items that must complement each other, such as flights and hotel booking, and items that can substitute for each other, such as bus transport or taxis.

- A trading agent should learn about which items sell quickly, which of the suppliers are reliable, where to find good deals, and what unanticipated events may occur.

- A trading agent faces severe communication limitations. In the time between finding that some item is available and coordinating the item with other items, the item may have been sold. This can sometimes be alleviated by sellers agreeing to hold some items (not to sell them to someone else in the meantime), but sellers will not be prepared to hold an item indefinitely if others want to buy it.

Because of the personalized nature of the trading agent, it should be able to do better than a generic purchaser that, for example, only offers packaged tours.

1.6.5 Smart House

A **smart house** is a house looks after itself and its inhabitants. It can be seen as a mix of the other applications.

A smart house is an inside-out robot. It has physical sensors and actuators. It should be able to sense where people, pets and objects are. It should be able to adjust lighting, sound, heat, etc., to suit the needs of its occupants, while reducing costs and minimizing environmental impacts. A smart home will not only have fixed sensors and actuators, but will be combined with mobile robots, and other actuators, such as arms on the kitchen walls to help with cooking, cleaning and finding ingredients.

A purchaser of a smart house may expect it to be able to clean floors, dishes and clothes and to put things where they are kept. It is easy to clean a floor with the assumption that everything small on the floor is garbage. It is much more difficult to know which of the small items are precious toys and which are junk that should be discarded, and this depends on the individual inhabitants and their age. Each person may have his or her own categorization of objects and where they are expected to be kept, which forces a smart house to adapt to the inhabitants.

A smart house also must act as a diagnostician. When something goes wrong, it should be able to determine what is the problem and fix it. It should also be able to observe the inhabitants and determine if there is something wrong, such as someone has been injured or there is a burglary.

Sometimes a smart house needs to act as a tutoring system. It may have to explain its actions to someone, and to do this it has to take into account the knowledge and the level of understanding of the person.

A smart house may also need to act as a purchasing agent. The house should notice when essential items, such as toilet paper, soap or essential food-stuff are running low and should order more. Given a decision about what food each inhabitant wants, it should make sure the ingredients are in stock. It might even need to decide when inessential items, such as junk food, should be kept in stock. It also might need to decide when to discard perishable items, without creating too much waste or putting people's health at risk.

A smart house would include energy management. For example, with solar energy providing power during daylight hours, it could determine whether to store the energy locally or buy and sell energy on the smart grid. It could manage appliances to minimize cost of energy, such as washing clothes when water and electricity are cheaper.

1.7   Overview of the Book

The rest of the book explores the design space defined by the dimensions of complexity. It considers each dimension separately, where this can be done sensibly.

Chapter 2 analyzes what is inside the black box of Figure 1.3 (page 12) and discusses the modular and hierarchical decomposition of intelligent agents.

Chapter 3 considers the simplest case of determining what to do in the case of a single agent that reasons with explicit states, no uncertainty, and has goals to be achieved, but with an indefinite horizon. In this case, the task of solving the goal can be abstracted to searching for a path in a graph. It is shown how extra knowledge of the domain can help the search.

Chapters 4 and 5 show how to exploit features. In particular, Chapter 4 considers how to find possible states given constraints on the assignments of values to features represented as variables. Chapter 5 presents reasoning with propositions in various forms.

Chapter 6 considers the task of planning, in particular representing and reasoning with feature-based representations of states and actions.

Chapter 7 shows how an agent can learn from past experiences and data. It covers the most common case of learning, namely supervised learning with features, where a set of observed target features are being learned.

Chapter 8 shows how to reason with uncertainty, in particular with probability and graphical models of independence.

Chapter 9 considers the task of planning with uncertainty, and Chapter 11 expands the case to multiple agents.

Chapter 10 introduces learning with uncertainty, and Chapter 12 deals with reinforcement learning.

Chapter 13 shows how to reason in terms of individuals and relations. Chapter 14 discusses how to enable semantic interoperability using what are called ontologies, and how to build knowledge-based systems. Chapter 15 shows how reasoning about individuals and relations can be combined with planning, learning, and probabilistic reasoning.

Chapter 16 reviews the design space of AI and shows how the material presented can fit into that design space. It also presents some ethical considerations involved in building intelligent agents.

1.8 Review

The following are the main points you should have learned from this chapter:

- Artificial intelligence is the study of computational agents that act intelligently.
- An agent acts in an environment and only has access to its abilities, its prior knowledge, its history of stimuli, and its goals and preferences.
- A physical symbol system manipulates symbols to determine what to do.
- A designer of an intelligent agent should be concerned about modularity, how to describe the world, how far ahead to plan, uncertainty in both perception and the effects of actions, the structure of goals or preferences, other agents, how to learn from experience, how the agent can reason while interacting with the environment, and the fact that all real agents have limited computational resources.
- To solve a task by computer, the computer must have an effective representation with which to reason.
- To know when it has solved a task, an agent must have a definition of what constitutes an adequate solution, such as whether it has to be optimal, approximately optimal, or almost always optimal, or whether a satisficing solution is adequate.
- In choosing a representation, an agent designer should find a representation that is as close as possible to the task, so that it is easy to determine what is represented and so it can be checked for correctness and be able to be maintained. Often, users want an explanation of why they should believe the answer.

1.9   References and Further Reading

The ideas in this chapter have been derived from many sources. Here, we will try to acknowledge those that are explicitly attributable to particular authors. Most of the other ideas are part of AI folklore; trying to attribute them to anyone would be impossible.

Levesque [2012] provides an accessible account of how thinking can be seen in terms of computation. Haugeland [1997] contains a good collection of articles on the philosophy behind artificial intelligence, including that classic paper of Turing [1950] that proposes the Turing test. Grosz [2012] and Cohen [2005] discuss the Turing test from a more modern perspective. Winograd schemas are described by Levesque [2014].

Nilsson [2010] and Buchanan [2005] provide accessible histories of AI. Chrisley and Begeer [2000] present many classic papers on AI.

The physical symbol system hypothesis was posited by Newell and Simon [1976]. Simon [1996] discusses the role of symbol systems in a multidisciplinary context. The distinctions between real, synthetic, and artificial intelligence are discussed by Haugeland [1985], who also provides useful introductory material on interpreted, automatic formal symbol systems and the Church–Turing thesis. Brooks [1990] and Winograd [1990] critique the symbol-system hypothesis. Nilsson [2007] evaluates the hypothesis in terms of such criticisms. Shoham [2016] argues for the importance of symbolic knowledge representation in modern applications.

The use of anytime algorithms is due to Horvitz [1989] and Boddy and Dean [1994]. See Dean and Wellman [1991], Zilberstein [1996], and Russell [1997] for introductions to bounded rationality.

For discussions on the foundations of AI and the breadth of research in AI see Kirsh [1991a], Bobrow [1993], and the papers in the corresponding volumes, as well as Schank [1990] and Simon [1995]. The importance of knowledge in AI is discussed in Lenat and Feigenbaum [1991], Smith [1991], Sowa [2000] and Brachman and Levesque [2004]

For overviews of cognitive science and the role that AI and other disciplines play in that field, see Gardner [1985], Posner [1989], and Stillings et al. [1987].

Wellman [2011] overviews research in trading agents. Sandholm [2007] describes how AI can be used for procurement of multiple goods with complex preferences.

A number of AI texts are valuable as reference books complementary to this book, providing a different perspective on AI. In particular, Russell and Norvig [2010] give a more encyclopedic overview of AI and provide an excellent complementary source for many of the topics covered in this book. They also provide an outstanding review of the scientific literature, which we do not try to duplicate.

The Association for the Advancement of Artificial Intelligence (AAAI) provides introductory material and news at their *AI Topics* website (https://aitopics.org/). *AI Magazine*, published by AAAI, often has excellent overview articles and descriptions of particular applications. *IEEE Intelligent Systems* also provides accessible articles on AI research.

There are many journals that provide in-depth research contributions and conferences where the most up-to-date research is found. These include the journals *Artificial Intelligence*, the *Journal of Artificial Intelligence Research*, *IEEE Transactions on Pattern Analysis and Machine Intelligence*, and *Computational Intelligence*, as well as more specialized journals such as *Neural Computation*, *Computational Linguistics*, *Machine Learning*, the *Journal of Automated Reasoning*, the *Journal of Approximate Reasoning*, *IEEE Transactions on Robotics and Automation*, and the *Theory and Practice of Logic Programming*. Most of the cutting-edge research is published first in conferences. Those of most interest to a general audience are the International Joint Conference on Artificial Intelligence (IJCAI), the AAAI Annual Conference, the European Conference on AI (ECAI), the Pacific Rim International Conference on AI (PRICAI), various national conferences, and many specialized conferences and workshops.

1.10   Exercises

Exercise 1.1 For each of the following, give five reasons why:

(a) A dog is more intelligent than a worm.

(b) A human is more intelligent than a dog.

(c) An organization is more intelligent than an individual human.

Based on these, give a definition of what "more intelligent" may mean.

Exercise 1.2 Give as many disciplines as you can whose aim is to study intelligent behavior of some sort. For each discipline, find out what aspect of behavior is investigated and what tools are used to study it. Be as liberal as you can regarding what defines intelligent behavior.

Exercise 1.3 Find out about two applications of AI (not classes of applications, but specific programs). For each application, write, at most, one typed page describing it. You should try to cover the following questions.

(a) What does the application actually do (e.g., control a spacecraft, diagnose a photocopier, provide intelligent help for computer users)?

(b) What AI technologies does it use (e.g., model-based diagnosis, belief networks, semantic networks, heuristic search, constraint satisfaction)?

(c) How well does it perform? (According to the authors or to an independent review? How does it compare to humans? How do the authors know how well it works?)

(d) Is it an experimental system or a fielded system? (How many users does it have? What expertise do these users require?)

(e) Why is it intelligent? What aspects of it makes it an intelligent system?

(f) [optional] What programming language and environment was it written in? What sort of user interface does it have?

(g) References: Where did you get the information about the application? To what books, articles, or web pages should others who want to know about the application refer?

Exercise 1.4 For each of the Winograd schemas in Example 1.2 (page 6), what knowledge is required to correctly answer the questions? Try to find a "cheap" method to find the answer, such as by comparing the number of results in a Google search for different cases. Try this for six other Winograd schemas of Davis [2015]. Try to construct an example of your own.

Exercise 1.5 Choose four pairs of dimensions that were not compared in Section 1.5.10 (page 31). For each pair, give one commonsense example of where the dimensions interact.

Chapter 2

Agent Architectures and Hierarchical Control

> *By a hierarchic system, or hierarchy, I mean a system that is composed of interrelated subsystems, each of the latter being in turn hierarchic in structure until we reach some lowest level of elementary subsystem. In most systems of nature it is somewhat arbitrary as to where we leave off the partitioning and what subsystems we take as elementary. Physics makes much use of the concept of "elementary particle," although the particles have a disconcerting tendency not to remain elementary very long ...*
>
> *Empirically a large proportion of the complex systems we observe in nature exhibit hierarchic structure. On theoretical grounds we would expect complex systems to be hierarchies in a world in which complexity had to evolve from simplicity.*
>
> – Herbert A. Simon [1996]

This chapter shows how an intelligent agent can perceive, reason, and act over time in an environment. In particular, it considers the internal structure of an agent. As Simon points out in the quote above, hierarchical decomposition is an important part of the design of complex systems such as intelligent agents. This chapter presents ways to design agents in terms of hierarchical decompositions and ways that agents can be built, taking into account the knowledge that an agent needs to act intelligently.

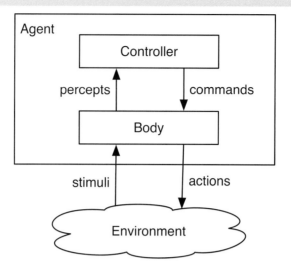

Figure 2.1: An agent system and its components

2.1 Agents

An **agent** is something that acts in an environment. An agent can, for example, be a person, a robot, a dog, a worm, a lamp, a computer program that buys and sells, or a corporation.

Agents interact with the environment with a **body**. An **embodied agent** has a *physical* body. A **robot** is an artificial **purposive** (page 13) embodied agent. Sometimes agents that act only in an information space are called robots or **bots**, but we just refer to those as agents.

Agents receive information through their **sensors**. An agent's actions depend on the information it receives from its sensors. These sensors may, or may not, reflect what is true in the world. Sensors can be noisy, unreliable, or broken, and even when sensors are reliable there still may be ambiguity about the world given the sensor readings. An agent must act on the information it has available. Often this information is very weak, for example, "sensor s appears to be producing value v."

Agents act in the world through their **actuators**, also called **effectors**. Actuators can also be noisy, unreliable, slow, or broken. What an agent controls is the message (command) it sends to its actuators. Agents often carry out actions to find more information about the world, such as opening a cupboard door to find out what is in the cupboard or giving students a test to determine their knowledge.

2.2   Agent Systems

Figure 2.1 depicts the general interaction between an agent and its environment. Together, the system consisting of the agent and the environment is known as an agent system.

An **agent system** is made up of an agent and the environment in which it acts. The agent receives **stimuli** from the environment and carries out **actions** in the environment.

An **agent** is made up of a **body** and a **controller**. The controller receives **percepts** from the body and sends **commands** to the body.

A body includes **sensors** that convert stimuli into percepts and **actuators** that convert commands into actions.

Stimuli include light, sound, words typed on a keyboard, mouse movements, and physical bumps. The stimuli can also include information obtained from a web page or from a database.

Common sensors include touch sensors, cameras, infrared sensors, sonar, microphones, keyboards, mice, and XML readers used to extract information from web pages. As a prototypical sensor, a camera senses light coming into its lens and converts it into a two-dimensional array of intensity values called **pixels**. Sometimes multiple pixel arrays represent different colors or multiple cameras. Such pixel arrays could be the percepts for our controller. More often, percepts consist of higher-level features such as lines, edges, and depth information. Often the percepts are more specialized – for example, the positions of bright orange dots, the part of the display a student is looking at, or the hand signals given by a human.

Actions include steering, accelerating wheels, moving links of arms, speaking, displaying information, or sending a post command to a website. Commands include low-level commands such as to set the voltage of a motor to some particular value, and high-level specifications of the desired motion of a robot, such as "stop" or "travel at 1 meter per second due east" or "go to room 103." Actuators, like sensors, are typically noisy. For example, stopping takes time; a robot, governed by the laws of physics, has momentum, and messages take time to travel. The robot may end up going only approximately 1 meter per second, approximately east, and both speed and direction may fluctuate. Even traveling to a particular room may fail for a number of reasons.

The controller is the brain of the agent. The rest of this chapter is about how to build controllers.

2.2.1   The Agent Function

Agents are situated in time; they receive sensory data in time and do actions in time. The action that an agent does at a particular time is a function of its inputs (page 11). We first consider the notion of time.

Let T be the set of **time** points. Assume that T is totally ordered and has some metric that can be used to measure the temporal distance between any two time points. Basically, we assume that T can be mapped to some subset of the real line.

T is **discrete** if there are only a finite number of time points between any two time points; for example, there is a time point every hundredth of a second, or every day, or there may be time points whenever interesting events occur. T is **dense** if there is always another time point between any two time points; this implies there must be infinitely many time points between any two points. Discrete time has the property that, for all times, except perhaps a last time, there is always a next time. Dense time does not have a "next time." Initially, we assume that time is discrete and goes on forever. Thus, for each time there is a next time. We write $t + 1$ as the next time after time t. The time points do not need to be equally spaced.

Assume that T has a starting point, which we arbitrarily call 0.

Suppose P is the set of all possible percepts. A **percept trace**, or **percept stream**, is a function from T into P. It specifies what is observed at each time.

Suppose C is the set of all commands. A **command trace** is a function from T into C. It specifies the command for each time point.

Example 2.1   Consider a household trading agent that monitors the price of some commodity (e.g., it checks online for special deals and for price increases for snacks or toilet paper) and how much the household has in stock. It must decide whether to order more and how much to order. The percepts are the price and the amount in stock. The command is the number of units the agent decides to order (which is zero if the agent does not order any). A percept trace specifies for each time point (e.g., each day) the price at that time and the amount in stock at that time. Percept traces are given in Figure 2.2 (on the next page). A command trace specifies how much the agent decides to order at each time point. An example command trace is given in Figure 2.3 (on the next page).

The action of actually buying depends on the command but may be different. For example, the agent could issue a command to buy 12 rolls of paper at a particular price. This does not mean that the agent actually buys 12 rolls because there could be communication problems, the store could have run out of paper, or the price could change between deciding to buy and actually buying. However, in this example we can see that the buy orders are all successfully executed, as the amount in stock went up immediately after the order to buy.

A percept trace for an agent is thus the sequence of all past, present, and future percepts received by the controller. A command trace is the sequence of all past, present, and future commands issued by the controller. The commands can be a function of the history of percepts. This gives rise to the concept of a **transduction**, a function from percept traces into command traces.

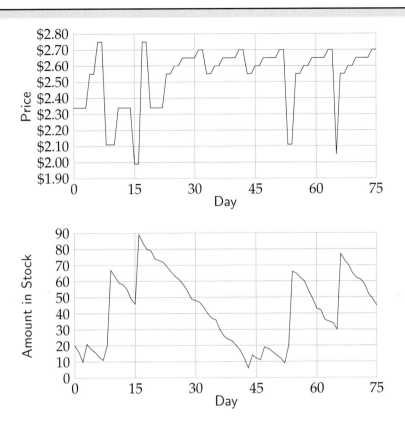

Figure 2.2: Percept traces for Example 2.1

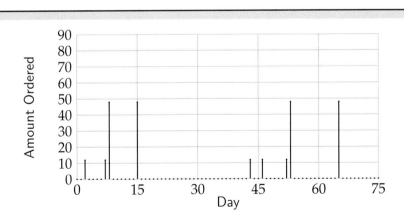

Figure 2.3: Command trace for Example 2.1

Because all agents are situated in time, an agent cannot actually observe full percept traces; at any time it has only experienced the part of the trace up to *now*. At time $t \in T$, an agent can only observe the value of the trace up to time t, and its commands cannot depend on percepts after time t.

A transduction is **causal** if, for all times t, the command at time t depends only on percepts up to and including time t. The causality restriction is needed because agents are situated in time; their command at any time cannot depend on future percepts.

A **controller** is an implementation of a causal transduction.

The **history** of an agent at time t is the percept trace of the agent for all times before or at time t and the command trace of the agent before time t.

Thus, a **causal transduction** maps the agent's history at time t into the command at time t. It can be seen as the most general specification of a controller.

Example 2.2   Continuing Example 2.1 (page 52), a causal transduction specifies, for each time, how much of the commodity the agent should buy depending on the price history, the history of how much of the commodity is in stock (including the current price and amount in stock) and the past history of buying.

An example of a causal transduction is as follows: buy four dozen rolls if there are fewer than five dozen in stock and the price is less than 90% of the average price over the last 20 days; buy a dozen rolls if there are fewer than a dozen in stock; otherwise, do not buy any.

Although a causal transduction is a function of an agent's history, it cannot be directly implemented because an agent does not have direct access to its entire history. It has access only to its current percepts and what it has remembered.

The **memory** or **belief state** of an agent at time t is all the information the agent has remembered from the previous times. An agent has access only to the history that it has encoded in its belief state. Thus, the belief state encapsulates all of the information about its history that the agent can use for current and future commands. At any time, an agent has access to its belief state and its current percepts.

The belief state can contain any information, subject to the agent's memory and processing limitations. This is a very general notion of belief.

Some instances of belief state include the following:

- The belief state for an agent that is following a fixed sequence of instructions may be a program counter that records its current position in the sequence.

- The belief state can contain specific facts that are useful – for example, where the delivery robot left a parcel when it went to find a key, or where it has already checked for the key. It may be useful for the agent to remember any information that it might need for the future that is reasonably stable and that cannot be immediately observed.

- The belief state could encode a model or a partial model of the state of the world. An agent could maintain its best guess about the current state of the world or could have a probability distribution over possible world states; see Section 8.5.2 (page 387).

- The belief state could be a representation of the dynamics of the world – how the world changes – and the meaning of its percepts. Given its percepts, the agent could reason about what is true in the world.

- The belief state could encode what the agent **desires**, the **goals** it still has to achieve, its **beliefs** about the state of the world, and its **intentions**, or the steps it intends to take to achieve its goals. These can be maintained as the agent acts and observes the world, for example, removing achieved goals and replacing intentions when more appropriate steps are found.

A controller maintains the agent's belief state and determine what command to issue at each time. The information it has available when it must do this are its belief state and its current percepts.

A **belief state transition function** for discrete time is a function

$$remember : S \times P \rightarrow S$$

where S is the set of belief states and P is the set of possible percepts; $s_{t+1} = remember(s_t, p_t)$ means that s_{t+1} is the belief state following belief state s_t when p_t is observed.

A **command function** is a function

$$command : S \times P \rightarrow C$$

where S is the set of belief states, P is the set of possible percepts, and C is the set of possible commands; $c_t = command(s_t, p_t)$ means that the controller issues command c_t when the belief state is s_t and when p_t is observed.

The belief-state transition function and the command function together specify a causal transduction for the agent. Note that a causal transduction is a function of the agent's history, which the agent does not necessarily have access to, but a command function is a function of the agent's belief state and percepts, which it does have access to.

Example 2.3 To implement the causal transduction of Example 2.2, a controller must keep track of the rolling history of the prices for the previous 20 days. By keeping track of the average (*average*), it can update the average using

$$average := average + \frac{new - old}{20}$$

where *new* is the new price and *old* is the oldest price remembered. It can then discard *old*. It must do something special for the first 20 days.

A simpler controller could, instead of remembering a rolling history in order to maintain the average, remember just a running estimate of the average and use that value as a surrogate for the oldest item. The belief state can then contain one real number (*ave*), with the state transition function

$$ave := ave + \frac{new - ave}{20}.$$

This controller is much easier to implement and is not as sensitive to what happened exactly 20 time units ago. It does not actually compute the average, as it is biased towards recent data. This way of maintaining estimates of averages is the basis for temporal differences in reinforcement learning (page 554).

If there are a finite number of possible belief states, the controller is called a **finite state controller** or a **finite state machine**. A **factored representation** is one in which the belief states, percepts, or commands are defined by features (page 24). If there are a finite number of features, and each feature can only have a finite number of possible values, the controller is a **factored finite state machine**. Richer controllers can be built using an unbounded number of values or an unbounded number of features. A controller that has an unbounded but countable number of states can compute anything that is computable by a Turing machine.

2.3   Hierarchical Control

One way that you could imagine building an agent depicted in Figure 2.1 (page 50) is to split the body into the sensors and actuators, with a complex perception system that feeds a description of the world into a reasoning engine implementing a controller that, in turn, outputs commands to the actuators. This turns out to be a bad architecture for intelligent systems. It is too slow and it is difficult to reconcile the slow reasoning about complex, high-level goals with the fast reaction that an agent needs for lower-level tasks such as avoiding obstacles. It also is not clear that there is a description of a world that is independent of what you do with it (see Exercise 2.1 (page 71)).

An alternative architecture is a hierarchy of controllers as depicted in Figure 2.4 (on the next page). Each layer sees the layers below it as a **virtual body** from which it gets percepts and to which it sends commands. The **planning horizon** (page 23) at the lower level is much shorter than the planning horizon at upper levels. The lower-level layers run much faster, react to those aspects of the world that need to be reacted to quickly, and deliver a simpler view of the world to the higher layers, hiding details that are not essential for the higher layers. People have to react to the world, at the lowest level, in fractions of

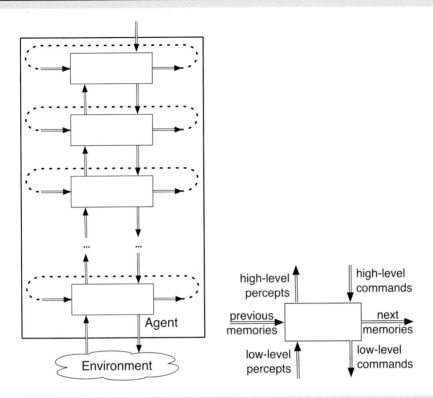

Figure 2.4: An idealized hierarchical agent system architecture. The unlabeled rectangles represent layers, and the double lines represent information flow. The dashed lines show how the output at one time is the input for the next time.

a second, but plan at the highest-level even for decades into the future. For example, the reason for doing some particular university course may be for the long-term career.

There is much evidence that people have multiple qualitatively different levels. Kahneman [2011] presents evidence for two distinct levels: **System 1**, the lower level, is fast, automatic, parallel, intuitive, instinctive, emotional, and not open to introspection, and **System 2**, the higher level, is slow, deliberate, serial, open to introspection, and based on reasoning.

In a hierarchical controller there can be multiple channels – each representing a feature – between layers and between layers at different times.

There are three types of inputs to each layer at each time:

- the features that come from the belief state, which are referred to as the remembered or previous values of these features

- the features representing the percepts from the layer below in the hierarchy

- the features representing the commands from the layer above in the hierarchy.

There are three types of outputs from each layer at each time:

- the higher-level percepts for the layer above
- the lower-level commands for the layer below
- the next values for the belief-state features.

An implementation of a layer specifies how the outputs of a layer are a function of its inputs. The definition of the **belief state transition function** (page 55) and the **command function** (page 55) can be extended to include higher-level commands as inputs, and each layer also requires a **percept function**, represented as *tell* below. Thus a layer implements:

$$remember : S \times P_l \times C_h \rightarrow S$$
$$command : S \times P_l \times C_h \rightarrow C_l$$
$$tell : S \times P_l \times C_h \rightarrow P_h$$

where S is the belief state, C_h is the set of commands from the higher layer, P_l is the set of percepts from the lower layer, C_l is the set of commands for the lower layer, P_h is the set of percepts for the higher layer.

Computing these functions can involve arbitrary computation, but the goal is to keep each layer as simple as possible.

To implement a controller, each input to a layer must get its value from somewhere. Each percept or command input should be connected to an output of some other layer. Other inputs come from the remembered beliefs. The outputs of a layer do not have to be connected to anything, or they could be connected to multiple inputs.

High-level reasoning, as carried out in the higher layers, is often discrete and qualitative, whereas low-level reasoning, as carried out in the lower layers, is often continuous and quantitative (see box on page 59). A controller that reasons in terms of both discrete and continuous values is called a **hybrid system**.

Example 2.4   Consider a delivery robot (page 36) able to carry out high-level navigation tasks while avoiding obstacles. The delivery robot is required to visit a sequence of named locations in the environment of Figure 1.7 (page 36), avoiding obstacles it may encounter.

Assume the delivery robot has wheels, like a car, and at each time can either go straight, turn right, or turn left. It cannot stop. The velocity is constant and the only command is to set the steering angle. Turning the wheels is instantaneous, but turning to a certain direction takes time. Thus, the robot can only travel straight ahead or go around in circular arcs with a fixed radius.

| Qualitative Versus Quantitative Representations |

Much of science and engineering considers **quantitative reasoning** with numerical quantities, using differential and integral calculus as the main tools. **Qualitative reasoning** is reasoning, often using logic, about qualitative distinctions rather than numerical values for given parameters.

Qualitative reasoning is important for a number of reasons.

- An agent may not know what the exact values are. For example, for the delivery robot to pour coffee, it may not be able to compute the optimal angle that the coffee pot needs to be tilted, but a simple control rule may suffice to fill the cup to a suitable level.
- The reasoning may be applicable regardless of the quantitative values. For example, you may want a strategy for a robot that works regardless of what loads are placed on the robot, how slippery the floors are, or what the actual charge is of the batteries, as long as they are within some normal operating ranges.
- An agent needs to do qualitative reasoning to determine which quantitative laws are applicable. For example, if the delivery robot is filling a coffee cup, different quantitative formulas are appropriate to determine where the coffee goes when the coffee pot is not tilted enough for coffee to come out, when coffee comes out into a non-full cup, and when the coffee cup is full and the coffee is soaking into the carpet.

Qualitative reasoning uses discrete values, which can take a number of forms:

- **Landmarks** are values that make qualitative distinctions in the individual being modeled. In the coffee example, some important qualitative distinctions include whether the coffee cup is empty, partially full, or full. These landmark values are all that is needed to predict what happens if the cup is tipped upside down or if coffee is poured into the cup.
- **Orders-of-magnitude reasoning** involves approximate reasoning that ignores minor distinctions. For example, a partially full coffee cup may be full enough to deliver, half empty, or nearly empty. These **fuzzy terms** have ill-defined borders.
- **Qualitative derivatives** indicate whether some value is increasing, decreasing, or staying the same.

A flexible agent needs to do qualitative reasoning before it does quantitative reasoning. Sometimes qualitative reasoning is all that is needed. Thus, an agent does not always need to do quantitative reasoning, but sometimes it needs to do both qualitative and quantitative reasoning.

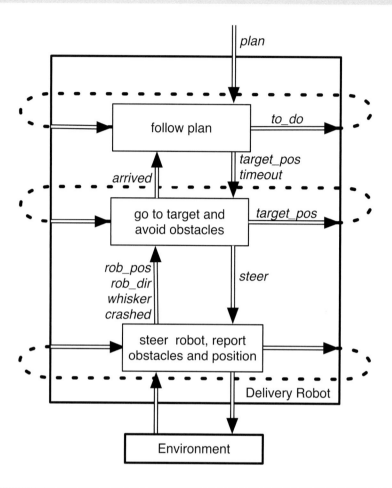

Figure 2.5: A hierarchical decomposition of the delivery robot

The robot has a position sensor that gives its current coordinates and orientation. It has a single whisker sensor that sticks out in front and slightly to the right and detects when it has hit an obstacle. In the example below, the whisker points $30°$ to the right of the direction the robot is facing. The robot does not have a map, and the environment can change with obstacles moving.

A layered controller for the delivery robot is shown in Figure 2.5. The robot is given a high-level plan to execute. The robot needs to sense the world and to move in the world in order to carry out the plan. The details of the lowest layer of the controller are not shown in this figure.

The top layer, called *follow plan*, is described in Example 2.6 (page 63). That layer takes in a plan to execute. The plan is a list of named locations to visit in sequence. The locations are selected in order. Each selected location becomes the current target. This layer determines the *x-y* coordinates of the target. These coordinates are the target position for the middle layer. The top layer knows about the names of locations, but the lower layers only know about coordinates.

The top layer maintains a belief state consisting of a list of names of locations that the robot still needs to visit. It issues commands to the middle layer to go to the current target position but not to spend more than *timeout* steps. The percepts for the top layer are whether the robot has arrived at the target position or not. So the top layer abstracts the details of the robot and the environment.

The middle layer, which could be called *go to target and avoid obstacles*, tries to keep traveling toward the current target position, avoiding obstacles. The middle layer is described in Example 2.5. The target position, *target_pos*, is received from the top layer. The middle layer needs to remember the current target position it is heading towards. When the middle layer has arrived at the target position or has reached the timeout, it signals to the top layer whether the robot has arrived at the target. When *arrived* becomes true, the top layer can change the target position to the coordinates of the next location on the plan.

The middle layer can access the robot's position, the robot's direction and whether the robot's whisker sensor is on or off. It can use a simple strategy of trying to head toward the target unless it is blocked, in which case it turns left.

The middle layer is built on a lower layer that provides a simple view of the robot. This lower layer could be called *steer robot and report obstacles and position*. It takes in steering commands and reports the robot's position, orientation, and whether the whisker sensor is on or off.

Inside a layer are features that can be functions of other features and of the inputs to the layers. In the graphical representation of a controller, there is an arc into a feature from the features or inputs on which it is dependent. The features that make up the belief state can be written to and read from memory.

In the controller code in the following two examples, **do**(C) means that C is the command for the lower level to do.

Example 2.5 The middle *go to location and avoid obstacles* layer steers the robot towards a target position while avoiding obstacles. The inputs and outputs of this layer are given in Figure 2.6 (on the next page).

The layer receives two high-level commands: a target position to head towards and a timeout, which is the number of steps it should take before giving up. It signals the higher layer when it has arrived or when the timeout is reached.

The robot has a single whisker sensor that detects obstacles touching the whisker. The one bit value that specifies whether the whisker sensor has hit an obstacle is provided by the lower layer. The lower layer also provides the robot position and orientation. All the robot can do is steer left by a fixed angle, steer right, or go straight. The aim of this layer is to make the robot head toward its current target position, avoiding obstacles in the process, and to report when it has arrived.

This layer of the controller needs to remember the target position and the number of steps remaining. The command function specifies the robot's steering direction as a function of its inputs and whether the robot has arrived.

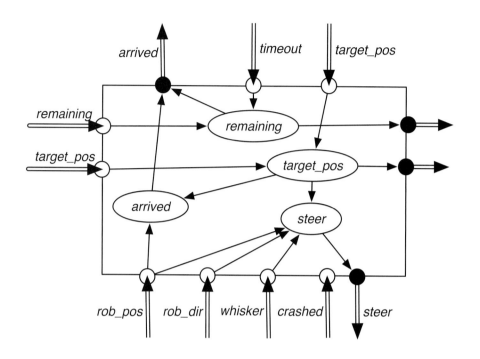

Figure 2.6: The middle layer of the delivery robot

The robot has arrived if its current position is close to the target position. Thus, *arrived* is function of the robot position and previous target position, and a threshold constant:

$$arrived() \equiv distance(target\_pos, rob\_pos) < threshold$$

where *distance* is the Euclidean distance, and *threshold* is a distance in the appropriate units.

The robot steers left if the whisker sensor is on; otherwise it heads toward the target position. This can be achieved by assigning the appropriate value to the *steer* variable, given an integer *timeout* and *target_pos*:

> *remaining* := *timeout*
> while not *arrived*() and *remaining* ≠ 0
>   if *whisker_sensor* = *on*
>   then *steer* := *left*
>   else if *straight_ahead*(*rob_pos*, *robot_dir*, *target_pos*)
>   then *steer* := *straight*
>   else if *left_of*(*rob_pos*, *robot_dir*, *target_pos*)
>   then *steer* := *left*

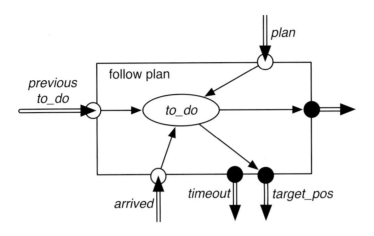

Figure 2.7: The top layer of the delivery robot controller

else *steer* := *right*

$do(steer)$

remaining := *remaining* − 1

tell upper layer *arrived*()

where *straight_ahead*(*rob_pos*, *robot_dir*, *target_pos*) is true when the robot is at *rob_pos*, facing the direction *robot_dir*, and when the current target position, *target_pos*, is straight ahead of the robot with some threshold (for later examples, this threshold is 11° of straight ahead). The function *left_of* tests if the target is to the left of the robot.

Example 2.6 The top layer, *follow plan*, is given a plan – a list of named locations to visit in order. These are the kinds of targets that could be produced by a planner, such as those that are developed in Chapter 6. The top layer must output target coordinates to the middle layer, and remember what it needs to carry out the plan. The layer is shown in Figure 2.7.

This layer remembers the locations it still has to visit. The *to_do* feature has as its value a list of all pending locations to visit.

Once the middle layer has signalled that the robot has arrived at its previous target or it has reached the timeout, the top layer gets the next target position from the head of the *to_do* list. The plan given is in terms of named locations, so these must be translated into coordinates for the middle layer to use. The following code shows the top layer as a function of the plan:

to_do := *plan*

timeout := 200

while not *empty*(*to_do*)

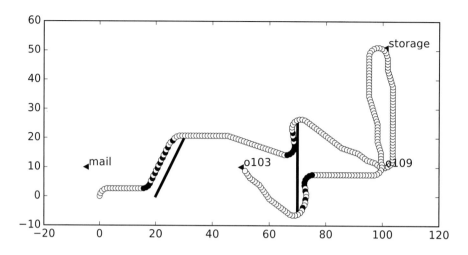

Figure 2.8: A simulation of the robot carrying out the plan of Example 2.6. The black lines are obstacles. The robot starts at position $(0,0)$ and follows the trajectory of the overlapping circles; the filled circles are when the whisker sensor is on. The robot goes to $o109$, *storage*, $o109$, and $o103$ in turn.

$$target\_pos := coordinates(first(to\_do))$$
$$do(timeout, target\_pos)$$
$$to\_do := rest(to\_do)$$

where $first(to\_do)$ is the first location in the to_do list, and $rest(to\_do)$ is the rest of the to_do list. The function $coordinates(loc)$ returns the coordinates of a named location loc. The controller tells the lower layer to go to the target coordinates, with a timeout here of 200 (which, of course, should be set appropriately). $empty(to\_do)$ is true when the to_do list is empty.

This layer determines the coordinates of the named locations. This could be done by simply having a database that specifies the coordinates of the locations. Using such a database is sensible if the locations do not move and are known a priori. If the locations can move, the lower layer must be able to tell the upper layer the current position of a location. See Exercise 2.7 (page 74).

A simulation of the plan $[goto(o109), goto(storage), goto(o109), goto(o103)]$ with two obstacles is given in Figure 2.8. The robot starts at position $(0,0)$ facing North, and the obstacles are shown with lines. The agent does not know about the obstacles before it starts.

Each layer is simple, and none model the full complexity of the problem. But, together they exhibit complex behavior.

2.4   Acting with Reasoning

The previous sections assumed that an agent has some belief state that it maintains through time. For an intelligent agent, the belief state can be complex, even for a single layer.

2.4.1   Agents Modeling the World

The definition of a belief state is very general and does not constrain what should be remembered by the agent. Often it is useful for the agent to maintain some model of the world, even if its model is incomplete and inaccurate. A **model** of a world is a representation of the state of the world at a particular time and/or the dynamics of the world.

At one extreme, a model may be so good that the agent can ignore its percepts. The agent can then determine what to do just by reasoning. This approach requires a model of both the state of the world and the dynamics of the world. Given the state at one time, and the dynamics, the state at the next time can be predicted. This process is known as **dead reckoning**. For example, a robot could maintain its estimate of its position and update the estimate based on its actions. When the world is dynamic or when there are noisy actuators (e.g., a wheel slips, the wheel is not of exactly the right diameter, or acceleration is not instantaneous), the noise accumulates, so that the estimates of position soon become so inaccurate that they are useless. However, if the model is accurate at some level of detail, it may still be useful. For example, finding a plan on a map is useful for an agent, even if the plan does not specify every action of the agent.

At the other extreme is a purely **reactive system** that bases its actions on the percepts, but does not update its internal belief state. The command function in this case is a function from percepts into actions. As an example, the middle layer of the robot in the previous section, if we ignore the timeout, could be considered to be a reactive system.

A more promising approach is to combine the agent's prediction of the world state with sensing information. This can take a number of forms:

- If both the noise of forward prediction and sensor noise are modeled, the next belief state can be estimated using Bayes' rule (page 353). This is known as **filtering** (page 388).

- With more complicated sensors such as vision, a model can be used to predict where visual features can be found, and then vision can be used to look for these features close to the predicted location. This makes the vision task much simpler and vision can greatly reduce the errors in position arising from forward prediction alone.

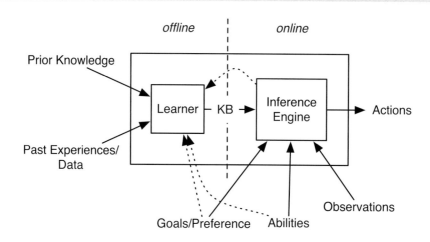

Figure 2.9: Offline and online decomposition of an agent

A control problem is **separable** if the best action can be obtained by first finding the best model of the world and then using that model to determine the best action. Unfortunately, most control problems are not separable. This means that the agent should consider multiple models to determine what to do. Usually, there is no "best model" of the world that is independent of what the agent will do with the model.

2.4.2   Knowledge and Acting

Experience in studying and building intelligent agents has shown that an intelligent agent requires some internal representation of its belief state. **Knowledge** is the information about a domain that is used for acting in that domain. Knowledge can include general knowledge that can be applied to particular situations as well as beliefs about a specific state. A **knowledge-based system** is a system that uses knowledge about a domain to act or to solve problems.

Some philosophers have defined knowledge as justified true belief. AI researchers tend to use the terms knowledge and belief more interchangeably. Knowledge tends to mean general and persistent information that is taken to be true over a longer period of time. Belief tends to mean more transient information that is revised based on new information. Often knowledge and beliefs come with measures of how much they should be believed. In an AI system, knowledge is typically not necessarily true and is justified only as being useful. The distinction between knowledge and belief often becomes blurred when one module of an agent may treat some information as true but another module may be able to revise that information.

Figure 2.9 shows a refinement of Figure 1.3 (page 12) for a knowledge-based agent. A **knowledge base**, KB, is built offline by a learner and is used online to determine the actions. This decomposition of an agent is orthogonal to the layered view of an agent; an intelligent agent requires both hierarchical organization and knowledge bases.

Online (page 14), when the agent is acting, the agent uses its knowledge base, its observations of the world, and its goals and abilities to choose what to do and to use its newly acquired information to update its knowledge base. The **knowledge base** is its **long-term memory**, where it keeps the knowledge that is needed to act in the future. This knowledge is learned from prior knowledge and from data and past experiences. The **belief state** (page 54) is the **short-term memory** of the agent, which maintains the model of current environment needed between time steps.

Offline, before the agent has to act, the agent use prior knowledge and past experiences (either its own past experiences or data it has been given) in what is called **learning** to build knowledge base that is useful for acting online. Researchers have traditionally considered the case involving lots of data and very general, or even uninformative, prior knowledge in the field of statistics. The case of rich prior knowledge and little or no data from which to learn has been studied under the umbrella of **expert systems**. For most non-trivial domains, the agent needs whatever information is available, and so it requires both rich prior knowledge and observations from which to learn.

The goals and abilities are given offline, online, or both, depending on the agent. For example, a delivery robot could have general goals of keeping the lab clean and not damaging itself or other objects, but it could be given delivery goals at runtime. The online computation can be made more efficient if the knowledge base is tuned for the particular goals and abilities. This is often not possible when the goals and abilities are only available at runtime.

Figure 2.10 (on the next page) shows more detail of the interface between the agents and the world.

2.4.3 Design Time and Offline Computation

The knowledge base required for online computation can be built initially at design time and then augmented offline by the agent.

In philosophy, ontology is the study of existence. An ontology is a theory about what exists, or what may exist, in a particular domain. In AI, an **ontology** is a specification of the meaning of the symbols used in an information system, where symbols refer to things that exist. An ontology specifies what exists and the vocabulary used to describe what exists.

In the simplest case, if an agent is using an explicit state-based representation with full observability, an ontology specifies the mapping between the state and the world. For example, the ontology would specify what holds in state 57; without the ontology, the state is just a meaningless number. In other

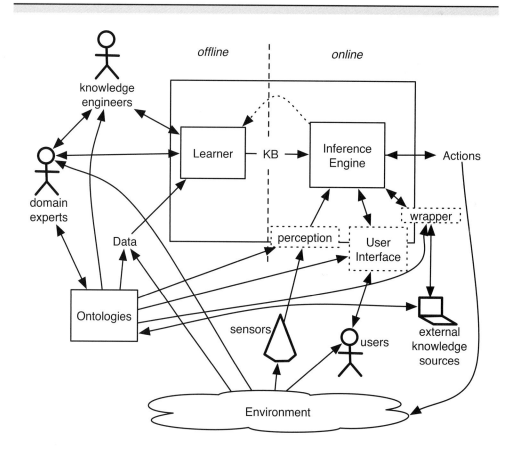

Figure 2.10: Internals of an agent, showing roles

cases, an ontology would define the features or the individuals and relationships. The computer can reason with the meaningless symbols, but to interact with the world, it needs to know how these symbols relate to the world. By sharing ontologies, people and computers can have meaningful interchanges.

Ontologies are typically built by communities, often independently of a particular knowledge base or specific application. It is this shared vocabulary that allows for effective communication and interoperation of the data from multiple sources (sensors, humans, and databases). Ontologies are discussed in Section 14.3 (page 655).

The ontology logically comes before the data and the prior knowledge: we require an ontology to have data or to have knowledge. Without an ontology, data are just sequences of bits. Without an ontology, a human does not know what to input; it is the ontology that specifies the meaning of the data.

The ontology specifies a level, or levels, of abstraction. If the ontology changes, the data must change. For example, a robot may have an ontology of obstacles (e.g., every physical object is an obstacle to be avoided). If the ontology is expanded to differentiate people, chairs, tables, coffee mugs, etc., different data about the world are required.

The knowledge base is typically built offline from a combination of expert knowledge and data. A **knowledge engineer** is a person who interacts with a **domain expert** to build a knowledge base. The knowledge engineer knows about intelligent systems, but not necessarily about the domain, and the domain expert knows about the domain, but not necessarily about how to specify knowledge.

Offline, the agent can combine the expert knowledge and whatever data is available. For example, it can compile parts of the knowledge base to allow more efficient inference. Offline, the system can be tested and debugged.

2.4.4   Online Computation

Online, the information about the particular situation becomes available, and the agent has to act. The information includes the observations of the domain and often the preferences or goals. The agent can get observations from sensors, users, and other information sources, such as websites, although it typically does not have access to the domain experts or knowledge engineer while acting.

An agent typically has much more time for offline computation than for online computation. During online computation it can take advantage of particular goals and particular observations.

For example, a medical diagnosis system only has the details of a particular patient online. Offline, it can acquire knowledge about how diseases and symptoms interact and do some debugging and compilation. It can only do the computation about a particular patient online.

Online the following roles are involved:

- A **user** is a person who has a need for expertise or has information about individual situations. Users typically are not experts in the domain of the knowledge base. They often do not know what information is needed by the system. Thus, it is unreasonable to expect them to volunteer everything that is true about a particular situation. A simple and natural interface must be provided because users do not typically understand the internal structure of the system. Users often, however, must make informed decisions based on the recommendation of the system; thus, they require an explanation of why the recommendation is appropriate.

- **Sensors** provide information about the environment. For example, a thermometer is a sensor that can provide the current temperature at the location of the thermometer. Sensors may be more sophisticated, such as a vision sensor. At the lowest level, a vision sensor may simply provide an array of 1920×1080 pixels at 50 frames per second. At a higher level, a vision system may be able to answer specific questions about the location of particular features, whether some type of individual is in the environment, or whether some particular individual is in the scene. An array of microphones can be used at a low level of abstraction to detect a sound of a particular frequency. Such an array may also be used as a component a speech understanding system.

Sensors come in two main varieties. A **passive sensor** continuously feeds information to the agent. Passive sensors include thermometers, cameras, and microphones. The designer can typically choose where the sensors are or where they are pointing, but they just feed the agent information. In contrast, an **active sensor** is controlled or queried for information. Examples of an active sensor include a medical probe able to answer specific questions about a patient or a test given to a student in an intelligent tutoring system. Often sensors that are passive sensors at lower levels of abstraction can be seen as active sensors at higher levels of abstraction. For example, a camera could be asked whether a particular person is in the room. To do this it may need to zoom in on the faces in the room, looking for distinguishing features of the person.

- An **external knowledge source**, such as a website or a database, might be asked questions and can provide the answer for a limited domain. An agent can ask a weather website for the temperature at a particular location or an airline website for the arrival time of a particular flight. The knowledge sources have various protocols and efficiency trade-offs. The interface between an agent and an external knowledge source is called a **wrapper**. A wrapper translates between the representation the agent uses and the queries the external knowledge source is prepared to handle. Often wrappers are designed so that the agent is able to ask the same query of multiple knowledge sources. For example, an agent may want to know about airplane arrivals, but different airlines or airports may require very different protocols to access that information. When websites and databases adhere to a common ontology, they can be used together because the same symbols have the same meaning. Having the same symbols mean the same thing is called **semantic interoperability**. When they use different ontologies, there must be mappings between the ontologies to allow them to interoperate.

2.5   Review

The main points you should have learned from this chapter are as follows:

- An agent system is composed of an agent and an environment.
- Agents have sensors and actuators to interact with the environment.

- An agent is composed of a body and interacting controllers.

- Agents are situated in time and must make decisions of what to do based on their history of interaction with the environment.

- An agent has direct access to what it has remembered (its belief state) and what it has just observed. At each point in time, an agent decides what to do and what to remember based on its belief state and its current observations.

- Complex agents are built modularly in terms of interacting hierarchical layers.

- An intelligent agent requires knowledge that is acquired at design time, offline or online.

2.6 References and Further Reading

The model of agent systems is based on the constraint nets of Zhang and Mackworth [1995] and Rosenschein and Kaelbling [1995]. The hierarchical control is based on Albus [1981] and the subsumption architecture of Brooks [1986]. *Turtle Geometry*, by Abelson and DiSessa [1981], investigates mathematics from the viewpoint of modeling simple reactive agents. Luenberger [1979] is a readable introduction to the classical theory of agents interacting with environments. Simon [1996] argues for the importance of hierarchical control. Kahneman [2011] provides compelling evidence for distinguishing two modes of human thought: fast, instinctive and emotional, versus slow, deliberate and rational, which he calls **Systems 1 and 2** to avoid oversimplification.

For more detail on agent control see Dean and Wellman [1991], Latombe [1991], and Agre [1995]. The methodology for building intelligent agents is discussed by Haugeland [1985], Brooks [1991], Kirsh [1991b], and Mackworth [1993].

Qualitative reasoning is described by Forbus [1996] and Kuipers [2001]. Weld and de Kleer [1990] contains many seminal papers on qualitative reasoning. See also Weld [1992] and related discussion in the same issue. For a more recent review see Price et al. [2006].

2.7 Exercises

Exercise 2.1 The start of Section 2.3 (page 56) argued that it was impossible to build a representation of a world independently of what the agent will do with it. This exercise lets you evaluate this argument.

Choose a particular world, for example, the things on top of your desk right now.

i) Get someone to list all of the individuals (things) that exist in this world (or try it yourself as a thought experiment).

ii) Try to think of twenty individuals that they missed. Make these as different from each other as possible. For example, the ball at the tip of the rightmost ball-point pen on the desk, the part of the stapler that makes the staples bend, or the third word on page 72 of a particular book on the desk.

iii) Try to find an individual that cannot be described using your natural language (such as a particular component of the texture of the desk).

iv) Choose a particular task, such as making the desk tidy, and try to write down all of the individuals in the world at a level of description relevant to this task.

Based on this exercise, discuss the following statements.

(a) What exists in a world is a property of the observer.

(b) We need ways to refer to individuals other than expecting each individual to have a separate name.

(c) Which individuals exist is a property of the task as well as of the world.

(d) To describe the individuals in a domain, you need what is essentially a dictionary of a huge number of words and ways to combine them, and this should be able to be done independently of any particular domain.

Exercise 2.2 Consider the top level controller of Example 2.6 (page 63)

(a) If the lower level reach the timeout without getting to the target position, what does the agent do?

(b) The definition of the target position means that, when the plan ends, the top level stops. This is not reasonable for the robot that can only change directions and cannot stop. Change the definition so that the robot keeps going.

Exercise 2.3 The obstacle avoidance implemented in Example 2.5 (page 61) can easily get stuck.

(a) Show an obstacle and a target for which the robot using the controller of Example 2.5 (page 61) would not be able to get around (and it will crash or loop).

(b) Even without obstacles, the robot may never reach its destination. For example, if the robot is close to its target position, but not close enough to have arrived, it may keep circling forever without reaching its target. Design a controller that can detect this situation and find its way to the target.

Exercise 2.4 Consider the "robot trap" in Figure 2.11.

(a) This question is to explore why it is so tricky for a robot to get to location g. Explain what the current robot does. Suppose one was to implement a robot that follows the wall using the "right-hand rule": the robot turns left when it hits an obstacle and keeps following a wall, with the wall always on its

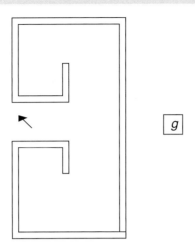

Figure 2.11: A robot trap

right. Is there a simple characterization of the situations in which the robot should keep following this rule or head towards the target?

(b) An intuition of how to escape such a trap is that, when the robot hits a wall, it follows the wall until the number of right turns equals the number of left turns. Show how this can be implemented, explaining the belief state, and the functions of the layer.

Exercise 2.5 If the current target location were to be moved, the middle layer of Example 2.5 (page 61) travels to the original position of that target and does not try to go to the new position. Change the controller so that the robot can adapt to targets moving.

Exercise 2.6 The current controller visits the locations in the *to_do* list sequentially.

(a) Change the controller so that it is opportunistic; when it selects the next location to visit, it selects the location that is closest to its current position. It should still visit all the locations.

(b) Give one example of an environment in which the new controller visits all the locations in fewer time steps than the original controller.

(c) Give one example of an environment in which the original controller visits all the locations in fewer time steps than the modified controller.

(d) Change the controller so that, at every step, the agent heads toward whichever target location is closest to its current position.

(e) Can the controller from part (d) get stuck and never reach a target in an example where the original controller will work? Either give an example in which it gets stuck and explain why it cannot find a solution, or explain why it gets to a goal whenever the original can.

Exercise 2.7 Change the controller so that the robot senses the environment to determine the coordinates of a location. Assume that the body can provide the coordinates of a named location.

Exercise 2.8 Suppose the robot has a battery that must be charged at a particular wall socket before it runs out. How should the robot controller be modified to allow for battery recharging?

Exercise 2.9 Suppose you have a new job and must build a controller for an intelligent robot. You tell your bosses that you just have to implement a command function and a state transition function. They are very skeptical. Why these functions? Why only these? Explain why a controller requires a command function and a state transition function, but not other functions. Use proper English. Be concise.

Part II

Reasoning, Planning and Learning with Certainty

Chapter 3

Searching for Solutions

Have you ever watched a crab on the shore crawling backward in search of the Atlantic Ocean, and missing? That's the way the mind of man operates.

– H. L. Mencken (1880–1956)

The previous chapter discussed how an agent perceives and acts, but not how its goals affect its actions. An agent could be programmed to act in the world to achieve a fixed goal or set of goals, but then it would not adapt to changing goals, and so would not be intelligent. An intelligent agent needs to reason about its abilities and its goals to determine what to do. This chapter casts the problem of an agent deciding how to solve a goal as the problem of searching to find a path in a graph. It presents a number of ways to solve such problems on a computer.

3.1 Problem Solving as Search

In the simplest case of an agent deciding what it should do, the agent has a state-based model of the world, with a goal to achieve and no uncertainty. This is either a flat (non-hierarchical) representation or a single level of a hierarchy. The agent is able to determine how to achieve its goal by searching in its representation of the world state space for a way to get from its current state to a state that satisfies its goal. Given a complete model, it tries to find a sequence of actions that will achieve its goal before it has to act in the world.

This problem can be abstracted to the mathematical problem of finding a path from the start node to a goal node in a directed graph. Many other problems can also be mapped to this abstraction, so it is worthwhile to consider this level of abstraction. Most of this chapter explores various algorithms for finding such paths.

Example 3.1 Computer maps provide path-finding: showing how to drive (or ride, walk or take transit) from one location to another. Finding the best route from a current location to a destination is a search problem. The state includes the location, and possibly the driving direction and speed. A legal route will include the roads (going the correct way down one-way streets) and intersections the traveler will traverse.

The best route could mean

- the shortest (least distance) route
- the quickest route
- the lowest-cost route that takes into account time, money (e.g, fuel and tolls) and the route's attractiveness.

Finding the shortest route is usually easiest to implement as computing distances from a map is usually straightforward.

Estimating the time it will take to travel is difficult. The route planner might need to take into account regular traffic volumes as well as known local conditions, such as roadworks or accidents. If the route planner is advising many people, and advises them all to take the same route, that route may become more congested because of the advice, and so it may be better for users to deliberately avoid the advice. The system could avoid this by telling different users different routes. It would be good for the system to guarantee that the user will not do better by ignoring the advice, but that is beyond the scope of this chapter.

Finding the best route that takes into account other preferences people may have is complicated. It is difficult to acquire these preferences and people may not even be able to articulate these preferences and trade-offs. But given the preferences, the problem reduces to one of searching, albeit with a complex cost function.

Another challenge is that a driver might not actually take the route suggested either by design, perhaps visiting a place off the suggested route, or by accident, such as taking a wrong turn, or where a road is closed. This is explored in Example 3.22 (page 117).

This notion of search is computation solely inside the agent. It is different from searching in the world, when an agent may have to act in the world, for example, a robot searching for keys, lifting up cushions, and so on. It is also different from searching the web, which involves searching for information by indexing huge amounts of data and trying to find the best response for each search query. Searching in this chapter means searching in an internal representation for a path to a goal.

Search underlies much of artificial intelligence. When an agent is given a problem, it is usually given only a description that lets it recognize a solution, not an algorithm to solve it. It has to search for a solution. The existence of NP-complete problems (page 88), with efficient means to recognize solutions but no efficient methods for finding them, indicates that searching is a necessary part of solving problems.

It is often believed that humans are able to use intuition to jump to solutions to difficult problems. However, humans cannot find optimal solutions to computationally difficult problems. Humans do not tend to solve general problems; instead they solve specific instances about which they may know much more than the underlying search space. They often do not find optimal solutions, but find **satisficing**, or good enough, solutions. Problems with little structure, or ones in which the structure cannot be related to the physical world, are very difficult for humans to solve. The existence of public key encryption codes, where the search space is clear and the test for a solution is given – which humans nevertheless have no hope of solving and computers cannot solve in a realistic time frame – demonstrates the difficulty of search.

The difficulty of search and the fact that humans are able to solve some search problems efficiently suggests that computer agents should exploit knowledge about special cases to guide them to a solution. This extra knowledge beyond the search space is called **heuristic knowledge**. This chapter considers one kind of heuristic knowledge in the form of an estimate of the cost from a node to a goal.

3.2 State Spaces

One general formulation of intelligent action is in terms of a **state space**. A **state** contains all of the information necessary to predict the effects of an action and to determine whether a state satisfies the goal. State-space searching assumes:

Dimensions (p. 31)
flat
states
indefinite horizon
fully observable
deterministic
goal directed
non-learning
single agent
offline
perfect rationality

- The agent has perfect knowledge of the state space and is planning for the case where it observes what state it is in: there is full observability.

- The agent has a set of actions that have known deterministic effects.

- The agent can determine whether a state satisfies the goal.

A **solution** is a sequence of actions that will get the agent from its current state to a state that satisfies the goal.

Example 3.2 Consider the robot delivery domain of Figure 3.1 (on the next page), where the only way a robot can get through a doorway is to push the door open in the direction shown. The task is to find a path from one location to another. Assuming that the agent can use a lower-level controller to get from

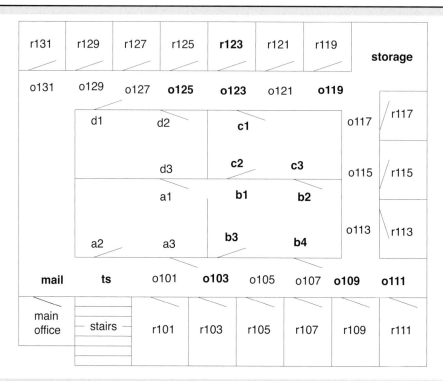

Figure 3.1: The delivery robot domain with interesting locations labeled

one location to a neighboring location, the actions can involve deterministic traveling between neighboring locations. This can be modeled as a state-space search problem, where the states are locations.

Consider an example problem with the robot outside room $r103$, at position $o103$, and the goal is to get to room $r123$. Thus, $r123$ is the only state that satisfies the goal. A solution is a sequence of actions that moves the robot from $o103$ to room $r123$.

Example 3.3 In a more complicated example, the delivery robot may have a number of parcels to deliver to various locations, where each parcel has its own delivery destination. In this case, the state may consist of the location of the robot, which parcels the robot is carrying, and the locations of the other parcels. The possible actions may be for the robot to move, to pick up parcels that are at the same location as the robot, or to put down some or all of the parcels it is carrying. A goal state may be one in which some specified parcels are at their desired locations. There may be many goal states because we may not care where the robot is or where some of the other parcels are in a goal state.

Notice that this representation has ignored many details, for example, how the robot is carrying the parcels (which may affect whether it can carry other parcels), the battery level of the robot, whether the parcels are fragile or damaged, and the color of the floor. By not having these as part of the state space, we assume that those details are not relevant to the problem at hand.

Example 3.4 In a tutoring system, a state may consist of the set of topics that the student knows. The action may be teaching a particular lesson, and the result of a teaching action may be that a student knows the topic of the lesson as long as the student knows the topics that are prerequisites for the lesson being taught. The aim is for a student to know a particular set of topics.

If the effect of teaching also depends on the aptitude of the student, this detail must be part of the state space as well. We do not have to model what the student is carrying if that does not affect the result of actions or whether the goal is achieved.

A **state-space problem** consists of

- a set of states

- a distinguished state called the **start state**

- for each state, a set of actions available to the agent in that state

- an **action function** that, given a state and an action, returns a new state

- a **goal** specified as a Boolean function, $goal(s)$, that is true when state s satisfies the goal, in which case we say that s is a **goal state**

- a criterion that specifies the quality of an acceptable solution. For example, any sequence of actions that gets the agent to the goal state may be acceptable, or there may be costs associated with actions and the agent may be required to find a sequence that has minimal total cost. A solution that is best according to some criterion is called an **optimal solution**. We do not always need an optimal solution, for example, we may be satisfied with any solution that is within 10% of optimal.

This framework is extended in subsequent chapters to include cases where the states have structure that can be exploited, where the state is not fully observable (e.g., the robot does not know where the parcels are initially, or the teacher does not know the aptitude of the student), where the actions are stochastic (e.g., the robot may overshoot, or a student perhaps does not learn a topic that is taught), and with complex preferences in terms of rewards and punishments, not just a set of goal states.

3.3   Graph Searching

In this chapter, the problem of finding a sequence of actions to achieve a goal is abstracted as searching for paths in directed graphs. To solve a problem, first define the underlying search space and then apply a search algorithm to that search space. Many problem-solving tasks are transformable into the problem of finding a path in a graph. Searching in graphs provides an appropriate abstract model of problem solving independent of a particular domain.

A directed graph consists of a set of nodes and a set of directed arcs between nodes. The idea is to find a path along these arcs from the start node to a goal node.

In representing a state-space problem, the states are represented as nodes, and the actions as arcs.

The abstraction is necessary because there may be more than one way to represent a problem as a graph. The examples in this chapter are in terms of state-space searching, where nodes represent states and arcs represent actions. Future chapters consider other ways to represent problem solving in terms of graph searching.

3.3.1   Formalizing Graph Searching

A **directed graph** consists of

- a set N of **nodes** and

- a set A of arcs, where an **arc** is an ordered pair of nodes.

In this definition, a node could be anything. There may be infinitely many nodes and arcs. We do not assume that a graph is represented explicitly; we require only a procedure to generate nodes and arcs as needed.

The arc $\langle n_1, n_2 \rangle$ is an **outgoing arc** from n_1 and an **incoming arc** to n_2.

A node n_2 is a **neighbor** of n_1 if there is an arc from n_1 to n_2; that is, if $\langle n_1, n_2 \rangle \in A$. Note that being a neighbor does not imply symmetry; just because n_2 is a neighbor of n_1 does not mean that n_1 is necessarily a neighbor of n_2. Arcs may be **labeled**, for example, with the action that will take the agent from one node to another or with the cost of an action or both.

A **path** from node s to node g is a sequence of nodes $\langle n_0, n_1, \ldots, n_k \rangle$ such that $s = n_0$, $g = n_k$, and $\langle n_{i-1}, n_i \rangle \in A$; that is, there is an arc from n_{i-1} to n_i for each i. Sometimes it is useful to view a path as the sequence of arcs, $\langle n_0, n_1 \rangle$, $\langle n_1, n_2 \rangle, \ldots, \langle n_{k-1}, n_k \rangle$, or a sequence of labels of these arcs. Path $\langle n_0, n_1, \ldots, n_i \rangle$ is an **initial part** of $\langle n_0, n_1, \ldots, n_k \rangle$, when $i \leq k$.

A **goal** is a Boolean function on nodes. If $goal(n)$ is true, we say that node n satisfies the goal, and n is a **goal node**.

To encode problems as graphs, one node is identified as the **start node**. A **solution** is a path from the start node to a node that satisfies the goal.

Sometimes there is a **cost** – a non-negative number – associated with arcs. We write the cost of arc $\langle n_i, n_j \rangle$ as $cost(\langle n_i, n_j \rangle)$.

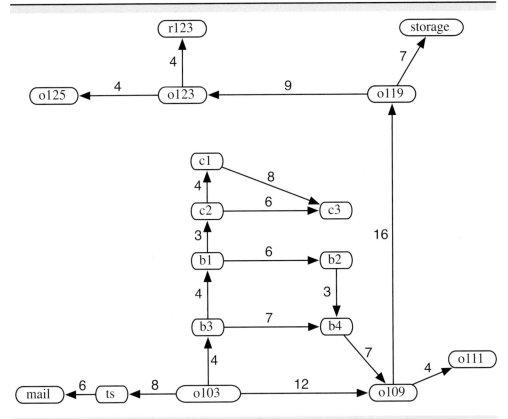

Figure 3.2: A graph with arc costs for the delivery robot domain

The costs of arcs induce a cost of paths. Given a path $p = \langle n_0, n_1, \ldots, n_k \rangle$, the cost of path p is the sum of the costs of the arcs in the path:

$$cost(p) = \sum_{i=1}^{k} cost(\langle n_{i-1}, n_i \rangle) = cost(\langle n_0, n_1 \rangle) + \cdots + cost(\langle n_{k-1}, n_k \rangle)$$

An **optimal solution** is one of the solutions that has the lowest cost. That is, an optimal solution is a path p from the start node to a goal node such that there is no path p' from the start node to a goal node where $cost(p') < cost(p)$.

Example 3.5 Consider the problem of the delivery robot finding a path from location $o103$ to location $r123$ in the domain shown in Figure 3.1 (page 80). In that figure, the interesting locations are named. For simplicity, we consider only the locations shown in bold and we initially limit the directions that the robot is able to travel. Figure 3.2 shows the resulting graph where the nodes represent locations and the arcs represent possible single steps between locations. In this figure, each arc is shown with the associated cost of getting from one location to the next.

In this graph, the nodes are $N = \{mail, ts, o103, b3, o109, \ldots\}$ and the arcs are $A = \{\langle ts, mail \rangle, \langle o103, ts \rangle, \langle o103, b3 \rangle, \langle o103, o109 \rangle, \ldots\}$. Node $o125$ has no neighbors. Node *ts* has one neighbor, namely *mail*. Node *o*103 has three neighbors, namely *ts*, *b*3, and *o*109.

There are three paths from *o*103 to *r*123:

$$\langle o103, o109, o119, o123, r123 \rangle$$
$$\langle o103, b3, b4, o109, o119, o123, r123 \rangle$$
$$\langle o103, b3, b1, b2, b4, o109, o119, o123, r123 \rangle$$

If *o*103 were the start node and *r*123 were the unique goal node, each of these three paths would be a solution to the graph-searching problem. The first of these is an optimal solution, with a solution cost of $12 + 16 + 9 + 4 = 41$.

A **cycle** is a nonempty path where the end node is the same as the start node – that is, $\langle n_0, n_1, \ldots, n_k \rangle$ such that $n_0 = n_k$. A directed graph without any cycles is called a **directed acyclic graph** (**DAG**). Note that this should be called an **acyclic directed graph**, because it is a directed graph that happens to be acyclic, not an acyclic graph that happens to be directed, but DAG sounds better than ADG!

A **tree** is a DAG where there is one node with no incoming arcs and every other node has exactly one incoming arc. The node with no incoming arcs is called the **root** of the tree. A node with no outgoing arcs is called a **leaf**. In a tree, neighbors are often called **children**, and we use the family-tree metaphor, with grandparents, siblings, and so on.

In many problems the search graph is not given explicitly, but is dynamically constructed as needed. For the search algorithms, all that is required is a way to generate the neighbors of a node and to determine if a node is a goal node.

The **forward branching factor** of a node is the number of outgoing arcs from the node. The **backward branching factor** of a node is the number of incoming arcs to the node. These factors provide measures for the complexity of graph algorithms. When we discuss the time and space complexity of the search algorithms, we assume that the branching factors are bounded, meaning they are all less than some postive integer.

Example 3.6 In the graph of Figure 3.2, the forward branching factor of node *o*103 is three because there are three outgoing arcs from node *o*103. The backward branching factor of node *o*103 is zero; there are no incoming arcs to node *o*103. The forward branching factor of *mail* is zero and the backward branching factor of *mail* is one. The forward branching factor of node *b*3 is two and the backward branching factor of *b*3 is one.

The branching factor is an important key component in the size of the graph. If the forward branching factor for each node is b, and the graph is a tree, there are b^n nodes that are n arcs away from the start node.

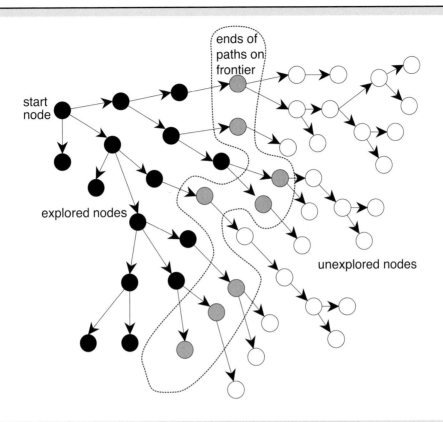

Figure 3.3: Problem solving by graph searching

3.4   A Generic Searching Algorithm

This section describes a generic algorithm to search for a solution path in a graph. The algorithm calls procedures that can be coded to implement various search strategies.

The intuitive idea behind the generic search algorithm, given a graph, a start node, and a goal predicate, is to explore paths incrementally from the start node. This is done by maintaining a **frontier** (or **fringe**) of paths from the start node. The frontier contains all of the paths that could form initial segments of paths from the start node to a goal node. (See Figure 3.3, where the frontier is the set of paths to the gray shaded nodes.) Initially, the frontier contains the trivial path containing just the start node, and no arcs. As the search proceeds, the frontier expands into the unexplored nodes until a goal node is encountered. Different search strategies are obtained by providing an appropriate implementation of the frontier.

The **generic search algorithm** is shown in Figure 3.4 (on the next page). The frontier is a set of paths. Initially, the frontier contains the path of zero cost consisting of just the start node. At each step, the algorithm removes a

1: **procedure** $Search(G, S, goal)$
2:     **Inputs**
3:         G: graph with nodes N and arcs A
4:         s: start node
5:         $goal$: Boolean function of nodes
6:     **Output**
7:         path from s to a node for which $goal$ is true
8:         or $\perp$ if there are no solution paths
9:     **Local**
10:         $Frontier$: set of paths
11:     $Frontier := \{\langle s \rangle\}$
12:     **while** $Frontier \neq \{\}$ **do**
13:         **select** and **remove** $\langle n_0, \ldots, n_k \rangle$ from $Frontier$
14:         **if** $goal(n_k)$ **then**
15:             **return** $\langle n_0, \ldots, n_k \rangle$
16:         $Frontier := Frontier \cup \{\langle n_0, \ldots, n_k, n \rangle : \langle n_k, n \rangle \in A\}$
17:     **return** $\perp$

Figure 3.4: Search: generic graph searching algorithm

path $\langle n_0, \ldots, n_k \rangle$ from the frontier. If $goal(n_k)$ is true (i.e., n_k is a goal node), it has **found a solution** and returns the path $\langle n_0, \ldots, n_k \rangle$. Otherwise, the path is extended by one more arc by finding the neighbors of n_k. For every neighbor n of n_k, the path $\langle n_0, \ldots, n_k, n \rangle$ is added to the frontier. This step is known as **expanding** the path $\langle n_0, \ldots, n_k \rangle$.

This algorithm has a few features that should be noted:

- Which path is selected at line 13 defines the search strategy. The selection of a path can affect the efficiency; see the box on page 88 for more details on the use of "select".

- It is useful to think of the *return* at line 15 as a temporary return, where a caller can **retry** the search to get another answer by continuing the while loop. This can be implemented by having a class that keeps the state of the search and a *search*() method that returns the next solution.

- If the procedure returns $\perp$ ("**bottom**"), there are no solutions, or no remaining solutions if the search has been retried.

- The algorithm only tests if a path ends in a goal node *after* the path has been selected from the frontier, not when it is added to the frontier. There are two important reasons for this. There could be a costly arc from a node on the frontier to a goal node. The search should not always return the path with this arc, because a lower-cost solution may exist. This is crucial when the lowest-cost path is required. A second reason is that it may be expensive to determine whether a node is a goal node, and so this should be delayed in case the computation is not necessary.

If the node at the end of the selected path is not a goal node and it has no neighbors, then extending the path means removing the path from the frontier. This outcome is reasonable because this path could not be part of a path from the start node to a goal node.

3.5   Uninformed Search Strategies

A problem determines the graph, the start node and the goal but not which path to select from the frontier. This is the job of a **search strategy**. A search strategy defines the order in which paths are selected from the frontier. It specifies which path is selected at line 13 of Figure 3.4. Different strategies are obtained by modifying how the selection of paths in the frontier is implemented.

This section presents four **uninformed search strategies** that do not take into account the location of the goal. Intuitively, these algorithms ignore where they are going until they find a goal and report success.

3.5.1   Breadth-First Search

In **breadth-first search** the frontier is implemented as a **FIFO** (first-in, first-out) **queue**. Thus, the path that is selected from the frontier is the one that was added earliest.

This approach implies that the paths from the start node are generated in order of the number of arcs in the path. One of the paths with the fewest arcs is selected at each iteration.

Example 3.7   Consider the tree-shaped graph in Figure 3.5 (page 89). Suppose the start node is the node at the top, and the children of a node are added in a left-to-right order. In breadth first search, the order in which the paths are expanded does not depend on the location of the goal. The nodes at the end of the first sixteen paths expanded are numbered in order of expansion in the figure. The shaded nodes are the nodes at the ends of the paths of the frontier after the first sixteen iterations.

Example 3.8   Consider breadth-first search from $o103$ in the graph given in Figure 3.2 (page 83). The only goal node is $r123$. Initially, the frontier is $[\langle o103 \rangle]$. This is extended by $o103$'s neighbors, making the frontier $[\langle o103, ts \rangle, \langle o103, b3 \rangle, \langle o103, o109 \rangle]$. These are the nodes one arc away from $o013$. The next three paths chosen are $\langle o103, ts \rangle$, $\langle o103, b3 \rangle$, and $\langle o103, o109 \rangle$, at which stage the frontier contains

$$[\langle o103, ts, mail \rangle, \langle o103, b3, b1 \rangle, \langle o103, b3, b4 \rangle,$$

Non-deterministic Choice

In many AI programs, we want to separate the definition of a solution from how it is computed. Usually, the algorithms are **non-deterministic**, which means that there are choices in the program that are left unspecified. There are two forms of non-determinism:

- In **don't-care non-determinism**, if one selection does not lead to a solution, neither will other selections. Don't-care non-determinism is used in resource allocation, where a number of requests occur for a limited number of resources, and a scheduling algorithm has to select who gets which resource at each time. Correctness should not be affected by the selection, but efficiency and termination may be. When there is an infinite sequence of selections, a selection mechanism is **fair** if a request that is repeatedly available to be selected will eventually be selected. The problem of an element being repeatedly not selected is called **starvation**. In this context, a **heuristic** is a rule-of-thumb that can be used to select a value.

- In **don't-know non-determinism**, just because one choice did not lead to a solution does not mean that other choices will not. Often we speak of an **oracle** that could specify, at each point, which choice will lead to a solution. Because our agent does not have such an oracle, it has to search through the space of alternate choices.

  Don't-know non-determinism plays a large role in computational complexity theory. A decision problem is a problem with a yes or no answer. The class P consists of decision problems solvable in time complexity polynomial in the size of the problem. The class NP, of nondeterministic polynomial time problems, contains decision problems that could be solved in polynomial time with an **oracle** that chooses the correct value at each choice in constant time or, equivalently, if a solution is verifiable in polynomial time. It is widely conjectured that $P \neq NP$, which would mean that no such oracle can exist. One pivotal result of complexity theory is that the hardest problems in the NP class are all equally complex; if one can be solved in polynomial time, they all can. These problems are **NP-complete**. A problem is **NP-hard** if it is at least as hard as an NP-complete problem.

  In a **non-deterministic procedure**, we pretend that an oracle makes an appropriate choice at each time. Thus, a **choose** statement will result in a choice that will led to success, or will **fail** if there are no such choices. A non-deterministic procedure may have multiple answers, where there are multiple choices that succeed, and will fail if there are no applicable choices. An explicit **fail** in the code indicates a choice that should not succeed.

In this book, we consistently use the term **select** for don't-care non-determinism and **choose** for don't-know non-determinism.

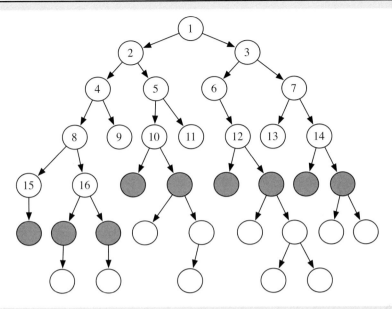

Figure 3.5: The order in which paths are expanded in breadth-first search

$\langle o103, o109, o111 \rangle$, $\langle o103, o109, o119 \rangle$].

These are the paths containing two arcs starting at $o103$. These five paths are the next paths on the frontier chosen, at which stage the frontier contains the paths of three arcs away from $o103$, namely,

$[\langle o103, b3, b1, c2 \rangle$, $\langle o103, b3, b1, b2 \rangle$, $\langle o103, b3, b4, o109 \rangle$,

$\langle o103, o109, o119, storage \rangle$, $\langle o103, o109, o119, o123 \rangle$].

Note how in breadth-first search each path on the frontier has either the same number of arcs or one more arc than the next element of the frontier that will be selected.

Suppose the branching factor of the search is b. If the next path to be selected on the frontier contains n arcs, there are at least b^{n-1} elements of the frontier. All of these paths contain n or $n+1$ arcs. Thus, both space and time complexities are exponential in the number of arcs of the path to a goal with the fewest arcs. This method is guaranteed, however, to find a solution if one exists and will find a solution with the fewest arcs.

Breadth-first search is useful when

- the problem is small enough so that space is not a problem (e.g., if you already need to store the graph) and
- you want a solution containing the fewest arcs.

It is a poor method when all solutions have many arcs or there is some heuristic knowledge available. It is not used very often for large problems where the graph is dynamically generated because of its exponential space complexity.

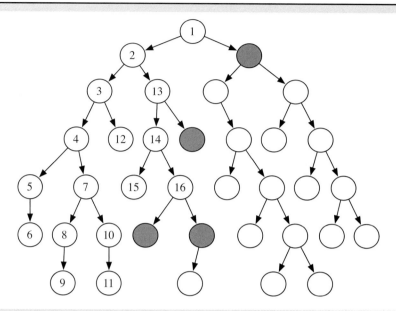

Figure 3.6: The order paths are expanded in depth-first search

3.5.2   Depth-First Search

In **depth-first search**, the frontier acts like a **LIFO** (last-in, first-out) **stack** of paths. In a stack, elements are added and removed from the top of the stack. Using a stack means that the path selected and removed from the frontier at any time is the last path that was added.

> **Example 3.9**   Consider the tree-shaped graph in Figure 3.6. Suppose the start node is the root of the tree (the node at the top). As depth-first search does not define the order of the neighbors, suppose for this graph that the children of each node are ordered from left to right, and they added to the stack in reverse order so that the path to the leftmost neighbor is added to the stack last (and so removed first).
>
> In depth-first search, like breadth-first search, the order in which the paths are expanded does not depend on the goal. The nodes at the end of the first sixteen paths expanded are numbered in order of expansion in Figure 3.6. The shaded nodes are the nodes at the ends of the paths on the frontier after the first sixteen steps, assuming none of the expanded paths end at a goal node.
>
> Notice how the first six paths expanded are all initial parts of a single path. The node at the end of this path has no neighbors. The next path expanded is a path that follows that path as long as possible and has one extra node.

Implementing the frontier as a stack results in paths being pursued in a depth-first manner – searching one path to its completion before trying an alternative path. This method is said to involve **backtracking**: the algorithm selects a first alternative at each node, and it *backtracks* to the next alternative when it has pursued all of the paths from the first selection. Some paths may be infinite when the graph has cycles or infinitely many nodes, in which case a depth-first search may never stop.

This algorithm does not specify the order in which the paths to the neighbors are added to the frontier. The efficiency of the algorithm is sensitive to this ordering.

Example 3.10 Consider depth-first search from $o103$ to $r123$ in the graph given in Figure 3.2 (page 83). In this example, the frontier is shown as a list of paths with the top of the stack at the left of the list.

Initially, the frontier contains the trivial path $\langle o103 \rangle$.

At the next stage, the frontier contains the paths:

$$[\langle o103, ts \rangle, \langle o103, b3 \rangle, \langle o103, o109 \rangle].$$

Next, the path $\langle o103, ts \rangle$ is selected because it is at the top of the stack. It is removed from the frontier and replaced by extending it by one arc, resulting in the frontier

$$[\langle o103, ts, mail \rangle, \langle o103, b3 \rangle, \langle o103, o109 \rangle].$$

Next, the path $\langle o103, ts, mail \rangle$ is removed from the frontier and is replaced by the set of paths that extend it by one arc, which is the empty set because *mail* has no neighbors. Thus, the resulting frontier is

$$[\langle o103, b3 \rangle, \langle o103, o109 \rangle].$$

At this stage, the path $\langle o103, b3 \rangle$ is the top of the stack. Notice what has happened: depth-first search has pursued all paths from *ts* and, when all of these paths were exhausted (there was only one), it backtracked to the next element of the stack. Next, $\langle o103, b3 \rangle$ is selected and is replaced in the frontier by the paths that extend it by one arc, resulting in the frontier

$$[\langle o103, b3, b1 \rangle, \langle o103, b3, b4 \rangle, \langle o103, o109 \rangle].$$

Then $\langle o103, b3, b1 \rangle$ is selected from the frontier and is replaced by all one-arc extensions, resulting in the frontier

$$[\langle o103, b3, b1, c2 \rangle, \langle o103, b3, b1, b2 \rangle, \langle o103, b3, b4 \rangle, \langle o103, o109 \rangle].$$

Now the first path is selected from the frontier and is extended by one arc, resulting in the frontier

$$[\langle o103, b3, b1, c2, c3 \rangle, \langle o103, b3, b1, c2, c1 \rangle,$$
$$\langle o103, b3, b1, b2 \rangle, \langle o103, b3, b4 \rangle, \langle o103, o109 \rangle].$$

Node $c3$ has no neighbors, and thus the search backtracks to the last alternative that has not been pursued, namely to the path to $c1$.

Eventually, it will find a path to $r123$ which goes through $b2$.

Suppose $\langle n_0, \ldots, n_k \rangle$ is the path selected on line 13 of Figure 3.4 (page 86). In depth-first search every other path on the frontier is of the form $\langle n_0, \ldots, n_i, m \rangle$, for some index $i < k$ and some node m that is a neighbor of n_i; that is, it follows the selected path for a number of arcs and then has exactly one extra node. Thus, the frontier contains only the current path and paths to neighbors of the nodes on this path. If the branching factor is b and the selected path on the frontier has k arcs, there can be at most $k * (b - 1)$ other paths on the frontier. These are the up to $(b - 1)$ alternative paths from each node. Therefore, for depth-first search, the space used at any stage is linear in the number of arcs from the start to the current node.

If there is a solution on the first branch searched, the time complexity is linear in the number of arcs in the path. In the worst case, depth-first search can get trapped on infinite branches and never find a solution, even if one exists, for infinite graphs or for graphs with cycles. If the graph is a finite tree, with the forward branching factor less than or equal to b and with all paths from the start having k or fewer arcs, the worst-case time complexity is $O(b^k)$.

Example 3.11 Consider the modification of the delivery graph presented in Figure 3.7 (page 94), in which the agent has much more freedom in moving between locations. An infinite path leads from ts to $mail$, back to ts, back to $mail$, and so forth. As presented, depth-first search follows this path forever, never considering alternative paths from $b3$ or $o109$. The frontiers for the first five iterations of the path-finding search algorithm using depth-first search are

$$[\langle o103 \rangle]$$
$$[\langle o103, ts \rangle, \langle o103, b3 \rangle, \langle o103, o109 \rangle]$$
$$[\langle o103, ts, mail \rangle, \langle o103, ts, o103 \rangle, \langle o103, b3 \rangle, \langle o103, o109 \rangle]$$
$$[\langle o103, ts, mail, ts \rangle, \langle o103, ts, o103 \rangle, \langle o103, b3 \rangle, \langle o103, o109 \rangle]$$
$$[\langle o103, ts, mail, ts, mail \rangle, \langle o103, ts, mail, ts, o103 \rangle, \langle o103, ts, o103 \rangle,$$
$$\langle o103, b3 \rangle, \langle o103, o109 \rangle]$$

Depth-first search can be improved by pruning paths with cycles (page 105).

Because depth-first search is sensitive to the order in which the neighbors are added to the frontier, care must be taken to do it sensibly. This ordering may be done statically (so that the order of the neighbors is fixed) or dynamically (where the ordering of the neighbors depends on the goal).

Depth-first search is appropriate when

- space is restricted

- many solutions exist, perhaps with long paths, particularly for the case where nearly all paths lead to a solution or

- the order in which the neighbors of a node are added to the stack can be tuned so that solutions are found on the first try.

Comparing Algorithms

Algorithms (including search algorithms) can be compared on
- the time taken,
- the space used, and
- the quality or accuracy of the results.

The time taken, space used, and accuracy of an algorithm are a function of the inputs to the algorithm. Computer scientists talk about the **asymptotic complexity** of algorithms, which specifies how the time or space grows with the input size of the algorithm. An algorithm has time (or space) complexity $O(f(n))$ – read "big-oh of $f(n)$" – for input size n, where $f(n)$ is some function of n, if there exist constants n_0 and k such that the time, or space, of the algorithm is less than $k * f(n)$ for all $n > n_0$. The most common types of functions are exponential functions such as 2^n, 3^n, or 1.015^n; polynomial functions such as n^5, n^2, n, or $n^{1/2}$; and logarithmic functions, $\log n$. In general, exponential algorithms get worse more quickly than polynomial algorithms which, in turn, are worse than logarithmic algorithms.

An algorithm has time or space complexity $\Omega(f(n))$ for input size n if there exist constants n_0 and k such that the time or space of the algorithm is greater than $k * f(n)$ for all $n > n_0$. An algorithm has time or space complexity $\Theta(f(n))$ if it has complexity $O(f(n))$ and $\Omega(f(n))$. Typically, you cannot give a $\Theta(f(n))$ complexity on an algorithm, because most algorithms take different times for different inputs. Thus, when comparing algorithms, one has to specify the class of problems that will be considered.

Algorithm A is better than B, using a measure of either time, space, or accuracy, could mean any one of:
- the worst case of A is better than the worst case of B
- A works better in practice, or the average case of A is better than the average case of B, where you average over typical problems
- there is a subclass of problems for which A is better than B, so that which algorithm is better depends on the problem
- for every problem, A is better than B.

The worst-case asymptotic complexity is often the easiest to show, but it is usually the least useful. Characterizing the subclass of problems for which one algorithm is better than another is usually the most useful, if it is easy to determine which subclass a given problem is in. Unfortunately, this characterization is usually very difficult to obtain.

Characterizing when one algorithm is better than the other can be done either theoretically using mathematics or empirically by building implementations. Theorems are only as valid as the assumptions on which they are based. Similarly, empirical investigations are only as good as the suite of test cases and the actual implementations of the algorithms. It is easy to disprove a conjecture that one algorithm is better than another for some class of problems by showing a counterexample, but it is usually much more difficult to prove such a conjecture.

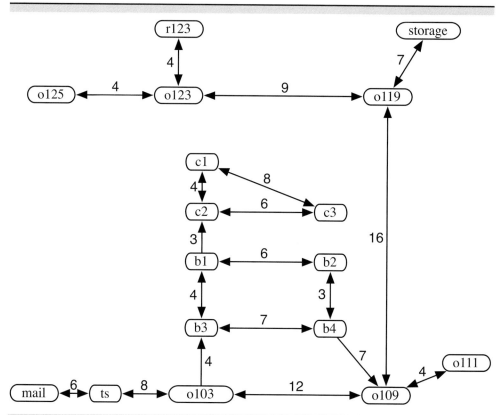

Figure 3.7: A graph, with cycles, for the delivery robot domain. Edges of the form $X \longleftrightarrow Y$ means there is an arc from X to Y and an arc from Y to X. That is, $\langle X, Y \rangle \in A$ and $\langle Y, X \rangle \in A$.

It is a poor method when

- it is possible to get caught in infinite paths, which occurs when the graph is infinite or when there are cycles in the graph

- solutions exist at shallow depth, because in this case the search may explore many long paths before finding the short solutions, or

- there are multiple paths to a node, for example, on a $n \times n$ grid, where all arcs go right or down, there are exponentially paths from the top-left node, but only n^2 nodes.

Depth-first search is the basis for a number of other algorithms, such as iterative deepening.

3.5.3   Iterative Deepening

Neither of the preceding methods is ideal. Breadth-first search, which guarantees that a path will be found, requires exponential space. Depth-first search may not halt on infinite graphs or graphs with cycles. One way to combine the space efficiency of depth-first search with the optimality of breadth-first search is to use **iterative deepening**. The idea is to recompute the elements of the breadth-first frontier rather than storing them. Each recomputation can be a depth-first search, which thus uses less space.

Iterative deepening repeatedly calls a **depth-bounded searcher**, a depth-first searcher that takes in an integer **depth bound** and never explores paths with more arcs than this depth bound. Iterative deepening first does a depth-first search to depth 1 by building paths of length 1 in a depth-first manner. If that does not find a solution, it can build paths to depth 2, then depth 3, and so on until a solution is found. When a search with depth-bound n fails to find a solution, it can throw away all of the previous computation and start again with a depth-bound of $n + 1$. Eventually, it will find a solution if one exists, and, as it is enumerating paths in order of the number of arcs, a path with the fewest arcs will always be found first.

To ensure it halts for finite graphs, iterative deepening search needs to distinguish between

- failure because the depth bound was reached and
- failure due to exhausting the search space.

In the first case, the search must be retried with a larger depth bound. In the second case, it is a waste of time to try again with a larger depth bound, because no path exists no matter what the depth, and so the whole search should fail.

Pseudocode for iterative deepening search, *ID_search*, is presented in Figure 3.8 (on the next page). The local procedure *Depth_bounded_search* implements a depth-bounded depth-first search (using recursion to keep the stack) that places a limit on the length of the paths for which it is searching. It either returns a path, or reaches the end of its code, and returns with no path. It uses a depth-first search to find paths of length $k + b$, where k is the path length of the given path from the start and b is a non-negative integer. The iterative deepening searcher calls *Depth_bounded_search* for increasing depth bounds. This program finds the paths to goal nodes in the same order as does breadth-first search. Note that it only needs to check for a goal when $b = 0$, because it knows that there are no solutions for lower bounds.

To ensure that iterative deepening search fails whenever breadth-first search would fail, it needs to keep track of when increasing the bound could help find an answer. A depth-bounded search **fails naturally** – it fails by exhausting the search space – if the search did not prune any paths due to the depth bound. In this case, the program can stop and report no paths. This is handled through the variable *hit_depth_bound* in Figure 3.8, which is false when *Depth_bounded_search* is called initially, and becomes true if the search is pruned due to the depth bound. If it is true at the end of a depth-bounded search, the

```
 1: procedure ID_search(G, s, goal)
 2:     Inputs
 3:         G: graph with nodes N and arcs A
 4:         s: start node
 5:         goal: Boolean function on nodes
 6:     Output
 7:         path from s to a node for which goal is true
 8:         or ⊥ if there is no such path
 9:     Local
10:         hit_depth_bound: Boolean
11:         bound: integer
12:         procedure Depth_bounded_search(⟨n₀, . . . , n_k⟩, b)
13:             Inputs
14:                 ⟨n₀, . . . , n_k⟩: path
15:                 b: integer, b ≥ 0
16:             Output
17:                 path to goal of length k + b if one exists
18:             if b > 0 then
19:                 for each arc ⟨n_k, n⟩ ∈ A do
20:                     res := Depth_bounded_search(⟨n₀, . . . , n_k, n⟩, b − 1)
21:                     if res is a path then
22:                         return res
23:             else if goal(n_k) then
24:                 return ⟨n₀, . . . , n_k⟩
25:             else if n_k has any neighbors then
26:                 hit_depth_bound := true
27:     bound := 0
28:     repeat
29:         hit_depth_bound := false
30:         res := Depth_bounded_search(⟨s⟩, bound)
31:         if res is a path then
32:             return res
33:         bound := bound + 1
34:     until not hit_depth_bound
```

Figure 3.8: *ID_search*: iterative deepening search

search failed due to hitting the depth bound, and so the depth bound can be increased, and another depth-bounded search is carried out.

The obvious problem with iterative deepening is the wasted computation that occurs at each step. This, however, may not be as bad as one might think, particularly if the branching factor is high. Consider the running time of the algorithm. Assume a constant branching factor of $b > 1$. Consider the search where the bound is k. At depth k, there are b^k nodes; each of these has been generated once. The nodes at depth $k - 1$ have been generated twice, those at depth $k - 2$ have been generated three times, and so on, and the nodes at depth 1 have been generated k times. Thus, the total number of paths expanded is

$$b^k + 2b^{k-1} + 3b^{k-2} + \cdots + kb = b^k(1 + 2b^{-1} + 3b^{-2} + \cdots + kb^{1-k})$$

$$< b^k \left(\sum_{i=1}^{\infty} ib^{(1-i)} \right)$$

$$= b^k \left(\frac{b}{b-1} \right)^2.$$

Breadth-first search expands $\sum_{i=1}^{k} b^i = \left(\frac{b^{k+1}-1}{b-1} \right) = b^k \left(\frac{b}{b-1} \right) - \frac{1}{b-1}$ nodes. Thus iterative deepening has an asymptotic overhead of $\frac{b}{(b-1)}$ times the cost of expanding the nodes at depth k using breadth-first search. Thus, when $b = 2$ there is an overhead factor of 2, and when $b = 3$ there is an overhead of 1.5. This algorithm is $O(b^k)$ and there cannot be an asymptotically better uninformed search strategy. Note that, if the branching factor is close to 1, this analysis does not work because then the denominator would be close to zero; see Exercise 3.9 (page 123).

3.5.4 Lowest-Cost-First Search

For many domains, arcs have non-unit costs, and the aim is to find an **optimal solution**, a solution such that no other solution has a lower total cost. For example, for a delivery robot, the cost of an arc may be resources (e.g., time, energy) required by the robot to carry out the action represented by the arc, and the aim is for the robot to solve a given goal using fewest resources. The cost for a tutoring system may be the time and effort required by a student. In each of these cases, the searcher should try to minimize the total cost of the path found to a goal.

The search algorithms considered thus far are not guaranteed to find the minimum cost paths; they have not used the arc cost information at all. Breadth-first search finds a solution with the fewest arcs first, but the distribution of arc costs may be such that a path with the fewest arcs is not one of minimal cost.

The simplest search method that is guaranteed to find a minimum cost path is **lowest-cost-first search**, which is similar to breadth-first search, but instead of expanding a path with the fewest number of arcs, it selects a path with the lowest cost. This is implemented by treating the frontier as a priority queue ordered by the *cost* function (page 82).

Example 3.12   Consider a lowest-cost-first search from $o103$ to $r123$ in the graph given in Figure 3.2 (page 83). In this example, the frontier is shown as a list of paths in order of cost, where paths are denoted by the node at the end of the path, with a subscript showing the cost of the path.

Initially, the frontier is $[o103_0]$. At the next stage it is $[b3_4, ts_8, o109_{12}]$. The path to $b3$ is selected, with the resulting frontier

$$[b1_8, ts_8, b4_{11}, o109_{12}].$$

The path to $b1$ is then selected, resulting in frontier

$$[ts_8, c2_{11}, b4_{11}, o109_{12}, b2_{14}].$$

Then the path to ts is selected, and the resulting frontier is

$$[c2_{11}, b4_{11}, o109_{12}, mail_{14}, b2_{14}].$$

Then $c2$ is selected, and so forth. Note how the lowest-cost-first search grows many paths incrementally, always expanding the path with lowest cost.

If the costs of the arcs are all greater than a positive constant (bounded arc costs) and the branching factor is finite, the lowest-cost-first search is guaranteed to find an optimal solution – a solution with lowest path cost – if a solution exists. Moreover, the first path to a goal that is expanded is a path with lowest cost. Such a solution is optimal, because the algorithm expands paths from the start node in order of path cost. If a better path to a goal existed than the first solution found, it would have been expanded from the frontier earlier.

The bounded arc cost is used to guarantee the lowest-cost search will find a solution, when one exists, in graphs with finite branching factor. Without such a bound there can be infinite paths with a finite cost. For example, there could be nodes $n_0, n_1, n_2, \ldots$ with an arc $\langle n_{i-1}, n_i \rangle$ for each $i > 0$ with cost $1/2^i$. Infinitely many paths of the form $\langle n_0, n_1, n_2, \ldots, n_k \rangle$ all have a cost of less than 1. If there is an arc from n_0 to a goal node with a cost equal to 1, it will never be selected. This is the basis of **Zeno's paradox** that Aristotle wrote about more than 2300 years ago.

Like breadth-first search, lowest-cost-first search is typically exponential in both space and time. It generates *all* paths from the start that have a cost less than the cost of a solution.

3.6   Heuristic Search

The search methods in the preceding section are **uninformed** (or blind) in that they do not take the goal into account until they expand a path that leads to a node that satisfies the goal. Heuristic information about which nodes are most promising can guide the search by changing which node is selected in line 13 of the generic search algorithm in Figure 3.4 (page 86).

A **heuristic function** $h(n)$, takes a node n and returns a non-negative real number that is an estimate of the cost of the least-cost path from node n to a goal node. The function $h(n)$ is an **admissible heuristic** if $h(n)$ is always less than or equal to the actual cost of a lowest-cost path from node n to a goal.

There is nothing magical about a heuristic function. It must use only information that can be readily obtained about a node. Typically there is a trade-off between the amount of work it takes to compute a heuristic value for a node and the accuracy of the heuristic value.

A standard way to derive a heuristic function is to solve a simpler problem and to use the cost to the goal in the simplified problem as the heuristic function of the original problem (see Section 3.6.2, (page 104)).

Example 3.13 For the graph of Figure 3.2 (page 83), if the cost is the distance traveled, the straight-line distance between the node and its closest goal can be used as the heuristic function.

The examples that follow assume the following heuristic function:

$$
\begin{aligned}
h(mail) &= 26 & h(ts) &= 23 & h(o103) &= 21 \\
h(o109) &= 24 & h(o111) &= 27 & h(o119) &= 11 \\
h(o123) &= 4 & h(o125) &= 6 & h(r123) &= 0 \\
h(b1) &= 13 & h(b2) &= 15 & h(b3) &= 17 \\
h(b4) &= 18 & h(c1) &= 6 & h(c2) &= 10 \\
h(c3) &= 12 & h(storage) &= 12
\end{aligned}
$$

This h function is an admissible heuristic because the h value is less than or equal to the exact cost of a lowest-cost path from the node to a goal. It is the exact cost for node $o123$. It is very much an underestimate of the cost to the goal for node $b1$, which seems to be close, but there is only a long route to the goal. It is very misleading for $c1$, which also seems close to the goal, but it has no path to the goal.

The h function can be extended to be applicable to paths by making the heuristic value of a path equal to the heuristic value of the node at the end of the path. That is:

$$h(\langle n_o, \ldots, n_k \rangle) = h(n_k)$$

A simple use of a heuristic function in depth-first search is to order the neighbors that are added to the stack representing the frontier. The neighbors can be added to the frontier so that the best neighbor is selected first. This is known as **heuristic depth-first search**. This search selects the locally best path, but it explores all paths from the selected path before it selects another path.

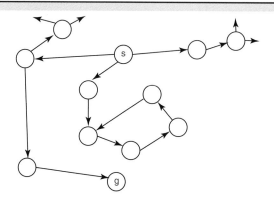

Figure 3.9: A graph that is bad for greedy best-first search

Although it is often used, it suffers from the problems of depth-first search, and is not guaranteed to find a solution and may not find an optimal solution.

Another way to use a heuristic function is to always select a path on the frontier with the lowest heuristic value. This is called **greedy best-first search**. This method sometimes works well. However, it can follow paths that look promising because they appear (according to the heuristic function) close to the goal, but the path explored may keep getting longer.

Example 3.14 Consider the graph shown in Figure 3.9, drawn to scale, where the cost of an arc is its length. The aim is to find the shortest path from s to g. Suppose the Euclidean straight line distance to the goal g is used as the heuristic function. A heuristic depth-first search will select the node below s and will never terminate. Similarly, because all of the nodes below s look good, a greedy best-first search will cycle between them, never trying an alternate route from s.

3.6.1 A^* Search

A^* **search** uses both path cost, as in lowest-cost-first, and heuristic information, as in greedy best-first search, in its selection of which path to expand. For each path on the frontier, A^* uses an estimate of the total path cost from the start node to a goal node constrained to follow that path initially. It uses $cost(p)$, the cost of the path found, as well as the heuristic function $h(p)$, the estimated path cost from the end of p to the goal.

For any path p on the frontier, define $f(p) = cost(p) + h(p)$. This is an estimate of the total path cost to follow path p then go to a goal node. If n is the node at the end of path p, this can be depicted as:

$$\underbrace{\underbrace{start \xoverset{actual}{\longrightarrow} n}_{cost(p)} \underbrace{\xoverset{estimate}{\longrightarrow} goal}_{h(p)}}_{f(p)}$$

If $h(n)$ is an admissible heuristic (page 99) and so never overestimates the cost from node n to a goal node, then $f(p)$ does not overestimate the path cost of going from the start node to a goal node via p.

A^* is implemented using the generic search algorithm (page 86), treating the frontier as a priority queue ordered by $f(p)$.

Example 3.15 Consider using A^* search in Example 3.5 (page 83) using the heuristic function of Example 3.13 (page 99). In this example, the paths on the frontier are shown using the final node of the path, subscripted with the f-value of the path. The frontier is initially $[o103_{21}]$, because $h(o103) = 21$ and the cost of the path is zero. It is replaced by its neighbors, forming the frontier

$$[b3_{21}, ts_{31}, o109_{36}].$$

The first element represents the path $\langle o103, b3 \rangle$; its f-value is $f(\langle o103, b3 \rangle) = cost(\langle o103, b3 \rangle) + h(b3) = 4 + 17 = 21$. Next $b3$ is selected and replaced by its neighbors, forming the frontier

$$[b1_{21}, b4_{29}, ts_{31}, o109_{36}].$$

Then the path to $b1$ is selected and replaced by its neighbors, forming the frontier

$$[c2_{21}, b2_{29}, b4_{29}, ts_{31}, o109_{36}].$$

Then the path to $c2$ is selected and replaced by its neighbors, forming

$$[c1_{21}, b2_{29}, b4_{29}, c3_{29}, ts_{31}, o109_{36}].$$

Up to this stage, the search has been continually exploring what seems to be the direct path to the goal. Next the path to $c1$ is selected and is replaced by its neighbor, forming the frontier

$$[b2_{29}, b4_{29}, c3_{29}, ts_{31}, c3_{35}, o109_{36}].$$

At this stage, there are two paths to the node $c3$ on the frontier. The path to $c3$ that does not go through $c1$ has a lower f-value than the one that does. Later (page 106), we consider how to prune one of these paths without giving up optimality.

There are three paths with the same f-value. The algorithm does not specify which is selected. Suppose it selects the path to the node with the smallest heuristic value (see Exercise 3.6 (page 122)), which is the path to $c3$. This node is removed from the frontier and has no neighbors so the resulting frontier is

$$[b2_{29}, b4_{29}, ts3_{31}, c3_{35}, o109_{36}].$$

Next $b2$ is selected resulting in the frontier

$$[b4_{29}, ts3_{31}, c3_{35}, b4_{35}, o109_{36}].$$

The first path to $b4$ is selected next and is replaced by its neighbors, forming

$$[ts3_{31}, c3_{35}, b4_{35}, o109_{36}, o109_{42}].$$

Note how A^* pursues many different paths from the start.

A lowest-cost path to the goal is eventually found. The algorithm is forced to try many different paths, because several of them temporarily seemed to have the lowest cost. It still does better than either lowest-cost-first search or greedy best-first search.

Example 3.16 Consider Figure 3.9 (page 100), which was a problematic graph for the other heuristic methods. Although it initially searches down from s because of the heuristic function, eventually the cost of the path becomes so large that it picks the node on an actual optimal path.

A search algorithm is **admissible** if, whenever a solution exists, it returns an optimal solution. To guarantee admissibility, some conditions on the graph and the heuristic must hold. The following theorem gives sufficient conditions for A^* to be admissible.

Proposition 3.1. (A^* admissibility) *If there is a solution, A^* using heuristic function h always returns an optimal solution, if*

- *the branching factor is finite (each node has a bounded number of neighbors),*
- *all arc costs are greater than some $\epsilon > 0$, and*
- *h is an **admissible heuristic** (page 99), which means that $h(n)$ is less than or equal to the actual cost of the lowest-cost path from node n to a goal node.*

Proof. **Part A:** *A solution will be found.* If the arc costs are all greater than some $\epsilon > 0$, we say the costs are **bounded above zero**. If this holds and with a finite branching factor, eventually, for all paths p in the frontier, $cost(p)$ will exceed any finite number and, thus, will exceed a solution cost if one exists (with each path having no greater than c/ϵ arcs, where c is the cost of an optimal solution). Because the branching factor is finite, only a finite number of paths must be expanded before the search could get to this point, but the A^* search would have found a solution by then. Bounding the arc costs above zero is a sufficient condition for A^* to avoid suffering from Zeno's paradox (page 98), as described for lowest-cost-first search.

Part B: *The first path to a goal selected is an optimal path.* h is admissible implies the f-value of a node on an optimal solution path is less than or equal to the cost of an optimal solution, which, by the definition of optimal, is less than the cost for any non-optimal solution. The f-value of a solution is equal to the cost of the solution if the heuristic is admissible. Because an element with minimum f-value is chosen at each step, a non-optimal solution can never be chosen while there is a path on the frontier that leads to an optimal solution. So, before it can select a non-optimal solution, A^* will have to pick all of the nodes on an optimal path, including an optimal solution. □

It should be noted that the admissibility of A^* does not ensure that every intermediate node selected from the frontier is on an optimal path from the start node to a goal node. Admissibility ensures that the first solution found will be optimal even in graphs with cycles. It does not ensure that the algorithm will not change its mind about which partial path is the best while it is searching.

To see how the heuristic function improves the efficiency of A^*, suppose c is the cost of a least-cost path from the start node to a goal node. A^*, with an admissible heuristic, expands all paths from the start node in the set (whose initial parts are also in the set):

$$\{p : cost(p) + h(p) < c\}$$

and some of the paths in the set

$$\{p : cost(p) + h(p) = c\}.$$

Increasing h while keeping it admissible, affects the efficiency of A^* if it reduces the size of the first of these sets. If the second set is large, there can be a great variability in the space and time of A^*. The space and time can be sensitive to the tie-breaking mechanism for selecting a path from those with the same f-value. It could, for example, select a path with minimal h-value or use a first-in last-out protocol (i.e., the same as a depth-first search) for these paths; see Exercise 3.6 (page 122).

Iterative Deepening A^*

Iterative deepening can also be applied to an A^* search. **Iterative Deepening A^* (IDA^*)** performs repeated depth-bounded depth-first searches. Instead of the bound being on the number of arcs in the path, it is a bound on the value of $f(n)$. The threshold is initially the value of $f(s)$, where s is the start node. IDA^* then carries out a depth-first depth-bounded search but never expands a path with a higher f-value than the current bound. If the depth-bounded search fails and the bound was reached, the next bound is the minimum of the f-values that exceeded the previous bound. IDA^* thus checks the same nodes as A^*, perhaps breaking ties differently, but recomputes them with a depth-first search instead of storing them.

If all that is required is an approximately optimal path, for example within δ of optimal, the bound can be δ plus the minimum of the f-values that exceeded the previous bound. This can make the search much more efficient in cases where the path lengths can be very close to each other.

3.6.2   Designing a Heuristic Function

An **admissible heuristic** (page 99) is a non-negative function h of nodes, where $h(n)$ is never greater than the actual cost of the shortest path from node n to a goal. The standard way to construct a heuristic function is to find a solution to a simpler problem, which is one with fewer constraints. A problem with fewer constraints is often easier to solve (and sometimes trivial to solve). An optimal solution to the simpler problem cannot have a higher cost than an optimal solution to the full problem because any solution to the full problem is a solution to the simpler problem.

In many spatial problems where the cost is distance and the solution is constrained to go via predefined arcs (e.g., road segments), the straight-line Euclidean distance between two nodes is an admissible heuristic because it is the solution to the simpler problem where the agent is not constrained to go via the arcs.

For many problems one can design a better heuristic function, as in the following examples.

Example 3.17   Consider the delivery robot of Example 3.3 (page 80), where the state space includes the parcels to be delivered. Suppose the cost function is the total distance traveled by the robot to deliver all the parcels. If the robot could carry multiple parcels, one possible heuristic function is the maximum of (a) and (b):

   (a) the maximum delivery distance for any of the parcels that are not at their destination and not being carried, where the delivery distance of a parcel is the distance to that parcel's location plus the distance from that parcel's location to its destination

   (b) the distance to the furthest destination for the parcels being carried.

This is not an overestimate because it is a solution to the simpler problem which is to ignore that it cannot travel though walls, and to ignore all but the most difficult parcel. Note that a maximum is appropriate here because the agent has to both deliver the parcels it is carrying and go to the parcels it is not carrying and deliver them to their destinations.

   If the robot could only carry one parcel, one possible heuristic function is the sum of the distances that the parcels must be carried plus the distance to the closest parcel. Note that the reference to the closest parcel does not imply that the robot will deliver the closest parcel first, but is needed to guarantee that the heuristic is admissible.

Example 3.18 In route planning of Example 3.1 (page 78), when minimizing time, a heuristic could use the straight-line distance from the current location to the goal divided by the maximum speed – assuming the user could drive straight to the destination at top speed.

A more sophisticated heuristic may take into account the different maximum speeds on highways and local roads. One admissible heuristic is the minimum of (a) and (b):

(a) the estimated minimum time required to drive straight to the destination on slower local roads

(b) the minimum time required to drive to a highway on slow roads, then drive on highways to a location close to the destination, then drive on local roads to the destination.

The minimum is appropriate here because the agent can go via highways or local roads, whichever is quicker.

In the above examples, determining the heuristic did not involve search. Once the problem is simplified, it could be solved using search, which should be simpler than the original problem. Note the simpler search problem needs to be solved multiple times, even perhaps for all nodes. It is often useful to cache these results into a **pattern database** that maps the nodes of the simpler problem into the heuristic value. In the simpler problem, there are often fewer nodes, and so multiple original nodes are mapped into a single simpler node, so this may be feasible.

3.7 Pruning the Search Space

The preceding algorithms can be improved by taking into account multiple paths to a node. We consider two pruning strategies. The simplest strategy is to prune cycles; if the goal is to find a least cost path, there is no use considering paths with cycles. The other strategy is only ever to consider one path to a node and to prune other paths to that node.

3.7.1 Cycle Pruning

A graph representing a search space may include cycles. For example, in the robot delivery domain of Figure 3.7 (page 94), the robot can go back and forth between nodes $o103$ and $o109$. Some of the aforementioned search methods can get trapped in cycles, continuously repeating the cycle and never finding an answer even in finite graphs. The other methods can loop through cycles, wasting time, but eventually still find a solution.

A simple method of pruning the search, while guaranteeing that a solution will be found in a finite graph, is to ensure that the algorithm does not consider neighbors that are already on the path from the start. **Cycle pruning** or **loop pruning** checks whether the last node on the path already appears earlier on the path from the start node to that node. Paths $\langle n_0, \ldots, n_k, n \rangle$, where $n \in \{n_0, \ldots, n_k\}$ are not added to the frontier at line 16 of Figure 3.4 (page 86) or are discarded when removed from the frontier.

The computational complexity of cycle pruning depends on which search method is used. For depth-first methods, the overhead can be as low as a constant factor, by storing the elements of the current path as a set (e.g., by maintaining a bit that is set when the node is in the path, or using a hash function). For the search strategies that maintain multiple paths – namely, all of those with exponential space in Figure 3.11 (page 109) – cycle pruning takes time linear in the length of the path being searched. These algorithms cannot do better than searching up the partial path being considered, checking to ensure they do not add a node that already appears in the path.

3.7.2 Multiple-Path Pruning

There is often more than one path to a node. If only one path is required, a search algorithm can prune from the frontier any path that leads to a node to which it has already found a path.

Multiple-path pruning is implemented by maintaining an **explored set** (traditionally called **closed list**) of nodes that are at the end of paths that have been expanded. The explored set is initially empty. When a path $\langle n_0, \ldots, n_k \rangle$ is selected at line 13 of Figure 3.4 (page 86), if n_k is already in the explored set, the path can be discarded. Otherwise, n_k is added to the explored set, and the algorithm proceeds as before.

This approach does not necessarily guarantee that the least-cost path is not discarded. Something more sophisticated may have to be done to guarantee that an optimal solution is found. To ensure that the search algorithm can still find a lowest-cost path to a goal, one of the following can be done:

- Make sure that the first path found to any node is a lowest-cost path to that node, then prune all subsequent paths found to that node.

- If the search algorithm finds a lower-cost path to a node than one already found, it could remove all paths that used the higher-cost path to the node (because these cannot be on an optimal solution). That is, if there is a path p on the frontier $\langle s, \ldots, n, \ldots, m \rangle$, and a path p' to n is found that has a lower cost than the portion of the path from s to n in p, then p can be removed from the frontier.

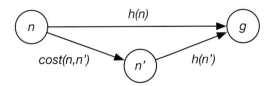

- Whenever the search finds a lower-cost path to a node than a path to that node already found, it could incorporate a new initial section on the paths that have extended the initial path. Thus, if there is a path $p = \langle s, \ldots, n, \ldots, m \rangle$ on the frontier, and a path p' to n is found with a cost lower than the portion of p from s to n, then p' can replace the initial part of p to n.

The first of these alternatives allows the use of the explored set without losing the ability to find an optimal path. The others require more sophisticated algorithms.

In lowest-cost-first search, the first path found to a node (i.e., when the node is selected from the frontier) is the lowest-cost path to the node. Pruning subsequent paths to that node cannot remove a lower-cost path to that node, and thus pruning subsequent paths to each node still enables an optimal solution to be found.

A^* (page 100) does not guarantee that when a path to a node is selected for the first time it is the lowest cost path to that node. Note that the admissibility theorem guarantees this for every path to a *goal* node but not for every path to any node. Whether it holds for all nodes depends on properties of the heuristic function.

A **consistent heuristic** is a non-negative function $h(n)$ on node n that satisfies the constraint $h(n) \leq cost(n, n') + h(n')$ for any two nodes n' and n, where $cost(n, n')$ is the cost of the least-cost path from n to n'. Note that if $h(g) = 0$ for any goal g, then a consistent heuristic is never an overestimate of the cost of going from a node n to a goal.

Consistency can be guaranteed if the heuristic function satisfies the **monotone restriction**: $h(n) \leq cost(n, n') + h(n')$ for any arc $\langle n, n' \rangle$. It is easier to check the monotone restriction as it only depends on the arcs, whereas consistency depends on all pairs of nodes.

Consistency and the monotone restriction can be understood in terms of the **triangle inequality**, which specifies that the length of any side of a triangle cannot be greater than the sum of lengths of the other two sides. In consistency, the estimated cost of going from n to a goal should not be more than the estimated cost of first going to n' then to a goal (see Figure 3.10). The heuristic function of Euclidean distance (the straight-line distance in a multidimensional Euclidean space) between two points when the cost function is distance is consistent. A heuristic function that is a solution to a simplified problem that has shorter solutions is also typically consistent.

With the monotone restriction, the f-values of the paths selected from the frontier are monotonically non-decreasing. That is, when the frontier is expanded, the f-values do not get smaller.

Proposition 3.2. *With a consistent heuristic, multiple-path pruning can never prevent A^* search from finding an optimal solution.*

That is, under the conditions of Proposition 3.1 (page 102), which guarantee A^* finds an optimal solution, if the heuristic function is consistent, A^* with multiple-path pruning will always find an optimal solution.

Proof. We show if the heuristic is consistent, when A^* expands a path p' to a node n', no other path to n' can have a lower cost than p'. Thus, the algorithm can prune subsequent paths to any node and will still find an optimal solution.

We use a proof by contradiction. Suppose the algorithm has selected a path p' to node n' for expansion, but there exists a lower-cost path to node n', which it has not found yet. Then there must be a path p on the frontier that is the initial part of the lower-cost path to n'. Suppose path p ends at node n. It must be that $f(p') \leq f(p)$, because p' was selected before p. This means that

$$cost(p') + h(p') \leq cost(p) + h(p).$$

If the path to n' via p has a lower cost than the path p'

$$cost(p) + cost(n, n') < cost(p')$$

where $cost(n, n')$ is the actual cost of the least cost path from node n to n'. From these two equations, it follows that

$$cost(n, n') < cost(p') - cost(p) \leq h(p) - h(p') = h(n) - h(n')$$

where the last inequality follows because $h(p)$ is defined to be $h(n)$. This cannot happen if $h(n) - h(n') \leq cost(n, n')$, which is the consistency condition. $\qquad \square$

A^* **search** in practice includes multiple-path pruning; if A^* is used without multiple-path pruning, the lack of pruning should be made explicit. It is up to the designer of a heuristic function to ensure that the heuristic is consistent, and so an optimal path will be found.

Multiple-path pruning subsumes cycle pruning, because a cycle is another path to a node and is therefore pruned. Multiple-path pruning can be done in constant time, by setting a bit on each node to which a path has been found if the graph is explicitly stored, or using a hash function. Multiple-path pruning is preferred over cycle pruning for breadth-first methods where virtually all of

Strategy	Selection from Frontier	Path found	Space
Breadth-first	First node added	Fewest arcs	Exponential
Depth-first	Last node added	No	Linear
Iterative deepening	—	Fewest arcs	Linear
Greedy best-first	Minimal $h(p)$	No	Exponential
Lowest-cost-first	Minimal $cost(p)$	Least cost	Exponential
A^*	Minimal $cost(p) + h(p)$	Least cost	Exponential
IDA^*	—	Least cost	Linear

"Path found" refers to guarantees about the path found (for graphs with finite branching factor and arc costs bounded above zero). The algorithms that guarantee to find a path with fewest arcs or least cost are complete. "No" means that it is not guaranteed to find a path in infinite graphs. Both depth-first search and greedy best-first search can fail to find a solution on finite graphs with cycles unless cycle pruning or multiple-path pruning is used.

Space refers to the space complexity, which is either "Linear" in the maximum number of arcs in a path expanded before a solution is found or "Exponential" in the number of arcs in a path expanded before a solution is found.

Iterative deepening is not an instance of the generic search algorithm, and so the iterative deepening methods do not have an entry for the selection from the frontier.

Figure 3.11: Summary of search strategies

the nodes considered have to be stored anyway. Depth-first search does not have to store all of the nodes at the end of paths already expanded; storing them in order to implement multiple-path pruning makes depth-first search exponential in space. For this reason, cycle pruning is preferred over multiple-path pruning for depth-first search.

Multiple path pruning is not appropriate for IDA^*, because the space required to store the explored set is typically more than the space required for A^*, thus defeating the purpose of iterative deepening. Loop pruning can be used with IDA^*. In domains where there are multiple paths to a node, IDA^* loses much of its effectiveness.

3.7.3 Summary of Search Strategies

Figure 3.11 summarizes the searching strategies presented so far.

A search algorithm is **complete** if it is guaranteed to find a solution if there is one. Those search strategies that are guaranteed to find a path with fewest arcs or the least cost are complete. They have worst-case time complexity which increases exponentially with the number of arcs on the paths explored. Whether there can be algorithms that are complete but better than exponential time complexity is related to the $P \neq NP$ question. The algorithms that are not guaranteed to halt (depth-first and greedy best-first) have an infinite worst-case time complexity.

Depth-first search used linear space with respect to the number of arcs in the paths explored, but is not guaranteed to find a solution even if one exists. Breadth-first, lowest-cost-first, and A^* may be exponential in both space and time, but are guaranteed to find a solution if one exists, even if the graph is infinite as long as there are finite branching factors and arc costs are bounded above zero. Iterative deepening and IDA^* reduce the space complexity at the cost of recomputing the elements on the frontier.

Lowest-cost-first, A^* and IDA^* searches are guaranteed to find a lowest-cost solution.

3.8   More Sophisticated Search

A number of refinements can be made to the preceding strategies. First, we present depth-first branch-and-bound search, which is guaranteed to find an optimal solution, and can take advantage of a heuristic function, like A^* search, but with the space advantages of depth-first search. We also present problem-reduction methods to break down a search problem into a number of smaller search problems, each of which may be much easier to solve. Finally, we show how dynamic programming can be used for finding paths from anywhere to a goal and for constructing heuristic functions.

3.8.1   Branch and Bound

Depth-first branch-and-bound search is a way to combine the space saving of depth-first search with heuristic information for finding optimal paths. It is particularly applicable when there are many paths to a goal. As in A^* search, the heuristic function $h(n)$ is non-negative and less than or equal to the cost of a lowest-cost path from n to a goal node.

The idea of a branch-and-bound search is to maintain the lowest-cost path to a goal found so far, and its cost. Suppose this cost is *bound*. If the search encounters a path p such that $cost(p) + h(p) \geq bound$, path p can be pruned. If a non-pruned path to a goal is found, it must be better than the previous best path. This new solution is remembered and *bound* is set to the cost of this new solution. The searcher then proceeds to search for a better solution.

Branch-and-bound search generates a sequence of ever-improving solutions. The final solution found is the optimal solution.

Branch-and-bound search is typically used with depth-first search, where the space saving of the depth-first search can be achieved. It can be implemented similarly to depth-bounded search, but where the bound is in terms of

1: **procedure** $DF\_branch\_and\_bound(G, s, goal, h, bound_0)$
2:    **Inputs**
3:       G: graph with nodes N and arcs A
4:       s: start node
5:       $goal$: Boolean function on nodes
6:       h: heuristic function on nodes
7:       $bound_0$: initial depth bound (can be ∞ if not specified)
8:    **Output**
9:       a lowest-cost path from s to a goal node if there is a solution with cost less than $bound_0$
10:       or $\perp$ if there is no solution with cost less than $bound_0$
11:    **Local**
12:       $best\_path$: path or $\perp$
13:       $bound$: non-negative real
14:       **procedure** $cbsearch(\langle n_0, \ldots, n_k \rangle)$
15:          **if** $cost(\langle n_0, \ldots, n_k \rangle) + h(n_k) < bound$ **then**
16:             **if** $goal(n_k)$ **then**
17:                $best\_path := \langle n_0, \ldots, n_k \rangle$
18:                $bound := cost(\langle n_0, \ldots, n_k \rangle)$
19:             **else**
20:                **for each** arc $\langle n_k, n \rangle \in A$ **do**
21:                    $cbsearch(\langle n_0, \ldots, n_k, n \rangle)$
22:    $best\_path := \perp$
23:    $bound := bound_0$
24:    $cbsearch(\langle s \rangle)$
25:    **return** $best\_path$

Figure 3.12: Depth-first branch-and-bound search

path cost and reduces as shorter paths are found. The algorithm remembers the lowest-cost path found and returns this path when the search finishes.

The algorithm is shown in Figure 3.12. The internal procedure *cbsearch*, for cost-bounded search, uses the global variables to provide information to the main procedure.

Initially, *bound* can be set to infinity, but it is often useful to set it to an overestimate, $bound_0$, of the path cost of an optimal solution. This algorithm will return an optimal solution – a lowest-cost path from the start node to a goal node – if there is a solution with cost less than the initial bound $bound_0$.

If the initial bound is slightly above the cost of a lowest-cost path, this algorithm can find an optimal path expanding no more arcs than A^* search without multiple-path pruning. This happens when the initial bound is such that the algorithm prunes any path that has a higher cost than a lowest-cost path. Once

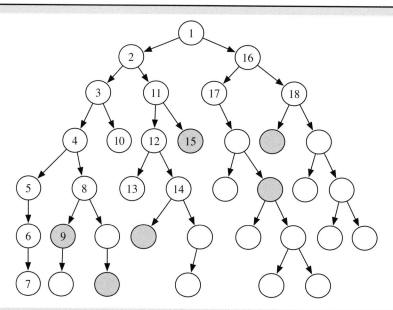

Figure 3.13: The paths expanded in depth-first branch-and-bound search. The shaded nodes are goal nodes.

it has found a path to the goal, it only explores paths whose f-value is lower than the path found. These are exactly the paths that A^* explores when it finds one solution.

If it returns $\bot$ when $bound_0 = \infty$, there are no solutions. If it returns $\bot$ when $bound_0$ is some finite value, it means no solution exists with cost less than $bound_0$. This algorithm can be combined with iterative deepening to increase the bound until either a solution is found or it can show there is no solution, using a method such as the use of *hit_depth_bound* in Figure 3.8 (page 96). See Exercise 3.13 (page 123).

Example 3.19 Consider the tree-shaped graph in Figure 3.13. The goal nodes are shaded. Suppose that each arc has cost 1, and there is no heuristic information (i.e., $h(n) = 0$ for each node n). In the algorithm, suppose $bound_0 = \infty$ and the depth-first search always selects the leftmost child first. This figure shows the order in which the nodes are checked to determine if they are a goal node. The nodes that are not numbered are not checked for being a goal node.

The subtree under the node numbered "5" does not have a goal and is explored fully (or up to depth $bound_0$ if it had a finite value). The ninth node checked is a goal node. It has a path cost of 5, and so the bound is set to 5. From then on, only paths with a cost of less than 5 are checked for being a solution. The fifteenth node checked is also a goal. It has a path cost of 3, and so the bound is reduced to 3. There are no other goal nodes found, and so the path to the node labeled 15 is returned. It is an optimal path. There is another optimal path that is pruned; the algorithm never checks the children of the node labeled with 18.

> If there were heuristic information, it could also be used to prune parts of the search space, as in A^* search.

Cycle pruning works well with depth-first branch and bound. Multiple-path pruning is not appropriate for depth-first branch and bound because storing the explored set defeats the space saving of the depth-first search. It is possible to have a bounded size explored set, for example, by only keeping the newest elements, which will enable some pruning.

3.8.2 Direction of Search

The size of the search space of the generic search algorithm, for a given pruning strategy, depends on the path length and the branching factor. Anything that can be done to reduce these can potentially give great savings.

If the following conditions hold:

- the set of goal nodes, $\{n : goal(n)\}$, is finite and can be generated

- for any node n the neighbors of n in the **inverse graph**, namely $\{n' : \langle n', n \rangle \in A\}$, can be generated

the graph search algorithm can either begin with the start node and search forward for a goal node, or begin with a goal node and search backward for the start node. In many applications the set of goal nodes or the inverse graph cannot easily be generated so backward search may not be feasible; indeed, sometimes the purpose of the search is to just find a goal node and not the path to it.

In **backward search**, the frontier starts with a node labeled *goal*. The neighbors of *goal* are the goal nodes, $\{n : goal(n)\}$. The neighbours of the other nodes are given in the in the inverse graph. The search stops when it finds the start node. Once *goal* is expanded, the frontier contains all of the goal nodes.

Forward search searches from the start node to the goal nodes in the original graph.

For those cases where the goal nodes and the inverse graph can be created, it may be more efficient to search in one direction than in the other. The size of the search space is typically exponential in the branching factor. It is often the case that forward and backward searches have different branching factors. A general principle is to search in the direction that has the smaller branching factor.

The following sections consider some other ways in which search efficiency can be improved for many search spaces.

Bidirectional Search

The idea of **bidirectional search** is to search forward from the start and backward from the goal simultaneously. When the two search frontiers intersect, the algorithm needs to construct a single path that extends from the start node through the frontier intersection to a goal node. It is a challenge to guarantee that the path found is optimal.

A new problem arises during a bidirectional search, namely ensuring that the two search frontiers actually meet. For example, a depth-first search in both directions is not likely to work at all unless one is extremely lucky because its small search frontiers are likely to pass each other by. Breadth-first search in both directions would be guaranteed to meet.

A combination of depth-first search in one direction and breadth-first search in the other would guarantee the required intersection of the search frontiers, but the choice of which to apply in which direction may be difficult. The decision depends on the cost of saving the breadth-first frontier and searching it to check when the depth-first method will intersect one of its elements.

There are situations where a bidirectional search results in substantial savings. For example, if the forward and backward branching factors of the search space are both b, and the goal is at depth k, then breadth-first search will take time proportional to b^k, whereas a symmetric bidirectional search will take time proportional to $2b^{k/2}$. This is an exponential saving in time, even though the time complexity is still exponential.

Island-Driven Search

One of the ways that search may be made more efficient is to identify a limited number of places where the forward search and backward search could meet. For example, in searching for a path from two rooms on different floors, it may be appropriate to constrain the search to first go to the elevator on one level, go to the appropriate level and then go from the elevator to the goal room. Intuitively, these designated positions are **islands** in the search graph, which are constrained to be on a solution path from the start node to a goal node.

When islands are specified, an agent can decompose the search problem into several search problems, for example, one from the initial room to the elevator, one from the elevator on one level to the elevator on the other level, and one from the elevator to the destination room. This reduces the search space by having three simpler problems to solve. Having smaller problems helps to reduce the combinatorial explosion of large searches and is an example of how extra knowledge about a problem is used to improve efficiency of search.

To find a path between s and g using islands:

1. identify a set of islands $i_0, ..., i_k$
2. find paths from s to i_0, from i_{j-1} to i_j for each j, and from i_k to g.

Each of these searching problems should be correspondingly simpler than the general problem and, therefore, easier to solve.

The identification of islands is extra knowledge which may be beyond that which is in the graph. The use of inappropriate islands may make the problem more difficult (or even impossible to solve). It may also be possible to identify an alternate decomposition of the problem by choosing a different set of islands and search through the space of possible islands. Whether this works in practice depends on the details of the problem. Island search sacrifices optimality unless one is able to guarantee that the isands are on an optimal path.

Searching in a Hierarchy of Abstractions

The notion of islands can be used to define problem-solving strategies that work at multiple levels of detail or multiple levels of abstraction.

The idea of searching in a hierarchy of abstractions first involves abstracting the problem, leaving out as many details as possible. A solution to the abstract problem can be seen as a partial solution to the original problem. For example, the problem of getting from one room to another requires the use of many instances of turning, but an agent would like to reason about the problem at a level of abstraction where the steering details are omitted. It is expected that an appropriate abstraction solves the problem in broad strokes, leaving only minor problems to be solved.

One way this can be implemented is to generalize island-driven search to search over possible islands. Once a solution is found at the island level, this information provides a heuristic function for lower levels. Information that is found at lower level can inform higher levels by changing the arc lengths. For example, the higher level may assume a particular distance between exit doors, but a lower-level search could find a better estimate of the actual distance.

The effectiveness of searching in a hierarchy of abstractions depends on how one decomposes and abstracts the problem to be solved. Once the problems are abstracted and decomposed, any of the search methods could be used to solve them. It is not easy, however, to recognize useful abstractions and problem decompositions.

3.8.3   Dynamic Programming

Dynamic programming is a general method for optimization that involves computing and storing partial solutions to problems. Solutions that have already been found can be retrieved rather than being recomputed. Dynamic programming algorithms are used throughout AI and computer science.

Dynamic programming can be used for finding paths in finite graphs by constructing a cost-to-goal function for nodes that gives the exact cost of a minimal-cost path from the node to a goal.

Let $cost\_to\_goal(n)$ be the actual cost of a lowest-cost path from node n to a goal; $cost\_to\_goal(n)$ can be defined as

$$cost\_to\_goal(n) = \begin{cases} 0 & \text{if } is\_goal(n), \\ \min_{\langle n,m \rangle \in A}(cost(\langle n,m \rangle) + cost\_to\_goal(m)) & \text{otherwise.} \end{cases}$$

The general idea is to build a table offline of the $cost\_to\_goal(n)$ value for each node. This is done by carrying out a lowest-cost-first search, with multiple-path pruning, from the goal nodes in the inverse graph (page 113), which is the graph with all arcs reversed. Rather than having a goal to search for, the dynamic programming algorithm records the $cost\_to\_goal$ values for each node found. It uses the inverse graph to compute the costs from each node to the goal and not the costs from the goal to each node. In essence, dynamic programming works backward from the goal, building the lowest-cost paths to the goal from each node in the graph.

Example 3.20   For the graph given in Figure 3.2 (page 83), $r123$ is a goal, so

$cost\_to\_goal(r123) = 0.$

Continuing with a lowest-cost-first search from $r123$:

$cost\_to\_goal(o123) = 4$

$cost\_to\_goal(o119) = 13$

$cost\_to\_goal(o109) = 29$

$cost\_to\_goal(b4) = 36$

$cost\_to\_goal(b2) = 39$

$cost\_to\_goal(o103) = 41$

$cost\_to\_goal(b3) = 43$

$cost\_to\_goal(b1) = 45$

At this stage the backward search halts. Notice that, if a node does not have a $cost\_to\_goal$ value, there is no path to the goal from that node.

A **policy** is a specification of which arc to take from each node. An **optimal policy** is a policy such that the cost of following that policy is not worse than the cost of following any other policy. Given a $cost\_to\_goal$ function, which is computed offline, a policy can be computed as follows: From node n it should go to a neighbor m that minimizes $cost(\langle n,m \rangle) + cost\_to\_goal(m)$. This policy will take the agent from any node to a goal along a lowest-cost path.

Either this neighbor can be recorded for all nodes offline, and the mapping from node to node is provided to the agent for online action, or the $cost\_to\_goal$ function is given to the agent and each neighbor can be computed online.

Dynamic programming takes time and space linear in the size of the graph to build the $cost\_to\_goal$ table. Once the $cost\_to\_goal$ function has been built, even if the policy has not been recorded, the time to determine which arc is optimal depends only on the number of neighbors for the node.

Example 3.21 Given the cost-to-goal of Example 3.20 for the goal of getting to $r123$, if the agent is at $o103$, it compares $4 + 43$ (the cost of going via $b3$) with $12 + 29$ (the cost of going straight to $o109$) and can determine to go next to $o109$. It does not need to consider going to ts as it knows there is no path from ts to $r123$.

Dynamic programming has the advantage that it specifies what to do for every node, and so can be used given a goal for any starting position.

Example 3.22 In route planning (see Example 3.1 (page 78)), we also might want to find a robust solution that can allow for dynamic online replanning by quickly adapting when the user deviates (intentionally or unintentionally) from the best route. It should be able to give the best route from the user's current location and driving direction.

It is even possible to adapt A^* for dynamic programming for cases where there is a known goal, and an initial starting position, but where the agent can deviate from the optimal path. One way this can be done is to carry out an A^* search (with multiple-path pruning) from the destination to the current location, in the inverse graph. When the user deviates from an optimal route, the other paths to the goal have often been explored, or can be generated to find a path from the current location.

Dynamic programming can be used to construct heuristic functions which can be used for A^* and branch-and-bound searches. One way to build a heuristic function is to simplify the problem (e.g., by leaving out some details) until the simplified problem is small enough. Dynamic programming can be used to find the cost of an optimal path to a goal in the simplified problem. This information forms a **pattern database** that can then be used as a heuristic for the original problem.

Dynamic programming is useful when

- the goal nodes are explicit (the previous methods only assumed a function that recognizes goal nodes)
- a lowest-cost path is needed
- the graph is finite and small enough to be able to store the *cost_to_goal* value for each node
- the goal does not change very often, and
- the policy is used a number of times for each goal, so that the cost of generating the *cost_to_goal* values can be amortized over many instances of the problem.

The main problems with dynamic programming are that

| Optimality of the A^* algorithm |

A search algorithm is **optimal** if no other search algorithm uses less time or space or expands fewer paths, while still guaranteeing solution quality. The optimal search algorithm would be one that picks the correct node at each choice. However, this specification is not effective because we cannot directly implement it. Whether such an algorithm is possible is related to whether $P \neq NP$. There seems to be a statement that can be proved.

Optimality of A^*: Among search algorithms that only use arc costs and a consistent heuristic, no algorithm expands fewer paths than A^* and guarantees to find a lowest-cost path.

Proof sketch: Given only the information about the arc costs and the heuristic information, unless the algorithm has expanded each path p, where $f(p)$ is less than the cost of an optimal path, it does not know whether p leads to a lower-cost path. More formally, suppose an algorithm A' found a path for a problem P where some path p was not expanded such that $f(p)$ was less than the solution found. Suppose there was another problem P', which was the same as P, except that there really was a path via p with cost $f(p)$. The algorithm A' cannot tell P' from P, because it did not expand the path p, so it would report the same solution for P' as for P, but the solution found for P would not be optimal for P' because the solution found has a higher cost than the path via p. Therefore, an algorithm is not guaranteed to find a lowest-cost path unless it explores all paths with f-values less than the value of an optimal path; that is, it must explore all the paths that A^* explores.

Counterexample: Although this proof seems reasonable, there are algorithms that explore fewer nodes. Consider an algorithm that does a forward A^*-like search and a backward dynamic programming search, where the steps are interleaved in some way (e.g., by alternating between the forward steps and the backward steps). The backward search builds a table of $cost\_to\_goal(n)$ values of the actual discovered cost from n to a goal, and it maintains a bound b, where it has explored all paths of cost less than b to a goal. The forward search uses a priority queue on $cost(p) + c(n)$, where n is the node at the end of the path p, and $c(n)$ is $cost\_to\_goal(n)$ if it has been computed; otherwise, $c(n)$ is $max(h(n), b)$. The intuition is that, if a path exists from the end of path p to a goal node, either it uses a path that has been discovered by the backward search or it uses a path that costs at least b. This algorithm is guaranteed to find a lowest-cost path and often expands fewer paths than A^* (see Exercise 3.11 (page 123)).

Conclusion: Having a counterexample would seem to mean that the optimality of A^* is false. However, the proof has some appeal and should not be dismissed outright. A^* is not optimal out of the class of all algorithms, but the proof is correct for the class of algorithms that only do forward search (with conditions related to tie-breaking). Lakatos [1976] discusses how proofs and refutations are common. Dechter and Pearl [1985] give a detailed analysis of conditions when A^* is optimal.

- it only works when the graph is finite and the table can be made small enough to fit into memory
- an agent must recompute a policy for each different goal, and
- the time and space required is linear in the size of the graph, where the graph size for finite graphs is typically exponential in the path length.

3.9   Review

The following are the main points you should have learned from this chapter:

- Many problems can be abstracted to the problem of finding paths in graphs.
- Breadth-first and depth-first searches can find paths in graphs without any extra knowledge beyond the graph.
- A^* search can use a heuristic function that estimates the cost from a node to a goal. If graph is not pathological (see Proposition 3.2 (page 108)) and the heuristic is admissible, A^* is guaranteed to find a lowest-cost path to a goal if one exists.
- Multiple-path pruning and cycle pruning can be used to make search more efficient.
- Iterative deepening and depth-first branch-and-bound searches can be used to find lowest-cost paths with less memory than methods, such as A^*, which store multiple paths.
- When graphs are small enough to store the nodes, dynamic programming records the actual cost of a lowest-cost path from each node to the goal, which can be used to find the next arc in an optimal path.

3.10   References and Further Reading

There is a vast literature on search techniques in operations research, computer science, and AI. Search was seen early on as one of the foundations of AI. The AI literature emphasizes the use of heuristics in search.

Basic search algorithms are discussed in Nilsson [1971]. For a detailed analysis of heuristic search see Pearl [1984]. The A^* algorithm was developed by Hart et al. [1968]. The optimality of A^* is investigated by Dechter and Pearl [1985]. Breadth-first search was invented by Moore [1959]. Lowest-cost-first search with multiple path pruning is known as Dijkstra's algorithm [Dijkstra, 1959]. Depth-first iterative deepening is described in Korf [1985]. Branch-and-bound search was developed in the operations research community and is described in Lawler and Wood [1966].

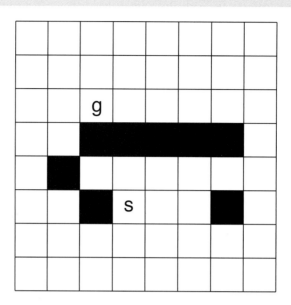

Figure 3.14: A grid-searching problem

Dynamic programming is a general algorithm that will be used as a dual to search algorithms in other parts of this book. See Cormen et al. [2001] for more details on the general class of dynamic programming algorithms.

The idea of using pattern databases as a source of heuristics for A^* search was proposed by Culberson and Schaeffer [1998] and further developed by Felner et al. [2004]. Minsky [1961] discussed islands and problem reduction.

3.11   Exercises

Exercise 3.1   Comment on the following quote: "One of the main goals of AI should be to build general heuristics applicable to any graph-searching problem."

Exercise 3.2   Which of the path-finding search procedures are fair in the sense that any element on the frontier will eventually be chosen? Consider this question for finite graphs without cycles, finite graphs with cycles, and infinite graphs (with finite branching factors).

Exercise 3.3   Consider the problem of finding a path in the grid shown in Figure 3.14 from the position s to the position g. A piece can move on the grid horizontally or vertically, one square at a time. No step may be made into a forbidden shaded area.

(a) On the grid shown in Figure 3.14, number the nodes expanded (in order) for a depth-first search from s to g, given that the order of the operators is up, left, right, and down. Assume there is cycle pruning. What is the first path found?

(b) On a copy of the same grid, number the nodes expanded, in order, for a greedy best-first search from s to g. Manhattan distance should be used as the evaluation function. The Manhattan distance between two points is the distance in the x-direction plus the distance in the y-direction. It corresponds to the distance traveled along city streets arranged in a grid. Assume multiple-path pruning. What is the first path found?

(c) On a copy of the same grid, number the nodes expanded, in order, for a heuristic depth-first search from s to g, given Manhattan distance as the evaluation function. Assume cycle pruning. What is the path found?

(d) Number the nodes in order for an A^* search, with multiple-path pruning, for the same grid. What is the path found?

(e) Show how to solve the same problem using dynamic programming. Give the *cost_to_goal* value for each node, and show which path is found.

(f) Based on this experience, discuss which algorithms are best suited for this problem.

(g) Suppose that the grid extended infinitely in all directions. That is, there is no boundary, but s, g, and the blocks are in the same positions relative to each other. Which methods would no longer find a path? Which would be the best method, and why?

Exercise 3.4 This question investigates using graph searching to design video presentations. Suppose there exists a database of video segments, together with their length in seconds and the topics covered, set up as follows:

Segment	Length	Topics covered
seg0	10	[welcome]
seg1	30	[skiing, views]
seg2	50	[welcome, artificial_intelligence, robots]
seg3	40	[graphics, dragons]
seg4	50	[skiing, robots]

Represent a node as a pair:

$$\langle To\_Cover, Segs \rangle,$$

where *Segs* is a list of segments that must be in the presentation, and *To_Cover* is a list of topics that also must be covered. Assume that none of the segments in *Segs* cover any of the topics in *To_Cover*.

The neighbors of a node are obtained by first selecting a topic from *To_Cover*. There is a neighbor for each segment that covers the selected topic. [Part of this exercise is to think about the exact structure of these neighbors.]

For example, given the aforementioned database of segments, the neighbors of the node $\langle [welcome, robots], [] \rangle$, assuming that *welcome* was selected, are $\langle [], [seg2] \rangle$ and $\langle [robots], [seg0] \rangle$.

Thus, each arc adds exactly one segment but can cover one or more topics. Suppose that the cost of the arc is equal to the time of the segment added.

The goal is to design a presentation that covers all of the topics in *MustCover*. The starting node is $\langle MustCover, [] \rangle$, and the goal nodes are of the form $\langle [], Presentation \rangle$. The cost of the path from a start node to a goal node is the time of the presentation. Thus, an optimal presentation is a shortest presentation that covers all of the topics in *MustCover*.

(a) Suppose that the goal is to cover the topics $[welcome, skiing, robots]$ and the algorithm always select the leftmost topic to find the neighbors for each node. Draw the search space expanded for a lowest-cost-first search until the first solution is found. This should show all nodes expanded, which node is a goal node, and the frontier when the goal was found.

(b) Give a non-trivial heuristic function h that is admissible. [Note that $h(n) = 0$ for all n is the trivial heuristic function.] Does it satisfy the monotone restriction for a heuristic function?

Exercise 3.5 Draw two different graphs, indicating start and goal nodes, for which forward search is better in one and backward search is better in the other.

Exercise 3.6 The A^* algorithm does not define what happens when multiple elements on the frontier have the same f-value. Compare the following tie-breaking conventions by first conjecturing which will work better, and then testing it on some examples. Try it on some examples where there are multiple optimal paths to a goal (such as finding a path from one corner of a rectangular grid to the far corner of a grid). Of the paths on the frontier with the same minimum f-value, select one:

  i) uniformly at random
 ii) that has been on the frontier the longest
iii) that was most recently added to the frontier.
 iv) with the smallest h-value
  v) with the least cost

The last two may require other tie-breaking conventions when the cost and h values are equal.

Exercise 3.7 What happens if the heuristic function is not admissible, but is still nonnegative? What can we say about the path found by A^* if the heuristic function

(a) is less than $1 + \epsilon$ times the least-cost path (e.g., is less than 10% greater than the cost of the least-cost path)

(b) is less than δ more than the least-cost path (e.g., is less than 10 units plus the cost of the optimal path)?

Develop a hypothesis about what would happen and show it empirically or prove your hypothesis. Does it change if multiple-path pruning is in effect or not?

Does loosening the heuristic in either of these ways improve efficiency? Try A^* search where the heuristic is multiplied by a factor $1 + \epsilon$, or where a cost δ is added to the heuristic, for a number of graphs. Compare these on the time taken (or the number of nodes expanded) and the cost of the solution found for a number of values of ϵ or δ.

Exercise 3.8 How can depth-first branch-and-bound be modified to find a path with a cost that is not more than, say, 10% greater than the least-cost path. How does this algorithm compare to A^* from the previous question?

Exercise 3.9 The overhead for iterative deepening with $b - 1$ on the denominator (page 97) is not a good approximation when $b \approx 1$. Give a better estimate of the complexity of iterative deepening when $b \approx 1$. (Hint: think about the case when $b = 1$.) How does this compare with A^* for such graphs? Suggest a way that iterative deepening can have a lower overhead when the branching factor is close to 1.

Exercise 3.10 Bidirectional search must be able to determine when the frontiers intersect. For each of the following pairs of searches specify how to determine when the frontiers intersect.

(a) Breadth-first search and depth-bounded depth-first search.

(b) Iterative deepening search and depth-bounded depth-first search.

(c) A^* and depth-bounded depth-first search.

(d) A^* and A^*.

Exercise 3.11 Consider the algorithm sketched in the counterexample of the box on page 118.

(a) When can the algorithm stop? (Hint: it does not have to wait until the forward search finds a path to a goal.)

(b) What data structures should be kept?

(c) Specify the algorithm in full.

(d) Show that it finds the optimal path.

(e) Give an example where it expands (many) fewer nodes than A^*.

Exercise 3.12 Give a statement of the optimality of A^* that specifies a class of algorithms for which A^* is optimal. Give the formal proof.

Exercise 3.13 The depth-first branch-and-bound of Figure 3.12 (page 111) is like a depth-bounded search in that it only finds a solution if there is a solution with cost less than *bound*. Show how this can be combined with an iterative deepening search to increase the depth bound if there is no solution for a particular depth bound. This algorithm must return $\perp$ in a finite graph if there is no solution. The algorithm should allow the bound to be incremented by an arbitrary amount and still return an optimal (least-cost) solution when there is a solution.

Chapter 4

Reasoning with Constraints

Every task involves constraint,
Solve the thing without complaint;
There are magic links and chains
Forged to loose our rigid brains.
Structures, strictures, though they bind,
Strangely liberate the mind.

– James Falen

Instead of reasoning explicitly in terms of states, it is typically better to describe states in terms of **features** and to reason in terms of these features. Features are described using **variables**. Often features are not independent and there are **hard constraints** that specify legal combinations of assignments of values to variables. As Falen's elegant poem emphasizes, the mind discovers and exploits constraints to solve tasks. In planning and scheduling an agent assigns a time for each action. These assignments must satisfy constraints on the order actions can be carried out and constraints specifying that the actions achieve a goal. Preferences over assignments are specified in terms of **soft constraints**. This chapter shows how to generate assignments that satisfy hard constraints and optimize soft constraints.

4.1 Possible Worlds, Variables, and Constraints

4.1.1 Variables and Worlds

Constraint satisfaction problems are described in terms of variables and possible worlds. A **possible world** is a possible way the world (the real world or some imaginary world) could be.

Possible worlds are described by algebraic variables. An **algebraic variable** is a symbol used to denote features of possible worlds. For this chapter, we refer to an algebraic variable simply as a **variable**. Algebraic variables are written starting with an upper-case letter. Each algebraic variable X has an associated **domain**, $dom(X)$, which is the set of values the variable can take.

A **discrete variable** is one whose domain is finite or countably infinite. A **binary variable** is a discrete variable with two values in its domain. One particular case of a binary variable is a **Boolean variable**, which is a variable with domain $\{true, false\}$. We can also have variables that are not discrete; for example, a variable whose domain corresponds to the real line or an interval of the real line is a **continuous variable**.

Given a set of variables, an **assignment** on the set of variables is a function from the variables into the domains of the variables. We write an assignment on $\{X_1, X_2, \ldots, X_k\}$ as $\{X_1=v_1, X_2=v_2, \ldots, X_k=v_k\}$, where v_i is in $dom(X_i)$. This assignment specifies that, for each i, variable X_i is assigned value v_i. A variable can only be assigned one value in an assignment. A **total assignment** assigns all of the variables. Assignments do not have to be total, but may be partial.

A **possible world** is defined to be a total assignment. That is, it is a function from variables into values that assigns a value to every variable. If world w is the assignment $\{X_1=v_1, X_2=v_2, \ldots, X_k=v_k\}$, we say that variable X_i has value v_i in world w.

Example 4.1   The variable *Class_time* may denote the starting time for a particular class. The domain of *Class_time* may be the following set of possible times:

$$dom(Class\_time) = \{8, 9, 10, 11, 12, 1, 2, 3, 4, 5\}.$$

The variable *Height_joe* may refer to the height of a particular person at a particular time and have as its domain the set of real numbers, in some range, that represent the height in centimeters. *Raining* may be a random variable with domain $\{true, false\}$, which has value *true* if it is raining at a particular time.

The assignment $\{Class\_time=11, Height\_joe=165, Raining=false\}$ specifies that the class starts at 11, Joe is 165cm tall and it is not raining.

Example 4.2   In the electrical environment of Figure 1.8 (page 38), there may be a variable for the position of each switch that specifies whether the switch is up or down. There may be a variable for each light that specifies whether it is lit or not. There may be a variable for each component specifying whether it is working properly or if it is broken. Some variables that the following examples use include:

- S_1_pos is a binary variable denoting the position of switch s_1 with domain $\{up, down\}$, where $S_1\_pos=up$ means switch s_1 is up, and $S_1\_pos=down$ means switch s_1 is down.

Symbols and Semantics

Algebraic variables are symbols.

Internal to a computer, a **symbol** is just a sequence of bits that is distinguished from other symbols. Some symbols have a fixed interpretation; for example, symbols that represent numbers and symbols that represent characters are predefined in most computer languages. Symbols with a meaning outside of the program (as opposed to variables in the program), but without a predefined meaning in the language, can be defined in many programming languages. In Java they are called *enumeration types*. Lisp refers to them as *atoms*. Python 3.4 introduced a symbol type called *enum*, but Python's strings are often used as symbols. Usually, symbols are implemented as indexes into a symbol table that gives the name to print out. The only operation performed on these symbols is equality to determine whether two symbols are the same. This can be implemented by comparing the indexes in the symbol table.

To a **user** of a computer, symbols have meanings. A person who inputs constraints or interprets the output of a program associates meanings with the symbols making up the constraints or the outputs. He or she associates a symbol with some concept or object in the world. For example, the variable *SamsHeight*, to the computer, is just a sequence of bits. It has no relationship to *SamsWeight* or *AlsHeight*. To a person, this variable may mean the height, in particular units, of a particular person at a particular time.

The meaning associated with a variable–value pair must satisfy the **clarity principle**: an **omniscient agent** – a fictitious agent who knows the truth and the meanings associated with all of the symbols – should be able to determine the value of each variable. For example, the *height of Hagrid* only satisfies the clarity principle if the particular person being referred to and the particular time are specified as well as the units. For example, one may want to reason about the height, in centimeters, of Hagrid in a particular scene at the start of the second Harry Potter movie. This is different from the height, in inches, of Hagrid at the end of the third movie (although they are, of course, related). To refer to Hagrid's height at two different times, you need two variables.

You should have a consistent meaning for any symbols you use. When stating constraints, you must have the same meaning for the same variable and the same values, and you can use this meaning to interpret the output.

The bottom line is that symbols have meanings because you give them meanings. For this chapter, assume that the computer does not know what the symbols mean. A computer can know what a symbol means if it perceives and manipulates the environment.

- S_1_st is a discrete variable denoting the status of switch s_1 with domain $\{ok, upside\_down, short, intermittent, broken\}$, where $S_1\_st=ok$ means switch s_1 is working normally, $S_1\_st=upside\_down$ means it is installed upside down, $S_1\_st=short$ means it is shorted and it allows electricity to flow whether it is up or down, $S_1\_st=intermittent$ means it is working intermittently, and $S_1\_st=broken$ means it is broken and does not allow electricity to flow.

- *Number_of_broken_switches* is an integer-valued variable denoting the number of switches that are broken.

- *Current_w_1* is a real-valued variable denoting the current, in amps, flowing through wire w_1. *Current_w_1*=1.3 means there are 1.3 amps flowing through wire w_1. We also allow inequalities between variables and constants; for example, *Current_w_1* $\geq$ 1.3 is true when there are at least 1.3 amps flowing through wire w_1.

A world specifies the position of every switch, the status of every device, and so on. For example, a world may be described as switch 1 is up, switch 2 is down, fuse 1 is okay, wire 3 is broken, etc.

Example 4.3 A classic example of a constraint satisfaction problem is a crossword puzzle. There are two different representations of crossword puzzles in terms of variables:

- In one representation, the variables are the numbered squares with the direction of the word (down or across), and the domains are the set of possible words that can be used. For example, *one_across* could be a variable with domain {'ant', 'big', 'bus', 'car', 'has'}. A possible world corresponds to an assignment of a word for each of the variables.

- In another representation of a crossword, the variables are the individual squares and the domain of each variable is the set of letters in the alphabet. For example, the top-left square could be a variable *p00* with domain $\{a,\dots,z\}$. A possible world corresponds to an assignment of a letter to each square.

Example 4.4 A trading agent, in planning a trip for a group of tourists, may be required to schedule a given set of activities. There could be two variables for each activity: one for the date, for which the domain is the set of possible days for the activity, and one for the location, for which the domain is the set of possible towns where it may occur. A possible world corresponds to an assignment of a date and a town for each activity.

An alternative representation may have the days as the variables, with domains the set of possible activity–location pairs.

The number of worlds is the product of the number of values in the domains of the variables.

Example 4.5   If there are two variables, A with domain $\{0,1,2\}$ and B with domain $\{true, false\}$, there are six possible worlds, which we name $w_0, \dots, w_5$ as follows

- $w_0 = \{A=0, B=true\}$
- $w_1 = \{A=0, B=false\}$
- $w_2 = \{A=1, B=true\}$
- $w_3 = \{A=1, B=false\}$
- $w_4 = \{A=2, B=true\}$
- $w_5 = \{A=2, B=false\}$

If there are n variables, each with domain size d, there are d^n possible worlds.

One main advantage of reasoning in terms of variables is the computational savings. Many worlds can be described by a few variables:

- 10 binary variables can describe $2^{10} = 1,024$ worlds

- 20 binary variables can describe $2^{20} = 1,048,576$ worlds

- 30 binary variables can describe $2^{30} = 1,073,741,824$ worlds

- 100 binary variables can describe $2^{100} = 1,267,650,600,228,229,401,496,$ $703,205,376$ worlds.

Reasoning in terms of thirty variables may be easier than reasoning in terms of more than a billion worlds. One hundred variables is not that many, but reasoning in terms of more than 2^{100} worlds explicitly is not possible. Many real-world problems have thousands, if not millions, of variables.

4.1.2   Constraints

In many domains, not all possible assignments of values to variables are permissible. A **hard constraint**, or simply **constraint**, specifies legal combinations of assignments of values to some of the variables.

A **scope** is a set of variables. A **relation** on a scope S is a function from assignments on S to $\{true, false\}$. That is, it specifies whether each assignment is true or false. A **constraint** c is a scope S and a relation on S. A constraint is said to **involve** each of the variables in its scope.

A constraint can be evaluated on any assignment that extends its scope. Consider constraint c on S. Assignment A on S', where $S \subseteq S'$, **satisfies** c if A, restricted to S, is mapped to $true$ by the relation. Otherwise, the constraint is **violated** by the assignment.

A possible world w **satisfies** a set of constraints if, for every constraint, the values assigned in w to the variables in the scope of the constraint satisfy the constraint. In this case, we say that the possible world is a **model** of the constraints. That is, a **model** is a possible world that satisfies all of the constraints.

Constraints are defined either by their **intension**, in terms of formulas, or by their **extension**, listing all the assignments that are true. Constraints defined extensionally can be seen as relations of legal assignments as in relational databases (page 747).

A **unary constraint** is a constraint on a single variable (e.g., $B \leq 3$). A **binary constraint** is a constraint over a pair of variables (e.g., $A \leq B$). In general, a k-ary constraint has a scope of size k. For example, $A + B = C$ is a 3-ary (ternary) constraint.

Example 4.6 Suppose a robot needs to schedule a set of activities for a manufacturing process, involving casting, milling, drilling, and bolting. Each activity has a set of possible times at which it may start. The robot has to satisfy various constraints arising from prerequisite requirements and resource use limitations. For each activity there is a variable that represents the time that it starts. For example, it could use D to represent the start time for the drilling, B for the start time of the bolting, and C the start time for the casting. Some constraints are that drilling must start before bolting, which translates into the constraint $D < B$. If casting and drilling must not start at the same time, this corresponds to the constraint $C \neq D$. If bolting must start exactly 3 time units after casting starts this corresponds to the constraint $B = C + 3$.

Example 4.7 Consider a constraint on the possible dates for three activities. Let A, B, and C be variables that represent the date of each activity. Suppose the domain of each variable is $\{1, 2, 3, 4\}$.

A constraint with scope $\{A, B, C\}$ could be described by its **intension**, using a logical formula to specify the legal assignments, such as

$$(A \leq B) \wedge (B < 3) \wedge (B < C) \wedge \neg(A = B \wedge C \leq 3),$$

where $\wedge$ means *and*, and $\neg$ means *not*. This formula says that A is on the same date or before B, and B is before day 3, B is before C, and it cannot be that A and B are on the same date and C is on or before day 3.

This constraint could instead have its relation defined its **extension**, as a table specifying the legal assignments:

A	B	C
2	2	4
1	1	4
1	2	3
1	2	4

The first assignment is $\{A=2, B=2, C=4\}$, which assigns A the value 2, B the value 2, and C the value 4. There are four legal assignments of the variables.

The assignment $\{A=1, B=2, C=3, D=3, E=1\}$ satisfies this constraint because that assignment restricted to the scope of the relation, namely $\{A=1, B=2, C=3\}$, is one of the legal assignments in the table.

Example 4.8 Consider the constraints for the two representations of crossword puzzles of Example 4.3 (page 128):

- For the case in which the domains are words, the constraint is that the letters where a pair of words intersect must be the same.

- For the representation in which the domains are the letters, the constraint is that each contiguous sequence of letters must form a legal word.

4.1.3 Constraint Satisfaction Problems

A **constraint satisfaction problem** (CSP) consists of

- a set of variables,
- a domain for each variable, and
- a set of constraints.

A finite CSP has a finite set of variables and a finite domain for each variable. Some of the methods considered in this chapter only work for finite CSPs, although some are designed for infinite, even continuous, domains.

Example 4.9 Suppose the delivery robot must carry out a number of delivery activities, a, b, c, d, and e. Suppose that each activity happens at any of times 1, 2, 3, or 4. Let A be the variable representing the time that activity a will occur, and similarly for the other activities. The variable domains, which represent possible times for each of the deliveries, are

$$dom(A) = \{1,2,3,4\}, \quad dom(B) = \{1,2,3,4\}, \quad dom(C) = \{1,2,3,4\},$$
$$dom(D) = \{1,2,3,4\}, \quad dom(E) = \{1,2,3,4\}.$$

Suppose the following constraints must be satisfied:

$$\{(B \neq 3), (C \neq 2), (A \neq B), (B \neq C), (C < D), (A = D),$$
$$(E < A), (E < B), (E < C), (E < D), (B \neq D)\}$$

It is instructive for you to try to find a model for this example; try to assign a value to each variable that satisfies these constraints.

Given a CSP, a number of tasks are useful:

- Determine whether or not there is a model.
- Find a model.
- Count the number of models.
- Enumerate all of the models.
- Find a best model, given a measure of how good models are.
- Determine whether some statement holds in all the models.

The multidimensional aspect of CSPs, where each variable is a separate dimension, makes these tasks difficult to solve, but also provides structure that can be exploited.

This chapter mostly considers the problem of finding a model. Some of the methods can also determine if there is no model, and can be adapted to finding all models. What may be more surprising is that some of the methods can find a model if one exists, but they cannot determine that there is no model if none exists.

CSPs are very common, so it is worth trying to find relatively efficient ways to solve them. Determining whether there is a model for a CSP with finite domains is NP-complete (see box on page 88) and no known algorithms exist to solve such problems that do not use exponential time in the worst case. However, just because a problem is NP-complete does not mean that all instances are difficult to solve. Many instances have structure to exploit.

4.2   Generate-and-Test Algorithms

A finite CSP could be solved by an exhaustive generate-and-test algorithm. The **assignment space**, D, is the set of total assignments. The algorithm returns one model or all models.

The **generate-and-test** algorithm to find one model is as follows: check each total assignment in turn; if an assignment is found that satisfies all of the constraints, return that assignment. A generate-and-test algorithm to find all models is the same except, instead of returning the first model found, it saves all of the models found.

Example 4.10   In Example 4.9 the assignment space is

$$D = \{\{A{=}1, B{=}1, C{=}1, D{=}1, E{=}1\},$$
$$\{A{=}1, B{=}1, C{=}1, D{=}1, E{=}2\}, \ldots,$$
$$\{A{=}4, B{=}4, C{=}4, D{=}4, E{=}4\}\}.$$

In this case there are $|D| = 4^5 = 1,024$ different assignments to be tested. If there were 15 variables instead of 5, there would be 4^{15}, which is about a billion, assignments to test. This method could not work for 30 variables.

If each of the n variable domains has size d, then D has d^n elements. If there are e constraints, the total number of constraints tested is $O(ed^n)$. As n becomes large, this very quickly becomes intractable, and so we must find alternative solution methods.

4.3 Solving CSPs Using Search

Generate-and-test algorithms assign values to all variables before checking the constraints. Because individual constraints only involve a subset of the variables, some constraints can be tested before all of the variables have been assigned values. If a partial assignment is inconsistent with a constraint, any total assignment that extends the partial assignment will also be inconsistent.

Example 4.11 In the delivery scheduling problem of Example 4.9 (page 131), the assignments $A=1$ and $B=1$ are inconsistent with the constraint $A \neq B$ regardless of the values of the other variables. If the variables A and B are assigned values first, this inconsistency can be discovered before any values are assigned to C, D, or E, thus saving a large amount of work.

An alternative to generate-and-test algorithms is to construct a search space for the search strategies of the previous chapter to use. The graph to search is defined as follows:

- The nodes are assignments of values to some subset of the variables.

- The neighbors of a node n are obtained by selecting a variable Y that is not assigned in node n and by having a neighbor for each assignment of a value to Y that does not violate any constraint.

  Suppose node n is the assignment $\{X_1=v_1,\ldots,X_k=v_k\}$. To find the neighbors of n, select a variable Y that is not in the set $\{X_1,\ldots,X_k\}$. For each value $y_i \in dom(Y)$, where $X_1=v_1,\ldots,X_k=v_k, Y=y_i$ is consistent with the constraints, the node $\{X_1=v_1,\ldots,X_k=v_k, Y=y_i\}$ is a neighbor of n.

- The start node is the empty assignment that does not assign a value to any variables.

- A goal node is a node that assigns a value to every variable. Note that this only exists if the assignment is consistent with all of the constraints.

In this case, it is not the path from the start node that is of interest, but the goal nodes.

Example 4.12 Suppose you have a very simple CSP with the variables A, B, and C, each with domain $\{1,2,3,4\}$. Suppose the constraints are $A < B$ and $B < C$. A possible search tree is shown in Figure 4.1 (on the next page). In this figure, a node corresponds to all of the assignments from the root to that node. The potential nodes that are pruned because they violate constraints are labeled with ✗.

The leftmost ✗ corresponds to the assignment $A=1$, $B=1$. This violates the $A < B$ constraint, and so it is pruned.

This CSP has four solutions. The leftmost one is $A=1$, $B=2$, $C=3$. The size of the search tree, and thus the efficiency of the algorithm, depends on which variable is selected at each time. A static ordering, such as always splitting on

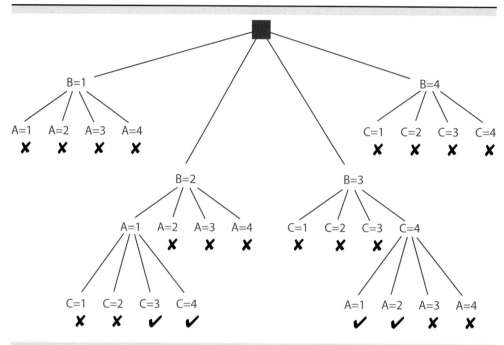

Figure 4.1: Search tree for the CSP of Example 4.12

A then *B* then *C*, is usually less efficient than the dynamic ordering used here, but it might be more difficult to find the best dynamic ordering than to find the best static ordering. The set of answers is the same regardless of the variable ordering.

There would be $4^3 = 64$ total assignments tested in a generate-and-test algorithm. For the search method, there are 8 total assignments generated, and 16 other partial assignments that were tested for consistency.

Searching this tree with a depth-first search, typically called **backtracking,** can be much more efficient than generate and test. Generate and test is equivalent to not checking constraints until reaching the leaves. Checking constraints higher in the tree can prune large subtrees that do not have to be searched.

4.4   Consistency Algorithms

Although depth-first search over the search space of assignments is usually a substantial improvement over generate and test, it still has various inefficiencies that can be overcome.

Example 4.13   In Example 4.12, the variables *A* and *B* are related by the constraint $A < B$. The assignment *A*=4 is inconsistent with each of the possible assignments to *B* because $dom(B) = \{1, 2, 3, 4\}$. In the course of the backtrack search (see Figure 4.1), this fact is rediscovered for different assignments to *B*

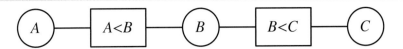

Figure 4.2: Constraint network for the CSP of Example 4.14

and C. This inefficiency can be avoided by the simple expedient of deleting 4 from $dom(A)$, once and for all. This idea is the basis for the consistency algorithms.

The consistency algorithms are best thought of as operating over the network of constraints formed by the CSP:

- There is a node for each variable. These nodes are drawn as circles or ovals.
- There is a node for each constraint. These nodes are drawn as rectangles.
- Associated with each variable, X, is a set D_X of possible values. This set of values is initially the domain of the variable.
- For every constraint c, and for every variable X in the scope of c, there is an arc $\langle X, c \rangle$.

Such a network is called a **constraint network**.

Example 4.14 Consider Example 4.12 (page 133). There are three variables A, B, and C, each with domain $\{1, 2, 3, 4\}$. The constraints are $A < B$ and $B < C$. In the constraint network, shown in Figure 4.2, there are four arcs:

$\langle A, A < B \rangle$
$\langle B, A < B \rangle$
$\langle B, B < C \rangle$
$\langle C, B < C \rangle$

Example 4.15 The constraint $X \neq 4$ has one arc:

$\langle X, X \neq 4 \rangle$

The constraint $X + Y = Z$ has three arcs:

$\langle X, X + Y = Z \rangle$
$\langle Y, X + Y = Z \rangle$
$\langle Z, X + Y = Z \rangle$

In the simplest case, when a constraint has just one variable in its scope, the arc is **domain consistent** if every value of the variable satisfies the constraint.

1: **procedure** $GAC(\langle Vs, dom, Cs \rangle)$
2:                              ▷ Returns arc consistent domains for CSP $\langle Vs, dom, Cs \rangle$
3:     **return** $GAC2(\langle Vs, dom, Cs \rangle, \{\langle X, c \rangle \mid c \in Cs \text{ and } X \in scope(c)\})$
4: **procedure** $GAC2(\langle Vs, dom, Cs \rangle, to\_do)$
5:     **while** $to\_do \neq \{\}$ **do**
6:         **select** and **remove** $\langle X, c \rangle$ from to_do
7:         let $\{Y_1, \ldots, Y_k\} = scope(c) \setminus \{X\}$
8:         $ND := \{x \mid x \in dom[X] \text{ and exists } y_1 \in dom[Y_1] \ldots y_k \in dom[Y_k] \text{ such}$
     that $c(X{=}x, Y_1{=}y_1, \ldots, Y_k{=}y_k)\}$
9:         **if** $ND \neq dom[X]$ **then**
10:             $to\_do := to\_do \cup \{\langle Z, c' \rangle \mid \{X, Z\} \subseteq scope(c'), c' \neq c, Z \neq X\}$
11:             $dom[X] := ND$
12:     **return** dom

Figure 4.3: Generalized arc consistency algorithm

Example 4.16   The constraint $B \neq 3$ has scope $\{B\}$. With this constraint, and with $D_B = \{1, 2, 3, 4\}$, the arc $\langle B, B \neq 3 \rangle$ is not domain consistent because $B{=}3$ violates the constraint. If the value 3 were removed from the domain of B, then it would be domain consistent.

Suppose constraint c has scope $\{X, Y_1, \ldots, Y_k\}$. Arc $\langle X, c \rangle$ is **arc consistent** if, for each value $x \in D_X$, there are values $y_1, \ldots, y_k$ where $y_i \in D_{Y_i}$, such that $c(X{=}x, Y_1{=}y_1, \ldots, Y_k{=}y_k)$ is satisfied. A network is arc consistent if all its arcs are arc consistent.

Example 4.17   Consider the network of Example 4.14 shown in Figure 4.2. None of the arcs are arc consistent. The first arc is not arc consistent because for $A{=}4$ there is no corresponding value for B for which $A < B$. If 4 were removed from the domain of A, then it would be arc consistent. The second arc is not arc consistent because there is no corresponding value for A when $B{=}1$.

If an arc $\langle X, c \rangle$ is *not* arc consistent, there are some values of X for which there are no values for $Y_1, \ldots, Y_k$ for which the constraint holds. In this case, all values of X in D_X for which there are no corresponding values for the other variables can be deleted from D_X to make the arc $\langle X, c \rangle$ consistent. When a value is removed from a domain, this may make some other arcs that were previously consistent no longer consistent.

The **generalized arc consistency (GAC)** algorithm is given in Figure 4.3. It makes the entire network arc consistent by considering a set to_do of potentially inconsistent arcs, the *to-do* arcs. The set to_do initially consists of all the arcs in the graph. While the set is not empty, an arc $\langle X, c \rangle$ is removed from the set and considered. If the arc is not arc consistent, it is made arc consistent by pruning the domain of variable X. All of the previously consistent arcs that could, as a result of pruning X, have become inconsistent are placed back into the set to_do. These are the arcs $\langle Z, c' \rangle$, where c' is a constraint different from c that involves X, and Z is a variable involved in c' other than X.

Example 4.18   Consider the algorithm GAC operating on the network from Example 4.14 (page 135), with constraints $A < B$, $B < C$. Initially, all of the arcs are in the to_do set. Here is one possible sequence of selections of arcs.

- Suppose the algorithm first selects the arc $\langle A, A < B \rangle$. For $A=4$, there is no value of B that satisfies the constraint. Thus, 4 is pruned from the domain of A. Nothing is added to to_do because there is no other arc not in to_do.
- Suppose that $\langle B, A < B \rangle$ is selected next. The value 1 is pruned from the domain of B. Again no arc is added to to_do.
- Suppose that $\langle B, B < C \rangle$ is selected next. The value 4 is removed from the domain of B. Because the domain of B has been reduced, the arc $\langle A, A < B \rangle$ must be added back into the to_do set because the domain of A could potentially be reduced further now that the domain of B is smaller.
- If the arc $\langle A, A < B \rangle$ is selected next, the value $A=3$ is pruned from the domain of A.
- The remaining arc on to_do is $\langle C, B < C \rangle$. The values 1 and 2 are removed from the domain of C. No arcs are added to to_do because C is not involved in any other constraints, and to_do becomes empty.

The algorithm then terminates with $D_A = \{1,2\}$, $D_B = \{2,3\}$, $D_C = \{3,4\}$. Although this has not fully solved the problem, it has greatly simplified it. For example, depth-first backtrackingsearch (page 133) would now solve the problem more efficiently.

Example 4.19 Consider applying GAC to the scheduling problem of Example 4.9 (page 131). The network shown in Figure 4.4 (on the next page) has already been made domain consistent (the value 3 has been removed from the domain of B and 2 has been removed from the domain of C). Suppose arc $\langle D, C < D \rangle$ is considered first. The arc is not arc consistent because $D=1$ is not consistent with any value for C in D_C, so 1 is deleted from D_D. D_D becomes $\{2,3,4\}$ and arcs $\langle A, A=D \rangle$, $\langle B, B \neq D \rangle$, and $\langle E, E < D \rangle$ could be added to to_do but they are in to_do already.

Suppose arc $\langle C, E < C \rangle$ is considered next; then D_C is reduced to $\{3,4\}$ and arc $\langle D, C < D \rangle$ goes back into the to_do set to be reconsidered.

Suppose arc $\langle D, C < D \rangle$ is next; then D_D is further reduced to the singleton $\{4\}$. Processing arc $\langle C, C < D \rangle$ prunes D_C to $\{3\}$. Making arc $\langle A, A = D \rangle$ consistent reduces D_A to $\{4\}$. Processing $\langle B, B \neq D \rangle$ reduces D_B to $\{1,2\}$. Then arc $\langle B, E < B \rangle$ reduces D_B to $\{2\}$. Finally, arc $\langle E, E < B \rangle$ reduces D_E to $\{1\}$. All arcs remaining in the queue are consistent, and so the algorithm terminates with the to_do set empty. The set of reduced variable domains is returned. In this case, the domains all have size 1 and there is a unique solution: $A=4$, $B=2$, $C=3$, $D=4$, $E=1$.

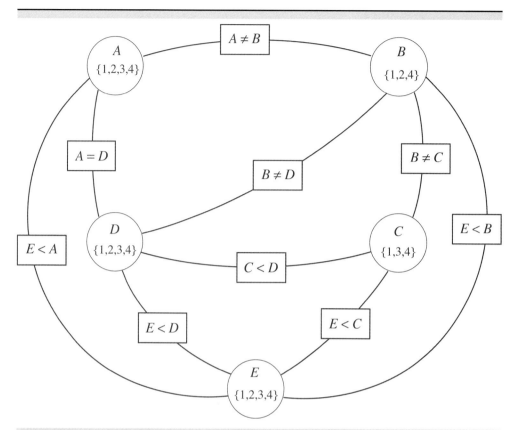

Figure 4.4: Domain-consistent constraint network. The variables are depicted as circles or ovals with their corresponding domain. The constraints are represented as rectangles. There is an arc between each variable and each constraint that involves that variable.

Regardless of the order in which the arcs are considered, the algorithm will terminate with the same result, namely, an arc consistent network and the same set of reduced domains. Three cases are possible, depending on the state of the network upon termination:

- In the first case, one domain becomes empty, indicating there is no solution to the CSP. Note that, as soon as any one domain becomes empty, all the domains of connected nodes will become empty before the algorithm terminates.

- In the second case, each domain has a singleton value, indicating that there is a unique solution to the CSP, as in Example 4.19.

- In the third case, every domain is non-empty and at least one has multiple values left in it. In this case, we do not know whether there is a solution or what the solutions look like (unless just a single domain has multiple values). Methods to solve the problem in this case are explored in the following sections.

The following example shows that it is possible for a network to be arc consistent even though there is no solution.

Example 4.20 Suppose there are three variables, A, B and C, each with the domain $\{1,2,3\}$. Consider the constraints $A = B$, $B = C$, and $A \neq C$. This is arc consistent: no domain can be pruned using any single constraint. However, there are no solutions. There is no assignment to the three variables that satisfies the constraints.

Consider the time complexity of the generalized arc consistency algorithm for binary constraints. Suppose there are c binary constraints, and the domain of each variable is of size d. There are $2c$ arcs. Checking an arc $\langle X, r(X, Y) \rangle$ involves, in the worst case, iterating through each value in the domain of Y for each value in the domain of X, which takes $O(d^2)$ time. This arc may need to be to be checked once for every element in the domain of Y, thus GAC for binary variables can be done in time $O(cd^3)$, which is linear in c, the number of constraints. The space used is $O(nd)$ where n is the number of variables and d is the domain size. Exercise 4.4 (page 170) explores the complexity of more general constraints.

Various extensions to arc consistency are also possible. The domains need not be finite; they may be specified using intensions, not just lists of their values. It is also possible to prune the constraints if the constraints are represented extensionally: if a value has been pruned for a variable X, this value can be pruned from all constraints that involve X. Higher-order consistency techniques, such as **path consistency**, consider k-tuples of variables at a time, not just pairs of variables that are connected by a constraint. For example, by considering all three variables, you can recognize that there is no solution in Example 4.20. These higher-order methods are often less efficient for solving a problem than using arc consistency augmented with the methods described below.

4.5 Domain Splitting

Another method for simplifying the network is **domain splitting** or **case analysis**. The idea is to split a problem into a number of disjoint cases and solve each case separately. The set of all solutions to the initial problem is the union of the solutions to each case.

In the simplest case, suppose there is a binary variable X with domain $\{t,f\}$. All of the solutions either have $X=t$ or $X=f$. One way to find all of the solutions is to set $X=t$, find all of the solutions with this assignment, and then assign $X=f$ and find all solutions with this assignment. Assigning a value to a variable gives a smaller *reduced* problem to solve. If we only want to find one solution, we can look for the solutions with $X=t$, and if we do not find any, we can look for the solutions with $X=f$.

If the domain of a variable has more than two elements, for example if the domain of A is $\{1,2,3,4\}$, there are a number of ways to split it

- Split the domain into a case for each value. For example, split A into the four cases $A=1$, $A=2$, $A=3$, and $A=4$.
- Always split the domain into two disjoint non-empty subsets. For example, split A into the two cases: $A \in \{1,2\}$ and the case $A \in \{3,4\}$.

The first approach makes more progress with one split, but the second may allow for more pruning with fewer steps. For example, if the same values for B can be pruned whether A is 1 or 2, the second case allows this fact to be discovered once and not have to be rediscovered for each element of A. This saving depends on how the domains are split.

Recursively solving the cases using domain splitting, recognizing when there is no solution based on the assignments, is equivalent to the search algorithm of Section 4.3 (page 133). We can be more efficient by interleaving arc consistency with the search.

One effective way to solve a CSP is to use arc consistency to simplify the network before each step of domain splitting. That is, to solve a problem,

- simplify the problem using arc consistency, and
- if the problem is not solved, select a variable whose domain has more than one element, split it, and recursively solve each case.

One thing to notice about this algorithm is that it does not require arc consistency to start from scratch after domain splitting. If the variable X has its domain split, *to_do* can start with just the arcs that are possibly no longer arc consistent as a result of the split. These are the arcs of the form $\langle Y, r \rangle$, where X appears in r and Y is not X.

Figure 4.5 (on the next page) shows how to solve a CSP with arc consistency and domain splitting. *CSP_Solver(CSP)* returns a solution to constraint satisfaction problem *CSP* if there is (at least) one, or *false* otherwise. Note that the "or" in line 16 is assumed to return the value of its first argument it is not false, and otherwise returns the value of the second argument.

It is possible to use essentially the same algorithm to find all solutions: line 7 should return the empty set, line 9 should return the set containing one element, and line 16 should return the union of the answers from each case.

Example 4.21 In Example 4.18 (page 137), arc consistency simplified the network, but did not solve the problem. After arc consistency had completed, there were multiple elements in the domains. Suppose B is split. There are two cases

- $B=2$. In this case $A=2$ is pruned. Splitting on C produces two of the answers.

1: **procedure** $CSP\_Solver(\langle Vs, dom, Cs \rangle)$
2:       ▷ Returns a solution to CSP $\langle Vs, dom, Cs \rangle$ or *false* if there is no solution
3:       **return** $Solve2(\langle Vs, dom, Cs \rangle, \{\langle X, c \rangle \mid c \in Cs \text{ and } X \in scope(c)\})$
4: **procedure** $Solve2(\langle Vs, dom, Cs \rangle, to\_do)$
5:       $dom_0 := GAC2(\langle Vs, dom, Cs \rangle, to\_do)$
6:       **if** there is a variable X such that $dom_0[X] = \{\}$ **then**
7:             **return** false
8:       **else if** for every variable X, $|dom_0[X]| = 1$ **then**
9:             **return** solution with each variable X having the value in $dom_0[X]$
10:      **else**
11:            select variable X such that $|dom_0[X]| > 1$
12:            partition $dom_0[X]$ into D_1 and D_2
13:            $dom_1 :=$ a copy of dom_0 but with $dom_1[X] = D_1$
14:            $dom_2 :=$ a copy of dom_0 but with $dom_2[X] = D_2$
15:            $to\_do := \{\langle Z, c' \rangle \mid \{X, Z\} \subseteq scope(c'), Z \neq X\}$
16:            **return** $Solve2(\langle Vs, dom_1, Cs \rangle, to\_do)$ **or** $Solve2(\langle Vs, dom_2, Cs \rangle, to\_do)$

Figure 4.5: Finding a model for a CSP using arc consistency and domain splitting

---

- $B=3$. In this case $C=3$ is pruned. Splitting on A produces the other two answers.

  This search tree should be contrasted with the search tree of Figure 4.1 (page 134). The search space with arc consistency is much smaller.

Domain splitting forms a search space from which any of the methods of Chapter 3 can be used. However, as it is only the solution and not the path that is of interest, and because the search space is finite, depth-first search is often used for these problems.

One other enhancement make domain splitting much more efficient when counting the number of solutions or finding all solutions. If assigning values to the variables disconnects the graph, each disconnected component can be solved separately. The solution to the complete problem is the cross product of the solutions to each component. This can save much computation when one is counting the number of solutions. For example, if one component has 100 solutions and the other component has 20 solutions, there are 2000 solutions. This is a more efficient way to count than finding each of the 2000 solutions separately.

4.6 Variable Elimination

Arc consistency simplifies the network by removing values of variables. A complementary method is **variable elimination** (**VE**), which simplifies the network by removing variables.

The idea of VE is to remove the variables one by one. When removing a variable X, VE constructs a new constraint on some of the remaining variables reflecting the effects of X on all of the other variables. This new constraint replaces all of the constraints that involve X, forming a reduced network that does not involve X. The new constraint is constructed so that any solution to the reduced CSP can be extended to a solution of the CSP that contains X. In addition to creating the new constraint, VE provides a way to construct a solution to the CSP that contains X from a solution to the reduced CSP.

The following algorithm is described using the relational algebra calculations of join and project (page 747).

When eliminating X, the influence of X on the remaining variables is through the constraint relations that involve X. First, the algorithm collects all of the constraints that involve X. Let the join of all of these relations be the relation $r_X(X, \overline{Y})$, where $\overline{Y}$ is the set of other variables in the scope of r_X. Thus $\overline{Y}$ is the set of all variables that are neighbors of X in the constraint graph. The algorithm then projects r_X onto $\overline{Y}$; this relation replaces all of the relations that involve X. It now has a reduced CSP that involves one less variable, which it solves recursively. Once it has a solution for the reduced CSP, it extends that solution to a solution for the original CSP by joining the solution with r_X.

When only one variable is left, it returns those domain elements that are consistent with the constraints on this variable.

Example 4.22   Consider a CSP that contains the variables A, B, and C, each with domain $\{1, 2, 3, 4\}$. Suppose the constraints that involve B are $A < B$ and $B < C$. There may be many other variables, but if B does not have any constraints in common with these variables, eliminating B will not impose any new constraints on these other variables. To remove B, first join on the relations that involve B:

A	B		B	C			A	B	C
1	2		1	2			1	2	3
1	3		1	3			1	2	4
1	4	$\bowtie$	1	4	$=$		1	3	4
2	3		2	3			2	3	4
2	4		2	4					
3	4		3	4					

To get the relation on A and C induced by B, project this join onto A and C, which gives

A	C
1	3
1	4
2	4

1: **procedure** $VE\_CSP(Vs, Cs)$
2:     **Inputs**
3:         Vs: a set of variables
4:         Cs: a set of constraints on Vs
5:     **Output**
6:         a relation containing all of the consistent variable assignments
7:     **if** Vs contains just one element **then**
8:         return the join of all the relations in Cs
9:     **else**
10:        **select** variable Xs to eliminate
11:        $Vs' := Vs \setminus \{X\}$
12:        $Cs_X := \{T \in Cs : T \text{ involves } X\}$
13:        **let** R be the join of all of the constraints in Cs_X
14:        **let** R' be R projected onto the variables other than X
15:        $S := VE\_CSP(Vs', (Cs \setminus Cs_X) \cup \{R'\})$
16:        **return** $R \bowtie S$

Figure 4.6: Variable elimination for finding all solutions to a CSP

This relation on A and C contains all of the information about the constraints on B that affect the solutions of the rest of the network.

The original constraints on B are replaced with the new constraint on A and C. VE then solves the rest of the network, which is now simpler because it does not involve the variable B. To generate one or all solutions, the algorithm remembers the joined relation on A, B, C to construct a solution that involves B from a solution to the reduced network.

Figure 4.6 gives a recursive algorithm for variable elimination, VE_CSP, to find all solutions for a CSP.

The base case of the recursion occurs when only one variable is left. In this case (line 8), a solution exists if and only if there are rows in the join of the final relations. Note that these relations are all relations on a single variable, and so they are the sets of legal values for this variable. The join of these relations is the intersection of these sets.

In the non-base case, a variable X is selected for elimination (line 10). Which variable is selected does not affect the correctness of the algorithm, but it may affect the efficiency. To eliminate variable X, the algorithm propagates the effect of X onto those variables that X is directly related to. This is achieved by joining all of the relations in which X is involved (line 13) and then projecting X out of the resulting relation (line 14). Thus, a simplified problem (with one less variable) has been created that can be solved recursively. To get the possible values for X, the algorithm joins the solution of the simplified problem with the relation R that defines the effect of X.

If you only wanted to find one solution, instead of returning $R \bowtie S$, the algorithm can return one element of the join. No matter which element it returns, that element is guaranteed to be part of a solution. If any value of R in this algorithm contains no tuples, there are no solutions.

The efficiency of the VE algorithm depends on the order in which variables are selected. The intermediate structure – which variables the intermediate relations are over – depends not on the actual content of relations but only on the graph structure of the constraint network. The efficiency of this algorithm can be determined by considering the graphical structure. In general, VE is efficient when the constraint network is sparse. The number of variables in the largest relation returned for a particular variable ordering is called the **treewidth** of the graph for that variable ordering. The treewidth of a graph is the minimum treewidth for any ordering. The complexity of VE is exponential in treewidth and linear in the number of variables. This can be compared to searching (see Section 4.3, (page 133)), which is exponential in the number of variables.

Finding an elimination ordering that results in the smallest treewidth is NP-hard. However, some good heuristics exist. The two most common are:

- **min-factor**: at each stage, select the variable that results in the smallest relation

- **minimum deficiency** or **minimum fill**: at each stage, select the variable that adds the fewest arcs to the remaining constraint network. The deficiency of a variable X is the number of pairs of variables that are in a relationship with X that are not in a relationship with each other. The intuition is that it is okay to remove a variable that results in a large relation as long as it does not make the network more complicated.

The minimum deficiency has usually been found empirically to give a smaller treewidth than min-factor, but it is more difficult to compute.

VE can also be combined with arc consistency; whenever VE removes a variable, arc consistency can be used to further simplify the problem. This approach can result in smaller intermediate tables.

4.7 Local Search

The preceding algorithms systematically search the space of assignments of values to variables. If the space is finite, they will either find a solution or report that no solution exists. Unfortunately, many spaces are too big for systematic search and are possibly even infinite. In any reasonable time, systematic search will have failed to consider enough of the space to give any meaningful results. This section and the next consider methods intended to work in these very large spaces. The methods do not systematically search the whole search space but they are designed to find solutions quickly on average. They do not

1: **procedure** *Local_search*(*Vs*, *dom*, *Cs*)
2:     **Inputs**
3:         *Vs*: a set of variables
4:         *dom*: a function such that *dom*(*X*) is the domain of variable *X*
5:         *Cs*: set of constraints to be satisfied
6:     **Output**
7:         total assignment that satisfies the constraints
8:     **Local**
9:         *A* an array of values indexed by variables in *Vs*
10:     **repeat**
11:         **for each** variable *X* in *Vs* **do**
12:             *A*[*X*] := a random value in *dom*(*X*);
13:         **while** not *stop_walk*() & *A* is not a satisfying assignment **do**
14:             Select a variable *Y* and a value $w \in dom(Y)$
15:             Set *A*[*Y*] := *w*
16:         **if** *A* is a satisfying assignment **then**
17:             **return** *A*
18:     **until** termination

Figure 4.7: Local search for finding a solution to a CSP

guarantee that a solution will be found even if one exists, and so they are not able to prove that no solution exists. They are often the method of choice for applications where solutions are known to exist or are very likely to exist.

Local search methods start with a total assignment of a value to each variable and try to improve this assignment iteratively by taking improving steps, by taking random steps, or by restarting with another total assignment. Many different local search techniques have been proposed. Understanding when these techniques work for different problems forms the focus of a number of research communities, in both operations research and AI.

A generic local search algorithm for CSPs is given in Figure 4.7. The array *A* specifies an assignment of a value to each variable. The first *for each* loop assigns a random value to each variable. The first time it is executed is called a **random initialization**. Each iteration of the outer loop is called a **try**. The second and subsequent assignments of a random value to each variable in line 11 and line 12 is a **random restart**. An alternative to random initialization is to use some more informed guess, utilizing some heuristic or prior knowledge, which is then iteratively improved.

The *while* loop (line 13 to line 15) does a **local search**, or a **walk**, through the assignment space. It considers a set of possible **successors** of the total assignment *A*, and selects one to be the next total assignment. In Figure 4.7, the possible successors of a total assignment are those assignments that differ in the assignment of a single variable.

This walk through assignments continues until either a satisfying assignment is found and returned or some stopping criterion is satisfied. The stopping criterion, the *stop_walk()* function in the algorithm, is used to decide when to stop the current local search and do a random restart, starting again with a new assignment. A stopping criterion could be as simple as stopping after a certain number of steps.

This algorithm is not guaranteed to halt. In particular, if the termination condition is false, it goes on forever if there is no solution, and, even if there is a solution, it is possible to get trapped in some region of the search space. An algorithm is **complete** if it guarantees to finds an answer whenever there is one. This algorithm can be complete or incomplete, depending on the selection and the stopping criterion.

One version of this algorithm is **random sampling**. In random sampling, the stopping criterion *stop_walk()* always returns *true* so that the *while* loop from line 13 is never executed. Random sampling keeps picking random assignments until it finds one that satisfies the constraints, and otherwise it does not halt. Random sampling is complete in the sense that, given enough time, it guarantees that a solution will be found if one exists, but there is no upper bound on the time it may take. It is typically very slow. The efficiency depends on the product of the domain sizes and how many solutions exist.

Another version is a **random walk** when *stop_walk()* is always false, and so there are no random restarts. In a random walk the *while* loop is only exited when it has found a satisfying assignment. In the *while* loop, random walk selects a variable and a value for that variable at random. Random walk is also complete in the same sense as random sampling. Each step takes less time than resampling all variables, but it can take more steps than random sampling, depending on how the solutions are distributed. When the domain sizes of the variables differ, a random walk algorithm can either select a variable at random and then a value at random, or select a variable–value pair at random. The latter is more likely to select a variable when it has a larger domain.

4.7.1 Iterative Best Improvement

Iterative best improvement is a local search algorithm that selects a successor of the current assignment that most improves some **evaluation function**. If there are several possible successors that most improve the evaluation function, one is chosen at random. When the aim is to minimize, this algorithm is called **greedy descent**. When the aim is to maximize a function, this is called **hill climbing** or **greedy ascent**. We only consider minimization; to maximize a quantity, you can minimize its negation.

Iterative best improvement requires a way to evaluate each total assignment. For constraint satisfaction problems, a common evaluation function is the number of constraints that are violated. A violated constraint is called a **conflict**. With the evaluation function being the number of conflicts, a solution is a total assignment with an evaluation of zero. Sometimes this evaluation function is refined by weighting some constraints more than others.

A **local optimum** is an assignment such that no possible successor improves the evaluation function. This is also called a local minimum in greedy descent, or a local maximum in greedy ascent. A **global optimum** is an assignment that has the best value out of all assignments. All global optima are local optima, but there can be many local optima that are not a global optimum.

If the heuristic function is the number of conflicts, a satisfiable CSP has a global optimum with a heuristic value of 0, and an unsatisfiable CPS has a global optimum with a value above 0. If the search reaches a local minimum with a value above 0, you do not know if it is a global minimum (which implies the CSP is unsatisfiable) or not.

Example 4.23 Consider the delivery scheduling in Example 4.9 (page 131). Suppose greedy descent starts with the assignment $A=2, B=2, C=3, D=2, E=1$. This assignment has an evaluation of 3, because it violates $A \neq B$, $B \neq D$, and $C < D$. One possible successor with the minimal evaluation has $B=4$ with an evaluation of 1 because only $C < D$ is unsatisfied. This assignment is selected. This is a local minimum. One possible successor with the fewest conflicts can be obtained by changing D to 4, which has an evaluation of 2. It can then change A to 4, with an evaluation of 2, and then change B to 2 with an evaluation of 0, and a solution is found.

The following gives a trace of the assignments through the walk:

A	B	C	D	E	evaluation
2	2	3	2	1	3
2	4	3	2	1	1
2	4	3	4	1	2
4	4	3	4	1	2
4	2	3	4	1	0

Different initializations, or different choices when multiple assignments have the same evaluation, give different sequences of assignments to the variables and possibly different results.

Iterative best improvement considers the best successor assignment even if it is equal to or even worse than the current assignment. This means that if there are two or more assignments that are possible successors of each other and are all local, but not global, optima, it will keep moving between these assignments, and never reach a global optimum. Thus, this algorithm is not complete.

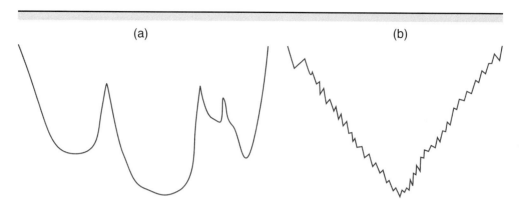

Figure 4.8: Two search spaces; find the minimum

4.7.2 Randomized Algorithms

Iterative best improvement randomly picks one of the best possible successors of the current assignment, but it can get stuck in local minima that are not global minima.

Randomness can be used to escape local minima that are not global minima in two main ways:

- **random restart** (page 145), in which values for all variables are chosen at random. This lets the search start from a completely different part of the search space.

- **random walk**, in which some random steps are taken interleaved with the optimizing steps. With greedy descent, this process allows for upward steps that may enable random walk to escape a local minimum that is not a global minimum.

A random walk is a local random move, whereas a random restart is a global random move. For problems involving a large number of variables, a random restart can be quite expensive.

A mix of iterative best improvement with random moves is an instance of a class of algorithms known as **stochastic local search**.

Unfortunately, it is very difficult to visualize the search space to understand what algorithms work because there are often thousands or millions of dimensions, each with a discrete, or even continuous, set of values. Some intuitions can be gleaned from lower-dimensional problems. Consider the two one-dimensional search spaces in Figure 4.8, where the objective is to find the minimum value. Suppose that a possible successor is obtained by a small step, either left or right of the current position. To find the global minimum in the search space (a), one would expect the greedy descent with random restart after a local optimum has been found to find the optimal value quickly. Once a random choice has found a point in the deepest valley, greedy descent quickly leads to the global minimum. One would not expect a random walk to work well in this example, because many random steps are required to exit one of the local, but not global, minima. However, for search space (b), a random restart quickly gets stuck on one of the jagged peaks and does not work very well. However, a random walk combined with greedy descent enables it to escape these local minima. A few random steps may be enough to escape a local minimum. Thus, one may expect that a random walk would work better in this search space. Because it is difficult to determine which method would work best from examining the problem, practitioners will evaluate many methods to see which one works well in practice for the particular problem. It is even possible that different parts of the search space have different characteristics.

4.7.3 Local Search Variants

There are many variants of iterative best improvement with randomness.

If the variables have small finite domains, a local search algorithm can consider all other values of the variable when considering the possible successors. If the domains are large, the cost of considering all other values may be too high. An alternative is to consider only a few other values, often the close values, for one of the variables. Sometimes quite sophisticated methods are used to select an alternative value.

As presented, the local search has no memory. It does not remember anything about the search as it proceeds. A simple way to use memory to improve a local search is use **tabu search** that prevents recently changed variable assignments from being changed again. The idea is, when selecting a variable to change, not to select a variable that was changed in the last t steps for some integer t, called the **tabu tenure**. If t is small, tabu search can be implemented by having a list of the recently changed variables. If t is larger it can be implemented by including, for each variable, the step at which the variable got its current value. Tabu search prevents cycling among a few assignments. The tabu tenure is one of the parameters that can be optimized. A tabu list of size 1 is equivalent to not allowing the same assignment to be immediately revisited.

Algorithms differ in how much work they require to guarantee the best improvement step. At one extreme, an algorithm can guarantee to select one of the new assignments with the best improvement out of all of the possible successors. At the other extreme, an algorithm can select a new assignment at random and reject the assignment if it makes the situation worse. It is often better to make a quick choice than to spend a lot of time making the best choice. Which of these methods works best is, typically, an empirical question; it is difficult to determine theoretically whether slow large steps are better than small quick steps for a particular problem domain. There are many possible variants of which successor to select, some of which are explored in the next sections.

Most Improving Step

The **most improving step** method always selects a variable–value pair that makes the best improvement. If there are many such pairs, one is chosen at random.

The naive way of implementing most improving step is, given a current total assignment, to linearly scan the variables, and for each variable X and for each value v in the domain of X that is different from the value X has in the current total assignment, comparing the current total assignment with the assignment that differed by just having $X=v$. Then select one of the variable–value pairs that results in the best improvement, even if that improvement is negative. Variables that do not appear in any constraints can be ignored. One step requires $O(ndr)$ evaluations of constraints, where n is the number of variables, d is the domain size, and r is the number of constraints for each variable.

A more sophisticated alternative is to have a priority queue of variable–value pairs with associated weights. For each variable X, and each value v in the domain of X such that X is not assigned to v in the current assignment, the pair $\langle X, v \rangle$ would be in the priority queue. The weight w of the pair $\langle X, v \rangle$ is the evaluation of the total assignment that is the same as the current total assignment, but with $X=v$ minus the evaluation of the current total assignment. This weight depends on values assigned to X and the neighbors of X in the constraint graph, but does not depend on the values assigned to other variables. At each stage, the algorithm selects a variable–value pair with minimum weight, which gives a successor with the biggest improvement.

Once a variable X has been given a new value, the weights of all variable–value pairs that participate in a constraint that has been made satisfied or made unsatisfied by the new assignment to X must have their weights reassessed and, if changed, they need to be reinserted into the priority queue.

The size of the priority queue is $n(d-1)$, where n is the number of variables and d is the average domain size. To insert or remove an element takes time $O(\log nd)$. The algorithm removes one element from the priority queue, adds another and updates the weights of at most rk variables, where r is the number of constraints per variable and k is the number of variables per constraint. The complexity of one step of this algorithm is $O(rkd \log nd)$, where n is the number of variables, d is the average domain size, and r is the number of constraints per variable.

This algorithm spends much time maintaining the data structures to ensure that the most improving step is taken at each time.

Two-Stage Choice

An alternative is to first select a variable and then select a value for that variable. The **two-stage choice** algorithm maintains a priority queue of variables, where the weight of a variable is the number of conflicts in which it participates. At each time, the algorithm selects a variable that participates in the maximum number of conflicts. Once a variable has been chosen, it can be assigned either a value that minimizes the number of conflicts or a value at random. For each constraint that becomes true or false as a result of this new assignment, the other variables participating in the constraint must have their weight reevaluated.

The complexity of one step of this algorithm is $O(rk \log n)$, where n is the number of variables and r is the number of constraints per variable, and k is the number of variables per constraint. Compared to selecting the best variable–value pair, this does less work for each step and so more steps are achievable for any given time period. However, the steps tend to give less improvement, giving a trade-off between the number of steps and the complexity per step.

Any Conflict

Instead of choosing the best variable, an even simpler alternative is to select any variable participating in a conflict. A variable that is involved in a conflict is a **conflicting variable**. In the **any-conflict algorithm**, at each step, one of the conflicting variables is selected at random. The algorithm assigns to the chosen variable one of the values that minimizes the number of violated constraints or a value at random.

There are two variants of this algorithm, which differ in how the variable to be modified is selected:

- In the first variant, a conflict is chosen at random, and then a variable that is involved in the conflict is chosen at random.

- In the second variant, a variable that is involved in a conflict is chosen at random.

These differ in the probability that a variable in a conflict is chosen. In the first variant, the probability variable is chosen depends on the number of conflicts it is involved in. In the second variant, all of the variables that are in conflicts are equally likely to be chosen.

Each of these algorithms requires maintaining data structures that enable a variable to be quickly selected at random. The data structure need to be maintained as variables change their values. The first variant requires a set of conflicts from which a random element is selected, such as a binary search tree. The complexity of one step of this algorithm is thus $O(r \log c)$, where r is the number of constraints per variable and c is the number of constraints, because in the worst case r constraints may need to be added or removed from the set of conflicts.

Simulated Annealing

The last method maintains no data structure of conflicts; instead it picks a variable and a new value for that variable at random and either rejects or accepts the new assignment.

Annealing is a metallurgical process where molten metals are slowly cooled to allow them to reach a low energy state, making them stronger. Simulated annealing is an analogous method for optimization. It is typically described in terms of thermodynamics. The random movement corresponds to high temperature; at low temperature, there is little randomness. **Simulated annealing** is a stochastic local search algorithm where the temperature is reduced slowly, starting from a random walk at high temperature eventually becoming pure greedy descent as it approaches zero temperature. The randomness should allow the search to jump out of local minima and find regions that have a low heuristic value; whereas the greedy descent will lead to local minima. At high temperatures, worsening steps are more likely than at lower temperatures.

Like the other methods, simulated annealing maintains a current total assignment. At each step, it picks a variable at random, then picks a value for that variable at random. If assigning that value to the variable does not increase the number of conflicts, the algorithm accepts the assignment of that value to the variable, resulting in a new current assignment. Otherwise, it accepts the assignment with some probability, depending on the temperature and how much worse the new assignment is than the current assignment. If the change is not accepted, the current assignment is unchanged.

To control whether worsening steps are accepted, there is a positive real-valued temperature T. Suppose A is the current total assignment. Suppose that $h(A)$ is the evaluation of assignment A to be minimized. For solving constraints, h is typically the number of conflicts. Simulated annealing selects a possible successor at random, which gives a new assignment A'. If $h(A') \leq h(A)$, it accepts the assignment and A' becomes the new assignment. Otherwise, the new assignment is accepted randomly, using a **Gibbs distribution** or **Boltzmann distribution**, with probability

$$e^{-(h(A')-h(A))/T}.$$

This is only used when $h(A') - h(A) > 0$, and so the exponent is always negative. If $h(A')$ is close to $h(A)$, the assignment is more likely to be accepted. If the temperature is high, the exponent will be close to zero, and so the probability will be close to 1. As the temperature approaches zero, the exponent approaches $-\infty$, and the probability approaches zero.

Temperature	Probability of acceptance		
	1-worse	2-worse	3-worse
10	0.9	0.82	0.74
1	0.37	0.14	0.05
0.25	0.018	0.0003	0.000006
0.1	0.00005	$2 * 10^{-9}$	$9 * 10^{-14}$

Figure 4.9: Probability of simulated annealing accepting worsening steps

Figure 4.9 shows the probability of accepting worsening steps at different temperatures. In this figure, k-worse means that $h(A') - h(A) = k$. For example, if the temperature is 10 (i.e., $T = 10$), a change that is one worse (i.e., if $h(A') - h(A) = 1$) will be accepted with probability $e^{-0.1} \approx 0.9$; a change that is two worse will be accepted with probability $e^{-0.2} \approx 0.82$. If the temperature T is 1, accepting a change that is one worse will happen with probability $e^{-1} \approx 0.37$. If the temperature is 0.1, a change that is one worse will be accepted with probability $e^{-10} \approx 0.00005$. At this temperature, it is essentially only performing steps that improve the value or leave it unchanged.

If the temperature is high, as in the $T = 10$ case, the algorithm tends to accept steps that only worsen a small amount; it does not tend to accept very large worsening steps. There is a slight preference for improving steps. As the temperature is reduced (e.g., when $T = 1$), worsening steps, although still possible, become much less likely. When the temperature is low (e.g., $T = 0.1$), it is very rare that it selects a worsening step.

Simulated annealing requires an **annealing schedule**, which specifies how the temperature is reduced as the search progresses. Geometric cooling is one of the most widely used schedules. An example of a geometric cooling schedule is to start with a temperature of 10 and multiply by 0.99 after each step; this will have a temperature of 0.07 after 500 steps. Finding a good annealing schedule is an art, and depends on the problem.

4.7.4 Evaluating Randomized Algorithms

It is difficult to compare randomized algorithms when they give a different result and a different run time each time they are run, even for the same problem. It is especially difficult when the algorithms sometimes do not find an answer; they either run forever or must be stopped at an arbitrary point.

Unfortunately, summary statistics, such as the mean or median run time, are not very useful. For example, comparing algorithms on the mean run time requires deciding how to average in unsuccessful runs, where no solution was found. If unsuccessful runs are ignored in computing the average, an algorithm that picks a random assignment and then stops would be the best algorithm;

it does not succeed very often, but when it does, it is very fast. Treating the non-terminating runs as having infinite time means all algorithms that do not find a solution will have infinite averages. A run that has not found a solution will need to be terminated. Using the time it was terminated in the average is more of a function of the stopping time than of the algorithm itself, although this does allow for a crude trade-off between finding some solutions fast versus finding more solutions.

If you were to compare algorithms using the median run time, you would prefer an algorithm that solves the problem 51% of the time but very slowly over one that solves the problem 49% of the time but very quickly, even though the latter is more useful. The problem is that the median (the 50th percentile) is just an arbitrary value; you could just as well consider the 47th percentile or the 87th percentile.

One way to visualize the run time of an algorithm for a particular problem is to use a **run-time distribution**, which shows the variability of the run time of a randomized algorithm on a single problem instance. The x-axis represents either the number of steps or the run time. The y-axis shows, for each value of x, the number of runs, or proportion of the runs, solved within that run time or number of steps. Thus, it provides a cumulative distribution of how often the problem was solved within some number of steps or run time. For example, you can find the run time of the 30th percentile of the runs by finding the x-value that maps to 30% on the y-scale. The run-time distribution can be plotted (or approximated) by running the algorithm for a large number of times (say, 100 times for a rough approximation or 1000 times for a reasonably accurate plot) and then by sorting the runs by run time.

> **Example 4.24** Four empirically generated run-time distributions for a single problem are shown in Figure 4.10 (on the next page). On the x-axis is the number of steps, using a logarithmic scale. On the y-axis is the number of instances that were successfully solved out of 1000 runs. This shows four run-time distributions on the same problem instance. Algorithms 1 and 2 solved the problem 40% of the time in 10 or fewer steps. Algorithm 3 solved the problem in about 50% of the runs in 10 or fewer steps. Algorithm 4 found a solution in 10 or fewer steps in about 12% of the runs. Algorithms 1 and 2 found a solution in about 58% of the runs. Algorithm 3 could find a solution about 80% of the time. Algorithm 4 always found a solution. This only compares the number of steps; the time taken would be a better evaluation but is more difficult to measure for small problems and depends on the details of the implementation.

One algorithm strictly dominates another for this problem if its run-time distribution is completely to the left (and above) the run-time distribution of the second algorithm. Often two algorithms are incomparable under this measure. Which algorithm is better depends on how much time an agent has before it needs to use a solution or how important it is to actually find a solution.

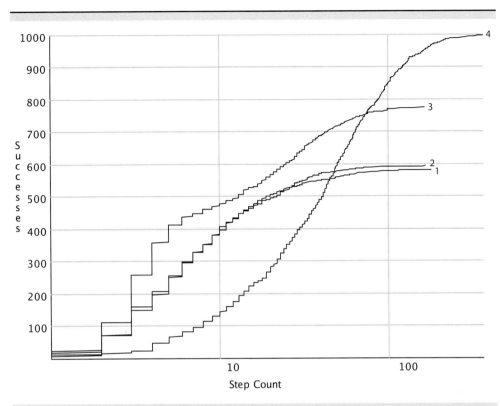

Figure 4.10: Run-time distributions. These are empirical run-time distributions of 1000 runs, with each run having a limit of 1000 steps. On the x-axis is the number of steps (using a logarithmic scale), and on the y-axis is the number of successes out of 1000 runs. This is for the sample CSP, "Scheduling Problem 1," of Alspace.org. Distributions 1 and 2 are two separate runs for the two-stage greedy descent. Distribution 3 is for the one-stage greedy descent. Distribution 4 is a greedy descent with random walk, where first a random variable that participates in a conflict (a red node in Alspace.org) is chosen, then the best value for this variable is chosen with a 50% chance and a random value is chosen otherwise.

Example 4.25 In the run-time distributions of Figure 4.10, Algorithm 3 dominates Algorithms 1 and 2. Algorithms 1 and 2 are actually different sets of runs of the same algorithm with the same settings. This shows the errors that are typical of multiple runs of the same stochastic algorithm on the same problem instance. Algorithm 3 is better than Algorithm 4 up to 60 steps, after which Algorithm 4 is better.

By looking at the graph, you can see that Algorithm 3 often solves the problem in its first four or five steps, after which it is not as effective. This may lead you to try to suggest using Algorithm 3 with a random restart after five steps and this does, indeed, dominate all of the algorithms for this problem instance, at least in the number of steps (counting a restart as a single step). However, because the random restart is an expensive operation, this algorithm may not be the most efficient. This also does not necessarily predict how well the algorithm will work in other problem instances.

4.7.5 Random Restart

It may seem like a randomized algorithm that only succeeds, say, 20% of the time is not very useful if you need an algorithm to succeed, say, 99% of the time. However, a randomized algorithm that succeeds some of the time can be extended to an algorithm that succeeds more often by running it multiple times, using a random restart, and reporting any solution found.

Whereas a random walk, and its variants, are evaluated empirically by running experiments, the performance of random restart can also be predicted ahead of time, because the runs following a random restart are independent of each other.

An algorithm that succeed with probability p, that is run n times or until a solution is found, will find a solution with probability $1 - (1 - p)^n$. It fails to find a solution if it fails for each retry, and each retry is independent of the others.

For example, an algorithm with $p = 0.5$ tried 5 times, will find a solution around 96.9% of the time; tried 10 times it will find a solution 99.9% of the time. If each run succeeded with a probability $p = 0.1$, running it 10 times will succeed 65% of the time, and running it 44 times will give a 99% success rate.

A run-time distribution allows us to predict how the algorithm will work with random restart after a certain number of steps. Intuitively, a random restart will repeat the lower left corner of the run-time distribution, suitably scaled down, at the stage where the restart occurs. A random restart after a certain number of greedy descent steps will make any algorithm that sometimes finds a solution into an algorithm that always finds a solution, given that one exists, if it is run for long enough.

A random restart can be expensive if there are many variables. A **partial restart** randomly assigns just some not all of the variables, say 100 variables, or 10% of the variables, to move to another part of the search space. While this is often effective, the above theoretical analysis does not work because the partial restarts are not independent of each other.

4.8 Population-Based Methods

The preceding local search algorithms maintain a single total assignment. This section considers algorithms that maintain multiple total assignments. The first method, beam search, maintains the best k assignments. The next algorithm, stochastic beam search, selects which assignments to maintain stochastically.

In genetic algorithms, which are inspired by biological evolution, the k assignments forming a population interact to produce the new population. In these algorithms, a total assignment of a value to each variable is called an **individual** and the set of current individuals is a **population**.

Beam search is a method similar to iterative best improvement, but it maintains up to k assignments instead of just one. It reports success when it finds a satisfying assignment. At each stage of the algorithm, it selects k best possible successors of the current individuals (or all of them if there are less than k) and picks randomly in the case of ties. It repeats with this new set of k total assignments.

Beam search considers multiple assignments at the same time. Beam search is useful for memory-bounded cases, where k can be selected depending on the memory available. The variants of stochastic local search presented earlier are also applicable to beam search; you can spend more time finding the best k, or spend less time and only approximate the best k.

Stochastic beam search is an alternative to beam search, which, instead of choosing the best k individuals, selects k of the individuals at random; the individuals with a better evaluation are more likely to be chosen. This is done by making the probability of being chosen a function of the evaluation function. A standard way to do this is to use a **Gibbs distribution** or **Boltzmann distribution** and to select an assignment A with probability proportional to

$$e^{-h(A)/T},$$

where $h(A)$ is an evaluation function and T is a temperature.

Stochastic beam search tends to allow more diversity in the k individuals than does plain beam search. As an analogy to evolution in biology, the evaluation function reflects the fitness of the individual; the fitter the individual, the more likely it is to pass its genetic material – here its variable assignment – onto the next generation. Stochastic beam search is like asexual reproduction; each individual gives slightly mutated children and then stochastic beam search proceeds with survival of the fittest. Note that under stochastic beam search it is possible for an individual to be selected multiple times at random.

Genetic algorithms further pursue the evolution analogy. Genetic algorithms are like stochastic beam searches, but each new element of the population is a combination of a pair of individuals – its parents. In particular, genetic algorithms use an operation known as **crossover** that select pairs of individuals and then create new offspring by taking some of the values for the offspring's variables from one of the parents and the rest of the values from the other parent, loosely analogous to how DNA is spliced in sexual reproduction.

A genetic algorithm is shown in Figure 4.11 (on the next page). This maintains a population of k individuals (where k is an even number). At each step, a new generation of individuals is generated via the following steps until a solution is found:

1: **procedure** *Genetic_algorithm*(Vs, dom, Cs, S, k)
2:    **Inputs**
3:       *Vs*: a set of variables
4:       *dom*: a function; $dom(X)$ is the domain of variable X
5:       *Cs*: set of constraints to be satisfied
6:       *S*: a cooling schedule for the temperature
7:       *k*: population size – an even integer
8:    **Output**
9:       total assignment that satisfies the constraints
10:    **Local**
11:       *Pop*: a set of assignments
12:       *T*: real
13:    $Pop :=\ k$ random total assignments
14:    T is assigned a value according to S
15:    **repeat**
16:       **if** some $A \in Pop$ satisfies all constraints in *Cs* **then**
17:          **return** A
18:       $Npop := \{\}$
19:       **repeat** $k/2$ **times**
20:          $A_1 := Random\_selection(Pop, T)$
21:          $A_1 := Random\_selection(Pop, T)$
22:          $N_1, N_2 := Crossover(A_1, A_2)$
23:          $Npop := Npop \cup \{mutate(N_1), mutate(N_2)\}$
24:       $Pop := Npop$
25:       T is updated according to S
26:    **until** termination
27: **procedure** *Random_selection*(Pop, T)
28:    select A from *Pop* with probability proportional to $e^{-h(A)/T}$
29:    **return** A
30: **procedure** *Crossover*(A_1, A_2)
31:    select integer i, $1 \leq i < |Vs|$ at random
32:    Let $N_1 := \{(X_j{=}v_j) \in A_1 \text{ for } j \leq i\} \cup \{(X_j{=}v_j) \in A_2 \text{ for } j > i\}$
33:    Let $N_2 := \{(X_j{=}v_j) \in A_2 \text{ for } j \leq i\} \cup \{(X_j{=}v_j) \in A_1 \text{ for } j > i\}$
34:    **return** N_1, N_2

Figure 4.11: Genetic algorithm for finding a solution to a CSP

- Randomly select pairs of individuals where the fitter individuals are more likely to be chosen. How much more likely a fit individual is to be chosen than a less fit individual depends on the difference in fitness levels and a temperature parameter.

- For each pair, perform a crossover.

- Randomly mutate some (very few) values by choosing other values for some randomly chosen variables. This is a random walk step.

It proceeds in this way until it has created k individuals, and then the operation proceeds to the next generation.

The new operation that occurs in genetic algorithms is called **crossover**. Uniform crossover takes two individuals (the parents) and creates two new individuals, called the **children**. The value for each variable in a child comes from one of the parents. A common method is **one-point crossover**, shown in the procedure *Crossover* in Figure 4.11, which assumes a total ordering of the variables. An index i is selected at random. One of the children is constructed by selecting the values for the variables up to i from one of the parents, and the values for variables after i from the other parent. The other child gets the other values. The effectiveness of the crossover depends on the total ordering of the variables. The ordering of the variables is part of the design of the genetic algorithm.

Example 4.26 Consider Example 4.9 (page 131) where the evaluation function to be minimized is the number of unsatisfied constraints. The individual $A=2$, $B=2$, $C=3$, $D=1$, $E=1$ has an evaluation of 4. It has a low value mainly because $E=1$. Its offspring that preserve this property will tend to have a lower evaluation than those that do not and, thus, will be more likely to survive. Other individuals may have low values for different reasons; for example, the individual $A=4$, $B=2$, $C=3$, $D=4$, $E=4$ also has an evaluation of 4. It is low mainly because of the assignment of values to the first four variables. Again, offspring that preserve this property will be fitter and more likely to survive than those that do not. If these two were to mate, some of the offspring would inherit the bad properties of both and would die off. Some, by chance, would inherit the good properties of both. These would then have a better chance of survival.

Efficiency is very sensitive to the variables used to describe the problem and the ordering of the variables. Getting this to work is an art. As with many other randomized algorithms, evolutionary algorithms have many degrees of freedom and, therefore, are difficult to configure or tune for good performance.

A large community of researchers are working on genetic algorithms to make them practical for real problems and there have been some impressive results. What we have described here is only one of the possible genetic algorithms.

4.9 Optimization

Instead of just having possible worlds satisfy constraints or not, we often have a **preference** relation over possible worlds, and we want a best possible world according to the preference.

An **optimization problem** is given

- a set of variables, each with an associated domain

- an **objective function** that maps total assignments to real numbers, and

- an **optimality criterion**, which is typically to find a total assignment that minimizes or maximizes the objective function.

The aim is to find a total assignment that is optimal according to the optimality criterion. For concreteness, we assume that the optimality criterion is to minimize the objective function.

A **constrained optimization problem** is an optimization problem that also has hard constraints specifying which variable assignments are possible. The aim is to find an optimal assignment that satisfies the hard constraints.

A huge literature exists on optimization. There are many techniques for particular forms of constrained optimization problems. For example, **linear programming** is the class of constrained optimization where the variables are real valued, the objective function is a linear function of the variables, and the hard constraints are linear inequalities. If the problem you are interested in solving falls into one of the classes for which there are more specific algorithms, or can be transformed into one, it is generally better to use those techniques than the more general algorithms presented here.

In a **constraint optimization problem**, the objective function is factored into a set of soft constraints. A **soft constraint** has a **scope** that is a set of variables. The soft constraint is a function from the domains of the variables in its scope into a real number, a **cost**. A typical optimality criterion is to choose a total assignment that minimizes the sum of the costs of the soft constraints.

Example 4.27 Suppose a number of delivery activities must be scheduled, similar to Example 4.9 (page 131), but, instead of hard constraints, there are preferences on times for the activities. The soft constraints are costs associated with combinations of times. The aim is to find a schedule with the minimum total sum of the costs.

Suppose variables A, C, D, and E have domain $\{1, 2\}$, and variable B has domain $\{1, 2, 3\}$. The soft constraints are

c_1:	A	B	Cost	c_2:	B	C	Cost	c_3:	B	D	Cost
	1	1	5		1	1	5		1	1	3
	1	2	2		1	2	2		1	2	0
	1	3	2		2	1	0		2	1	2
	2	1	0		2	2	4		2	2	2
	2	2	4		3	1	2		3	1	2
	2	3	3		3	2	0		3	2	4

Thus, the scope of c_1 is $\{A, B\}$, the scope of c_2 is $\{B, C\}$, and the scope of c_3 is $\{B, D\}$. Suppose there are also constraints $c_4(C, E)$ and $c_5(D, E)$.

Soft constraints can be added pointwise. The sum of two soft constraints is a soft constraint with scope that is the union of their scopes. The cost of any assignment to variables in the scope is the sum of the costs of the constraints being added on that assignment.

Example 4.28 Consider functions c_1 and c_2 in the previous example. $c_1 + c_2$ is a function with scope $\{A, B, C\}$, given by

$c_1 + c_2$:	A	B	C	Cost
	1	1	1	10
	1	1	2	7
	1	2	1	2
	...	...	...	...

The second value is computed as follows:

$$(c_1 + c_2)(A=1, B=1, C=2) = c_1(A=1, B=1) + c_2(B=1, C=2)$$
$$= 5 + 2$$
$$= 7$$

Hard constraints can be modeled as having a cost of infinity for violating a constraint. As long as the cost of an assignment is finite, it does not violate a hard constraint. An alternative is to use a large number – larger than the sum of the soft constraints could be – as the cost of violating a hard constraint. Then optimization can be used to find a solution with the fewest number of violated hard constraints and, among those, one with the lowest cost.

Optimization problems have one difficulty that goes beyond constraint satisfaction problems. It is difficult to know whether an assignment is optimal. Whereas, for a CSP, an algorithm can check whether an assignment is a solution by just considering the assignment and the constraints, in optimization problems an algorithm can only determine whether an assignment is optimal by comparing it to other assignments.

Many of the methods for solving hard constraints can be extended to optimization problems, as outlined in the following sections.

4.9.1 Systematic Methods for Optimization

One way to find the minimal assignment, corresponding to **generate and test** (page 132), is to compute the sum of the soft constraints and to select an assignment with minimum value. This is infeasible for large problems.

Arc consistency (page 136) can be generalized to optimization problems by allowing pruning of dominated assignments. Suppose $c_1, \ldots, c_k$ are the soft constraints that involve X. Let $c = c_1 + \cdots + c_k$. Suppose $Y_1, \ldots, Y_m$ are the variables, other than X, that are involved in c. A value v for variable X is **strictly dominated** if, for all values $y_1, \ldots, y_k$ of $Y_1, \ldots, Y_m$, some value v' of X exists such that $c(X=v', Y_1=y_1, \ldots, Y_m=y_m) < c(X=v, Y_1=y_1, \ldots, Y_m=y_m)$. Pruning strictly dominated values does not remove a minimal solution. The pruning of domains can be done repeatedly, as in the GAC algorithm (page 136).

Weakly dominated has the same definition as strictly dominated, but with "less than" replaced by "less than or equal to." If only one solution is required, weakly dominated values can be pruned sequentially. Which weakly dominated values are removed may affect which optimal solution is found, but removing a weakly dominated value does not remove all optimal solutions. As with arc consistency for hard constraints, pruning (strictly or weakly) dominated values may greatly simplify the problem but does not, by itself, always solve the problem.

Domain splitting (page 139) is used to build a search tree. A node is an assignment of a value to a subset of the variables. The neighbors of a node are obtained by selecting a variable X that is not assigned in the node to split; there is a neighbor of the node for each value of X. Assigning a value to X allows the constraints that involve X to be simplified and values for other variables to be pruned due to hard constraints or to domination. The arc cost is the evaluation of the soft constraints that are able to be evaluated. A goal node is one where all of the variables are assigned.

By assigning costs as soon as a soft constraint is able to be evaluated, search algorithms such as A^* or branch-and-bound can be used to find a minimal solution. These methods require each arc cost to be non-negative. To achieve this, the lowest cost in each soft constraint – even if it is negative – is subtracted from each of the costs in the soft constraint. This cost then needs to be added to the cost of a final solution.

Example 4.29 Suppose X and Y are variables with domain $\{0, 1\}$. The constraint

X	Y	Cost
0	0	-4
0	1	-1
1	0	5
1	1	6

1: **procedure** $VE\_SC(Vs, Cs)$
2:     **Inputs**
3:         Vs: set of variables
4:         Cs: set of soft constraints
5:     **Output**
6:         an optimal assignment to Vs.
7:     **if** Vs contains a single element or Cs contains a single constraint **then**
8:         let C be the sum of the constraints in Cs
9:         **return** assignment with minimum value in C
10:     **else**
11:         select $X \in Vs$ according to some elimination ordering
12:         $R = \{C \in Cs : C \text{ involves } X\}$
13:         let T be the sum of the constraints in R
14:         $N := \min_X T$
15:         $S := VE\_SC(Vs \setminus \{X\}, Cs \setminus R \cup \{N\})$
16:         $X_{opt} := \arg\min_X T(S)$
17:         **return** $S \cup \{X = X_{opt}\}$

Figure 4.12: Variable elimination for optimizing with soft constraints

is converted into nonnegative form by subtracting -4 (i.e., adding 4) to each cost, so the costs range from 0 to 10, rather than from -4 to 6. The 4 is then subtracted from the cost of the solution.

Variable elimination (page 141) can also be used for soft constraints. The variables are eliminated one at a time. A variable X is eliminated as follows. Let R be the set of constraints that involve X. Compute, T, a new constraint whose scope is the union of the scopes of the constraints in R and whose value is the sum of the values of R. Let $V = scope(T) \setminus \{X\}$. For each value of the variables in V, select a value of X that minimizes T, resulting in a new soft constraint, N, with scope V. The constraint N replaces the constraints in R. This results in a new problem, with fewer variables and a new set of constraints, which can be solved recursively. A solution, S, to the reduced problem is an assignment to the variables in V. Thus, $T(S)$, the constraint T under the assignment S, is a function of X. An optimal value for X is obtained by choosing a value that results in the minimum value of $T(S)$.

Figure 4.12 gives pseudocode for the variable elimination with soft constraints (VE_SC) algorithm. The elimination ordering can be given a priori or may be computed on the fly, for example, using the elimination ordering heuristics discussed for VE_CSP (page 144). It is possible to implement VE_SC without storing T and by only constructing an extensional representation of N.

Example 4.30 Consider Example 4.27 (page 160). First consider eliminating

A. It appears in only one constraint, $c_1(A, B)$. Eliminating A gives

$$c_6(B) = \arg\min_A c_1(A, B):$$

B	Cost
1	0
2	2
3	2

The constraint $c_1(A, B)$ is replaced by $c_6(B)$.

Suppose B is eliminated next. B appears in three constraints: $c_2(B, C)$, $c_3(B, D)$, and $c_6(B)$. These three constraints are added, giving

$$c_2(B, C) + c_3(B, D) + c_6(B):$$

B	C	D	Cost
1	1	1	8
1	1	2	5
	...		
2	1	1	4
2	1	2	4
	...		
3	1	1	6
3	1	2	8

The constraints c_2, c_3, and c_6 are replaced by

$$c_7(C, D) = \min_B (c_2(B, C) + c_3(B, D) + c_6(B)):$$

C	D	Cost
1	1	4
1	2	4
	...	

There are now three remaining constraints: $c_4(C, E)$, $c_5(D, E)$, and $c_7(C, D)$. These can be optimized recursively.

Suppose the recursive call returns the solution $C=1, D=2, E=2$. An optimal value for B is the value with the minimum in $c_2(B, C=1) + c_3(B, D=2) + c_6(B)$, which is $B=2$.

From $c_1(A, B)$, the value of A that minimizes $c_1(A, B=2)$ is $A=1$. Thus, an optimal solution is $A=1, B=2, C=1, D=2, E=2$, with a cost of 4.

The complexity of VE_SC depends on the structure of the constraint graph, as it does with hard constraints (page 144). Sparse graphs may result in small intermediate constraints in VE algorithms, including VE_SC. Densely connected graphs result in large intermediate constraints.

4.9.2   Local Search for Optimization

Local search is directly applicable to optimization problems, where the local search is used to minimize the objective function, rather than find a solution. The algorithm runs for a certain amount of time (perhaps including random restarts to explore other parts of the search space), always keeping the best assignment found thus far, and returning this as its answer.

Local search for optimization has one extra complication that does not arise when there are only hard constraints. With only hard constraints, the algorithm has found a solution when there are no conflicts. For optimization, is difficult to determine whether the best total assignment found is the best possible solution. A **local optimum** is a total assignment that is at least as good, according to the optimality criterion, as any of its possible successors. A **global optimum** is a total assignment that is at least as good as all of the other total assignments. Without systematically searching the other assignments, the algorithm may not know whether the best assignment found so far is a global optimum or whether a better solution exists in a different part of the search space.

When using local search to solve constrained optimization problems, with both hard and soft constraints, it is often useful to allow the algorithm to violate hard constraints on the way to a solution. This is done by making the cost of violating a hard constraint some large, but finite value.

Continuous Domains

For optimization with continuous domains, a local search becomes more complicated because it is not obvious what the possible successor of a total assignment are.

For optimization where the evaluation function is continuous and differentiable, **gradient descent** can be used to find a minimum value, and **gradient ascent** can be used to find a maximum value. Gradient descent is like walking downhill and always taking a step in the direction that goes down the most; this is the direction a rock will tumble if let loose. The general idea is that the successor of a total assignment is a step downhill in proportion to the slope of the evaluation function h. Thus, gradient descent takes steps in each direction proportional to the negative of the partial derivative in that direction.

In one dimension, if X is a real-valued variable with the current value of v, the next value should be

$$v - \eta * \left(\frac{dh}{dX} \right) (v),$$

- η, the **step size**, is the constant of proportionality that determines how fast gradient descent approaches the minimum. If η is too large, the algorithm can overshoot the minimum; if η is too small, progress becomes very slow.

- $\frac{dh}{dX}$, the derivative of h with respect to X, is a function of X and is evaluated for $X=v$. This is equal to $\lim_{\epsilon \to 0} (h(X = v + \epsilon) - h(X = v))/\epsilon$

Example 4.31   Figure 4.13 (on the next page) shows a typical example for finding a local minimum of a one-dimensional function. It starts at a position marked as 1. The derivative is a big positive value, so it takes a step to the left

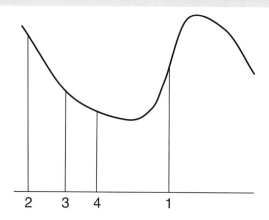

Figure 4.13: Gradient descent

to position 2. Here the derivative is negative, and closer to zero, so it takes a smaller step to the right to position 3. At position 3, the derivative is negative and closer to zero, so it takes a smaller step to the right. As it approaches the local minimum value, the slope becomes closer to zero and it takes smaller steps.

For multidimensional optimization, when there are many variables, gradient descent takes a step in each dimension proportional to the partial derivative of that dimension. If $\langle X_1, \ldots, X_n \rangle$ are the variables that have to be assigned values, a total assignment corresponds to a tuple of values $\langle v_1, \ldots, v_n \rangle$. The successor of the total assignment $\langle v_1, \ldots, v_n \rangle$ is obtained by moving in each direction in proportion to the slope of h in that direction. The new value for X_i is

$$v_i - \eta * \left(\frac{\partial h}{\partial X_i} \right) (v_1, \ldots, v_n),$$

where η is the **step size**. The partial derivative, $\frac{\partial h}{\partial X_i}$, is a function of $X_1, \ldots, X_n$. Applying it to the point $(v_1, \ldots, v_n)$ gives

$$\left(\frac{\partial h}{\partial X_i} \right)(v_1, \ldots, v_n) = \lim_{\epsilon \to 0} \frac{h(v_1, \ldots, v_i + \epsilon, \ldots, v_n) - h(v_1, \ldots, v_i, \ldots, v_n)}{\epsilon}.$$

If the partial derivative of h can be computed analytically, it is usually good to do so. If not, it can be estimated using a small value of ϵ.

Gradient descent is used for parameter learning (page 292), in which there may be thousands or even millions of real-valued parameters to be optimized. There are many variants of this algorithm. For example, instead of using a constant step size, the algorithm could do a binary search to determine a locally optimal step size.

For smooth functions, where there is a minimum, if the step size is small enough, gradient descent will converge to a local minimum. If the step size is too big, it is possible that the algorithm will diverge. If the step size is too small the algorithm will be very slow. If there is a unique local minimum, gradient descent, with a small enough step size, will converge to that global minimum. When there are multiple local minima, not all of which are global minima, it may need to search to find a global minimum, for example by doing a random restart (page 145) or a random walk (page 148). These are not guarantee to find a global minimum unless the whole search space is exhausted, but are often as good as we can get.

4.10 Review

The following are the main points you should have learned from this chapter:

- Instead of reasoning explicitly in terms of worlds or states, it is almost always much more efficient for an agent to reason in terms of variables or features.

- Constraint satisfaction problems are represented as a set of variables, domains for the variables, and a set of hard and/or soft constraints. A solution is an assignment of a value to each variable that satisfies a set of hard constraints or optimizes the sum of the soft constraints.

- Arc consistency and search can often be combined to find assignments that satisfy some constraints or to show that there is no assignment.

- Stochastic local search can be used to find satisfying assignments, but not to show there are no satisfying assignments. The efficiency depends on the trade-off between the time taken for each improvement and how much the value is improved at each step. Some method must be used to allow the search to escape local minima that are not solutions.

- Optimization can use systematic methods when the constraint graph is sparse. Local search can also be used, but the added problem arises of not knowing when the search is at a global optimum.

4.11 References and Further Reading

Constraint satisfaction techniques are described in Dechter [2003] and Freuder and Mackworth [2006]. The *GAC* algorithm was invented by Mackworth [1977].

Variable elimination for propositional satisfiability was proposed by Davis and Putnam [1960]. VE for optimization has been called **non-serial dynamic programming** and was invented by Bertelè and Brioschi [1972].

1	2	3
4		
5		

Words:
add, age, aid, aim, air,
are, arm, art, bad, bat,
bee, boa, dim, ear, eel,
eft, lee, oaf

Figure 4.14: A crossword puzzle to be solved with six words

Stochastic local search is described by Spall [2003] and Hoos and Stützle [2004]. The any-conflict algorithm is based on Minton et al. [1992]. Simulated annealing was invented by Kirkpatrick et al. [1983].

Genetic algorithms were pioneered by Holland [1975]. A huge literature exists on genetic algorithms; for overviews see Goldberg [1989], Koza [1992], Mitchell [1996], Bäck [1996], Whitley [2001], and Goldberg [2002].

4.12 Exercises

Exercise 4.1 Consider the crossword puzzle shown in Figure 4.14.

You must find six three-letter words: three words read across (*1-across, 4-across, 5-across*) and three words read down (*1-down, 2-down, 3-down*). Each word must be chosen from the list of 18 possible words shown. Try to solve it yourself, first by intuition, then by hand using first domain consistency and then arc consistency.

There are at least two ways to represent the crossword puzzle shown in Figure 4.14 as a constraint satisfaction problem.

The first is to represent the word positions (*1-across, 4-across,* etc.) as variables, with the set of words as possible values. The constraints are that the letter is the same where the words intersect.

The second is to represent the nine squares as variables. The domain of each variable is the set of letters of the alphabet, $\{a, b, \ldots, z\}$. The constraints are that there is a word in the word list that contains the corresponding letters. For example, the top-left square and the center-top square cannot both have the value a, because there is no word starting with aa.

(a) Give an example of pruning due to domain consistency using the first representation (if one exists).

(b) Give an example of pruning due to arc consistency using the first representation (if one exists).

(c) Are domain consistency plus arc consistency adequate to solve this problem using the first representation? Explain.

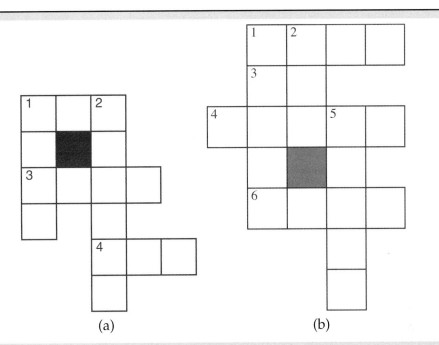

Figure 4.15: Two crossword puzzles

(d) Give an example of pruning due to domain consistency using the second representation (if one exists).

(e) Give an example of pruning due to arc consistency using the second representation (if one exists).

(f) Are domain consistency plus arc consistency adequate to solve this problem using the second representation?

(g) Which representation leads to a more efficient solution using consistency-based techniques? Give the evidence on which you are basing your answer.

Exercise 4.2 Suppose you have a relation $v(N, W)$ that is true if there is a vowel (one of: a, e, i, o, u) as the N-th letter of word W. For example, $v(2, cat)$ is true because there is a vowel ("a") as the second letter of the word "cat"; $v(3, cat)$ is false, because the third letter of "cat" is "t", which is not a vowel; and $v(5, cat)$ is also false because there is no fifth letter in "cat".

Suppose the domain of N is $\{1, 3, 5\}$ and the domain of W is $\{added, blue, fever, green, stare\}$.

(a) Is the arc $\langle N, v \rangle$ arc consistent? If so, explain why. If not, show what element(s) can be removed from a domain to make it arc consistent.

(b) Is the arc $\langle W, v \rangle$ arc consistent? If so, explain why. If not, show what element(s) can be removed from a domain to make it arc consistent.

Exercise 4.3 Consider the crossword puzzles shown in Figure 4.15. The possible words for (a) are:

ant, big, bus, car, has, book, buys, hold, lane, year, ginger, search, symbol, syntax.

The available words for (b) are

at, eta, be, hat, he, her, it, him, on, one, desk, dance, usage, easy, dove, first, else, loses, fuels, help, haste, given, kind, sense, soon, sound, this, think.

(a) Draw the constraint graph nodes for the positions (*1-across*, *2-down*, etc.) and words for the domains, after it has been made domain consistent

(b) Give an example of pruning due to arc consistency.

(c) What are the domains after arc-consistency has halted?

(d) Consider the dual representation, in which the squares on the intersection of words are the variables. The domains of the variable contain the letters that could go in these positions. Give the domains after this network has been made arc consistent. Does the result after arc consistency in this representation correspond to the result in part (c)?

(e) Show how variable elimination solves the crossword problem. Start from the arc-consistent network from part (c).

(f) Does a different elimination ordering affect the efficiency? Explain.

Exercise 4.4 Consider the complexity for generalized arc consistency beyond the binary case considered in the text (page 139). Suppose there are n variables, c constraints, where each constraint involves k variables, and the domain of each variable is of size d. How many arcs are there? What is the worst-case cost of checking one arc as a function of c, k and d? How many times must an arc be checked? Based on this, what is the time complexity of GAC as a function of c, k and d? What is the space complexity?

Exercise 4.5 Consider how stochastic local search can solve Exercise 4.3. You should use the "stochastic local search" Alspace.org applet or the book's Python code to answer this question. Start with the arc-consistent network.

(a) How well does random walking work?

(b) How well does hill climbing work?

(c) How well does the combination work?

(d) Which (range of) parameter settings works best? What evidence did you use to answer this question?

Exercise 4.6

Consider a scheduling problem, where there are five activities to be scheduled in four time slots. Suppose we represent the activities by the variables A, B, C, D, and E, where the domain of each variable is $\{1, 2, 3, 4\}$ and the constraints are $A > D, D > E, C \neq A, C > E, C \neq D, B \geq A, B \neq C,$ and $C \neq D + 1$.

[Before you start this, try to find the legal schedule(s) using your own intuitions.]

(a) Show how backtracking solves this problem. To do this, you should draw the search tree generated to find all answers. Indicate clearly the valid schedule(s). Make sure you choose a reasonable variable ordering.

To indicate the search tree, write it in text form with each branch on one line. For example, suppose we had variables X, Y, and Z with domains t, f and constraints $X \neq Y$ and $Y \neq Z$. The corresponding search tree is written as:

```
X=t Y=t failure
    Y=f Z=t solution
        Z=f failure
X=f Y=t Z=t failure
        Z=f solution
    Y=f failure
```

[Hint: It may be easier to write a program to generate such a tree for a particular problem than to do it by hand.]

(b) Show how arc consistency solves this problem. To do this you must

- draw the constraint graph;
- show which elements of a domain are deleted at each step, and which arc is responsible for removing the element;
- show explicitly the constraint graph after arc consistency has stopped; and
- show how splitting a domain can be used to sove this problem.

Exercise 4.7 Which of the following methods can

(a) determine that there is no model, if there is not one

(b) find a model if one exists

(c) find all models?

The methods to consider are

i) arc consistency with domain splitting

ii) variable elimination

iii) stochastic local search

iv) genetic algorithms.

Exercise 4.8 Modify arc consistency with domain splitting to return all of the models and not just one. Give the algorithm.

Exercise 4.9 Give the algorithm for variable elimination to return one of the models rather than all of them. How is finding one easier than finding all?

Exercise 4.10 Explain how arc consistency with domain splitting can be used to count the number of models. If domain splitting results in a disconnected graph, how can this be exploited by the algorithm?

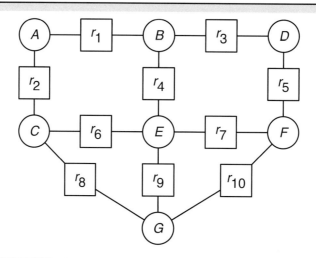

Figure 4.16: Abstract constraint network

Exercise 4.11 Modify VE to count the number of models, without enumerating them all. [Hint: You do not need the backward pass, but instead you can pass forward the number of solutions there would be.]

Exercise 4.12 Consider the constraint graph of Figure 4.16 with named binary constraints. r_1 is a relation on A and B, which we can write as $r_1(A, B)$, and similarly for the other relations. Consider solving this network using VE.

(a) Suppose you were to eliminate variable A. Which constraints are removed? A constraint is created on which variables? (You can call this r_{11}.)

(b) Suppose you were to subsequently eliminate B (i.e., after eliminating A). Which relations are removed? A constraint is created on which variables?

Exercise 4.13 Pose and solve the crypt-arithmetic problem $SEND + MORE = MONEY$ as a CSP. In a crypt-arithmetic problem, each letter represents a different digit, the leftmost digit cannot be zero (because then it would not be there), and the sum must be correct considering each sequence of letters as a base ten numeral. In this example, you know that $Y = (D + E)$ mod 10 and that $E = (N + R + ((D + E) \div 10))$ mod 10, and so on.

Chapter 5

Propositions and Inference

For when I am presented with a false theorem, I do not need to examine or even to know the demonstration, since I shall discover its falsity a posteriori by means of an easy experiment, that is, by a calculation, costing no more than paper and ink, which will show the error no matter how small it is ...

And if someone would doubt my results, I should say to him: "Let us calculate, Sir," and thus by taking to pen and ink, we should soon settle the question.

– Gottfried Wilhelm Leibniz [1677]

This chapter considers a simple form of a knowledge base that is told what facts and rules hold in the world. An agent can use such a knowledge base, together with its observations, to determine what else must be true in the world. When queried about what must be true given a knowledge base, it answers the query without enumerating the possible worlds, or even generating any possible worlds. This chapter presents a number of reasoning formalisms that use propositions. They differ in what is being proved, what background knowledge must be provided, and how observations are handled.

5.1 Propositions

Statements about the world provide constraints about what could be true. Constraints could be specified **extensionally** (page 130) as tables of legal assignments to variables, or **intensionally** (page 130) in terms of formulas. For many domains propositions provide a suitable language for providing intensional constraints.

There are a number of reasons for using propositions for specifying constraints and queries:

- It is often more concise and readable to give a logical statement about the relationship among some variables than to use an extensional representation.

- The form of the knowledge can be exploited to make reasoning more efficient.

- They are modular, so small changes to the problem result in small changes to the knowledge base. This also means that a knowledge base is easier to debug than for other representations.

- The kind of queries an agent may have to answer may be richer than single assignments of values to variables.

- This language is extended to reason about individuals and relations in Chapter 13.

We first give the syntax and the semantics of a language called the **propositional calculus**.

5.1.1 Syntax of Propositional Calculus

A **proposition** is a sentence, written in a language, that has a truth value (i.e., it is true or false) in a world. A proposition is built from atomic propositions using logical connectives.

An **atomic proposition**, or just an **atom**, is a symbol (page 127). We use the convention that propositions consist of letters, digits and the underscore (_) and start with a lower-case letter.

For example, ai_is_fun, lit_l_1, $live\_outside$, $mimsy$ and $sunny$ are all atoms.

Propositions can be built from simpler propositions using logical connectives. A **proposition** or **logical formula** is either

- an atomic proposition or

- a **compound proposition** of the form

$\neg p$	"not p"	**negation** of p
$p \wedge q$	"p and q"	**conjunction** of p and q
$p \vee q$	"p or q"	**disjunction** of p and q
$p \rightarrow q$	"p implies q"	**implication** of q from p
$p \leftarrow q$	"p if q"	**implication** of p from q
$p \leftrightarrow q$	"p if and only if q"	**equivalence** of p and q

where p and q are propositions.

The operators $\neg$, $\wedge$, $\vee$, $\rightarrow$, $\leftarrow$ and $\leftrightarrow$ are **logical connectives**.

Parentheses can be used to make logical formulae unambiguous. When parentheses are omitted, the precedence of the operators is in the order they

p	q	$\neg p$	$p \wedge q$	$p \vee q$	$p \leftarrow q$	$p \rightarrow q$	$p \leftrightarrow q$
true	true	false	true	true	true	true	true
true	false	false	false	true	true	false	false
false	true	true	false	true	false	true	false
false	false	true	false	false	true	true	true

Figure 5.1: Truth table defining $\neg$, $\wedge$, $\vee$, $\leftarrow$, $\rightarrow$, and $\leftrightarrow$

are given above. Thus, a compound proposition can be disambiguated by adding parentheses to the subexpressions in the order the operations are defined above. For example,

$$\neg a \vee b \wedge c \rightarrow d \wedge \neg e \vee f$$

is an abbreviation for

$$((\neg a) \vee (b \wedge c)) \rightarrow ((d \wedge (\neg e)) \vee f).$$

5.1.2 Semantics of the Propositional Calculus

Semantics defines the meaning of the sentences of a language. When the sentences are about a (real or imagined) world, semantics specifies how to put symbols of the language into correspondence with the world.

The semantics of propositional calculus is defined below. Intuitively, atoms have meaning to someone and are either true or false in interpretations. The truth of atoms gives the truth of other propositions in interpretations.

An **interpretation** consists of a function π that maps atoms to $\{true, false\}$. If $\pi(a) = true$, atom a is **true** in the interpretation, or the interpretation assigns *true* to a. If $\pi(a) = false$, atom a is **false** in the interpretation. Sometimes it is useful to think of π as the set of the atoms that map to *true*, and the rest of the atoms map to *false*.

Whether a compound proposition is true in an interpretation is inferred using the truth table of Figure 5.1 from the truth values of the components of the proposition.

Note that truth values are only defined with respect to interpretations; propositions may have different truth values in different interpretations.

Example 5.1 Suppose there are three atoms: *ai_is_fun*, *happy*, and *light_on*.

Suppose interpretation I_1 assigns *true* to *ai_is_fun*, *false* to *happy*, and *true* to *light_on*. That is, I_1 is defined by the function π_1

$$\pi_1(ai\_is\_fun)=true, \quad \pi_1(happy)=false, \quad \pi_1(light\_on)=true.$$

Then

- *ai_is_fun* is true in I_1
- $\neg ai\_is\_fun$ is false in I_1
- *happy* is false in I_1
- $\neg happy$ is true in I_1
- *ai_is_fun* $\lor$ *happy* is true in I_1
- *ai_is_fun* $\leftarrow$ *happy* is true in I_1
- *happy* $\leftarrow$ *ai_is_fun* is false in I_1
- *ai_is_fun* $\leftarrow$ *happy* $\land$ *light_on* is true in I_1.

Suppose interpretation I_2 assigns *false* to *ai_is_fun*, *true* to *happy*, and *false* to *light_on*:

- *ai_is_fun* is false in I_2
- $\neg ai\_is\_fun$ is true in I_2
- *happy* is true in I_2
- $\neg happy$ is false in I_2
- *ai_is_fun* $\lor$ *happy* is true in I_2
- *ai_is_fun* $\leftarrow$ *happy* is false in I_2
- *ai_is_fun* $\leftarrow$ *light_on* is true in I_2
- *ai_is_fun* $\leftarrow$ *happy* $\land$ *light_on* is true in I_2.

A **knowledge base** is a set of propositions that are stated to be true. An element of the knowledge base is an **axiom**.

A **model** of a knowledge base *KB* is an interpretation in which all the propositions in *KB* are true.

If *KB* is a knowledge base and g is a proposition, g is a **logical consequence** of *KB*, written as

$$KB \models g$$

if g is true in every model of *KB*. Thus $KB \not\models g$, meaning g is not a logical consequence of *KB*, when there is a model of *KB* in which g is false.

That is, $KB \models g$ means no interpretation exists in which *KB* is true and g is false. The definition of logical consequence places no constraints on the truth value of g in an interpretation where *KB* is false.

If $KB \models g$ we also say g **logically follows** from *KB*, or *KB* **entails** g.

Example 5.2 Suppose *KB* is the following knowledge base:

sam_is_happy.

ai_is_fun.

worms_live_underground.

night_time.

bird_eats_apple.

apple_is_eaten $\leftarrow$ *bird_eats_apple.*

switch_1_is_up $\leftarrow$ *sam_is_in_room* $\land$ *night_time.*

Given this knowledge base,

$KB \models bird\_eats\_apple.$

$KB \models apple\_is\_eaten.$

KB does not entail $switch\_1\_is\_up$ as there is a model of the knowledge base where $switch\_1\_is\_up$ is false. Note that $sam\_is\_in\_room$ must be false in that interpretation.

The Human's View of Semantics

The description of semantics does not tell us why semantics is interesting or how it can be used as a basis to build intelligent systems. The basic idea behind the use of logic is that, when a **knowledge base designer** has a particular world to characterize, the designer can choose that world as an **intended interpretation**, choose meanings for the symbols with respect to that world, and write propositions about what is true in that world. When the system computes a logical consequence of a knowledge base, the designer can interpret this answer with respect to the intended interpretation. A designer should communicate this meaning to other designers and users so that they can also interpret the answer with respect to the meaning of the symbols.

The logical entailment "$KB \models g$" is a semantic relation between a set of propositions (KB) and a proposition it entails, g. Both KB and g are symbolic, and so they can be represented in the computer. The meaning may be with reference to the world, which is typically not symbolic. The $\models$ relation is not about computation or proofs; it provides the specification of what follows from some statements about what is true.

The methodology used by a knowledge base designer to represent a world can be expressed as follows:

Step 1 A knowledge base designer chooses a task domain or world to represent, which is the intended interpretation. This could be some aspect of the real world (for example, the structure of courses and students at a university, or a laboratory environment at a particular point in time), some imaginary world (such as the world of Alice in Wonderland, or the state of the electrical environment if a switch breaks), or an abstract world (for example, the world of numbers and sets).

Step 2 The knowledge base designer selects atoms to represent propositions of interest. Each atom has a precise meaning with respect to the intended interpretation.

Step 3 The knowledge base designer **tells** the system propositions that are true in the intended interpretation. This is often called **axiomatizing the domain**, where the given propositions are the **axioms** of the domain.

Step 4 The knowledge base designer can now **ask** questions about the intended interpretation. The system can answer these questions. The designer is able to interpret the answers using the meaning assigned to the symbols.

Within this methodology, the designer does not actually tell the computer anything until step 3. The first two steps are carried out in the head of the designer.

Designers should document the meanings of the symbols so that they can make their representations understandable to other people, so that they remember what each symbol means, and so that they can check the truth of the given propositions. A specification of meaning of the symbols is called an **ontology**. Ontologies can be informally specified in comments, but they are increasingly specified in formal languages to enable semantic interoperability – the ability to use symbols from different knowledge bases together. Ontologies are discussed in detail in Chapter 14.

Step 4 can be carried out by people as long as they understand the meaning of the symbols. Other people who know the meaning of the symbols in the question and the answer, and who trust the knowledge base designer to have told the truth, can interpret answers to their questions as being correct in the world under consideration.

The Computer's View of Semantics

The knowledge base designer who provides information to the system has an intended interpretation and interprets symbols according to that intended interpretation. The designer states knowledge, in terms of propositions, about what is true in the intended interpretation. The computer does not have access to the intended interpretation – only to the propositions in the knowledge base. Let *KB* be a given knowledge base. As will be shown, the computer is able to tell if some statement is a logical consequence of *KB*. The intended interpretation is a model of the axioms if the knowledge base designer has been truthful according to the meaning assigned to the symbols. Assuming the intended interpretation is a model of *KB*, if a proposition is a logical consequence of *KB*, it is true in the intended interpretation because it is true in all models of *KB*.

The concept of logical consequence seems like exactly the right tool to infer implicit information from an axiomatization of a world. Suppose *KB* represents the knowledge about the intended interpretation; that is, the intended interpretation is a model of *KB*, and that is all the system knows about the intended interpretation. If $KB \models g$, then g must be true in the intended interpretation, because it is true in all models of the knowledge base. If $KB \not\models g$, meaning g is not a logical consequence of *KB*, there is a model of *KB* in which g is false. As far as the computer is concerned, the intended interpretation may be the model of *KB* in which g is false, and so it does not know whether g is true in the intended interpretation.

Given a knowledge base, the models of the knowledge base correspond to all of the ways that the world could be, given that the knowledge base is true.

Example 5.3 Consider the knowledge base of Example 5.2 (page 176). The user could interpret these symbols as having some meaning. The computer does not know the meaning of the symbols, but it can still draw conclusions based on what it has been told. It can conclude that *apple_is_eaten* is true in the intended interpretation. It cannot conclude *switch_1_is_up* because it does not know if *sam_is_in_room* is true or false in the intended interpretation.

If the knowledge base designer tells lies – some axioms are false in the intended interpretation – the computer's answers are not guaranteed to be true in the intended interpretation.

It is very important to understand that, until we consider computers with perception and the ability to act in the world, the computer does not know the meaning of the symbols. It is the human that gives the symbols meaning. All the computer knows about the world is what it is told about the world. However, because the computer can provide logical consequences of the knowledge base, it can draw conclusions that are true in the world.

5.2 Propositional Constraints

Chapter 4 shows how to reason with constraints. Logical formulas provide a concise form of constraints with structure that can be exploited.

The class of **propositional satisfiability** problems have:

- Boolean variables: a **Boolean variable** (page 126) is a variable with domain $\{true, false\}$. If X is a Boolean variable, we write $X = true$ as its lower-case equivalent, x, and write $X = false$ as $\neg x$. Thus, given a Boolean variable *Happy*, the proposition *happy* means *Happy* $= true$, and $\neg happy$ means *Happy* $= false$.

- Clausal constraints: a **clause** is an expression of the form $l_1 \vee l_2 \vee \cdots \vee l_k$, where each l_i is a literal. A **literal** is an atom or the negation of an atom; thus a literal is an assignment of a value to a Boolean variable. A clause is satisfied in a possible world if and only if at least one of the literals that makes up the clause is true in that possible world.

  If $\neg a$ appear in a clause, the atom a is said to appear negatively in the clause. If a appears unnegated in a clause, it is said to appear positively in a clause.

In terms of the propositional calculus, a set of clauses is a restricted form of logical formulas. Any propositional formula can be converted into clausal form.

In terms of constraints (page 129), a clause is a constraint on a set of Boolean variables that rules out one of the assignments from consideration – the assignment that makes all literals false.

Example 5.4   The clause $happy \lor sad \lor \neg living$ is a constraint among the variables $Happy$, Sad, and $Living$, which is true if $Happy$ has value $true$, Sad has value $true$, or $Living$ has value $false$. The atoms $happy$ and sad appear positively in the clause, and $living$ appears negatively in the clause.

The assignment $\neg happy$, $\neg sad$, $living$ violates the constraint of clause $happy \lor sad \lor \neg living$. It is the only assignment of these three variables that violates this clause.

It is possible to convert any finite CSP into a propositional satisfiable problem:

- A CSP variable Y with domain $\{v_1, \dots, v_k\}$ can be converted into k Boolean variables $\{Y_1, \dots, Y_k\}$, where Y_i is true when Y has value v_i and is false otherwise. Each Y_i is called an **indicator variable**. Thus k atoms, $y_1, \dots, y_k$, are used to represent the CSP variable.

- There are constraints that specify that y_i and y_j cannot both be true when $i \neq j$. There is a constraint that one of the y_i must be true. Thus, the knowledge base contains the clauses: $\neg y_i \lor \neg y_j$ for $i < j$ and $y_1 \lor \cdots \lor y_k$.

- There is a clause for each false assignment in each constraint, which specifies which assignments to the Y_i are not allowed by the constraint. Often these clauses can be combined resulting in simpler constraints. For example, the clauses $a \lor b \lor c$ and $a \lor b \lor \neg c$ can be combined to $a \lor b$.

5.2.1   Clausal Form for Consistency Algorithms

Consistency algorithms (page 134) can be made more efficient for propositional satisfiability problems than for general CSPs. When there are only two values, pruning a value from the domain is equivalent to assigning the opposite value. Thus, if X has domain $\{true, false\}$, pruning $true$ from the domain of X is the same as assigning X to have value $false$.

Arc consistency can be used to prune the set of values and the set of constraints. Assigning a value to a Boolean variable can simplify the set of constraints:

- If X is assigned $true$, all of the clauses with $X = true$ become redundant; they are automatically satisfied. These clauses can be removed. Similarly, if X is assigned $false$, clauses containing $X = false$ can be removed.

- If X is assigned $true$, any clause with $X = false$ can be simplified by removing $X = false$ from the clause. Similarly, if X is assigned $false$, then

$X = true$ can be removed from any clause it appears in. This step is called **unit resolution**.

If, after pruning the clauses, there is a clause that contains just one assignment, $Y = v$, the other value can be removed from the domain of Y. This is a form of arc consistency. If all of the assignments are removed from a clause, the constraints are unsatisfiable.

Example 5.5   Consider the clause $\neg x \vee y \vee \neg z$. If X is assigned to *true*, the clause can be simplified to $y \vee \neg z$. If Y is then assigned to *false*, the clause can be simplified to $\neg z$. Thus, *true* can be pruned from the domain of Z.

If, instead, X is assigned to *false*, the clause can be removed.

If a variable has the same value in all remaining clauses, and the algorithm must only find one model, it can assign that value to that variable. For example, if variable Y only appears as $Y = true$ (i.e., $\neg y$ is not in any clause), then Y can be assigned the value *true*. That assignment does not remove all of the models; it only simplifies the problem because the set of clauses remaining after setting $Y = true$ is a subset of the clauses that would remain if Y were assigned the value *false*. A variable that only has one value in all of the clauses is called a **pure literal**.

It turns out that pruning the domains and constraints, domain splitting, and assigning pure literals is a very efficient algorithm, as long as the data structures are indexed to carry out these tasks efficiently. It is called the **DPLL** algorithm, after its authors.

5.2.2   Exploiting Propositional Structure in Local Search

Stochastic local search (page 144) is simpler, and so can be faster, for CSPs that are in the form of propositional satisfiability problems (page 179), with Boolean variables and clausal constraints. It can be made more efficient for the following reasons:

- Because only one alternative value exists for each assignment to a variable, the algorithm does not have to search through the alternative values.
- Changing any value in an unsatisfied clause makes the clause satisfied. As a result, it is easy to satisfy a clause, but this may make other clauses unsatisfied.
- If a variable is changed to be true, only those clauses where it appears negatively can become unsatisfied, and all of the clauses where it appears positively must become satisfied. Conversely, if a variable is changed to be false, only those clauses where it appears positively can become unsatisfied, and all of the clauses where it appears negatively must become satisfied. This enables fast indexing of clauses.

- The search space is expanded. In particular, before a solution has been found, more than one of the indicator variables for a variable Y could be true (which corresponds to Y having multiple values) or all of the indicator variables could be false (which corresponds to Y having no values). This can mean that some assignments that were local minima in the original problem may not be local minima in the new representation.

- Satisfiability has been studied much more extensively than most other types of CSPs and more efficient solvers exist because more of the space of potential algorithms has been explored by researchers.

Whether converting a particular CSP to a satisfiability problem makes search performance better is an empirical question.

5.3   Propositional Definite Clauses

The rest of this chapter considers some restricted languages and reasoning tasks that are useful and can be efficiently implemented.

The language of **propositional definite clauses** is a sublanguage of propositional calculus that does not allow uncertainty or ambiguity. In this language, propositions have the same meaning as in propositional calculus, but not all compound propositions are allowed in a knowledge base.

The **syntax** of propositional definite clauses is defined as follows:

- An **atomic proposition** or **atom** is the same as in propositional calculus.

- A **definite clause** is of the form

    $$h \leftarrow a_1 \wedge \ldots \wedge a_m.$$

    where h is an atom, the **head** of the clause, and each a_i is an atom. It can be read "h if a_1 and ... and a_m".

    If $m > 0$, the clause is called a **rule**, where $a_1 \wedge \ldots \wedge a_m$ is the **body** of the clause.

    If $m = 0$ the arrow can be omitted and the clause is called an **atomic clause** or **fact**. The clause has an **empty body**.

- A **knowledge base** is a set of definite clauses.

Example 5.6   The elements of the knowledge base in Example 5.2 (page 176) are all definite clauses.

The following are *not* definite clauses:

    ¬apple_is_eaten.

    apple_is_eaten $\wedge$ bird_eats_apple.

    sam_is_in_room $\wedge$ night_time $\leftarrow$ switch_1_is_up.

    Apple_is_eaten $\leftarrow$ Bird_eats_apple.

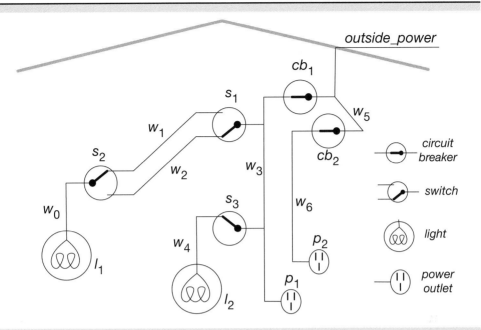

Figure 5.2: An electrical environment with components named

happy ∨ *sad* ∨ ¬*alive*.

The fourth statement is not a definite clause because an atom must start with a lower-case letter.

A definite clause $h \leftarrow a_1 \wedge \ldots \wedge a_m$ is false in interpretation I (page 175) if $a_1 \ldots a_m$ are all true in I and h is false in I; otherwise the definite clause is true in I.

Note that a definite clause is a restricted form of a clause (page 179). For example, the definite clause

$$a \leftarrow b \wedge c \wedge d.$$

is equivalent to the clause

$$a \vee \neg b \vee \neg c \vee \neg d.$$

In general, a definite clause is equivalent to a clause with exactly one positive literal (non-negated atom). Propositional definite clauses cannot represent disjunctions of atoms (e.g., $a \vee b$) or disjunctions of negated atoms (e.g., $\neg c \vee \neg d$).

Example 5.7 Consider how to axiomatize the electrical environment of Figure 5.2 following the methodology for the user's view of semantics (page 177). This axiomatization will allow us to simulate the electrical system. It will be expanded in later sections to let us diagnose faults based on observed symptoms.

The representation will be used to determine whether lights are on or off, based on switch positions and the status of circuit breakers. The agent is not concerned here with the color of the wires, the design of the switches, the length or weight of the wire, the date of manufacture of the lights and the wires, or any of the other myriad details one could imagine about the domain.

We must choose a level of abstraction. The aim is to represent the domain at the most general level that will enable the agent to solve the problems it must solve. We also want to represent the domain at a level that the agent will have information about. For example, we could represent the actual voltages and currents, but exactly the same reasoning would be done if this were a 12-volt DC system or a 120-volt AC system; the voltages and frequencies are irrelevant for questions about how switches affect whether lights are on. Instead, we represent this domain at a commonsense level that non-electricians may use to describe the domain, in terms of wires being live and currents flowing from the outside through wires to the lights, and that circuit breakers and light switches connect wires if they are turned on and working.

We have to choose what to represent. Suppose we want to represent propositions about whether lights are lit, whether wires are live, whether switches are up or down, and whether components are broken.

We then choose atoms with a specific meaning in the world. We can use descriptive names for these, such as up_s_2 to represent whether switch s_2 is up and $live\_l_1$ to represent whether light l_1 is live (i.e., has power coming into it). The computer does not know the meaning of these names and does not have access to the components of the atom's name.

At this stage, we have not told the computer anything. It does not know what the atoms are, let alone what they mean.

Once we have decided which symbols to use and what they mean, we tell the system, using definite clauses, background knowledge about what is true in the world. The simplest forms of definite clauses are those without bodies – the atomic clauses – such as

$light\_l_1$.

$light\_l_2$.

ok_l_1.

ok_l_2.

ok_cb_1.

ok_cb_2.

$live\_outside$.

The designer may look at part of the domain and know that light l_1 is live if wire w_0 is live, because they are connected together, but may not know whether w_0 is live. Such knowledge is expressible in terms of rules:

$live\_l_1 \leftarrow live\_w_0$.

$live\_w_0 \leftarrow live\_w_1 \land up\_s_2$.

$$live\_w_0 \leftarrow live\_w_2 \wedge down\_s_2.$$
$$live\_w_1 \leftarrow live\_w_3 \wedge up\_s_1.$$
$$live\_w_2 \leftarrow live\_w_3 \wedge down\_s_1.$$
$$live\_l_2 \leftarrow live\_w_4.$$
$$live\_w_4 \leftarrow live\_w_3 \wedge up\_s_3.$$
$$live\_p_1 \leftarrow live\_w_3.$$
$$live\_w_3 \leftarrow live\_w_5 \wedge ok\_cb_1.$$
$$live\_p_2 \leftarrow live\_w_6.$$
$$live\_w_6 \leftarrow live\_w_5 \wedge ok\_cb_2.$$
$$live\_w_5 \leftarrow live\_outside.$$
$$lit\_l_1 \leftarrow light\_l_1 \wedge live\_l_1 \wedge ok\_l_1.$$
$$lit\_l_2 \leftarrow light\_l_2 \wedge live\_l_2 \wedge ok\_l_2.$$

At run time, the user is able to input the observations of the current switch positions, such as

$$down\_s_1.$$

$$up\_s_2.$$

$$up\_s_3.$$

The knowledge base consists of all of the definite clauses, whether specified as background knowledge or as observations.

5.3.1 Questions and Answers

One reason to build a description of a real or imaginary world is to be able to determine what else must be true in that world. After the computer is given a knowledge base about a particular domain, a user might like to ask the computer questions about that domain. The computer can answer whether or not a proposition is a logical consequence of the knowledge base. If the user knows the meaning of the atoms, the user can interpret the answer in terms of the domain.

A **query** is a way of asking whether a proposition is a logical consequence of a knowledge base. Once the system has been provided with a knowledge base, a query is used to ask whether a formula is a logical consequence of the knowledge base. Queries have the form

ask b.

where b is a an atom or a conjunction of atoms (analogous to the body of a rule (page 182)).

A query is a question that has the **answer** "*yes*" if the body is a logical consequence of the knowledge base, or the answer "*no*" if the body is not a consequence of the knowledge base. The latter does not mean that *body* is false in the intended interpretation but rather that it is impossible to determine whether it is true or false based on the knowledge provided.

Example 5.8 Once the computer has been told the knowledge base of Example 5.7 (page 183), it can answer queries such as

   ask $light\_l_1$.

for which the answer is *yes*. The query

   ask $light\_l_6$.

has answer *no*. The computer does not have enough information to know whether or not l_6 is a light. The query

   ask lit_l_2.

has answer *yes*. This atom is true in all models.

   The user can interpret this answer with respect to the intended interpretation.

5.3.2 Proofs

So far, we have specified what an answer is, but not how it can be computed. The definition of $\models$ (page 176) specifies which propositions should be logical consequences of a knowledge base but not how to compute them. The problem of **deduction** is to determine if some proposition is a logical consequence of a knowledge base. Deduction is a specific form of **inference**.

   A **proof** is a mechanically derivable demonstration that a proposition logically follows from a knowledge base. A **theorem** is a provable proposition. A **proof procedure** is a – possibly non-deterministic – algorithm for deriving consequences of a knowledge base. (See the box on page 88 for a description of non-deterministic choice.)

   Given a proof procedure, $KB \vdash g$ means g can be **proved** or **derived** from knowledge base KB.

   A proof procedure's quality can be judged by whether it computes what it is meant to compute.

   A proof procedure is **sound** with respect to a semantics if everything that can be derived from a knowledge base is a logical consequence of the knowledge base. That is, if $KB \vdash g$, then $KB \models g$.

   A proof procedure is **complete** with respect to a semantics if there is a proof of each logical consequence of the knowledge base. That is, if $KB \models g$, then $KB \vdash g$.

   We present two ways to construct proofs for propositional definite clauses: a bottom-up procedure and a top-down procedure.

```
1: procedure Prove_DC_BU(KB)
2:     Inputs
3:         KB: a set of definite clauses
4:     Output
5:         Set of all atoms that are logical consequences of KB
6:     Local
7:         C is a set of atoms
8:     C := {}
9:     repeat
10:        select "h ← a₁ ∧ ... ∧ aₘ" in KB where aᵢ ∈ C for all i, and h ∉ C
11:        C := C ∪ {h}
12:     until no more definite clauses can be selected
13:     return C
```

Figure 5.3: Bottom-up proof procedure for computing consequences of KB

Bottom-Up Proof Procedure

A **bottom-up proof procedure** can be used to derive all logical consequences of a knowledge base. It is called bottom-up as an analogy to building a house, where each part of the house is built on the structure already completed. The bottom-up proof procedure builds on atoms that have already been established. It should be contrasted with a top-down approach (page 189), which starts from a query and tries to find definite clauses that support the query. Sometimes we say that a bottom-up procedure is **forward chaining** on the definite clauses, in the sense of going forward from what is known rather than going backward from the query.

The general idea is based on one **rule of derivation**, a generalized form of the rule of inference called **modus ponens**:

If "$h \leftarrow a_1 \wedge \ldots \wedge a_m$" is a definite clause in the knowledge base, and each a_i has been derived, then h can be derived.

An atomic clause (page 182) corresponds to the case of $m = 0$; modus ponens can always immediately derive any atomic clauses in the knowledge base.

Figure 5.3 gives a procedure for computing the **consequence set** C of a set KB of definite clauses. Under this proof procedure, if g is an atom, $KB \vdash g$ if $g \in C$ at the end of the *Prove_DC_BU* procedure. For a conjunction, $KB \vdash g_1 \wedge \cdots \wedge g_k$, if $\{g_1, \ldots, g_k\} \subseteq C$.

Example 5.9 Suppose the system is given the knowledge base KB:

$a \leftarrow b \wedge c.$

$b \leftarrow d \wedge e.$

$b \leftarrow g \wedge e.$

$c \leftarrow e.$

$d.$

$e.$

$f \leftarrow a \wedge g.$

One trace of the value assigned to C in the bottom-up procedure is

$\{\}$

$\{d\}$

$\{e, d\}$

$\{c, e, d\}$

$\{b, c, e, d\}$

$\{a, b, c, e, d\}.$

The algorithm terminates with $C = \{a, b, c, e, d\}$. Thus, $KB \vdash a$, $KB \vdash b$, and so on.

The last rule in KB is never used. The bottom-up proof procedure cannot derive f or g. This is as it should be because there is a model of the knowledge base in which f and g are both false.

The proof procedure of Figure 5.3 has a number of interesting properties:

Soundness Every atom in C is a logical consequence of KB. That is, if $KB \vdash g$ then $KB \models g$. To show this, assume that there is an atom in C that is not a logical consequence of KB. If such an atom exists, let h be first atom added to C that is not true in every model of KB. Suppose I is a model of KB in which h is false. Because h has been generated, there must be some definite clause in KB of the form $h \leftarrow a_1 \wedge \ldots \wedge a_m$ such that $a_1 \ldots a_m$ are all in C (which includes the case where h is an atomic clause and so $m = 0$). Because h is the first atom added to C that is not true in all models of KB, and the a_i are generated before h, all of the a_i true in I. This clause's head is false in I, and its body is true in I. Therefore, by the definition of truth of clauses, this clause is false in I. This is a contradiction to the fact that I is a model of KB. Thus, every element of C is a logical consequence of KB.

Complexity The algorithm of Figure 5.3 halts, and the number of times the loop is repeated is bounded by the number of definite clauses in KB. This is easily seen because each definite clause is only used at most once. Thus, the time complexity of the bottom-up proof procedure is linear in the size of the knowledge base if it indexes the definite clauses so that the inner loop is carried out in constant time.

Fixed Point The final C generated in the algorithm of Figure 5.3 is called a **fixed point** because any further application of the rule of derivation does not change C. C is the **least fixed point** because there is no smaller fixed point.

Let I be the interpretation in which every atom in the least fixed point is true and every atom not in the least fixed point is false. To show that I must be a model of KB, suppose "$h \leftarrow a_1 \wedge \ldots \wedge a_m$" $\in KB$ is false in I. The only way this could occur is if $a_1, \ldots, a_m$ are in the fixed point, and h is not in the fixed point. By construction, the rule of derivation can be used to add h to the fixed point, a contradiction to it being the fixed point. Therefore, there can be no definite clause in KB that is false in an interpretation defined by a fixed point. Thus, I is a model of KB.

I is the **minimal model** in the sense that it has the fewest true propositions. Every other model must also assign the atoms in C to be true.

Completeness Suppose $KB \models g$. Then g is true in every model of KB, so it is true in the minimal model, and so it is in C, and so $KB \vdash g$.

Top-Down Proof Procedure

An alternative proof method is to search *backward* or *top-down* from a query to determine whether it is a logical consequence of the given definite clauses. This procedure is called **propositional definite clause resolution** or **SLD resolution**, where SL stands for Selecting an atom using a Linear strategy, and D stands for Definite clauses. It is an instance of the more general **resolution** method.

The top-down proof procedure can be understood in terms of answer clauses. An **answer clause** is of the form

$$yes \leftarrow a_1 \wedge a_2 \wedge \ldots \wedge a_m$$

where *yes* is a special atom. Intuitively, *yes* is going to be true exactly when the answer to the query is "yes."

If the query is

$$ask \ q_1 \wedge \ldots \wedge q_m$$

the initial answer clause is

$$yes \leftarrow q_1 \wedge \ldots \wedge q_m$$

Given an answer clause, the top-down algorithm selects an atom in the body of the answer clause. Suppose it selects a_1. The atom selected is called a **subgoal**. The algorithm proceeds by doing steps of **resolution**. In one step of resolution, it chooses a definite clause in KB with a_1 as the head. If there is no such clause, the algorithm fails.

Note the use of **select** and **choose** (box on page 88). Any atom in the body can be selected, and if one selection does not lead to a proof, other selections do not need to be tried. When choosing a clause, the algorithm may need to search for a choice that makes the proof succeed.

The **resolvent** of the above answer clause on the selection a_1 with the definite clause

$$a_1 \leftarrow b_1 \wedge \ldots \wedge b_p$$

is the answer clause

$$yes \leftarrow b_1 \wedge \ldots \wedge b_p \wedge a_2 \wedge \ldots \wedge a_m$$

That is, the subgoal in the answer clause is replaced by the body of the chosen definite clause.

An **answer** is an answer clause with an empty body ($m = 0$). That is, it is the answer clause $yes \leftarrow$.

An **SLD derivation** of a query "ask $q_1 \wedge \ldots \wedge q_k$" from knowledge base KB is a sequence of answer clauses $\gamma_0, \gamma_1, \ldots, \gamma_n$ such that

- γ_0 is the answer clause corresponding to the original query, namely the answer clause $yes \leftarrow q_1 \wedge \ldots \wedge q_k$
- γ_i is the resolvent of γ_{i-1} with a definite clause in KB
- γ_n is an answer.

Another way to think about the algorithm is that the top-down algorithm maintains a collection G of atoms to prove. Each atom that must be proved is a **subgoal**. Initially, G is the set of atoms in the query. A clause $a \leftarrow b_1 \wedge \ldots \wedge b_p$ means subgoal a can be replaced by subgoals $b_1, \ldots, b_p$. The G to be proved corresponds to the answer clause $yes \leftarrow G$.

Figure 5.4 (on the next page) specifies a non-deterministic procedure for solving a query. It follows the definition of a derivation. In this procedure, G is the set of atoms in the body of the answer clause. The procedure is non-deterministic: at line 12 has to *choose* a definite clause to resolve against. If there are choices that result in G being the empty set, the algorithm returns yes; otherwise it fails, and the answer is no.

This algorithm treats the body of a clause as a set of atoms and G is also a set of atoms. An alternative is to have G as an ordered list of atoms, perhaps with an atom appearing more than once.

Example 5.10 Suppose the system is given the knowledge base:

$$a \leftarrow b \wedge c.$$
$$b \leftarrow d \wedge e.$$
$$b \leftarrow g \wedge e.$$
$$c \leftarrow e.$$
$$d.$$
$$e.$$

1: **non-deterministic procedure** *Prove_DC_TD(KB, Query)*
2:     **Inputs**
3:         *KB*: a set of definite clauses
4:         *Query*: a set of atoms to prove
5:     **Output**
6:         *yes* if *KB* $\models$ *Query* and the procedure fails otherwise
7:     **Local**
8:         *G* is a set of atoms
9:     *G* := *Query*
10:    **repeat**
11:        **select** an atom *a* in *G*
12:        **choose** definite clause "*a* ← *B*" in *KB* with *a* as head
13:        *G* := *B* ∪ (*G* \ {*a*})
14:    **until** *G* = {}
15:    **return** *yes*

Figure 5.4: Top-down definite clause proof procedure

$$f \leftarrow a \land g.$$

It is asked the query:

ask *a*.

The following shows a derivation that corresponds to a sequence of assignments to *G* in the repeat loop of Figure 5.4. Here we have written *G* in the form of an answer clause, and always selected the leftmost atom in the body:

$$yes \leftarrow a$$
$$yes \leftarrow b \land c$$
$$yes \leftarrow d \land e \land c$$
$$yes \leftarrow e \land c$$
$$yes \leftarrow c$$
$$yes \leftarrow e$$
$$yes \leftarrow$$

The following shows a sequence of choices, where the second definite clause for *b* was chosen. This choice does not lead to a proof.

$$yes \leftarrow a$$
$$yes \leftarrow b \land c$$
$$yes \leftarrow g \land e \land c$$

If *g* is selected, there are no rules that can be chosen. This proof attempt is said to *fail*.

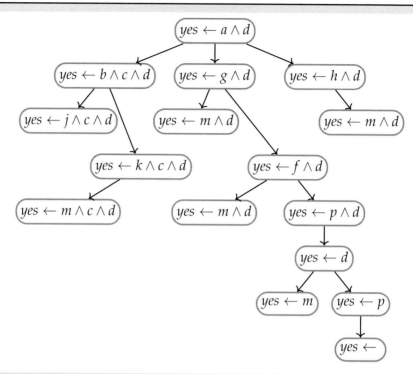

Figure 5.5: A search graph for a top-down derivation

The non-deterministic top-down algorithm of Figure 5.4 together with a selection strategy induces a search graph. Each node in the search graph represents an answer clause. The neighbors of a node $yes \leftarrow a_1 \wedge \ldots \wedge a_m$, where a_1 is the selected atom, represent all of the possible answer clauses obtained by resolving on a_1. There is a neighbor for each definite clause whose head is a_1. The goal nodes of the search are of the form $yes \leftarrow$.

Example 5.11   Given the knowledge base

$$
\begin{array}{lll}
a \leftarrow b \wedge c. & a \leftarrow g. & a \leftarrow h. \\
b \leftarrow j. & b \leftarrow k. & d \leftarrow m. \\
d \leftarrow p. & f \leftarrow m. & f \leftarrow p. \\
g \leftarrow m. & g \leftarrow f. & k \leftarrow m. \\
h \leftarrow m. & p. &
\end{array}
$$

and the query

ask $a \wedge d$.

the search graph for an SLD derivation, assuming the leftmost atom is selected in each answer clause, is shown in Figure 5.5.

The search graph is not defined statically, because this would require anticipating every possible query. Instead, the search graph is dynamically constructed as needed. All that is required is a way to generate the neighbors of a node. Selecting an atom in the node's answer clause defines a set of neighbors: the node has a neighbor for each clause with the selected atom as its head.

Any of the search methods of Chapter 3 can be used to search the search space. Because we are only interested in whether the query is a logical consequence, we just require a path to a goal node; an optimal path is not necessary. The search space depends on the query and which atom is selected at each node.

When the top-down procedure has derived the answer, the rules used in the derivation can be used in a bottom-up proof procedure to infer the query. Similarly, a bottom-up proof of an atom can be used to construct a corresponding top-down derivation. This equivalence can be used to show the soundness and completeness of the top-down proof procedure. As defined, the top-down proof procedure may spend extra time re-proving the same atom multiple times, whereas the bottom-up procedure proves each atom only once. However, the bottom-up procedure proves every atom, but the top-down procedure proves only atoms that are relevant to the query.

It is possible that the proof procedure can get into an infinite loop, as in the following example (without cycle pruning).

Example 5.12 Consider the knowledge base and query:

$g \leftarrow a$.

$a \leftarrow b$.

$b \leftarrow a$.

$g \leftarrow c$.

c.

ask g.

Atoms g and c are the only atomic logical consequences of this knowledge base, and the bottom-up proof procedure will halt with fixed point $\{c, g\}$. However, the top-down proof procedure with a depth-first search will go on indefinitely, and not halt if the first clause for g is chosen, and there is no cycle pruning.

The algorithm requires a selection strategy to decide which atom to select at each time. In the above examples the leftmost atom a_1 was selected, but any atom could be selected. Which atom is selected affects the efficiency and perhaps even whether the algorithm terminates if there is no cycle pruning. The best selection strategy is to select the atom that is most likely to fail. Ordering the atoms and selecting the leftmost atom is a common strategy, because this lets someone who is providing the rules provide heuristic knowledge about which atom to select.

5.4   Knowledge Representation Issues

5.4.1   Background Knowledge and Observations

An **observation** (page 14) is information received online from users, sensors, or other knowledge sources. For this chapter, assume an observation is a set of atomic propositions, which are implicitly conjoined. Observations do not provide rules directly. The background knowledge in a knowledge base allows the agent to do something useful with these observations.

In many reasoning frameworks, the observations are added to the background knowledge. But in other reasoning frameworks (e.g, in abduction, probabilistic reasoning, and learning), observations are treated separately from background knowledge.

Users (page 69) cannot be expected to tell us everything that is true. First, they do not know what is relevant, and second, they do not know what vocabulary to use. An **ontology** (page 67) that specifies the meaning of the symbols, and a graphical user interface to allow the user to click on what is true, may help to solve the vocabulary problem. However, many problems are too big; what is relevant depends on other things that are true, and there are too many possibly relevant truths to expect the user to specify everything that is true, even with a sophisticated user interface.

Similarly, passive sensors (page 69) may be able to provide direct observations of conjunctions of atomic propositions, but active sensors may have to be queried by the agent for the information that is necessary for a task.

5.4.2   Querying the User

At design time or offline, there is typically no information about particular cases. This information arrives online (page 69) as observations from users, sensors, and external knowledge sources. For example, a medical diagnosis program may have knowledge represented as definite clauses about the possible diseases and symptoms but it would not have knowledge about the actual symptoms manifested by a particular patient. One would not expect that the user would want to, or even be able to, volunteer all of the information about a particular case because often the user does not know what information is relevant or know the syntax of the representation language. Users typically prefer to answer explicit questions put to them in a more natural language or using a graphical user interface.

A simple way to acquire information from a user is to incorporate an **ask-the-user** mechanism into the top-down proof procedure (page 189). In such a mechanism, an atom is **askable** if the user may know the truth value at run time. The top-down proof procedure, when it has selected an atom to prove, either can use a clause in the knowledge base to prove it, or, if the atom is askable, can ask the user whether or not the atom is true. The user is thus only asked about atoms that are relevant for the query. There are three classes of atoms that can be selected:

- atoms for which the user is not expected to know the answer, so the system never asks
- askable atoms for which the user has not already provided an answer; in this case, the user should be asked for the answer, and the answer should be recorded
- askable atoms for which the user has already provided an answer; in this case, that answer should be used, and the user should not be asked again about this atom.

A bottom-up proof procedure can also be adapted to ask a user, but it should avoid asking about all askable atoms; see Exercise 5.5 (page 230).

Note the symmetry between the roles of the user and the roles of the system. They can both ask questions and give answers. At the top level, the user asks the system a question, and at each step the system asks a question, which is answered either by finding the relevant definite clauses or by asking the user. The whole interaction can be characterized by a protocol of questions and answers between two agents, the user and the system.

Example 5.13 In the electrical domain of Example 5.7 (page 183), one would not expect the designer of the house to know the switch positions (whether each switch is up or down) or expect the user to know which switches are connected to which wires. It is reasonable that all of the definite clauses of Example 5.7, except for the switch positions, should be given by the designer. The switch positions can then be made askable.

Here is a possible dialog, where the user asks a query and answers yes or no to the system's questions. The user interface here is minimal to show the basic idea; a real system would use a more sophisticated user-friendly interface.

ailog: ask lit_l_1.
Is up_s_1 true? no.
Is $down\_s_1$ true? yes.
Is $down\_s_2$ true? yes.
Answer: lit_l_1.

The system only asks the user questions that the user is able to answer and that are relevant to the task at hand.

Instead of answering questions, it is sometimes preferable for a user to be able to specify that there is something strange or unusual going on. For example, patients may not be able to specify everything that is true about them but can specify what is unusual. Patients that come to a doctor because their left knee hurts, should not be expected them to specify that their left elbow does not hurt and, similarly, for every other part that does not hurt. It may be possible for a sensor to specify that something has changed in a scene, even though it may not be able to recognize what is in a scene.

Given that a user has specified everything that is exceptional, an agent can often infer something from the lack of knowledge. The normality will be a **default** that can be overridden with exceptional information. This idea of allowing for defaults and exceptions to the defaults is explored in Section 5.6 (page 212).

5.4.3   Knowledge-Level Explanation

The explicit use of semantics allows explanation and debugging at the **knowledge level** (page 21). To make a system usable by people, the system cannot just give an answer and expect the user to believe it. Consider the case of a system advising doctors who are legally responsible for the treatment that they carry out based on the diagnosis. The doctors must be convinced that the diagnosis is appropriate. The system must be able to justify that its answer is correct. The same mechanism can be used to explain how the system found a result and to debug the knowledge base.

Three complementary means of interrogation are used to explain the relevant knowledge: (1) a **how question** is used to explain how an answer was proved, (2) a **why question** is used to ask the system why it is asking the user a question, and (3) a **whynot question** is used to ask why an atom was not proven.

To explain how an answer was proved, a "how" question can be asked by a user when the system has returned the answer. The system provides the definite clause used to deduce the answer. For any atom in the body of the definite clause, the user can ask how the system proved that atom.

The user can ask "why" in response to being asked a question. The system replies by giving the rule that produced the question. The user can then ask why the head of that rule was being proved. Together these rules allow the user to traverse a proof or a partial proof of the top-level query.

A "whynot" question can be used to ask why a particular atom was not proven.

How Did the System Prove an Atom?

The first explanation procedure allows the user to ask "how" an atom was proved. If there is a proof for g, either g must be an atomic clause or there must be a rule

$$g \leftarrow a_1 \wedge \ldots \wedge a_k$$

such that each a_i has been proved.

If the system has proved g, and the user asks how in response, the system can display the clause that was used to prove g. If this clause was a rule, the user could then ask

how i.

which will give the rule that was used to prove a_i. The user can continue using the how command to explore how g was proved.

Example 5.14 In the axiomatization of Example 5.7 (page 183), the user can ask the query ask lit_l_2. In response to the system proving this query, the user can ask how. The system would reply:

$lit\_l_2 \leftarrow$
$\qquad light\_l_2 \land$
$\qquad live\_l_2 \land$
$\qquad ok\_l_2.$

This is the top-level rule used to prove lit_l_2. To find out how $live\_l_2$ was proved, the user can ask

how 2.

The system can return the rule used to prove $live\_l_2$, namely,

$live\_l_2 \leftarrow$
$\qquad live\_w_4.$

To find how $live\_w_4$ was proved, the user can ask

how 1.

The system presents the rule

$live\_w_4 \leftarrow$
$\qquad live\_w_3 \land$
$\qquad up\_s_3.$

To find how first atom in the body was proved, the user can ask

how 1.

The first atom, $live\_w_3$, was proved using the following rule:

$live\_w_3 \leftarrow$
$\qquad live\_w_5 \land$
$\qquad ok\_cb_1.$

To find how the second atom in the body was proved, the user can ask

how 2.

The system will report that ok_cb_1 is explicitly given.

Notice that the explanation here was only in terms of the knowledge level, and it only gave the relevant definite clauses it has been told. The user does not have to know anything about the proof procedure or the actual computation.

A method to implement how questions is presented in Section 14.4.5 (page 681).

Why Did the System Ask a Question?

Another useful explanation is for why a question was asked. This is useful for a number of reasons:

- We want the system to appear intelligent, transparent and trustworthy. Knowing why a question was asked will increase a user's confidence that the system is working sensibly.

- One of the main measures of complexity of an interactive system is the number of questions asked of a user, which should be kept to a minimum. Knowing why a question was asked will help the knowledge designer reduce this complexity.

- An irrelevant question is usually a symptom of a deeper problem.

- The user may learn something from the system by knowing why the system is doing something. This learning is much like an apprentice asking a master why the master is doing something.

When the system asks the user a question (q), there must be a rule used by the system that contains q in the body. The user can ask

why.

This is read as "Why did you ask me that question?" The answer can be the rule that contains q in the body. If the user asks why again, the system should explain why the atom at the head of the rule was asked, and so forth. Repeatedly asking why will eventually give the path of subgoals to the top-level query. If all of these rules are reasonable, this justifies why the system's question to the user is reasonable.

Example 5.15   Consider the dialog of Example 5.13 (page 195). The following shows how repeated use of why can repeatedly find higher-level subgoals. The following dialog is for the query ask lit_l_1, with user asking the initial query, and responding with "why".

> ailog: ask lit_l_1.
> Is up_s_1 true? why.
> up_s_1 is used in the rule $live\_w_1 \leftarrow live\_w_3 \wedge up\_s_1$: why.
> $live\_w_1$ is used in the rule $live\_w_0 \leftarrow live\_w_1 \wedge up\_s_2$: why.
> $live\_w_0$ is used in the rule $live\_l_1 \leftarrow live\_w_0$: why.

> $live\_l_1$ is used in the rule $lit\_l_1 \leftarrow light\_l_1 \wedge live\_l_1 \wedge ok\_l_1$: why.
> Because that is what you asked me!

Typically, how and why are used together; how moves from higher-level to lower-level subgoals, and why moves from lower-level to higher-level subgoals. Together they let the user traverse a **proof tree**, where nodes are atoms, and a node together with its children corresponds to a clause in the knowledge base.

Example 5.16   As an example of the need to combine how and why, consider the previous example where the user asked why up_s_1. The system gave the following rule:

$$live\_w_1 \leftarrow live\_w_3 \wedge up\_s_1.$$

This means that up_s_1 was asked because the system wants to know $live\_w_1$ and is using this rule to try to prove up_s_1. The user may think it is reasonable that the system wants to know $live\_w_1$ but may think it is inappropriate that up_s_1 be asked because the user may doubt that $live\_w_3$ should have succeeded. In this case it is useful for the user to ask how $live\_w_3$ was derived.

5.4.4   Knowledge-Level Debugging

Just as with other software, knowledge bases may have errors and omissions. Domain experts and knowledge engineers must be able to debug a knowledge base and add knowledge. In knowledge-based systems, debugging is difficult because the domain experts and users who have the domain knowledge required to detect a bug do not necessarily know anything about the internal working of the system, nor do they want to. Standard debugging tools, such as providing traces of the execution, are inappropriate because they require a knowledge of the mechanism by which the answer was produced. In this section, we show how the idea of semantics (page 175) enables debugging facilities for knowledge-based systems. Whoever is debugging the system is required only to know the meaning of the symbols and whether specific atoms are true or not, and does not need to know the proof procedure. This is the kind of knowledge that a domain expert and a user may have.

Knowledge-level debugging is the process of finding errors in knowledge bases with reference only to what the symbols mean and what is true in the world. One of the goals of building knowledge-based systems that are usable by a range of domain experts is that a discussion about the correctness of a knowledge base should be a discussion about the knowledge domain. For example, debugging a medical knowledge base should involve questions of medicine that medical experts, who are not expected to be experts in AI, can answer. Similarly, debugging a knowledge base about house wiring should be with reference to the particular house, not about the internals of the system reasoning with the knowledge base.

Four types of non-syntactic errors arise in rule-based systems.

- An incorrect answer is produced; that is, some atom that is false in the intended interpretation was derived.

- An answer that was not produced; that is, the proof failed on a particular true atom when it should have succeeded.

- The program gets into an infinite loop.

- The system asks irrelevant questions.

Ways to debug the first three types of error are examined below. Irrelevant questions can be investigated using the why questions as described earlier.

Incorrect Answers

An **incorrect answer** is an answer that has been proved yet is false in the intended interpretation. It is also called a **false-positive error**. An incorrect answer is only produced by a sound proof procedure if an incorrect definite clause was used in the proof.

Assume that whoever is debugging the knowledge base, such as a domain expert or a user, knows the intended interpretation of the symbols of the language and is able to determine whether a particular proposition is true or false in the intended interpretation. The person does not have to know how the answer was computed. To debug an incorrect answer, a domain expert needs only to answer yes-or-no questions.

Suppose there is an atom g that was proved yet is false in the intended interpretation. Then there must be a rule $g \leftarrow a_1 \wedge \ldots \wedge a_k$ in the knowledge base that was used to prove g. Either

- one of the a_i is false in the intended interpretation, in which case it can be debugged in the same way, or

- all of the a_i are true in the intended interpretation; in this case, the definite clause $g \leftarrow a_1 \wedge \ldots \wedge a_k$ must be incorrect.

This leads to an algorithm, presented in Figure 5.6 (on the next page), to **debug false positives**, namely to find a false clause in a knowledge base when an atom that is false in the intended interpretation is derived. This only requires the person debugging the knowledge base to be able to answer yes-or-no questions.

This procedure can also be carried out by the use of the how command (page 196). Given a proof for an atom g that is false in the intended interpretation, a user can ask how g was proved. This will return the definite clause that was used in the proof. If the clause was a rule, the user could use how to ask about an atom in the body that was false in the intended interpretation.

1: **procedure** *Debug_false(g, KB)*
2:     **Inputs**
3:         *KB* a knowledge base
4:         *g* an atom: $KB \vdash g$ and *g* is false in intended interpretation
5:     **Output**
6:         clause in *KB* that is false
7:     Find definite clause $g \leftarrow a_1 \wedge \ldots \wedge a_k \in KB$ used to prove *g*
8:     **for each** a_i **do**
9:         ask user whether a_i is true
10:        **if** user specifies a_i is false **then**
11:            **return** *Debug_false*(a_i, KB)
12:    **return** $g \leftarrow a_1 \wedge \ldots \wedge a_k$

Figure 5.6: An algorithm to debug false positive answers

This will return the rule that was used to prove that atom. The user repeats this until a definite clause is found where all of the elements of the body are true (or there are no elements in the body). This is the incorrect definite clause.

Example 5.17   Consider Example 5.7 (page 183), involving the electrical domain, but assume there is a bug in the knowledge base. Suppose that the domain expert or user had inadvertently said that whether w_1 is connected to w_3 depends on the status of s_3 instead of s_1 (see Figure 5.2 (page 183)). Thus, the knowledge includes the following incorrect rule:

$live\_w_1 \leftarrow live\_w_3 \wedge up\_s_3.$

All of the other axioms are the same as in Example 5.7. Given this axiom set, the atom lit_l_1 can be derived, which is false in the intended interpretation. Consider how a user would go about finding this incorrect definite clause when they detected this incorrect answer.

Given that lit_l_1 is false in the intended interpretation, they ask how it was derived, which will give the following rule:

$lit\_l_1 \leftarrow light\_l_1 \wedge live\_l_1 \wedge ok\_l_1.$

They check the atoms in the body of this rule. $light\_l_1$ and ok_l_1 are true in the intended interpretation, but $live\_l_1$ is false in the intended interpretation. So they ask

how 2.

The system presents the rule

$live\_l_1 \leftarrow live\_w_0.$

$live\_w_0$ is false in the intended interpretation, so they ask

how 1.

The system presents the rule

$$live\_w_0 \leftarrow live\_w_1 \wedge up\_s_2.$$

$live\_w_1$ is false in the intended interpretation, so they ask

how 1.

The system presents the rule

$$live\_w_1 \leftarrow live\_w_3 \wedge up\_s_3.$$

Both elements of the body are true in the intended interpretation, so this is a buggy rule.

The user or domain expert can find the buggy definite clause without having to know the internal workings of the system or how the proof was computed. They only require knowledge about the intended interpretation and the disciplined use of how.

Missing Answers

The second type of error occurs when an expected answer is not produced. This manifests itself by a failure when an answer is expected. An atom g that is true in the domain, but is not a consequence of the knowledge base, is called a **false-negative error**. The preceding algorithm does not work in this case; there is no proof. We must look for why there is no proof for g.

An appropriate answer is not produced only if a definite clause or clauses are missing from the knowledge base. By knowing the intended interpretation of the symbols and by knowing what queries should succeed (i.e, what is true in the intended interpretation), a domain expert can debug a missing answer. Given a **false negative**, an atom that failed when it should have succeeded, Figure 5.7 (on the next page) shows how to **debug** the knowledge base to find an atom for which there is a missing definite clause.

Suppose g is an atom that should have a proof, but which fails. Because the proof for g fails, the bodies of all of the definite clauses with g in the head fail.

- Suppose one of these definite clauses for g should have resulted in a proof; this means all of the atoms in the body must be true in the intended interpretation. Because the body failed, there must be an atom in the body that fails. This atom is then true in the intended interpretation, but fails. So we can recursively debug it.

- Otherwise, there is no definite clause applicable to proving g, so the user must add a definite clause for g.

A **whynot question** can be used by the user to ask why some g was not proved. The system can ask the relevant questions to implement *Debug_missing*.

1: **procedure** *Debug_missing*(*g*, *KB*)
2:     **Inputs**
3:         *KB* a knowledge base
4:         *g* an atom: $KB \not\vdash g$ and *g* is true in the intended interpretation
5:     **Output**
6:         atom for which there is a clause missing
7:     **if** there is a definite clause $g \leftarrow a_1 \wedge \ldots \wedge a_k \in KB$ such that all a_i are true in the intended interpretation **then**
8:         **select** a_i that cannot be proved
9:         **return** *Debug_missing*(a_i, *KB*)
10:    **else**
11:        **return** *g*

Figure 5.7: An algorithm for debugging missing answers (false negatives)

Example 5.18   Suppose that, for the axiomatization of the electrical domain in Example 5.7 (page 183), the world of Figure 5.2 (page 183) actually had s_2 down. Thus, it is missing the definite clause specifying that s_2 is down. The axiomatization of Example 5.7 fails to prove lit_l_1 when it should succeed. Consider how to find the bug.

lit_l_1 failed, so the system finds all of the rules with lit_l_1 in the head. There is one such rule:

$$lit\_l_1 \leftarrow light\_l_1 \wedge live\_l_1 \wedge ok\_l_1.$$

The user can then verify that all of the elements of the body are true. $light\_l_1$ and ok_l_1 can both be proved, but $live\_l_1$ fails, so the user debugs this atom. There is one rule with $live\_l_1$ in the head:

$$live\_l_1 \leftarrow live\_w_0.$$

The atom $live\_w_0$ cannot be proved, but the user verifies that it is true in the intended interpretation. So the system find the rules for $live\_w_0$:

$$live\_w_0 \leftarrow live\_w_1 \wedge up\_s_2.$$
$$live\_w_0 \leftarrow live\_w_2 \wedge down\_s_2.$$

The user can determine that the body of the second rule is true. There is a proof for $live\_w_2$, but there are no clauses for $down\_s_2$, so this atom is returned. The correction is to add an appropriate clause, by stating it as a fact or providing a rule for it.

Infinite Loops

Example 5.12 (page 193) shows an example where the top-down derivation can loop. There can be an infinite loop only if the knowledge base is cyclic, where a knowledge base is **cyclic** if there is an atom a such that there is a sequence of definite clauses of the form

$$a \leftarrow \ldots a_1 \ldots$$
$$a_1 \leftarrow \ldots a_2 \ldots$$
$$\ldots$$
$$a_n \leftarrow \ldots a \ldots$$

(where if $n = 0$ there is a single definite clause with a in the head and body).

A knowledge base is **acyclic** if there is an assignment of natural numbers (non-negative integers) to the atoms so that the atoms in the body of a definite clause are assigned a lower number than the atom in the head. There cannot be an infinite loop in an acyclic knowledge base.

To detect a cyclic knowledge base, the top-down proof procedure can be modified to maintain the set of all **ancestors** for each atom in the proof.

Initially, the set of ancestors of each atom is empty. When the rule

$$a \leftarrow a_1 \wedge \ldots \wedge a_k$$

is used to prove a, the ancestors of a_i will be the ancestors of a together with a. That is,

$$ancestors(a_i) = ancestors(a) \cup \{a\}.$$

The proof can fail if an atom is in its set of ancestors. This failure only occurs if the knowledge base is cyclic. This is a refined version of cycle pruning used in search (page 105), with each atom having its own set of ancestors.

A cyclic knowledge base is often a sign of a bug. When writing a knowledge base, it is often useful to ensure an acyclic knowledge base by identifying a value that is being reduced at each iteration. For example, in the electrical domain, the number of steps away from the outside of the house is meant to be reduced by one each time through the loop.

Note that the bottom-up proof procedure does not get into an infinite loop, because it selects a rule only when the head has not been derived.

5.5   Proving by Contradiction

Definite clauses can be used in a proof by contradiction by allowing rules that give contradictions. For example, in the electrical wiring domain (page 183), it is useful to be able to specify that some prediction, such as that light l_2 is on, is not true. This will enable diagnostic reasoning to deduce that some switches, lights, or circuit breakers are broken.

5.5.1 Horn Clauses

The definite clause language does not allow a contradiction to be stated. However, a simple expansion of the language can allow proof by contradiction.

An **integrity constraint** is a clause of the form

$$false \leftarrow a_1 \wedge \ldots \wedge a_k.$$

where the a_i are atoms and *false* is a special atom that is false in all interpretations.

A **Horn clause** is either a definite clause (page 182) or an integrity constraint. That is, a Horn clause has either *false* or a normal atom as its head.

Integrity constraints allow the system to prove that some conjunction of atoms is false in all models of a knowledge base. Recall (page 174) that $\neg p$ is the **negation** of p, which is true in an interpretation when p is false in that interpretation, and $p \vee q$ is the **disjunction** of p and q, which is true in an interpretation if p is true or q is true or both are true in the interpretation. The integrity constraint $false \leftarrow a_1 \wedge \ldots \wedge a_k$ is logically equivalent to $\neg a_1 \vee \ldots \vee \neg a_k$.

A Horn clause knowledge base can imply negations of atoms, as shown in Example 5.19.

Example 5.19 Consider the knowledge base KB_1:

$$false \leftarrow a \wedge b.$$
$$a \leftarrow c.$$
$$b \leftarrow c.$$

The atom c is false in all models of KB_1. To see this, suppose instead that c is true in model I of KB_1. Then a and b would both be true in I (otherwise I would not be a model of KB_1). Because *false* is false in I and a and b are true in I, the first clause is false in I, a contradiction to I being a model of KB_1. Thus $\neg c$ is true in all models of KB_1, which can be written as

$$KB_1 \models \neg c$$

Although the language of Horn clauses does not allow disjunctions and negations to be input, disjunctions of negations of atoms can be derived, as the following example shows.

Example 5.20 Consider the knowledge base KB_2:

$$false \leftarrow a \wedge b.$$
$$a \leftarrow c.$$
$$b \leftarrow d.$$
$$b \leftarrow e.$$

Either c is false or d is false in every model of KB_2. If they were both true in some model I of KB_2, both a and b would be true in I, so the first clause would be false in I, a contradiction to I being a model of KB_2. Similarly, either c is false or e is false in every model of KB_2. Thus,

$$KB_2 \models \neg c \vee \neg d$$
$$KB_2 \models \neg c \vee \neg e.$$

A set of clauses is **unsatisfiable** if it has no models. A set of clauses is provably **inconsistent** with respect to a proof procedure if *false* can be derived from the clauses using that proof procedure. If a proof procedure is sound and complete, a set of clauses is provably inconsistent if and only if it is unsatisfiable.

It is always possible to find a model for a set of definite clauses. The interpretation with all atoms true is a model of any set of definite clauses. Thus, a definite-clause knowledge base is always satisfiable. However, a set of Horn clauses can be unsatisfiable.

Example 5.21   The set of clauses $\{a, false \leftarrow a\}$ is unsatisfiable. There is no interpretation that satisfies both clauses. Both a and $false \leftarrow a$ cannot be true in any interpretation.

Both the top-down and the bottom-up proof procedures can be used to prove inconsistency, by using *false* as the query.

5.5.2   Assumables and Conflicts

Reasoning from contradictions is a very useful tool. For many activities it is useful to know that some combination of assumptions is incompatible. For example, it is useful in planning to know that some combination of actions an agent is contemplating is impossible. When designing a new artifact, it us useful to know that some combination of components cannot work together.

In a diagnostic application it is useful to be able to prove that some components working normally is inconsistent with the observations of the system. Consider a system that has a description of how it is supposed to work and some observations. If the system does not work according to its specification, a diagnostic agent should identify which components could be faulty.

To carry out these tasks it is useful to be able to make assumptions that can be proven to be false.

An **assumable** is an atom that can be assumed in a proof by contradiction. A proof by contradiction derives a disjunction of the negation of assumables.

With a Horn clause knowledge base and explicit assumables, if the system can prove a contradiction from some assumptions, it can extract those combinations of assumptions that cannot all be true. Instead of proving a query, the system tries to prove *false*, and collects the assumables that are used in a proof.

If *KB* is a set of Horn clauses, a **conflict** of *KB* is a set of assumables that, given *KB*, implies *false*. That is, $C = \{c_1, \ldots, c_r\}$ is a conflict of *KB* if

$$KB \cup \{c_1, \ldots, c_r\} \models false.$$

In this case, an **answer** is

$$KB \models \neg c_1 \vee \ldots \vee \neg c_r.$$

A **minimal conflict** is a conflict such that no strict subset is also a conflict.

Example 5.22   In Example 5.20 (page 205), if $\{c, d, e, f, g, h\}$ is the set of assumables, then $\{c, d\}$ and $\{c, e\}$ are minimal conflicts of KB_2; $\{c, d, e, h\}$ is also a conflict, but not a minimal conflict.

In the examples that follow, assumables are specified using the assumable keyword followed by one or more assumable atoms separated by commas.

5.5.3   Consistency-Based Diagnosis

Making assumptions about what is working normally, and deriving what components could be abnormal, is the basis of **consistency-based diagnosis**. Suppose a **fault** is something that is wrong with a system. The aim of consistency-based diagnosis is to determine the possible faults based on a model of the system and observations of the system. By making the absence of faults assumable, conflicts can be used to prove what is wrong with the system.

Example 5.23   Consider the house wiring example depicted in Figure 5.2 (page 183) and represented in Example 5.7 (page 183). A background knowledge base suitable for consistency-based diagnosis is given in Figure 5.8 (on the next page). Normality assumptions, specifying that switches, circuit breakers, and lights must be ok to work as expected, are added to the clauses. There are no clauses for the *ok* atoms, but they are made assumable.

The user is able to observe the switch positions and whether a light is lit or dark.

A light cannot be both lit and dark. This knowledge is stated in the following integrity constraints:

$$false \leftarrow dark\_l_1 \wedge lit\_l_1.$$
$$false \leftarrow dark\_l_2 \wedge lit\_l_2.$$

Suppose the user observes that all three switches are up, and that l_1 and l_2 are both dark. This is represented by the atomic clauses

$$up\_s_1.$$
$$up\_s_2.$$
$$up\_s_3.$$

$light\_l_1$.

$light\_l_2$.

$live\_outside$.

$live\_l_1 \leftarrow live\_w_0$.

$live\_w_0 \leftarrow live\_w_1 \wedge up\_s_2 \wedge ok\_s_2$.

$live\_w_0 \leftarrow live\_w_2 \wedge down\_s_2 \wedge ok\_s_2$.

$live\_w_1 \leftarrow live\_w_3 \wedge up\_s_1 \wedge ok\_s_1$.

$live\_w_2 \leftarrow live\_w_3 \wedge down\_s_1 \wedge ok\_s_1$.

$live\_l_2 \leftarrow live\_w_4$.

$live\_w_4 \leftarrow live\_w_3 \wedge up\_s_3 \wedge ok\_s_3$.

$live\_p_1 \leftarrow live\_w_3$.

$live\_w_3 \leftarrow live\_w_5 \wedge ok\_cb_1$.

$live\_p_2 \leftarrow live\_w_6$.

$live\_w_6 \leftarrow live\_w_5 \wedge ok\_cb_2$.

$live\_w_5 \leftarrow live\_outside$.

$lit\_l_1 \leftarrow light\_l_1 \wedge live\_l_1 \wedge ok\_l_1$.

$lit\_l_2 \leftarrow light\_l_2 \wedge live\_l_2 \wedge ok\_l_2$.

$false \leftarrow dark\_l_1 \wedge lit\_l_1$.

$false \leftarrow dark\_l_2 \wedge lit\_l_2$.

assumable $ok\_cb_1, ok\_cb_2, ok\_s_1, ok\_s_2, ok\_s_3, ok\_l_1, ok\_l_2$.

Figure 5.8: Knowledge for Example 5.23

$dark\_l_1$.

$dark\_l_2$.

Given the knowledge of Figure 5.8 together with the observations, there are two minimal conflicts:

$\{ok\_cb_1, ok\_s_1, ok\_s_2, ok\_l_1\}$

$\{ok\_cb_1, ok\_s_3, ok\_l_2\}$.

Thus, it follows that

$KB \models \neg ok\_cb_1 \vee \neg ok\_s_1 \vee \neg ok\_s_2 \vee \neg ok\_l_1$

$KB \models \neg ok\_cb_1 \vee \neg ok\_s_3 \vee \neg ok\_l_2$,

which means that at least one of the components cb_1, s_1, s_2, or l_1 must not be ok, and least one of the components cb_1, s_3, or l_2 must not be ok.

Given the set of all conflicts, a user can determine what may be wrong with the system being diagnosed. However, given a set of conflicts, it is often difficult to determine whether all of the conflicts could be explained by a few faults. Some of the questions that a user may want to know are whether all of the conflicts could be accounted for a by a single fault or a pair of faults.

Given a set of conflicts, a **consistency-based diagnosis** is a set of assumables that has at least one element in each conflict. A **minimal diagnosis** is a diagnosis such that no subset is also a diagnosis. For one of the diagnoses, all of its elements must be false in the world being modeled.

Example 5.24 In Example 5.23 (page 207), the disjunction of the negation of the two conflicts is a logical consequence of the clauses. Thus, the conjunction

$$(\neg ok\_cb_1 \lor \neg ok\_s_1 \lor \neg ok\_s_2 \lor \neg ok\_l_1)$$
$$\land (\neg ok\_cb_1 \lor \neg ok\_s_3 \lor \neg ok\_l_2)$$

follows from the knowledge base. This conjunction of disjunctions in **conjunctive normal form (CNF)** can be distributed into **disjunctive normal form (DNF)**, a disjunction of conjunctions, here of negated atoms:

$$\neg ok\_cb_1 \lor$$
$$(\neg ok\_s_1 \land \neg ok\_s_3) \lor (\neg ok\_s_1 \land \neg ok\_l_2) \lor$$
$$(\neg ok\_s_2 \land \neg ok\_s_3) \lor (\neg ok\_s_2 \land \neg ok\_l_2) \lor$$
$$(\neg ok\_l_1 \land \neg ok\_s_3) \lor (\neg ok\_l_1 \land \neg ok\_l_2).$$

Thus, either cb_1 is broken or there is at least one of six double faults.

The propositions that are disjoined together correspond to the seven minimal diagnoses: $\{ok\_cb_1\}$, $\{ok\_s_1, ok\_s_3\}$, $\{ok\_s_1, ok\_l_2\}$, $\{ok\_s_2, ok\_s_3\}$, $\{ok\_s_2, ok\_l_2\}$, $\{ok\_l_1, ok\_s_3\}$, $\{ok\_l_1, ok\_l_2\}$. The system has proved that one of these combinations must be faulty.

5.5.4 Reasoning with Assumptions and Horn Clauses

This section presents a bottom-up implementation and a top-down implementation for finding conflicts in Horn clause knowledge bases.

Bottom-Up Implementation

The bottom-up implementation is an augmented version of the bottom-up algorithm for definite clauses presented in Section 5.3.2 (page 187).

The modification to that algorithm is that the conclusions are pairs $\langle a, A \rangle$, where a is an atom and A is a set of assumables that imply a in the context of Horn clause knowledge base KB.

Initially, the conclusion set C is $\{\langle a, \{a\} \rangle : a \text{ is assumable}\}$. Clauses can be used to derive new conclusions. If there is a clause $h \leftarrow b_1 \land \ldots \land b_m$ such that for each b_i there is some A_i such that $\langle b_i, A_i \rangle \in C$, then $\langle h, A_1 \cup \ldots \cup A_m \rangle$ can be

---

1: **procedure** *Prove_conflict_BU(KB, Assumables)*
2:     **Inputs**
3:         *KB*: a set of Horn clauses
4:         *Assumables*: a set of atoms that can be assumed
5:     **Output**
6:         set of conflicts
7:     **Local**
8:         *C* is a set of pairs of an atom and a set of assumables
9:     $C := \{\langle a, \{a\} \rangle : a \text{ is assumable}\}$
10:    **repeat**
11:        **select** clause "$h \leftarrow b_1 \wedge \ldots \wedge b_m$" in *KB* such that
12:            $\langle b_i, A_i \rangle \in C$ for all i and
13:            $\langle h, A \rangle \notin C$ where $A = A_1 \cup \ldots \cup A_m$
14:        $C := C \cup \{\langle h, A \rangle\}$
15:    **until** no more selections are possible
16:    **return** $\{A : \langle false, A \rangle \in C\}$

Figure 5.9: Bottom-up proof procedure for computing conflicts

---

added to C. Note that this covers the case of atomic clauses, with $m = 0$, where $\langle h, \{\} \rangle$ is added to C.

Figure 5.9 gives code for the algorithm. This algorithm is sometimes called an **assumption-based truth maintenance system (ATMS)**, particularly when it is combined with the incremental addition of clauses and assumables.

When the pair $\langle false, A \rangle$ is generated, the assumptions A form a conflict.

One refinement of this program is to prune supersets of assumptions. If $\langle a, A_1 \rangle$ and $\langle a, A_2 \rangle$ are in C, where $A_1 \subset A_2$, then $\langle a, A_2 \rangle$ can be removed from C or not added to C. There is no reason to use the extra assumptions to imply a. Similarly, if $\langle false, A_1 \rangle$ and $\langle a, A_2 \rangle$ are in C, where $A_1 \subseteq A_2$, then $\langle a, A_2 \rangle$ can be removed from C because A_1 and any superset – including A_2 – are inconsistent with the clauses given, and so nothing more can be learned from considering such sets of assumables.

> **Example 5.25** Consider the axiomatization of Figure 5.8 (page 208), discussed in Example 5.23 (page 207).
>
>   Initially, in the algorithm of Figure 5.9, C has the value
>
> $$\{\langle ok\_l_1, \{ok\_l_1\} \rangle, \langle ok\_l_2, \{ok\_l_2\} \rangle, \langle ok\_s_1, \{ok\_s_1\} \rangle, \langle ok\_s_2, \{ok\_s_2\} \rangle,$$
> $$\langle ok\_s_3, \{ok\_s_3\} \rangle, \langle ok\_cb_1, \{ok\_cb_1\} \rangle, \langle ok\_cb_2, \{ok\_cb_2\} \rangle\}.$$
>
> The following shows a sequence of values added to C under one sequence of selections:
>
> $\langle live\_outside, \{\} \rangle$

$\langle connected\_to\_w5, outside, \{\}\rangle$

$\langle live\_w5, \{\}\rangle$

$\langle connected\_to\_w3, w5, \{ok\_cb_1\}\rangle$

$\langle live\_w3, \{ok\_cb_1\}\rangle$

$\langle up\_s_3, \{\}\rangle$

$\langle connected\_to\_w4, w3, \{ok\_s_3\}\rangle$

$\langle live\_w4, \{ok\_cb_1, ok\_s_3\}\rangle$

$\langle connected\_to\_l_2, w4, \{\}\rangle$

$\langle live\_l_2, \{ok\_cb_1, ok\_s_3\}\rangle$

$\langle light\_l_2, \{\}\rangle$

$\langle lit\_l_2, \{ok\_cb_1, ok\_s_3, ok\_l_2\}\rangle$

$\langle dark\_l_2, \{\}\rangle$

$\langle false, \{ok\_cb_1, ok\_s_3, ok\_l_2\}\rangle$.

Thus, the knowledge base entails

$$\neg ok\_cb_1 \vee \neg ok\_s_3 \vee \neg ok\_l_2.$$

The other conflict can be found by continuing the algorithm.

Top-Down Implementation

The top-down implementation is similar to the top-down definite clause interpreter described in Figure 5.4 (page 191), except the top-level query is to prove *false*, and the assumables encountered in a proof are not proved but collected.

The algorithm is shown in Figure 5.10 (on the next page). Different choices can lead to different conflicts being found. If no choices are available, the algorithm fails.

Example 5.26   Consider the representation of the circuit in Example 5.23 (page 207). The following is a sequence of the values of G for one sequence of selections and choices that leads to a conflict:

$\{false\}$

$\{dark\_l_1, lit\_l_1\}$

$\{lit\_l_1\}$

$\{light\_l_1, live\_l_1, ok\_l_1\}$

$\{live\_l_1, ok\_l_1\}$

$\{live\_w_0, ok\_l_1\}$

$\{live\_w_1, up\_s_2, ok\_s_2, ok\_l_1\}$

$\{live\_w_3, up\_s_1, ok\_s_1, up\_s_2, ok\_s_2, ok\_l_1\}$

$\{live\_w_5, ok\_cb_1, up\_s_1, ok\_s_1, up\_s_2, ok\_s_2, ok\_l_1\}$

$\{live\_outside, ok\_cb_1, up\_s_1, ok\_s_1, up\_s_2, ok\_s_2, ok\_l_1\}$

1: **non-deterministic procedure** *Prove_conflict_TD(KB, Assumables)*
2:    **Inputs**
3:        *KB*: a set Horn clauses
4:        *Assumables*: a set of atoms that can be assumed
5:    **Output**
6:        A conflict
7:    **Local**
8:        *G* is a set of atoms (that implies false)
9:    $G := \{false\}$
10:   **repeat**
11:       **select** an atom a in G such that $a \notin$ *Assumables*
12:       **choose** clause "$a \leftarrow B$" in *KB* with a as head
13:       $G := (G \setminus \{a\}) \cup B$
14:   **until** $G \subseteq$ *Assumables*
15:   **return** G

Figure 5.10: Top-down Horn clause interpreter to find conflicts

$$\{ok\_cb_1, up\_s_1, ok\_s_1, up\_s_2, ok\_s_2, ok\_l_1\}$$
$$\{ok\_cb_1, ok\_s_1, up\_s_2, ok\_s_2, ok\_l_1\}$$
$$\{ok\_cb_1, ok\_s_1, ok\_s_2, ok\_l_1\}.$$

The set $\{ok\_cb_1, ok\_s_1, ok\_s_2, ok\_l_1\}$ is returned as a conflict. Different choices of the clause to use can lead to another answer.

5.6   Complete Knowledge Assumption

A database is often complete in the sense that anything not implied is false.

Example 5.27   You may want the user to specify which switches are up and which circuit breakers are broken so that the system can conclude that any switch not mentioned as up is down and any circuit breaker not specified as broken is ok. Thus, down is the default value of switches, and ok is the default value for circuit breakers. It is easier for users to communicate using defaults than it is to specify the seemingly redundant information about which switches are down and which circuit breakers are ok. To reason with such defaults, an agent must assume it has complete knowledge; a switch's position is not mentioned because it is down, not because the agent does not know whether it is up or down.

The given definite-clause logic does not allow the derivation of a conclusion from a lack of knowledge or a failure to prove. It does not assume that the knowledge is complete. In particular, the negation of an atom can never be a logical consequence of a definite-clause knowledge base.

The **complete knowledge assumption** assumes that, for every atom, the clauses with the atom as the head cover all the cases when the atom is true. Under this assumption, an agent can conclude that an atom is false if it cannot derive that the atom is true. This is also called the **closed-world assumption**. It can be contrasted with the **open-world assumption**, which is that the agent does not know everything and so cannot make any conclusions from a lack of knowledge. The closed-world assumption requires that everything relevant about the world is known to the agent.

Suppose the clauses for atom a are

$$a \leftarrow b_1.$$

$$\vdots$$

$$a \leftarrow b_n.$$

where an atomic clause a is treated as the rule $a \leftarrow true$. The complete knowledge assumption specifies that if a is true in some interpretation then one of the b_i must be true in that interpretation; that is,

$$a \rightarrow b_1 \vee \ldots \vee b_n.$$

Because the clauses defining a are equivalent to

$$a \leftarrow b_1 \vee \ldots \vee b_n$$

the meaning of the clauses can be seen as the conjunction of these two propositions, namely, the equivalence:

$$a \leftrightarrow b_1 \vee \ldots \vee b_n$$

where $\leftrightarrow$ is read as "if and only if" (see Figure 5.1 (page 175)). This equivalence is called **Clark's completion** of the clauses for a. Clark's completion of a knowledge base is the completion for each atom in the knowledge base.

Clark's completion means that if there are no rules for an atom a, the completion of this atom is $a \leftrightarrow false$, which means that a is false.

Example 5.28 Consider the clauses from Example 5.7 (page 183):

$down\_s_1.$

$up\_s_2.$

$ok\_cb_1.$

$live\_l_1 \leftarrow live\_w_0.$

$live\_w_0 \leftarrow live\_w_1 \wedge up\_s_2.$

$live\_w_0 \leftarrow live\_w_2 \wedge down\_s_2.$

$live\_w_1 \leftarrow live\_w_3 \wedge up\_s_1.$

$live\_w_2 \leftarrow live\_w_3 \wedge down\_s_1.$

$live\_w_3 \leftarrow live\_outside \wedge ok\_cb_1$.

$live\_outside$.

Suppose that these are the only clauses for the atoms in the heads of these clauses, and there are no clauses for up_s_1 or $down\_s_2$. The completion of these atoms is

$down\_s_1 \leftrightarrow true$.

$up\_s_1 \leftrightarrow false$.

$up\_s_2 \leftrightarrow true$.

$down\_s_2 \leftrightarrow false$.

$ok\_cb_1 \leftrightarrow true$.

$live\_l_1 \leftrightarrow live\_w_0$.

$live\_w_0 \leftrightarrow (live\_w_1 \wedge up\_s_2) \vee (live\_w_2 \wedge down\_s_2)$.

$live\_w_1 \leftrightarrow live\_w_3 \wedge up\_s_1$.

$live\_w_2 \leftrightarrow live\_w_3 \wedge down\_s_1$.

$live\_w_3 \leftrightarrow live\_outside \wedge ok\_cb_1$.

$live\_outside \leftrightarrow true$.

This implies that up_s_1 is false, $live\_w_1$ is false and $live\_w_2$ is true.

With the completion, the system can derive negations, and so it is useful to extend the language to allow negations in the body of clauses. A **literal** is either an atom or the negation of an atom. The definition of a definite clause (page 182) can be extended to allow literals in the body rather than just atoms. We write the negation of atom a under the complete knowledge assumption as $\sim a$ to distinguish it from classical negation that does not assume the completion. This negation is often called **negation as failure**.

Under negation as failure, body g is a consequence of the knowledge base KB if $KB' \models g$, where KB' is Clark's completion of KB. A negation $\sim a$ in the body of a clause or the query becomes $\neg a$ in the completion. That is, a query follows from a knowledge base under the complete knowledge assumption means that the query is a logical consequence of the completion of the knowledge base.

Example 5.29 Consider the axiomatization of Example 5.7 (page 183). Representing a domain can be made simpler by expecting the user to tell the system only what switches are up and by the system concluding that a switch is down if it has not been told the switch is up. This can be done by adding the following rules:

$down\_s_1 \leftarrow \sim up\_s_1$.

$down\_s_2 \leftarrow \sim up\_s_2$.

$down\_s_3 \leftarrow \sim up\_s_3$.

Similarly, the system may conclude that the circuit breakers are ok unless it has been told they are broken:

$ok\_cb_1 \leftarrow {\sim}broken\_cb_1.$

$ok\_cb_2 \leftarrow {\sim}broken\_cb_2.$

Although this may look more complicated than the previous representation, it means that is it easier for the user to specify what is occurring in a particular situation. The user has to specify only what is up and what is broken. This may save time if being down is normal for switches and being ok is normal for circuit breakers.

To represent the state of Figure 5.2 (page 183), the user specifies

$up\_s_2.$

$up\_s_3.$

The system can infer that s_1 must be down and both circuit breakers are ok.

The completion of the knowledge base consisting of the clauses above is

$down\_s_1 \leftrightarrow \neg up\_s_1.$

$down\_s_2 \leftrightarrow \neg up\_s_2.$

$down\_s_3 \leftrightarrow \neg up\_s_3.$

$ok\_cb_1 \leftrightarrow \neg broken\_cb_1.$

$ok\_cb_2 \leftrightarrow \neg broken\_cb_2.$

$up\_s_1 \leftrightarrow false.$

$up\_s_2 \leftrightarrow true.$

$up\_s_3 \leftrightarrow true.$

$broken\_cb_1 \leftrightarrow false.$

$broken\_cb_2 \leftrightarrow false.$

Notice that atoms that are in the bodies of clauses but are not in the head of any clauses are false in the completion.

Recall that a knowledge base is **acyclic** (page 204) if there is an assignment of natural numbers (non-negative integers) to the atoms so that the atoms in the body of a clause are assigned a lower number than the atom in the head. With negation as failure, non-acyclic knowledge bases become semantically problematic.

The following knowledge base is not acyclic:

$a \leftarrow {\sim}b.$

$b \leftarrow {\sim}a.$

Clark's completion of this knowledge base is equivalent to $a \leftrightarrow \neg b$, which just specifies that a and b have different truth values but not which one is true.

The following knowledge base is also not acyclic:

$a \leftarrow {\sim}a.$

Clark's completion of this knowledge base is $a \leftrightarrow \neg a$, which is logically inconsistent.

Clark's completion of an acyclic knowledge base is always consistent and always gives a unique truth value to each atom. For the rest of this chapter, we assume that the knowledge bases are acyclic.

5.6.1 Non-monotonic Reasoning

A logic is **monotonic** if any proposition that can be derived from a knowledge base can also be derived when extra propositions are added to the knowledge base. That is, adding knowledge does not reduce the set of propositions that can be derived. The definite clause logic is monotonic.

A logic is **non-monotonic** if some conclusions can be invalidated by adding more knowledge. The logic of definite clauses with negation as failure is non-monotonic. Non-monotonic reasoning is useful for representing defaults. A **default** is a rule that can be used unless it overridden by an exception.

For example, to say that b is normally true if c is true, a knowledge base designer can write a rule of the form

$$b \leftarrow c \wedge \sim ab\_a.$$

where ab_a is an atom that means abnormal with respect to some aspect a. Given c, the agent can infer b unless it is told ab_a. Adding ab_a to the knowledge base can prevent the conclusion of b. Rules that imply ab_a can be used to prevent the default under the conditions of the body of the rule.

Example 5.30 Suppose the purchasing agent is investigating purchasing holidays. A resort may be adjacent to a beach or away from a beach. This is not symmetric; if the resort were adjacent to a beach, the knowledge provider would specify this. Thus, it is reasonable to have the clause

$$away\_from\_beach \leftarrow \sim on\_beach.$$

This clause enables an agent to infer that a resort is away from the beach if the agent is not told it is on a beach.

A **cooperative system** tries to not mislead. If we are told the resort is on the beach, we would expect that resort users would have access to the beach. If they have access to a beach, we would expect them to be able to swim at the beach. Thus, we would expect the following defaults:

$$beach\_access \leftarrow on\_beach \wedge \sim ab\_beach\_access.$$

$$swim\_at\_beach \leftarrow beach\_access \wedge \sim ab\_swim\_at\_beach.$$

A cooperative system would tell us if a resort on the beach has no beach access or if there is no swimming. We could also specify that, if there is an enclosed bay and a big city, then there is no swimming, by default:

$$ab\_swim\_at\_beach \leftarrow enclosed\_bay \wedge big\_city \wedge \sim ab\_no\_swimming\_near\_city.$$

We could say that British Columbia is abnormal with respect to swimming near cities:

$$ab\_no\_swimming\_near\_city \leftarrow in\_BC \wedge \sim ab\_BC\_beaches.$$

Given only the preceding rules, an agent infers *away_from_beach*. If it is then told *on_beach*, it can no longer infer *away_from_beach*, but it can now infer *beach_access* and *swim_at_beach*. If it is also told *enclosed_bay* and *big_city*, it can no longer infer *swim_at_beach*. However, if it is then told *in_BC*, it can then infer *swim_at_beach*.

By having defaults of what is normal, a user can interact with the system by telling it what is abnormal, which allows for economy in communication. The user does not have to state the obvious.

One way to think about non-monotonic reasoning is in terms of **arguments**. The rules can be used as components of arguments, in which the negated abnormality gives a way to undermine arguments. Note that, in the language presented, only positive arguments exist that can be undermined. In more general theories, there can be positive and negative arguments that attack each other.

5.6.2   Proof Procedures for Negation as Failure

Bottom-Up Procedure

The bottom-up procedure for negation as failure is a modification of the bottom-up procedure for definite clauses (page 187). The difference is that it can add literals of the form $\sim p$ to the set C of consequences that have been derived; $\sim p$ is added to C when it can determine that p must fail.

Failure can be defined recursively: p **fails** when every body of a clause with p as the head fails. A body fails if one of the literals in the body fails. An atom b_i in a body fails if $\sim b_i$ can be derived. A negation $\sim b_i$ in a body fails if b_i can be derived.

Figure 5.11 (on the next page) gives a bottom-up negation-as-failure interpreter for computing consequents of a ground *KB*. Note that this includes the case of a clause with an empty body (in which case $m = 0$, and the atom at the head is added to C) and the case of an atom that does not appear in the head of any clause (in which case its negation is added to C).

Example 5.31   Consider the following clauses:

$p \leftarrow q \wedge \sim r.$

$p \leftarrow s.$

$q \leftarrow \sim s.$

$r \leftarrow \sim t.$

$t.$

```
1: procedure Prove_NAF_BU(KB)
2:     Inputs
3:         KB: a set of clauses that can include negation as failure
4:     Output
5:         set of literals that follow from the completion of KB
6:     Local
7:         C is a set of literals
8:     C := {}
9:     repeat
10:         either
11:             select r ∈ KB such that
12:                 r is "h ← b₁ ∧ ... ∧ bₘ"
13:                 bᵢ ∈ C for all i, and
14:                 h ∉ C;
15:             C := C ∪ {h}
16:         or
17:             select h such that ∼h ∉ C and
18:                 where for every clause "h ← b₁ ∧ ... ∧ bₘ" ∈ KB
19:                     either for some bᵢ, ∼bᵢ ∈ C
20:                     or some bᵢ = ∼g and g ∈ C
21:             C := C ∪ {∼h}
22:     until no more selections are possible
```

Figure 5.11: Bottom-up negation as failure proof procedure

$$s \leftarrow w.$$

The following is a possible sequence of literals added to C:

$$t$$

$$\sim r$$

$$\sim w$$

$$\sim s$$

$$q$$

$$p$$

where t is derived trivially because it is given as an atomic clause; $\sim r$ is derived because $t \in C$; $\sim w$ is derived as there are no clauses for w, and so the "for every clause" condition of line 18 of Figure 5.11 trivially holds. Literal $\sim s$ is derived as $\sim w \in C$; and q and p are derived as the bodies are all proved.

```
 1: non-deterministic procedure Prove_NAF_TD(KB, Query)
 2:     Inputs
 3:         KB: a set of clauses that can include negation as failure
 4:         Query: a set of literals to prove
 5:     Output
 6:         yes if completion of KB entails Query and fail otherwise
 7:     Local
 8:         G is a set of literals
 9:     G := Query
10:     repeat
11:         select literal l ∈ G
12:         if l is of the form ∼a then
13:             if Prove_NAF_TD(KB, a) fails then
14:                 G := G \ {l}
15:             else
16:                 fail
17:         else
18:             choose clause "l ← B" in KB with l as head
19:             G := G \ {l} ∪ B
20:     until G = {}
21:     return yes
```

Figure 5.12: Top-down negation as failure interpreter

Top-Down Negation-as-Failure Procedure

The top-down procedure for the complete knowledge assumption proceeds by **negation as failure**. It is similar to the top-down definite-clause proof procedure of Figure 5.4 (page 191). This is a non-deterministic procedure (see the box on page 88) that can be implemented by searching over choices that succeed. When a negated atom $\sim a$ is selected, a new proof for atom a is started. If the proof for a fails, $\sim a$ succeeds. If the proof for a succeeds, the algorithm fails and must make other choices. The algorithm is shown in Figure 5.12.

> **Example 5.32** Consider the clauses from Example 5.31 (page 217). Suppose the query is ask p.
>
> Initially, $G = \{p\}$.
>
> Using the first rule for p, G becomes $\{q, \sim r\}$.
>
> Selecting q, and replacing it with the body of the third rule, G becomes $\{\sim s, \sim r\}$.
>
> It then selects $\sim s$ and starts a proof for s. This proof for s fails, and thus G becomes $\{\sim r\}$.
>
> It then selects $\sim r$ and tries to prove r. In the proof for r, there is the subgoal $\sim t$, and so it tries to prove t. This proof for t succeeds. Thus, the proof for $\sim t$

fails and, because there are no more rules for r, the proof for r fails. Therefore, the proof for $\sim r$ succeeds.

> G is empty and so it returns *yes* as the answer to the top-level query.

Note that this implements **finite failure**, because it makes no conclusion if the proof procedure does not halt. For example, suppose there is just the rule $p \leftarrow p$. The algorithm does not halt for the query ask p. The completion, $p \leftrightarrow p$, gives no information. Even though there may be a way to conclude that there will never be a proof for p, a sound proof procedure should not conclude $\sim p$, as it does not follow from the completion.

5.7   Abduction

Abduction is a form of reasoning where assumptions are made to explain observations. For example, if an agent were to observe that some light was not working, it hypothesizes what is happening in the world to explain why the light was not working. An intelligent tutoring system could try to explain why a student gives some answer in terms of what the student understands and does not understand.

The term **abduction** was coined by Peirce (1839–1914) to differentiate this type of reasoning from **deduction**, which involves determining what logically follows from a set of axioms, and **induction**, which involves inferring general relationships from examples.

In abduction, an agent hypothesizes what may be true about an observed case. An agent determines what implies its observations – what could be true to make the observations true. Observations are trivially implied by contradictions (as a contradiction logically implies everything), so we want to exclude contradictions from our explanation of the observations.

To formalize abduction, we use the language of Horn clauses and assumables (page 206). The system is given

- a knowledge base, KB, which is a set of of Horn clauses, and

- a set A of atoms, called the **assumables**, which are the building blocks of hypotheses.

Instead of adding observations to the knowledge base, observations must be explained.

A **scenario** of $\langle KB, A \rangle$ is a subset H of A such that $KB \cup H$ is satisfiable. $KB \cup H$ is **satisfiable** if a model exists in which every element of KB and every element H is true. This happens if no subset of H is a conflict of KB.

An **explanation** of proposition g from $\langle KB, A \rangle$ is a scenario that, together with KB, implies g.

That is, an explanation of proposition g is a set H, $H \subseteq A$ such that

$$KB \cup H \models g$$
$$KB \cup H \not\models false.$$

A **minimal explanation** of g from $\langle KB, A \rangle$ is an explanation H of g from $\langle KB, A \rangle$ such that no strict subset of H is also an explanation of g from $\langle KB, A \rangle$.

Example 5.33 Consider the following simplistic knowledge base and assumables for a diagnostic assistant:

> $bronchitis \leftarrow influenza$.
> $bronchitis \leftarrow smokes$.
> $coughing \leftarrow bronchitis$.
> $wheezing \leftarrow bronchitis$.
> $fever \leftarrow influenza$.
> $fever \leftarrow infection$.
> $soreThroat \leftarrow influenza$.
> $false \leftarrow smokes \wedge nonsmoker$.
> assumable $smokes, nonsmoker, influenza, infection$.

If the agent observes *wheezing*, there are two minimal explanations:

> $\{influenza\}$ and $\{smokes\}$

These explanations imply *bronchitis* and *coughing*.
  If *wheezing* ∧ *fever* is observed, the minimal explanations are

> $\{influenza\}$ and $\{smokes, infection\}$.

If *wheezing* ∧ *nonsmoker* was observed, there is one minimal explanation:

> $\{influenza, nonsmoker\}$.

The other explanation of *wheezing* is inconsistent with being a non-smoker.

Example 5.34 Consider the knowledge base:

> $alarm \leftarrow tampering$.
> $alarm \leftarrow fire$.
> $smoke \leftarrow fire$.

If *alarm* is observed, there are two minimal explanations:

> $\{tampering\}$ and $\{fire\}$.

If *alarm* ∧ *smoke* is observed, there is one minimal explanation:

> {*fire*}.

Notice how, when *smoke* is observed, there is no need to hypothesize *tampering* to explain *alarm*; it has been **explained away** by *fire*.

Determining what is going on inside a system based on observations about the behavior is the problem of **diagnosis** or **recognition**. In **abductive diagnosis**, the agent hypothesizes diseases or malfunctions, as well as that some parts are working normally, to explain the observed symptoms.

This differs from consistency-based diagnosis (page 207) (CBD) in the following ways:

- In CBD, only normal behavior needs to be represented, and the hypotheses are assumptions of normal behavior. In abductive diagnosis, faulty behavior as well as normal behavior needs to be represented, and the assumables need to be for normal behavior and for each fault (or different behavior).

- In abductive diagnosis, observations need to be explained. In CBD observations are added to the knowledge base, and *false* is proved.

Abductive diagnosis requires more detailed modeling and gives more detailed diagnoses, because the knowledge base has to be able to actually prove the observations from the knowledge base and the assumptions. Abductive diagnosis is also used to diagnose systems in which there is no normal behavior. For example, in an intelligent tutoring system, by observing what a student does, the tutoring system can hypothesize what the student understands and does not understand, which can guide the actions of the tutoring system.

Abduction can also be used for **design**, in which the query to be explained is a design goal and the assumables are the building blocks of the designs. The explanation is the design. Consistency means that the design is possible. The implication of the design goal means that the design provably achieved the design goal.

Example 5.35 Consider the electrical domain of Figure 5.2 (page 183). Similar to the representation of the example for consistency-based diagnosis in Example 5.23 (page 207), we axiomatize what follows from the assumptions of what may be happening in the system. In abductive diagnosis, we must axiomatize what follows both from faults and from normality assumptions. For each atom that could be observed, we axiomatize how it could be produced.

A user could observe that l_1 is lit or is dark. We must write rules that axiomatize how the system must be to make these true. Light l_1 is lit if it is ok and there is power coming in. The light is dark if it is broken or there is no power. The system can assume l_1 is ok or broken, but not both:

> $lit\_l_1 \leftarrow live\_w_0 \land ok\_l_1.$
>
> $dark\_l_1 \leftarrow broken\_l_1.$
>
> $dark\_l_1 \leftarrow dead\_w_0.$
>
> assumable $ok\_l_1.$
>
> assumable $broken\_l_1.$
>
> $false \leftarrow ok\_l_1 \land broken\_l_1.$

Wire w_0 is live or dead depending on the switch positions and whether the wires coming in are alive or dead:

> $live\_w_0 \leftarrow live\_w_1 \land up\_s_2 \land ok\_s_2.$
>
> $live\_w_0 \leftarrow live\_w_2 \land down\_s_2 \land ok\_s_2.$
>
> $dead\_w_0 \leftarrow broken\_s_2.$
>
> $dead\_w_0 \leftarrow up\_s_2 \land dead\_w_1.$
>
> $dead\_w_0 \leftarrow down\_s_2 \land dead\_w_2.$
>
> assumable $ok\_s_2.$
>
> assumable $broken\_s_2.$
>
> $false \leftarrow ok\_s_2 \land broken\_s_2.$

The other wires are axiomatized similarly. Some of the wires depend on whether the circuit breakers are ok or broken:

> $live\_w_3 \leftarrow live\_w_5 \land ok\_cb_1.$
>
> $dead\_w_3 \leftarrow broken\_cb_1.$
>
> $dead\_w_3 \leftarrow dead\_w_5.$
>
> assumable $ok\_cb_1.$
>
> assumable $broken\_cb_1.$
>
> $false \leftarrow ok\_cb_1 \land broken\_cb_1.$

For the rest of this example, we assume that the other light and wires are represented analogously.

The outside power can be live or the power can be down:

> $live\_w_5 \leftarrow live\_outside.$
>
> $dead\_w_5 \leftarrow outside\_power\_down.$
>
> assumable $live\_outside.$
>
> assumable $outside\_power\_down.$
>
> $false \leftarrow live\_outside \land outside\_power\_down.$

The switches can be assumed to be up or down:

> assumable $up\_s_1.$
>
> assumable $down\_s_1.$

$false \leftarrow up\_s_1 \wedge down\_s_1$.

There are two minimal explanations of lit_l_1:

    $\{live\_outside, ok\_cb_1, ok\_l_1, ok\_s_1, ok\_s_2, up\_s_1, up\_s_2\}$

    $\{live\_outside, ok\_cb_1, ok\_l_1, ok\_s_1, ok\_s_2, down\_s_1, down\_s_2\}$.

This could be seen in design terms as a way to make sure the light is on: put both switches up or both switches down, and ensure the switches all work. It could also be seen as a way to determine what is going on if the agent observed that l_1 is lit; one of these two scenarios must hold.

There are ten minimal explanations of $dark\_l_1$:

    $\{broken\_l_1\}$

    $\{broken\_s_2\}$

    $\{down\_s_1, up\_s_2\}$

    $\{broken\_s_1, up\_s_2\}$

    $\{broken\_cb_1, up\_s_1, up\_s_2\}$

    $\{outside\_power\_down, up\_s_1, up\_s_2\}$

    $\{down\_s_2, up\_s_1\}$

    $\{broken\_s_1, down\_s_2\}$

    $\{broken\_cb_1, down\_s_1, down\_s_2\}$

    $\{down\_s_1, down\_s_2, outside\_power\_down\}$

There are six minimal explanations of $dark\_l_1 \wedge lit\_l_2$:

    $\{broken\_l_1, live\_outside, ok\_cb_1, ok\_l_2, ok\_s_3, up\_s_3\}$

    $\{broken\_s_2, live\_outside, ok\_cb_1, ok\_l_2, ok\_s_3, up\_s_3\}$

    $\{down\_s_1, live\_outside, ok\_cb_1, ok\_l_2, ok\_s_3, up\_s_2, up\_s_3\}$

    $\{broken\_s_1, live\_outside, ok\_cb_1, ok\_l_2, ok\_s_3, up\_s_2, up\_s_3\}$

    $\{down\_s_2, live\_outside, ok\_cb_1, ok\_l_2, ok\_s_3, up\_s_1, up\_s_3\}$

    $\{broken\_s_1, down\_s_2, live\_outside, ok\_cb_1, ok\_l_2, ok\_s_3, up\_s_3\}$

Notice how the explanations cannot include $outside\_power\_down$ or $broken\_cb_1$ because they are inconsistent with the explanation of l_2 being lit.

Both the bottom-up and top-down implementations for assumption-based reasoning with Horn clauses can be used for abduction. The bottom-up algorithm of Figure 5.9 (page 210) computes the minimal explanations for each atom; at the end of the repeat loop, C contains the minimal explanations of each atom (as well as potentially some non-minimal explanations). The refinement of pruning dominated explanations (page 210) can also be used. The top-down algorithm (page 212) can be used to find the explanations of any g by first generating the conflicts and, using the same code and knowledge base, proving g instead of $false$. The minimal explanations of g are the minimal sets of assumables collected to prove g such that no subset is a conflict.

5.8 Causal Models

A **primitive atom** is an atom that is defined using facts. A **derived atom** is an atom that is defined using rules. Typically, the designer writes axioms for the derived atoms and then expects a user to specify which primitive atoms are true. Thus, a derived atom will be inferred as necessary from the primitive atoms and other atoms that can be derived.

The designer of an agent must make many decisions when designing a knowledge base for a domain. For example, consider two propositions, a and b, both of which are true. There are many choices of how to write this. A designer could specify both a and b as atomic clauses, treating both as primitive. A designer could have a as primitive and b as derived, stating a as an atomic clause and giving the rule $b \leftarrow a$. Alternatively, the designer could specify the atomic clause b and the rule $a \leftarrow b$, treating b as primitive and a as derived. These representations are logically equivalent; they cannot be distinguished logically. However, they have different effects when the knowledge base is changed. Suppose a was no longer true for some reason. In the first and third representations, b would still be true, and in the second representation b would no longer true.

A **causal model**, or a model of **causality**, is a representation of a domain that predicts the results of interventions. An **intervention** is an action that forces a variable to have a particular value. That is, an intervention changes the value in some way other than manipulating other variables in the model.

To predict the effect of interventions, a causal model represents how the cause implies its effect. When the cause is changed, its effect should be changed. An **evidential model** represents a domain in the other direction – from effect to cause. Note that we do not assume that there is "the cause" of an effect; rather there are propositions, which together may cause the effect to become true.

Example 5.36   In the electrical domain depicted in Figure 5.2 (page 183), consider the relationship between switches s_1 and s_2 and light l_1. Assume all components are working properly. Light l_1 is lit whenever both switches are up or both switches are down. Thus,

$$lit\_l_1 \leftrightarrow (up\_s_1 \leftrightarrow up\_s_2). \tag{5.1}$$

This is logically equivalent to

$$up\_s_1 \leftrightarrow (lit\_l_1 \leftrightarrow up\_s_2).$$

This formula is symmetric between the three propositions; it is true if and only if an odd number of the propositions are true. However, in the world, the relationship between these propositions is not symmetric. Suppose both switches were up and the light was lit. Putting s_1 down does not make s_2 go down to preserve lit_l_1. Instead, putting s_1 down makes lit_l_1 false, and up_s_2 remains true.

Thus, to predict the result of interventions, we require more than proposition (5.1) above.

A causal model is

$$lit\_l_1 \leftarrow up\_s_1 \wedge up\_s_2.$$
$$lit\_l_1 \leftarrow {\sim}up\_s_1 \wedge {\sim}up\_s_2.$$

The completion of this is equivalent to proposition (5.1); however, it makes reasonable predictions when one of the values is changed. Changing one of the switch positions changes whether the light is lit, but changing whether the light is lit (by some other mechanism) does not change whether the switches are up or down.

An evidential model is

$$up\_s_1 \leftarrow lit\_l_1 \wedge up\_s_2.$$
$$up\_s_1 \leftarrow {\sim}lit\_l_1 \wedge {\sim}up\_s_2.$$

This can be used to answer questions about whether s_1 is up based on the position of s_2 and whether l_1 is lit. Its completion is also equivalent to formula (5.1). However, it does not accurately predict the effect of interventions.

For most purposes, it is preferable to use a causal model of the world as it is more transparent, stable and modular than an evidential model.

5.9   Review

The following are the main points you should have learned from this chapter:

- Representing constraints in terms of propositions often enables constraint reasoning to be more efficient.

- A definite clause knowledge base can be used to specify atomic clauses and rules about a domain when there is no uncertainty or ambiguity.

- Given a set of statements that are claimed to be true about a domain, the logical consequences characterize what else must be true.

- A sound and complete proof procedure can be used to determine the logical consequences of a knowledge base.

- Bottom-up and top-down proof procedures can be proven to be sound and complete.

- Proof by contradiction can be used to make inference from a Horn clause knowledge base.

- Negation as failure can be used to make conclusions assuming complete knowledge.

- Abduction can be used to explain observations.

- Consistency-based diagnosis and abductive diagnosis are alternative methods for troubleshooting systems.

- A causal model predicts the effect of interventions.

5.10 References and Further Reading

Propositional logic has a long history; the semantics for propositional logic presented here is based on that of Tarski [1956]. For introductions to logic see Copi et al. [2016] for an informal overview, Enderton [1972] and Mendelson [1987] for more formal approaches, and Bell and Machover [1977] for advanced topics. For in-depth presentations on the use of logic in AI see the multivolume *Handbook of Logic in Artificial Intelligence and Logic Programming* [Gabbay et al., 1993].

The DPLL algorithm (page 181) is by Davis et al. [1962]. Levesque [1984] describes the tell-ask protocol for knowledge bases. Consistency-based diagnosis was formalized by de Kleer et al. [1992].

Much of the foundation of definite and Horn clause reasoning was developed in the context of a richer first-order logic that is presented in Chapter 13 and is studied under the umbrella of **logic programming**. Resolution was developed by Robinson [1965]. SLD resolution was pioneered by Kowalski [1974] and Colmerauer et al. [1973], building on previous work by Green [1969], Hayes [1973], and Hewitt [1969]. The fixed point semantics was developed by van Emden and Kowalski [1976]. For more detail on the semantics and properties of logic programs see Lloyd [1987].

The work on negation as failure (page 212) is based on the work of Clark [1978]. Apt and Bol [1994] provide a survey of different techniques and semantics for handling negation as failure. The bottom-up negation-as-failure proof procedure is based on the **truth maintenance system** (**TMS**) of Doyle [1979], who also considered incremental addition and removal of clauses; see Exercise 5.15 (page 236). The use of abnormality for default reasoning was advocated by McCarthy [1986].

The abduction framework presented here is based on the **assumption-based truth maintenance system** (**ATMS**) of de Kleer [1986] and on Theorist [Poole et al., 1987]. Abduction has been used for diagnosis [Peng and Reggia, 1990], natural language understanding [Hobbs et al., 1993], and temporal reasoning [Shanahan, 1989]. Kakas et al. [1993] and Kakas and Denecker [2002] review abductive reasoning. For an overview of the work of Peirce, who first characterized abduction, see Burch [2008]. The bottom-up Horn implementation for finding explanations is based on the ATMS [de Kleer, 1986]. The ATMS is more sophisticated in that it considers the problem of incremental addition of clauses and assumables also; see Exercise 5.16 (page 236).

Dung [1995] presents an abstract framework for arguments that provides a foundation for much of the work in this area. Chesnevar et al. [2000] and Besnard and Hunter [2008] survey work on arguments.

Causal models are discussed by Pearl [2009] and Spirtes et al. [2001].

5.11   Exercises

Some of these exercises can use AILog, a simple logical reasoning system that implements all of the reasoning discussed in this chapter. It is available from the book website (http://artint.info). Many of these can also be done in Prolog.

Exercise 5.1 Suppose we want to be able to reason about an electric kettle plugged into one of the power outlets for the electrical domain of Figure 5.2 (page 183). Suppose a kettle must be plugged into a working power outlet, it must be turned on, and it must be filled with water, in order to heat.

Write axioms in terms of definite clauses that let the system determine whether kettles are heating. AILog code for the electrical environment is available from the book website.

You must

- give the intended interpretation of all symbols used

- write the clauses so they can be loaded into AILog

- show that the resulting knowledge base runs in AILog.

Exercise 5.2 Consider the domain of house plumbing shown in Figure 5.13.

In this diagram, p_1, p_2, and p_3 are cold water pipes; t_1, t_2, and t_3 are taps; d_1, d_2, and d_3 are drainage pipes.

Suppose you have the following atoms

- *pressurized_p_i* is true if pipe p_i has mains pressure in it
- *on_t_i* is true if tap t_i is on
- *off_t_i* is true if tap t_i is off
- *wet_b* is true if b is wet (b is either the sink, bath or floor)
- *flow_p_i* is true if water is flowing through p_i
- *plugged_sink* is true if the sink has the plug in
- *plugged_bath* is true if the bath has the plug in
- *unplugged_sink* is true if the sink does not have the plug in
- *unplugged_bath* is true if the bath does not have the plug in.

A definite-clause axiomatization for how water can flow down drain d_1 if taps t_1 and t_2 are on and the bath is unplugged is

pressurized_p_1.

pressurized_p_2 $\leftarrow$ *on_t_1* $\wedge$ *pressurized_p_1*.

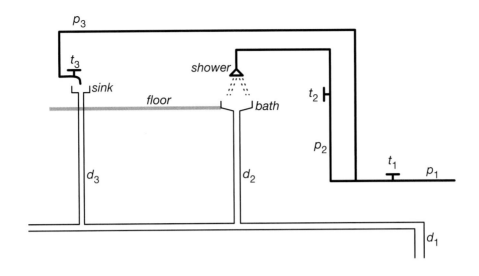

Figure 5.13: The plumbing domain

$flow\_shower \leftarrow on\_t_2 \wedge pressurized\_p_2.$

$wet\_bath \leftarrow flow\_shower.$

$flow\_d_2 \leftarrow wet\_bath \wedge unplugged\_bath.$

$flow\_d_1 \leftarrow flow\_d_2.$

$on\_t_1.$

$on\_t_2.$

$unplugged\_bath.$

(a) Finish the axiomatization for the sink in the same manner as the axiomatization for the bath. Test it in AILog.

(b) What information would you expect the a resident of a house to be able to provide that the plumber who installed the system, who is not at the house, cannot? Change the axiomatization so that questions about this information are asked of the user.

(c) Axiomatize how the floor is wet if the sink overflows or the bath overflows. They overflow if the plug is in and water is flowing in. You may invent new atomic propositions as long as you give their intended interpretation. (Assume that the taps and plugs have been in the same positions for one hour; you do not have to axiomatize the dynamics of turning on the taps and inserting and removing plugs.) Test it in AILog.

(d) Suppose a hot water system is installed to the left of tap t_1. This has another tap in the pipe leading into it and supplies hot water to the shower and the sink (there are separate hot and cold water taps for each). Add this to your axiomatization. Give the denotation for all propositions you invent. Test it in AILog.

Exercise 5.3 Consider the following knowledge base:

$a \leftarrow b \wedge c.$

$a \leftarrow e \wedge f.$

$b \leftarrow d.$

$b \leftarrow f \wedge h.$

$c \leftarrow e.$

$d \leftarrow h.$

$e.$

$f \leftarrow g.$

$g \leftarrow c.$

(a) Give a model of the knowledge base.

(b) Give an interpretation that is not a model of the knowledge base.

(c) Give two atoms that are logical consequences of the knowledge base.

(d) Give two atoms that are not logical consequences of the knowledge base.

Exercise 5.4 Consider the knowledge base *KB*:

$a \leftarrow b \wedge c.$

$b \leftarrow d.$

$b \leftarrow e.$

$c.$

$d \leftarrow h.$

$e.$

$f \leftarrow g \wedge b.$

$g \leftarrow c \wedge k.$

$j \leftarrow a \wedge b.$

(a) Show how the bottom-up proof procedure works for this example. Give all logical consequences of *KB*.

(b) *f* is not a logical consequence of *KB*. Give a model of *KB* in which *f* is false.

(c) *a* is a logical consequence of *KB*. Give a top-down derivation for the query ask *a*.

Exercise 5.5 A bottom-up proof procedure can incorporate an ask-the-user mechanism by asking the user about every askable atom. How can a bottom-up proof

procedure still guarantee proof of all (non-askable) atoms that are a logical consequence of a definite-clause knowledge base without asking the user about every
askable atom?

Exercise 5.6   This question explores how having an explicit semantics can be
used to debug programs. The file `elect_bug2.ail` in the AILog distribution on
the book website is an axiomatization of the electrical wiring domain of Figure
5.2 (page 183), but it contains a buggy clause (one that is false in the intended
interpretation shown in the figure). The aim of this exercise is to use AILog to
find the buggy clause, given the denotation of the symbols given in Example 5.7
(page 183). To find the buggy rule, you do not even need to look at the knowledge
base! (You can look at the knowledge base to find the buggy clause if you like, but
that will not help you in this exercise.) All you must know is the meaning of the
symbols in the program and what is true in the intended interpretation.

The query $lit_{-}l_1$ can be proved, but it is false in the intended interpretation. Use
the *how* questions of AILog to find a clause whose head is false in the intended
interpretation and whose body is true. This is a buggy rule.

Exercise 5.7   Consider the following knowledge base and assumables aimed to
explain why people are acting suspiciously:

> $goto\_forest \leftarrow walking.$
>
> $get\_gun \leftarrow hunting.$
>
> $goto\_forest \leftarrow hunting.$
>
> $get\_gun \leftarrow robbing.$
>
> $goto\_bank \leftarrow robbing.$
>
> $goto\_bank \leftarrow banking.$
>
> $fill\_withdrawal\_form \leftarrow banking.$
>
> $false \leftarrow banking \land robbing.$
>
> $false \leftarrow wearing\_good\_shoes \land goto\_forest.$
>
> assumable $walking, hunting, robbing, banking.$

(a) Suppose *get_gun* is observed. What are all of the minimal explanations for
this observation?

(b) Suppose *get_gun* ∧ *goto_bank* is observed. What are all of the minimal explanations for this observation?

(c) Is there something that could be observed to remove one of these as a minimal explanation? What must be added to be able to explain this?

(d) What are the minimal explanations of *goto_bank*?

(e) What are the minimal explanations of *goto_bank* ∧ *get_gun* ∧ *fill_withdrawal_form*?

Exercise 5.8   Suppose there are four possible diseases a particular patient may
have: p, q, r, and s. p causes spots. q causes spots. Fever could be caused by one
(or more) of q, r, or s. The patient has spots and fever. Suppose you have decided
to use abduction to diagnose this patient based on the symptoms.

(a) Show how to represent this knowledge using Horn clauses and assumables.

(b) Show how to diagnose this patient using abduction. Show clearly the query and the resulting answer(s).

(c) Suppose also that p and s cannot occur together. Show how that changes your knowledge base from part (a). Show how to diagnose the patient using abduction with the new knowledge base. Show clearly the query and the resulting answer(s).

Exercise 5.9 Consider the following clauses and integrity constraints:

$$false \leftarrow a \wedge b.$$
$$false \leftarrow c.$$
$$a \leftarrow d.$$
$$a \leftarrow e.$$
$$b \leftarrow d.$$
$$b \leftarrow g.$$
$$b \leftarrow h.$$
$$c \leftarrow h.$$

Suppose the assumables are $\{d, e, f, g, h, i\}$. What are the minimal conflicts?

Exercise 5.10 Deep Space One (http://nmp.jpl.nasa.gov/ds1/) was a spacecraft launched by NASA in October 1998 that used AI technology for its diagnosis and control. For more details, see Muscettola et al. [1998] or http://ti.arc.nasa.gov/tech/asr/planning-and-scheduling/remote-agent/ (although these references are not necessary to complete this question).

Figure 5.14 depicts a part of the actual DS1 engine design. To achieve thrust in an engine, fuel and oxidizer must be injected. The whole design is highly redundant to ensure its operation even in the presence of multiple failures (mainly stuck or inoperative valves). Note that whether the valves are black or white, and whether or not they have a bar are irrelevant for this question.

Each valve can be ok (or not) and can be open (or not). The aim of this question is to axiomatize the domain so that we can do two tasks.

(a) Given an observation of the lack of thrust in an engine and given which valves are open, using consistency-based diagnosis, determine what could be wrong.

(b) Given the goal of having thrust and given the knowledge that some valves are ok, determine which valves should be opened.

For each of these tasks, you must think about what the clauses are in the knowledge base and what is assumable.

The atoms should be of the following forms

- $open\_V$ is true if valve V is open. This the atoms should be $open\_v_1$, $open\_v_2$, and so on.

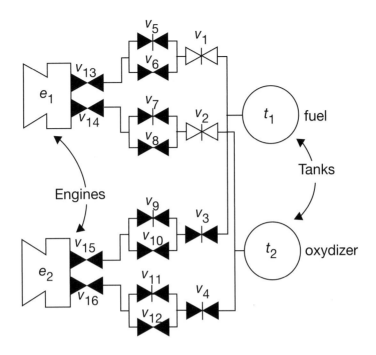

Figure 5.14: Deep Space One engine design

- *ok_V* is true if valve *V* is working properly.

- *pressurized_V* is true if the output of valve *V* is pressurized with gas. You should assume that *pressurized_t₁* and *pressurized_t₂* are true.

- *thrust_E* is true if engine *E* has thrust.

- *thrust* is true if no thrust exists in either engine.

- *nothrust* is true if there is no thrust.

To make this manageable, only write rules for the input into engine e_1. Test your code using AILog on a number of examples.

Exercise 5.11 Consider using abductive diagnosis on the problem in the previous question, with the following elaborations.

- Valves can be *open* or *closed*. Some of valves may be specified as open or closed.

- A valve can be *ok*, in which case the gas will flow if the valve is open and not if it is closed; *broken*, in which case gas never flows; *stuck*, in which case gas flows independently of whether the valve is open or closed; or *leaking*, in which case gas flowing into the valve leaks out instead of flowing through.

- There are three gas sensors that can detect gas leaking (but not which gas); the first gas sensor detects gas from the rightmost valves ($v_1, \ldots, v_4$), the second gas sensor detects gas from the center valves ($v_5, \ldots, v_{12}$), and the third gas sensor detects gas from the leftmost valves ($v_{13}, \ldots, v_{16}$).

(a) Axiomatize the domain so the system can explain thrust or no thrust in engine e_1 and the presence of gas in one of the sensors. For example, it should be able to explain why e_1 is thrusting. It should be able to explain why e_1 is not thrusting and there is a gas detected by the third sensor.

(b) Test your axiomatization on some non-trivial examples.

(c) Some of the queries have many explanations. Suggest how the number of explanations could be reduced or managed so that the abductive diagnoses are more useful.

Exercise 5.12 AILog has *askables*, which are atoms that are asked of the user, and *assumables*, which are collected in an answer.

Imagine you are axiomatizing the plumbing in your home and you have an axiomatization similar to that of Exercise 5.2 (page 228). You are axiomatizing the domain for a new tenant who is going to sublet your home and may want to determine what may be going wrong with the plumbing (before calling you or the plumber).

There are some atoms that you will know the rules for, some that the tenant will know, and some that neither will know. Divide the atomic propositions into these three categories, and suggest which should be made askable and which should be assumable. Show what the resulting interaction will look like under your division.

Exercise 5.13 This question explores how integrity constraints and consistency-based diagnosis can be used in a purchasing agent that interacts with various information sources on the web. The purchasing agent will ask a number of the information sources for facts. However, information sources are sometimes wrong. It is useful to be able to automatically determine which information sources may be wrong when a user gets conflicting information.

This question uses meaningless symbols such as $a, b, c, \ldots$, but in a real domain there will be meaning associated with the symbols, such as a meaning "there is skiing in Hawaii" and z meaning "there is no skiing in Hawaii" or a meaning "butterflies do not eat anything" and z meaning "butterflies eat nectar". We will use meaningless symbols in this question because the computer does not have access to the meanings and must simply treat them as meaningless symbols.

Suppose the following information sources and associated information are provided.

Source s_1: Source s_1 claims the following clauses are true:

$$a \leftarrow h.$$
$$d \leftarrow c.$$

Source s_2**:** Source s_2 claims the following clauses are true:

$$e \leftarrow d.$$
$$f \leftarrow k.$$
$$z \leftarrow g.$$
$$j.$$

Source s_3**:** Source s_3 claims the following clause is true:

$$h \leftarrow d.$$

Source s_4**:** Source s_4 claims the following clauses are true:

$$a \leftarrow b \wedge e.$$
$$b \leftarrow c.$$

Source s_5**:** Source s_5 claims the following clause is true:

$$g \leftarrow f \wedge j.$$

Yourself: Suppose that you know that the following clauses are true:

$$false \leftarrow a \wedge z.$$
$$c.$$
$$k.$$

Not every source can be believed, because together they produce a contradiction.

(a) Code the knowledge provided by the users into AILog using assumables. To use a clause provided by one of the sources, you must assume that the source is reliable.

(b) Use the program to find the conflicts about what sources are reliable. (To find conflicts you can just ask *false*.)

(c) Suppose you would like to assume that as few sources as possible are unreliable. Which single source, if it was unreliable, could account for a contradiction (assuming all other sources were reliable)?

(d) Which pairs of sources could account for a contradiction (assuming all other sources are reliable) such that no single one of them could account for the contradiction?

Exercise 5.14 Suppose you have a job at a company that is building online teaching tools. Because you have taken an AI course, your boss wants to know your opinion on various options under consideration.

They are planning on building an intelligent tutoring system for teaching elementary physics (e.g., mechanics and electromagnetism). One of the things that the system must do is to diagnose errors that a student may be making.

For each of the following, answer the explicit questions and use proper English. Answering parts not asked or giving more than one answer when only one is asked for will annoy the boss. The boss also does not like jargon, so please use straightforward English.

The boss has heard of consistency-based diagnosis and abductive diagnosis but wants to know what they involve *in the context of building an intelligent tutoring system for teaching elementary physics*.

(a) Explain what knowledge (about physics and about students) is required for consistency-based diagnosis.

(b) Explain what knowledge (about physics and about students) is required for abductive diagnosis.

(c) What is the main advantage of using abductive diagnosis over consistency-based diagnosis in this domain?

(d) What is the main advantage of consistency-based diagnosis over abductive diagnosis in this domain?

Exercise 5.15 Consider the bottom-up negation-as-failure proof procedure of Figure 5.11 (page 218). Suppose we want to allow for incremental addition and deletion of clauses. How does C change as a clause is added? How does C change if a clause is removed?

Exercise 5.16 Suppose you are implementing a bottom-up Horn clause explanation reasoner and you want to incrementally add clauses or assumables. When a clause is added, how are the minimal explanations affected? When an assumable is added, how are the minimal explanations affected?

Exercise 5.17 Figure 5.15 (on the next page) shows a simplified redundant communication network between an unmanned spacecraft (sc) and a ground control center (gc). There are two indirect high-bandwidth (high-gain) links that are relayed through satellites (s_1, s_2) to different ground antennae (a_1, a_2). Furthermore, there is a direct, low-bandwidth (low-gain) link between the ground control center's antenna (a_3) and the spacecraft. The low-gain link is affected by atmospheric disturbances – it works if there are no disturbances (no_dist) – and the spacecraft's low-gain transmitter (sc_lg) and antenna 3 are ok. The high-gain links always work if the spacecraft's high-gain transmitter (sc_hg), the satellites' antennae (s_1_ant, s_2_ant), the satellites' transmitters (s_1_trans, s_2_trans), and the ground antennae (a_1, a_2) are ok.

To keep matters simple, consider only messages from the spacecraft going through these channels to the ground control center.

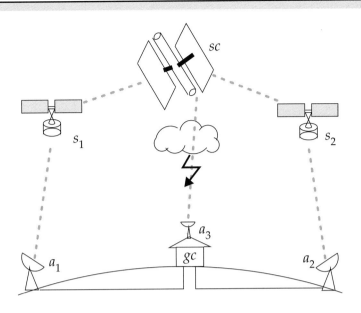

Figure 5.15: A space communication network

The following knowledge base formalizes the part of the communication network we are interested in:

$$send\_signal\_lg\_sc \leftarrow ok\_sc\_lg \land alive\_sc.$$
$$send\_signal\_hg\_sc \leftarrow ok\_sc\_hg \land alive\_sc.$$
$$get\_signal\_s_1 \leftarrow send\_signal\_hg\_sc \land ok\_s_1\_ant.$$
$$get\_signal\_s_2 \leftarrow send\_signal\_hg\_sc \land ok\_s_2\_ant.$$
$$send\_signal\_s_1 \leftarrow get\_signal\_s_1 \land ok\_s_1\_trans.$$
$$send\_signal\_s_2 \leftarrow get\_signal\_s_2 \land ok\_s_2\_trans.$$
$$get\_signal\_gc \leftarrow send\_signal\_s_1 \land ok\_a_1.$$
$$get\_signal\_gc \leftarrow send\_signal\_s_2 \land ok\_a_2.$$
$$get\_signal\_gc \leftarrow send\_signal\_lg\_sc \land ok\_a_3 \land no\_dist.$$

Ground control is worried, because it has not received a signal from the spacecraft (no_signal_gc). It knows for sure that all ground antennae are ok (i.e., ok_a_1, ok_a_2, and ok_a_3) and satellite s_1's transmitter is ok ($ok\_s_1\_trans$). It is not sure about the state of the spacecraft, its transmitters, the satellites' antennae, s_2's transmitter, and atmospheric disturbances.

(a) Specify a set of assumables and an integrity constraint that model the situation.

(b) Using the assumables and the integrity constraints from part (a), what is the set of minimal conflicts?

(c) What is the consistency-based diagnosis for the given situation? In other words, what are the possible combinations of violated assumptions that could account for why the control center cannot receive a signal from the spacecraft?

Exercise 5.18

(a) Explain why NASA may want to use abduction rather than consistency-based diagnosis for the domain of Exercise 5.17 (page 236).

(b) Suppose that an atmospheric disturbance *dist* could produce static or no signal in the low-bandwidth signal. To receive the static, antenna a_3 and the spacecraft's low-bandwidth transmitter *sc_lg* must be working. If a_3 or *sc_lg* are not working or *sc* is dead, there is no signal. What rules and assumables must be added to the knowledge base of Exercise 5.17 so that we can explain the possible observations *no_signal_gc*, *get_signal_gc*, or *static_gc*? You may ignore the high-bandwidth links. You may invent any symbols you need.

Chapter 6

Planning with Certainty

He who every morning plans the transaction of the day and follows out that plan, carries a thread that will guide him through the maze of the most busy life. But where no plan is laid, where the disposal of time is surrendered merely to the chance of incidence, chaos will soon reign.

– Victor Hugo (1802–1885)

Planning is the process of finding a sequence of actions to achieve a goal. Because an agent does not usually achieve its goals in one step, what it should do at any time depends on what it will do in the future. What it will do in the future depends on the state it is in, which, in turn, depends on what it has done in the past. This chapter presents three representation of actions and their effects, and four offline algorithms for an agent to find a plan to achieve its goals from a given state.

This chapter makes the following simplifying assumptions:

- There is a single agent.
- The agent's actions are deterministic and the agent can predict the consequences of its actions.
- There are no exogenous events beyond the control of the agent that change the state of the environment.
- The environment is fully observable; thus, the agent can observe the current state of the environment.
- Time progresses discretely from one state to the next.
- Goals are predicates of states that must be achieved.

Some of these assumptions are relaxed in the following chapters.

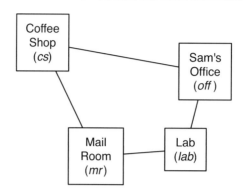

Features to describe states

RLoc – Rob's location

RHC – Rob has coffee

SWC – Sam wants coffee

MW – Mail is waiting

RHM – Rob has mail

Actions

mc – move clockwise

mcc – move counterclockwise

puc – pickup coffee

dc – deliver coffee

pum – pickup mail

dm – deliver mail

Figure 6.1: The delivery robot domain

6.1 Representing States, Actions, and Goals

To reason about what to do, assume an agent has goals, a model of the environment, and a model of its actions.

A deterministic **action** is a partial function from states to states. It is partial because not every action is able to be carried out in every state. For example, a robot cannot pick up a particular object if it is nowhere near the object. The **precondition** of an action specifies when the action can be carried out. The **effect** of an action specifies the resulting state.

> **Example 6.1** Consider a delivery robot (page 34) with mail and coffee to deliver. Assume a simplified problem domain with four locations as shown in Figure 6.1. The robot, called Rob, can buy coffee at the coffee shop, pick up mail in the mail room, move, and deliver coffee and/or mail. Delivering the coffee to Sam's office will stop Sam from wanting coffee. There could be mail waiting at the mail room to be delivered to Sam's office. This domain is quite simple, yet it is rich enough to demonstrate many of the issues in representing actions and in planning.
>
> The state is described in terms of the following features.
> - *RLoc*, the robot's location, which is one of the coffee shop (*cs*), Sam's office (*off*), the mail room (*mr*), or the laboratory (*lab*).

- *RHC*, whether the robot has coffee. The atom *rhc* means Rob has coffee (i.e., *RHC=true*) and ¬*rhc* means Rob does not have coffee (i.e., *RHC=false*).
- *SWC*, whether Sam wants coffee. The atom *swc* means Sam wants coffee and ¬*swc* means Sam does not want coffee.
- *MW*, whether mail is waiting at the mail room. The atom *mw* means there is mail waiting and ¬*mw* means there is no mail waiting.
- *RHM*, whether the robot is carrying the mail. The atom *rhm* means Rob has mail, and ¬*rhm* means Rob does not have mail.

Rob has six actions.

- Rob can move clockwise (*mc*).
- Rob can move counterclockwise (*mcc*).
- Rob can pick up coffee if Rob is at the coffee shop. Let *puc* mean that Rob picks up coffee. The precondition of *puc* is ¬*rhc* ∧ *RLoc=cs*; that is, Rob can pick up coffee in any state where its location is *cs*, and it is not already holding coffee. The effect of this action is to make *RHC* true. It does not affect the other features.
- Rob can deliver coffee if Rob is carrying coffee and is at Sam's office. Let *dc* mean that Rob delivers coffee. The precondition of *dc* is *rhc* ∧ *RLoc=off*. The effect of this action is to make *RHC* true and make *SWC* false. Note that Rob can deliver coffee whether or not Sam wants it.
- Rob can pick up mail if Rob is at the mail room and there is mail waiting there. Let *pum* mean Rob picks up the mail.
- Rob can deliver mail if Rob is carrying mail and at Sam's office. Let *dm* mean Rob delivers mail.

Assume that it is only possible for Rob to do one action at a time. We assume that a lower-level controller is able to implement these actions, as described in Chapter 2.

6.1.1 Explicit State-Space Representation

One possible representation of the effect and precondition of actions is to explicitly enumerate the states and, for each state, specify the actions that are possible in that state and, for each state–action pair, specify the state that results from carrying out the action in that state. This would require a table such as the following:

State	Action	Resulting State
s_7	act_{47}	s_{94}
s_7	act_{14}	s_{83}
s_{94}	act_5	s_{33}
...	...	...

The first tuple in this relation specifies that it is possible to carry out action act_{47} in state s_7 and, if it were to be carried out in state s_7, the resulting state would be s_{94}.

Thus, this is the explicit representation of a graph, where the nodes are states and the acts are actions. This is called a **state-space graph**. This is the sort of graph that was used in Chapter 3. Any of the algorithms of Chapter 3 can be used to search the space.

Example 6.2 In Example 6.1 (page 240), the states are the quintuples specifying the robot's location, whether the robot has coffee, whether Sam wants coffee, whether mail is waiting, and whether the robot is carrying the mail. For example, the tuple

$$\langle lab, \neg rhc, swc, \neg mw, rhm \rangle$$

represents the state where Rob is at the Lab, Rob does not have coffee, Sam wants coffee, there is no mail waiting, and Sam has mail. The tuple

$$\langle lab, rhc, swc, mw, \neg rhm \rangle$$

represents the state where Rob is at the Lab carrying coffee, Sam wants coffee, there is mail waiting, and Rob is not holding any mail.

In this example, there are $4 \times 2 \times 2 \times 2 \times 2 = 64$ states. Intuitively, all of them are possible, even if one would not expect that some of them would be reached by an intelligent robot.

There are six actions, not all of which are applicable in each state.

The actions are defined in terms of the state transitions:

State	Action	Resulting State
$\langle lab, \neg rhc, swc, \neg mw, rhm \rangle$	mc	$\langle mr, \neg rhc, swc, \neg mw, rhm \rangle$
$\langle lab, \neg rhc, swc, \neg mw, rhm \rangle$	mcc	$\langle off, \neg rhc, swc, \neg mw, rhm \rangle$
$\langle off, \neg rhc, swc, \neg mw, rhm \rangle$	dm	$\langle off, \neg rhc, swc, \neg mw, \neg rhm \rangle$
$\langle off, \neg rhc, swc, \neg mw, rhm \rangle$	mcc	$\langle cs, \neg rhc, swc, \neg mw, rhm \rangle$
$\langle off, \neg rhc, swc, \neg mw, rhm \rangle$	mc	$\langle lab, \neg rhc, swc, \neg mw, rhm \rangle$
...	...	...

This table shows the transitions for two of the states. The complete representation includes the transitions for the other 62 states.

This is not a good representation for three main reasons:

- There are usually too many states to represent, to acquire, and to reason with.

- Small changes to the model mean a large change to the representation. Adding another feature means changing the whole representation. For example, to model the level of power in the robot, so that it can recharge itself in the Lab, every state has to change.

- It does not represent the structure of states; there is much structure and regularity in the effects of actions that is not reflected in the state transitions. For example, most actions do not affect whether Sam wants coffee, but this fact needs to be repeated for every state.

An alternative is to model how the actions affect the features.

6.1.2 The STRIPS Representation

The **STRIPS representation** is an action-centric representation which, for each action, specifies when the action can occur and the effects of the action. STRIPS, which stands for "STanford Research Institute Problem Solver," was the planner used in Shakey, one of the first robots built using AI technology.

To represent a planning problem in STRIPS, first divide the features that describe the state of the world into **primitive** and **derived** features. The STRIPS representation is used to specify the values of primitive features in a state based on the previous state and the action taken by the agent. Definite clauses are used to determine the value of derived features from the values of the primitive features in any given state.

The **STRIPS representation** for an action consists of

- the **precondition**, a set of assignments of values to features that must hold for the action to occur, and

- the **effect**, a set of assignments of values to primitive features that specifies the features that change, and the values they change to, as the result of the action.

The **precondition** of an action is a proposition – the conjunction of the elements of the set – that must be true before the action is able to be carried out. In terms of constraints, the robot is constrained so it can only choose an action for which the precondition holds.

Example 6.3 In Example 6.1 (page 240), the action of Rob to pick up coffee (*puc*) has precondition $\{cs, \neg rhc\}$. That is, Rob must be at the coffee shop (*cs*), not carrying coffee ($\neg rhc$) to carry out the *puc* action. As a constraint, this means that *puc* is not available for any other location or when *rhc* is true.

The action to move clockwise is always possible. Its precondition is the empty set, $\{\}$, which represents the proposition *true*.

The STRIPS representation is based on the idea that most things are not affected by a single action. The semantics relies on the **STRIPS assumption**: the values of all of the primitive features not mentioned in the effects of the action are unchanged by the action.

Primitive feature X has value v after action *act* if action *act* was possible (its preconditions hold) and $X = v$ is in the effect of *act* or if X is not mentioned in the effect of *act*, and X had value v immediately before *act*. The values of non-primitive features can be derived from the values of the primitive features for each time.

Example 6.4 In Example 6.1 (page 240), the action of Rob to pick up coffee (*puc*) has the following STRIPS representation:

precondition $\{cs, \neg rhc\}$

effect $\{rhc\}$

That is, in order to be able to pick up coffee, the robot must be at the coffee shop and not have coffee. After the action, *rhc* holds (i.e., *RHC=true*). All other feature values are unaffected by this action.

Example 6.5 The action of delivering coffee (*dc*) can be defined by

precondition $\{off, rhc\}$

effect $\{\neg rhc, \neg swc\}$

The robot can deliver coffee when it is in the office and has coffee. The robot does not have coffee after the action, and Sam does not want coffee after the action. Thus, the effects are to make *RHC=false* and *SWC=false*. Note that, according this model, the robot can deliver coffee whether Sam wants coffee or not; in either case, Sam does not want coffee immediately after the action.

STRIPS cannot directly define **conditional effects**, where the effect of an action depends on what is true initially. However, conditional effects can be modeled by introducing new actions, as shown in the following example.

Example 6.6 Consider representing the action *mc* to move clockwise. The effect of *mc*, where the robot ends up, depends on the robot's location before *mc* was carried out.

To represent this in the STRIPS representation, we can construct multiple actions that differ in what is true initially. For example, the action *mc_cs* (move clockwise from coffee shop) has a precondition $\{RLoc=cs\}$ and effect $\{RLoc=off\}$. The action *mc_off* (move clockwise from office) has a precondition $\{RLoc=off\}$ and effect $\{RLoc=lab\}$. STRIPS thus requires four move clockwise actions (one for each location) and four move counterclockwise actions.

6.1.3 Feature-Based Representation of Actions

Whereas STRIPS is an action-centric representation, a feature-centric representation is more flexible, as it allows for conditional effects, and non-local effects.
    A **feature-based representation of actions** models

- the precondition of each action
- for each feature, the feature values in the next state as a function of the feature values of the previous state and the action.

The feature-based representation of actions uses definite clauses to specify the value of each variable in the state resulting from an action. The bodies of these rules can include propositions about the action carried out and propositions about values of features in the previous state. We assume these propositions can be equalities and inequalities between features and values.
    The rules have two forms:

- A **causal rule** specifies when a feature gets a new value.

- A **frame rule** specifies when a feature keeps its value.

It is useful to think of these as two separate cases: what makes the feature change its value, and what makes it keep its value.

Example 6.7   In Example 6.1 (page 240), Rob's location depends on its previous location and where it moved. Let $RLoc'$ be the variable that specifies the location in the resulting state. The following rules specify the conditions under which Rob is at the coffee shop:

$$RLoc'=cs \leftarrow RLoc=off \wedge Act=mcc.$$
$$RLoc'=cs \leftarrow RLoc=mr \wedge Act=mc.$$
$$RLoc'=cs \leftarrow RLoc=cs \wedge Act \neq mcc \wedge Act \neq mc.$$

The first two rules are causal rules and the last rule is a frame rule.

Whether the robot has coffee in the resulting state depends on whether it has coffee in the previous state and its action. A causal rule specifies that picking up the coffee causes the robot to have coffee in the next time step:

$$rhc' \leftarrow Act=puc.$$

A frame rule specifies that the robot having coffee persists unless the robot delivers the coffee.

$$rhc' \leftarrow rhc \wedge Act \neq dc.$$

The rule implicitly implies that the robot cannot drop the coffee, drink it or lose it, and the coffee cannot be stolen.

The feature-based representation is more powerful than the STRIPS representation; it can represent anything representable in STRIPS, but can also represent conditional effects. It may be more verbose because it requires explicit frame axioms, which are implicit in the STRIPS representation.

The mapping from STRIPS to the feature-based representation for Boolean features is as follows. If the effect of an action act is $\{e_1, \ldots, e_k\}$, the STRIPS representation is equivalent to the causal rules

$$e'_i \leftarrow act.$$

for each e_i that is made true by the action and the frame rules

$$c' \leftarrow c \wedge act.$$

for each condition c that does not involve a variable on the effects list. Thus each e_i that assigns a feature to be false does not result in a rule. The precondition of each action is the same in both representations. Non-Boolean features may require multiple rules for the different values of the feature.

A **conditional effect** of an action depends on the value of other features. The feature-based representation is able to specify conditional effects, whereas STRIPS cannot represent these directly. Example 6.6 (page 244) shows how to represent in STRIPS the action moving clockwise, where the effect depends on the previous state, by inventing new actions. Example 6.7 shows how the feature-based representation can represent actions without needing to invent those new actions by adding conditions to the rules. The feature-based representation also allows for non-local effects, as in the following example.

Example 6.8 Suppose that all of the actions make the robot dirty, except for the *wash* action that makes the robot clean. In STRIPS this would entail having dirty as an effect of every action. In the feature-based representation, we could add a rule that robot is dirty after every action that is not *wash*:

$$robot\_dirty' \leftarrow Act \neq wash.$$

6.1.4   Initial States and Goals

In a typical planning problem, where the world is fully observable and deterministic, the initial state is defined by specifying the value for each feature for the initial state.

There are several different kinds of **goals**:

- An **achievement goal** is a proposition that must be true in the final state.
- A **maintenance goal** is a proposition that must be true in every state through which the agent passes. These are often **safety goals** – the goal of staying away from bad states.
- A **transient goal** is a proposition that must be achieved somewhere in the plan.
- A **resource goal** is the goal of minimizing some resource in the plan. For example, the goal may be to minimize fuel consumption or the time required to execute the plan.

In the rest of this chapter, we concentrate on achievement goals, where the goal is a set of assignment of values to features, all of which must hold in the final state.

6.2   Forward Planning

A deterministic **plan** is a sequence of actions to achieve a **goal** from a given starting state. A deterministic **planner** produces a plan given an initial world description, a specification of the actions available to the agent, and a goal description.

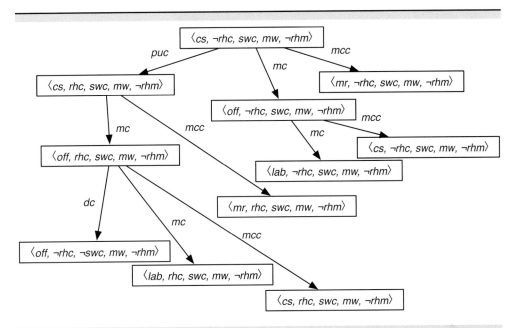

Figure 6.2: Part of the search space for a state-space planner

A forward planner treats the planning problem as a path planning problem in the **state-space graph**. In a state-space graph, nodes are states, and arcs correspond to actions from one state to another. The arcs coming out of a state *s* correspond to all of the legal actions that can be carried out in that state. That is, for each state, there is an arc for each action *a* whose precondition holds in state *s*. A plan is a path from the initial state to a state that satisfies the achievement goal.

A **forward planner** searches the state-space graph from the initial state looking for a state that satisfies a goal description. It can use any of the search strategies described in Chapter 3.

The search graph is defined as follows:

Dimensions (p. 31)
flat
states
indefinite horizon
fully observable
deterministic
goal directed
non-learning
single agent
offline
perfect rationality

- The nodes are states of the world, where a state is a total assignment of a value to each feature.

- The arcs correspond to actions. In particular, an arc from node *s* to *s′*, labeled with action *act*, means *act* is possible in *s* and carrying out *act* in state *s* results in state *s′*.

- The start node is the initial state.

- The goal condition for the search, *goal(s)*, is true if state *s* satisfies the achievement goal.

- A path corresponds to a plan that achieves the goal.

Example 6.9   For the running example, a state can be represented as a quintuple

$$\langle Loc, RHC, SWC, MW, RHM \rangle$$

of values for the respective variables.

Figure 6.2 shows part of the search space (without showing the loops) starting from the state where Rob is at the coffee shop, Rob does not have coffee, Sam wants coffee, there is mail waiting, and Rob does not have mail. The search space is the same irrespective of the goal state.

Using a forward planner is not the same as making an explicit state-based representation of the actions (page 241), because the relevant part of the graph is created dynamically from the representations of the actions.

A complete search strategy, such as A^* with multiple-path pruning or depth-first branch-and-bound, is guaranteed to find a solution. The complexity of the search space is defined by the forward branching factor (page 82) of the graph. The branching factor is the set of all possible actions at any state, which may be quite large. For the simple robot delivery domain, the branching factor is three for the initial situation and is up to four for other situations. This complexity may be reduced by finding good heuristics, so that not all of the space is searched if there is a solution.

For a forward planner, a heuristic function for a state is an estimate of the cost of solving the goal from the state.

Example 6.10   For the delivery robot plan, if all actions have a cost of 1, a possible admissible heuristic function (page 99) given a particular goal, is the maximum of:

- the distance from the robot location in the state s to the goal location, if there is one, and

- the distance from the robot's location in the state s to the coffee shop plus three (because the robot has to, at least, get to the coffee shop, pick up the coffee, get to the office and deliver the coffee) if the goal includes *SWC=false* and state s has *SWC=true* and *RHC=false*.

A state can be represented as either

(a) *a complete world description*, in terms of an assignment of a value to each primitive proposition, or

(b) *a path from an initial state*; that is, by the sequence of actions that were used to reach that state from the initial state. In this case, what holds in a state is computed from the axioms that specify the effects of actions.

Choice (a) involves computing a whole new world description for each world created, whereas (b) involves computing what holds in a state as needed. Alternative (b) may save on space (particularly if there is a complex world description) and may allow faster creation of a new node, it may be slower to determine what actually holds in any given world. Each representation requires a way to determine whether two states are the same if cycle pruning or multiple-path pruning are used.

State-space searching has been presented as a forward search method, but it is also possible to search backward (page 113) from the set of states that satisfy the goal. Typically, the goal does not fully specify a state, so there may be many goal states that satisfy the goal. If there are multiple states, create a node, *goal*, that has, as neighbors, all of the goal states, and use this as the start node for backward search. Once *goal* is expanded, the frontier has as many elements as there are goal states, which can be very large, making backward search in the state space impractical.

6.3 Regression Planning

It is often more efficient to search in a different search space – one where the nodes are not states but rather are subgoals to be achieved. A **subgoal** is an assignment to some of the features.

Regression planning is searching in the graph defined by the following:

Dimensions (p. 31)
flat
features
indefinite horizon
fully observable
deterministic
goal directed
non-learning
single agent
offline
perfect rationality

- The nodes are subgoals.

- The arcs correspond to actions. In particular, an arc from node g to g', labeled with action *act*, means

  - *act* is the last action that is carried out before subgoal g is achieved, and

  - node g' is a subgoal that must be true immediately before *act* so that g is true immediately after *act*.

- The start node is the planning goal to be achieved.

- The goal condition for the search, $goal(g)$, is true if g is true of the initial state.

Given a node that represents subgoal g, a neighbor of g exists for every action *act* such that

- *act* is **possible**, it is possible for *act* to be carried out and for g to be true immediately after *act* and

- *act* is **useful**, *act* achieves part of g.

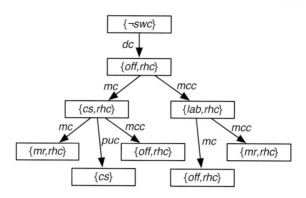

Figure 6.3: Part of the search space for a regression planner

Consider the subgoal $g = \{X_1=v_1,\ldots,X_n=v_n\}$. In terms of the STRIPS representation, *act* is useful for solving g if, for some i, $X_i=v_i$ is an effect of action *act*. Immediately before *act*, the preconditions of *act*, as well as any $X_k=v_k$ not achieved by *act*, must hold. Thus the neighbor of subgoal g on the arc labeled with *act* is the subgoal *precondition*(*act*) $\cup$ ($g \setminus$ *effects*(*act*)), as long as *act* is possible. Action *act* is possible if:

- for each $X_j=v_j$ in g, there is no effect $X_j=v_j'$ of *act* where $v_j' \neq v_j$ and

- *precondition*(*act*) $\cup$ ($g \setminus$ *effects*(*act*)) does not include two different assignments to any feature.

Example 6.11 Suppose the goal is to achieve ¬*swc*. Therefore, the start node is $\{\neg swc\}$. If this is true in the initial state, the planner stops. If not, it chooses an action that achieves ¬*swc*. In this case, there is only one such action: *dc*. The precondition of *dc* is $\{off, rhc\}$. Thus, there is one arc:

$$\langle \{\neg swc\}, \{off, rhc\}\rangle \text{ labeled with } dc.$$

Consider the node $\{off, rhc\}$. There are two actions that can achieve *off*, namely *mc* from *cs* and *mcc* from *lab*. There is one action that can achieve *rhc*, namely *puc*. However, *puc* has as precondition $\{cs, \neg rhc\}$, but *cs* and *off* are inconsistent (because they involve different assignments to the variable *RLoc*). Therefore, *puc* is not a possible last action; it is not possible that, immediately after *puc*, the condition $\{off, rhc\}$ holds.

Figure 6.3 shows the first three levels of the search space (without cycle pruning or multiple-path pruning). Note that the search space is the same no matter what the initial state is. The starting state has two roles: to serve as a stopping criterion and as a source of heuristics.

If a subgoal contains a number of assignments, regression can often determine which of the assignments to achieve last, as in the following example.

Example 6.12 Suppose the goal is for Sam to not want coffee and for the robot to have coffee: $\{\neg swc, rhc\}$. The last action cannot be dc to achieve $\neg swc$, because this achieves $\neg rhc$. The only last action must be puc to achieve rhc. Thus, the resulting subgoal is $\{\neg swc, cs\}$. Again, the last action before this subgoal cannot be to achieve $\neg swc$ because this has as a precondition off, which is inconsistent with cs. Therefore, the second-to-last action must be a move action to achieve cs.

In terms of the feature-based representation of actions, an action act is useful if there is a causal rule that achieves $X_i=v_i$ for some i, using action act. The neighbor of this node along the arc labeled with action act is the proposition

$$precondition(act) \wedge body(X_1=v_1, act) \wedge \cdots \wedge body(X_n=v_n, act)$$

where $body(X_i=v_i, act)$ is the set of assignments of variables in the body of a rule that specifies when $X_i=v_i$ is true immediately after act. There is no such neighbor if there is no corresponding rule for some i, or if the proposition is inconsistent (i.e., assigns different values to a variable). Note that, if multiple rules are applicable for the same action, there will be multiple neighbors.

Search algorithms such as A^* and branch-and-bound can make use of heuristic knowledge. For a regression planner, the heuristic value of a node is an estimate of the cost to achieve the subgoal represented by the node from the initial state. This form of heuristic as an estimate of the cost of achieving a subgoal from a state is the same as used in a forward planner. So, for example, the heuristic of Example 6.10 (page 248) could also be used for a regression planner. However, an effective heuristic for a regression planner may not be very useful for a forward planner, and vice versa (see Exercise 6.4 (page 262)).

One problem that arises in regression planning is that a subgoal may not be achievable. Deciding whether a subgoal is achievable is often difficult to infer from the definitions of the actions. For example, consider the restriction that an object cannot be at two different places at the same time; sometimes this is not explicitly represented and is only implicit in the effects of an action, and the fact that the object is only in one position initially. It is possible to have domain knowledge to prune nodes that can be shown to be inconsistent.

Cycle pruning and multiple-path pruning may be incorporated into a regression planner. The regression planner does not have to visit exactly the same node to prune the search. If the subgoal represented by a node n is a superset of a subgoal on the path to n, node n can be pruned. Similarly, for multiple-path pruning, see Exercise 6.10 (page 264).

A regression planner commits to a total ordering of actions, even if no particular reason exists for one ordering over another. This commitment to a total ordering tends to increase the complexity of the search space if the actions do not interact much or at all. For example, a regression planner would test each permutation of a sequence of actions when it may be possible to show that no ordering can succeed.

6.4   Planning as a CSP

In forward planning, the search is constrained by the initial state and only uses the goal as a stopping criterion and as a source for heuristics. In regression planning, the search is constrained by the goal and only uses the start state as a stopping criterion and as a source for heuristics. By converting the problem to a constraint satisfaction problem (CSP), the initial state can be used to prune what is not reachable and the goal to prune what is not useful. The CSP will be defined for a finite number of steps; the number of steps can be adjusted to find the shortest plan. One of the CSP methods from Chapter 4 can then be used to solve the CSP and thus find a plan.

> Dimensions (p. 31
> flat
> features
> finite horizon
> fully observable
> deterministic
> goal directed
> non-learning
> single agent
> offline
> perfect rationality

To construct a CSP from a planning problem, first choose a fixed planning **horizon**, which is the number of time steps over which to plan. Suppose the horizon is k. The CSP has the following variables:

- a **state variable** for each feature and each time from 0 to k. If there are n features for a horizon of k, there are $n * (k + 1)$ state variables. The domain of the state variable is the domain of the corresponding feature.

- an **action variable**, $Action_t$, for each time t in the range 0 to $k - 1$. The domain of $Action_t$ is the set of all possible actions. The value of $Action_t$ represents the action that takes the agent from the state at time t to the state at time $t + 1$.

There are several types of constraints:

- A **precondition constraint** between a state variable at time t and the variable $Action_t$ constrains what actions are legal at time t.

- An **effect constraint** between $Action_t$ and a state variable at time $t + 1$ constrains the values of a state variable that is a direct effect of the action.

- A **frame constraint** among a state variable at time t, the variable $Action_t$, and the corresponding state variable at time $t + 1$ specifies when the variable that does not change as a result of an action has the same value before and after the action.

- An **initial-state constraint** constrains a variable on the initial state (at time 0). The initial state is represented as a set of domain constraints on the state variables at time 0.

- A **goal constraint** constrains the final state to be a state that satisfies the achievement goal. These are domain constraints on the variables that appear in the goal.

- A **state constraint** is a constraint among variables at the same time step. These can include physical constraints on the state or can ensure that states that violate maintenance goals (page 246) are forbidden. This is extra knowledge beyond the power of the feature-based or STRIPS representations of the action.

The STRIPS representation gives precondition, effect and frame constraints for each time t as follows:

- For each $Var=v$ in the precondition of action A, there is a precondition constraint

$$Var_t=v \leftarrow Action_t=A$$

that specifies that if the action is to be A, Var_t must have value v immediately before. This constraint is violated when $Action_t=A$ and $Var_t \neq v$, and thus is is equivalent to $\neg(Var_t \neq v \wedge Action_t=A)$.

- For each $Var=v$ in the effect of action A, there is an effect constraint

$$Var_{t+1}=v \leftarrow Action_t=A$$

which is violated when $Var_{t+1} \neq v \wedge Action_t=A$, and thus is equivalent to $\neg(Var_{t+1} \neq v \wedge Action_t=A)$.

- For each Var, there is a frame constraint, where As is the set of actions that include Var in the effect of the action:

$$Var_{t+1}=Var_t \leftarrow Action_t \notin As$$

which specifies that the feature Var has the same value before and after any action that does not affect Var.

Example 6.13 Figure 6.4 (on the next page) shows a CSP representation of the delivery robot example, with a planning horizon of $k = 2$. There are three copies of the state variables: one at time 0, the initial state; one at time 1; and one at time 2, the final state. There are action variables for times 0 and 1.

Precondition constraints: The constraints to the left of the action variable for each time are the precondition constraints. There is a separate constraint for each element of the precondition of the action.

The precondition for the action deliver coffee, dc, is $\{RLoc=off, rhc\}$; the robot has to be in the office and it must have coffee. Thus there are two precondition constraints for delivers coffee:

$$RLoc_t=office \leftarrow Action_t=dc$$
$$RHC_t=true \leftarrow Action_t=dc$$

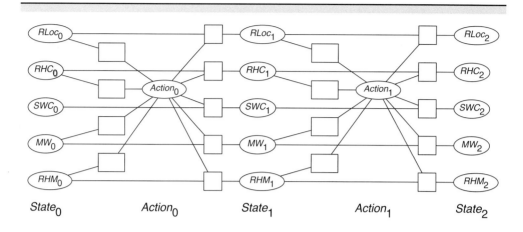

$RLoc_i$ – Rob's location MW_i – Mail is waiting
RHC_i – Rob has coffee RHM_i – Rob has mail
SWC_i – Sam wants coffee $Action_i$ – Rob's action

Figure 6.4: The delivery robot CSP planner for a planning horizon of $k = 2$

Effect constraints: The effect of delivering coffee (dc) is $\{\neg rhc, \neg swc\}$. Therefore there are two effect constraints

$$RHC_{t+1}=\text{false} \leftarrow Action_t=dc$$
$$SWC_{t+1}=\text{office} \leftarrow Action_t=dc$$

Frame constraints: Rob has mail (rhm) is not one of the effects of delivering coffee (dc). Thus there is a frame constraint

$$RHM_{t+1}=RHM_t \leftarrow Act_t=dc$$

which is violated when $RHM_{t+1} \neq RHM_t \wedge Act_t=dc$.

Example 6.14 Consider finding a plan to get Sam coffee, where initially, Sam wants coffee but the robot does not have coffee. This can be represented as initial-state constraints: $SWC_0=\text{true}$ and $RHC_0=\text{false}$.

With a planning horizon of 2, the goal is represented as the domain constraint $SWC_2=\text{false}$, and there is no solution.

With a planning horizon of 3, the goal is represented as the domain constraint $SWC_3=\text{false}$. This has many solutions, all with $RLoc_0=cs$ (the robot has to start in the coffee shop), $Action_0=puc$ (the robot has to pick up coffee initially), $Action_1=mc$ (the robot has to move to the office), and $Action_2=dc$ (the robot has to deliver coffee at time 2).

The CSP representation assumes a fixed planning horizon (i.e., a fixed number of steps). To find a plan over any number of steps, the algorithm can be run for a horizon of $k = 0, 1, 2, \ldots$ until a solution is found. For the stochastic local search algorithm, it is possible to search multiple horizons at once, searching for all horizons, k from 0 to n, and allowing n to vary slowly. When solving the CSP using arc consistency and domain splitting, it is sometimes possible to determine that trying a longer plan will not help. That is, by analyzing why no solution exists for a horizon of n steps, it may be possible to show that there can be no plan for any length greater than n. This will enable the planner to halt when there is no plan. See Exercise 6.11 (page 264).

6.4.1 Action Features

So far we have assumed that actions are atomic and that an agent can only do one action at any time. For the CSP representation, it can be useful to describe the actions in terms of features – to have a factored representation of actions as well as a factored representation of states. The features representing actions are called **action features** and the features representing states are called **state features**. The action features can be considered as actions in themselves that are carried out in the same time step.

In this case, there can be an extra set of constraints called **action constraints** to specify which action features cannot co-occur. These are sometimes called mutual exclusion or **mutex constraints**.

Example 6.15 Another way to model the actions of Example 6.1 (page 240) is that, at each step, Rob gets to choose

- whether it will pick up coffee. Let *PUC* be a Boolean variable that is true when Rob picks up coffee.

- whether it will deliver coffee. Let *DelC* be a Boolean variable that is true when Rob delivers coffee.

- whether it will pick up mail. Let *PUM* be a Boolean variable that is true when Rob picks up mail.

- whether it will deliver mail. Let *DelM* be a Boolean variable that is true when Rob delivers mail.

- whether it moves. Let *Move* be a variable with domain $\{mc, mcc, nm\}$ that specifies whether Rob moves clockwise, moves counterclockwise, or does not move (*nm* means "not move").

Thus the agent can be seen as doing more than one action in a single stage. For some of the actions at the same stage, the robot can do them in any order, such as delivering coffee and delivering mail. Some of the actions at the same stage need to be carried out in a particular order, for example, the agent must move after the other actions.

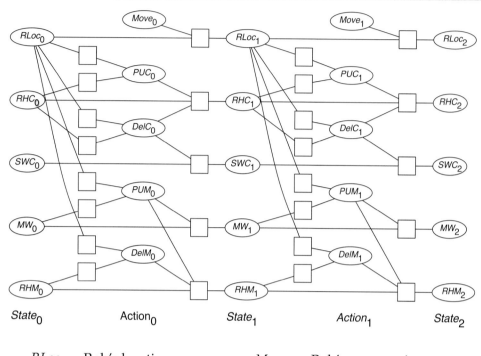

$RLoc_i$ – Rob's location	$Move_i$ – Rob's move action
RHC_i – Rob has coffee	PUC_i – Rob picks up coffee
SWC_i – Sam wants coffee	$DelC$ – Rob delivers coffee
MW_i – Mail is waiting	PUM_i – Rob picks up mail
RHM_i – Rob has mail	$DelM_i$ – Rob delivers mail

Figure 6.5: The delivery robot CSP planner with factored actions

Example 6.16 Consider finding a plan to get Sam coffee, where initially, Sam wants coffee but the robot does not have coffee. The initial state can be represented as two domain constraints: $SWC_0=true$ and on $RHC_0=false$. The goal is that Sam no longer wants coffee, $SWC_k=false$.

With a planning horizon of 2, the CSP is shown in Figure 6.5. The goal is represented as the domain constraint $SWC_2=false$, there is a solution $RLoc_0=cs$ (the robot has to start in the coffee shop), $PUC_0=true$ (the robot has to pick up coffee initially), $Move_0=mc$ (the robot has to move to the office), and $DC_1=true$ (the robot has to deliver coffee at time 1).

Note that in the representation without factored actions, the problem cannot be solved with a horizon of 2; it requires a horizon of 3, as there are no concurrent actions.

6.5 Partial-Order Planning

The forward and regression planners enforce a total ordering on actions at all stages of the planning process. The CSP planner commits to the particular time that the action will be carried out. This means that those planners have to commit to an ordering of actions when adding them to a partial plan, even if there is no particular reason to put one action before another.

Dimensions (p. 31)
flat
features
indefinite horizon
fully observable
deterministic
goal directed
non-learning
single agent
offline
perfect rationality

A **partial-order planner** maintains a partial ordering between actions and only commits to an ordering between actions when forced. This is sometimes also called a **non-linear planner**, which is a misnomer because such planners often produce a linear plan.

Because the same action may be used a number of times in the same plan, for example, the robot may need to move clockwise a number of times, the partial ordering will be between **action instances**, where an action instance is just a pair of an action and an integer, which we will write as *act#i*. By the preconditions and effects of the action instance, we mean the precondition and the effects of the action.

A partial ordering is a binary relation that is transitive and asymmetric. A **partial-order plan** is a set of action instances together with a partial ordering between them, representing a "before" relation on action instances. Write $act_0 < act_1$ if action instance act_0 is before action instance act_1 in the partial order. This means that the action of act_0 must occur before the action of act_1. The aim of the planner is to produce a partial ordering of the action instances so that any total ordering consistent with the partial ordering will solve the goal from the initial state.

There are two special action instances, *start*, that achieves the relations that are true in the initial state, and *finish*, whose precondition is the goal to be solved. Every other action instance is after *start* and before *finish* in the partial ordering. The use of these as action instances means that the algorithm does not require special cases for the initial situation and for the goals. When the preconditions of *finish* are achieved, the goal is solved.

Any action instance, other than *start* or *finish*, will be in a partial-order plan to achieve a precondition of an action instance in the plan. Each precondition P of an action instance act_1 in the plan is either true in the initial state, and so achieved by *start*, or there will be an action instance act_0 in the plan that achieves P. The action instance act_0 that achieves P must be before act_1; that is, $act_0 < act_1$. To be correct, the algorithm must also ensure that nothing makes P false in between act_0 and act_1.

A **causal link** is a triple $\langle act_0, P, act_1 \rangle$, where act_0 and act_1 are action instances and P is a *Var=val* assignment that is in the precondition of act_1, and in the effect of act_0. This means that act_0 makes P hold for act_1. With this causal link, any other action instance that makes P false must either be before act_0 or after act_1.

Informally, a partial-order planner works as follows. Begin with the action instances *start* and *finish* and the partial order *start* $<$ *finish*. The planner maintains an agenda that is a set of $\langle P, A \rangle$ pairs, where A is an action instance in the plan and P is a variable-value assignment that is a precondition of A that remains to be achieved. Initially, the agenda contains pairs $\langle G, finish \rangle$, where G is an assignment that must be true in the goal state.

At each stage in the planning process, a pair $\langle G, act_1 \rangle$ is chosen from the agenda, where P is in the precondition for action instance act_1. Then an action instance, act_0, is chosen to achieve P. That action instance is either already in the plan – it could be the *start* action, for example – or it is a new action instance that is added to the plan. Action instance act_0 must happen before act_1 in the partial order. The planner adds a causal link that records that act_0 achieves P for action act_1. Any action in the plan that makes P false must happen either before act_0 or after act_1. If act_0 is a new action, its preconditions are added to the agenda, and the process continues until the agenda is empty.

The algorithm *Partial_order_planner* is given in Figure 6.6 (on the next page). This is a non-deterministic procedure. The "choose" and the "either … or … " form choices that must be searched over. There are two choices that require search:

- which action is chosen to achieve P and

- whether an action instance that deletes P happens before act_0 or after act_1.

The function *add_const*$(A_0 < A_1, Constraints)$ returns the constraints formed by adding the constraint $A_0 < A_1$ to *Constraints*, and it fails if $A_0 < A_1$ is incompatible with *Constraints*. There are many ways this function can be implemented. See Exercise 6.12.

The function *protect*$(\langle A_0, G, A_1 \rangle, A)$ checks whether $A \neq A_0$, $A \neq A_1$ and the effect of A is inconsistent with G. If so, either $A < A_0$ is added to the set of constraints or $A_1 < A$ is added to the set of constraints. This is a non-deterministic choice that is searched over.

Example 6.17 Consider the goal of Sam not wanting coffee and no mail waiting (i.e., $\neg swc \wedge \neg mw$), where in the initial state Rob is in the lab, Sam wants coffee, Rob does not have coffee, there is mail waiting and Rob does not have mail, i.e., $RLoc{=}lab, swc, \neg rhc, mw, \neg rhm$.

We will write instances of action *Act* as *Act#n* where n is a unique integer. Initially the agenda is

$$\{\langle \neg swc, finish \rangle, \langle \neg mw, finish \rangle\}.$$

Suppose $\langle \neg swc, finish \rangle$ is chosen and removed from the agenda. One action can achieve $\neg swc$, namely deliver coffee, dc, with preconditions *off* and *rhc*. So

1: **non-deterministic procedure** *Partial_order_planner(As, Gs)*
2:   **Inputs**
3:     *As*: possible actions
4:     *Gs*: goal, aset of variable-value assignments to achieve
5:   **Output**
6:     linear plan to achieve *Gs*
7:   **Local**
8:     *Agenda*: set of $\langle P, A \rangle$ pairs where P is an atom and A an action instance
9:     *Actions*: set of action instances in the current plan
10:     *Constraints*: set of temporal constraints on action instances
11:     *CausalLinks*: set of $\langle act_0, P, act_1 \rangle$ triples
12:   $Agenda := \{ \langle G, \text{\textit{finish}} \rangle : G \in Gs \}$
13:   $Actions := \{ start, finish \}$
14:   $Constraints := \{ start < finish \}$
15:   $CausalLinks := \{ \}$
16:   **repeat**
17:     select and remove $\langle G, act_1 \#i \rangle$ from *Agenda*
18:     **either**
19:       choose $act_0 \#j \in Actions$ such that act_0 achieves G
20:     **Or**
21:       choose $act_0 \in As$ such that act_0 achieves G
22:       select unique integer j
23:       $Actions := Actions \cup \{ act_0 \#j \}$
24:       $Constraints := add\_const(start < act_0 \#j, Constraints)$
25:       **for each** $CL \in CausalLinks$ **do**
26:         $Constraints := protect(CL, act_0 \#j, Constraints)$
27:       $Agenda := Agenda \cup \{ \langle P, act_0 \#j \rangle : P$ is a precondition of $act_0 \}$
28:     $Constraints := add\_const(act_0 \#j < act_1 \#i, Constraints)$
29:     $new\_cl := \langle act_0 \#j, G, act_1 \#i \rangle$
30:     $CausalLinks := CausalLinks \cup \{ new\_cl \}$
31:     **for each** $A \in Actions$ **do**
32:       $Constraints := protect(new\_cl, A, Constraints)$
33:   **until** $Agenda = \{ \}$
34:   **return** total ordering of *Actions* consistent with *Constraints*

Figure 6.6: Partial-order planner

it inserts an instance, say $dc\#6$, into the plan. After the first time through the **repeat** loop, *Agenda* contains

$$\{\langle\mathit{off},dc\#6\rangle\,,\langle\mathit{rhc},dc\#6\rangle\,,\langle\neg\mathit{mw},\mathit{finish}\rangle\}.$$

At this stage, the value of *Constraints* is $\{\mathit{start}\ <\ \mathit{finish},\mathit{start}\ <\ dc\#6,dc\#6\ <\ \mathit{finish}\}$. There is one causal link, $\langle dc\#6,\ \neg\mathit{swc},\mathit{finish}\rangle$. This causal link means that no action that undoes $\neg\mathit{swc}$ is allowed to happen between $dc\#6$ and *finish*.

Suppose $\langle\neg\mathit{mw},\mathit{finish}\rangle$ is chosen from the agenda. One action can achieve this, *pum*, with precondition $\{\mathit{mw},\mathit{RLoc}{=}mr\}$. The algorithm constructs a new action instance, say *pum#7*. The causal link $\langle\mathit{pum\#7},\ \neg\mathit{mw},\mathit{finish}\rangle$ is added to the set of causal links; $\langle\mathit{mw},\mathit{pum\#7}\rangle$ and $\langle\mathit{mr},\mathit{pum\#7}\rangle$ are added to the agenda.

Suppose $\langle\mathit{mw},\mathit{pum\#7}\rangle$ is chosen from the agenda. The action *start* achieves *mw*, because *mw* is true initially. The causal link $\langle\mathit{start},\mathit{mw},\mathit{pum\#7}\rangle$ is added to the set of causal links. Nothing is added to the agenda.

At this stage, there is no ordering imposed between $dc\#6$ and *pum#7*.

Suppose $\langle\mathit{off},dc\#6\rangle$ is removed from the agenda. There are two actions that can achieve *off*: *mc_cs* with preconditions *cs*, and *mcc_lab* with preconditions *lab*. The algorithm searches over these choices. Suppose it chooses the action instance *mc_cs#9*. The causal link $\langle\mathit{mc\_cs\#9},\mathit{off},dc\#6\rangle$ is added.

The first violation of a causal link occurs when a move action is used to achieve $\langle\mathit{mr},\mathit{pum\#7}\rangle$. This action violates the causal link $\langle\mathit{mc\_cs\#9},\mathit{off},dc\#6\rangle$, and so must happen after $dc\#6$ (the robot goes to the mail room after delivering coffee) or before *mc_cs#9*.

Eventually, it finds a plan of action instances, such as:

$$\mathit{start};\mathit{mc\_lab\#15};\mathit{pum\#7};\mathit{mc\_mr\#40};\mathit{puc\#11};\mathit{mc\_cs\#9};dc\#6;\mathit{finish}$$

This is the only total ordering consistent with the partial ordering.

A partial order planner works particularly well when no ordering of actions can achieve a goal, as it does not need to search over all permutations of the actions. It also works well when many orderings can solve the goal, in which case it can find a flexible plan for the robot.

6.6 Review

The following are the main points you should have learned from this chapter:

- Planning is the process of choosing a sequence of actions to achieve a goal.

- An action is a partial function from a state to a state. Two representations for actions that exploit structure in states are the STRIPS representation, which is an action-centric representation, and the feature-based representation of actions, which is a feature-centric representation.

- Planning algorithms can be used to convert a planning problem into a search problem.

- A forward planner searches in the state space from the initial state to a goal state.

- A regression planner searches backwards from the goal, where each node in the search space is a subgoal to be achieved.

- A planning problem for a fixed horizon can be represented as a CSP, and any of the CSP algorithms can be used to solve it. The planner may need to search over horizons to find a plan.

- A partial-order planner does not enforce an ordering between actions unless there is a reason to make such an ordering.

6.7 References and Further Reading

There is much ongoing research into how to plan sequences of actions. Geffner and Bonet [2013] and Yang [1997] present overviews of automated planning.

The STRIPS representation was developed by Fikes and Nilsson [1971].

Forward planning with good heuristics [Bacchus and Kabanza, 1996] is the basis for the most efficient algorithms [Geffner and Bonet, 2013]. (See Exercise 6.4 (on the next page).)

Regression planning was pioneered by Waldinger [1977]. The use of weakest preconditions is based on the work of Dijkstra [1976], where it was used to define the semantics of imperative programming languages. This should not be too surprising because the commands of an imperative language are actions that change the state of the computer.

Planning as CSP is based on Graphplan [Blum and Furst, 1997] and Satplan [Kautz and Selman, 1996] and is also investigated by Lopez and Bacchus [2003] and van Beek and Chen [1999]. Bryce and Kambhampati [2007] surveys the field.

Partial-order planning was introduced in Sacerdoti's [1975] NOAH and followed up in Tate's [1977] NONLIN system, Chapman's [1987] TWEAK algorithm, and McAllester and Rosenblitt's [1991] systematic non-linear planning (SNLP) algorithm. See Weld [1994] for an overview of partial-order planning and see Kambhampati et al. [1995] for a comparison of the algorithms. The version presented here is basically SNLP (but see Exercise 6.14).

See Wilkins [1988] for a discussion on practical issues in planning. See Weld [1999], McDermott and Hendler [1995], and Nau [2007] and associated papers for a recent overview.

6.8   Exercises

Exercise 6.1 Consider the planning domain in Figure 6.1 (page 240).

  (a) Give the STRIPS representations for the pick up mail (*pum*) and deliver mail
      (*dm*) actions.

  (b) Give the feature-based representation of the *MW* and *RHM* features.

Exercise 6.2 Change the representation of the delivery robot world of Example
6.1 (page 240) so that the robot cannot carry both *mail* and *coffee* at the same time.
Test it on an example that gives a different solution than the original representation.

Exercise 6.3 Suppose the robot cannot carry both *mail* and *coffee* at the same
time, but the robot can carry a box in which it can place objects (so it can carry the
box and the box can hold the mail and coffee). Suppose boxes can be picked up
and dropped off at any location. Give the STRIPS representation for the resulting
problem and test it on the problem of starting from the lab with mail waiting, the
robot must deliver coffee and the mail to Sam's office.

Exercise 6.4 This exercise involves designing a heuristic function than is better
than the heuristic of Example 6.10 (page 248).

  (a) For each of the forward and regression planners, test how efective each of the
      individual parts of the heuristic for Example 6.10 is, as well as the maximum.
      Explain why the results you observed occurred.

  (b) Give an admissible heuristic function for the forward planner that expands
      fewer nodes than the forward planner does with that heuristic.

  (c) Give an admissible heuristic function for the regression planner that ex-
      pands fewer nodes than the regression planner does with that heuristic.

An implementation of the heuristic can be found in `stripsHeuristic.py` in http:
//artint.info/AIPython/aipython.zip

Exercise 6.5 Suppose we must solve planning problems for cleaning a house.
Various rooms can be dusted (making the room dust-free) or swept (making the
room have a clean floor), but the robot can only sweep or dust a room if it is in that
room. Sweeping causes a room to become dusty (i.e., not dust-free). The robot can
only dust a room if the dustcloth is clean; but dusting rooms that are extra-dusty,
like the garage, cause the dustcloth to become dirty. The robot can move directly
from any room to any other room.

Assume there are only two rooms, the garage – which, if it is dusty, is extra-
dusty – and the living room – which is not extra-dusty. Assume the following
features

  • *Lr_dusty* is true when the living room is dusty.

  • *Gar_dusty* is true when the garage is dusty.

  • *Lr_dirty_floor* is true when the living room floor is dirty.

  • *Gar_dirty_floor* is true when the garage floor is dirty.

- *Dustcloth_clean* is true when the dust cloth is clean.
- *Rob_loc* is the location of the robot, with values $\{garage, lr\}$.

Suppose the robot can do one of the following actions at any time:

- *move*: move to the other room
- *dust*: dust the room the robot is in, as long as the room is dusty and the dustcloth is clean
- *sweep*: sweep the floor the robot is in.

(a) Give the STRIPS representation for *dust*. [Hint: because STRIPS cannot represent conditional effects, you may need to use two separate actions that depend on the robot's location.]

(b) Give the feature-based representation for *lr_dusty*

(c) Suppose that the initial state is that the robot is in the garage, both rooms are dusty but have clean floors and the goal is to have both rooms not dusty. Draw the first two levels (with two actions, so the root has children and grandchildren) of a forward planner with multiple-path pruning, showing the actions (but you do not have to show the states). Show explicitly what nodes are pruned through multiple-path pruning.

(d) Pick two of the states at the second level (after two actions) and show what is true in those states

(e) Suppose that the initial state is that the robot is in the garage, both rooms are dusty but have clean floors and the goal is to have both rooms not dusty. Draw the first two levels (with two actions, so the root has children and grandchildren) of a regression planner showing the actions but you do not have to show what the nodes represent.

(f) Pick two of the nodes at the second level (after two actions) and show what the subgoal is at those nodes.

(g) Draw the CSP for a planning horizon of two. Describe each constraint in English by specifying which values are (in)consistent.

(h) In designing the actions, the above description made one choice of what to include as preconditions of the actions. Consider the choices of whether to have the room is dusty as a precondition for cleaning the room, and whether to have the floor is dirty as a precondition for sweeping. Do these choices make a difference to (i) the shortest plan, (ii) the size of the search space for a forward planner or (iii) the size of the search space for a regression planner?

Exercise 6.6 Suppose you have a STRIPS representation for actions a_1 and a_2, and you want to define the STRIPS representation for the composite action $a_1; a_2$, which means that you do a_1 then do a_2.

(a) What are the effects for this composite action?

(b) When is the composite action impossible? (That is, when is it impossible for a_2 to be immediately after a_1?)

(c) Assuming the action is not impossible, what are the preconditions for this composite action?

(d) Using the delivery robot domain of Example 6.1 (page 240), give the STRIPS representation for the composite action *puc; mc*.

(e) Give the STRIPS representation for the composite action *puc; mc; dc* made up of three primitive actions.

(f) Give the STRIPS representation for the composite action *mcc; puc; mc; dc* made up of four primitive actions.

Exercise 6.7 In a forward planner, you can represent a state in terms of the sequence of actions that lead to that state.

(a) Explain how to check whether the precondition of an action is satisfied, given such a representation.

(b) Explain how to do cycle pruning (page 105) in such a representation. You can assume that all of the states are legal. (Some other program has ensured that the preconditions hold.)

[Hint: Consider the composite action (Exercise 6.6) consisting of the first k or the last k actions at any stage.]

Exercise 6.8 Explain how the regression planner can be extended to include maintenance goals, for the STRIPS representation. Assume a maintenance goal is a disjunction of assignments of values to variables.

Exercise 6.9 For the delivery robot domain, give a nontrivial admissible heuristic function for the regression planner. A nontrivial heuristic function is nonzero for some nodes, and always nonnegative. Does it satisfy the monotone restriction?

Exercise 6.10 Explain how multiple-path pruning can be incorporated into a regression planner. When can a node be pruned? See the discusion on page 251.

Exercise 6.11 Give a condition for the CSP planner that, when arc consistency with search fails at some horizon, implies there can be no solutions for any longer horizon. [Hint: Think about a very long horizon where the forward search and the backward search do not influence each other.] Implement it.

Exercise 6.12 To implement the function *add_constraint*($A_0 < A_1$, *Constraints*) used in the partial-order planner, you have to choose a representation for a partial ordering. Implement the following as different representations for a partial ordering.

(a) Represent a partial ordering as a set of less-than relations that entail the ordering – for example, as the list $[1 < 2, 2 < 4, 1 < 3, 3 < 4, 4 < 5]$.

(b) Represent a partial ordering as the set of all the less-than relations entailed by the ordering – for example, as the list $[1 < 2, 2 < 4, 1 < 4, 1 < 3, 3 < 4, 1 < 5, 2 < 5, 3 < 5, 4 < 5]$.

(c) Represent a partial ordering as a set of pairs $\langle E, L \rangle$, where E is an element in the partial ordering and L is the list of all elements that are after E in the partial ordering. For every E, there exists a unique term of the form $\langle E, L \rangle$.

An example of such a representation is $[\langle 1, [2,3,4,5]\rangle, \langle 2, [4,5]\rangle, \langle 3, [4,5]\rangle, \langle 4, [5]\rangle, \langle 5, []\rangle]$.

For each of these representations, how big can the partial ordering be? How easy is it to check for consistency of a new ordering? How easy is it to add a new less-than ordering constraint? Which do you think would be the most efficient representation? Can you think of a better representation?

Exercise 6.13 The selection algorithm used in the partial-order planner is not very sophisticated. It may be sensible to order the selected subgoals. For example, in the robot world, the robot should try to achieve a *carrying* subgoal before an *at* subgoal because it may be sensible for the robot to try to carry an object as soon as it knows that it should carry it. However, the robot does not necessarily want to move to a particular place unless it is carrying everything it is required to carry. Implement a selection algorithm that incorporates such a heuristic. Does this selection heuristic actually work better than selecting, say, the last added subgoal? Can you think of a general selection algorithm that does not require each pair of subgoals to be ordered by the knowledge engineer?

Exercise 6.14 The SNLP algorithm is the same as the partial-order planner presented here but, in the *protect* procedure, the condition is

$$A \neq A_0 \text{ and } A \neq A_1 \text{ and } (A \text{ deletes } G \text{ or } A \text{ achieves } G).$$

This enforces *systematicity*, which means that for every linear plan there is a unique partial-ordered plan. Explain why systematicity may or may not be a good thing (e.g., discuss how it changes the branching factor or reduces the search space). Test the different algorithms on different examples.

Chapter 7

Supervised Machine Learning

> *Who so neglects learning in his youth, loses the past and is dead for the future.*

> – Euripides (484 BC – 406 BC), Phrixus, Frag. 927

Learning is the ability of an agent to improve its behavior based on experience. This could mean the following

- The range of behaviors is expanded; the agent can do more.
- The accuracy on tasks is improved; the agent can do things better.
- The speed is improved; the agent can do things faster.

The ability to learn is essential to any intelligent agent. As Euripides pointed out, learning involves an agent remembering its past in a way that is useful for its future.

This chapter considers the problem of making a prediction as supervised learning: given a set of training examples made up of input–output pairs, predict the output of a new example where only the inputs are given. We explore four approaches to learning: choosing a single hypothesis that fits the training examples well, predicting directly from the training examples, selecting the subset of a hypothesis space consistent with the training examples, or (in Section 10.4 (page 512)) predicting based on the posterior probability distribution of hypotheses conditioned on the training examples.

Chapter 10 considers learning probabilistic models. Chapter 12 covers reinforcement learning. Section 15.2 (page 701) considers learning relational representations.

7.1 Learning Issues

The following components are part of any learning problem:

Task The behavior or task that is being improved

Data The experiences that are used to improve performance in the task, usually in the form of a sequence of examples

Measure of improvement How the improvement is measured – for example, new skills that were not present initially, increasing accuracy in prediction, or improved speed

Consider the agent internals of Figure 2.9 (page 66). The problem of **learning** is to take in prior knowledge and data (e.g., about the experiences of the agent) and to create an internal representation (the knowledge base) that is used by the agent as it acts.

Learning techniques face the following issues:

Task Virtually any task for which an agent can get data or experiences can be learned. The most commonly studied learning task is **supervised learning**: given some input features, some target features, and a set of **training examples** where the input features and the target features are specified, predict the value of target features for new examples given their values on the input features. This is called **classification** when the target features are discrete and **regression** when the target features are continuous.

Other learning tasks include learning classifications when the examples do not have targets defined (unsupervised learning), learning what to do based on rewards and punishments (reinforcement learning), learning to reason faster (analytic learning), and learning richer representations such as logic programs (inductive logic programming).

Feedback Learning tasks can be characterized by the feedback given to the learner. In **supervised learning**, what has to be learned is specified for each training example. Supervised classification occurs when a trainer provides the classification for each example. Supervised learning of actions occurs when the agent is given immediate feedback about the value of an action in the current situation. **Unsupervised learning** occurs when no classifications are given and the learner must discover categories and regularities in the data. Feedback often falls between these extremes, such as in **reinforcement learning**, where the feedback in terms of rewards and punishments occurs after a sequence of actions. This leads to the **credit assignment problem** of determining which actions were responsible for the rewards or punishments. For example, a user could give rewards to the delivery robot without telling it exactly what it is being rewarded for. The robot then must either learn what it is being rewarded for or learn which actions are preferred in which situations. It is possible that it can learn which actions to perform without actually determining which consequences of the actions are responsible for rewards.

Representation For an agent to use its experiences, the experiences must affect the agent's internal representation. This internal representation could be the raw experiences themselves, but it is typically a compact representation that generalizes the data.

The problem of inferring an internal representation based on examples is called **induction** in contrast to **deduction** (page 186), which is deriving consequences of a knowledge base, and **abduction** (page 220), which is hypothesizing what may be true about a particular case.

There are two principles that are at odds in choosing a representation:

- *The richer the representation, the more useful it is for subsequent problem solving.* For an agent to learn a way to solve a task, the representation must be rich enough to express a way to solve the task.

- *The richer the representation, the more difficult it is to learn.* A very rich representation is difficult to learn because it requires a great deal of data, and often many different hypotheses are consistent with the data.

The representations required for intelligence are a compromise between many desiderata. The ability to learn the representation is one of them, but it is not the only one.

Much of machine learning is studied in the context of particular representations (e.g., decision trees, neural networks, or case bases). This chapter presents some standard representations to show the common features behind learning.

Online and offline In **offline learning**, all of the training examples are available to an agent before it needs to act. In **online learning**, training examples arrive as the agent is acting. An agent that learns online requires some representation of its previously seen examples before it has seen all of its examples. As new examples are observed, the agent must update its representation. Typically, an agent never sees all of the examples it could possibly see. **Active learning** is a form of online learning in which the agent acts to acquire useful examples from which to learn. In active learning, the agent reasons about which examples would be useful to learn from and acts to collect those examples.

Measuring success Learning is defined in terms of improving performance based on some measure. To know whether an agent has learned, we must define a measure of success. The measure is usually not how well the agent performs on the training data, but how well the agent performs for new data.

In classification, being able to correctly classify all training examples is not the goal. For example, consider predicting a Boolean (true/false) feature based on a set of examples. Suppose that there were two agents P and N. Agent P claims that all of the negative examples seen are the only negative examples and that every other instance is positive. Agent N claims that the positive examples in the training set are the only positive examples and that every other instance is negative. Both agents correctly classify every example in the training set but disagree on every other example. Success in learning should not be judged on correctly classifying the training set but on being able to correctly classify unseen examples. Thus, the learner must **generalize**: go beyond the specific given examples to classify unseen examples.

A standard way to evaluate a learning procedure is to divide the examples into **training examples** and **test examples**. A representation is built using the training examples, and the predictive accuracy is measured on the test examples. To properly evaluate the method, the test cases should not be known while the training is occurring. Of course, using a test set is only an approximation of what is wanted; the real measure is its performance on some future task.

Bias The tendency to prefer one hypothesis over another is called a **bias**. Consider the agents N and P defined earlier. Saying that a hypothesis is better than N's or P's hypothesis is not something that is obtained from the data – both N and P accurately predict all of the data given – but is something external to the data. Without a bias, an agent will not be able to make any predictions on unseen examples. The hypotheses adopted by P and N disagree on all further examples, and, if a learning agent cannot choose some hypotheses as better, the agent will not be able to resolve this disagreement. To have any inductive process make predictions on unseen data, an agent requires a bias. What constitutes a good bias is an empirical question about which biases work best in practice; we do not imagine that either P's or N's biases work well in practice.

Learning as search Given a representation and a bias, the problem of learning can be reduced to one of search. Learning is a search through the space of possible representations, trying to find the representation or representations that best fit the data given the bias. Unfortunately, the search spaces are typically prohibitively large for systematic search, except for the simplest of examples. Nearly all of the search techniques used in machine learning can be seen as forms of local search (page 144) through a space of representations. The definition of the learning algorithm then becomes one of defining the search space, the evaluation function, and the search method.

Noise In most real-world situations, the data are not perfect. There can be

noise where the observed features are not adequate to predict the classification, **missing data** where the observations of some of the features for some or all of the examples are missing, and **errors** where some of the features have been assigned wrong values. One of the important properties of a learning algorithm is its ability to handle noisy data in all of its forms.

Interpolation and extrapolation For domains with a natural interpretation of "between," such as where the features are about time or space, **interpolation** involves making a prediction between cases for which there are data. **Extrapolation** involves making a prediction that goes beyond the seen examples. Extrapolation is usually much less accurate than interpolation. For example, in ancient astronomy, the Ptolemaic system and the heliocentric system of Copernicus made detailed models of the movement of solar system in terms of epicycles (cycles within cycles). The parameters for the models could be made to fit the data very well and they were very good at interpolation; however, the models were very poor at extrapolation. As another example, it is often easy to predict a stock price on a certain day given data about the prices on the days before and the days after that day. It is very difficult to predict the price that a stock will be tomorrow, and it would be very profitable to be able to do so. An agent must be careful if its test cases mostly involve interpolating between data points, but the learned model is used for extrapolation.

7.2 Supervised Learning

One learning task is **supervised learning**, where there is a set of examples, and a set of features, partitioned into input features and target features. The aim is to predict the values of the target features from the input features.

A **feature** is a function from examples into a value. If e is an example, and F is a feature, $F(e)$ is the value of feature F for example e. The **domain** of a feature is the set of values it can return. Note that this is the *range* of the function, but is traditionally called the *domain*.

In a supervised learning task, the learner is given

- a set of **input features**, $X_1, \ldots, X_n$

- a set of **target features**, $Y_1, \ldots, Y_k$

- a set of **training examples**, where the values for the input features and the target features are given for each example, and

- a set of **test examples**, where only the values for the input features are given.

Why Should We Believe an Inductive Conclusion?

When learning from data, an agent makes predictions beyond what the data give it. From observing the sun rising each morning, people predict that the sun will rise tomorrow. From observing unsupported objects repeatedly falling, a child may conclude that unsupported objects always fall (until she comes across helium-filled balloons). From observing many swans, all of which were black, someone may conclude that all swans are black. From the data of Figure 7.1 (on the next page), an algorithm may learn a representation that predicts the user action for a case where the author is unknown, the thread is new, the length is long, and it was read at work. The data do not tell us what the user does in this case. The question arises of why an agent should ever believe any conclusion that is not a logical consequence of its knowledge.

When an agent adopts a bias, or chooses a hypothesis, it is going beyond the data – even making the same prediction about a new case that is identical to an old case in all measured respects goes beyond the data. So why should an agent believe one hypothesis over another? By what criteria can it possibly go about choosing a hypothesis?

The most common method is to choose the simplest hypothesis that fits the data by appealing to **Ockham's razor**. William of Ockham was an English philosopher who was born in about 1285 and died, apparently of the plague, in 1349. (Note that "Occam" is the French spelling of the English town "Ockham" and is often used.) He argued for economy of explanation: "What can be done with fewer [assumptions] is done in vain with more."

Why should one believe the simplest hypothesis when which hypothesis is simplest depends on the language used to express the hypothesis?

First, it is reasonable to assume that there is structure in the world and that an agent should discover this structure to act appropriately. A reasonable way to discover the structure of the world is to search for it. An efficient search strategy is to search from simpler hypotheses to more complicated ones. If there is no structure to be discovered, nothing will work! The fact that much structure has been found in the world (e.g., all of the structure discovered by physicists) would lead us to believe that this is not a futile search.

The fact that simplicity is language dependent should not necessarily make us suspicious. Language has evolved because it is useful; it allows people to express the structure of the world. Thus, we would expect that simplicity in everyday language would be a good measure of complexity.

The most important reason for believing inductive hypotheses is that it is useful to believe them. An agent that does not learn that it should not fling itself from heights will not survive long. The "simplest hypothesis" heuristic is useful because it works.

Example	Author	Thread	Length	Where_read	User_action
e_1	known	new	long	home	skips
e_2	unknown	new	short	work	reads
e_3	unknown	followup	long	work	skips
e_4	known	followup	long	home	skips
e_5	known	new	short	home	reads
e_6	known	followup	long	work	skips
e_7	unknown	followup	short	work	skips
e_8	unknown	new	short	work	reads
e_9	known	followup	long	home	skips
e_{10}	known	new	long	work	skips
e_{11}	unknown	followup	short	home	skips
e_{12}	known	new	long	work	skips
e_{13}	known	followup	short	home	reads
e_{14}	known	new	short	work	reads
e_{15}	known	new	short	home	reads
e_{16}	known	followup	short	work	reads
e_{17}	known	new	short	home	reads
e_{18}	unknown	new	short	work	reads
e_{19}	unknown	new	long	work	?
e_{20}	unknown	followup	short	home	?

Figure 7.1: Examples of a user's preferences. These are some training and test examples obtained from observing a user deciding whether to read articles posted to a threaded discussion website depending on whether the author is known or not, whether the article started a new thread or was a follow-up, the length of the article, and whether it is read at home or at work. $e_1, \ldots, e_{18}$ are the training examples. The aim is to make a prediction for the user action on e_{19}, e_{20}, and other, currently unseen, examples.

The aim is to predict the values of the target features for the test examples and as-yet-unseen examples.

Example 7.1 Figure 7.1 shows training and test examples typical of a classification task. The aim is to predict whether a person reads an article posted to a threaded discussion website given properties of the article. The input features are *Author*, *Thread*, *Length*, and *Where_read*. There is one target feature, *User_action*. The domain of *Author* is {*known, unknown*}, the domain of *Thread* is {*new, followup*}, and so on.

There are eighteen training examples, each of which has a value for all of the features. In this data set, *Author*(e_{11})=*unknown*, *Thread*(e_{11})=*followup*, and *UserAction*(e_{11})=*skips*.

There are two test examples, e_{19} and e_{20}, where the user action is unknown.

Example	X	Y
e_1	0.7	1.7
e_2	1.1	2.4
e_3	1.3	2.5
e_4	1.9	1.7
e_5	2.6	2.1
e_6	3.1	2.3
e_7	3.9	7
e_8	2.9	?
e_9	5.0	?

Figure 7.2: Training and test examples for a regression task

Example 7.2   Figure 7.2 shows some data for a regression task, where the aim is to predict the value of feature Y on examples for which the value of feature X is provided. This is a regression task because Y is a real-valued feature. Predicting a value of Y for example e_8 is an interpolation problem, as its value for the input feature is between the values of the training examples. Predicting a value of Y for the example e_9 is an extrapolation problem, because its X value is outside the range of the training examples.

7.2.1   Evaluating Predictions

A **point estimate** for target feature Y on example e is a prediction of the value of $Y(e)$. Let $\widehat{Y}(e)$ be the predicted value for target feature Y on example e. The **error** for this example on this feature is a measure of how close $\widehat{Y}(e)$ is to $Y(e)$.

For regression, when the target feature Y is real valued, both $\widehat{Y}(e)$ and $Y(e)$ are real numbers that can be compared arithmetically.

For classification, when the target feature Y is a discrete function, there are a number of alternatives:

- When the domain of Y is binary, one value can be associated with 0, the other value with 1, and a prediction can be some real number. For Boolean features, with domain {*false, true*}, we associate 0 with *false* and 1 with *true*. The predicted value could be any real number or could be restricted to be 0 or 1. Here we assume that the prediction can be any real number, except where explicitly noted. The predicted and actual values can be compared numerically. There is nothing special about {0, 1} for binary features; it is possible to use {−1, 1} or to use zero and non-zero.

- In a **cardinal feature** the values are mapped to real numbers. This is appropriate when values in the domain of Y are totally ordered, and the differences between the values are meaningful. In this case, the predicted and actual values can be compared on this scale.

Often, mapping values to the real line is not appropriate even when the values are totally ordered; for example, suppose the values are *short*, *medium*, and *long*. The prediction that the value is "either *short* or *long*" is very different from the prediction that the value is *medium*. When the domain of a feature is totally ordered, but the differences between the values are not comparable, the feature is called an **ordinal feature**.

- For a totally ordered feature, either cardinal or ordinal, and for a given value v, a Boolean feature can be constructed as a **cut**: a new feature that has value 1 when $Y \leq v$ and 0 otherwise. Which cut-values are used to construct features may be chosen according to the data or be selected a priori. Note that a cut for the maximal value in the domain, if there is one, is redundant as it is always true. It is also possible to construct a cut using less-than rather than less-than-or-equal to. Combining cuts allows for features that are true for intervals.

- When Y is discrete with domain $\{v_1, \ldots, v_k\}$, where $k > 2$, a separate prediction can be made for each v_i. This can be modeled by having a binary **indicator variable** (page 180), Y_i, associated with each value v_i, where $Y_i(e) = 1$ if $Y(e) = v_i$, and $Y_i(e) = 0$ otherwise. For each example, e, exactly one of $Y_1(e) \ldots Y_k(e)$ will be 1 and the others will be 0. A prediction gives k real numbers – one real number for each Y_i.

Example 7.3   A trading agent wants to learn a person's preference for the length of holidays. The holiday can be for 1, 2, 3, 4, 5, or 6 days.

One representation is to have a real-valued variable Y that is the number of days in the holiday.

Another representation is in terms of indicator variables, $Y_1, \ldots, Y_6$, where Y_i represents the proposition that the person would like to stay for i days. For each example, $Y_i=1$ when there are i days in the holiday, and $Y_i=0$ otherwise.

The following are five data points using these two representations:

Example	Y		Example	Y_1	Y_2	Y_3	Y_4	Y_5	Y_6
e_1	1		e_1	1	0	0	0	0	0
e_2	6		e_2	0	0	0	0	0	1
e_3	6		e_3	0	0	0	0	0	1
e_4	2		e_4	0	1	0	0	0	0
e_5	1		e_5	1	0	0	0	0	0

A third representation is to have a binary cut feature of $Y \leq i$ for various values of i:

Example	$Y \leq 1$	$Y \leq 2$	$Y \leq 3$	$Y \leq 4$	$Y \leq 5$
e_1	1	1	1	1	1
e_2	0	0	0	0	0
e_3	0	0	0	0	0
e_4	0	1	1	1	1
e_5	1	1	1	1	1

A prediction for a new example e in the first representation can be any real number, such as $\widehat{Y}(e)=3.2$.

In the second representation, the learner would predict a value for each Y_i for each example. One such prediction may be, for each example e, predict $\widehat{Y_1}(e)=0.5$, $\widehat{Y_2}(e)=0.3$, $\widehat{Y_3}(e)=0.1$, $\widehat{Y_4}(e)=0.1$, $\widehat{Y_5}(e)=0.1$, and $\widehat{Y_6}(e)=0.5$. This is a prediction that the person may like 1 day or 6 days, but will like a stay of 3, 4, or 5 days much less.

In the third representation, the learner could predict a value for $Y \leq i$ for each value of i. One such prediction may be to predict $Y \leq 1$ with value 0.4, $Y \leq i$ with 0.6, for the other values for i. It is not rational to predict, for example, that $Y \leq 2$ but not $Y \leq 4$, because one implies the other.

In the following measures of **prediction error**, Es is a set of examples and **T** is a set of target features. For target feature $Y \in \mathbf{T}$ and example $e \in Es$, the actual value is $Y(e)$ and the predicted value is $\widehat{Y}(e)$.

- The **0/1 error** on Es is the sum of the number of predictions that are wrong:

$$\sum_{e \in Es} \sum_{Y \in \mathbf{T}} Y(e) \neq \widehat{Y}(e) \, ,$$

  where $Y(e) \neq \widehat{Y}(e)$ is 0 when false, and 1 when true. This is the number of incorrect predictions. It does not take into account how wrong the predictions are, just whether they are correct or not.

- The **absolute error** on Es is the sum of the absolute differences between the actual and predicted values on each example:

$$\sum_{e \in Es} \sum_{Y \in \mathbf{T}} \left| Y(e) - \widehat{Y}(e) \right| .$$

  This is always non-negative, and is only zero when all the predictions exactly fit the observed values. Unlike for the 0/1 error, close predictions are better than far-away predictions.

- The **sum-of-squares error** on Es is

$$\sum_{e \in Es} \sum_{Y \in \mathbf{T}} (Y(e) - \widehat{Y}(e))^2.$$

  This measure treats large errors as much worse than small errors. For example, an error of 2 on an example is as bad as 4 errors of 1, and an error

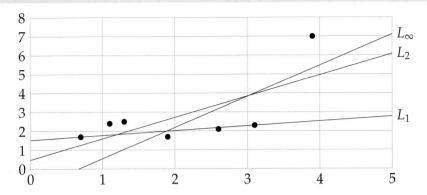

Figure 7.3: Linear regression predictions for a simple prediction example. Filled circles are the training examples. L_1 is the prediction that minimizes the absolute error of the training examples. L_2 is the prediction that minimizes the sum-of-squares error of the training examples. L_∞ is the prediction that minimizes the worst-case error of the training examples. See Example 7.4.

of 10 on one example is as bad as 100 errors of 1. Minimizing sum-of-squares error is equivalent to minimizing the **root-mean-square (RMS) error**, obtained by dividing by the number of examples and taking the square root. Taking the square root and dividing by a constant do not affect which predictions are minimal.

- The **worst-case error** on Es is the maximum absolute difference:

$$\max_{e \in Es} \max_{Y \in \mathbf{T}} \left| Y(e) - \widehat{Y}(e) \right|.$$

In this case, the learner is evaluated by how bad it can be.

These are often described in terms of the **norms** of the difference between the predicted and actual values. The $0/1$ error is the L_0 **error**, the absolute error is the L_1 **error**, the sum-of-squares error is the square of the L_2 **error**, and the worst-case error is the L_∞ **error**. The sum-of-squares error is often written as L_2^2, as the L_2 norm takes the square root of the sum of squares. Taking square roots does not affect which value is the minimum. Note that the L_0 error does not fit the mathematical definition of a norm.

Example 7.4 Consider the data of Figure 7.2 (page 274). Figure 7.3 shows a plot of the training data (filled circles) and three lines, L_1, L_2, and L_∞, that predict the Y-value for all X points. L_1 is the line that minimizes the absolute error, L_2 is the line that minimizes the sum-of-squares error, and L_∞ minimizes the worst-case error of the training examples.

As no three points are collinear, any line through any pair of the points minimizes the $0/1$, L_0, error.

Lines L_1 and L_2 give similar predictions for $X=1.1$; namely, L_1 predicts 1.805 and L_2 predicts 1.709, whereas the data contain a data point $(1.1, 2.4)$. L_∞ predicts 0.7. They give predictions within 1.5 of each other when interpolating in the range $[1, 3]$. Their predictions diverge when extrapolating from the data. L_1 and L_∞ give very different predictions for $X=5$.

An **outlier** is an example that does not follow the pattern of the other examples. The difference between the lines that minimize the various error measures is most pronounced in how they handle outliers. The point $(3.9, 7)$ can be seen as an outlier as the other points are approximately in a line.

The prediction with the least worse-case error for this example, L_∞, only depends on three data points, $(1.1, 2.4)$, $(3.1, 2.3)$, and $(3.9, 7)$, each of which has the same worst-case error for prediction L_∞. The other data points could be at different locations, as long as they are not farther away from L_∞ than these three points.

The prediction that minimizes the absolute error, L_1, does not change as a function of the actual Y-value of the training examples, as long as the points above the line stay above the line, and those below the line stay below. For example, the prediction that minimizes the absolute error would be the same, even if the last data point was $(3.9, 107)$ instead of $(3.9, 7)$.

Prediction L_2 is sensitive to all of the data points; if the Y-value for any point changes, the line that minimizes the sum-of-squares error will change. Changes to outliers will have more effect on the line than changes to points close to the line.

For the special case where the domain of Y is $\{0, 1\}$, and the prediction is in the range $[0, 1]$ (and so for Boolean domains where *true* is treated as 1, and *false* as 0), the following can also be used to evaluate predictions:

- The **likelihood of the data** is the probability of the data when the predicted value is interpreted as a probability, and each of the examples are predicted independently:

$$\prod_{e\in Es}\prod_{Y\in \mathbf{T}} \widehat{Y}(e)^{Y(e)}(1 - \widehat{Y}(e))^{(1-Y(e))}.$$

  One of $Y(e)$ and $(1 - Y(e))$ is 1, and the other is 0. Thus, this product uses $\widehat{Y}(e)$ when $Y(e)=1$ and $(1 - \widehat{Y}(e))$ when $Y(e)=0$. A better prediction is one with a higher likelihood. The model with the greatest likelihood is the **maximum likelihood model**.

- The **log-likelihood** is the logarithm of the likelihood, which is:

$$\sum_{e\in Es}\sum_{Y\in \mathbf{T}} \left(Y(e)\log\widehat{Y}(e) + (1 - Y(e))\log(1 - \widehat{Y}(e))\right).$$

  A better prediction is one with a higher log-likelihood. To make this into an error term to minimize, the **log loss** is the negative of the log-likelihood divided by the number of examples.

The log loss is closely related to the notion of **entropy** (on the next page). The log loss can be seen as the average number of bits it will take to encode the data given a code that is based on $\widehat{Y}(e)$ treated as a probability.

Example 7.5 Consider the length of holiday data of Example 7.3 (page 275). Suppose there are no input features, so all of the examples get the same prediction.

In the first representation, the prediction that minimizes the sum of absolute errors on the training data presented in Example 7.3 is 2, with an error of 10. The prediction that minimizes the sum-of-squares error on the training data is 3.2. The prediction the minimizes the worst-case error is 3.5.

For the second representation, the prediction that minimizes the sum of absolute errors for the training examples is to predict 0 for each Y_i. The prediction that minimizes the sum-of-squares error for the training examples is $Y_1=0.4$, $Y_2=0.1$, $Y_3=0$, $Y_4=0$, $Y_5=0$, and $Y_6=0.4$. This is also the prediction that maximizes the likelihood of the training data. The prediction that minimizes the worst-case error for the training examples is to predict 0.5 for Y_1, Y_2, and Y_6 and to predict 0 for the other features.

Thus, which prediction is preferred depends on how the prediction is represented and how it will be evaluated.

7.2.2 Types of Errors

Not all errors are equal; the consequences of some errors may be much worse than others. For example, it may be much worse to predict a patient does not have a disease that the patient actually has, so that the patient does not get appropriate treatment, than it is predict that a patient has a disease the patient does not actually have, which will force the patient to undergo further tests.

A prediction can be seen as an action of a predicting agent. The agent should choose the best prediction according to the costs associated with the errors. What an agent should do when faced with decisions under uncertainty is discussed in Chapter 9. The actions may be more than true or false, but may be more complex, such as "watch for worsening symptoms" or "go and see a specialist."

Consider a simple case where the domain of the target feature is Boolean (which we can consider as "positive" and "negative") and the predictions are restricted to be Boolean. One way to evaluate a prediction independently of the decision is to consider the four cases between the predicted value and the actual value:

	actual positive (*ap*)	actual negative (*an*)
predict positive (*pp*)	true positive (*tp*)	false positive (*fp*)
predict negative (*pn*)	false negative (*fn*)	true negative (*tn*)

$$\boxed{\text{Information Theory}}$$

A **bit** is a binary digit. Because a bit has two possible values (0 and 1), it can be used to distinguish two items. Two bits can distinguish four items, each associated with either 00, 01, 10, or 11. In general, n bits can distinguish 2^n items. Thus, we can distinguish n items with $\log_2 n$ bits. It may be surprising, but we can do better than this using probabilities.

Consider this code to distinguish the elements of the set $\{a, b, c, d\}$, with $P(a) = \frac{1}{2}$, $P(b) = \frac{1}{4}$, $P(c) = \frac{1}{8}$, and $P(d) = \frac{1}{8}$:

a	0	c	110
b	10	d	111

This code sometimes uses 1 bit, sometimes 2 bits and sometimes uses 3 bits. On average, it uses

$$P(a) * 1 + P(b) * 2 + P(c) * 3 + P(d) * 3 = \frac{1}{2} + \frac{2}{4} + \frac{3}{8} + \frac{3}{8} = 1\frac{3}{4} \text{ bits.}$$

For example, the string *aacabbda* with 8 characters has code 00110010101110, which uses 14 bits.

With this code, $-\log_2 P(a) = 1$ bit is required to distinguish a from the other symbols. Distinguishing b uses $-\log_2 P(b) = 2$ bits. Distinguishing c or d requires $-\log_2 P(c) = 3$ bits.

It is possible to build a code that, to identify x, requires $-\log_2 P(x)$ bits (or the integer greater than this). Suppose there is a sequence of symbols we want to transmit or store and we know the probability distribution over the symbols. A symbol x with probability $P(x)$ can use $-\log_2 P(x)$ bits. To transmit a sequence, each symbol requires, on average,

$$\sum_x -P(x) * \log_2 P(x)$$

bits to send it. This is called the **information content** or **entropy** of the distribution. This value just depends on the probability distribution of the symbols.

Analogous to conditioning in probability (page 350), the expected number of bits it takes to describe a distribution for x given evidence e is

$$\sum_x -P(x \mid e) * \log_2 P(x \mid e).$$

For a test that can distinguish the cases where α is true from the cases where α is false, the expected information after the test is

$$-P(\alpha) * \sum_x P(x \mid \alpha) * \log_2 P(x \mid \alpha) - P(\neg\alpha) * \sum_x P(x \mid \neg\alpha) * \log_2 P(x \mid \neg\alpha).$$

The entropy of the distribution minus the expected information after the test is called the **information gain** of the test.

A **false-positive error** or **type I error** is a positive prediction that is wrong (i.e., the predicted value is true, and the actual value is false). A **false-negative error** or **type II error** is a negative prediction that is wrong (i.e., the predicted value is false, and the actual value is true).

A **predictor** or predicting agent could, at one extreme, choose to only claim a positive prediction for an example when it is sure the example is actually positive. At the other extreme, it could claim a positive prediction for an example unless it is sure the example is actually negative. It could also make predictions between these extremes. We can separate the question of whether a predicting agent has a good learning algorithm from whether it makes good predictions based on preferences or costs that are outside the learner.

For a given predictor for a given set of examples, suppose tp is the number of true positives, fp is the number of false positives, fn is the number of false negatives, and tn is the number of true negatives. The following measures are often used:

- The **precision** is $\frac{tp}{tp+fp}$ the proportion of positive predictions that are actual positives.

- The **recall** or **true-positive rate** is $\frac{tp}{tp+fn}$ the proportion of actual positives that are predicted to be positive.

- The **false-positive rate** is $\frac{fp}{fp+tn}$ the proportion of actual negatives predicted to be positive.

An agent should try to maximize precision and recall and to minimize the false-positive rate; however, these goals are incompatible. An agent can maximize precision and minimize the false-positive rate by only making positive predictions it is sure about. However, this choice worsens recall. To maximize recall, an agent can be risky in making predictions, which makes precision smaller and the false-positive rate larger.

To compare predictors for a given set of examples, an **ROC space**, or **receiver operating characteristic** space, plots the false-positive rate against the true-positive rate. Each predictor for these examples becomes a point in the space.

A **precision-recall space** plots the precision against the recall. Each of these approaches may be used to compare learning algorithms independently of the actual costs of the prediction errors.

Example 7.6   Consider a case where there are 100 examples that are actually positive (ap) and 1000 examples that are actually negative (an). Figure 7.4 (on the next page) shows the performance of six possible predictors for these 1100 examples. Predictor (a) predicts 70 of the positive examples correctly and 850 of the negative examples correctly. Predictor (e) predicts every example

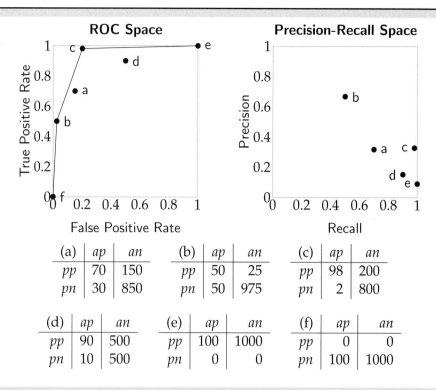

Figure 7.4: Six predictors in the ROC space and the precision-recall space

as positive, and (f) predicts all examples as negative. The precision for (f) is undefined.

The recall (true positive rate) of (a) is 0.7, the false positive rate is 0.15, and the precision is $70/220 \approx 0.318$. Predictor (c) has a recall of 0.98, a false-positive rate of 0.2 and a precision of $98/298 \approx 0.329$. Thus (c) is better than (a) in terms of precision and recall, but is worse in terms of the false positive rate. If false positives were much more important than false negatives, then (a) would be better than (c). This dominance is reflected in the ROC space, but not the precision-recall space.

In the ROC space, any predictor lower and to the right of another predictor is worse than the other predictor. For example, (d) is worse than (c); there would be no reason to choose (d) if (c) were available as a predictor. Any predictor that is below the upper envelope of predictors (shown with line segments in Figure 7.4), is dominated by the other predictors. For example, although (a) is not dominated by (b) or by (c) it is dominated by the randomized predictor: with probability 0.5 use the prediction of (b), else use the prediction of (c). This randomized predictor would expect to have 26 false negatives and 112.5 false positives.

7.2.3 Point Estimates with No Input Features

The simplest case for learning is when there are no input features and where there is a single target feature. This is the base case for many of the learning algorithms and corresponds to the case where all inputs are ignored. In this case, a learning algorithm predicts a single value for the target feature for all of the examples. The prediction that minimizes the error depends on the error that is being minimized.

Suppose Es is a set of examples and Y is a numeric feature. The best an agent can do is to make a single point estimate, v, for all examples. The errors for this case are

The 0/1 error on Es of prediction v is $\sum_{e \in Es} Y(e) \neq v$.

The sum-of-squares error on Es of prediction v is $\sum_{e \in Es} (Y(e) - v)^2$.

The absolute error on Es of prediction v is $\sum_{e \in Es} |Y(e) - v|$.

The worst-case error on Es of prediction v is $\max_{e \in Es} |Y(e) - v|$.

Proposition 7.1. *Suppose V is the multiset of values of $Y(e)$ for $e \in Es$.*

(a) *A prediction that minimizes the 0/1 error is a **mode**; one of the values that appears most often. When there are multiple modes, any can be chosen.*

(b) *The prediction that minimizes the sum-of-squares error on Es is the **mean** of V (the average value).*

(c) *The absolute error is minimized by any median of V. A **median** is the middle number when the values are sorted; a number m such that half or more of values of V less than or equal to m and half or more are greater than or equal to m. For example, for the numbers $\{3, 4, 6, 17\}$, any number between 4 and 6 is a median.*

(d) *The value that minimizes the worst-case error is $(max + min)/2$, where max is the maximum value and min is the minimum value.*

Proof. The details of the proof are left as an exercise. The proof sketch is as follows.

(a) This should be obvious.

(b) Differentiate the formula for the sum-of-squares error with respect to v and set to zero. This is elementary calculus.

(c) The absolute error is a piecewise linear function of v. The slope for a value that is not in V depends on the number of elements greater minus the number of elements less than that value: v is a minimum if there are the same number of elements greater than v as there are less than v.

(d) This prediction has a worst-case error of $(max - min)/2$; increasing or decreasing the prediction will increase the error.

$\square$

Prediction measure	Measure of prediction p for the training data	Optimal prediction for training data
0/1 error	n_1 if $p = 1$ else n_0 if $p = 0$	0 if $n_0 > n_1$ else 1
absolute error	$n_0 p + n_1(1 - p)$	0 if $n_0 > n_1$ else 1
sum squares	$n_0 p^2 + n_1(1 - p)^2$	$\frac{n_1}{n_0 + n_1}$
worst case	$\begin{cases} p \text{ if } n_1 = 0 \\ 1 - p \text{ if } n_0 = 0 \\ \max(p, 1 - p) \text{ otherwise} \end{cases}$	$\begin{cases} 0 \text{ if } n_1 = 0 \\ 1 \text{ if } n_0 = 0 \\ 0.5 \text{ otherwise} \end{cases}$
likelihood	$p^{n_1}(1 - p)^{n_0}$	$\frac{n_1}{n_0 + n_1}$
log-likelihood	$n_1 \log p + n_0 \log(1 - p)$	$\frac{n_1}{n_0 + n_1}$

Figure 7.5: Optimal prediction for binary classification where the training data consist of n_0 examples of 0 and n_1 examples of 1, with no input features

When the target feature has domain $\{0, 1\}$, the training examples can be summarized in two numbers: n_0, the number of examples with the value 0, and n_1, the number of examples with value 1. The prediction for each new case is the same number, p.

The optimal prediction p depends on the optimality criteria. The value of the optimality criteria for the training examples can be computed analytically and can be optimized analytically. The results are summarized in Figure 7.5.

Notice that optimizing the absolute error means predicting the median, which in this case is also the mode. The error is linear in p, and so has a minimum at one of the ends.

The optimal prediction for the training data for the other criteria is to predict the **empirical frequency**: the proportion of 1s in the training data, namely $\frac{n_1}{n_0 + n_1}$. This can be seen as a prediction of the **probability**. The empirical frequency is often called the **maximum-likelihood estimate**.

This analysis does not specify the optimal prediction for the test data. We would *not* expect the empirical frequency of the training data to be the optimal prediction for the test data for maximizing the likelihood or minimizing the entropy. If $n_0 = 0$ or if $n_1 = 0$, all of the training data are classified the same. However, if just one of the test examples is not classified in this way, the likelihood would be 0 (its lowest possible value) and the entropy would be infinite. This is an example of overfitting (page 298). See Exercise 7.1 (page 333).

7.3 Basic Models for Supervised Learning

A learned model is a function from the input features to the target features. Most supervised learning methods take the input features, the target features, and the training data and return a compact representation of a function that can be used for future prediction. An alternative to this is case-based reasoning (page 320), which uses the examples directly rather than building a model. Learning methods differ in which representations are considered for representing the function. This section considers some basic models from which other composite models are built. Section 7.6 (page 316) considers more sophisticated models that are built from these basic models.

7.3.1 Learning Decision Trees

A decision tree is a simple representation for classifying examples. Decision tree learning is one of the simplest useful techniques for supervised classification learning. For this section, assume there is a single discrete target feature called the **classification**. Each element of the domain of the classification is called a **class**.

A **decision tree** or a **classification tree** is a tree in which

- each internal (non-leaf) node is labeled with a condition, a Boolean function of examples

- each internal node has two children, one labeled with *true* and the other with *false*

- each leaf of the tree is labeled with a point estimate on the class.

To classify an example, filter it down the tree, as follows. Each condition encountered in the tree is evaluated and the arc corresponding to the result is followed. When a leaf is reached, the classification corresponding to that leaf is returned. A decision tree corresponds to a nested if-then-else structure in a programming language.

Example 7.7 Figure 7.6 (on the next page) shows two possible decision trees for the examples of Figure 7.1 (page 273). Each decision tree can be used to classify examples according to the user's action. To classify a new example using the tree on the left, first determine the length. If it is long, predict *skips*. Otherwise, check the thread. If the thread is new, predict *reads*. Otherwise, check the author and predict *reads* only if the author is known. This decision tree can correctly classify all examples in Figure 7.1 (page 273).

The tree corresponds to the program defining $\widehat{UserAction}(e)$:

define $\widehat{UserAction}(e)$:
   if $long(e)$: return *skips*

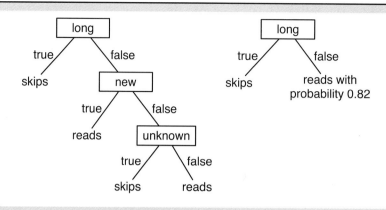

Figure 7.6: Two decision trees

else if *new*(*e*): return *reads*
else if *unknown*(*e*): return *skips*
else: return *reads*

   The tree on the right makes probabilistic predictions when the length is
not *long*. In this case, it predicts *reads* with probability 0.82 and so *skips* with
probability 0.18.

   To use decision trees as a target representation, there are a number of questions that arise:

- Given some training examples, what decision tree should be generated?
  Because a decision tree can represent any function of discrete input features, the bias that is necessary is incorporated into the preference of one
  decision tree over another. One proposal is to prefer the smallest tree
  that is consistent with the data, which could mean the tree with the least
  depth or the tree with the fewest nodes. Which decision trees are the best
  predictors of unseen data is an empirical question.

- How should an agent go about building a decision tree? One way is to
  search the space of decision trees for the smallest decision tree that fits the
  data. Unfortunately, the space of decision trees is enormous (see Exercise
  7.5 (page 335)). A practical solution is to carry out a greedy search on the
  space of decision trees, with the goal of minimizing the error. This is the
  idea behind the algorithm described below.

Searching for a Good Decision Tree

The algorithm *Decision_tree_learner* of Figure 7.7 (on the next page) builds a decision tree from the top down as follows. The input to the algorithm is a set of
input conditions (Boolean functions of examples that use only input features), a

```
1:  procedure Decision_tree_learner(Cs, Y, Es)
2:      Inputs
3:          Cs: set of possible conditions
4:          Y: target feature
5:          Es: set of training examples
6:      Output
7:          function to predict a value of Y for an example
8:      if stopping criterion is true then
9:          let v = point_estimate(Y, Es)
10:         define T(e) = v
11:         return T
12:     else
13:         pick condition c ∈ Cs
14:         true_examples := {e ∈ Es : c(e)}
15:         t₁ := Decision_tree_learner(Cs \ {c}, Y, true_examples)
16:         false_examples := {e ∈ Es : ¬c(e)}
17:         t₀ := Decision_tree_learner(Cs \ {c}, Y, false_examples)
18:         define T(e) = if c(e) then t₁(e) else t₀(e)
19:         return T
```

Figure 7.7: Decision tree learner

target feature, and a set of training examples. If the input features are Boolean, they can be used directly as the conditions.

A decision tree can be seen as a simple branching program, taking in an example and returning a prediction for that example, either

- a prediction that ignores the input conditions (a leaf) or
- of the form "if $c(e)$ then $t_1(e)$ else $t_0(e)$" where t_1 and t_0 are decision trees; t_1 is the tree that is used when the condition c is true of example e, and t_0 is the tree used when $c(e)$ is false.

The learning algorithm mirrors this recursive decomposition of a tree. The learner first tests whether a stopping criterion is true. If the stopping criterion is true, it determines a point estimate (page 274) for Y, which is either a value for Y or a probability distribution over the values for Y. The function $point\_estimate(Y, Es)$ returns a value for Y that can be predicted for all examples Es, ignoring the input features (page 283). The algorithm returns a function that returns that point estimate for any example. This is a leaf of the tree.

If the stopping criterion is not true, the learner picks a condition c to split on, it partitions the training examples into those examples e with $c(e)$ true and those examples with $\neg c(e)$ true (i.e., $c(e) = \mathit{False}$). It recursively builds a subtree for these sets of examples. It then returns a function that, given an example, tests whether c is true of the example, and then uses the prediction from the appropriate subtree.

Example 7.8 Consider applying *Decision_tree_learner* to the classification data of Figure 7.1 (page 273). The initial call is

decisionTreeLearner({*Author, Thread, Length, Where_read*}, *User_action*,
  {$e_1, e_2, \ldots, e_{18}$}).

Suppose the stopping criterion is not true and the algorithm picks the condition *Length* = *long* to split on. It then calls

decisionTreeLearner({*Where_read, Thread, Author*}, *User_action*,
  {$e_1, e_3, e_4, e_6, e_9, e_{10}, e_{12}$}).

All of these examples agree on the user action; therefore, the algorithm returns the prediction *skips*. The second step of the recursive call is

decisionTreeLearner({*Where_read, Thread, Author*}, *User_action*,
  {$e_2, e_5, e_7, e_8, e_{11}, e_{13}, e_{14}, e_{15}, e_{16}, e_{17}, e_{18}$}).

Not all of the examples agree on the user action, so assuming the stopping criterion is false, the algorithm picks a condition to split on. Suppose it picks *Thread* = *new*. Eventually, this recursive call returns the function on example *e* in the case when *Length* is *short*:

if *new*(*e*) then *reads*
              else if *unknown*(*e*) then *skips* else *reads*

The final result is the function of Example 7.7 (page 285).

The learning algorithm of Figure 7.7 leaves three choices unspecified:

- The stopping criterion is not defined. The learner needs to stop when there are no input conditions, or when all of the examples have the same classification. A number of criteria have been suggested for stopping earlier:

  - Minimum child size: do not split more if one of the children will have fewer examples than a threshold.

  - Minimum number of examples at a node: stop splitting if there are fewer examples than some threshold. With a minimum child size, we know we can stop with fewer than twice the minimum child size, but the threshold may be higher than this.

  - The improvement of the criteria being optimized must be above a threshold. For example, the information gain may need to be above some threshold.

  - Maximum depth: do not split more if the depth reaches a maximum.

- What should be returned at the leaves is not defined. This is a point estimate (page 274) that ignores all of the input conditions (except the ones on the path that lead to this leaf). This prediction is typically the most likely classification, the median value, the mean value, or a probability distribution over the classifications. See Exercise 7.8 (page 335).

- Which condition to pick to split on is not defined. The aim is to pick a condition that will result in the smallest tree. The standard way to do this is to pick the **myopically optimal** or **greedy optimal** split; if the learner were only allowed one split, pick whichever condition would result in the best classification if that were the only split. For likelihood, entropy, or when minimizing the log loss (page 278), the myopically optimal split is the one that gives the maximum **information gain** (page 280). Sometimes information gain is used even when the optimality criterion is some other error measure.

Example 7.9 In the running example of learning the user action from the data of Figure 7.1 (page 273), suppose you want to maximize the likelihood of the prediction or, equivalently, minimize the log loss. In this example, we myopically choose a split that minimizes the log loss.

Without any splits, the optimal prediction on the training set is the empirical frequency (page 284). There are 9 examples with $User\_action=reads$ and 9 examples with $User\_action=skips$, and so $known$ is predicted with probability 0.5. The log loss is equal to $(-18 * log_2 0.5)/18 = 1$.

Consider splitting on $Author$. This partitions the examples into $[e_1, e_4, e_5, e_6, e_9, e_{10}, e_{12}, e_{13}, e_{14}, e_{15}, e_{16}, e_{17}]$ with $Author=known$ and $[e_2, e_3, e_7, e_8, e_{11}, e_{18}]$ with $Author=unknown$, each of which is evenly split between the different user actions. The optimal prediction for each partition is again 0.5, and so the log loss after the split is again 1. In this case, finding out whether the author is known, by itself, provides no information about what the user action will be.

Splitting on $Thread$ partitions the examples into $[e_1, e_2, e_5, e_8, e_{10}, e_{12}, e_{14}, e_{15}, e_{17}, e_{18}]$ with $Thread=new$ and $[e_3, e_4, e_6, e_7, e_9, e_{11}, e_{13}, e_{16}]$ with $Thread=followup$. The examples with $Thread=new$, contains 3 examples with $User\_action=skips$ and 7 examples with $User\_action=reads$, thus the optimal prediction for these is to predict reads with probability $7/10$. The examples with $Thread = followup$, have 2 $reads$ and 6 $skips$. Thus the best prediction for these is to predict $reads$ with probability $2/8$. The log loss after the split is

$$- (3 * log_2(3/10) + 7 * log_2(7/10) + 2 * log_2(2/8) + 6 * log_2(6/8))/18$$
$$\approx 15.3/18 \approx 0.85$$

Splitting on $Length$ divides the examples into $[e_1, e_3, e_4, e_6, e_9, e_{10}, e_{12}]$ and $[e_2, e_5, e_7, e_8, e_{11}, e_{13}, e_{14}, e_{15}, e_{16}, e_{17}, e_{18}]$. The former all agree on the value of $User\_action$ and predict with probability 1. The user action divides the second set $9 : 2$, and so the log loss is

$$-(7 * log_2 1 + 9 * log_2 9/11 + 2 * log_2 2/11)/18 \approx 7.5/18 \approx 0.417$$

> Therefore, splitting on *Length* is better than splitting on *Thread* or *Author*, when myopically optimizing the log loss.

In the algorithm of Figure 7.7 (page 287), Boolean input features can be used directly as the conditions. Non-Boolean input features can be handled in two ways:

- Expand the algorithm to allow multiway splits. To split on a multivalued variable, there would be a child for each value in the domain of the variable. This means that the representation of the decision tree becomes more complicated than the simple if-then-else form used for binary features. There are two main problems with this approach. The first is what to do with values of a feature for which there are no training examples. The second is that for most myopic splitting heuristics, including information gain, it is generally better to split on a variable with a larger domain because it produces more children and so can fit the data better than splitting on a feature with a smaller domain. However, splitting on a feature with a smaller domain keeps the representation more compact. A 4-way split, for example, is equivalent to 3 binary splits; they both result in 4 leaves. See Exercise 7.6 (page 335).

- Partition the domain of an input feature into two disjoint subsets, as with ordinal features (page 275) or indicator variables (page 275)

  If the domain of input variable X is totally ordered, a cut (page 275) of the domain can be used as the condition. That is, the children could correspond to $X \leq v$ and $X > v$ for some value v. To pick the optimal value for v, sort the examples on the value of X, and sweep through the examples to consider each split value and pick the best. See Exercise 7.7 (page 335).

  When the domain of X is discrete and does not have a natural ordering, a split can be performed on arbitrary subsets of the domain. When the target is Boolean, each value of X has a proportion of the target feature that is true. A myopically optimal split will be between values when the values are sorted according to this probability of the target feature.

A major problem of the preceding algorithm is **overfitting** the data. Overfitting occurs when the algorithm tries to fit distinctions that appear in the training data but do not appear in the test set. Overfitting is discussed more fully in Section 7.4 (page 298).

There are two principal ways to overcome the problem of overfitting in decision trees:

- Restrict the splitting to split only when the split is useful, such as only when the training-set error reduces by more than some threshold.
- Allow unrestricted splitting and then prune the resulting tree where it makes unwarranted distinctions.

The second method often work better in practice. One reason is that it is possible that two features together predict well but one of them, by itself, is not very useful, as shown in the following example.

Example 7.10 Matching pennies is a game where two coins are tossed and the player wins if both coins come up heads or both coins come up tails, and loses if the coins are different. Suppose the aim is to predict whether a game of matching pennies is won or not. The input features are A, whether the first coin is heads or tails; B, whether the second coin is heads or tails; and C, whether there is cheering. The target feature, W, is true when there is a win. Suppose cheering is correlated with winning. This example is tricky because A by itself provides no information about W, and B by itself provides no information about W. However, together they perfectly predict W. A myopic split may first split on C, because this provides the most myopic information. If all the agent is told is C, this is much more useful than A or B. However, if the tree eventually splits on A and B, the split on C is not needed. Pruning can remove C as part of the tree, whereas stopping early will keep the split on C.

A discussion of how to trade off model complexity and fit to the data is presented in Section 7.4 (page 298).

7.3.2 Linear Regression and Classification

Linear functions provide a basis for many learning algorithms. This section first covers regression – the problem of predicting a real-valued function from training examples – then considers the discrete case of classification.

Linear regression is the problem of fitting a linear function to a set of training examples, in which the input and target features are numeric.

Suppose the input features, $X_1, \ldots, X_n$, are all numeric and there is a single target feature Y. A **linear function** of the input features is a function of the form

$$\widehat{Y}^{\overline{w}}(e) = w_0 + w_1 * X_1(e) + \cdots + w_n * X_n(e)$$
$$= \sum_{i=0}^{n} w_i * X_i(e)$$

where $\overline{w} = \langle w_0, w_1, \ldots, w_n \rangle$ is a tuple of weights. To make w_0 not be a special case, we invent a new feature, X_0, whose value is always 1.

Suppose Es is a set of examples. The sum-of-squares error (page 276) on examples Es for target Y is

$$error(Es, \overline{w}) = \sum_{e \in Es} (Y(e) - \widehat{Y}^{\overline{w}}(e))^2$$
$$= \sum_{e \in Es} \left(Y(e) - \sum_{i=0}^{n} w_i * X_i(e) \right)^2. \tag{7.1}$$

In this linear case, the weights that minimize the error can be computed analytically (see Exercise 7.10 (page 336)). A more general approach, which can be used for wider classes of functions, is to compute the weights iteratively.

Gradient descent (page 165) is an iterative method to find the minimum of a function. Gradient descent for minimizing *error* starts with an initial set of weights; in each step, it decreases each weight in proportion to its partial derivative:

$$w_i := w_i - \eta * \frac{\partial}{\partial w_i} error(Es, \overline{w})$$

where η, the gradient descent step size, is called the **learning rate**. The learning rate, as well as the features and the data, is given as input to the learning algorithm. The partial derivative specifies how much a small change in the weight would change the error.

The sum-of-squares error for a linear function is convex and has a unique local minimum, which is the global minimum. As gradient descent with small enough step size will converge to a local minimum, this algorithm will converge to the global minimum.

Consider minimizing the sum-of-squares error. The partial derivative of the error in Equation (7.1) with respect to weight w_i is

$$\frac{\partial}{\partial w_i} error(Es, \overline{w}) = \sum_{e \in Es} -2 * \delta(e) * X_i(e) \qquad (7.2)$$

where $\delta(e) = Y(e) - \widehat{Y^{\overline{w}}}(e)$.

Gradient descent will update the weights after sweeping through all examples. An alternative is to update each weight after each example. Each example e can update each weight w_i using:

$$w_i := w_i + \eta * \delta(e) * X_i(e), \qquad (7.3)$$

where we have ignored the constant 2, because we assume it is absorbed into the learning rate η.

Figure 7.8 (on the next page) gives an algorithm, *Linear_learner*(Xs, Y, Es, η), for learning the weights of a linear function that minimize the **sum-of-squares error** (page 276). This algorithm returns a function that makes predictions on examples. In the algorithm, $X_0(e)$ is defined to be 1 for all e.

Termination is usually after some number of steps, when the error is small or when the changes get small.

Updating the weights after each example does not strictly implement gradient descent because the weights are changing beween examples. To implement gradient descent, we should save up all of the changes and update the weights after all of the examples have been processed. The algorithm presented in Figure 7.8 (on the next page) is called **incremental gradient descent** because the

1: **procedure** *Linear_learner*(Xs, Y, Es, η)
2:     **Inputs**
3:         Xs: set of input features, $Xs = \{X_1, \ldots, X_n\}$
4:         Y: target feature
5:         Es: set of training examples
6:         η: learning rate
7:     **Output**
8:         function to make prediction on examples
9:     **Local**
10:         $w_0, \ldots, w_n$: real numbers
11:     initialize $w_0, \ldots, w_n$ randomly
12:     **define** $pred(e) = \sum_i w_i * X_i(e)$
13:     **repeat**
14:         **for each** example e in Es **do**
15:             $error := Y(e) - pred(e)$
16:             $update := \eta * error$
17:             **for each** $i \in [0, n]$ **do**
18:                 $w_i := w_i + update * X_i(e)$
19:     **until** termination
20:     **return** *pred*

Figure 7.8: Incremental gradient descent for learning a linear function

weights change while it iterates through the examples. If the examples are selected at random, this is called **stochastic gradient descent**. These incremental methods have cheaper steps than gradient descent and so typically become more accurate more quickly when compared to saving all of the changes to the end of the examples. However, it is not guaranteed that they will converge as individual examples can move the weights away from the minimum.

Batched gradient descent updates the weights after a batch of examples. The algorithm computes the changes to the weights after every example, but only applies the changes after the batch. If a batch is all of the examples, it is equivalent to gradient descent. If a batch consists of just one example, it is equivalent to incremental gradient descent. It is typical to start with small batches to learn quickly and then increase the batch size so that it converges.

A similar algorithm can be used for other error functions that are (almost always) differentiable and where the derivative has some signal (is not 0). For the absolute error, which is not differentiable at zero, the derivative can be defined to be zero at that point because the error is already at a minimum and the weights do not have to change. See Exercise 7.9 (page 336). It does not work for other errors such as the 0/1 error, where the derivative is either 0 (almost everywhere) or undefined.

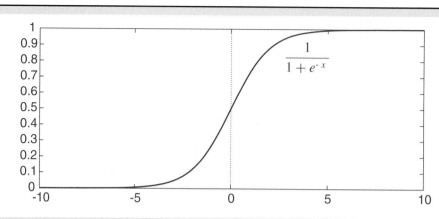

Figure 7.9: The sigmoid or logistic function

Squashed Linear Functions

Consider binary classification, where the domain of the target variable is $\{0, 1\}$. Multiple binary target variables can be learned separately.

The use of a linear function does not work well for such classification tasks; a learner should never make a prediction of greater than 1 or less than 0. However, a linear function could make a prediction of, say, 3 for one example just to fit other examples better.

A **squashed linear function** is of the form

$$\widehat{Y^{\overline{w}}}(e) = f(w_0 + w_1 * X_1(e) + \cdots + w_n * X_n(e))$$
$$= f(\sum_i w_i * X_i(e))$$

where f, an **activation function**, is a function from the real line $[-\infty, \infty]$ into some subset of the real line, such as $[0, 1]$.

A prediction based on a squashed linear function is a **linear classifier**.

A simple activation function is the **step function**, $step_0(x)$, defined by

$$step_0(x) = \begin{cases} 1 & \text{if } x \geq 0 \\ 0 & \text{if } x < 0. \end{cases}$$

A step function was the basis for the **perceptron** [Rosenblatt, 1958], which was one of the early methods developed for learning. It is difficult to adapt gradient descent to step functions because gradient descent takes derivatives and step functions are not differentiable.

If the activation is (almost everywhere) differentiable, gradient descent can be used to update the weights. The step size might need to converge to zero to guarantee convergence.

One differentiable activation function is the **sigmoid** or **logistic function**:

$$sigmoid(x) = \frac{1}{1 + e^{-x}}.$$

This function, depicted in Figure 7.9, squashes the real line into the interval $(0, 1)$, which is appropriate for classification because we would never want to make a prediction of greater than 1 or less than 0. It is also differentiable, with a simple derivative – namely, $\frac{d}{dx} sigmoid(x) = sigmoid(x) * (1 - sigmoid(x))$.

The problem of determining weights for the sigmoid of a linear function that minimize an error on a set of examples is called **logistic regression**.

To optimize the **log loss** (page 278) error for logistic regression, minimize the negative log-likelihood

$$LL(E, \overline{w}) = - \left(\sum_{e \in Es} \left(Y(e) * \log \widehat{Y}(e) + (1 - Y(e)) * \log(1 - \widehat{Y}(e)) \right) \right)$$

where $\widehat{Y}(e) = sigmoid \left(\sum_{i=0}^{n} w_i * X_i(e) \right)$.

$$\frac{\partial}{\partial w_i} LL(E, \overline{w}) = \sum_{e \in E} -\delta(e) * X_i(e)$$

where $\delta(e) = Y(e) - \widehat{Y}^{\overline{w}}(e)$. This is, essentially, the same as Equation (7.2) (page 292), the only differences being the definition of the predicted value and the constant "2" which can be absorbed into the step size.

The *Linear_learner* algorithm of Figure 7.8 (page 293) can be modified to carry out logistic regression to minimize log loss by changing the prediction to be $sigmoid(\sum_i w_i * X_i(e))$. The algorithm is show in Figure 7.10 (on the next page).

Example 7.11 Consider learning a squashed linear function for classifying the data of Figure 7.1 (page 273). One function that correctly classifies the examples is

$$\widehat{Reads}(e) = sigmoid(-8 + 7 * Short(e) + 3 * New(e) + 3 * Known(e)) ,$$

where f is the sigmoid function. A function similar to this can be found with about 3000 iterations of gradient descent with a learning rate $\eta = 0.05$. According to this function, $\widehat{Reads}(e)$ is true (the predicted value for example e is closer to 1 than 0) if and only if $Short(e)$ is true and either $New(e)$ or $Known(e)$ is true. Thus, the linear classifier learns the same function as the decision tree learner. To see how this works, see the "mail reading" example of the Neural AIspace.org applet.

To minimize **sum-of-squares error** (page 276), instead, the prediction is the same, but the derivative is different. In particular, line 16 of Figure 7.10 should become

$$update := \eta * error * pred(e) * (1 - pred(e)) .$$

```
1:  procedure Logistic_regression_learner(Xs, Y, Es, η)
2:      Inputs
3:          Xs: set of input features, Xs = {X_1, ..., X_n}
4:          Y: target feature
5:          Es: set of training examples
6:          η: learning rate
7:      Output
8:          function to make prediction on examples
9:      Local
10:         w_0, ..., w_n: real numbers
11:     initialize w_0, ..., w_n randomly
12:     define pred(e) = sigmoid(∑_i w_i * X_i(e))
13:     repeat
14:         for each example e in Es in random order do
15:             error := Y(e) − pred(e)
16:             update := η * error
17:             for each i ∈ [0, n] do
18:                 w_i := w_i + update * X_i(e)
19:     until termination
20:     return pred
```

Figure 7.10: Stochastic gradient descent for logistic regression

Consider each input feature as a dimension; if there are n features, there will be n dimensions. A **hyperplane** in an n-dimensional space is a set of points that all satisfy a constraint that some linear function of the variables is zero. The hyperplane forms an $(n-1)$-dimensional space. For example, in a (two-dimensional) plane, a hyperplane is a line, and in a three-dimensional space, a hyperplane is a plane. A classification is **linearly separable** if there exists a hyperplane where the classification is true on one side of the hyperplane and false on the other side.

The *Logistic_regression_learner* algorithm can learn any linearly separable classification. The error can be made arbitrarily small for arbitrary sets of examples if, and only if, the target classification is linearly separable. The hyperplane is the set of points where $\sum_i w_i * X_i = 0$ for the learned weights $\overline{w}$. On one side of this hyperplane, the prediction is greater than 0.5; on the other side, the prediction is less than 0.5.

Example 7.12 Figure 7.11 (on the next page) shows linear separators for "or" and "and". The dashed line separates the positive (true) cases from the negative (false) cases. One simple function that is not linearly separable is the **exclusive-or** (xor) function. There is no straight line that separates the positive examples

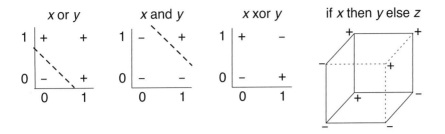

Figure 7.11: Linear separators for Boolean functions

from the negative examples. As a result, a linear classifier cannot represent, and therefore cannot learn, the exclusive-or function.

Consider a learner with three input features x, y and z, each with domain $\{0,1\}$. Suppose that the ground truth is the function "if x then y else z". This is depicted on the right of Figure 7.11 by a cube in the standard coordinates, where the x, y and z range from 0 to 1. This function is not linearly separable.

Often it is difficult to determine a priori whether a data set is linearly separable.

Example 7.13 Consider the data set of Figure 7.12 (a), which is used to predict whether a person likes a holiday as a function of whether there is culture, whether the person has to fly, whether the destination is hot, whether there is music, and whether there is nature. In this data set, the value 1 means true and 0 means false. The linear classifier requires the numerical representation.

After 10,000 iterations of gradient descent with a learning rate of 0.05, the prediction found is (to one decimal point)

$$lin(e) = 2.3 * Culture(e) + 0.01 * Fly(e) - 9.1 * Hot(e)$$
$$- 4.5 * Music(e) + 6.8 * Nature(e) + 0.01$$
$$\widehat{Likes}(e) = sigmoid(lin(e)) \, .$$

The linear function lin and the prediction for each example are shown in Figure 7.12 (on the next page) (b). All but four examples are predicted reasonably well, and for those four it predicts a value of approximately 0.5. This function is quite stable with different initializations. Increasing the number of iterations makes it predict the other tuples more accurately, but does not improve on these four. This data set is not linearly separable.

When the domain of the target variable has more than two values – there are more than two classes – indicator variables (page 275) can be used to convert the classification to binary variables. These binary variables could be learned separately. The predictions of the individual classifiers can be combined to give

Culture	Fly	Hot	Music	Nature	Likes
0	0	1	0	0	0
0	1	1	0	0	0
1	1	1	1	1	0
0	1	1	1	1	0
0	1	1	0	1	0
1	0	0	1	1	1
0	0	0	0	0	0
0	0	0	1	1	1
1	1	1	0	0	0
1	1	0	1	1	1
1	1	0	0	0	1
1	0	1	0	1	1
0	0	0	1	0	0
1	0	1	1	0	0
1	1	1	1	0	0
1	0	0	1	0	0
1	1	1	0	1	0
0	0	0	0	1	1
0	1	0	0	0	1

lin	$\widehat{Likes}$
−9.09	0.00011
−9.08	0.00011
−4.48	0.01121
−6.78	0.00113
−2.28	0.09279
4.61	0.99015
0.01	0.50250
2.31	0.90970
−6.78	0.00113
4.62	0.99024
2.32	0.91052
0.01	0.50250
−4.49	0.01110
−11.29	0.00001
−11.28	0.00001
−2.19	0.10065
0.02	0.50500
6.81	0.99890
0.02	0.50500

(a)   (b)

Figure 7.12: Predicting what holiday a person likes (a) training data (b) prediction

a prediction for the target variable. Because exactly one of the values must be true for each example, a learner should not predict that more than one will be true or that none will be true. Suppose we separately learned the predicted values for $Y_1 \dots Y_k$ are $q_1 \dots q_k$, where the $q_i \geq 0$. A learner that predicts a probability distribution could predict $Y = y_i$ with probability $q_i / \sum_j q_j$. A learner that must make a definitive prediction can predict the mode, a y_i for which q_i is the maximum.

7.4 Overfitting

Overfitting occurs when the learner makes predictions based on regularities that appear in the training examples but do not appear in the test examples or in the world from which the data is taken. It typically happens when the model tries to find signal in randomness – there are spurious correlations in the training data that are not reflected in the problem domain as a whole – or when the learner becomes overconfident in its model. This section outlines methods to detect and avoid overfitting.

Example 7.14 Consider a website where people submit ratings for restaurants from 1 to 5 stars. Suppose the website designers would like to display the best restaurants, which are those restaurants that future patrons would like the most. It is extremely unlikely that a restaurant that has many ratings, no matter how outstanding it is, will have an average of 5 stars, because that would require all of the ratings to be 5 stars. However, given that 5 star ratings are not that uncommon, it would be quite likely that a restaurant with just one rating will have 5 stars. If the designers used the average rating, the top rated restaurants will be ones with very few ratings, and these are unlikely to be the best restaurants. Similarly, restaurants with few ratings but all low are unlikely to be as bad as the ratings indicate.

The phenomenon that extreme predictions will not perform as well on test cases is analogous to **regression to the mean**. Regression to the mean was discovered by Galton [1886], who called it *regression to mediocrity*, after discovering that the offspring of plants with larger than average seeds are more like average seeds their parents are. In both of the restaurant and the seeds cases, this occurs because ratings, or the size, will be a mix of quality and luck (e.g., who gave the rating or what genes the seeds had). Restaurants that have a very high rating will have to be high in quality and be lucky (and be very lucky if the quality is not very high). More data averages out the luck; it is very unlikely that someones luck does not run out. Similarly, the seed offspring do not inherit the part of the size of the seed that was due to random fluctuations.

Overfitting is also caused by **model complexity**: a more complex model, with more parameters, can virtually always fit data better than a simple model.

Example 7.15 A polynomial of degree k is of the form:

$$y = w_0 + w_1 * x + w_2 * x^2 + \cdots + w_k * x^k$$

The linear learner (page 293) can be used unchanged to learn the weights of the polynomial that minimize the sum-of-squares error, simply by using $1, x, x^2, \ldots, x^k$ as the input features to predict y.

Figure 7.13 (on the next page) shows polynomials up to degree 4 for the data of Figure 7.2 (page 274). Higher-order polynomials can fit the data better than lower-order polynomials, but that does not make them better on the training set.

Notice how the higher-order polynomials get more extreme in extrapolation. All of the polynomials, except the degree 0 polynomials, go to plus or minus infinity as x gets bigger or smaller, which is almost never what you want. Moreover, if the maximum value of k for which $w_k \neq 0$ is even, then as x approaches plus or minus infinity, the predictions will have the same sign, going to either plus infinity or minus infinity. The degree 4 polynomial in the figure approaches ∞ as x gets smaller, which does not seems reasonable given the data. If the maximum value of k for which $w_k \neq 0$ is odd, then as x approaches plus or minus infinity, the predictions will have opposite signs.

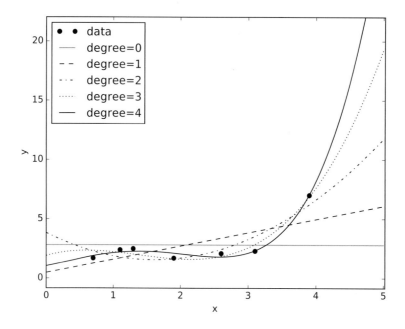

Figure 7.13: Fitting polynomials to the data of Figure 7.2 (page 274)

You need to be careful to use an appropriate step size to use gradient descent for such fitting polynomials. If x is close to zero ($|x| \ll 1$) then x^k can be tiny, and if is x is large ($|x| \gg 1$) then x^k can be enormous. Suppose x in Figure 7.2 (page 274) is in centimeters. If x were in millimeters (so $x(e_7) = 39$), then the coefficient of x^4 would have a huge effect on the error. If x were in meters (where $x(e_7) = 0.039$), the coefficient of x^4 would have very little effect on the error.

Example 7.14 showed how more data can allow for better predictions. Example 7.15 showed how complex models can lead to overfitting the data. We would like large amounts of data to make good predictions. However, even when we have so-called **big data**, the number of (potential) features tends to grow as well as the number of data points. For example, once there is a detailed enough description of patients, even if all of the people in the world were included, there would be no two patients that are identical in all respects.

The test set error is caused by:

- **bias**, the error due to the algorithm finding an imperfect model. The bias is low when the model learned is close to the **ground truth**, the process in the world that generated the data. The bias can be divided into **representation bias** caused by the representation not containing a hypothesis close to the ground truth, and a **search bias** caused by the algorithm not searching enough of the space of hypotheses to find the appropriate hypothesis. For example, with discrete features, a decision tree can represent any function, and so has a low representation bias. With a large number of features, there are too many decision trees to search systematically, and decision tree learning can have a large search bias. Linear regression, if solved directly using the analytic solution, has a large representation bias, and zero search bias. There would also be a search bias if the gradient descent algorithm was used.

- **variance**, the error due to a lack of data. A more complicated model, with more parameters to tune will require more data. Thus with a fixed amount of data, there is a **bias–variance trade-off**; we can have a complicated model which could be accurate, but we do not have enough data to estimate it appropriately (with low bias and high variance), or a simpler model that cannot be accurate, but we can estimate the parameters reasonably well given the data (with high bias and low variance).

- **noise** the inherent error due to the data depending on features not modeled or because the process generating the data is inherently stochastic.

Overfitting results in **overconfidence**, where the learner is more confident in its prediction than the data warrants. For example, in the predictions in Figure 7.12 (page 298), the probabilities are much more extreme than could be justified by the data. The first prediction, that there is approximately a 1 in 10000 chance of being true, does not seem to be reasonable given only 19 examples. This overconfidence is reflected in test data, as in the following example.

> **Example 7.16**   Figure 7.14 (on the next page) shows a typical plot of how the sum-of-squares error changes with the number of iterations of gradient descent. The sum-of-squares error on the training set decreases as the number of iterations increases. For the test set, the error reaches a minimum and then increases as the number of iterations increases. As it fits to the training examples, it becomes more confident in its imperfect model, and so errors in the test set become bigger.

The following sections discuss three ways to avoid overfitting. The first explicitly allows for regression to the mean, and can be used for cases where the representations are simple. The second provides an explicit trade-off between model complexity and fitting the data. The third approach is to use some of the training data to detect overfitting.

7.4.1   Pseudocounts

For many of the prediction measures, the optimal prediction on the training data is the mean (the average value). In the case of Boolean data (assuming true

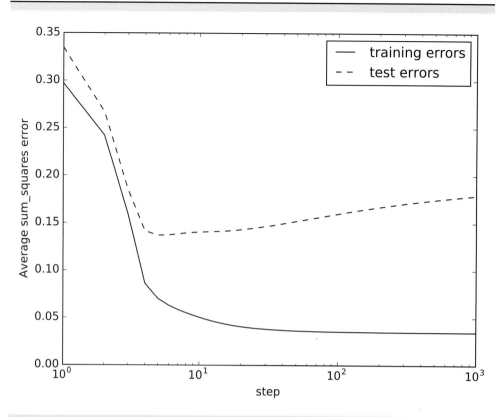

Figure 7.14: Training set error as a function of number of steps. On the x-axis is the step count of a run of a learner using gradient descent. On the y-axis is the average sum-of-squares error (the sum-of-squares error divided by the number of examples) for the training set (solid line) and the test set (dashed line).

is represented as 1, and false as 0), the mean can be interpreted as a probability. However, the empirical mean, the mean of the training set, is typically not a good estimate of the probability of new cases. For example, just because an agent has not observed some value of a variable does not mean that the value should be assigned a probability of zero, which means it is impossible. Similarly, if we are to make predictions for the future grades of a student, the average grade of a student may be appropriate to predict the future grades of the student if the student has taken many courses, but may not be appropriate for a student with just one grade recorded, and is not appropriate for a student with no grades recorded (where the average is undefined).

A simple way both to solve the zero-probability problem and to take prior knowledge into account is to use a real-valued **pseudocount** or **prior count** to which the training data is added.

Suppose the examples are values $v_1 \ldots v_n$ and you want to make a prediction for the next v, which we will write as $\widehat{v}$.

One prediction is the average. Suppose a_n is the average of the first n values, then:

$$a_n = \frac{v_1 + \cdots + v_{n-1} + v_n}{n}$$

$$= \frac{n-1}{n} * a_{n-1} + \frac{v_n}{n}$$

$$= a_{n-1} + \frac{v_n - a_{n-1}}{n}.$$

The **running average** keeps the current average of all of the data points seen. It can be implemented by storing the current average, a, and the number of values seen, n. When a new value v arrives, n is incremented and $(v - a)/n$ is added to a.

When $n = 0$ assume you use prediction a_0 (which you cannot get from data as there are no data for this case). A prediction that takes into account **regression to the mean** is to use:

$$\widehat{v} = \frac{v_1 + \cdots + v_n + c * a_0}{n + c}$$

where c is a constant, which is the pseudocount of the number of assumed fictional data points. If $c = 0$, the prediction is the average value. The value of c can control the amount of regression to the mean. This can be implemented using the running average by initializing a with a_0 and n with c.

Example 7.17   Consider how to better estimate the ratings of restaurants in Example 7.14 (page 299). The aim is to predict the average rating over the test data, not the average rating of the seen ratings.

You can use the existing data about other restaurants to make estimates about the new cases, assuming that the new cases are like the old. Before seeing anything, it may be reasonable to use the average rating of the restaurants as value for a_0. This would be like assuming that a new restaurant is like an average restaurant (which may or may not be a good assumption). Suppose you are most interested in being accurate for top-rated restaurants. To estimate c, consider a restaurant with a single 5-star rating. You could expect this restaurant to be like the other restaurants with a 5-star rating. Let a' be the average rating of the restaurants with a 5-star rating (where the average is weighted by the number of ratings of 5 stars each restaurant has). Then you would expect that a restaurant with a single 5-star rating would be like the others and have this rating, and so $a' = a_0 + (5 - a_0)/(c + 1)$. You can then solve for c.

Suppose the average rating is 3, and the average rating for the restaurants with a 5-star rating is 4.5. Solving $4.5 = 3 + (5 - 3)/(c + 1)$ gives $c = 1/3$. If the average for 5-star restaurants was instead 3.5, then c would be 3. See Exercise 7.12 (page 336).

Example 7.18   Consider the following thought experiment (or, better yet, implement it). First select a number p randomly from the range $[0, 1]$. Suppose this is the ground truth for the probability that $Y = 1$ for a variable Y with domain $\{0, 1\}$. Then generate n training examples (page 403) with $P(Y{=}1) = p$, for a number for values of n, such as $1, 2, 3, 4, 5, 10, 20, 100, 1000$. Let n_1 be the number of samples with $Y = 1$ and so there are $n_0 = n - n_1$ samples with $Y = 0$. The learning problem for this scenario is: from n_0 and n_1 create an estimator $\hat{p}$ that can be used to predict new cases. Then generate some (e.g., 100) test cases from the same p. The aim is to produce the estimator $\hat{p}$ with the smallest error on the test cases. If you repeat this 1000 times, you will get a good idea of what is going on.

If you try this, with log-likelihood you will find that $\hat{p} = n_1 / (n_0 + n_1)$ works very poorly; one reason is that if either n_0 or n_1 is 0, and that value appears in the test set, the likelihood of the test set will be 0, which is the worst it could possibly be! It turns out that **Laplace smoothing** (page 489), defined by $\hat{p} = (n_1 + 1)/(n_0 + n_1 + 2)$, has the maximum likelihood of all estimators on the test set. $\hat{p} = (n_1 + 1)/(n_0 + n_1 + 2)$ also works better than $\hat{p} = n_1/(n_0 + n_1)$ for sum-of-squares error.

If you were to select p from some distribution other than the uniform distribution, adding 1 to the numerator and 2 from the denominator may not result in the best predictor.

7.4.2   Regularization

Ockham's razor (page 272) specifies that we should prefer simpler models over more complex models. Instead of just optimizing fit-to-data, as done in Section 7.2.1 (page 274), we can optimize fit-to-data plus a term that rewards simplicity and penalizes complexity. The penalty term is a **regularizer**.

The typical form for a regularizer is to find a hypothesis h to minimize:

$$\left(\sum_e error(e, h) \right) + \lambda * regularizer(h) \tag{7.4}$$

where the $error(e, h)$ is the error of example e for hypothesis h, which specifies how well hypothesis h fits example e. The **regularization parameter**, λ, trades off fit-to-data and model simplicity, and $regularizer(h)$ is a penalty term that penalizes complexity or deviation from the mean. Notice that as the number of examples increases the leftmost sum tends to dominate and the regularizer has little effect. The regularizer has most effect when there are few examples. The regularization parameter is needed because the error and complexity terms are typically in different units. The regularization parameter can be chosen by prior knowledge, past experience with similar problems or by cross validation (page 306).

For example, in learning a decision tree one complexity measure is the number of splits in the decision tree (which is one less than the number of leaves for a binary decision tree). When building a decision tree, we could optimize the sum-of-squares error plus a function of the size of the decision tree, minimizing

$$\left(\sum_{e \in Es} (Y(e) - \widehat{Y}(e))^2 \right) + \lambda * |tree|$$

where $|tree|$ is the number of splits in the tree. When splitting, a single split is worthwhile if it reduces the sum-of-squares error by λ.

For models where there are real-valued parameters, an L_2 **regularizer**, penalizes the sum of squares of the parameters. To optimize the sum-of-squares error for linear regression (page 291) with an L_2 regularizer, minimize

$$\left(\sum_{e \in Es} \left(Y(e) - \sum_{i=0}^{n} w_i * X_i(e) \right)^2 \right) + \lambda \left(\sum_{i=0}^{n} w_i^2 \right)$$

which is known as **ridge regression**.

To optimize the log loss (page 278) error for logistic regression (page 295) with an L_2 regularizer, minimize

$$- \left(\sum_{e \in Es} \left(Y(e) \log \widehat{Y}(e) + (1 - Y(e)) \log(1 - \widehat{Y}(e)) \right) \right) + \lambda \left(\sum_{i=0}^{n} w_i^2 \right)$$

where $\widehat{Y}(e) = sigmoid \left(\sum_{i=0}^{n} w_i * X_i(e) \right)$.

An L_2 regularization is implemented by adding

$$w_i := w_i - \eta * (\lambda / |Es|) * w_i$$

after line 18 of Figure 7.8 (page 293) or after line 18 of Figure 7.10 (page 296) (in the scope of both "for each"). This divides by the number of examples ($|Es|$) because it is carried out once for each example. It is also possible to regularize after each iteration through all of the examples, in which case the regularizer should not divide by the number of examples. Note that $\eta * \lambda / |Es|$ does not change as so should be computed once and stored.

An L_1 **regularizer** adds a penalty for the sum of the absolute values of the parameters.

Adding an L_1 regularizer to the log loss entails minimizing

$$- \left(\sum_{e \in Es} \left(Y(e) \log \widehat{Y}(e) + (1 - Y(e)) \log(1 - \widehat{Y}(e)) \right) \right) + \lambda \left(\sum_{i=0}^{n} |w_i| \right).$$

The partial derivative of the sum of absolute values with respect to w_i is the sign of w_i, either 1 or -1 (defined as $sign(w_i) = w_i / |w_i|$), at every point except at 0. We do not need to make a step at 0, because the value is already a minimum. To implement an L_1 regularizer, each parameter is moved towards zero by a constant, except if that constant would change the sign of the parameter, in which case the parameter becomes zero. Thus, an L_1 regularizer can be incorporated into the logistic regression gradient descent algorithm of Figure 7.10 (page 296) by adding after line 18 (in the scope of both "for each"):

$$w_i := sign(w_i) * max(0, |w_i| - \eta * \lambda / |Es|)$$

This is called **iterative soft-thresholding** and is a special case of the *proximal-gradient method*.

An L_1 regularizer when there are many features tends to make many weights zero, which means the corresponding feature is ignored. This is a way to implement **feature selection**. An L_2 regularizer tends to make all of the parameters smaller, but not zero.

7.4.3 Cross Validation

The problem with the previous methods is that they require a notion of simplicity to be known before the agent has seen any data. It would seem that an agent should be able to determine, from the data, how complicated a model needs to be. Such a method could be used when the learning agent has no prior information about the world.

The idea of **cross validation** is to use part of the training data as a surrogate for test data. In the simplest case, we split the training set into two: a set of examples to train with, and a **validation set**. The agent trains using the new training set. Prediction on the validation set is used to determine which model to use.

Consider a graph such as the one in Figure 7.14 (page 302). The error on the training set gets smaller as the size of the tree grows. However, on the test set the error typically improves for a while and then starts to get worse. The idea of cross validation is to choose a parameter setting or a representation in which the error of the validation set is a minimum. The hypothesis is that this is where the error on the test set is also at a minimum.

The validation set that is used as part of training is not the same as the test set. The test set is used to evaluate how well the learning algorithm works as a whole. It is cheating to use the test set as part of learning. Remember that the aim is to predict examples that the agent has not seen. The test set acts as a surrogate for these unseen examples, and so it cannot be used for training or validation.

Typically, we want to train on as many examples as possible, because then we get better models. However, a bigger training set results in a smaller validation set, and a small validation set may fit well, or not fit well, just by luck.

The method of *k*-**fold cross validation** allows us to reuse examples for both training and validation, but still use all of the data for training. It can be used

Regularization, Pseudocounts and Probabilistic Mixtures

Consider the simplest case of a learner that takes a sequence Es of examples $e_1 \ldots e_n$, with no input features. Suppose you regularize to some default value m, and so penalize the difference from m. The regularizers in Section 7.4.2 (page 304) regularize to 0.

Consider the following programs that do stochastic gradient descent with L_2 regularization in different ways. Each takes in the data set Es, the value for m, the learning rate η and the regularization parameter λ.

procedure $Learn_0(Es, m, \eta, \lambda)$
    $p := m$
    repeat
        for each $e_i \in Es$ **do**
            $p := p - \eta * (p - e_i)$
            $p := p - \eta * \lambda * (p - m)$
    until termination
    return p

procedure $Learn_1(Es, m, \eta, \lambda)$
    $p := m$
    repeat
        for each $e_i \in Es$ **do**
            $p := p - \eta * (p - e_i)$
            $p := p - \eta * \lambda * (p - m)$
    until termination
    return p

The programs differ as to whether the regularization happens for each element of the data set or for the whole data set at each iteration.

Program $Learn_0$ minimizes

Program $Learn_1$ minimizes

$$\left(\sum_i (p - e_i)^2 \right) + \lambda (p - m)^2$$

$$\sum_i \left((p - e_i)^2 + \lambda (p - m)^2 \right)$$

which is minimal when

which is minimal when

$$p = \frac{m\lambda + \sum_i e_i}{\lambda + n}.$$

$$p = \frac{\lambda}{1 + \lambda} m + \frac{1}{1 + \lambda} \frac{\sum_i e_i}{n}.$$

Program $Learn_0$ is equivalent to having a **pseudocount** (page 302) with λ extra examples, each with value m.

Program $Learn_1$ is equivalent to a probabilistic mixture of m and the average of the data.

For a fixed number of examples, n, these can be mapped into each other; λ for $Learn_1$ is λ for $Learn_0$ divided by n. They act differently when the number of examples varies, for example, in cross validation, when using a single λ for multiple data sets, or in more complicated cases such as collaborative filtering (page 706).

For a fixed λ, with n varying, they are qualitatively different. In $Learn_0$, as the number of examples increases the regularization gets less and less important. In $Learn_1$, m has the same effect on the prediction, no matter what n is. Using the strategy of $Learn_0$ is appropriate if the examples are independent of each other, where it is appropriate that enough examples will dominate any prior model. The strategy of $Learn_1$ may appropriate if there is some chance the whole data set is misleading.

to tune parameters that control the model complexity, or otherwise affect the model learned. It has the following steps:

- Partition the training examples randomly into k sets, of approximately equal size, called **folds**.

- To evaluate a parameter setting, train k times for that parameter setting, each time using one of the folds as the validation set and the remaining folds for training. Thus each fold is used as a validation set exactly once. The accuracy is evaluated using the validation set. For example, if $k = 10$, then 90% of the training examples are used for training and 10% of the examples for validation. It does this 10 times, so each example is used once in a validation set.

- Optimize parameter settings based on the error on each example when it is used in the validation set.

- Return the model with the selected parameter settings, trained on all of the data.

Example 7.19   One of the possible parameters for the decision tree learner is the minimum number of examples that needs to be in the data set to split, so the stopping criterion for the decision tree learner of Figure 7.7 (page 287) will be true if the number of examples is less than *min_number_examples*. If this threshold is too small, the decision tree learner will tend to overfit, and if it is too large it will tend not to generalize.   Figure 7.15 (on the next page) shows the validation error for 5-fold cross validation as a function of the parameter *min_number_examples*. For each point on the x-axis, the decision tree was run 5 times, and the average sum-of-squares error was computed for the validation set. The error is at a minimum at 39, and so this is selected as the best value for this parameter. This plot also shows the error on the test set for trees with various settings for the minimum number of examples, and 39 is a reasonable parameter setting based on the test set.

At one extreme, when k is the number of training examples, k-fold cross validation becomes **leave-one-out cross validation**. With n examples in the training set, it learns n times; for each example e, it uses the other examples as training set, and evaluates on e. This is not practical if each training is done independently, because it increases the complexity by the number of training examples. However, if the model from one run can be adjusted quickly when one example is removed and another added, this can be very effective.

7.5   Neural Networks and Deep Learning

Neural networks are a popular target representation for learning. These networks are inspired by the **neurons** in the brain but do not actually simulate

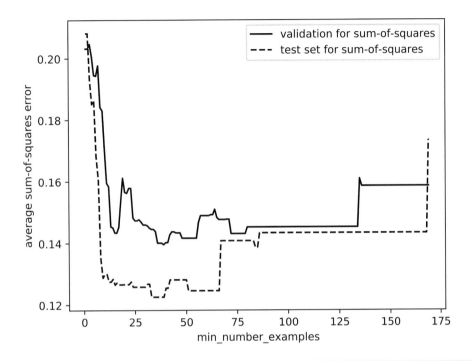

Figure 7.15: Validation error and test set error for determining the minimum number of examples needed to split in a decision tree learner.

neurons. Artificial neural networks typically contain many fewer than the approximately 10^{11} neurons that are in the human brain, and the artificial neurons, called **units**, are much simpler than their biological counterparts. Neural networks have had considerable success in low-level reasoning for which there is abundant training data such as for image interpretation, speech recognition and machine translation. One reason is that they are very flexible and can invent features.

Artificial neural networks are interesting to study for a number of reasons:

- As part of neuroscience, to understand real neural systems, researchers are simulating the neural systems of simple animals such as worms, which promises to lead to an understanding about which aspects of neural systems are necessary to explain the behavior of these animals.

- Some researchers seek to automate not only the functionality of intelligence (which is what the field of artificial intelligence is about) but also the mechanism of the brain, suitably abstracted. One hypothesis is that the only way to build the functionality of the brain is by using the mechanism of the brain. This hypothesis can be tested by attempting to build intelligence using the mechanism of the brain, as well as attempting it without using the mechanism of the brain. Experience with building other machines, such as flying machines (page 10), which use the same principles, but not the same mechanism, that birds use to fly, would indicate that this hypothesis may not be true. However, it is interesting to test the hypothesis.

- The brain inspires a new way to think about computation that contrasts with traditional computers. Unlike conventional computers, which have a few processors and a large but essentially inert memory, the brain consists of a huge number of asynchronous distributed processes, all running concurrently with no master controller. Conventional computers are not the only architecture available for computation. Indeed, current neural network systems are often implemented on massively parallel architectures.

- As far as learning is concerned, neural networks provide a different measure of simplicity as a learning bias than, for example, decision trees. Multilayer neural networks, like decision trees, can represent any function of a set of discrete features. However, the functions that correspond to simple neural networks do not necessarily correspond to simple decision trees. Which is better, in practice, is an empirical question that can be tested on different problem domains.

There are many different types of neural networks. This book considers **feed-forward neural networks**. Feed-forward networks can be seen as a hierarchy consisting of linear functions interleaved with **activation functions** (page 294).

Neural networks can have multiple input features and multiple target features. These features are all real valued. Discrete features can be transformed into indicator variables (page 275) or ordinal features (page 275). The inputs feed into layers of **hidden units**, which can be considered as features that are never directly observed, but are useful for prediction. Each of these units is a simple function of the units in a lower layer. These layers of hidden units feed ultimately into predictions of the target features.

A typical architecture is shown in Figure 7.16 (on the next page). There are **layers** of units (shown as circles). On the bottom layer are the input units for the input features. On the top is the output layer that makes predictions for the target variables.

Each layer of units is a function of the previous layer. Each example has a value for each unit. We consider three kinds of layers:

- An **input layer** consists of a unit for each input feature. This layer gets its value for an example from the value for the corresponding input feature for that example.

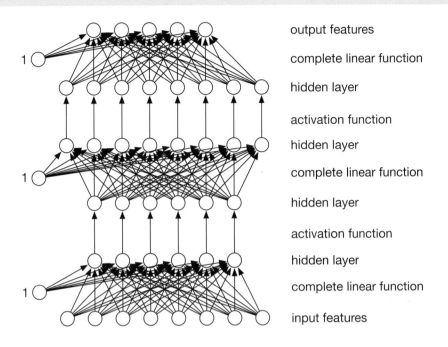

output features

complete linear function

hidden layer

activation function

hidden layer

complete linear function

hidden layer

activation function

hidden layer

complete linear function

input features

Figure 7.16: A deep neural network

- A **complete linear layer**, where each output o_j is a linear function of the input values v_i to the layer (and, as in linear regression (page 291), an extra constant input that has value "1" is added) defined by

$$o_j = \sum_i w_{ji} v_i$$

for weights w_{ji} that are learned. There is a weight for every input–output pair of the layer. In the diagram of Figure 7.16 there is a weight for every arc for the linear functions.

- An **activation layer**, where each output o_i is a function of the corresponding input value, v_i; thus $o_i = f(v_i)$ for activation function f. Typical activation functions are the **sigmoid** (page 294): $f(x) = 1/(1 + e^{-x})$ and the **rectified linear unit** (ReLU): $f(x) = max(0, x)$. An activation function should be (almost everywhere) differentiable.

For regression, where the prediction can be any real number, it is typical for the last layer to be a complete linear layer, as this allows the full range of values. For binary classification, where the output values can be mapped to $\{0, 1\}$, it is typical for the output to be a sigmoid function of its inputs; one reason is that we never not want to predict a value greater than one or less than zero.

There is no point in having linear layers adjacent to each other because a linear function of a linear function is a linear function.

Back-propagation implements stochastic gradient descent for all weights. Recall that **stochastic gradient descent** (page 293) involves updating each weight w by $\frac{\partial}{\partial w} error(e)$, for each example e.

There are two properties of differentiation used in back-propagation:

- **Linear rule**: the derivative of a linear function, $aw + b$, is given by:

$$\frac{\partial}{\partial w}(aw + b) = a$$

  so the derivative is the number that is multiplied by w in the linear function.

- **Chain rule**: if g is a function of w and function f, which does not depend on w, is applied to $g(w)$, then

$$\frac{\partial}{\partial w} f(g(w)) = f'(g(w)) * \frac{\partial}{\partial w} g(w)$$

  where f' is the derivative of f.

Learning consists of two passes through the network for each example:

- Prediction: given the values on the inputs for each layer, compute a value for the outputs of the layer.

- Back-propagation: go backwards through the layers to update all of the weights of the network (the weights in the linear layers).

Treating each layer as a separate module, each layer has to implement the forward prediction and, in the back-propagation pass, update the weights in the layer and provide an error term for the lower levels. Back-propagation is an implementation of the chain rule that computes the derivative for all weights with one backward sweep through the network.

To make this more modular, an extra **error layer**, can sit above the network. For each example, this layer takes as inputs the prediction of the network on the target features for that example and the actual values of the target features for the example, and outputs an error that is fed into the final layer. Suppose the output of the final layer is an array *values* of predictions, such that *values*[*j*] is a prediction of the *j*th target feature, and the observed value for the current example in the training set is $Y[j]$. The sum-of-squares error for a particular example is

$$error = \sum_j (values[j] - Y[j])^2.$$

Consider a generic weight w somewhere in the network. Note that *values*[j] (potentially) depends on w and $Y[j]$ does not

$$\frac{\partial}{\partial w}error = \sum_j 2(values[j] - Y[j])\frac{\partial}{\partial w}values[j]$$

The **error** that is back-propagated for the sum-of-squares error is $Y[j] - values[j]$ (where the 2 is absorbed into the step size). Back-propagation is used to update the value of each weight w when it has computed this value for w. Note that this is the negative of the derivative, so we can think of this as gradient ascent; the reason to do this is that it is easy to remember that a positive error means that the value needs to be increased, and a negative error means the value needs to be decreased. Minimizing another error function, such as the log loss (page 278), would result in different initial errors.

The input to each layer in the back-propagation phase is an error term for each of its output units. This is the product of the weights from the higher layers (the product of the $f'(g(w))$ terms in the chain rule) to compute derivative of the error. For a linear layer, each weight is updated by the value of the incoming error multiplied by the input value associated with that weight. Each layer must also pass the error signal to the lower level. The chain rule specifies that error passed back to the lower level is the error into the layer multiplied by the derivative of the function of the layer.

Figure 7.17 (on the next page) shows the algorithm for a neural network learner that carries out back-propagation for networks with multiple layers of units. The variable *layers* is a sequence of layers, where the lowest layer has the same number of inputs as there are input features. Each subsequent layer has the number of inputs that is equal to the number of outputs of the previous layer. The number of output units of the final layer is the same as the number of target features.

For the linear layers, the back-propagation algorithm is similar to the linear learner of Figure 7.8 (page 293), but the algorithm also takes into account multiple linear layers and activation layers. Intuitively, for each example, back-propagation involves simulating the network on that example. At each stage *values* contains the values of one layer to be input to the next layer. The derivative of the sum-of-squares errors for the outputs becomes the first value of error. This error is then passed back through the layers. This algorithm computes the derivative of each weight with one sweep back through the network.

> **Example 7.20** Consider training a network on the data of Figure 7.12 (page 298). There are five input features and one output feature. Figure 7.18 (page 315) shows a neural network represented by the following layers:
>
> [*Linear_complete_layer*(5, 2), *Sigmoid_layer*(2),
>   *Linear_complete_layer*(2, 1), *Sigmoid_layer*(1)]

Each layer implements:

Output_values(*inputs*) which returns the output values for the input values
Backprop(*error*), where error is an array of a value for each output unit, updates
the weights and returns an array of errors for the input units.

```
1: class Sigmoid_layer(n_i)                                          ▷ n_i is # inputs
2:     procedure Output_values(input)            ▷ input is array with length n_i
3:         output[i] := 1/(1 + e^{-input[i]}) for each 0 ≤ i < n_i
4:         return output

5:     procedure Backprop(error)                 ▷ error is array with length n_i
6:         input_error[i] := output[i] * (1 − output[i]) * error[i] for each i
7:         return input_error

8:
9: class Linear_complete_layer(n_i, n_o)         ▷ n_i is # inputs, n_o is #outputs
10:     Create weight w_{ji} for each 0 ≤ j < n_o and each 0 ≤ i ≤ n_i
11:     procedure Output_values(input)           ▷ input is array with length n_i
12:         define input[n] to be 1
13:         output[j] := Σ_{i=0}^{n} w_{ji} * input[i] for each j
14:         return output

15:     procedure Backprop(error)                 ▷ error is array with length n_o
16:         w_{ji} := w_{ji} + η * input[i] * error[j] for each i, j, for learning rate η
17:         input_error[i] := Σ_j w_{ji} * error[j] for each i
18:         return input_error

19:
20: procedure Sum_sq_error_layer(Ys, predicted)  ▷ returns initial Backprop error
21:     return [Ys[j] − predicted[j] for each output unit j]
22: procedure Neural_network_learner(Xs, Ys, Es, layers, η)
23:     Inputs
24:         Xs: set of input features, Xs = {X_1, ..., X_n}
25:         Ys: target features
26:         Es: set of examples from which to learn
27:         layers: a sequence of layers
28:         η: learning rate (gradient descent step size)

29:     repeat
30:         for each example e in Es in random order do
31:             values[i] := X_i(e) for each input unit i
32:             for each layer from lowest to highest do
33:                 values := layer.Output_values(values)

34:             error := Sum_sq_error_layer(Ys(e), values)
35:             for each layer from highest to lowest do
36:                 error := layer.Backprop(error)

37:     until termination
```

Figure 7.17: Back-propagation for a multilayer neural network

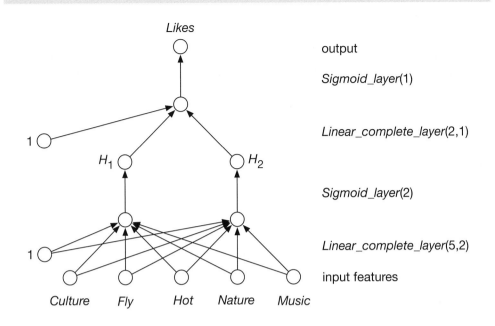

Figure 7.18: A neural network for Example 7.20 (page 313)

The lowest layer is a complete linear layer that takes five inputs and produces two outputs. The next sigmoid layer takes the sigmoid of these two outputs. Then a linear layer takes these and produces one linear output. The sigmoid of this output is the prediction of the network.

One run of back-propagation with the learning rate $\eta = 0.05$, and taking 10,000 steps, learns weights that accurately predict the training data. Each example e gives (where weight are given to two significant digits):

$$H_1(e) = sigmoid(-2.0 * Culture(e) - 4.4 * Fly(e) + 2.5 * Hot(e)$$
$$+ 2.4 * Music(e) - 6.1 * Nature(e) + 1.6)$$

$$H_2(e) = sigmoid(-0.7 * Culture(e) + 3.0 * Fly(e) + 5.8 * Hot(e)$$
$$+ 2.0 * Music(e) - 1.7 * Nature(e) - 5.0)$$

$$\widehat{Likes}(e) = sigmoid(-8.5 * H_1(e) - 8.8 * H_2(e) + 4.4).$$

Different runs can give quite different weights. For small examples like this, it is instructive to try to interpret the target; see Example 7.16 (page 337).

The use of neural networks may seem to challenge the **physical symbol system hypothesis** (page 19), which relies on symbols having meaning. Part of the appeal of neural networks is that, although meaning is attached to the input and target units, the designer does not associate a meaning with the hidden units. What the hidden units actually represent is something that is learned. After a neural network has been trained, it is often possible to look inside the network to determine what a particular hidden unit actually represents. Sometimes it is easy to express concisely in language what it represents, but often it is not. However, arguably, the computer has an internal meaning; it can explain its internal meaning by showing how examples map into the values of the hidden unit, or by turning on one of the units in a layer and then simulating the rest of the network.

Using multiple layers in a neural network can be seen as a form of hierarchical modeling (page 56), in what has become known as **deep learning**. **Convolutional neural networks** are specialized for vision tasks, and **recurrent neural networks** are used for time series. A typical real-world network can have 10 to 20 layers with hundreds of millions of weights, which can take hours or days or months to learn on machines with thousands of cores.

7.6   Composite Models

Decision trees, and (squashed) linear functions provide the basis for many other supervised learning techniques. Although decision trees can represent any discrete function, many simple functions have very complicated decision trees. Linear functions and linear classifiers by themselves are very restricted in what they can represent. However, layers of linear functions, separated by non-linear activation functions, forming neural networks, can approximate many more functions (including discrete functions and continuous functions over a compact set).

One way to make the linear function more powerful is to have the inputs to the linear function be some non-linear function of the original inputs. Adding these new features can increase the dimensionality, making some functions that were not linear (or linearly separable) in the lower-dimensional space linear in the higher-dimensional space.

Example 7.21   The exclusive-or function, x_1 xor x_2, is linearly separable in the space where the dimensions are x_1, x_2, and $x_1 x_2$, where $x_1 x_2$ is a feature that is true when both x_1 and x_2 are true. To visualize this, consider Figure 7.11 (page 297); with the product as the third dimension, the top-right point will be lifted out of the page, allowing for a linear separator (in this case a plane) to go underneath it.

A **kernel function** is a function that is applied to the input features to create new features. For example, a product of features could either replace or augment the existing features. Adding such features can allow for linear separators where there was none before. Another example is, for a feature x, adding x^2 and x^3 to the features allows the learner to find the best degree-3 polynomial fit. Note that when the feature space is augmented, overfitting can become more of a problem.

Neural networks (page 308) allow the inputs to the (squashed) linear function to be a squashed linear function with weights to be tuned. Having multiple layers of squashed linear functions as inputs to (squashed) linear functions allows more complex functions to be represented.

Another nonlinear representation is a **regression tree**, which is a decision tree with a (squashed) linear function at the leaves of the decision tree. This can represent a piecewise linear approximation. It is even possible to have neural networks or other classifiers at the leaves of the decision tree. To classify a new example, the example is filtered down the tree, and the classifier at the leaves is then used to classify the example.

Another possibility is to use a number of classifiers that have each been trained on the data and to combine these using some mechanism such as voting or averaging. These techniques are known as ensemble learning (on the next page).

7.6.1   Random Forests

One simple yet effective composite model is to have an averaging over decision trees, known as a **random forest**. The idea is to have a number of decision trees, each of which can make a prediction on each example, and to aggregate the predictions of the trees to make a prediction of the forest for each example.

In order to make this work effectively, the trees that make up the forest need to make diverse predictions. There are a number of ways that we can ensure

---

| Are some linear separators better than others? |

A **support vector machine (SVM)** is used for classification. It uses functions of the original inputs as the inputs of the linear function. These functions are called **kernel functions**. Many different kernel functions are used. An example kernel function is the product of original features. Adding the products of features is enough to enable the representation of the exclusive-or function. Increasing the dimensionality can, however, cause overfitting. An SVM constructs a decision surface, which is a hyperplane that divides the positive and negative examples in this higher-dimensional space. Define the **margin** to be the minimum distance from the decision surface to any of the examples. An SVM finds the decision surface with maximum margin. The examples that are closest to the decision surface are those that support (or hold up) the decision surface. In particular, these examples, if removed, would change the decision surface. Overfitting is avoided because these support vectors define a surface that can be defined in fewer parameters than there are examples. For detailed description of SVMs see the references at the end of this chapter.

diversity:

- A subset of the features could be used for each tree. Rather than using all of the features, a random subset of, say one third of the features could be used for each tree.

- Instead of splitting on the best feature, the tree could choose the best from a smaller set of candidate features at each split. The set of features to choose from could change for each tree or even for each node.

- Each tree could use a different subset of the examples to train on. Suppose there are m training examples. If there are many examples, each tree could use just a few of them. In **bagging** a random subset (with replacement) of m examples is selected for each tree to train on. In each of these sets, some examples are not chosen, and some are duplicated. On average, each set contains about 63% of the original examples.

Once the trees have been trained, a prediction can use the average of the predictions of the tree for a probabilistic prediction. Alternatively, each tree can vote with its most likely classification, and the prediction with the most votes can be used.

7.6.2 Ensemble Learning

In **ensemble learning**, an agent takes a number of learners and combines their predictions to make a prediction for the ensemble. The algorithms being combined are called **base-level algorithms**. Random forests are an example of an ensemble method, where the base-level algorithm is decision tree, and the predictions from the individual trees are averaged or are used to vote for a prediction.

In **boosting**, there is a sequence of learners in which each one learns from the errors of the previous ones. The features of a boosting algorithm are:

- There is a sequence of **base learners** (that can be different from each other or the same as each other), such as small decision trees, or (squashed) linear functions

- Each learner is trained to fit the examples that the previous learners did not fit well

- The final prediction is a mix (e.g., sum, weighted average or mode) of the predictions of each learner.

The base learners can be **weak learners**, in that they do not need to be very good; they just need to better than random. These weak learners are then

---

1: **procedure** *Boosting_learner*(Xs, Y, Es, L, k)
2:       **Inputs**
3:             Xs: set of input features
4:             Y: target feature
5:             Es: set of examples from which to learn
6:             L: base learner
7:             k: number of components in the ensemble
8:       **Output**
9:             function to make prediction on examples
10:     $mean := \sum_{e \in Es} Y(e) / |Es|$
11:     define $p_0(e) = mean$
12:     **for each** i from 1 to k **do**
13:           let $E_i = \{\langle Xs(e), Y(e) - p_{i-1}(e) \rangle$ for $e \in Es\}$
14:           let $d_i = L(E_i)$
15:           define $p_i(e) = p_{i-1}(e) + d_i(e)$
16:     **return** p_k

Figure 7.19: Functional gradient boosting regression learner

boosted to be components in the ensemble that performs better than any of them.

A simple boosting algorithm is **functional gradient boosting** which can be used for regression, as follows. The final prediction, as a function of the inputs, is the sum

$$p_0(X) + d_1(X) + \cdots + d_k(X)$$

where $p_0(X)$ is an initial prediction, say the mean, and each d_i is the difference from the previous prediction. Let the ith prediction be $p_i(X) = p_0(X) + d_1(X) + \cdots + d_i(X)$. Then $p_i(X) = p_{i-1}(X) + d_i(X)$. Each d_i is constructed so that the error of p_i is minimal, given that p_{i-1} is fixed. At each stage, the base learner learns d_i to minimize

$$\sum_e error(Y_i(e) - p_i(e)) = \sum_e error(Y_i(e) - p_{i-1}(e) - d_i(e)).$$

The ith learner can learn $d_i(e)$ to best fit $Y_i(e) - p_{i-1}(e)$. This is equivalent to learning from a modified data set, where the previous prediction is subtracted from the actual value of the training set. In this way, each learner is made to correct the errors of the previous prediction.

The algorithm is shown in Figure 7.19. Each p_i is a function that, given an example, returns a prediction for that example. E_i is a new set of examples, where for each $e \in Es$, the latest prediction, $p_{i-1}(e)$, is subtracted from the value of the target feature $Y(e)$. The new learner is therefore learning from the errors

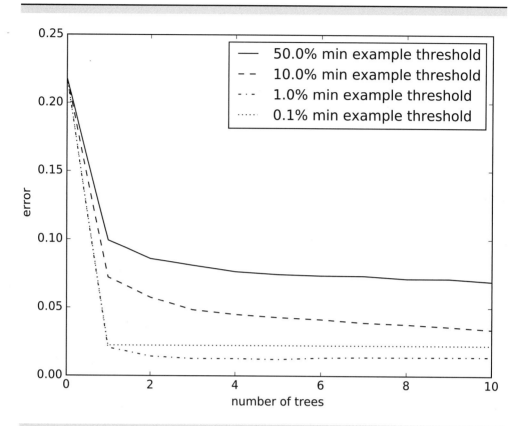

Figure 7.20: Error of functional gradient boosting of decision trees

of the old learner. Note that E_i does not need to be stored; the examples in E_i can be generated as needed. The function d_i is computed by applying the base learner to the examples E_i.

Example 7.22   Figure 7.20 shows a plot of the sum-of-squares error as the number of trees increases for functional gradient boosting of decision trees. The different lines are for different thresholds for the minimum number of examples required for a split, as a proportion of the total examples. At one tree, it is just the decision tree algorithm. Boosting makes the tree with a 1% threshold eventually better than with a 0.1% threshold, even though they are about the same for a single tree. The code is available from the book website.

7.7   Case-Based Reasoning

The previous methods tried to find a compact representation of the data to be used for future prediction. In **case-based reasoning**, the training examples, the **cases**, are stored and accessed to solve a new problem. To get a prediction for a new example, those cases that are similar, or close to, the new example are used to predict the value of the target features of the new example. This is at one extreme of the learning problem where, unlike decision trees and neural networks, relatively little work must be done offline, and virtually all of the work is performed at query time.

Case-based reasoning is used for classification and for regression. It is also applicable when the cases are complicated, such as in legal cases, where the cases are complex legal rulings, and in planning, where the cases are previous solutions to complex problems.

If the cases are simple, one algorithm that works well is to use the k-**nearest neighbors** for some given number k. Given a new example, the k training examples that have the input features closest to that example are used to predict the target value for the new example. The prediction could be the mode, average, or some interpolation between the prediction of these k training examples, perhaps weighting closer examples more than distant examples.

For this method to work, a distance metric is required that measures the closeness of two examples. First define a metric for the domain of each feature, in which the values of the features are converted to a numerical scale that is used to compare values. Suppose $X_i(e)$ is a numerical representation of the value of feature X_i for the example e. Then $(X_i(e_1) - X_i(e_2))$ is the difference between example e_1 and e_2 on the dimension defined by feature X_i. The **Euclidean distance**, the square root of the sum of the squares of the dimension differences, could be used as the distance between two examples. One important issue is the relative scales of different dimensions; increasing the scale of one dimension increases the importance of that feature. Let w_i be a non-negative real-valued parameter that specifies the weight of feature X_i. The distance between examples e_1 and e_2 is then

$$d(e_1, e_2) = \sqrt{\sum_i w_i * (X_i(e_1) - X_i(e_2))^2}\, .$$

The feature weights could be provided as input. It is also possible to learn these weights. The learning agent would try to find weights that minimize the error in predicting the value of each element of the training set, based on every other instance in the training set. This is an instance of **leave-one-out cross validation**.

Example 7.23   Consider using case-based reasoning on the data of Figure 7.1 (page 273). Rather than converting the data to a secondary representation as in decision tree or neural network learning, case-based reasoning uses the examples directly to predict the value for the user action in a new case.

Suppose a learning agent wants to classify example e_{20}, for which the author is unknown, the thread is a follow-up, the length is short, and it is read at home. First the learner tries to find similar cases. There is an exact match in example e_{11}, so it may want to predict that the user does the same action as for example e_{11} and thus skips the article. It could also include other close examples.

Consider classifying example e_{19}, where the author is unknown, the thread is new, the length is long, and it was read at work. In this case there are no exact matches. Consider the close matches. Examples e_2, e_8, and e_{18} agree on the features *Author*, *Thread*, and *Where_read*. Examples e_{10} and e_{12} agree on *Thread*, *Length*, and *Where_read*. Example e_3 agrees on *Author*, *Length*, and *Where_read*. Examples e_2, e_8, and e_{18} predict *Reads*, but the other examples predict *Skips*. So what should be predicted? The decision tree algorithm says that *Length* is the best predictor, and so e_2, e_8, and e_{18} should be ignored. For the sigmoid linear learning algorithm, the parameter values in Example 7.11 (page 295) similarly predict that the reader skips the article. A case-based reasoning algorithm to predict whether the user will or will not read this article must determine the relative importance of the dimensions.

One of the problems in case-based reasoning is accessing the relevant cases. A ***kd*-tree** is a way to index the training examples so that training examples that are close to a given example can be found quickly. Like a decision tree, a *kd*-tree splits on input features, but at the leaves are subsets of the training examples. In building a *kd*-tree from a set of examples, the learner tries to find an input feature that partitions the examples into set of approximately equal size and then builds *kd*-trees for the examples in each partition. This division stops when there are only few examples at each leaf. A new example is filtered down the tree, as in a decision tree. The exact matches will be at the leaf found. However, the examples at the leaves of the *kd*-tree could possibly be quite distant from the example to be classified; they agree on the values down the branch of the tree but could disagree on the values of all other features. The same tree is used to search for those examples that have one feature different from those tested in the tree, by allowing for one branch of a different value to be used when filtering a new case down the tree. See Exercise 7.20 (page 338).

Case-based reasoning is also applicable when the cases are more complicated, for example, when they are legal cases or previous solutions to planning problems. In this scenario, the cases are carefully chosen and edited to be useful. Case-based reasoning consists of a cycle of the following four steps:

Retrieve Given a new case, retrieve similar cases from the case base.

Reuse Adapt the retrieved cases to fit to the new case.

Revise Evaluate the solution and revise it based on how well it works.

Retain Decide whether to retain this new case in the case base.

If the case retrieved works for the current situation, it should be used. Otherwise, it may need to be adapted. The revision may involve other reasoning techniques, such as using the proposed solution as a starting point to search for a solution, or a human could do the adaptation in an interactive system. The new case and the solution can then be saved if retaining it will help in the future.

Example 7.24 A common example of a case-based reasoning system is a help desk that users call with problems to be solved. Case-based reasoning could be used by the diagnostic assistant to help users diagnose problems on their computer systems. When users give a description of a problem, the closest cases in the case base are retrieved. The diagnostic assistant could recommend some of these to the user, adapting each case to the user's particular situation. An example of adaptation is to change the recommendation based on what software the user has, what method they use to connect to the Internet, and the model of the printer. If one of the adapted cases works, that case is added to the case base, to be used when another user asks a similar question. In this way, all of the common different cases will eventually be in the case base.

If none of the cases found works, some other method is attempted to solve the problem, perhaps by adapting other cases or having a human help diagnose the problem. When the problem is finally solved, the solution is added to the case base.

A case can be removed from the case base if similar cases all give the same recommendation. In particular, C is redundant and can be removed if there are cases C_i such that any case that uses C as the closest case, would, if C were not there, use one of the C_i, and these would give the same recommendation.

7.8 Learning as Refining the Hypothesis Space

So far, learning involves either choosing the best representation, such as the best decision tree or the best values for weights in a neural network, or predicting the value of the target features of a new case from a database of previous cases. This section considers a different notion of learning, namely learning as delineating those hypotheses that are consistent with the examples. Rather than choosing a hypothesis, the aim is to find a description of all hypotheses that are consistent with the data. This investigation will shed light on the role of a bias (page 270) and provide a mechanism for a theoretical analysis of the learning problem.

We make three assumptions:

- There is a single Boolean target feature, Y.

- The hypotheses make definitive predictions, predicting true or false for each example, rather than probabilistic predictions.

- There is no noise in the data.

Given these assumptions, it is possible to write a hypothesis in terms of a proposition, where the primitive propositions are assignments to the input features.

Example 7.25   The decision tree of Figure 7.6 (page 286) can be seen as a representation *reads* defined by the proposition

$$\widehat{Reads}(e) \leftrightarrow Short(e) \wedge (New(e) \vee Known(e)) .$$

This is the prediction that the person read an article if and only if the article is short and either new or known.

The goal is to try to find a proposition on the input features that correctly classifies the training examples.

Example 7.26 Consider a trading agent trying to infer which articles a user reads based on keywords for the article. Suppose the learning agent has the following data:

article	Crime	Academic	Local	Music	Reads
a_1	true	false	false	true	true
a_2	true	false	false	false	true
a_3	false	true	false	false	false
a_4	false	false	true	false	false
a_5	true	true	false	false	true

The aim is to learn which articles the user reads.

In this example, *Reads* is the target feature, and the aim is to find a definition such as

$$\widehat{Reads}(e) \leftrightarrow Crime(e) \wedge (\neg Academic(e) \vee \neg Music(e)) .$$

This definition may be used to classify the training examples as well as future examples.

Hypothesis space learning assumes the following sets

- I, the **instance space**, is the set of all possible examples.
- $\mathcal{H}$, the **hypothesis space**, is a set of Boolean functions on the input features.
- $Es \subseteq I$ is the set of **training examples**. Values for the input features and the target feature are given for the training example.

If $h \in \mathcal{H}$ and $i \in I$, then $h(i)$ is the value that h predicts for i.

Example 7.27 In Example 7.26, I is the set of the $2^5 = 32$ possible examples, one for each combination of values for the features.

The hypothesis space $\mathcal{H}$ could be all Boolean combinations of the input features or could be more restricted, such as conjunctions or propositions defined in terms of fewer than three features.

> In Example 7.26, the training examples are $Es = \{a_1, a_2, a_3, a_4, a_5\}$. The target feature is *Reads*. Because the table specifies some of the values of this feature, and the learner will make predictions on unseen cases, the learner requires a bias (page 270). In hypothesis space learning, the bias is imposed by the hypothesis space.

Hypothesis h is **consistent** with a set of training examples Es if the value predicted by h is the value of the target feature Y for each example in Es. That is, if $\forall e \in Es, h(e) = Y(e)$.

The problem in hypothesis space learning is to find the set of elements of $\mathcal{H}$ that is consistent with all of the training examples.

> **Example 7.28** Consider the data of Example 7.26, and suppose $\mathcal{H}$ is the set of conjunctions of literals. An example hypothesis in $\mathcal{H}$ that is consistent with the set $\{a_1\}$ that consists of a single example is $\widehat{Reads(e)} \leftrightarrow \neg academic(e) \wedge music(e)$. This hypothesis means that the person reads an article if and only if the article is not academic and it is about music. This concept is not the target concept because it is inconsistent with $\{a_1, a_2\}$.

7.8.1 Version-Space Learning

Rather than enumerating all of the hypotheses, the set of elements of $\mathcal{H}$ consistent with all of the examples can be found more efficiently by imposing some structure on the hypothesis space.

Hypothesis h_1 is a **more general hypothesis** than hypothesis h_2 if h_2 implies h_1. In this case, h_2 is a **more specific hypothesis** than h_1. Any hypothesis is both more general than itself and more specific than itself.

> **Example 7.29** The hypothesis $\neg academic \wedge music$ is more specific than *music* and is also more specific than $\neg academic$. Thus, *music* is more general than $\neg academic \wedge music$. The most general hypothesis is *true*. The most specific hypothesis is *false*.

The "more general than" relation forms a partial ordering over the hypothesis space. The version-space algorithm that follows exploits this partial ordering to search for hypotheses that are consistent with the training examples.

Given hypothesis space $\mathcal{H}$ and examples Es, the **version space** is the subset of $\mathcal{H}$ that is consistent with the examples.

The **general boundary** of a version space, G, is the set of maximally general members of the version space (i.e., those members of the version space such that no other element of the version space is more general). The **specific boundary** of a version space, S, is the set of maximally specific members of the version space.

These concepts are useful because the general boundary and the specific boundary completely determine the version space, as shown by the following proposition.

Proposition 7.2. *The version space is the set of $h \in \mathcal{H}$ such that h is more general than an element of S and more specific than an element of G.*

Candidate Elimination Learner

The **candidate elimination learner** incrementally builds the version space given a hypothesis space $\mathcal{H}$ and a set Es of examples. The examples are added one by one; each example possibly shrinks the version space by removing the hypotheses that are inconsistent with the example. The candidate elimination algorithm does this by updating the general and/or the specific boundary for each new example. This is described in Figure 7.21 (on the next page).

Example 7.30   Consider how the candidate elimination algorithm handles Example 7.26 (page 324), where $\mathcal{H}$ is the set of conjunctions of literals.

Before it has seen any examples, $G_0 = \{true\}$ – the user reads everything – and $S_0 = \{false\}$ – the user reads nothing. Note that *true* is the empty conjunction and *false* is the conjunction of an atom and its negation.

After considering the first example, a_1, $G_1 = \{true\}$ and

$$S_1 = \{crime \wedge \neg academic \wedge \neg local \wedge music\}.$$

Thus, the most general hypothesis is that the user reads everything, and the most specific hypothesis is that the user only reads articles exactly like this one.

After considering the first two examples, $G_2 = \{true\}$ and

$$S_2 = \{crime \wedge \neg academic \wedge \neg local\}.$$

Since a_1 and a_2 disagree on music, but have the same prediction it can be concluded that music cannot be relevant.

After considering the first three examples, the general boundary becomes

$$G_3 = \{crime, \neg academic\}$$

and $S_3 = S_2$. Now there are two most general hypotheses; the first is that the user reads anything about crime, and the second is that the user reads anything non-academic.

After considering the first four examples,

$$G_4 = \{crime, \neg academic \wedge \neg local\}$$

and $S_4 = S_3$.

After considering all five examples,

$$G_5 = \{crime\},$$

1: **procedure** *Candidate_elimination_learner*(*Xs*, *Y*, *Es*, $\mathcal{H}$)
2:    **Inputs**
3:        *Xs*: set of input features, $Xs = \{X_1, \ldots, X_n\}$
4:        *Y*: Boolean target feature
5:        *Es*: set of examples from which to learn
6:        $\mathcal{H}$: hypothesis space
7:    **Output**
8:        general boundary $G \subseteq \mathcal{H}$
9:        specific boundary $S \subseteq \mathcal{H}$ consistent with *Es*
10:    **Local**
11:        *G*: set of hypotheses in $\mathcal{H}$
12:        *S*: set of hypotheses in $\mathcal{H}$
13:    Let $G = \{true\}$, $S = \{false\}$;
14:    **for each** $e \in Es$ **do**
15:        **if** $Y(e) = true$ **then**
16:            Elements of *G* that classify *e* as negative are removed from *G*;
17:            Each element *s* of *S* that classifies *e* as negative is removed and replaced by the minimal generalizations of *s* that classify *e* as positive and are less general than some member of *G*;
18:            Non-maximal hypotheses are removed from *S*;
19:        **else**
20:            Elements of *S* that classify *e* as positive are removed from *S*;
21:            Each element *g* of *G* that classifies *e* as positive is removed and replaced by the minimal specializations of *g* that classifies *e* as negative and are more general than some member of *S*.
22:            Non-minimal hypotheses are removed from *G*.

Figure 7.21: Candidate elimination algorithm

$$S_5 = \{crime \wedge \neg local\}.$$

Thus, after five examples, only two hypotheses exist in the version space. They differ only in their prediction on an example that has *crime* $\wedge$ *local* true. If the target concept can be represented as a conjunction, only an example with *crime* $\wedge$ *local* true will change *G* or *S*. This version space can make predictions about all other examples.

The Bias Involved in Version-Space Learning

Recall (page 270) that a bias is necessary for any learning to generalize beyond the training data. There must have been a bias in Example 7.30 because, after observing only five of the 16 possible assignments to the input variables, an agent was able to make predictions about examples it had not seen.

The bias involved in version-space learning is a called a **language bias** or a **restriction bias** because the bias is obtained from restricting the allowable hypotheses. For example, a new example with crime false and music true will be classified as false (the user will not read the article), even though no such example has been seen. The restriction that the hypothesis must be a conjunction of literals is enough to predict its value.

This bias should be contrasted with the bias involved in decision tree learning (page 285). A decision tree can represent any Boolean function. Decision tree learning involves a **preference bias**, in that some Boolean functions are preferred over others; those with smaller decision trees are preferred over those with larger decision trees. A decision tree learning algorithm that builds a single decision tree top-down also involves a **search bias** in that the decision tree returned depends on the search strategy used.

The candidate elimination algorithm is sometimes said to be an **unbiased learning algorithm** because the learning algorithm does not impose any bias beyond the language bias involved in choosing $\mathcal{H}$. It is easy for the version space to collapse to the empty set, for example, if the user reads an article with crime false and music true. This means that the target concept is not in $\mathcal{H}$. Version-space learning is not tolerant to noise; just one misclassified example can throw off the whole system.

The **bias-free hypothesis space** is where $\mathcal{H}$ is the set of all Boolean functions. In this case, G always contains one concept: the concept which says that all negative examples have been seen and every other example is positive. Similarly, S contains the single concept which says that all unseen examples are negative. The version space is incapable of concluding anything about examples it has not seen; thus, it cannot generalize. Without a language bias or a preference bias, no generalization and, therefore, no learning will occur.

7.8.2 Probably Approximately Correct Learning

Rather than just studying different learning algorithms that happen to work well, **computational learning theory** investigates general principles that can be proved to hold for classes of learning algorithms.

Some relevant questions that we can ask about a theory of computational learning include the following:

- Is the learner guaranteed to converge to the correct hypothesis as the number of examples increases?

- How many examples are required to identify a concept?

- How much computation is required to identify a concept?

In general, the answer to the first question is "no," unless it can be guaranteed that the examples always eventually rule out all but the correct hypothesis. An adversary out to trick the learner could choose examples that do not help discriminate correct hypotheses from incorrect hypotheses. If an adversary cannot be ruled out, a learner cannot guarantee to find a consistent hypothesis. However, given randomly chosen examples, a learner that always chooses a consistent hypothesis can get arbitrarily close to the correct concept. This requires a notion of closeness and a specification of what is a randomly chosen example.

Consider a learning algorithm that chooses a hypothesis consistent with all of the training examples. Assume a probability distribution over possible examples and that the training examples and the test examples are chosen from the same distribution. The distribution does not have to be known. We will prove a result that holds for all distributions.

The **error of hypothesis** $h \in \mathcal{H}$ on instance space I, written $error(I,h)$, is defined to be the probability of choosing an element i of I such that $h(i) \neq Y(i)$, where $h(i)$ is the predicted value of target variable Y on possible example i, and $Y(i)$ is the actual value of Y on example i. That is,

$$error(I,h) = P(h(i) \neq Y(i) \mid i \in I) \, .$$

An agent typically does not know P or $Y(i)$ for all i and, thus, does not actually know the error of a particular hypothesis.

Given $\epsilon > 0$, hypothesis h is **approximately correct** if $error(I,h) \leq \epsilon$.

We make the following assumption.

Assumption 7.3. *The training and test examples are chosen independently from the same probability distribution as the population.*

It is still possible that the examples do not distinguish hypotheses that are far away from the concept. It is just very unlikely that they do not. A learner that chooses a hypothesis consistent with the training examples is **probably approximately correct** if, for an arbitrary number δ ($0 < \delta \leq 1$), the algorithm is not approximately correct in at most δ of the cases. That is, the hypothesis generated is approximately correct at least $1 - \delta$ of the time.

Under the preceding assumption, for arbitrary ϵ and δ, we can guarantee that an algorithm that returns a consistent hypothesis will find a hypothesis with error less than ϵ, in at least $1 - \delta$ of the cases. Moreover, this result does not depend on the probability distribution.

Proposition 7.4. *Given Assumption 7.3, if a hypothesis is consistent with at least*

$$\frac{1}{\epsilon} \left(\ln |\mathcal{H}| + \ln \frac{1}{\delta} \right)$$

training examples, it has error at most ϵ, at least $1 - \delta$ of the time.

Proof. Suppose $\epsilon > 0$ and $\delta > 0$ are given. Partition the hypothesis space $\mathcal{H}$ into

$$\mathcal{H}_0 = \{h \in \mathcal{H} : error(I, h) \le \epsilon\}$$
$$\mathcal{H}_1 = \{h \in \mathcal{H} : error(I, h) > \epsilon\} \,.$$

We want to guarantee that the learner does not choose an element of $\mathcal{H}_1$ in more than δ of the cases.

Suppose $h \in \mathcal{H}_1$, then

$P(h$ is wrong for a single example$) \ge \epsilon$

$P(h$ is correct for a single example$) \le 1 - \epsilon$

$P(h$ is correct for m random examples$) \le (1 - \epsilon)^m.$

Therefore,

$P(\mathcal{H}_1$ contains a hypothesis that is correct for m random examples$)$
$$\le |\mathcal{H}_1| \, (1 - \epsilon)^m$$
$$\le |\mathcal{H}| \, (1 - \epsilon)^m$$
$$\le |\mathcal{H}| \, e^{-\epsilon m}$$

using the inequality $(1 - \epsilon) \le e^{-\epsilon}$ if $0 \le \epsilon \le 1$.

If we ensure that $|\mathcal{H}| e^{-\epsilon m} \le \delta$, we guarantee that $\mathcal{H}_1$ does not contain a hypothesis that is correct for m examples in more than δ of the cases. So H_0 contains all of the correct hypotheses in all but δ of the cases.

Solving for m gives

$$m \ge \frac{1}{\epsilon} \left(\ln |\mathcal{H}| + \ln \frac{1}{\delta} \right)$$

which proves the proposition. $\square$

The number of examples required to guarantee this error bound is called the **sample complexity**. The number of examples required according to this proposition is a function of ϵ, δ, and the size of the hypothesis space.

Example 7.31 Suppose the hypothesis space $\mathcal{H}$ is the set of conjunctions of literals on n Boolean variables. In this case $|\mathcal{H}| = 3^n + 1$ because, for each conjunction, each variable is in one of three states: (1) it is unnegated in the conjunction, (2) it is negated, or (3) it does not appear; the "+1" is needed to represent false, which is the conjunction of any atom and its negation. Thus, the sample complexity is $\frac{1}{\epsilon} \left(n \ln 3 + \ln \frac{1}{\delta} \right)$ examples, which is polynomial in n, $\frac{1}{\epsilon}$, and $\ln \frac{1}{\delta}$.

If we want to guarantee at most a 5% error 99% of the time and have 30 Boolean variables, then $\epsilon = 1/20$, $\delta = 1/100$, and $n = 30$. The bound says that we can guarantee this performance if we find a hypothesis that is consistent with $20 * (30 \ln 3 + \ln 100) \approx 752$ examples. This is much fewer than the number of possible instances, which is $2^{30} = 1,073,741,824$, and the number of hypotheses, which is $3^{30} + 1 = 205,891,132,094,650$.

Example 7.32 If the hypothesis space $\mathcal{H}$ is the set of all Boolean functions on n variables, then $|\mathcal{H}| = 2^{2^n}$; thus, we require $\frac{1}{\epsilon}\left(2^n \ln 2 + \ln \frac{1}{\delta}\right)$ examples. The sample complexity is exponential in n.

If we want to guarantee at most a 5% error 99% of the time and have 30 Boolean variables, then $\epsilon = 1/20$, $\delta = 1/100$, and $n = 30$. The bound says that we can guarantee this performance if we find a hypothesis consistent with $20 * (2^{30} \ln 2 + \ln 100) \approx 14,885,222,452$ examples.

Consider the third question raised at the start of this section, namely, how quickly can a learner find the probably approximately correct hypothesis. First, if the sample complexity is exponential in the size of some parameter (e.g., n above), the computational complexity must be exponential because an algorithm must at least consider each example. To show an algorithm with polynomial complexity, you need to find a hypothesis space with polynomial sample complexity and show that the algorithm uses polynomial time for each example.

7.9 Review

The following are the main points you should have learned from this chapter:

- Learning is the ability of an agent to improve its behavior based on experience.
- Supervised learning is the problem of predicting the target of a new input, given a set of input–target pairs.
- Given some training examples, an agent builds a representation that can be used for new predictions.
- Linear classifiers and decision tree classifiers are representations which are the basis for more sophisticated models.
- Overfitting occurs when a prediction fits the training set well but does not fit the test set or future predictions.

7.10 References and Further Reading

For good overviews of machine learning see Briscoe and Caelli [1996], Mitchell [1997], Duda et al. [2001], Bishop [2008], Hastie et al. [2009] and Murphy [2012]. Halevy et al. [2009] discuss big data. Domingos [2012] overviews issues in machine learning. The UCI machine learning repository [Lichman, 2013] is a collection of classic machine learning data sets.

The collection of papers by Shavlik and Dietterich [1990] contains many classic learning papers. Michie et al. [1994] give empirical evaluation of many learning algorithms on multiple problems. Davis and Goadrich [2006] discusses precision, recall, and ROC curves. Settles [2012] overviews active learning.

The approach to combining expert knowledge and data was proposed by Spiegelhalter et al. [1990].

Decision tree learning is discussed by Breiman et al. [1984] and Quinlan [1986]. For an overview of a more mature decision tree learning tool see Quinlan [1993].

Ng [2004] compares L_1 and L_2 regularization for logistic regression.

Goodfellow et al. [2016] provide a modern overview of neural networks and deep learning. For classic overviews of neural networks see Hertz et al. [1991] and Bishop [1995]. McCulloch and Pitts [1943] defines a formal neuron, and Minsky [1952] showed how such representations can be learned from data. Rosenblatt [1958] introduced the perceptron. Back-propagation is introduced in Rumelhart et al. [1986]. LeCun et al. [1998] describe how to effectively implement back-propagation. Minsky and Papert [1988] analyze the limitations of neural networks. LeCun et al. [2015] review how multilayer neural networks have been used for deep learning in many applications. Hinton et al. [2012] review neural networks for speech recognition, Goldberg [2016] for natural language processing, and Krizhevsky et al. [2012] for vision. Rectified linear units are discussed by Glorot et al. [2011]. Nocedal and Wright [2006] provides practical advice on gradient descent and related methods. Karimi et al. [2016] analyze how many iterations of stochastic gradient descent are needed.

Random forests were introduced by Breiman [2001], and are compared by Dietterich [2000a] and Denil et al. [2014]. For reviews of ensemble learning see Dietterich [2002]. Boosting is described in Schapire [2002] and Meir and Rätsch [2003].

For overviews of case-based reasoning see Kolodner and Leake [1996] and López [2013]. For a review of nearest-neighbor algorithms, see Duda et al. [2001] and Dasarathy [1991]. The dimension-weight learning nearest-neighbor algorithm is from Lowe [1995].

Version spaces were defined by Mitchell [1977]. PAC learning was introduced by Valiant [1984]. The analysis here is due to Haussler [1988]. Kearns and Vazirani [1994] give a good introduction to computational learning theory and PAC learning. For more details on version spaces and PAC learning, see Mitchell [1997].

For research results on machine learning, see the journals *Journal of Machine Learning Research (JMLR)*, *Machine Learning*, the annual *International Conference* on *Machine Learning (ICML)*, the *Proceedings of the Neural Information Processing Society (NIPS)*, or general AI journals such as *Artificial Intelligence* and the *Journal of Artificial Intelligence Research*, and many specialized conferences and journals.

7.11 Exercises

Exercise 7.1 The aim of this exercise is to prove and extend the table of Figure 7.5 (page 284).

(a) Prove the optimal predictions for training data of Figure 7.5. To do this, find the minimum value of the absolute error, the sum-of-squares error, the entropy, and the value that gives the maximum likelihood. The maximum or minimum value is either an end point or where the derivative is zero.

(b) To determine the best prediction for the test data, assume that the data cases are generated stochastically according to some true parameter p_0. Try the following for a number of different values for $p_0 \in [0, 1]$. Generate k training examples (try various values for k, some small, say 2, 3 or 5, and some large, say 1000) by sampling with probability p_0; from these training examples generate n_0 and n_1. Generate a test set that contains many test cases using the same parameter p_0. Which of the following gives a lower error on the test set for each of the optimality criteria: sum of absolute values, sum of squares, and likelihood (or log loss)

  i) the mode

  ii) $n_1 / (n_0 + n_1)$

  iii) if $n_1 = 0$, use 0.001, if $n_0 = 0$, use 0.999, else use $n_1 / (n_0 + n_1)$. Try this for different numbers when the counts are zero.

  iv) $(n_1 + 1)/(n_0 + n_1 + 2)$

  v) $(n_1 + \alpha)/(n_0 + n_1 + 2\alpha)$ for different values of $\alpha > 0$

  vi) another predictor that is a function of n_0 and n_1.

  You may have to generate many different training sets for each parameter. (For the mathematically sophisticated, try to prove what the optimal predictor is for each criterion.)

Exercise 7.2 In the context of a point estimate of a feature with domain $\{0, 1\}$ with no inputs, it is possible for an agent to make a stochastic prediction with a parameter $p \in [0, 1]$ such that the agent predicts 1 with probability p and predicts 0 otherwise. For each of the following error measures, give the expected error on a training set with n_0 occurrences of 0 and n_1 occurrences of 1 (as a function of p). What is the value of p that minimizes the error? Is this worse or better than the prediction of Figure 7.5 (page 284)?

(a) Sum of absolute errors

(b) Sum-of-squares error

Example	Comedy	Doctors	Lawyers	Guns	Likes
e_1	false	true	false	false	false
e_2	true	false	true	false	true
e_3	false	false	true	true	true
e_4	false	false	true	false	false
e_5	false	false	false	true	false
e_6	true	false	false	true	false
e_7	true	false	false	false	true
e_8	false	true	true	true	true
e_9	false	true	true	false	false
e_{10}	true	true	true	false	true
e_{11}	true	true	false	true	false
e_{12}	false	false	false	false	false

Figure 7.22: Training examples for Exercise 7.3

(c) Worst-case error

Exercise 7.3 Suppose we have a system that observes a person's TV watching habits in order to recommend other TV shows the person may like. Suppose that we have characterized each show by whether it is a comedy, whether it features doctors, whether it features lawyers, and whether it has guns. Suppose we are given the examples of Figure 7.22 about whether the person likes various TV shows. We want to use this data set to learn the value of *Likes* (i.e., to predict which TV shows the person would like based on the attributes of the TV show).

You may find the AIspace.org applets useful for this assignment. (Before you start, see if you can see the pattern in what shows the person likes.)

(a) Suppose the error is the sum of absolute errors. Give the optimal decision tree with only one node (i.e., with no splits). What is the error of this tree?

(b) Do the same as in part (a), but with the sum-of-squares error.

(c) Suppose the error is the sum of absolute errors. Give the optimal decision tree of depth 2 (i.e., the root node is the only node with children). For each leaf in the tree, give the examples that are filtered to that node. What is the error of this tree?

(d) Do the same as in part (c) but with the sum-of-squares error.

(e) What is the smallest tree that correctly classifies all training examples? Does a top-down decision tree that optimizes the information gain at each step represent the same function?

(f) Give two instances not appearing in the examples of Figure 7.22 and show how they are classified using the smallest decision tree. Use this to explain the bias inherent in the tree. (How does the bias give you these particular predictions?)

(g) Is this data set linearly separable? Explain why or why not.

Exercise 7.4 Consider the decision tree learning algorithm of Figure 7.7 (page 287) and the data of Figure 7.1 (page 273). Suppose, for this question, the stopping criterion is that all of the examples have the same classification. The tree of Figure 7.6 (page 286) was built by selecting a feature that gives the maximum information gain. This question considers what happens when a different feature is selected.

(a) Suppose you change the algorithm to always select the first element of the list of features. What tree is found when the features are in the order [*Author, Thread, Length, WhereRead*]? Does this tree represent a different function than that found with the maximum information gain split? Explain.

(b) What tree is found when the features are in the order [*WhereRead, Thread, Length, Author*]? Does this tree represent a different function than that found with the maximum information gain split or the one given for the preceding part? Explain.

(c) Is there a tree that correctly classifies the training examples but represents a different function than those found by the preceding algorithms? If so, give it. If not, explain why.

Exercise 7.5 The aim of this exercise is to determine the size of the space of decision trees. Suppose there are n binary features in a learning problem. How many different decision trees are there? How many different functions are represented by these decision trees? Is it possible that two different decision trees give rise to the same function?

Exercise 7.6 Extend the decision tree learning algorithm of Figure 7.7 (page 287) to allow for multiway splits for discrete variables. Assume that the inputs are the input features, the target feature and the training examples. A split is on the values of a feature.

One problem that must be overcome is when no examples correspond to one particular value of a selected feature. You must make a reasonable prediction for this case.

Exercise 7.7 Implement a decision tree learner that handles input features with ordered domains. You can assume that any numerical feature is ordered. The condition should be a cut on a single variable, such as $X \leq v$, which partitions the training examples according to the value v. A cut-value can be chosen for a feature X by sorting the examples on the value of X, and sweeping through the examples in order. While sweeping through the examples, the evaluation of each partition should be computed from the evaluation of the previous partition. Does this work better than, for example, selecting the cuts arbitrarily?

Exercise 7.8 The decision tree learning algorithm of Figure 7.7 (page 287) has to stop if it runs out of features and not all examples agree.

Suppose that you are building a decision tree for a Boolean target feature and you have come to the stage where there are no remaining input features to split on and there are examples in the training set, n_1 of which are positive and n_0 of which are negative. Consider the strategies

i) Return whichever value has the most examples – return *true* if $n_1 > n_0$, *false* if $n_1 < n_0$, and either if $n_1 = n_0$.

ii) Return the empirical frequency, $n_1 / (n_0 + n_1)$.

iii) Return $(n_1 + 1)/(n_0 + n_1 + 2)$.

For each of the following objectives predict which of the strategies will have the smallest error on a test set.

(a) Minimize the sum of the absolute differences between the value of the example ($1 = true$ and $0 = false$) and the predicted values in the tree (either $1 = true$ and $0 = false$ or the probability).

(b) Minimize the sum of the squares of the differences in values.

(c) Maximize the log-likelihood of the data.

Explain your predictions, test it on some data sets, and report as to whether your prediction holds.

Exercise 7.9 Show how gradient descent can be used for learning a linear function that minimizes the absolute error. [Hint: Do a case analysis of the error; for each example the absolute value is either the positive or the negative of the value. What is appropriate when the value is zero?]

Exercise 7.10 Consider Equation (7.1) (page 291), which gives the error of a linear prediction.

(a) Give a formula for the weights that minimize the error for the case where $n = 2$ (i.e., when there are only two input feature). [Hint: For each weight, differentiate with respect to that weight and set to zero.]

(b) Why is it hard to minimize the error analytically when using a sigmoid function as an activation function, for $n = 2$? (Why doesn't the same method as in part (a) work?)

Exercise 7.11 Suppose you want to optimize the sum-of-squares error (page 276) for the sigmoid of a linear function.

(a) Modify the algorithm of Figure 7.8 (page 293) so that the update is proportional to the gradient of the sum-of-suares error. Note that this question assumes you know differential calculus, in particular, the chain rule for differentiation.

(b) Does this work better than the algorithm that minimizes log loss when evaluated according to the sum-of-squares error?

Exercise 7.12 Consider how to estimate the quality of restaurant from the ratings of 1 to 5 stars as in Example 7.17 (page 303).

(a) What would this predict for a restaurant that has two 5-star ratings? How would you test from the data whether this is a reasonable prediction?

(b) Suppose you wanted not to optimize just for the 5-star restaurants, but for all restaurants. How can this be done?

(c) Can c, as computed in Example 7.17, be negative? Give a scenario where this might occur.

(d) Why might we choose not to use the average rating for a_0? What else might you use? [Hint: A new restaurant may be quite different from a well-established restaurant. Hint: Picking a restaurant at random, and then a rating at random will have a different average than picking a rating at random.]

It might be useful to try this on some real data. For example, Movielens makes a data set of movie ratings available, which can be used to test such hypotheses (albeit on movies, not restaurants).

Exercise 7.13 Consider the update step for the L_2 regularizer for linear or logistic regression (page 305). It is possible to update the weights due to the regularization inside the "for each" loops in Figure 7.8 (page 293). Does this actually minimize the ridge regression formula? How must λ be modified? Does this work better in practice?

Exercise 7.14 Suggest how the update for the L_1 regularizer could be carried out once per example rather than after all examples have been considered. Which do you think would work better, and why? Does this work better or worse in practice than updating once per example?

Exercise 7.15 It is possible to define a regularizer to minimize $\sum_e (error_h(e) + \lambda * regularizer_h)$ rather than Formula (7.4) (page 304). How is this different than the existing regularizer? [Hint: Think about how this affects multiple data sets or for cross validation.]

Suppose λ is set by k-fold cross validation, and then the model is learned for the whole data set. How would the algorithm be different for the original way(s) of defining a regularizer and this alternative way? [Hint: There is a different number of examples used for the regularization than there is the full data set; does this matter?] Which works better in practice?

Exercise 7.16 Consider the parameters learned for the neural network in Example 7.20 (page 313). Give a logical formula (or a decision tree) representing the Boolean function that is the value for the hidden units and the output units. This formula should not refer to any real numbers. [Suppose that, in the output of a neural network, any value greater than 0.5 is considered true and any less than 0.5 is false (i.e., any positive value before the activation function is true, and a negative value is false). Also consider whether intermediate values of the hidden units matter.]

[Hint: One brute-force method is to go through the 16 combinations of values for the inputs to each hidden unit and determine the truth value of the output. A better method is to try to understand the functions themselves.]

Does the neural network learn the same function as a decision tree with classifications at the leaves? If not, what is the smallest decision tree that represents the same function?

Exercise 7.17 Run the Alspace.org neural network learner on the data of Figure 7.1 (page 273).

(a) Suppose that you decide to use any predicted value from the neural network greater than 0.5 as true, and any value less than 0.5 as false. How many examples are misclassified initially? How many examples are misclassified after 40 iterations? How many examples are misclassified after 80 iterations?

(b) Try the same example and the same initial values, with different step sizes for the gradient descent. Try at least $\eta = 0.1$, $\eta = 1.0$, and $\eta = 5.0$. Comment on the relationship between step size and convergence.

(c) Given the final parameter values you found, give a logical formula for what each of the units is computing. [Hint: As a brute-force method, for each of the units, build the truth tables for the input values and determine the output for each combination, then simplify the resulting formula]. Is it always possible to find such a formula?

(d) All of the parameters were set to different initial values. What happens if the parameter values are all set to the same (random) value? Test it out for this example, and hypothesize what occurs in general.

(e) For the neural network algorithm, comment on the following stopping criteria.

  i) Learn for a limited number of iterations, where the limit is set initially.

  ii) Stop when the sum-of-squares error is less than 0.25. Explain why 0.25 may be an appropriate number.

  iii) Stop when the derivatives all become within some ϵ of zero.

  iv) Split the data into training data and validation data, train on the training data and stop when the error on the validation data increases.

  Which would you expect to better handle overfitting? Which criteria guarantee the gradient descent will stop? Which criteria would guarantee that, if it stops, the network can be used to predict the test data accurately?

Exercise 7.18 In the neural net learning algorithm, the parameters are updated for each example. To compute the derivative accurately, the parameters should be updated only after all examples have been seen. Implement such a learning algorithm and compare it to the incremental algorithm, with respect to both rate of convergence and to speed of the algorithm.

Exercise 7.19 How does a neural network with hidden units as rectified linear units (page 311) ($f(z) = max(0, z)$) compare to a neural network with sigmoid hidden units? This should be tested on more than one data set. Make sure that the output unit is appropriate for the data set(s).

Exercise 7.20

(a) Draw a *kd*-tree for the data of Figure 7.1 (page 273). The topmost feature to split on should be the one that most divides the examples into two equal classes. (Do not split on *UserAction*.) Show which training examples are at which leaf nodes.

(b) Show the locations in this tree that contain the closest training examples to a new case where the author is unknown, the thread is new, the length is long, and it was read at work.

(c) Based on this example, discuss which examples should be returned from a lookup on a *kd*-tree. Why is this different from a lookup on a decision tree?

Exercise 7.21 Implement a nearest-neighbor learning system that stores the training examples in a *kd*-tree and uses the neighbors that differ in the fewest number of features, weighted evenly. How well does this work in practice?

Part III

Reasoning, Learning and Acting with Uncertainty

Chapter 8

Reasoning with Uncertainty

> *It is remarkable that a science which began with the consideration of games of chance should become the most important object of human knowledge ... The most important questions of life are, for the most part, really only problems of probability ...*
>
> *The theory of probabilities is at bottom nothing but common sense reduced to calculus.*

– Pierre Simon de Laplace [1812]

Agents in real environments are inevitably forced to make decisions based on incomplete information. Even when an agent senses the world to find out more information, it rarely finds out the exact state of the world. For example, a doctor does not know exactly what is going on inside a patient, a teacher does not know exactly what a student understands, and a robot does not know what is in a room it left a few minutes ago. When an intelligent agent must act, it has to use whatever information it has. This chapter considers reasoning with uncertainty that arises whenever an agent is not omniscient. This is used in Chapter 9 as a basis for acting with uncertainty. This chapter starts with probability, shows how to represent the world by making appropriate independence assumptions, and shows how to reason with such representations.

8.1 Probability

To make a good decision, an agent cannot simply assume what the world is like and act according to that assumption. It must consider multiple hypotheses when making a decision. Consider the following example.

> **Example 8.1** Many people consider it sensible to wear a seat belt when traveling in a car because, in an accident, wearing a seat belt reduces the risk of serious injury. However, consider an agent that commits to assumptions and bases its decision on these assumptions. If the agent assumes it will not have an accident, it will not bother with the inconvenience of wearing a seat belt. If it assumes it will have an accident, it will not go out. In neither case would it wear a seat belt! A more intelligent agent may wear a seat belt because the inconvenience of wearing a seat belt is far outweighed by the increased risk of injury or death if it has an accident. It does not stay at home too worried about an accident to go out; the benefits of being mobile, even with the risk of an accident, outweigh the benefits of the extremely cautious approach of never going out. The decisions of whether to go out and whether to wear a seat belt depend on the likelihood of having an accident, how much a seat belt helps in an accident, the inconvenience of wearing a seat belt, and how important it is to go out. The various trade-offs may be different for different agents. Some people do not wear seat belts, and some people do not go in cars because of the risk of accident.

Reasoning with uncertainty has been studied in the fields of probability theory and decision theory. Probability is the calculus of **gambling**. When an agent makes decisions and is uncertain about the outcomes of its actions, it is gambling on the outcomes. However, unlike a gambler at the casino, an agent that has to survive in the real world cannot opt out and decide not to gamble; whatever it does – including doing nothing – involves uncertainty and risk. If it does not take the probabilities of possible outcomes into account, it will eventually lose at gambling to an agent that does. This does not mean, however, that making the best decision guarantees a win.

Many of us learn probability as the theory of tossing coins and rolling dice. Although this may be a good way to present probability theory, probability is applicable to a much richer set of applications than coins and dice. In general, probability is a calculus for belief designed for making decisions.

The view of probability as a measure of belief is known as **Bayesian probability** or **subjective probability**. The term *subjective* means "belonging to the subject" (as opposed to *arbitrary*). For example, suppose there are three agents, Alice, Bob, and Chris, and one six-sided die that has been tossed, that they all agree is fair. Suppose Alice observes that the outcome is a "6" and tells Bob that the outcome is even, but Chris knows nothing about the outcome. In this case, Alice has a probability of 1 that the outcome is a "6," Bob has a probability of $\frac{1}{3}$ that it is a "6" (assuming Bob believes Alice), and Chris may have probability of $\frac{1}{6}$ that the outcome is a "6." They all have different probabilities because they all have different knowledge. The probability is about the outcome of this particular toss of the die, not of some generic event of tossing dice.

We are assuming that the uncertainty is **epistemological** – pertaining to an agent's beliefs of the world – rather than **ontological** – how the world is.

For example, if you are told that someone is very tall, you know they have some height but you only have vague knowledge about the actual value of their height.

Probability theory is the study of *how knowledge affects belief*. Belief in some proposition, α, is measured in terms of a number between 0 and 1. The probability of α is 0 means that α is believed to be definitely false (no new evidence will shift that belief), and the probability of α is 1 means that α is believed to be definitely true. Using 0 and 1 is purely a convention. If an agent's probability of α is greater than zero and less than one, this does not mean that α is true to some degree but rather that the agent is ignorant of whether α is true or false. The probability reflects the agent's ignorance.

8.1.1   Semantics of Probability

Probability theory is built on the foundation of worlds and variables (page 125). The variables in probability theory are referred to as **random variables**. The term *random variable* is somewhat of a misnomer because it is neither random nor variable. As discussed in Section 4.1 (page 125), worlds could be described in terms of variables; a world is a function that maps each variable to its value. Alternatively, variables could be described in terms of worlds; a variable is a function from worlds into the **domain** of the variable.

Variables will be written starting with an uppercase letter. Each variable has a **domain** which is the set of values that the variable can take. A Boolean variable is a variable with domain {*true,false*}. We will write the assignment of *true* to a variable as the lower-case variant of the variable, e.g., *Happy=true* is written as *happy* and *Fire=true* is *fire*. A **discrete variable** has a domain that is a finite or countable set.

A **primitive proposition** (page 173) is an assignment of a value to a variable, or an inequality between variables and values or between variables (e.g., $A = true$, $X < 7$ or $Y > Z$). Propositions are built from primitive propositions using logical connectives (page 174).

This chapter mainly considers discrete variables with finite domains. The examples will have few variables, but modern applications may have thousands, millions or even billions of variables (or even infinitely many variables). For example, a world could consist of the symptoms, diseases and test results for all of the patients and care providers in a hospital throughout time. The model effectively goes on forever into the future, but we will only ever reason about a finite past and future. We might be able to answer questions about the probability that a patient with a particular combination of symptoms may come into the hospital in the next few years. There are infinitely many worlds whenever some variables have infinite domains or there are infinitely many variables.

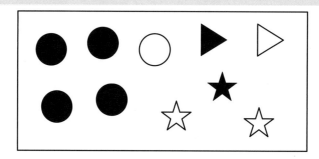

Figure 8.1: Ten worlds described by variables *Filled* and *Shape*

We first define a probability over finite sets of worlds with finitely many variables and use this to define the probability of propositions.

A **probability measure** is a function P from worlds into the non-negative real numbers such that,

$$\sum_{w \in \Omega} P(w) = 1$$

where Ω is the set of all **possible worlds**.

The use of 1 as the probability of the set of all of the worlds is just by convention. You could just as well use 100.

The definition of P is extended to cover propositions. The **probability** of proposition α, written $P(\alpha)$, is the sum of the probabilities of possible worlds in which α is true. That is,

$$P(\alpha) = \sum_{\omega \,:\, \alpha \text{ is true in } \omega} P(\omega).$$

Note that this definition is consistent with the probability of worlds, because if proposition α completely describes a single world, the probability of α and the probability of the world are equal.

Example 8.2 Consider the ten worlds of Figure 8.1, with Boolean variable *Filled*, and with variable *Shape* with domain $\{circle, triangle, star\}$. Each world is defined by its shape, whether it's filled and its position. Suppose the probability of each of these 10 worlds is 0.1, and any other worlds have probability 0. Then $P(Shape{=}circle) = 0.5$ and $P(Filled{=}false) = 0.4$. $P(Shape{=}circle \wedge Filled{=}false) = 0.1$

If X is a random variable, a **probability distribution**, $P(X)$, over X is a function from the domain of X into the real numbers such that, given a value $x \in domain(X)$, $P(x)$ is the probability of the proposition $X{=}x$. A probability distribution over a set of variables is a function from the values of those variables into a probability. For example, $P(X, Y)$ is a probability distribution over

X and Y such that $P(X=x, Y=y)$, where $x \in domain(X)$ and $y \in domain(Y)$, has the value $P(X=x \wedge Y=y)$, where $X=x \wedge Y=y$ is a proposition and P is the function on propositions defined above. Whether P refers to a function on propositions or a probability distribution should be clear from context.

If $X_1 \ldots X_n$ are all of the random variables, then an assignment to all of the random variables corresponds to a world, and the probability of the proposition defining a world is equal to the probability of the world. The distribution over all worlds, $P(X_1, \ldots, X_n)$ is called the **joint probability distribution**.

8.1.2 Axioms for Probability

The preceding section gave a semantic definition of probability. An axiomatic definition specifies axioms. These are axioms one may want for a calculus of belief, and we show they are satisfied by probability.

Suppose P is a function from propositions into real numbers that satisfies the following three **axioms of probability**:

Axiom 1 $0 \le P(\alpha)$ for any proposition α. That is, the belief in any proposition cannot be negative.

Axiom 2 $P(\tau) = 1$ if τ is a tautology. That is, if τ is true in all possible worlds, its probability is 1.

Axiom 3 $P(\alpha \vee \beta) = P(\alpha) + P(\beta)$ if α and β are contradictory propositions; that is, if $\neg(\alpha \wedge \beta)$ is a tautology. In other words, if two propositions cannot both be true (they are mutually exclusive), the probability of their disjunction is the sum of their probabilities.

These axioms are meant to be intuitive properties that we would like to have of any reasonable measure of belief. If a measure of belief follows these intuitive axioms, it is covered by probability theory. Note that empirical frequencies (page 284) – propositions about the proportion of examples in a data set – obey these axioms, and so follow the rules of probability, but that does not mean that all probabilities are empirical frequencies (or obtained from them).

These axioms form a sound and complete axiomatization of the meaning of probability. Soundness means that probability, as defined by the possible-worlds semantics, follows these axioms. Completeness means that any system of beliefs that obeys these axioms has a probabilistic semantics.

Proposition 8.1. *If there are a finite number of finite discrete random variables, Axioms 1, 2, and 3 are sound and complete with respect to the semantics.*

It is easy to check that these axioms are true of the semantics. Conversely, the axioms can be used to compute any probability from the probability of worlds, because the descriptions of two worlds are mutually exclusive. The full proof is left as an exercise. (See Exercise 8.2 (page 416).)

Beyond Finitely Many Worlds

The definition of probability given in this chapter works when there are finitely many worlds.

There are infinitely many worlds when

- the domain of a variable is infinite, for example the domain of a variable *height* might be the set of nonnegative real numbers or

- there are infinitely many variables, for example, there might be a variable for the location of a robot for every millisecond from now infinitely into the future

When there are infinitely many worlds, probability is defined on a measure over sets of worlds. A **probability measure** is a nonnegative function μ from sets of worlds into the real numbers, that satisfies the axioms: $\mu(S_1 \cup S_2) = \mu(S_1) \cup \mu(S_2)$ if $S_1 \cap S_2 = \{\}$, and $\mu(\Omega) = 1$ where Ω is the set of all worlds. μ does not have to be defined over all sets of worlds, just those defined by logical formulas. The probability of proposition α is defined by $P(\alpha) = \mu(\{w : \alpha \text{ is true in } w\})$.

Variables with continuous domains typically do not have a probability distribution, because the probability of a set of worlds can be non-zero even though the measure of each individual world is 0. For variables with real-valued domains, a **probability density function**, written as p, is a function from reals into non-negative reals that integrates to 1. The probability that a real-valued random variable X has value between a and b is given by

$$P(a \leq X \leq b) = \int_a^b p(X)\, \mathrm{d}X.$$

This allows the probability of any formula about intervals and less than to be well defined. It is possible that, for every real number a, $P(X = a) = P(a \leq X \leq a) = 0$.

A **parametric distribution** is one where the probability or density function is described by a formula. Although not all distributions can be described by formulas, all of the ones that are able to be represented are. Sometimes statisticians use the term **parametric** to mean a distribution described using a fixed, finite number of parameters. A **non-parametric distribution** is one where the number of parameters is not fixed. (Oddly, non-parametric typically means "many parameters".)

Another common method is to consider only **discretizations** of finitely many worlds. For example, only consider height to the nearest centimeter or micron, and only consider heights up to some finite number (e.g., a kilometer). Or only consider the location of the robot for a millennium. While there might be a lot of worlds, there are only finitely many. A challenge is to define representations that work for any (fine enough) discretization.

Proposition 8.2. *The following hold for all propositions α and β*

(a) *Negation of a proposition:*

$$P(\neg\alpha) = 1 - P(\alpha).$$

(b) *If $\alpha \leftrightarrow \beta$, then $P(\alpha) = P(\beta)$. That is, logically equivalent propositions have the same probability.*

(c) *Reasoning by cases:*

$$P(\alpha) = P(\alpha \wedge \beta) + P(\alpha \wedge \neg\beta).$$

(d) *If V is a random variable with domain D, then, for all propositions α,*

$$P(\alpha) = \sum_{d \in D} P(\alpha \wedge V = d).$$

(e) *Disjunction for non-exclusive propositions:*

$$P(\alpha \vee \beta) = P(\alpha) + P(\beta) - P(\alpha \wedge \beta).$$

Proof. (a) The propositions $\alpha \vee \neg\alpha$ and $\neg(\alpha \wedge \neg\alpha)$ are tautologies. Therefore, $1 = P(\alpha \vee \neg\alpha) = P(\alpha) + P(\neg\alpha)$. Rearranging gives the desired result.

(b) If $\alpha \leftrightarrow \beta$, then $\alpha \vee \neg\beta$ is a tautology, so $P(\alpha \vee \neg\beta) = 1$. α and $\neg\beta$ are contradictory statements, so Axiom 3 gives $P(\alpha \vee \neg\beta) = P(\alpha) + P(\neg\beta)$. Using part (a), $P(\neg\beta) = 1 - P(\beta)$. Thus, $P(\alpha) + 1 - P(\beta) = 1$, and so $P(\alpha) = P(\beta)$.

(c) The proposition $\alpha \leftrightarrow ((\alpha \wedge \beta) \vee (\alpha \wedge \neg\beta))$ and $\neg((\alpha \wedge \beta) \wedge (\alpha \wedge \neg\beta))$ are tautologies. Thus, $P(\alpha) = P((\alpha \wedge \beta) \vee (\alpha \wedge \neg\beta)) = P(\alpha \wedge \beta) + P(\alpha \wedge \neg\beta)$.

(d) The proof is analogous to the proof of part (c).

(e) $(\alpha \vee \beta) \leftrightarrow ((\alpha \wedge \neg\beta) \vee \beta)$ is a tautology. Thus,

$$\begin{aligned} P(\alpha \vee \beta) &= P((\alpha \wedge \neg\beta) \vee \beta) \\ &= P(\alpha \wedge \neg\beta) + P(\beta). \end{aligned}$$

Part (c) shows $P(\alpha \wedge \neg\beta) = P(\alpha) - P(\alpha \wedge \beta)$. Thus,

$$P(\alpha \vee \beta) = P(\alpha) + P(\beta) - P(\alpha \wedge \beta).$$

$\square$

8.1.3   Conditional Probability

Probability is a measure of belief. Beliefs need to be updated when new evidence is observed.

The measure of belief in proposition h given proposition e is called the **conditional probability** of h **given** e, written $P(h \mid e)$.

A proposition e representing the conjunction of *all* of the agent's **observations** of the world is called **evidence**. Given evidence e, the conditional probability $P(h \mid e)$ is the agent's **posterior probability** of h. The probability $P(h)$ is the **prior probability** of h and is the same as $P(h \mid true)$ because it is the probability before the agent has observed anything.

The evidence used for the posterior probability is *everything* the agent observes about a particular situation. Everything observed, and not just a few select observations, must be conditioned on to obtain the correct posterior probability.

Example 8.3   For the diagnostic assistant, the prior probability distribution over possible diseases is used before the diagnostic agent finds out about the particular patient. Evidence is obtained through discussions with the patient, observing symptoms, and the results of lab tests. Essentially any information that the diagnostic assistant finds out about the patient is evidence. The assistant updates its probability to reflect the new evidence in order to make informed decisions.

Example 8.4   The information that the delivery robot receives from its sensors is its evidence. When sensors are noisy, the evidence is what is known, such as the particular pattern received by the sensor, not that there is a person in front of the robot. The robot could be mistaken about what is in the world but it knows what information it received.

Semantics of Conditional Probability

Evidence e, where e is a proposition, will rule out all possible worlds that are incompatible with e. Like the definition of logical consequence, the given proposition e selects the possible worlds in which e is true. As in the definition of probability, we first define the conditional probability over worlds, and then use this to define a probability over propositions.

Evidence e induces a new probability $P(w \mid e)$ of world w given e. Any world where e is false has conditional probability 0, and the remaining worlds are normalized so that the probabilities of the worlds sum to 1:

$$P(w \mid e) = \begin{cases} c * P(w) & \text{if} \quad e \text{ is true in world } w \\ 0 & \text{if} \quad e \text{ is false in world } w \end{cases}$$

where c is a constant (that depends on e) that ensures the posterior probability of all worlds sums to 1.

For $P(w \mid e)$ to be a probability measure over worlds for each e:

$$
\begin{aligned}
1 &= \sum_{w} P(w \mid e) \\
&= \sum_{w : e \text{ is true in } w} P(w \mid e) + \sum_{w : e \text{ is false in } w} P(w \mid e) \\
&= \sum_{w : e \text{ is true in } w} c * P(w) + 0 \\
&= c * P(e)
\end{aligned}
$$

Therefore, $c = 1/P(e)$. Thus, the conditional probability is only defined if $P(e) > 0$. This is reasonable, as if $P(e) = 0$, e is impossible.

The conditional probability of proposition h given evidence e is the sum of the conditional probabilities of the possible worlds in which h is true. That is,

$$
\begin{aligned}
P(h \mid e) &= \sum_{w : h \text{ is true in } w} P(w \mid e) \\
&= \sum_{w : h \wedge e \text{ is true in } w} P(w \mid e) + \sum_{w : \neg h \wedge e \text{ is true in } w} P(w \mid e) \\
&= \sum_{w : h \wedge e \text{ is true in } w} \frac{1}{P(e)} * P(w) + 0 \\
&= \frac{P(h \wedge e)}{P(e)}.
\end{aligned}
$$

The last form above is typically given as the definition of conditional probability. Here we have derived it as a consequence of a more basic definition.

> **Example 8.5** As in Example 8.2, consider the worlds of Figure 8.1 (page 346), each with probability 0.1. Given the evidence *Filled=false*, only 4 worlds have a non-zero posterior probability. $P(Shape=circle \mid Filled=false) = 0.25$ and $P(Shape=star \mid Filled=false) = 0.5$.

A **conditional probability distribution**, written $P(X \mid Y)$ where X and Y are variables or sets of variables, is a function of the variables: given a value $x \in domain(X)$ for X and a value $y \in domain(Y)$ for Y, it gives the value $P(X = x \mid Y = y)$, where the latter is the conditional probability of the propositions.

The definition of conditional probability allows the decomposition of a conjunction into a product of conditional probabilities:

Proposition 8.3. *(Chain rule) For any propositions $\alpha_1, \ldots, \alpha_n$:*

$$
\begin{aligned}
P(\alpha_1 \wedge \alpha_2 \wedge \ldots \wedge \alpha_n) = &P(\alpha_1) * \\
&P(\alpha_2 \mid \alpha_1) * \\
&P(\alpha_3 \mid \alpha_1 \wedge \alpha_2) *
\end{aligned}
$$

Background Knowledge and Observation

The difference between background knowledge and observation was described in Section 5.4.1 (page 194). When reasoning with uncertainty, the background model is described in terms of a probabilistic model, and the observations form evidence that must be conditioned on.

Within probability, there are two ways to state that a is true:

- The first is to state that the probability of a is 1 by writing $P(a) = 1$.

- The second is to condition on a, which involves using a on the right-hand side of the conditional bar, as in $P(\cdot \mid a)$.

The first method states that a is true in all possible worlds. The second says that the agent is only interested in worlds where a happens to be true.

Suppose an agent was told about a particular animal:

$$P(\textit{flies} \mid \textit{bird}) = 0.8,$$
$$P(\textit{bird} \mid \textit{emu}) = 1.0,$$
$$P(\textit{flies} \mid \textit{emu}) = 0.001.$$

If the agent determines the animal is an emu, it cannot add the statement $P(\textit{emu}) = 1$. No probability distribution satisfies these four assertions. If emu were true in all possible worlds, it would not be the case that in 0.8 of the possible worlds, the individual flies. The agent, instead, must condition on the fact that the individual is an emu.

To build a probability model, a knowledge base designer takes some knowledge into consideration and builds a probability model based on this knowledge. All knowledge acquired subsequently must be treated as observations that are conditioned on.

Suppose proposition k represents an agent's observations up to some time. The agent's subsequent belief states can be modeled by either of the following:

- construct a probability model for the agent's belief before it had observed k and then condition on the evidence k conjoined with the subsequent evidence e (i.e, for each proposition α use $P(\alpha \mid e \wedge k)$)

- construct a probability model, call it P_k, which models the agent's beliefs after observing k, and then condition on subsequent evidence e (i.e., use $P_k(\alpha \mid e)$ for proposition α).

All subsequent probabilities will be identical no matter which construction was used. Building P_k directly is sometimes easier because the model does not have to cover the cases of when k is false. Sometimes, however, it is easier to build P and condition on k.

What is important is that there is a coherent stage where the probability model is reasonable and every subsequent observation is conditioned on.

$$\vdots$$

$$P(\alpha_n \mid \alpha_1 \wedge \cdots \wedge \alpha_{n-1})$$

$$= \prod_{i=1}^{n} P(\alpha_i \mid \alpha_1 \wedge \cdots \wedge \alpha_{i-1}),$$

where the right-hand side is assumed to be zero if any of the products are zero (even if some of them are undefined).

Note that any theorem about unconditional probabilities can be converted into a theorem about conditional probabilities by adding the same evidence to each probability. This is because the conditional probability measure is a probability measure. For example, case (e) of Proposition 8.2 (page 349) implies $P(\alpha \vee \beta \mid k) = P(\alpha \mid k) + P(\beta \mid k) - P(\alpha \wedge \beta \mid k)$.

Bayes' Rule

An agent using probability updates its belief when it observes new evidence. A new piece of evidence is conjoined to the old evidence to form the complete set of evidence. Bayes' rule specifies how an agent should update its belief in a proposition based on a new piece of evidence.

Suppose an agent has a current belief in proposition h based on evidence k already observed, given by $P(h \mid k)$, and subsequently observes e. Its new belief in h is $P(h \mid e \wedge k)$. Bayes' rule tells us how to update the agent's belief in hypothesis h as new evidence arrives.

Proposition 8.4. *(Bayes' rule) As long as $P(e \mid k) \neq 0$,*

$$P(h \mid e \wedge k) = \frac{P(e \mid h \wedge k) * P(h \mid k)}{P(e \mid k)}.$$

This is often written with the background knowledge k implicit. In this case, if $P(e) \neq 0$, then

$$P(h \mid e) = \frac{P(e \mid h) * P(h)}{P(e)}.$$

$P(e \mid h)$ is the **likelihood** and $P(h)$ is the **prior probability** of the hypothesis h. Bayes' rule states that the **posterior probability** is proportional to the likelihood times the prior.

Proof. The commutativity of conjunction means that $h \wedge e$ is equivalent to $e \wedge h$, and so they have the same probability given k. Using the rule for multiplication in two different ways,

$$P(h \wedge e \mid k) = P(h \mid e \wedge k) * P(e \mid k)$$
$$= P(e \wedge h \mid k) = P(e \mid h \wedge k) * P(h \mid k).$$

The theorem follows from dividing the right-hand sides by $P(e \mid k)$, which is not 0 by assumption.   □

Often, Bayes' rule is used to compare various hypotheses (different h_is). The denominator $P(e \mid k)$ is a constant that does not depend on the particular hypothesis, and so when comparing the relative posterior probabilities of hypotheses, the denominator can be ignored.

To derive the posterior probability, the denominator may be computed by reasoning by cases. If H is an exclusive and covering set of propositions representing all possible hypotheses, then

$$P(e \mid k) = \sum_{h \in H} P(e \wedge h \mid k)$$
$$= \sum_{h \in H} P(e \mid h \wedge k) * P(h \mid k).$$

Thus, the denominator of Bayes' rule is obtained by summing the numerators for all the hypotheses. When the hypothesis space is large, computing the denominator is computationally difficult.

Generally, one of $P(e \mid h \wedge k)$ or $P(h \mid e \wedge k)$ is much easier to estimate than the other. Bayes' rule is used to compute one from the other.

Example 8.6   In medical diagnosis, the doctor observes a patient's symptoms, and would like to know the likely diseases. Thus the doctor would like $P(Disease \mid Symptoms)$. This is difficult to assess as it depends on the context (e.g., some diseases are more prevalent in hospitals). It is typically more easy to assess $P(Symtoms \mid Disease)$ as how the disease gives rise to the symptoms is typically less context dependent. These two are related by Bayes' rule, where the prior probability of the disease, $P(Disease)$, reflects the context.

Example 8.7   The diagnostic assistant may need to know whether the light switch s_1 of Figure 1.8 (page 38) is broken or not. You would expect that the electrician who installed the light switch in the past would not know if it is broken now, but would be able to specify how the output of a switch is a function of whether there is power coming into the switch, the switch position, and the status of the switch (whether it is working, shorted, installed upside-down, etc.). The prior probability for the switch being broken depends on the maker of the switch and how old it is. Bayes' rule lets an agent infer the status of the switch given the prior and the evidence.

Example 8.8   Suppose an agent has information about the reliability of fire alarms. It may know how likely it is that an alarm will work if there is a fire. To determine the probability that there is a fire, given that there is an alarm, Bayes' rule gives:

$$P(fire \mid alarm) = \frac{P(alarm \mid fire) * P(fire)}{P(alarm)}$$

$$= \frac{P(alarm \mid fire) * P(fire)}{P(alarm \mid fire) * P(fire) + P(alarm \mid \neg fire) * P(\neg fire)}$$

where $P(alarm \mid fire)$ is the probability that the alarm worked, assuming that there was a fire. It is a measure of the alarm's reliability. The expression $P(fire)$ is the probability of a fire given no other information. It is a measure of how fire-prone the building is. $P(alarm)$ is the probability of the alarm sounding, given no other information. $P(fire \mid alarm)$ is more difficult to directly represent because it depends, for example, on how much vandalism there is in the neighborhood.

8.1.4   Expected Values

The expected value of a numerical function on worlds is the function's average value, averaged over all possible worlds.

Let f be a function on worlds. f could select the value of one of the random variables, it could be the number of bits used to describe the world, or it could be some measure of how much an agent likes the world.

The **expected value** of f, written $\mathcal{E}_P(f)$, with respect to probability P is

$$\mathcal{E}_P(f) = \sum_{\omega \in \Omega} f(\omega) * P(\omega)$$

Other Possible Measures of Belief

Justifying other measures of belief is problematic. Consider, for example, the proposal that the belief in $\alpha \wedge \beta$ is some function of the belief in α and the belief in β. Such a measure of belief is called **compositional**. To see why this is not sensible, consider the single toss of a fair coin. Compare the case where α is "the coin will land heads", β_1 is "the coin will land tails" and β_2 is "the coin will land heads." The belief in β_1 would be the same as the belief in β_2. But the belief in $\alpha \wedge \beta_1$, which is impossible, is very different from the belief in $\alpha \wedge \beta_2$, which is the same as α.

The conditional probability $P(f \mid e)$ is very different from the probability of the implication $P(e \rightarrow f)$. The latter is the same as $P(\neg e \vee f)$, which is the measure of the interpretations for which f is true or e is false. For example, suppose there is a domain where birds are relatively rare, and non-flying birds are a small proportion of the birds. Here $P(\neg flies \mid bird)$ would be the proportion of birds that do not fly, which would be low. $P(bird \rightarrow \neg flies)$ is the same as $P(\neg bird \vee \neg flies)$, which would be dominated by non-birds and so would be high. Similarly, $P(bird \rightarrow flies)$ would also be high, the probability also being dominated by the non-birds. It is difficult to imagine a situation where the probability of an implication is the kind of knowledge that is appropriate or useful.

One special case is if α is a proposition, and f is the function that has value 1 when α is true, and 0 otherwise, then $\mathcal{E}_P(f) = P(\alpha)$.

Example 8.9 In an electrical domain, if *number_of_broken_switches* is the number of switches broken,

$$\mathcal{E}_P(\textit{number\_of\_broken\_switches})$$

would give the expected number of broken switches given by probability distribution P. If the world acted according to the probability distribution P, this would give the long-run average number of broken switches. If there were three switches, each with a probability of 0.7 being broken, the expected number of broken switches is:

$$0 * 0.3^3 + 1 * 3 * 0.7 * 0.3^2 + 2 * 3 * 0.7^2 * 0.3 + 3 * 0.7^3 = 2.01$$

where 3 is in the middle two products because there are 3 worlds with 1 switch broken, and 3 worlds with 2 switches broken.

In a manner analogous to the semantic definition of conditional probability (page 350), the **conditional expected value** of f conditioned on evidence e, written $\mathcal{E}(f \mid e)$, is

$$\mathcal{E}(f \mid e) = \sum_{\omega \in \Omega} f(\omega) * P(\omega \mid e).$$

Example 8.10 The expected number of broken switches given that light l_1 is not lit is given by

$$\mathcal{E}(\textit{number\_of\_broken\_switches} \mid \neg lit(l_1)).$$

This is obtained by averaging the number of broken switches over all of the worlds in which light l_1 is not lit.

If a variable is Boolean, with *true* represented as 1 and *false* as 0, the expected value is the probability of the variable. Thus any algorithms for expected values can also be used to compute probabilities, and any theorems about expected values are also directly applicable to probabilities.

8.1.5   Information

The **information theory** box on page 280 discussed how to represent information using **bits**. For $x \in domain(X)$, it is possible to build a code that, to identify x uses $- \log_2 P(x)$ bits (or the integer greater than this). The expected number of bits to transmit a value for X is then

$$H(X) = \sum_{x \in domain(X)} -P(X=x) * \log_2 P(X=x)$$

This is the **information content** or **entropy** of random variable X.

[Note that, unlike the notation used elsewhere in the book, H is a function of the variable, not a function of the values of the variable. Thus, for a variable X, the entropy $H(X)$ is a number, unlike $P(X)$ which a function that given a value for X, returns a number.]

The entropy of X given the observation $Y = y$ is

$$H(X \mid Y{=}y) = \sum_x -P(X{=}x \mid Y{=}y) * \log_2 P(X{=}x \mid Y{=}y).$$

Before observing Y, the expectation over Y:

$$H(X \mid Y) = \sum_y P(Y{=}y) * \sum_x -P(X{=}x \mid (Y{=}y) * \log_2 P(X{=}x \mid (Y{=}y)$$

is called **conditional entropy** of X given Y.

For a test that determines the value of Y, the **information gain** from this test is $H(X) - H(X \mid Y)$, which is the number of bits used to describe X minus the expected number of bits to describe X after learning Y. The information gain is never negative.

Example 8.11 Suppose spinning a wheel in a game can produces a number in the set $\{1, 2, \ldots, 8\}$, each with equal probability. Let S be the outcome of a spin. Then $H(S) = -\sum_{i=1}^{8} \frac{1}{8} * \log_2 \frac{1}{8} = 3$ bits.

Suppose there is a sensor G that detects whether the outcome is greater than 6. $G{=}true$ if $H > 6$. Then $H(S \mid G) = -0.25 \log_2 \frac{1}{2} - 0.75 \log_2 \frac{1}{6} = 2.19$. The information gain of G is thus $3 - 2.19 = 0.81$ bits. A fraction of a bit makes sense in that it is possible to design a code that uses 219 bits to predict 100 outcomes.

For an "even" sensor E, where $E{=}true$ if H is even, $H(S \mid E) = -0.5 \log_2 \frac{1}{4} - 0.5 \log_2 \frac{1}{4} = 2$. The information gain of E is thus 1 bit.

The notion of information is used for a number of tasks:

- In diagnosis, an agent could choose a test that provides the most information.

- In decision tree learning (page 285), information theory provides a useful criterion for choosing which property to split on: split on the property that provides the greatest information gain. The elements it must distinguish are the different values in the target concept, and the probabilities are obtained from the proportion of each value in the training set remaining at each node.

- In Bayesian learning (page 512), information theory provides a basis for deciding which is the best model given some data.

8.2   Independence

The axioms of probability are very weak and provide few constraints on allowable conditional probabilities. For example, if there are n binary variables, there are $2^n - 1$ numbers to be assigned to give a complete probability distribution from which arbitrary conditional probabilities can be derived. To determine any probability, you may have to start with an enormous database of probabilities.

A useful way to limit the amount of information required is to assume that each variable only directly depends on a few other variables. This uses assumptions of conditional independence. Not only does it reduce how many numbers are requires to specify a model, but also the independence structure may be exploited for efficient reasoning.

As long as the value of $P(h \mid e)$ is not 0 or 1, the value of $P(h \mid e)$ does not constrain the value of $P(h \mid f \wedge e)$. This latter probability could have any value in the range $[0, 1]$. It is 1 when f implies h, and it is 0 if f implies $\neg h$. A common kind of qualitative knowledge is of the form $P(h \mid e) = P(h \mid f \wedge e)$, which specifies f is irrelevant to the probability of h given that e is observed. This idea applies to random variables, as in the following definition.

Random variable X is **conditionally independent** of random variable Y **given** a set of random variables Zs if

$$P(X \mid Y, Zs) = P(X \mid Zs)$$

whenever the probabilities are well defined. This means that for all $x \in domain(X)$, for all $y \in domain(Y)$, and for all $z \in domain(Zs)$, if $P(Y = y \wedge Zs = z) > 0$,

$$P(X = x \mid Y = y \wedge Zs = z) = P(X = x \mid Zs = z).$$

That is, given a value of each variable in Zs, knowing Y's value does not affect the belief in the value of X.

Example 8.12   Consider a probabilistic model of students and exams. It is reasonable to assume that the random variable *Intelligence* is independent of *Works_hard*, given no observations. If you find that a student works hard, it does not tell you anything about their intelligence.

The answers to the exam (the variable *Answers*) would depend on whether the student is intelligent and works hard. Thus, given *Answers*, *Intelligent* would be dependent on *Works_hard*; if you found someone had insightful answers, and did not work hard, your belief that they are intelligent would go up.

The grade on the exam (variable *Grade*) should depend on the student's answers, not on the intelligence or whether the student worked hard. Thus *Grade* would be independent of *Intelligence* given *Answers*. However, if the answers were not observed, *Intelligence* will affect *Grade* (because highly intelligent students would be expected to have different answers than not so intelligent students); thus *Grade* is dependent on *Intelligence* given no observations.

Reducing the Numbers

Two main approaches are used to overcome the need for so many numbers to specify a probability distribution:

Independence Assume that the knowledge of the truth of one proposition does not affect the agent's belief in another proposition in the context of other propositions.

Maximum entropy or random worlds Assume that probabilities are as uniform as possible given the available information.

The distinction between allowing representations of independence and using maximum entropy or random worlds highlights an important difference between views of a knowledge representation:

- The first view is that a knowledge representation provides a high-level modeling language that lets us model a domain in a reasonably natural way. According to this view, it is expected that knowledge representation designers prescribe how to use the representation language by providing a user manual on how to describe domains of interest.

- The second view is that a knowledge representation should allow someone to add whatever knowledge they may have about a domain. The knowledge representation should fill in the rest in a commonsense manner. According to this view, it is unreasonable for a knowledge representation designer to specify how particular knowledge should be encoded.

Judging a knowledge representation by the wrong criteria does not result in a fair assessment.

A belief network (on the next page) is a representation of a particular independence among variables. Belief networks should be viewed as a modeling language. Many domains are concisely and naturally represented by exploiting the independencies that belief networks compactly represent.

Once the network structure and the domains of the variables for a belief network are defined, which numbers are required (the conditional probabilities) are prescribed. The user cannot simply add arbitrary conditional probabilities but must follow the network's structure. If the numbers required of a belief network are provided and are locally consistent, the whole network will be consistent.

In contrast, the maximum entropy or random worlds approaches infer the most random worlds that are consistent with a probabilistic knowledge base. They form a probabilistic knowledge representation of the second type. For the random worlds approach, any numbers that happen to be available are added and used. However, if you allow someone to add arbitrary probabilities, it is easy for the knowledge to be inconsistent with the axioms of probability. Moreover, it is difficult to justify an answer as correct if the assumptions are not made explicit.

Proposition 8.5. *The following four statements are equivalent, as long as the conditional probabilities are well defined*

1. *X is conditionally independent of Y given Z.*

2. *Y is conditionally independent of X given Z.*

3. $P(X = x \mid Y = y \wedge Z = z) = P(X = x \mid Y = y' \wedge Z = z)$ *for all values x, y, y' and z. That is, in the context that you are given a value for Z, changing the value of Y does not affect the belief in X.*

4. $P(X, Y \mid Z) = P(X \mid Z)P(Y \mid Z)$.

The proof is left as an exercise. See Exercise 8.3 (page 416).

Variables X and Y are **unconditionally independent** if $P(X, Y) = P(X)P(Y)$, that is, if they are conditionally independent given no observations. Note that X and Y being unconditionally independent does not imply they are conditionally independent given some other information Z.

Conditional independence is a useful assumption that is often natural to assess and can be exploited in inference. It is very rare that we would have a table of probabilities of worlds and assess independence numerically.

8.3   Belief Networks

The notion of conditional independence is used to give a concise representation of many domains. The idea is that, given a random variable X, there may be a few variables that directly affect the X's value, in the sense that X is conditionally independent of other variables given these variables. The set of locally affecting variables is called the **Markov blanket**. This locality is exploited in a belief network.

A **belief network** is a directed model of conditional dependence among a set of random variables. The conditional independence in a belief network takes in an ordering of the variables, and results in a directed graph.

To define a belief network on a set of random variables, $\{X_1, \ldots, X_n\}$, first select a total ordering of the variables, say, $X_1, \ldots, X_n$. The chain rule (Proposition 8.3 (page 351)) shows how to decompose a conjunction into conditional probabilities:

$$P(X_1 = v_1 \wedge X_2 = v_2 \wedge \cdots \wedge X_n = v_n)$$
$$= \prod_{i=1}^{n} P(X_i = v_i \mid X_1 = v_1 \wedge \cdots \wedge X_{i-1} = v_{i-1}).$$

Or, in terms of random variables and probability distributions,

$$P(X_1, X_2, \ldots, X_n) = \prod_{i=1}^{n} P(X_i \mid X_1, \ldots, X_{i-1}).$$

Define the **parents** of random variable X_i, written $parents(X_i)$, to be a minimal set of predecessors of X_i in the total ordering such that the other predecessors of X_i are conditionally independent of X_i given $parents(X_i)$. Thus X_i **probabilistically depends on** each of its parents, but is independent of its other predecessors. That is, $parents(X_i) \subseteq \{X_1, \ldots, X_{i-1}\}$ such that

$$P(X_i \mid X_1, \ldots, X_{i-1}) = P(X_i \mid parents(X_i)).$$

When there are multiple minimal sets of predecessors satisfying this condition, any minimal set may be chosen to be the parents. There can be more than one minimal set only when some of the predecessors are deterministic functions of others.

Putting the chain rule and the definition of parents together gives:

$$P(X_1, X_2, \ldots, X_n) = \prod_{i=1}^{n} P(X_i \mid parents(X_i)).$$

The probability over all of the variables, $P(X_1, X_2, \ldots, X_n)$, is called the **joint probability distribution**. A belief network defines a **factorization** of the joint probability distribution into a product of conditional probabilities.

A **belief network**, also called a **Bayesian network**, is an acyclic directed graph (DAG), where the nodes are random variables. There is an arc from each element of $parents(X_i)$ into X_i. Associated with the belief network is a set of conditional probability distributions that specify the conditional probability of each variable given its parents (which includes the prior probabilities of those variables with no parents).

Thus, a belief network consists of

- a DAG, where each node is labeled by a random variable
- a domain for each random variable, and
- a set of conditional probability distributions giving $P(X \mid parents(X))$ for each variable X.

A belief network is acyclic by construction. How the chain rule decomposes a conjunction depends on the ordering of the variables. Different orderings can result in different belief networks. In particular, which variables are eligible to be parents depends on the ordering, as only predecessors in the ordering can be parents. Some of the orderings may result in networks with fewer arcs than other orderings.

Example 8.13 Consider the four variables of Example 8.12 (page 358), with the ordering: *Intelligent, Works_hard, Answers, Grade*. Consider the variables in order. *Intelligent* does not have any predecessors in the ordering, so it has no parents, thus $parents(Intelligent) = \{\}$. *Works_hard* is independent of *Intelligent*, and so it too has no parents. *Answers* depends on both *Intelligent* and *Works_hard*, so

$$parents(Answers) = \{Intelligent, Works\_hard\}.$$

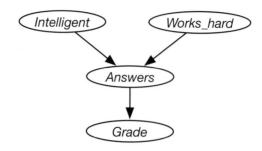

Figure 8.2: Belief network for exam answering of Example 8.13

Grade is independent of *Intelligent* and *Works_hard* given *Answers* and so

$$parents(Grade) = \{Answers\}.$$

The corresponding belief network is given in Figure 8.2.

This graph defines the decomposition of the joint distribution:

$$P(Intelligent, Works\_hard, Answers, Grade)$$
$$= P(Intelligent) * P(Works\_hard) * P(Answers \mid Intelligent, Works\_hard)$$
$$* P(Grade \mid Answers)$$

In the examples below, the domains of the variables are simple, for example the domain of *Answers* may be {*insightful, clear, superficial, vacuous*} or it could be the actual text answers.

The independence of a belief network, according to the definition of parents, is that each variable is independent of all of the variables that are not descendants of the variable (its non-descendants) given the variable's parents.

8.3.1 Observations and Queries

A belief network specifies a joint probability distribution from which arbitrary conditional probabilities can be derived. The most common probabilistic inference task is to compute the **posterior distribution** of a **query variable**, or variables, given some evidence, where the evidence is a conjunction of assignment of values to some of the variables.

Example 8.14   Before there are any observations, the distribution over intelligence is $P(Intelligent)$, which is provided as part of the network. To determine the distribution over grades, $P(Grade)$, requires inference.

If a grade of A is observed, the posterior distribution of *Intelligent* is given by:

$$P(Intelligent \mid Grade{=}A).$$

If it was also observed that *Works_hard* is false, the posterior distribution of *Intelligent* is:

$$P(Intelligent \mid Grade=A \wedge Works\_hard=false).$$

Although *Intelligent* and *Works_hard* are independent given no observations, they are dependent given the grade. This might explain why some people claim they did not work hard to get a good grade; it increases the probability they are intelligent.

8.3.2 Constructing Belief Networks

To represent a domain in a belief network, the designer of a network must consider the following questions:

- What are the relevant variables? In particular, the designer must consider

  - what the agent may observe in the domain. Each feature that may be observed should be a variable, because the agent must be able to condition on all of its observations.

  - what information the agent is interested in knowing the posterior probability of. Each of these features should be made into a variable that can be queried.

  - other **hidden variables** or **latent variables** that will not be observed or queried but make the model simpler. These variables either account for dependencies, reduce the size of the specification of the conditional probabilities, or better model how the world is assumed to work.

- What values should these variables take? This involves considering the level of detail at which the agent should reason to answer the sorts of queries that will be encountered.

  For each variable, the designer should specify what it means to take each value in its domain. What must be true in the world for a (non-hidden) variable to have a particular value should satisfy the **clarity principle** (page 127): an omniscient agent should be able to know the value of a variable. It is a good idea to explicitly document the meaning of all variables and their possible values. The only time the designer may not want to do this for hidden variables whose values the agent will want to learn from data (see Section 10.3.2, (page 509)).

- What is the relationship between the variables? This should be expressed by adding arcs in the graph to define the parent relation.

- How does the distribution of a variable depend on its parents? This is expressed in terms of the conditional probability distributions.

Example 8.15 Suppose you want to use the diagnostic assistant to diagnose whether there is a fire in a building and whether there has been some tampering with equipment based on noisy sensor information and possibly conflicting explanations of what could be going on. The agent receives a report from Sam about whether everyone is leaving the building. Suppose Sam's report is noisy: Sam sometimes reports leaving when there is no exodus (a false positive), and sometimes does not report when everyone is leaving (a false negative). Suppose the leaving only depends on the fire alarm going off. Either tampering or fire could affect the alarm. Whether there is smoke only depends on whether there is fire.

Suppose we use the following variables in the following order:

- *Tampering* is true when there is tampering with the alarm.
- *Fire* is true when there is a fire.
- *Alarm* is true when the alarm sounds.
- *Smoke* is true when there is smoke.
- *Leaving* is true if there are many people leaving the building at once.
- *Report* is true if Sam reports people leaving. *Report* is false if there is no report of leaving.

Assume the following conditional independencies:

- *Fire* is conditionally independent of *Tampering* (given no other information).
- *Alarm* depends on both *Fire* and *Tampering*. That is, we are making no independence assumptions about how *Alarm* depends on its predecessors given this variable ordering.
- *Smoke* depends only on *Fire* and is conditionally independent of *Tampering* and *Alarm* given whether there is a *Fire*.
- *Leaving* only depends on *Alarm* and not directly on *Fire* or *Tampering* or *Smoke*. That is, *Leaving* is conditionally independent of the other variables given *Alarm*.
- *Report* only directly depends on *Leaving*.

The belief network of Figure 8.3 (on the next page) expresses these dependencies. This network represents the factorization

$$P(Tampering, Fire, Alarm, Smoke, Leaving, Report)$$
$$= P(Tampering) * P(Fire) * P(Alarm \mid Tampering, Fire)$$
$$* P(Smoke \mid Fire) * P(Leaving \mid Alarm) * P(Report \mid Leaving).$$

Note that the alarm is not a smoke alarm, which would affected by the smoke, and not directly by the fire, but rather is a heat alarm that is directly

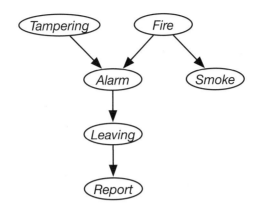

Figure 8.3: Belief network for report of leaving of Example 8.15

affected by the fire. This is made explicit in the model in that the *Alarm* is independent of *Smoke* given *Fire*.

We also must define the domain of each variable. Assume that the variables are Boolean; that is, they have domain {*true, false*}. We use the lower-case variant of the variable to represent the true value and use negation for the false value. Thus, for example, *Tampering = true* is written as *tampering*, and *Tampering = false* is written as ¬*tampering*.

The examples that follow assume the following conditional probabilities:

$P(tampering) = 0.02$ $\qquad P(smoke \mid fire) = 0.9$

$P(fire) = 0.01$ $\qquad P(smoke \mid \neg fire) = 0.01$

$P(alarm \mid fire \wedge tampering) = 0.5$ $\qquad P(leaving \mid alarm) = 0.88$

$P(alarm \mid fire \wedge \neg tampering) = 0.99$ $\qquad P(leaving \mid \neg alarm) = 0.001$

$P(alarm \mid \neg fire \wedge tampering) = 0.85$ $\qquad P(report \mid leaving) = 0.75$

$P(alarm \mid \neg fire \wedge \neg tampering) = 0.0001$ $\quad P(report \mid \neg leaving) = 0.01$

Before any evidence arrives, the probability is given by the priors. The following probabilities follow from the model (all of the numbers here are to about three decimal places):

$P(tampering) = 0.02$

$P(fire) = 0.01$

$P(report) = 0.028$

$P(smoke) = 0.0189$

Observing a report gives the following:

$P(tampering \mid report) = 0.399$

$P(fire \mid report) = 0.2305$

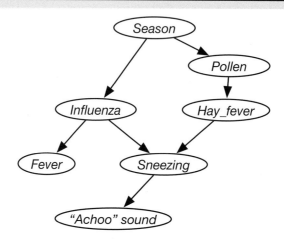

Figure 8.4: Belief network for Example 8.16

$P(smoke \mid report) = 0.215$

As expected, the probabilities of both *tampering* and *fire* are increased by the report. Because the probability of *fire* is increased, so is the probability of *smoke*.
   Suppose instead that *smoke* alone was observed:

$P(tampering \mid smoke) = 0.02$
$P(fire \mid smoke) = 0.476$
$P(report \mid smoke) = 0.320$

Note that the probability of *tampering* is not affected by observing *smoke*; however, the probabilities of *report* and *fire* are increased.
   Suppose that both *report* and *smoke* were observed:

$P(tampering \mid report \wedge smoke) = 0.0284$
$P(fire \mid report \wedge smoke) = 0.964$

Observing both makes *fire* even more likely. However, in the context of the *report*, the presence of *smoke* makes *tampering* less likely. This is because the *report* is **explained away** by *fire*, which is now more likely.
   Suppose instead that *report*, but not *smoke*, was observed:

$P(tampering \mid report \wedge \neg smoke) = 0.501$
$P(fire \mid report \wedge \neg smoke) = 0.0294$

In the context of the *report*, *fire* becomes much less likely and so the probability of *tampering* increases to explain the *report*.
   This example illustrates how the belief net independence assumption gives commonsense conclusions and also demonstrates how explaining away is a consequence of the independence assumption of a belief network.

Example 8.16 Consider the problem of diagnosing why someone is sneezing and perhaps has a fever. Sneezing could be because of influenza or because of hay fever. They are not independent, but are correlated due to the season. Suppose hay fever depends on the season because it depends on the amount of pollen, which in turn depends on the season. The agent does not get to observe sneezing directly, but rather observed just the "Achoo" sound. Suppose fever depends directly on influenza. These dependency considerations lead to the belief network of Figure 8.4.

Example 8.17 Consider the wiring example of Figure 1.8 (page 38). Suppose we decide to have variables for whether lights are lit, for the switch positions, for whether lights and switches are faulty or not, and for whether there is power in the wires. The variables are defined in Figure 8.5 (on the next page).

We order the variables so that each variable has few parents. In this case there seems to be a natural causal order where, for example, the variable for whether a light is lit comes after variables for whether the light is working and whether there is power coming into the light.

Whether light l_1 is lit depends only on whether there is power in wire w_0 and whether light l_1 is working properly. Other variables, such as the position of switch s_1, whether light l_2 is lit, or who is the Queen of Canada, are irrelevant. Thus, the parents of L_1_lit are W_0 and L_1_st.

Consider variable W_0, which represents whether there is power in wire w_0. If we knew whether there was power in wires w_1 and w_2, and we knew the position of switch s_2 and whether the switch was working properly, the value of the other variables (other than L_1_lit) would not affect our belief in whether there is power in wire w_0. Thus, the parents of W_0 should be S_2_Pos, S_2_st, W_1, and W_2.

Figure 8.5 (on the next page) shows the resulting belief network after the independence of each variable has been considered. The belief network also contains the domains of the variables, as given in the figure, and conditional probabilities of each variable given its parents.

For the variable W_1, the following conditional probabilities must be specified:

$$P(W_1 = live \mid S_1\_pos = up \wedge S_1\_st = ok \wedge W_3 = live)$$
$$P(W_1 = live \mid S_1\_pos = up \wedge S_1\_st = ok \wedge W_3 = dead)$$
$$P(W_1 = live \mid S_1\_pos = up \wedge S_1\_st = upside\_down \wedge W_3 = live)$$
$$\vdots$$
$$P(W_1 = live \mid S_1\_pos = down \wedge S_1\_st = broken \wedge W_3 = dead).$$

There are two values for S_1_pos, five values for S_1_ok, and two values for W_3, so there are $2 * 5 * 2 = 20$ different cases where a value for the conditional probability of $W_1 = live$ must be specified. As far as probability theory is concerned, the probability for $W_1 = live$ for these 20 cases could be assigned arbitrarily.

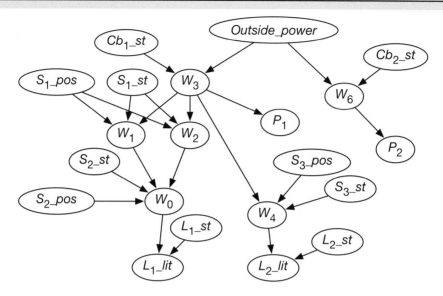

- For each wire w_i, there is a random variable, W_i, with domain $\{live, dead\}$, which denotes whether there is power in wire w_i. $W_i = live$ means wire w_i has power. $W_i = dead$ means there is no power in wire w_i.

- *Outside_power* with domain $\{live, dead\}$ denotes whether there is power coming into the building.

- For each switch s_i, variable S_i_pos denotes the position of s_i. It has domain $\{up, down\}$.

- For each switch s_i, variable S_i_st denotes the state of switch s_i. It has domain $\{ok, upside\_down, short, intermittent, broken\}$. $S_i\_st = ok$ means switch s_i is working normally. $S_i\_st = upside\_down$ means switch s_i is installed upside-down. $S_i\_st = short$ means switch s_i is shorted and acting as a wire. $S_i\_st = broken$ means switch s_i is broken and does not allow electricity to flow.

- For each circuit breaker cb_i, variable Cb_i_st has domain $\{on, off\}$. $Cb_i\_st = on$ means power could flow through cb_i and $Cb_i\_st = off$ means that power could not flow through cb_i.

- For each light l_i, variable L_i_st with domain $\{ok, intermittent, broken\}$ denotes the state of the light. $L_i\_st = ok$ means light l_i will light if powered, $L_i\_st = intermittent$ means light l_i intermittently lights if powered, and $L_i\_st = broken$ means light l_i does not work.

Figure 8.5: Belief network for the electrical domain of Figure 1.8

Of course, knowledge of the domain constrains what values make sense. The values for $W_1 = dead$ can be computed from the values for $W_1 = live$ for each of these cases.

Because the variable S_1_st has no parents, it requires a prior distribution, which can be specified as the probabilities for all but one of the values; the remaining value is derived from the constraint that all of the probabilities sum to 1. Thus, to specify the distribution of S_1_st, four of the following five probabilities must be specified:

$P(S_1\_st = ok)$

$P(S_1\_st = upside\_down)$

$P(S_1\_st = short)$

$P(S_1\_st = intermittent)$

$P(S_1\_st = broken)$

The other variables are represented analogously.

Such a network is used in a number of ways:

- By conditioning on the knowledge that the switches and circuit breakers are ok, and on the values of the outside power and the position of the switches, this network simulates how the lighting should work.

- Given values of the outside power and the position of the switches, the network can infer the probability of any outcome, such as how likely it is that l_1 is lit.

- Given values for the switches and whether the lights are lit, the posterior probability that each switch or circuit breaker is in any particular state can be inferred.

- Given some observations, the network may be used to determine the most likely position of switches.

- Given some switch positions, some outputs, and some intermediate values, the network may be used to determine the probability of any other variable in the network.

Note the independence assumption embedded in this model. The DAG specifies that the lights, switches, and circuit breakers break independently. To model dependencies among how the switches break, you could add more arcs and perhaps more variables. For example, if some lights do not break independently because they come from the same batch, you could add an extra node modeling the batch, and whether it is a good batch or a bad batch, which is made a parent of the L_i_st variables for each light L_i from that batch. The lights now break dependently. When you have evidence that one light is broken, the probability that the batch is bad may increase and thus make it more likely that other lights from that batch are broken. If you are not sure whether the lights are indeed from the same batch, you could add variables representing this, too. The important point is that the belief network provides a specification of independence that lets us model dependencies in a natural and direct manner.

The model implies that there is no possibility of shorts in the wires or that the house is wired differently from the diagram. For example, it implies that w_0 cannot be shorted to w_4 so that wire w_0 gets power from wire w_4. You could add extra dependencies that let each possible short be modeled. An alternative is to add an extra node that indicates that the model is appropriate. Arcs from this node would lead to each variable representing power in a wire and to each light. When the model is appropriate, you could use the probabilities of Example 8.17 (page 367). When the model is inappropriate, you could, for example, specify that each wire and light works at random. When there are weird observations that do not fit in with the original model – they are impossible or extremely unlikely given the model – the probability that the model is inappropriate will increase.

8.4 Probabilistic Inference

The most common probabilistic inference task is to compute the **posterior distribution** of a query variable or variables given some evidence. Unfortunately, even the problem of estimating the posterior probability in a belief network within an absolute error (of less than 0.5), or within a constant multiplicative factor, is NP-hard (page 88), so general efficient implementations will not be available. Computing the prior probability or the posterior probability of a variable is in a complexity class called *#NP* (pronounced "sharp-NP").

The main approaches for probabilistic inference in belief networks are:

Exact inference where the probabilities are computed exactly. A simple way is to enumerate the worlds that are consistent with the evidence. It is possible to do much better than this by exploiting the structure of the network. The variable elimination algorithm is an exact algorithm that uses dynamic programming and exploits conditional independence.

Approximate inference where probabilities are only approximated. These methods are characterized by the different guarantees they provide:

- They produce **guaranteed bounds** on the probabilities. That is, they return a range $[l, u]$ where the exact probability p is guaranteed to have $l \leq p \leq u$. An anytime algorithm may guarantee that l and u get closer to each other as time (and perhaps space) increases.

- They produce **probabilistic bounds** on the error produced. Such algorithms might guarantee that the error, for example, is within 0.1 of the correct answer 95% of the time. They might also have guarantees that, as time increases, probability estimates will converge to the exact probability. Some even have guarantees of the rates of convergence. Stochastic simulation (page 402) is a common method with such guarantees.

Belief Networks and Causality

Belief networks have often been called **causal networks** and provide representation of **causality** that takes noise and probabilities into account. Recall (page 225) that a causal model predicts the result of interventions, where an **intervention** is an action to change the value of a variable using a mechanism outside of the model (e.g., putting a light switch up, or artificially reducing the amount of pollen).

To build a causal model of a domain given a set of random variables, create the arcs as follows. For each pair of random variables X and Y, make X a parent of Y if intervening on X (perhaps in some context of other variables) causes Y to have a different value (even probabilistically), and the effect of X on Y cannot be accounted for by having other variables Z so that X affects Z and Z affects Y. The belief network of Figure 8.5 (page 368) is such a causal network. You would expect that a causal model built in this way would obey the independence assumption of the belief network. Thus, all of the conclusions of the belief network would be valid.

You would also expect such a graph to be acyclic; you do not want something eventually causing itself. This assumption is reasonable if you consider that the random variables represent particular events rather than event types. For example, consider a causal chain that "being stressed" causes you to "work inefficiently," which, in turn, causes you to "be stressed." To break the apparent cycle, we represent "being stressed" at different stages as different random variables that refer to different times. Being stressed in the past causes you to not work well at the moment which causes you to be stressed in the future. The variables should satisfy the **clarity principle** (page 127) and have a well-defined meaning. The variables should not be seen as event types.

The belief network itself has nothing to say about causation, and it can represent non-causal independence, but it seems particularly appropriate for modeling causality. Adding arcs that represent local causality tends to produce a small belief network.

A **causal network** models interventions in the following way. If someone were to artificially force a variable to have a particular value, the variable's descendants – but no other variables – would be affected. In Example 8.16 (page 367), **intervening** to add or remove pollen would affect hay fever, sneezing and the sound, but not the other variables. This contrasts with **observing** pollen which provides evidence of the season, and so the probability of all variables would be affected by the observation.

Finally, see how the causality in belief networks relates to the causal and evidential reasoning discussed in Section 5.8 (page 225). A causal belief network is a way of axiomatizing in a causal direction. Reasoning in belief networks corresponds to abducing to causes and then predicting from these.

- They could make a best effort to produce an approximation that may be good enough, even though there may be cases where they do not work very well. One such class of techniques is called **variational inference**, where the idea is to find an approximation to the problem that is easy to compute. First choose a class of representations that are easy to compute. This class could be as simple as the set of disconnected belief networks (with no arcs). Next try to find a member of the class that is closest to the original problem. That is, find an easy-to-compute distribution that is as close as possible to the posterior distribution to be computed. Thus, the problem reduces to an optimization problem of minimizing the error, followed by a simple inference problem.

This book presents the variable elimination method and some stochastic simulation methods.

8.4.1   Variable Elimination for Belief Networks

The **variable elimination** (VE) algorithm, as used for finding solutions to CSPs (page 141) and for optimization with soft constraints (page 163), can be adapted to find the posterior distribution for a variable in a belief network given conjunctive evidence. Many of the efficient exact methods are variants of this algorithm.

The algorithm is based on the notion that a belief network specifies a factorization of the joint probability distribution (page 361).

Before we provide the algorithm, we define factors and the operations that will be performed on them. Recall that $P(X \mid Y)$ is a function from variables (or sets of variables) X and Y into the real numbers that, given a value for X and a value for Y, returns the conditional probability of the value for X, given the value for Y. A function of variables is called a factor. The VE algorithm for belief networks manipulates factors to compute posterior probabilities.

Conditional Probability Tables

A conditional probability, $P(Y \mid X_1, \ldots, X_k)$ is a function from the variables $Y, X_1, \ldots, X_k$ into non-negative numbers that satisfies the constraints that for each assignment of values to all of $X_1, \ldots, X_k$ the values for Y sum to 1. That is, given values to all of the variables, the function returns a number that satisfies the constraint:

$$\forall x_1 \ldots \forall x_k \sum_{y \in domain(Y)} P(Y{=}y \mid X_1{=}x_1, \ldots, X_k{=}x_k) = 1 \tag{8.1}$$

With a finite set of variables with finite domains, conditional probabilities can be implemented as arrays. If there is an ordering of the variables (e.g.,

Fire	P(smoke | Fire)
true	0.9
false	0.01

Fire	Tampering	P(alarm | Fire, Tampering)
true	true	0.5
true	false	0.99
false	true	0.85
false	false	0.0001

X	Y	P(Z=t | X, Y)
t	t	0.1
t	f	0.2
f	t	0.4
f	f	0.3

Figure 8.6: Conditional probability tables

alphabetical) and the values in the domains are mapped into non-negative integers, there is a unique representation of each factor as a one-dimensional array that is indexed by natural numbers. This representation for a conditional probability is called a **conditional probability table** or **CPT**.

If the child variable is treated the same as the parent variables, the information is redundant; more numbers are specified than is required and a table could be inconsistent if it does not satisfy the above constraint. Using the redundant representation is common, but the following two methods are also used to specify and store probabilities:

- Store **unnormalized probabilities**, which are non-negative numbers that are proportional to the probability. The probability can be computed by normalizing: dividing each value by the sum of the values, summing over all values for the domain of Y.

- Store the probability for all-but-one of the values of Y. In this case, the probability of this other value can be computed to obey the constraint above. In particular, if Y is binary, we only need to represent the probability for one value, say $Y = true$, and the probability for other other value, $Y = false$, can be computed from this.

Example 8.18 Figure 8.6 shows three conditional probabilities tables. On the top left is $P(Smoke \mid Fire)$ and on the top right is $P(Alarm \mid Fire, Tampering)$, from Example 8.15 (page 364), which use Boolean variables.

These tables do not specify the probability for the child being false. This can be computed from the given probabilities, for example,

$$P(Alarm=false \mid Fire=false, Tampering=true) = 1 - 0.85 = 0.15$$

On the bottom is a simple example, with domains $\{t,f\}$, which will be used in the following examples.

Given a total ordering of the parents, such as *Fire* is before *Tampering* in the right table, and a total ordering of the values, such as *true* is before *false*, the table can be specified by giving the array of numbers in lexicographic order, such as $[0.5, 0.99, 0.85, 0.0001]$.

Factors

A **factor** is a function from a set of random variables into a number. A factor f on variables $X_1, \ldots, X_j$ is written as $f(X_1, \ldots, X_j)$. The variables $X_1, \ldots, X_j$ are the variables **of** the factor f, and f is a factor **on** $X_1, \ldots, X_j$.

Conditional probabilities are factors that also obey the constraint of Equation (8.1) (page 372). This section describes some operations on factors, including conditioning, multiplying factors and summing out variables. The operations can be used for conditional probabilities, but do not necessarily result in conditional probabilities.

Suppose $f(X_1, \ldots, X_j)$ is a factor and each v_i is an element of the domain of X_i. $f(X_1 = v_1, X_2 = v_2, \ldots, X_j = v_j)$ is a number that is the value of f when each X_i has value v_i. Some of the variables of a factor can be assigned to values to make a new factor on the other variables. This operation is called **conditioning** on the values of the variables that are assigned. For example, $f(X_1 = v_1, X_2, \ldots, X_j)$, sometimes written as $f(X_1, X_2, \ldots, X_j)_{X_1 = v_1}$, where v_1 is an element of the domain of variable X_1, is a factor on $X_2, \ldots, X_j$.

Example 8.19 Figure 8.7 (on the next page) shows a factor $r(X, Y, Z)$ on variables X, Y and Z as a table. This assumes that each variable is binary with domain $\{t,f\}$. This factor could be obtained from the last conditional probability table given in Figure 8.6. Figure 8.7 also gives a table for the factor $r(X=t, Y, Z)$, which is a factor on Y, Z. Similarly, $r(X=t, Y, Z=f)$ is a factor on Y, and $r(X=t, Y=f, Z=f)$ is a number.

Factors can be multiplied together. Suppose f_1 and f_2 are factors, where f_1 is a factor that contains variables $X_1, \ldots, X_i$ and $Y_1, \ldots, Y_j$, and f_2 is a factor with variables $Y_1, \ldots, Y_j$ and $Z_1, \ldots, Z_k$, where $Y_1, \ldots, Y_j$ are the variables in common to f_1 and f_2. The **product** of f_1 and f_2, written $f_1 * f_2$, is a factor on the union of the variables, namely $X_1, \ldots, X_i, Y_1, \ldots, Y_j, Z_1, \ldots, Z_k$, defined by:

$$(f_1 * f_2)(X_1, \ldots, X_i, Y_1, \ldots, Y_j, Z_1, \ldots, Z_k)$$
$$= f_1(X_1, \ldots, X_i, Y_1, \ldots, Y_j) * f_2(Y_1, \ldots, Y_j, Z_1, \ldots, Z_k).$$

Example 8.20 Figure 8.8 (on the next page) shows the product of $f_1(A, B)$ and $f_2(B, C)$, which is a factor on A, B, C. Note that $(f_1 * f_2)(A=t, B=f, C=f) = f_1(A=t, B=f) * f_2(B=f, C=f) = 0.9 * 0.4 = 0.36$.

X	Y	Z	val
t	t	t	0.1
t	t	f	0.9
t	f	t	0.2
t	f	f	0.8
f	t	t	0.4
f	t	f	0.6
f	f	t	0.3
f	f	f	0.7

$r(X,Y,Z) =$ (above table)

Y	Z	val
t	t	0.1
t	f	0.9
f	t	0.2
f	f	0.8

$r(X=t,Y,Z) =$ (above table)

Y	val
t	0.9
f	0.8

$r(X=t,Y,Z=f) =$ (above table)

$$r(X=t,Y=f,Z=f) = 0.8$$

Figure 8.7: An example factor and assignments

A	B	val
t	t	0.1
t	f	0.9
f	t	0.2
f	f	0.8

$f_1 =$ (above table)

B	C	val
t	t	0.3
t	f	0.7
f	t	0.6
f	f	0.4

$f_2 =$ (above table)

A	B	C	val
t	t	t	0.03
t	t	f	0.07
t	f	t	0.54
t	f	f	0.36
f	t	t	0.06
f	t	f	0.14
f	f	t	0.48
f	f	f	0.32

$f_1 * f_2 =$ (above table)

Figure 8.8: Multiplying factors

The remaining operation is to sum out a variable in a factor. Given factor $f(X_1, \ldots, X_j)$, summing out a variable, say X_1, results in a factor on the other variables, $X_2, \ldots, X_j$, defined by

$$\left(\sum_{X_1} f\right)(X_2, \ldots, X_j) = f(X_1 = v_1, X_2, \ldots, X_j) + \cdots + f(X_1 = v_k, X_2 \ldots, X_j),$$

where $\{v_1, \ldots, v_k\}$ is the set of possible values of variable X_1.

Example 8.21 Figure 8.9 (on the next page) gives an example of summing out variable B from a factor $f_3(A, B, C)$, which is a factor on A, C. Notice how

$$\left(\sum_B f_3\right)(A = t, C = f) = f_3(A = t, B = t, C = f) + f_3(A = t, B = f, C = f)$$

$$= 0.07 + 0.36$$

$$= 0.43$$

$$
f_3 =
\begin{array}{ccc|c}
A & B & C & \text{val} \\
\hline
t & t & t & 0.03 \\
t & t & f & 0.07 \\
t & f & t & 0.54 \\
t & f & f & 0.36 \\
f & t & t & 0.06 \\
f & t & f & 0.14 \\
f & f & t & 0.48 \\
f & f & f & 0.32 \\
\end{array}
\qquad
\sum_B f_3 =
\begin{array}{cc|c}
A & C & \text{val} \\
\hline
t & t & 0.57 \\
t & f & 0.43 \\
f & t & 0.54 \\
f & f & 0.46 \\
\end{array}
$$

Figure 8.9: Summing out a variable from a factor

Variable Elimination

Given evidence $Y_1 = v_1, \ldots, Y_j = v_j$, and query variable or variables Q, the problem of computing the posterior distribution on Q can be reduced to the problem of computing the probability of conjunctions:

$$
\begin{aligned}
P(Q \mid Y_1 = v_1, \ldots, Y_j = v_j) &= \frac{P(Q, Y_1 = v_1, \ldots, Y_j = v_j)}{P(Y_1 = v_1, \ldots, Y_j = v_j)} \\
&= \frac{P(Q, Y_1 = v_1, \ldots, Y_j = v_j)}{\sum_Q P(Q, Y_1 = v_1, \ldots, Y_j = v_j)}.
\end{aligned}
$$

The algorithm computes the factor $P(Q, Y_1 = v_1, \ldots, Y_j = v_j)$ and normalizes. Note that this is a factor only of Q; given a value for Q, it returns a number that is the probability of the conjunction of the evidence and the value for Q.

Suppose the variables of the belief network are $X_1, \ldots, X_n$. To compute the factor $P(Q, Y_1 = v_1, \ldots, Y_j = v_j)$, sum out the other variables from the joint distribution. Suppose $Z_1, \ldots, Z_k$ is an enumeration of the other variables in the belief network, that is,

$$
\{Z_1, \ldots, Z_k\} = \{X_1, \ldots, X_n\} \setminus \{Q, Y_1, \ldots, Y_j\}
$$

and the variables Z_i are ordered according to an **elimination ordering**.

The probability of Q conjoined with the evidence is

$$
p(Q, Y_1 = v_1, \ldots, Y_j = v_j) = \sum_{Z_k} \cdots \sum_{Z_1} P(X_1, \ldots, X_n)_{Y_1 = v_1, \ldots, Y_j = v_j}.
$$

By the chain rule (page 351) and the definition of a belief network,

$$
P(X_1, \ldots, X_n) = \prod_{i=1}^{n} P(X_i \mid parents(X_i))
$$

where $parents(X_i)$ is the set of parents of variable X_i.

The belief network inference problem is thus reduced to a problem of summing out a set of variables from a product of factors. The distribution law specifies that a sum of products such as $xy + xz$, can be simplified by distributing out the common factors (here x), which results in $x(y + z)$. The resulting form is more efficient to compute. Distributing out common factors is the essence of the VE algorithm. The elements multiplied together are called "factors" because of the use of the term in algebra. Initially, the factors represent the conditional probability distributions, but the intermediate factors are just functions on variables created by adding and multiplying factors.

To compute the posterior distribution of a query variable given observations

1. Construct a factor for each conditional probability distribution.

2. Eliminate each of the non-query variables:

   - if the variable is observed, its value is set to the observed value in each of the factors in which the variable appears,

   - otherwise the variable is summed out.

3. Multiply the remaining factors and normalize.

To sum out a variable Z from a product $f_1, \ldots, f_k$ of factors, first partition the factors into those not containing Z, say $f_1, \ldots, f_i$, and those containing Z, $f_{i+1}, \ldots, f_k$; then distribute the common factors out of the sum:

$$\sum_Z f_1 * \cdots * f_k = f_1 * \cdots * f_i * \left(\sum_Z f_{i+1} * \cdots * f_k \right).$$

VE explicitly constructs a representation (in terms of a multidimensional array, a tree, or a set of rules) of the rightmost factor.

Figure 8.10 (on the next page) gives pseudocode for the VE algorithm. The elimination ordering could be given a priori or computed on the fly. It is worthwhile to select observed variables first in the elimination ordering, because eliminating these simplifies the problem.

This algorithm assumes that the query variable is not observed. If it is observed to have a particular value, its posterior probability is just 1 for the observed value and 0 for the other values.

Example 8.22 Consider Example 8.15 (page 364) with the query

$P(\textit{Tampering} \mid \textit{Smoke} = \textit{true} \wedge \textit{Report} = \textit{true}).$

1: **procedure** $VE\_BN(Vs, Ps, e, Q)$
2:     **Inputs**
3:         Vs: set of variables
4:         Ps: set of factors representing the conditional probabilities
5:         e: the evidence, a variable-value assignment to some of the variables
6:         Q: a query variable
7:     **Output**
8:         posterior distribution on Q
9:     $Fs := Ps$ ▷ Fs is the current set of factors
10:    **for each** $X \in Vs - \{Q\}$ using some elimination ordering **do**
11:        **if** X is observed **then**
12:            **for each** $F \in Fs$ that involves X **do**
13:                **assign** X in F to its observed value in e
14:        **else**
15:            $Rs := \{F \in Fs : F$ involves $X\}$
16:            let T be the product of the factors in Rs
17:            $N := \sum_X T$
18:            $Fs := Fs \setminus Rs \cup \{N\}$
19:        let T be the product of the factors in Fs
20:        $N := \sum_Q T$
21:        **return** T/N

Figure 8.10: Variable elimination for belief networks

Suppose it first eliminates the observed variables, *Smoke* and *Report*. After these are eliminated, the following factors remain:

ConditionalProbability	Factor
$P(Tampering)$	$f_0(Tampering)$
$P(Fire)$	$f_1(Fire)$
$P(Alarm \mid Tampering, Fire)$	$f_2(Tampering, Fire, Alarm)$
$P(Smoke = yes \mid Fire)$	$f_3(Fire)$
$P(Leaving \mid Alarm)$	$f_4(Alarm, Leaving)$
$P(Report = yes \mid Leaving)$	$f_5(Leaving)$

Suppose *Fire* is next in the elimination ordering. To eliminate *Fire*, collect all of the factors containing *Fire*, namely $f_1(Fire)$, $f_2(Tampering, Fire, Alarm)$, and $f_3(Fire)$, multiply them together, and sum out *Fire* from the resulting factor. Call this factor $F_6(Tampering, Alarm)$. At this stage, Fs contains the factors:

$$f_0(Tampering), f_4(Alarm, Leaving), f_5(Leaving), f_6(Tampering, Alarm).$$

Suppose *Alarm* is eliminated next. VE multiplies the factors containing *Alarm* and sums out *Alarm* from the product, giving a factor, call it f_7:

$$f_7(Tampering, Leaving) = \sum_{Alarm} f_4(Alarm, Leaving) * f_6(Tampering, Alarm)$$

Fs then contains the factors:

$$f_0(Tampering), f_5(Leaving), f_7(Tampering, Leaving).$$

Eliminating *Leaving* results in the factor

$$f_8(Tampering) = \sum_{Leaving} f_5(Leaving) * f_7(Tampering, Leaving).$$

To determine the distribution over *Tampering*, multiply the remaining factors, giving

$$f_9(Tampering) = f_0(Tampering) * f_8(Tampering).$$

The posterior distribution over tampering is given by

$$\frac{f_9(Tampering)}{\sum_{Tampering} f_9(Tampering)}.$$

Note that the denominator is the prior probability of the evidence, namely $P(Smoke = true \wedge Report = true)$

Example 8.23   Consider the same network as in the previous example but with the following query:

$$P(Alarm \mid Fire{=}true).$$

When *Fire* is eliminated, the factor $P(Fire)$ becomes a factor of no variables; it is just a number, $P(Fire{=}true)$.

Suppose *Report* is eliminated next. It is in one factor, which represents $P(Report \mid Leaving)$. Summing over all of the values of *Report* gives a factor on *Leaving*, all of whose values are 1. This is because $P(Report{=}true \mid Leaving{=}v) + P(Report{=}false \mid Leaving{=}v) = 1$ for any value v of *Leaving*.

If *Leaving* is eliminated next, a factor that is all 1 is multiplied by a factor representing $P(Leaving \mid Alarm)$ and *Leaving* is summed out. This, again, results in a factor all of whose values are 1.

Similarly, eliminating *Smoke* results in a factor of no variables, whose value is 1. Note that even if smoke had also been observed, eliminating *Smoke* would result in a factor of no variables, which would not affect the posterior distribution on *Alarm*.

Eventually, there is only the factor on *Alarm* that represents its prior probability and a constant factor that will cancel in the normalization.

To speed up the inference, variables that are irrelevant to answer a query given the observations can be **pruned**. In particular, any node that has no observed or queried descendants and is itself not observed or queried may be pruned. This may result in a smaller network with fewer factors and variables.

For example, to compute $P(Alarm \mid Fire=true)$, the variables *Report*, *Leaving* and *Smoke* may be pruned.

The complexity of the algorithm depends on a measure of complexity of the network. The size of a tabular representation of a factor is exponential in the number of variables in the factor. The **treewidth** of a network, given an elimination ordering, is the maximum number of variables in a factor created by summing out a variable when using the elimination ordering. The **treewidth** of a belief network is the minimum treewidth over all elimination orderings. The treewidth depends only on the graph structure and is a measure of the sparseness of the graph. The complexity of VE is exponential in the treewidth and linear in the number of variables. Finding the elimination ordering with minimum treewidth is NP-hard, but there are some good elimination ordering heuristics, as discussed for CSP VE (page 144).

Example 8.24   Consider the belief network of Figure 8.4 (page 366). To compute the probability of *Sneezing*, the variables *Fever* and *"Achoo"sound* may be pruned, as they have no children and are not observed or queried. Summing out *Season* involves multiplying the factors

$$P(Season), P(Pollen \mid Season), P(Influenza \mid Season)$$

and results in a factor on *Influenza* and *Pollen*. The treewidth of this belief network is two; there is an ordering of the variables that only constructs factors of size one or two, and there is no ordering of the variables that has a smaller treewidth.

The **moral graph** of a belief network is the undirected graph where there is an arc between any two nodes that appear in the same initial factor. This is obtained by "marrying" the parents of a node, and removing the directions. If we prune as outlined in the previous paragraph, moralize the graph, and remove all observed variables, only those variables connected to the query in this graph are relevant to answering the query. The other variables can be pruned.

Many modern exact algorithms use what is essentially variable elimination, and they speed it up by preprocessing as much as possible into a secondary structure before any evidence arrives. This is appropriate when, for example, the same belief network may be used for many different queries, and where observations are added incrementally. The algorithms save intermediate results so that evidence is incrementally added. Unfortunately, extensive preprocessing, allowing arbitrary sequences of observations and deriving the posterior on each variable, precludes pruning the network. So for each application you need to choose whether you will save more by pruning irrelevant variables for each query and observation or by preprocessing before you have any observations.

8.4.2 Representing Conditional Probabilities and Factors

A conditional probability distribution is a function on variables; given an assignment to the values of the variables, it gives a number. A **factor** is a function of a set of variables; the variables it depends on are the **scope** of the factor. Thus a conditional probability is a factor, as it is a function on variables. This section explores some variants for representing factors and conditional probabilities. Some of the representations are for arbitrary factors and some are specific to conditional probabilities.

Factors do not have to be implemented as conditional probability tables (page 373). The resulting tabular representation is often too large when there are many parents. Often, structure in conditional probabilities can be exploited.

One such structure exploits **context-specific independence**, where one variable is conditionally independent of another, given a particular value of the third variable.

Example 8.25 Suppose a robot can go outside or get coffee (so the *Action* has domain {*go_out*, *get_coffee*}. Whether it gets wet (variable *Wet*) depends on whether there is rain (variable *Rain*) in the context that it went out or on whether the cup was full (variable *Full*) if it got coffee. Thus *Wet* is independent of *Rain* given *Action=get_coffee*, but is dependent on *Rain* given *Action=go_out*. Also, *Wet* is independent of *Full* given *Action=go_out*, but is dependent on *Full* given *Action=get_coffee*.

Context-specific independence may be exploited in a representation by not requiring numbers that are not needed. A simple representation for conditional probabilities that models context-specific independence is a **decision tree** (page 285), where the parents in a belief network correspond to the input features and the child corresponds to the target feature. Another representation is in terms of definite clauses (page 182) with probabilities. Context-specific independence could also be represented as tables that have contexts that specify when they should be used, as in the following example.

Example 8.26 The conditional probability $P(Wet \mid Action, Rain, Full)$ could be represented as a decision tree, as definite clauses with probabilities, or as tables with contexts:

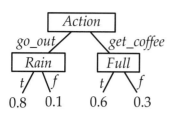

Rain	Wet	Prob
t	t	0.8
t	f	0.2
f	t	0.1
f	f	0.9

go_out :

Full	Wet	Prob
t	t	0.6
t	f	0.4
f	t	0.3
f	f	0.7

get_coffee :

$$wet \leftarrow go\_out \wedge rain : 0.8$$
$$wet \leftarrow go\_out \wedge \neg rain : 0.1$$
$$wet \leftarrow get\_coffee \wedge full : 0.6$$
$$wet \leftarrow get\_coffee \wedge \neg full : 0.3$$

Another common representation is a **noisy-or**, where the child is true if one of the parents is activated and each parent has a probability of activation. So the child is an "or" of the activations of the parents. The noisy-or is defined as follows. If X has Boolean parents $V_1, \ldots, V_k$, the probability is defined by $k+1$ parameters $p_0, \ldots, p_k$. We invent k new Boolean variables $A_0, A_1, \ldots, A_k$, where for each $i > 0$, A_i has V_i as its only parent. Define $P(A_i{=}true \mid V_i{=}true) = p_i$ and $P(A_i{=}true \mid V_i{=}false) = 0$. The bias term, A_0 has $P(A_0) = p_0$. The variables $A_0, \ldots, A_k$ are the parents of X, and the conditional probability is that $P(X \mid A_0, A_1, \ldots, A_k)$ is 1 if any of the A_i are true and is 0 if all of the A_i are false. Thus p_0 is the probability of X when all of V_i are false; the probability of X increases if more of the V_i become true.

Example 8.27 Suppose the robot could get wet from rain or coffee. There is a probability that it gets wet from rain if it rains, and a probability that it gets wet from coffee if it has coffee, and a probability that it gets wet for other reasons. The robot gets wet if it gets wet from one of them, giving the "or". We could have, $P(wet\_from\_rain \mid rain) = 0.3$, $P(wet\_from\_coffee \mid coffee) = 0.2$ and, for the bias term, $P(wet\_for\_other\_reasons) = 0.1$. The robot is wet if it wet from rain, wet from coffee, or wet for other reasons.

A **log-linear model** is a model where probabilities are specified as a product of terms. When the terms are non-zero (they are all strictly positive), the log of a product is the sum of logs. The sum of terms is often a convenient term to work with. To see how such a form is used to represent conditional probabilities, we can write the conditional probability in the following way:

$$P(h \mid e) = \frac{P(h \wedge e)}{P(h \wedge e) + P(\neg h \wedge e)}$$
$$= \frac{1}{1 + P(\neg h \wedge e)/P(h \wedge e)}$$

$$= \frac{1}{1 + e^{-(\log P(h \wedge e)/P(\neg h \wedge e))}}$$
$$= sigmoid(\log odds(h \mid e))$$

- The **sigmoid function**, $sigmoid(x) = 1/(1 + e^{-x})$, plotted in Figure 7.9 (page 294), has been used previously in this book for logistic regression (page 295) and neural networks (page 311).

- The **conditional odds** (as often used by bookmakers in gambling) is

$$odds(h \mid e) = \frac{P(h \wedge e)}{P(\neg h \wedge e)}$$
$$= \frac{P(e \mid h)}{P(e \mid \neg h)} * \frac{P(h)}{P(\neg h)}$$

where $\frac{P(h)}{P(\neg h)} = \frac{P(h)}{1-P(h)}$ is the **prior odds** and $\frac{P(e|h)}{P(e|\neg h)}$ is the **likelihood ratio**. For a fixed h, it is often useful to represent $P(e \mid h)/P(e \mid \neg h)$ as a product of terms, and so the log is a sum of terms.

The **logistic regression** (page 295) model of a conditional probability $P(X \mid Y_1, \ldots, Y_k)$ is of the form

$$P(x \mid Y_1, \ldots, Y_k) = sigmoid\left(\sum_i w_i * Y_i\right)$$

where Y_i is assumed to have domain $\{0, 1\}$. (Assume a dummy input Y_0 which is always 1.) This corresponds to a decomposition of the conditional probability, where the probabilities are a product of terms for each Y_i.

Note that $P(X \mid Y_1=0, \ldots, Y_k=0) = sigmoid(w_0)$. Thus w_0 determines the probability when all of the parents are zero. Each w_i specifies a value that should be added as Y_i changes. If Y_i is Boolean with values $\{0, 1\}$, then $P(X \mid Y_1-0, \ldots, Y_i-1, \ldots, Y_k=0) = sigmoid(w_0 \mid w_i)$. The logistic regression model makes the independence assumption that the influence of each parent on the child does not depend on the other parents. Learning logistic regression models was the topic of Section 7.3.2 (page 291).

Example 8.28 To represent the probability of *wet* given whether there is rain, coffee, kids, or whether the robot has a coat may be given by:

$P(wet \mid Rain, Coffee, Kids, Coat)$
$\quad = sigmoid(-1.0 + 2.0 * Rain + 1.0 * Coffee + 0.5 * Kids - 1.5 * Coat)$

This implies the following conditional probabilities

$\quad P(wet \mid \neg rain \wedge \neg coffee \wedge \neg kids \wedge \neg coat) = sigmoid(-1.0) = 0.27.$

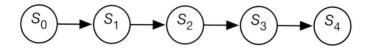

Figure 8.11: A Markov chain as a belief network

$P(wet \mid rain \land \neg coffee \land \neg kids \land \neg coat) = sigmoid(1.0) = 0.73.$
$P(wet \mid rain \land \neg coffee \land \neg kids \land coat) = sigmoid(-0.5) = 0.38.$

This requires fewer parameters than the $2^4 = 16$ parameters required for a tabular representation, but makes more independence assumptions.

Noisy-or and logistic regression models are similar, but different. Noisy-or is typically used when the causal assumption that a variable is true if it is caused to be true by one of the parents, is appropriate. Logistic regression is used when the various parents add-up to influence the child.

8.5 Sequential Probability Models

Special types of belief networks with repeated structure are used for reasoning about time and other sequences, such as sequences of words in a sentence. Such probabilistic models may have an unbounded number of random variables. Reasoning with time is essential for agents in the world. Reasoning about sentences with unbounded size is important for understanding language.

8.5.1 Markov Chains

A **Markov chain** is a belief network with random variables in a sequence, where each variable only directly depends on its predecessor in the sequence. Markov chains are used to represent sequences of values, such as the sequence of states in a dynamic system or the sequence of words in a sentence. Each point in the sequence is called **stage**.

Figure 8.11 shows a generic Markov chain as a belief network. The network has 5 stages, but does not have to stop at stage 4; it can extend indefinitely. The belief network conveys the independence assumption

$$P(S_{i+1} \mid S_0, \ldots, S_i) = P(S_{i+1} \mid S_i),$$

which is called the **Markov assumption**.

Often the sequences are in time and, S_t represents the **state** at time t. Intuitively, S_t conveys all of the information about the history that could affect the future states. The independence assumption of the Markov chain can be seen as "the future is conditionally independent of the past given the present."

A Markov chain is a **stationary model** or **time-homogenous model** if the variables all have the same domain, and the transition probabilities are the same for each stage, i.e.,

for all $i \geq 0$, $P(S_{i+1} \mid S_i) = P(S_1 \mid S_0)$

To specify a stationary Markov chain, two conditional probabilities are provided:

- $P(S_0)$ specifies the initial conditions
- $P(S_{i+1} \mid S_i)$ specifies the **dynamics**, which is the same for each $i \geq 0$.

Stationary Markov chains are of interest for the following reasons:

- They provide a simple model that is easy to specify.
- The assumption of stationarity is often the natural model, because the dynamics of the world typically does not change in time. If the dynamics does change in time, it is usually because of some other feature that could also be modeled.
- The network extends indefinitely. Specifying a small number of parameters gives an infinite network. You can ask queries or make observations about any arbitrary points in the future or the past.

To determine the probability distribution of state S_i, variable elimination can be used to sum out the preceding variables. The variables after S_i are irrelevant to the probability of S_i and need not be considered. To compute $P(S_i \mid S_k)$, where $i > k$, only the variables between S_i and S_k need to be considered, and if $i < k$, only the variables less than k need to be considered.

A **stationary distribution** of a Markov chain is a distribution of the states such that if it holds at one time, it holds at the next time. Thus P is a stationary distribution if for each state s, $P(S_{t+1}{=}s) = P(S_t{=}s)$. Thus,

$$P(S_i{=}s) = \sum_{S_i} P(S_{i+1}{=}s \mid S_i) * P(S_i)$$

A Markov chain is **ergodic** if, for any two states s_1 and s_2 in the domain of S_i, there is a non-zero probability of eventually reaching s_2 from s_1. A Markov chain is **periodic** with period p if the difference between the times when it visits the same state is always divisible by p. For example, consider the Markov chain with states the integers 0 to 9, and at each time it either adds 1 or adds 9 (modulo 10), each with probability 0.5. This Markov chain is periodic with period 2; if it starts in an even state at time 0, it will be in an even state at even times, and in an odd state at odd times. If the only period of a Markov chain is a period of 1, then the Markov chain is **aperiodic**.

$\boxed{\text{Pagerank}}$

Google's initial search engine [Brin and Page, 1998] was based on **Pagerank**. Pagerank [Page et al., 1999] is a probability measure over web pages where the most influential web pages have the highest probability. It is based on a Markov chain of a random web surfer who starts on a random page, and with some probability d picks a random page that is linked from the current page, and otherwise (if the current page has no outgoing links or with probability $1 - d$) picks a page at random. The Markov chain is defined as follows:

- The domain of S_i is the set of all web pages.

- $P(S_0)$ is the uniform distribution of web pages: $P(S_0 = p_j) = 1/N$ for each web page p_j, where N is the number of web pages.

- The transition is defined as follows:

$$P(S_{i+1} = p_j \mid S_i = p_k)$$

$$= (1-d)/N + d * \begin{cases} 1/n_k & \text{if } p_k \text{ links to } p_j \\ 1/N & \text{if } p_k \text{ has no links} \\ 0 & \text{otherwise} \end{cases}$$

  where there are N web pages and there n_k links on page p_k. The way to think about this is that p_k is the current web page, and p_j is the next web page. If p_k has no outgoing links, then p_j is a page at random, which is the effect of the middle case. If p_k has outgoing links, with probability d the surfer picks a random page linked from p_k, and otherwise picks a page at random.

- $d \approx 0.85$ is the probability someone picks a link on the current page.

This Markov chain converges to a distribution over web pages. Page et al. [1999] reported the search engine had converged to "a reasonable tolerance" for $i = 52$ with 322 million links.

Pagerank provides a measure of influence. To get a high Pagerank, a web page should be linked from other pages with a high Pagerank. It is difficult, yet not impossible, to manipulate Pagerank for selfish reasons. One could try to artificially boost Pagerank for a specific page, by creating many pages that point to that page, but it is difficult for those referring pages to also have a high pagerank.

In the initial reported version, Brin and Page [1998] used 24 million web pages and 76 million links. The web is more complex now with many pages being dynamically generated, and search engines use much more sophisticated algorithms.

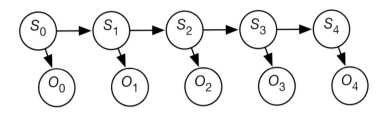

Figure 8.12: A hidden Markov model as a belief network

If a Markov chain is ergodic and aperiodic, then there is a unique stationary distribution, and this is the **equilibrium distribution** that will be approached from any starting state. Thus for any distribution over S_0, the distribution over S_i will get closer and closer to the equilibrium distribution, as i gets larger.

8.5.2 Hidden Markov Models

A **hidden Markov model (HMM)** is an augmentation of a Markov chain to include observations. A hidden Markov model includes the state transition of the Markov chain, and adds to it observations at each time that depend on the state at the time. These observations can be **partial** in that different states map to the same observation and **noisy** in that the same state stochastically maps to different observations at different times.

The assumptions behind an HMM are:

- The state at time $t + 1$ only directly depends on the state at time t for $t \geq 0$, as in the Markov chain.

- The observation at time t only directly depends on the state at time t.

The observations are modeled using the variable O_t for each time t whose domain is the set of possible observations. The belief network representation of an HMM is depicted in Figure 8.12. Although the belief network is shown for five stages, it extends indefinitely.

A stationary HMM includes the following probability distributions:

- $P(S_0)$ specifies initial conditions
- $P(S_{t+1} \mid S_t)$ specifies the dynamics
- $P(O_t \mid S_t)$ specifies the sensor model.

Example 8.29 Suppose you want to keep track of an animal in a triangular enclosure using sound. You have three microphones that provide unreliable (noisy) binary information at each time step. The animal is either near one of the 3 vertices of the triangle or close to the middle of the triangle. The state has domain $\{m, c_1, c_2, c_3\}$ where m means the animal is in the middle and c_i means the animal is in corner i.

The dynamics of the world is a model of how the state at one time depends on the previous time. If the animal is in a corner it stays in the same corner with probability 0.8, goes to the middle with probability 0.1 or goes to one of the other corners with probability 0.05 each. If it is in the middle, it stays in the middle with probability 0.7, otherwise it moves to one of the corners, each with probability 0.1.

The sensor model specifies the probability of detection by each microphone given the state. If the animal is in a corner, it will be detected by the microphone at that corner with probability 0.6, and will be independently detected by each of the other microphones with a probability of 0.1. If the animal is in the middle, it will be detected by each microphone with a probability of 0.4.

Initially the animal is in one of the four states, with equal probability.

There are a number of tasks that are common for HMMs.

The problem of **filtering** or belief-state **monitoring** is to determine the current state based on the current and previous observations, namely to determine

$$P(S_i \mid O_0, \ldots, O_i).$$

All state and observation variables after S_i are irrelevant because they are not observed and can be ignored when this conditional distribution is computed.

Example 8.30 Consider filtering for Example 8.29.

The following table gives the observations for each time, and the resulting state distribution. There are no observations at time 0.

Time	Observation			Posterior State Distribution			
	Mic#1	Mic#2	Mic#3	$P(m)$	$P(c_1)$	$P(c_2)$	$P(c_3)$
0	–	–	–	0.25	0.25	0.25	0.25
1	0	1	1	0.46	0.019	0.26	0.26
2	1	0	1	0.64	0.084	0.019	0.26

Thus, even with only two time steps of noisy observations from initial ignorance, it is very sure that the animal is not at corner 1 or corner 2. It is most likely that the animal is in the middle.

Note that the posterior at any time only depended on the observations up to that time. Filtering does not take into account future observations that provide more information about the initial state.

The problem of **smoothing** is to determine a state based on past and future observations. Suppose an agent has observed up to time k and wants to determine the state at time i for $i < k$; the smoothing problem is to determine

$$P(S_i \mid O_0, \ldots, O_k).$$

All of the variables S_i and V_i for $i > k$ can be ignored.

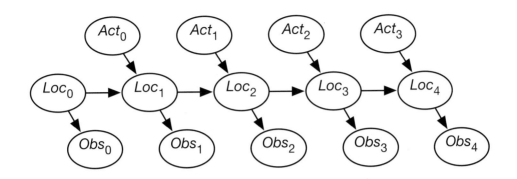

Figure 8.13: A belief network for localization

Localization

Suppose a robot wants to determine its location based on its history of actions and its sensor readings. This is the problem of **localization**. Figure 8.13 shows a belief-network representation of the localization problem. There is a variable Loc_i for each time i, which represents the robot's location at time i. There is a variable Obs_i for each time i, which represents the robot's observation made at time i. For each time i, there is a variable Act_i that represents the robot's action at time i. In this section, assume that the robot's actions are observed. (The case in which the robot chooses its actions is discussed in Chapter 9).

This model assumes the following dynamics: At time i, the robot is at location Loc_i, it observes Obs_i, then it acts, it observes its action Act_i, and time progresses to time $i + 1$, where it is at location Loc_{i+1}. Its observation at time t only depends on the state at time t. The robot's location at time $t + 1$ depends on its location at time t and its action at time t. Its location at time $t + 1$ is conditionally independent of previous locations, previous observations, and previous actions, given its location at time t and its action at time t.

The localization problem is to determine the robot's location as a function of its observation history:

$$P(Loc_t \mid Obs_0, Act_0, Obs_1, Act_1, \ldots, Act_{t-1}, Obs_t).$$

Example 8.31 Consider the domain depicted in Figure 8.14 (on the next page). There is a circular corridor, with 16 locations numbered 0 to 15. The robot is at one of these locations at each time. This is modeled with, for every time i, a variable Loc_i with domain $\{0, 1, \ldots, 15\}$.

- There are doors at positions 2, 4, 7, and 11 and no doors at other locations.
- The robot has a sensor that noisily senses whether or not it is in front of a door. This is modeled with a variable Obs_i for each time i, with domain

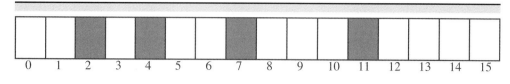

Figure 8.14: Localization domain

{*door*, *nodoor*}. Assume the following conditional probabilities:

$$P(Obs_t{=}door \mid atDoor_t) = 0.8$$
$$P(Obs_t{=}door \mid notAtDoor_t) = 0.1$$

where $atDoor_t$ is true when the robot is at states 2, 4, 7, or 11 at time t, and $notAtDoor_t$ is true when the robot is at the other states.

Thus, the observation is partial in that many states give the same observation and it is noisy in the following way: in 20% of the cases in which the robot is at a door, the sensor falsely gives a negative reading. In 10% of the cases where the robot is not at a door, the sensor records that there is a door.

- The robot can, at each time, move left, move right, or stay still. Assume that the *stay still* action is deterministic, but the dynamics of the moving actions are stochastic. Just because the robot carries out the *goRight* action does not mean that it actually goes one step to the right – it is possible that it stays still, goes two steps right, or even ends up at some arbitrary location (e.g., if someone picks up the robot and moves it). Assume the following dynamics, for each location L:

$$P(Loc_{t+1}{=}L \mid Act_t{=}goRight \wedge Loc_t{=}L) = 0.1$$
$$P(Loc_{t+1}{=}L+1 \mid Act_t{=}goRight \wedge Loc_t{=}L) = 0.8$$
$$P(Loc_{t+1}{=}L+2 \mid Act_t{=}goRight \wedge Loc_t{=}L) = 0.074$$
$$P(Loc_{t+1}{=}L' \mid Act_t{=}goRight \wedge Loc_t{=}L) = 0.002 \text{ for any other location } L'.$$

All location arithmetic is modulo 16. The action *goLeft* works the same way but to the left.

The robot starts at an unknown location and must determine its location.

It may seem as though the domain is too ambiguous, the sensors are too noisy, and the dynamics is too stochastic to do anything. However, it is possible to compute the probability of the robot's current location given its history of actions and observations.

Figure 8.15 (on the next page) gives the robot's probability distribution over its locations, assuming it starts with no knowledge of where it is and experiences the following observations: observe door, go right, observe no door, go right, and then observe door. Location 4 is the most likely current location, with posterior probability of 0.42. That is, in terms of the network of Figure 8.13:

$$P(Loc_2 = 4 \mid Obs_0 = door, Act_0 = goRight, Obs_1 = nodoor,$$

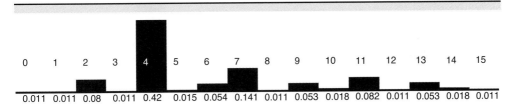

0.011 0.011 0.08   0.011 0.42   0.015 0.054 0.141 0.011 0.053 0.018 0.082 0.011 0.053 0.018 0.011

Figure 8.15: A distribution over locations. The locations are numbered from 0 to 15. The number at the bottom gives the posterior probability that the robot is at the location after the particular sequence of actions and observations given in Example 8.31 (page 389). The height of the bar is proportional to the posterior probability.

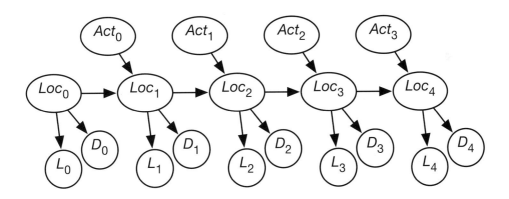

Figure 8.16: Localization with multiple sensors

$$Act_1 = goRight, Obs_2 = door) = 0.42$$

Location 7 is the second most likely current location, with posterior probability of 0.141. Locations 0, 1, 3, 8, 12, and 15 are the least likely current locations, with posterior probability of 0.011.

You can see how well this works for other sequences of observations by using the applet at the book website.

Example 8.32   Let us augment Example 8.31 (page 389) with another sensor. Suppose that, in addition to a door sensor, there is also a light sensor. The light sensor and the door sensor are conditionally independent given the state. Suppose the light sensor is not very informative; it only gives yes-or-no information about whether it detects any light, and this is very noisy, and depends on the location.

This is modeled in Figure 8.16 using the following variables:

- Loc_t is the robot's location at time t

- Act_t is the robot's action at time t
- D_t is the door sensor value at time t
- L_t is the light sensor value at time t.

Conditioning on both L_i and D_i lets it combine information from the light sensor and the door sensor. This is an instance of **sensor fusion**. It is not necessary to define any new mechanisms for sensor fusion given the belief-network model; standard probabilistic inference combines the information from both sensors.

8.5.3   Algorithms for Monitoring and Smoothing

Any standard belief-network algorithms, such as variable elimination, can be used to carry out monitoring or smoothing. However, it is possible to take advantage of the fact that time moves forward and that the agent is getting observations in time and is interested in its state at the current time.

In **belief monitoring** or **filtering**, an agent computes the probability of the current state given the history of observations. In terms of the HMM of Figure 8.12 (page 387), for each i, the agent wants to compute $P(S_i \mid o_0, \dots, o_i)$, which is the distribution over the state at time i given the particular observation of $o_0, \dots, o_i$. This is done using **variable elimination** (page 372):

$$
\begin{aligned}
P(S_i \mid o_0, \dots, o_i) &\propto P(S_i, o_0, \dots, o_i) \\
&= P(o_i \mid S_i) P(S_i, o_0, \dots, o_{i-1}) \\
&= P(o_i \mid S_i) \sum_{S_{i-1}} P(S_i, S_{i-1}, o_0, \dots, o_{i-1}) \\
&= P(o_i \mid S_i) \sum_{S_{i-1}} P(S_i \mid S_{i-1}) P(S_{i-1}, o_0, \dots, o_{i-1}) \\
&\propto P(o_i \mid S_i) \sum_{S_{i-1}} P(S_i \mid S_{i-1}) P(S_{i-1} \mid o_0, \dots, o_{i-1}). \quad (8.2)
\end{aligned}
$$

Suppose the agent has computed the previous belief based on the observations received up until time $i - 1$. That is, it has a factor representing $P(S_{i-1} \mid o_0, \dots, o_{i-1})$. This is just a factor on S_{i-1}. To compute the next belief, it multiplies this by $P(S_i \mid S_{i-1})$, sums out S_{i-1}, multiplies this by the factor $P(o_i \mid S_i)$, and normalizes.

Multiplying a factor on S_{i-1} by the factor $P(S_i \mid S_{i-1})$ and summing out S_{i-1} is an instance of **matrix multiplication**. Multiplying the result by $P(o_i \mid S_i)$ is called the **dot product**. Matrix multiplication and dot product are simple instances of variable elimination.

Example 8.33   Consider the domain of Example 8.31 (page 389). An observation of a door involves multiplying the probability of each location L by $P(door \mid Loc = L)$ and renormalizing. A move right involves, for each state,

> doing a forward simulation of the move-right action in that state weighted by
> the probability of being in that state.

Smoothing is the problem of computing the probability distribution of a state variable in an HMM given past and future observations. The use of future observations can make for more accurate predictions. Given a new observation, it is possible to update all previous state estimates with one sweep through the states using variable elimination; see Exercise 8.17 (page 422).

8.5.4 Dynamic Belief Networks

The state at a particular time need not be represented as a single variable. It is often more natural to represent the state in terms of features.

A **dynamic belief network** (**DBN**) is a discrete time belief network with regular repeated structure. It is like a (hidden) Markov model, but the states and the observations are represented in terms of features. If F is a feature, we write F_t as the random variable that represented the value of variable F at time t. A dynamic belief network makes the following assumptions:

- The set of features is the same at each time.
- For any time $t > 0$, the parents of variable F_t are variables at time t or time $t - 1$, such that the graph for any time is acyclic. The structure does not depend on the value of t (except $t = 0$ is a special case).
- The conditional probability distribution of how each variable depends on its parents is the same for every time $t > 0$. This is called a **stationary model**.

Thus, a dynamic belief network specifies a belief network for time $t = 0$, and for each variable F_t specifies $P(F_t \mid parents(F_t))$, where the parents of F_t are in the same or previous time steps. This is specified for t as a free parameter; the conditional probabilities can be used for any time $t > 0$. As in a belief network, directed cycles are not allowed.

The model for a dynamic belief network is represented as a **two-step belief network**, which represents the variables at the first two times (times 0 and 1). That is, for each feature F there are two variables, F_0 and F_1. The set of parents of F_0, namely $parents(F_0)$ can only include variables for time 0. The resulting graph must be acyclic. Associated with the network are the probabilities $P(F_0 \mid parents(F_0))$ and $P(F_1 \mid parents(F_1))$.

The two-step belief network is **unfolded** into a belief network by replicating the structure for subsequent times. In the unfolded network, $P(F_i \mid parents(F_i))$, for $i > 1$, has exactly the same structure and the same conditional probability values as $P(F_1 \mid parents(F_1))$.

> **Example 8.34** Suppose a trading agent (page 41) wants to model the dynamics of the price of a commodity such as printer paper. To represent this domain,

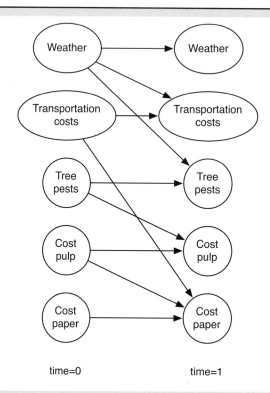

time=0   time=1

Figure 8.17: Two-stage dynamic belief network for paper pricing

the designer models variables affecting the price and the other variables. Suppose the cost of pulp and the transportation costs directly affect the price of paper. The transportation costs are affected by the weather. The pulp cost is affected by the prevalence of tree pests, which in turn depend on the weather. Suppose that each variable depends on its value at the previous time step. A two-stage dynamic belief network representing these dependencies is shown in Figure 8.17.

According to this figure, the variables are initially independent.

This two-stage dynamic belief network can be expanded into a regular dynamic belief network by replicating the nodes for each time step, and the parents for future steps are a copy of the parents for the time 1 variables. An expanded belief network for a horizon of 3 is shown in Figure 8.18 (on the next page). The subscripts represent the time that the variable is referring to.

8.5.5   Time Granularity

One of the problems with the definition of an HMM or a dynamic belief network is that the model depends on the time granularity. The **time granularity** specifies how often a dynamic system transitions from one state to the next. The time granularity could either be fixed, for example each day or each thir-

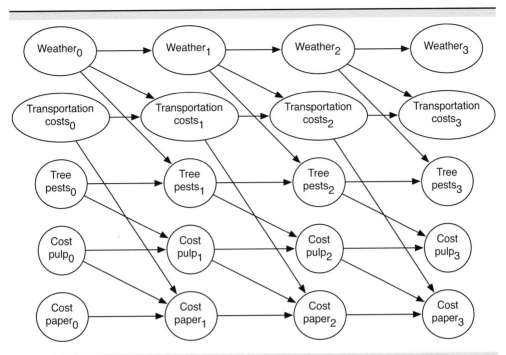

Figure 8.18: Expanded dynamic belief network for paper pricing

tieth of a second, or it could be event based, where a time step occurs when something interesting occurs. If the time granularity were to change, for example from daily to hourly, the conditional probabilities would also change.

One way to model the dynamics independently of the time granularity is to model **continuous time**, where for each variable and each value for the variable, the following are specified:

- a distribution of how long the variable is expected to keep that value (e.g., an exponential decay) and
- what value it will transition to when its value changes.

Given a **discretization** of time, where time moves from one state the next in discrete steps, a dynamic belief network can be constructed from this information. If the discretization of time is fine enough, ignoring multiple value transitions in each time step will result only in small errors.

8.5.6 Probabilistic Models of Language

Markov chains are the basis of simple language models, which have proved to be very useful in various **natural language processing** tasks in daily use.

Assume that a **document** is a sequence of sentences, where a **sentence** is a sequence of **words**. Here we want to consider the sorts of sentences that people may speak to a system or ask as a query to a help system. We do not assume

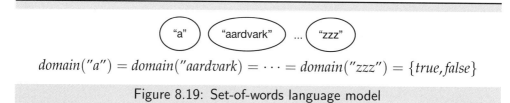

$$domain("a") = domain("aardvark) = \cdots = domain("zzz") = \{true, false\}$$

Figure 8.19: Set-of-words language model

they are grammatical, and often contain words, such as "thx" or "zzz", which may not be typically thought of as words.

In the **set-of-words** model, a sentence (or a document) is treated as the set of words that appear in the sentence, ignoring the order of the words or whether the words are repeated. For example, the sentence "how can I phone my phone" would be treated as the set {"can", "how", "I", "my", "phone"}.

To represent the set-of-words model as a belief network, as in Figure 8.19, there is a Boolean random variable for each word. In this figure, the words are independent of each other (but they do not have to be). This belief network requires the probability of each word appearing in a sentence: $P("a")$, $P("aardvark")$, ..., $P("zzz")$. To condition on the sentence "how can I phone my phone", all of the words in the sentence are assigned true, and all of the other words are assigned false. Words that are not defined in the model are either ignored, or are given a default (small) probability. The probability of sentence S is $\left(\prod_{w \in S} P(w)\right) * \left(\prod_{w \notin S}(1 - P(w))\right)$.

A set-of-words model is not very useful by itself, but is often used as part of a larger model, as in the following example.

Example 8.35 Suppose we want to develop a **help system** to determine which help page users are interested in based on the keywords they give in a query to a help system.

The system will observe the words that the user gives. Instead of modeling the sentence structure, assume that the set of words used in a query will be sufficient to determine the help page.

The aim is to determine which help page the user wants. Suppose that the user is interested in one and only one help page. Thus, it seems reasonable to have a node H with domain the set of all help pages, $\{h_1, \ldots, h_k\}$.

One way this could be represented is as a **naive Bayes classifier**. A naive Bayes classifier is a belief network that has a single node – the class – that directly influences the other variables, and the other variables are independent of each other given the class. Figure 8.20 (on the next page) shows a naive Bayes classifier for the help system where H, the help page the user is interested in, is the class, and the other nodes represent the words used in the query. This network embodies the independence assumption: the words used in a query depend on the help page the user is interested in, and the words are conditionally independent of each other given the help page.

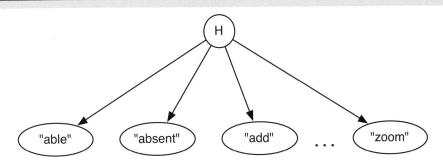

Figure 8.20: Naive belief network with a set-of-words model for a help system

This network requires $P(h_i)$ for each help page h_i, which specifies how likely it is that a user would want this help page given no information. This network assumes the user is interested in exactly one help page, and so $\sum_i P(h_i) = 1$.

The network also requires, for each word w_j and for each help page h_i, the probability $P(w_j \mid h_i)$. These may seem more difficult to acquire but there are a few heuristics available. The sum of these values should be the average number of words in a query. We would expect words that appear in the help page to be more likely to be used when asking for that help page than words not in the help page. There may also be keywords associated with the page that may be more likely to be used. There may also be some words that are just used more, independently of the help page the user is interested in. Example 10.5 (page 493) shows how to learn the probabilities of this network from experience.

To condition on the set of words in a query, the words that appear in the query are observed to be true and the words that are not in the query are observed to be false. For example, if the help text was "the zoom is absent", the words "the", "zoom", "is", and "absent" would be observed to be true, and the other words would be observed to be false. Once the posterior for H has been computed, the most likely few help topics can be shown to the user.

Some words, such as "the" and "is", may not be useful in that they have the same conditional probability for each help topic and so, perhaps, would be omitted from the model. Some words that may not be expected in a query could also be omitted from the model.

Note that the conditioning included the words that were not in the query. For example, if page h_{73} was about printing problems, we may expect that people who wanted page h_{73} would use the word "print". The non-existence of the word "print" in a query is strong evidence that the user did not want page h_{73}.

The independence of the words given the help page is a strong assumption. It probably does not apply to words like "not", where which word "not" is associated with is very important. There may even be words that are complementary, in which case you would expect users to use one and not the other (e.g., "type" and "write") and words you would expect to be used together (e.g., "go" and "to"); both of these cases violate the independence assumption.

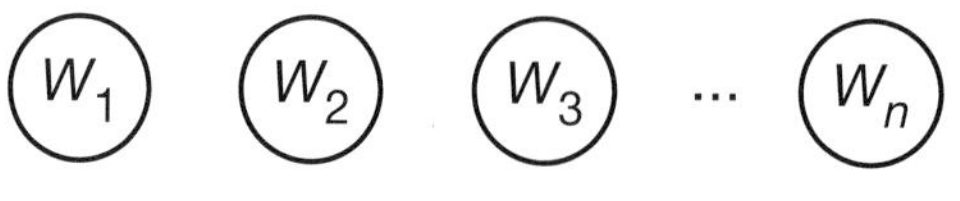

$$domain(W_i) = \{"a", "aarvark", \ldots, "zzz", "\perp", "?"\}$$

Figure 8.21: Bag-of-words or unigram language model

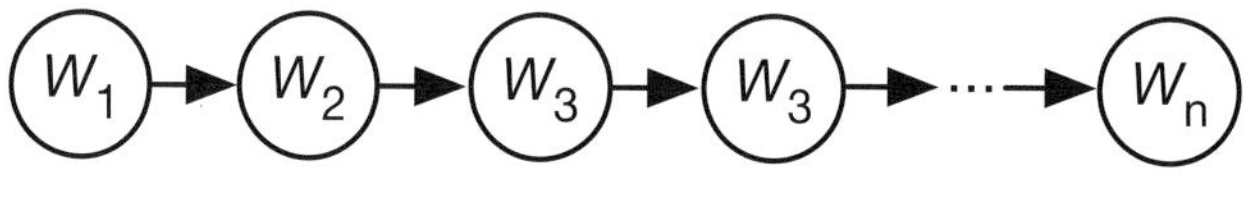

$$domain(W_i) = \{"a", "aarvark", \ldots, "zzz", "\perp", "?"\}$$

Figure 8.22: Bigram language model

It is an empirical question as to how much violating the assumptions hurts the usefulness of the system.

In a **bag-of-words** or **unigram** model, a sentence is treated as a multiset of words, representing the number of times a word is used in a sentence, but not the order of the words. Figure 8.21 shows how to represent a unigram as a belief network. For the sequence of words, there is a variable W_i for each position i, with domain of each variable the set of all words, such as $\{"a", "aardvark", \ldots, "zzz"\}$. The domain is often augmented with a symbol, "$\perp$", representing the end of the sentence, and with a symbol "?" representing a word that is not in the model.

To condition on the sentence "how can I phone my phone", the word W_1 is observed to be "how", the variable W_2 is observed to be "can", etc. Word W_7 is assigned $\perp$. Both W_4 and W_6 are assigned the value "phone". There are no variables W_8 onwards.

The unigram model assumes a stationary distribution, where the prior distribution of W_i is the same for each i. The value of $P(W_i = w)$ is the probability that a randomly chosen word is w. More common words have a higher probability than less common words.

In a **bigram model**, the probability of each word depends on the previous word in the sentence. It is called a bigram model because it depends on pairs of words. Figure 8.22 shows the belief network representation of a bigram model. This needs a specification of $P(W_i \mid W_{i-1})$.

To make W_1 not be a special case, we introduce a new word $\perp$; intuitively $\perp$ is the "word" between sentences. For example, $P("cat" \mid \perp)$ is the probability that the word "cat" is the first word in a sentence. $P(\perp \mid "cat")$ is the probability that the sentence ends after the the word "cat".

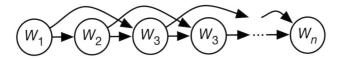

$$domain(W_i) = \{"a","aarvark",\ldots,"zzz","\bot","?"\}$$

Figure 8.23: Trigram language model

Word	P_1	Word	P_2	Word	P_3
the	0.0464	same	0.01023	time	0.15236
of	0.0294	first	0.00733	as	0.04638
and	0.0228	other	0.00594	way	0.04258
to	0.0197	most	0.00558	thing	0.02057
in	0.0156	world	0.00428	year	0.00989
a	0.0152	time	0.00392	manner	0.00793
is	0.00851	two	0.00273	in	0.00739
that	0.00806	whole	0.00197	day	0.00705
for	0.00658	people	0.00175	kind	0.00656
was	0.00508	great	0.00102	with	0.00327

Unigram, bigram and trigram probabilities derived from the Google books Ngram viewer (https://books.google.com/ngrams/) for the year 2000. P_1 is $P(Word)$ for the top 10 words, which are found by using the query "*" in the viewer. P_2 is part of a bigram model that represents $P(Word \mid "the")$ for the top 10 words. This is derived from the query "the *" in the viewer. P_3 is part of a trigram model; the probabilities given represent $P(Word \mid "the","same")$, which is derived from the query "the same *" in the viewer.

Figure 8.24: Some of the most-likely n-grams

In a **trigram** model, each triple of words is modeled. This is represented as a belief network in Figure 8.23. This requires $P(W_i \mid W_{i-2}, W_{i-1})$; the probability of each word given the previous two words.

In general, in an **n-gram** model, the probability of each word given the previous $n - 1$ words is modeled. This requires considering each sequence of n words, and so the complexity of representing this as a table grows with w^n where w is the number of words. Figure 8.24 shows some common unigram, bigram and trigram probabilities.

The conditional probabilities are typically not represented as tables, because the tables would be too large, and because it is difficult to assess the probability of a previously unknown word, or the probability of the next word given a previously unknown word or given an uncommon phrase. Instead one

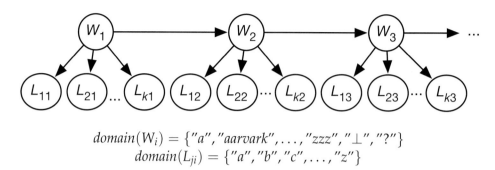

$$domain(W_i) = \{"a", "aarvark", \ldots, "zzz", "\perp", "?"\}$$
$$domain(L_{ji}) = \{"a", "b", "c", \ldots, "z"\}$$

Figure 8.25: Predictive typing model

could use context specific independence (page 381), such as, for trigram models, represent the probability of the next work conditioned on some of the pairs of words, and if none of these hold, use $P(W_i \mid W_{i-1})$, as in a bigram model. For example, the phrase "frightfully green" is not common, and so to compute the probability of the next word, $P(W \mid "frightfully", "green")$, it is typical to use $P(W \mid "green")$, which is easier to assess and learn.

Any of these models could be used in the help system of Example 8.35 (page 396), instead of the set-of-words model used there. These models may be combined to give more sophisticated models, as in the following example.

Example 8.36 Consider the problem of spelling correction as users type into a phone's onscreen keyboard to create sentences. Figure 8.25 gives a predictive typing model that does this (and more).

The variable W_i is the ith word in the sentence. The domain of each W_i is the set of all words. This uses a bigram model for words, and assumes $P(W_i \mid W_{i-1})$ is provided as the language model. A stationary model is typically appropriate.

The L_{ji} variable represents the jth letter in word i. The domain of each L_{ji} is the set of characters that could be typed. This uses a unigram model for each letter given the word, but it would not be a stationary model, as for example, the probability distribution of the first letter given the word "print" is different from the probability distribution of the second letter given the word "print". We would expect $P(L_{ji} = c \mid W_i = w)$ to be close to 1 if the jth letter of word w is c. The conditional probability could incorporate common misspellings and common typing errors (e.g., switching letters, or if someone tends to type slightly higher on the phone's screen).

For example, $P(L_{1j} = "p" \mid W_j = "print")$ would be close to 1, but not equal to 1, as the user could have mistyped. Similarly, $P(L_{2j} = "r" \mid W_j = "print")$ would be high. The distribution for the second letter in the word, $P(L_{2j} \mid W_j = "print")$, could take into account mistyping adjacent letters ("e" and "t" are adjacent to "r" on the standard keyboard), and missing letters (maybe "i" is more

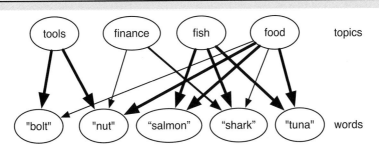

Figure 8.26: Simple topic model with a set-of-words. The thickness of the lines indicates the strength of the connection. See Example 8.37.

likely because it is the third letter in "print"). In practice, these probabilities are typically extracted from data of people typing known sentences, without needing to model why the errors occurred.

The word model allows the system to predict the next word even if no letters have been typed. Then as letters are typed, it predicts the word, based on the previous words and the typed letters, even if some of the letters are mistyped. For example, if the user types "I cannot pint", it might be more likely that the last word is "print" than it is "pint" because of the way the model combines of all of the evidence.

A **topic model** predicts the topics of a document from the sentences typed. Knowing the topic of a document helps people find the document or similar documents even if they do not know what words are in the document.

Example 8.37 Figure 8.26 shows a simple topic model based on a set-of-words language model. There is a set of topics which are a priori independent of each other (four are given). The words are independent of each other given the topic. We assume a noisy-or (page 382) model for how the words depend on the topics.

The **noisy-or** model can be represented by having a variable for each topic word pair where the word is relevant for the topic. For example the *tools_bolt* variable represents the probability that the word *bolt* is in the document because the topic is *tools*. This variable has probability zero if the topic is not *tools* and has the probability that the word would appear when the topic is *tools* (and there are no other relevant topics). The word *bolt* would appear, with probability 1 if *tools_bolt* is true or if an analogous variable, *food_bolt* is true, and with a small probability otherwise (the probability that it appears without one of the topics). Thus, each topic–word pair where the word is relevant to the topic is modeled by a single weight. In Figure 8.26, the higher weights are show by thicker lines.

Given the words, the topic model is used to infer the distribution over topics. Once a number of words that are relevant a topic are given, the topic becomes more likely, and so other words related to that topic also become more likely. Indexing documents by the topic lets us find relevant documents even if different words are used to look for a document.

This model is based on **Google**'s Rephil, which has 12,000,000 words (where common phrases are treated as words), 900,000 topics and 350 million topic-word pairs with non-zero probability.

It is possible to mix these patterns, for example by using the current topics to predict the word in a predictive typing model with a topic model.

Models based on *n*-grams cannot represent all of the subtleties of natural language, as exemplified by the following example.

Example 8.38   Consider the sentence:

A tall man with a big hairy cat drank the cold milk.

In English, this is unambiguous; the man drank the milk. Consider how an *n*-gram might fare with such a sentence. The problem is that the subject ("man") is far away from the verb ("drank"). It is also plausible that the cat drank the milk. It is easy to think of variants of this sentence where the "man" is arbitrarily far away from the subject and so would not be captured by any *n*-gram. How to handle such sentences is discussed in Section 13.6 (page 612).

8.6   Stochastic Simulation

Many problems are too big for exact inference, so one must resort to **approximate inference** (page 370). One of the most effective methods is based on generating random samples from the (posterior) distribution that the network specifies.

Stochastic simulation is based on the idea that a set of samples can be mapped to and from probabilities. For example, the probability $P(a) = 0.14$ means that out of 1000 samples, about 140 will have a true. Inference can be carried out by going from probabilities into samples and from samples into probabilities.

The following sections consider three problems:

- how to generate samples,

- how to infer probabilities from samples, and

- how to incorporate observations.

These form the basis for methods that use sampling to compute the posterior distribution of a variable in a belief network, including rejection sampling, importance sampling, particle filtering and Markov chain Monte Carlo.

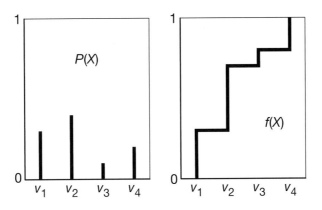

Figure 8.27: A cumulative probability distribution

8.6.1 Sampling from a Single Variable

The simplest case is to generate the probability distribution of a single variable. This is the base case the other methods build on.

From Probabilities to Samples

To generate samples from a single discrete or real-valued variable, X, first totally order the values in the domain of X. For discrete variables, if there is no natural order, just create an arbitrary ordering. Given this ordering, the **cumulative probability distribution** is a function of x, defined by $f(x) = P(X \leq x)$.

To generate a random sample for X, select a random number y in the domain $[0, 1]$. We select y from a uniform distribution to ensure that each number between 0 and 1 has the same chance of being chosen. Let v be the value of X that maps to y in the cumulative probability distribution. That is, v is the element of *domain*(X) such that $f(v) = y$ or, equivalently, $v = f^{-1}(y)$. Then, $X = v$ is a random sample of X, chosen according to the distribution of X.

Example 8.39   Consider a random variable X with domain $\{v_1, v_2, v_3, v_4\}$. Suppose $P(X{=}v_1) = 0.3$, $P(X{=}v_2) = 0.4$, $P(X{=}v_3) = 0.1$, and $P(X{=}v_4) = 0.2$. First, totally order the values, say $v_1 < v_2 < v_3 < v_4$. Figure 8.27 shows $P(X)$, the distribution for X, and $f(X)$, the cumulative distribution for X. Consider value v_1; 0.3 of the domain of f maps back to v_1. Thus, if a sample is uniformly selected from the Y-axis, v_1 has a 0.3 chance of being selected, v_2 has a 0.4 chance of being selected, and so forth.

From Samples to Probabilities

Probabilities can be estimated from a set of samples using the sample average. The **sample average** of a proposition α is the number of samples where α is true divided by the total number of samples. The sample average approaches the true probability as the number of samples approaches infinity by the **law of large numbers**.

Hoeffding's inequality provides an estimate of the error of the sample average as the probability given n samples, with the guarantee of the following proposition.

Proposition 8.6 (Hoeffding). *Suppose p is the true probability, and s is the sample average from n independent samples; then*

$$P(|s - p| > \epsilon) \leq 2e^{-2n\epsilon^2}.$$

This theorem can be used to determine how many samples are required to guarantee a **probably approximately correct** estimate of the probability. To guarantee that the error is *always* less than some $\epsilon < 0.5$, infinitely many samples are required. However, if you are willing to have an error greater than ϵ in δ of the cases, solve $2e^{-2n\epsilon^2} < \delta$ for n, which gives

$$n > \frac{-\ln\frac{\delta}{2}}{2\epsilon^2}.$$

For example, suppose you want an error less than 0.1, nineteen times out of twenty; that is, you are only willing to tolerate an error bigger than 0.1 in 5% of the cases. You can use Hoeffding's bound by setting ϵ to 0.1 and $\delta = 0.05$, which gives $n > 184$. Thus, you guarantee such bounds on the error with 185 samples. If you want an error of less than 0.01 in at least 95% of the cases, 18,445 samples could be used. If you want an error of less than 0.1 in 99% of the cases, 265 samples could be used.

8.6.2   Forward Sampling in Belief Networks

Forward sampling is a way to generate a sample of every variable in a belief network so that each sample is generated in proportion to its probability. This enables us to estimate the prior probability of any variable.

Suppose $X_1, \ldots, X_n$ is a total ordering of the variables so that the parents of each variable come before the variable in the total order. Forward sampling draws a sample of all of the variables by drawing a sample of each variable $X_1, \ldots, X_n$ in order. First, it samples X_1 using the cumulative distribution, as described above. For each of the other variables, due to the total ordering of variables, when it comes time to sample X_i, it already has values for all of X_i's parents. It now samples a value for X_i from the distribution of X_i given the

Sample	Tampering	Fire	Alarm	Smoke	Leaving	Report
s_1	false	true	true	true	false	false
s_2	false	false	false	false	false	false
s_3	false	true	true	true	true	true
s_4	false	false	false	false	false	true
s_5	false	false	false	false	false	false
s_6	false	false	false	false	false	false
s_7	true	false	false	true	true	true
s_8	true	false	false	false	false	true
...						
s_{1000}	true	false	true	true	false	false

Figure 8.28: Sampling for a belief network

values already assigned to the parents of X_i. Repeating this for every variable generates a sample containing values for all of the variables. The probability distribution of a query variable is estimated by considering the proportion of the samples that have assigned each value of the variable.

Example 8.40 To create a set of samples for the belief network of Figure 8.3 (page 365), suppose the variables are ordered: *Tampering, Fire, Alarm, Smoke, Leaving, Report*. First the algorithm samples *Tampering*, using the cumulative distribution (page 403). Suppose it selects *Tampering=false*. Then it samples *Fire* using the same method. Suppose it selects *Fire=true*. Then it samples a value for *Alarm*, using the distribution $P(Alarm \mid Tampering=false, Fire=true)$. Suppose it selects *Alarm=true*. Next, it samples a value for *Smoke* using $P(Smoke \mid Fire=true)$. And so on for the other variables. It has thus selected a value for each variable and created the first sample of Figure 8.28. Notice that it has selected a very unlikely combination of values. This does not happen very often; it happens in proportion to how likely the sample is. It repeats this until it has enough samples. In Figure 8.28, it generated 1000 samples.

The probability that *Report=true* is estimated from the proportion of the samples where the variable *Report* has value *true*.

8.6.3 Rejection Sampling

Given some evidence e, rejection sampling estimates $P(h \mid e)$ using the formula

$$P(h \mid e) = \frac{P(h \wedge e)}{P(e)}.$$

This is computed by considering only the samples where e is true and by determining the proportion of these in which h is true. The idea of **rejection sampling** is that samples are generated as before, but any sample where e is false

Sample	Tampering	Fire	Alarm	Smoke	Leaving	Report	
s_1	false	false	true	false	✗		
s_2	false	true	false	true	false	false	✔
s_3	false	true	true	false	✗		
s_4	false	true	false	true	false	false	✔
s_5	false	true	true	true	true	true	✗
s_6	false	false	false	true	false	false	✔
s_7	true	false	false	false	✗		
s_8	true	true	true	true	true	true	✗
...							
s_{1000}	true	false	true	false	✗		

Figure 8.29: Rejection sampling for $P(tampering \mid smoke \wedge \neg report)$

is rejected. The proportion of the remaining, non-rejected, samples where h is true is an estimate of $P(h \mid e)$. If the evidence is a conjunction of assignments of values to variables, a sample is rejected when any variable is assigned a value different from its observed value.

Example 8.41 Figure 8.29 shows how rejection sampling is used to estimate $P(tampering \mid smoke \wedge \neg report)$. Any sample with *Smoke=false* is rejected. The sample is rejected without considering any more variables. Any sample with *Report=true* is rejected. The sample average from the remaining samples (those marked with ✔) is used to estimate the posterior probability of *tampering*.

Because $P(smoke \wedge \neg report) = 0.0128$, we would expect about 13 samples out of the 1000 to have $smoke \wedge \neg report$ true; the other 987 samples would have $smoke \wedge \neg report$ false, and so would be rejected. Thus, 13 is used as n in Hoeffding's inequality, which, for example, guarantees an error for any probability computed from these samples of less than 0.25 in about 86% of the cases, which is not very accurate.

The error in the probability of h depends on the number of samples that are not rejected, which proportional to $P(e)$. Hoeffding's inequality can be used to estimate the error of rejection sampling, where n is the number of non-rejected samples. Therefore, the error depends on $P(e)$.

Rejection sampling does not work well when the evidence is unlikely. This may not seem like that much of a problem because, by definition, unlikely evidence is unlikely to occur. But, although this may be true for simple models, for complicated models with complex observations, every possible observation may be unlikely. Also, for many applications, such as in diagnosis, the user is interested in determining the probabilities because unusual observations are involved.

8.6.4 Likelihood Weighting

Instead of creating a sample and then rejecting it, it is possible to mix sampling with inference to reason about the probability that a sample would be rejected. In **importance sampling** methods, each sample has a weight, and the sample average is computed using the weighted average of samples. **Likelihood weighting** is a form of importance sampling where the variables are sampled in the order defined by a belief network, and evidence is used to update the weights. The weights reflect the probability that a sample would not be rejected.

Example 8.42 Consider the belief network of Figure 8.3 (page 365). In this $P(fire) = 0.01$, $P(smoke \mid fire) = 0.9$ and $P(smoke \mid \neg fire) = 0.01$. Suppose *Smoke=true* is observed, and another descendant of *Fire* is queried.

Starting with 1000 samples, approximately 10 will have *Fire=true*, and the other 990 samples will have *Fire=false*. In rejection sampling, of the 990 with *Fire=false*, 1%, which is approximately 10, will have *Smoke=true* and so will not be rejected. The remaining 980 samples will be rejected. Of the 10 with *Fire=true*, about 9 will not be rejected. Thus about 98% of the samples are rejected.

Instead of rejecting so many samples, the samples with *Fire=true* are weighted by 0.9 and the samples with *Fire=false* are weighted with 0.01. This potentially give a much better estimate of any of the probabilities that use these samples.

Figure 8.30 (on the next page) shows the details of the likelihood weighting for computing $P(Q \mid e)$ for query variable Q and evidence e. The *for* loop (from line 15) creates a sample containing a value for all of the variables. Each observed variable changes the weight of the sample by multiplying by the probability of the observed value given the assignment of the parents in the sample. The variables not observed are sampled according the probability of the variable given its parents in the sample. Note that the variables are sampled in an order to ensure that the parents of a variable have been assigned in the sample before the variable is selected.

To extract the distribution of the query variable Q, the algorithm maintain an array *counts*, such that *counts*[v] is the sum of the weights of the samples where $Q = v$. This algorithm can also be adapted to the case where the query is some complicated condition on the values; we just have to count the cases where the condition is true and those where the condition is false.

Example 8.43 Suppose we want to use likelihood weighting to compute $P(Tampering \mid smoke \wedge \neg report)$.

The following table gives a few samples. In this table, *s* is the sample; *e* is $\neg smoke \wedge report$. The weight is $P(e \mid s)$, which is equal to $P(smoke \mid Fire) * P(\neg report \mid Leaving)$, where the value for *Fire* and *Leaving* are from the sample.

1: **procedure** *Likelihood_weighting*(B, e, Q, n):
2:    **Inputs**
3:       B: belief network
4:       e: the evidence; a variable-value assignment to some of the variables
5:       Q: query variable
6:       n: number of samples to generate
7:    **Output**
8:       posterior distribution on Q
9:    **Local**
10:       array *sample*[*var*], where *sample*[*var*] $\in$ *domain*(*var*)
11:       real array *counts*[*k*] for $k \in domain(Q)$, initialized to 0
12:    **repeat** n **times**
13:       *sample* := {}
14:       *weight* := 1
15:       **for each** variable X in B, in order **do**
16:          **if** $X = v$ is in e **then**
17:             *sample*[X] := v
18:             *weight* := *weight* $* P(X = v \mid parents(X))$
19:          **else**
20:             *sample*[X] := a random sample from $P(X \mid parents(X))$
21:       v := *sample*[Q]
22:       *counts*[v] := *counts*[v] + *weight*
23:    **return** *counts*$/ \sum_v counts[v]$

Figure 8.30: Likelihood weighting for belief network inference

Tampering	Fire	Alarm	Smoke	Leaving	Report	weight
false	*true*	*false*	*true*	*true*	*false*	$0.9 * 0.25 = 0.225$
true	*true*	*true*	*true*	*false*	*false*	$0.9 * 0.99 = 0.891$
false	*false*	*false*	*true*	*true*	*false*	$0.01 * 0.25 = 0.0025$
false	*true*	*false*	*true*	*false*	*false*	$0.9 * 0.99 = 0.891$

$P(tampering \mid \neg smoke \wedge report)$ is estimated from the weighted proportion of the samples that have *Tampering* true.

8.6.5   Importance Sampling

Likelihood weighting is an instance of **importance sampling**. Importance sampling algorithms have the following characteristics:

- Samples are weighted.

- The samples do not need to come from the actual distribution, but can be from (almost) any distribution, with the weights adjusted to reflect the difference between the distributions.

- Some variables can be summed out and some sampled.

This freedom to sample from a different distribution allows the algorithm to choose better sampling distributions to give better estimates.

Stochastic simulation can be used to compute the expected value (page 355) of real-valued variable f under probability distribution P using:

$$\mathcal{E}_P(f) = \sum_w f(w) * P(w)$$

$$\approx \frac{1}{n} \sum_s f(s)$$

where s is a sample that is sampled with probability P, and n is the number of samples. The estimate gets more accurate as the number of samples grows.

Suppose it is difficult to sample with the distribution P, but it is easy to sample from a distribution Q. We adapt the previous equation to estimate the expected value from P, by sampling from Q using:

$$\mathcal{E}_P(f) = \sum_w f(w) * P(w)$$

$$= \sum_w f(w) * (P(w)/Q(w)) * Q(w)$$

$$\approx \frac{1}{n} \sum_s f(s) * P(s)/Q(s)$$

where the last sum is over n samples selected according the distribution Q. The distribution Q is called a **proposal distribution**. The only restriction on Q is that it should not be zero for any cases where P is not zero (i.e., if $Q(c) = 0$ then $P(c) = 0$).

Recall (page 355) that for Boolean variables, with *true* represented as 1 and *false* as 0, the expected value is the probability. So the methods here can be used to compute probabilities.

The algorithm of Figure 8.30 can be adapted to use a proposal distribution as follows: in line 20, it should sample from $Q(X \mid parents(X))$, and in a new line after that, it updates the value of *weight* by multiplying it by $P(X \mid parents(X))/Q(X \mid parents(X))$.

Example 8.44 In the running alarm example, $P(smoke) = 0.0189$. As explained in Example 8.42 (page 407), if the algorithm samples according to the prior probability, *Smoke=true* would only be true in about 19 samples out of 1000. Likelihood weighting ended up with a few samples with high weights and many samples with low weights, even though the samples represented similar number of cases.

Suppose, instead of sampling according to the probability, the proposal distribution with $Q(fire) = 0.5$ is used. Then $Fire=true$ is sampled 50% of the time. According to the model $P(fire) = 0.01$, thus each sample with $Fire=true$ is weighted by $0.01/0.5 = 0.02$ and each sample with $Fire=false$ is weighted by $0.99/0.5 = 1.98$.

With importance sampling with Q as the proposal distribution, half of the samples will have $Fire=true$, and the model specifies $P(smoke \mid fire) = 0.9$. Given the evidence e, these will be weighted by $0.9 * 0.02 = 0.018$. The other half of the samples will have $A=false$, and the model specifies $P(smoke \mid \neg fire) = 0.01$. These samples will have a weighting of $0.01 * 1.98 = 0.0198$. Notice how all of the samples have weights of the same order of magnitude. This means that the estimates from these are much more accurate.

Importance sampling can also be combined with exact inference. Not all variables need to be sampled. Those not sampled can be summed out by variable elimination.

The best proposal distribution is one where the samples have approximately equal weight. This occurs when sampling from the posterior distribution. In **adaptive importance sampling** the proposal distribution is modified to approximate the posterior probability of the variable being sampled.

8.6.6 Particle Filtering

Importance sampling enumerates the samples one at a time and, for each sample, assigns a value to each variable. It is also possible to start with all of the samples and, for each variable, generate a value for that variable for each sample. For example, for the data of Figure 8.28 (page 405), the same data could be generated by generating all of the samples for *Tampering* before generating the samples for *Fire*. The **particle filtering** algorithm or **sequential Monte Carlo** generates all the samples for one variable before moving to the next variable. It does one sweep through the variables, and for each variable it does a sweep through all of the samples. This algorithm is advantageous when variables are generated dynamically and when there are unboundedly many variables, as in the sequential models (page 384). It also allows for a new operation of resampling.

In particle filtering, the samples are called particles. A **particle** is a *variable-value* dictionary, where a **dictionary** is a representation of a partial function from keys into values; here the key is a variable and the particle maps to its value. A particle has an associated weight. A set of particles is a **population**.

The algorithm starts with a population of n empty dictionaries. The algorithm repeatedly selects a variable according to an ordering where a variable is selected after its parents. If the variable is not observed, for each particle, a value for the variable for that particle is sampled from the distribution of the variable given the assignment of the particle. If the variable is observed, each

---

1: **procedure** *Particle_filtering*(B, e, Q, n):
2:     **Inputs**
3:         B: belief network
4:         e: the evidence; a variable-value assignment to some of the variables
5:         Q: query variable
6:         n: number of samples to generate

7:     **Output**
8:         posterior distribution on Q
9:     **Local**
10:         *particles* is a set of particles
11:         array *counts*$[k]$ where k in *domain*(Q)

12:     *particles* := list of n empty particles
13:     **for each** variable X in B, in order **do**
14:         **if** $X = v$ is observed in e **then**
15:             **for each** *part* in *particles* **do**
16:                 *part*$[X] := v$
17:                 *weight*$[part]$:= *weight* $* P(X = v \mid part[parents(X)])$
18:             *particles* := n particles selected from *particles* according to *weight*
19:         **else**
20:             **for each** *part* in *particles* **do**
21:                 sample v from distribution $P(X \mid part[parents(X)])$
22:                 *part*$[X] := v$
23:     **for each** v in *domain*(Q) **do**
24:         *counts*$[v]$:= (number of *part* in *particles* s.th. *part*$[Q] = v$)$/n$
25:     **return** *counts*

Figure 8.31: Particle filtering for belief network inference

---

particle's weight is updated by multiplying by the probability of the observation given the assignment of the particle.

Given a population of n particles, **resampling** generates a new population of n particles, each with the same weight. Each particle is selected with probability proportional to its weight. Resampling can be implemented in the same way that random samples for a single random variable are generated (page 403), but particles, rather than values, are selected. Some particles may be selected multiple times and others might not be selected at all.

The particle filtering algorithm is shown in Figure 8.31. Line 16 assigns X its observed value. Line 17, which is used when X observed, updates the weights of the particles according to the probability of the observation on X. Line 22 assigns X a value sampled from the distribution of X given the values of its parents in the particle.

This algorithm resamples after each observation. It is also possible to re-sample less often, for example, after a number of variables are observed.

Importance sampling is equivalent to particle filtering without resampling. The principal difference is the order in which the particles are generated. In particle filtering, each variable is sampled for all particles, whereas, in importance sampling, each particle (sample) is sampled for all variables before the next particle is considered.

Particle filtering has two main advantages over importance sampling. First, it can be used for an unbounded number of variables, as in hidden Markov models (page 387) and dynamic belief networks (page 393). Second, resampling enables the particles to better cover the distribution over the variables. Whereas importance sampling will result in some particles that have very low probability, with only a few of the particles covering most of the probability mass, resampling lets many particles more uniformly cover the probability mass.

Example 8.45   Consider using particle filtering to compute $P(tampering \mid smoke \wedge report)$ for the belief network of Figure 8.3 (page 365). First generate the particles $s_1, \ldots, s_{1000}$. Suppose it first samples *Fire*. Out of the 1000 particles, about 10 will have *Fire* = *true* and about 990 will have *Fire* = *false* (as $P(fire) = 0.01$). It then absorbs the evidence *Smoke* = *true*. Those particles with *Fire* = *true* will be weighted by 0.9 as $P(smoke \mid fire) = 0.9$ and those particles with *Fire* = *false* will be weighted by 0.01 as $P(smoke \mid \neg fire) = 0.01$. It then resamples; each particle is chosen in proportion to its weight. The particles with *Fire* = *true* will be chosen in the ratio $990 * 0.01 : 10 * 0.9$. Thus, about 524 particles will be chosen with *Fire* = *true*, and the remainder with *Fire* = *false*. The other variables are sampled, in turn, until *Report* is observed, and the particles are resampled. At this stage, the probability of *Tampering* = *true* will be the proportion of the samples with tampering being true.

Note that in particle filtering the particles are not independent, so Hoeffding's inequality (page 404) is not directly applicable.

8.6.7   Markov Chain Monte Carlo

The previously described methods went forward through the network (parents were sampled before children), and were not good at passing information back through the network. The method described in this section can sample variables in any order.

A **stationary distribution** (page 385) of a Markov chain (page 384) is a distribution of its variables that is not changed by the transition function of the Markov chain. If the Markov chain mixes enough, there is a unique stationary distribution, which can be approached by running the Markov chain long enough. The idea behind **Markov chain Monte Carlo (MCMC)** methods to generate samples from a distribution (e.g., the posterior distribution given a

```
 1: procedure Gibbs_sampling(B, e, Q, n, burn_in):
 2:     Inputs
 3:         B: belief network
 4:         e: the evidence; a variable-value assignment to some of the variables
 5:         Q: query variable
 6:         n: number of samples to generate
 7:         burn_in: number of samples to discard initially
 8:     Output
 9:         posterior distribution on Q
10:     Local
11:         array sample[var], where sample[var] ∈ domain(var)
12:         real array counts[k] for k ∈ domain(Q), initialized to 0
13:     initialize sample[X] = e[X] if X observed, otherwise assign randomly
14:     repeat burn_in times
15:         for each non-observed variable X, in any order do
16:             sample[X] := a random sample from P(X | markov_blanket(X))
17:     repeat n times
18:         for each non-observed variable X, in any order do
19:             sample[X] := a random sample from P(X | markov_blanket(X))
20:         v := sample[Q]
21:         counts[v] := counts[v] + 1
22:     return counts / ∑_v counts[v]
```

Figure 8.32: Gibbs sampling for belief network inference

belief network) is to construct a Markov chain with the desired distribution as its (unique) stationary distribution and then sample from the Markov chain; these samples will be distributed according to the desired distribution. We typically discard the first few samples in a **burn-in** period, as these samples may be far from the stationary distribution.

One way to create a Markov chain from a belief network with observations, is to use **Gibbs sampling**. The idea is to clamp observed variables to the values they were observed to have, and sample the other variables. Each variable is sampled from the distribution of the variable given the current values of the other variables. Note that each variable only depends on the values of the variables in its Markov blanket (page 360). The **Markov blanket** of a variable X in a belief network contains X's parents, X's children, and the other parents of X's children; these are all of the variables that appear in factors with X.

Figure 8.32 gives pseudocode for Gibbs sampling. The only ill-defined part is to randomly sample $P(X \mid markov\_blanket(X))$. This can be computed by noticing that for each value of X, the probability $P(X \mid markov\_blanket(X))$ is the product of the values of the factors in which X appears projected onto the current value of all of the other variables.

Gibbs sampling will approach the correct probabilities as long as there are no zero probabilities. How quickly it approaches the distribution depends on how quickly the probabilities mix (how much of the probability space is explored), which depends on how extreme the probabilities are. Gibbs sampling works well when the probabilities are not extreme.

Example 8.46 As a problematic case for Gibbs sampling, consider a simple example with three Boolean variables A, B, C, with A as the parent of B, and B as the parent of C. Suppose $P(a) = 0.5$, $P(b \mid a) = 0.99$, $P(b \mid \neg a) = 0.0.1$, $P(c \mid b) = 0.99$, $P(c \mid \neg b) = 0.0.1$. There are no observations and the query variable is C. The two assignments with all variables having the same value are equally likely and are much more likely than the other assignments. Gibbs sampling will quickly get to one of these assignments, and will take a long time to transition to the other assignments (as it requires some very unlikely choices). If 0.99 and 0.01 were replaced by numbers closer to 1 and 0, it would take even longer to converge.

8.7   Review

The following are the main points you should have learned from this chapter:

- Probability is a measure of belief in a proposition.
- The posterior probability is used to update an agent's beliefs based on evidence.
- A Bayesian belief network is a representation of conditional independence of random variables.
- Exact inference can be carried out efficiently for sparse graphs (with low treewidth) by variable elimination.
- A hidden Markov model or a dynamic belief network can be used for probabilistic reasoning about sequences, such as changes over time or words in sentences, with applications such as robot localization and extracting information from language.
- Stochastic simulation is used for approximate inference.

8.8   References and Further Reading

Introductions to probability theory from an AI perspective, and belief (Bayesian) networks, are by Pearl [1988], Jensen [1996], Castillo et al. [1996], Koller and Friedman [2009], and Darwiche [2009]. Halpern [2003] overviews the foundations of probability.

Variable elimination for evaluating belief networks is presented in Zhang and Poole [1994], Dechter [1996], Darwiche [2009] and Dechter [2013]. Treewidth is discussed by Bodlaender [1993].

For comprehensive reviews of information theory, see Cover and Thomas [1991], MacKay [2003], and Grünwald [2007].

For discussions of causality, see Pearl [2009] and Spirtes et al. [2001].

Brémaud [1999] describes theory and applications of Markov chains. HMMs are described by Rabiner [1989]. Dynamic Bayesian networks were introduced by Dean and Kanazawa [1989]. Markov localization and other issues on the relationship of probability and robotics are described by Thrun et al. [2005]. The use of particle filtering for localization is due to Dellaert et al. [1999].

Manning and Schütze [1999] and Jurafsky and Martin [2008] present probabilistic and statistical methods for natural language. The topic model of Example 8.37 is based on Google's Rephil described by Murphy [2012].

For introductions to stochastic simulation, see Rubinstein [1981] and Andrieu et al. [2003]. Likelihood weighting in belief networks is based on Henrion [1988]. Importance sampling in belief networks is based on Cheng and Druzdzel [2000], who also consider how to learn the proposal distribution. There is a collection of articles on particle filtering in Doucet et al. [2001].

The annual Conference on Uncertainty in Artificial Intelligence, and the general AI conferences, provide up-to-date research results.

8.9 Exercises

Exercise 8.1 Bickel et al. [1975] report on gender biases for graduate admissions at UC Berkeley. This example is based on that case, but the numbers are fictional.

There are two departments, which we will call *dept#*1 and *dept#*2 (so *Dept* is a random variable with values *dept#*1 and *dept#*2) which students can apply to. Assume students apply to one, but not both. Students have a gender (male or female), and are either admitted or not. Consider the table of the percent of students in each category of Figure 8.33 (on the next page).

In the semantics of possible worlds, we will treat the students as possible worlds, each with the same measure.

(a) What is $P(Admitted=true \mid Gender=male)$?
    What is $P(Admitted=true \mid Gender=female)$?
    Which gender is more likely to be admitted?

(b) What is $P(Admitted=true \mid Gender=male, Dept=dept\#1)$?
    What is $P(Admitted=true \mid Gender=female, Dept=dept\#1)$?
    Which gender is more likely to be admitted to *dept#*1?

(c) What is $P(Admitted=true \mid Gender=male, Dept=dept\#2)$?
    What is $P(Admitted=true \mid Gender=female, Dept=dept\#2)$?
    Which gender is more likely to be admitted to *dept#*2?

Dept	Gender	Admitted	Percent
dept#1	*male*	*true*	32
dept#1	*male*	*false*	18
dept#1	*female*	*true*	7
dept#1	*female*	*false*	3
dept#2	*male*	*true*	5
dept#2	*male*	*false*	14
dept#2	*female*	*true*	7
dept#2	*female*	*false*	14

Figure 8.33: Counts for students in departments

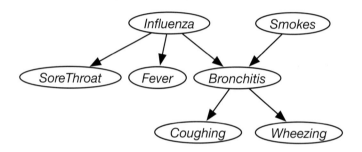

Figure 8.34: A simple diagnostic belief network

(d) This is an instance of Simpson's paradox. Why is it a paradox? Explain why it happened in this case.

(e) Give another scenario where Simpson's paradox occurs.

Exercise 8.2 Prove Proposition 8.1 (page 347) for finitely many worlds, namely that the axioms of probability (Section 8.1.2) are sound and complete with respect to the semantics of probability. [Hint: For soundness, show that each of the axioms is true based on the semantics. For completeness, construct a probability measure from the axioms.]

Exercise 8.3 Using only the axioms of probability and the definition of conditional independence, prove Proposition 8.5 (page 360).

Exercise 8.4 Consider the belief network of Figure 8.34. This the "Simple diagnostic example" in the AIspace belief network tool at http://www.aispace.org/bayes/. For each of the following, first predict the answer based on your intuition, then run the belief network to check it. Explain the result you found by carrying out the inference.

(a) The posterior probabilities of which variables change when *Smokes* is observed to be true? That is, give the variables X such that $P(X \mid Smoke=true) \neq P(X)$.

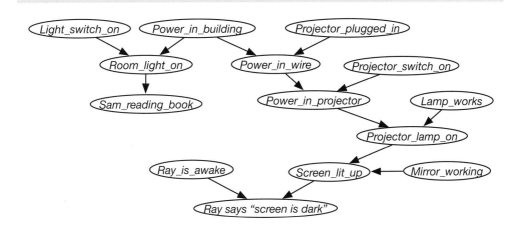

Figure 8.35: Belief network for an overhead projector

(b) Starting from the original network, the posterior probabilities of which variables change when *Fever* is observed to be true? That is, specify the X where $P(X \mid Fever=true) \neq P(X)$.

(c) Does the probability of *Fever* change when *Wheezing* is observed to be true? That is, is $P(Fever \mid Wheezing=true) \neq P(Fever)$? Explain why (in terms of the domain, in language that could be understood by someone who did not know about belief networks).

(d) Suppose *Wheezing* is observed to be true. Does the observing *Fever* change the probability of *Smokes*? That is, is $P(Smokes \mid Wheezing) \neq P(Smokes \mid Wheezing, Fever)$? Explain why (in terms that could be understood by someone who did not know about belief networks).

(e) What could be observed so that subsequently observing *Wheezing* does not change the probability of *SoreThroat*. That is, specify a variable or variables X such that $P(SoreThroat \mid X) = P(SoreThroat \mid X, Wheezing)$, or state that there are none. Explain why.

(f) Suppose *Allergies* could be another explanation of *Sore Throat*. Change the network so that *Allergies* also affects *Sore Throat* but is independent of the other variables in the network. Give reasonable probabilities.

(g) What could be observed so that observing *Wheezing* changes the probability of *Allergies*? Explain why.

(h) What could be observed so that observing *Smokes* changes the probability of *Allergies*? Explain why.

Note that parts (a), (b), and (c) only involve observing a single variable.

Exercise 8.5 Consider the belief network of Figure 8.35, which extends the electrical domain to include an overhead projector. Answer the following questions about how knowledge of the values of some variables would affect the probability of another variable.

(a) Can knowledge of the value of *Projector_plugged_in* affect your belief in the value of *Sam_reading_book*? Explain.

(b) Can knowledge of *Screen_lit_up* affect your belief in *Sam_reading_book*? Explain.

(c) Can knowledge of *Projector_plugged_in* affect your belief in *Sam_reading_book* given that you have observed a value for *Screen_lit_up*? Explain.

(d) Which variables could have their probabilities changed if just *Lamp_works* was observed?

(e) Which variables could have their probabilities changed if just *Power_in_projector* was observed?

Exercise 8.6 Kahneman [2011, p. 166] gives the following example.

A cab was involved in a hit-and-run accident at night. Two cab companies, Green and Blue, operate in the city. You are given the following data:

- 85% of the cabs in the city are Green and 15% are Blue.

- A witness identified the cab as Blue. The court tested the reliability of the witness in the circumstances that existed on the night of the accident and concluded that the witness correctly identifies each one of the two colors 80% of the time and fails 20% of the time.

What is the probability that the cab involved in the accident was Blue?

(a) Represent this story as a belief network. Explain all variables and conditional probabilities. What is observed, what is the answer?

(b) Suppose there were three independent witnesses, two of which claimed the cab was Blue and one of whom claimed the cab was Green. Show the corresponding belief network. What is the probability the cab was Blue? What if all three claimed the cab was Blue?

(c) Suppose it was found that the two witnesses who claimed the cab was Blue were not independent, but there was a 60% chance they colluded. (What might this mean?) Show the corresponding belief network, and the relevant probabilities. What is the probability that the cab is Blue, (both for the case where all three witnesses claim that cab was Blue and the case where the other witness claimed the cab was Green)?

(d) In a variant of this scenario, Kahneman [2011, p. 167] replaced the first condition with: "The two companies operate the same number of cabs, but Green cabs are involved in 85% of the accidents." How can this new scenario be represented as a belief network? Your belief network should allow observations about whether there is an accident as well as the color of the taxi. Show examples of inferences in your network. Make reasonable choices for anything that is not fully specified. Be explicit about any assumptions you make.

Exercise 8.7 Represent the same scenario as in Exercise 5.8 (page 231) using a belief network. Show the network structure. Give all of the initial factors, making reasonable assumptions about the conditional probabilities (they should follow the story given in that exercise, but allow some noise). Give a qualitative explanation of why the patient has spots and fever.

Exercise 8.8 Suppose you want to diagnose the errors school students make when adding multidigit binary numbers. Consider adding two two-digit numbers to form a three-digit number.

That is, the problem is of the form:

$$
\begin{array}{ccc}
 & A_1 & A_0 \\
+ & B_1 & B_0 \\
\hline
C_2 & C_1 & C_0
\end{array}
$$

where A_i, B_i, and C_i are all binary digits.

(a) Suppose you want to model whether students know binary addition and whether they know how to carry. If students know how, they usually get the correct answer, but sometimes make mistakes. Students who do not know how to do the appropriate task simply guess.

What variables are necessary to model binary addition and the errors students could make? You must specify, in words, what each of the variables represents. Give a DAG that specifies the dependence of these variables.

(b) What are reasonable conditional probabilities for this domain?

(c) Implement this, perhaps by using the AIspace.org belief-network tool. Test your representation on a number of different cases.

You must give the graph, explain what each variable means, give the probability tables, and show how it works on a number of examples.

Exercise 8.9 In this question, you will build a belief network representation of the Deep Space 1 (DS1) spacecraft considered in Exercise 5.10 (page 232). Figure 5.14 (page 233) depicts a part of the actual DS1 engine design.

Consider the following scenario.

- Valves are *open* or *closed*.

- A value can be *ok*, in which case the gas will flow if the valve is open and not if it is closed; *broken*, in which case gas never flows; *stuck*, in which case gas flows independently of whether the valve is open or closed; or *leaking*, in which case gas flowing into the valve leaks out instead of flowing through.

- There are three gas sensors that can detect whether gas is leaking (but not which gas); the first gas sensor detects gas from the rightmost valves ($v_1 \ldots v_4$), the second gas sensor detects gas from the center valves ($v_5 \ldots v_{12}$), and the third gas sensor detects gas from the leftmost valves ($v_{13} \ldots v_{16}$).

(a) Build a belief-network representation of the domain. You only must consider the topmost valves (those that feed into engine e_1). Make sure there are appropriate probabilities.

(b) Test your model on some non-trivial examples.

Exercise 8.10 Consider the following belief network:

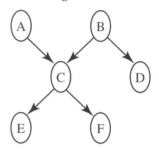

with Boolean variables (we write $A{=}true$ as a and $A{=}false$ as $\neg a$) and the following conditional probabilities:

$$P(a) = 0.9 \qquad\qquad P(d \mid b) = 0.1$$
$$P(b) = 0.2 \qquad\qquad P(d \mid \neg b) = 0.8$$
$$P(c \mid a, b) = 0.1 \qquad\qquad P(e \mid c) = 0.7$$
$$P(c \mid a, \neg b) = 0.8 \qquad\qquad P(e \mid \neg c) = 0.2$$
$$P(c \mid \neg a, b) = 0.7 \qquad\qquad P(f \mid c) = 0.2$$
$$P(c \mid \neg a, \neg b) = 0.4 \qquad\qquad P(f \mid \neg c) = 0.9$$

(a) Compute $P(e)$ using variable elimination (VE). You should first prune irrelevant variables. Show the factors that are created for a given elimination ordering.

(b) Suppose you want to compute $P(e \mid \neg f)$ using VE. How much of the previous computation is reusable? Show the factors that are different from those in part (a).

Exercise 8.11 Explain how to extend VE to allow for more general observations and queries. In particular, answer the following.

(a) How can the VE algorithm be extended to allow observations that are disjunctions of values for a variable (e.g., of the form $X = a \lor X = b$)?

(b) How can the VE algorithm be extended to allow observations that are disjunctions of values for different variables (e.g., of the form $X = a \lor Y = b$)?

(c) How can the VE algorithm be extended to allow for the probability on a set of variables (e.g., asking for the $P(X, Y \mid e)$)?

Exercise 8.12 In a nuclear research submarine, a sensor measures the temperature of the reactor core. An alarm is triggered ($A = true$) if the sensor reading is abnormally high ($S = true$), indicating an overheating of the core ($C = true$). The alarm and/or the sensor could be defective ($S\_ok = false$, $A\_ok = false$), which

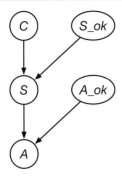

Figure 8.36: Belief network for a nuclear submarine

causes them to malfunction. The alarm system is modeled by the belief network of Figure 8.36.

(a) What are the initial factors for this network? For each factor, state what it represents and what variables it is a function of.

(b) Show how VE can be used to compute the probability that the core is over-heating, given that the alarm does not go off; that is, $P(c \mid \neg a)$. For each variable eliminated, show which variable is eliminated, which factor(s) are removed, and which factor(s) are created, including what variables each factor is a function of. Explain how the answer is derived from the final factor.

(c) Suppose we add a second, identical sensor to the system and trigger the alarm when either of the sensors reads a high temperature. The two sensors break and fail independently. Give the corresponding extended belief network.

Exercise 8.13 In this exercise, we continue Exercise 5.14 (page 236).

(a) Explain what knowledge (about physics and about students) a belief-network model requires.

(b) What is the main advantage of using belief networks over using abductive diagnosis or consistency-based diagnosis in this domain?

(c) What is the main advantage of using abductive diagnosis or consistency-based diagnosis over using belief networks in this domain?

Exercise 8.14 Suppose Kim has a camper van (a mobile home) and likes to keep it at a comfortable temperature and noticed that the energy use depended on the elevation. Kim knows that the elevation affects the outside temperature. Kim likes the camper warmer at higher elevation. Note that not all of the variables directly affect electrical usage.

(a) Show how this can be represented as a causal network, using the variables "Elevation", "Electrical Usage", "Outside Temperature", "Thermostat Setting".

(b) Give an example where intervening has an effect different from conditioning for this network.

Exercise 8.15 The aim of this exercise is to extend Example 8.29 (page 387). Suppose the animal is either sleeping, foraging or agitated.

If the animal is sleeping at any time, it does not make a noise, does not move and at the next time point it is sleeping with probability 0.8 or foraging or agitated with probability 0.1 each.

If the animal is foraging or agitated, it tends to remain in the same state of composure (with probability 0.8) move to the other state of composure with probability 0.1 or go to sleep with probability 0.1.

If the animal is foraging in a corner, it will be detected by the microphone at that corner with probability 0.5, and if the animal is agitated in a corner it will be detected by the microphone at that corner with probability 0.9. If the animal is foraging in the middle, it will be detected by each of the microphones with probability 0.2. If it is agitated in the middle it will be detected by each of the microphones with probability 0.6. Otherwise the microphones have a false positive rate of 0.05.

(a) Represent this as a two-stage dynamic belief network. Draw the network, give the domains of the variables and the conditional probabilities.

(b) What independence assumptions are embedded in the network?

(c) Implement either variable elimination or particle filtering for this problem.

(d) Does being able to hypothesize the internal state of the agent (whether it is sleeping, foraging, or agitated) help localization? Explain why.

Exercise 8.16 Suppose Sam built a robot with five sensors and wanted to keep track of the location of the robot, and built a hidden Markov model (HMM) with the following structure (which repeats to the right):

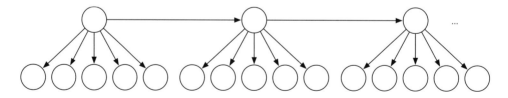

(a) What probabilities does Sam need to provide? You should label a copy of the diagram, if that helps explain your answer.

(b) What independence assumptions are made in this model?

(c) Sam discovered that the HMM with five sensors did not work as well as a version that only used two sensors. Explain why this may have occurred.

Exercise 8.17 Consider the problem of filtering in HMMs (page 392).

(a) Give a formula for the probability of some variable X_j given future and past observations. You can base this on Equation (8.2) (page 392). This should involve obtaining a factor from the previous state and a factor from the next state and combining them to determine the posterior probability of X_k.

[Hint: Consider how VE, eliminating from the leftmost variable and eliminating from the rightmost variable, can be used to compute the posterior distribution for X_j.]

(b) Computing the probability of all of the variables can be done in time linear in the number of variables by not recomputing values that were already computed for other variables. Give an algorithm for this.

(c) Suppose you have computed the probability distribution for each state S_1, ..., S_k, and then you get an observation for time $k+1$. How can the posterior probability of each variable be updated in time linear in k? [Hint: You may need to store more than just the distribution over each S_i.]

Exercise 8.18 Which of the following algorithms suffers from underflow (real numbers that are too small to be represented using double precision floats): rejection sampling, importance sampling, particle filtering? Explain why. How could underflow be avoided?

Exercise 8.19

(a) What are the independence assumptions made in the naive Bayes classifier for the help system of Example 8.35 (page 396).

(b) Are these independence assumptions reasonable? Explain why or why not.

(c) Suppose we have a topic-model network like the one of Figure 8.26 (page 401), but where all of the topics are parents of all of the words. What are all of the independencies of this model?

(d) Give an example where the topics would not be independent.

Exercise 8.20 Suppose you get a job where the boss is interested in localization of a robot that is carrying a camera around a factory. The boss has heard of variable elimination, rejection sampling, and particle filtering and wants to know which would be most suitable for this task. You must write a report for your boss (using proper English sentences), explaining which one of these technologies would be most suitable. For the two technologies that are not the most suitable, explain why you rejected them. For the one that is most suitable, explain what information is required by that technology to use it for localization:

(a) VE (i.e., exact inference as used in HMMs),

(b) rejection sampling, or

(c) particle filtering.

Exercise 8.21 How well does particle filtering work for Example 8.46 (page 414)? Try to construct an example where Gibbs sampling works much better than particle filtering. [Hint: Consider unlikely observations after a sequence of variable assignments.]

Chapter 9

Planning with Uncertainty

A plan is like the scaffolding around a building. When you're putting up the exterior shell, the scaffolding is vital. But once the shell is in place and you start to work on the interior, the scaffolding disappears. That's how I think of planning. It has to be sufficiently thoughtful and solid to get the work up and standing straight, but it cannot take over as you toil away on the interior guts of a piece. Transforming your ideas rarely goes according to plan.

– Twyla Tharp [2003]

In the quote above, Tharp is referring to dance, but the same idea holds for any agent when there is uncertainty. An agent cannot just plan a fixed sequence of steps; the result of planning needs to be more sophisticated. Planning must take into account the fact that an agent in the real world does not know what will actually happen when it acts. An agent should plan to react to its environment.

What an agent should do at any time depends on what it will do in the future. When an agent cannot precisely predict the effects of its actions, what it will do in the future depends on what it does now and what it will observe before it acts.

With uncertainty, an agent typically cannot guarantee to satisfy its goals, and even trying to maximize the probability of achieving a goal may not be sensible. For example, an agent whose goal is to minimize the probability of injury in a car accident would not get into a car or walk down a sidewalk or even go to the ground floor of a building, each of which increases the probability of being injured in a car accident, however slightly. An agent that does not guarantee to satisfy a goal can fail in many ways, some of which may be much worse than others.

This chapter is about how to take planning, reacting, observing, succeeding and failing into account simultaneously.

An agent's decision on what to do depends on three things:

- *the agent's ability.* The agent has to select from the options available to it.

- *what the agent believes and observes.* An agent might like to condition its action on what is true in the world, but it only has access to the world via its sensors. When an agent has to decide what to do, it only has access to what it has remembered and what it observes (page 54). Sensing the world updates an agent's beliefs. Beliefs and observations are the only information about the world available to an agent at any time.

- *the agent's preferences.* When an agent must reason with uncertainty, it has to consider not only what is most likely to happen but also what may happen. Some possible outcomes may have much worse consequences than others. The simple notion of a "goal" considered in Chapter 6, is not adequate when reasoning under uncertainty because the designer of an agent must specify trade-offs between different outcomes. For example, if an action results in a good outcome most of the time, but sometimes results in a disastrous outcome, it must be compared with performing an alternative action that results in the good outcome less often and the disastrous outcome less often and some mediocre outcome most of the time. Decision theory specifies how to trade off the desirability of outcomes with the probabilities of those outcomes.

9.1   Preferences and Utility

What an agent decides to do should depend on its preferences. In this section, we specify some intuitive properties of preferences and give some consequences of those properties. The properties that we give are **axioms of rationality** from which we prove a theorem about how to measure these preferences. You should consider whether each axiom is reasonable for a **rational agent** to follow; if you accept them all as reasonable, you should accept their consequences. If you do not accept the consequences, you should question which of the axioms to give up.

9.1.1   Axioms for Rationality

An agent chooses actions based on their **outcomes**. Outcomes are whatever the agent has preferences over. If an agent does not prefer any outcome to any other outcome, it does not matter what the agent does. Initially, we consider outcomes without considering the associated actions. Assume there are only a finite number of outcomes.

We define a preference relation over outcomes. Suppose o_1 and o_2 are outcomes. We say that o_1 is **weakly preferred** to outcome o_2, written $o_1 \succeq o_2$, if outcome o_1 is at least as desirable as outcome o_2.

Define $o_1 \sim o_2$ to mean $o_1 \succeq o_2$ and $o_2 \succeq o_1$. That is, $o_1 \sim o_2$ means outcomes o_1 and o_2 are equally preferred. In this case, we say that the agent is **indifferent** between o_1 and o_2.

Define $o_1 \succ o_2$ to mean $o_1 \succeq o_2$ and $o_2 \not\succeq o_1$. That is, the agent weakly prefers outcome o_1 to outcome o_2, but does not weakly prefer o_2 to o_1, and is not indifferent between them. In this case, we say that o_1 is **strictly preferred** to outcome o_2.

Typically, an agent does not know the outcome of its actions. A **lottery** is defined to be a finite distribution over outcomes, written as

$$[p_1 : o_1, p_2 : o_2, \ldots, p_k : o_k],$$

where each o_i is an outcome and p_i is a non-negative real number such that

$$\sum_i p_i = 1.$$

The lottery specifies that outcome o_i occurs with probability p_i. In all that follows, assume that outcomes may include lotteries. This includes lotteries where the outcomes are also lotteries, and so on recursively (called lotteries over lotteries).

Axiom 9.1. *(Completeness) An agent has preferences between all pairs of outcomes:*

$$o_1 \succeq o_2 \text{ or } o_2 \succeq o_1.$$

The rationale for this axiom is that an agent must act; if the actions available to it have outcomes o_1 and o_2 then, by acting, it is explicitly or implicitly preferring one outcome over the other.

Axiom 9.2. *(Transitivity) Preferences must be transitive:*

if $o_1 \succeq o_2$ and $o_2 \succeq o_3$ then $o_1 \succeq o_3$.

To see why this is reasonable, suppose it is false, in which case $o_1 \succeq o_2$ and $o_2 \succeq o_3$ and $o_3 \succ o_1$. Because o_3 is strictly preferred to o_1, the agent should be prepared to pay some amount to get from o_1 to o_3. Suppose the agent has outcome o_3; then o_2 is at least as good so the agent would just as soon have o_2. o_1 is at least as good as o_2 so the agent would just as soon have o_1 as o_2. Once the agent has o_1 it is again prepared to pay to get to o_3. It has gone through a cycle of preferences and paid money to end up where it is. This cycle that involves paying money to go through it is known as a **money pump** because, by going through the loop enough times, the amount of money that agent must pay can exceed any finite amount. It seems reasonable to claim that being prepared to pay money to cycle through a set of outcomes is irrational; hence, a rational agent should have transitive preferences.

It follows from the transitivity and completeness axioms that transitivity holds for mixes of $\succ$ and $\succeq$, so that if one or both of the preferences in the premise of the transitivity axiom is strict, then the conclusion is strict. That is, if $o_1 \succ o_2$ and $o_2 \succeq o_3$ then $o_1 \succ o_3$. Also, if $o_1 \succeq o_2$ and $o_2 \succ o_3$ then $o_1 \succ o_3$. See Exercise 9.1 (page 476).

Axiom 9.3. *(Monotonicity) An agent prefers a larger chance of getting a better outcome than a smaller chance of getting the better outcome. That is, if $o_1 \succ o_2$ and $p > q$ then*

$$[p : o_1, (1 - p) : o_2] \succ [q : o_1, (1 - q) : o_2].$$

Note that, in this axiom, $\succ$ between outcomes represents the agent's preference, whereas $>$ between p and q represents the familiar comparison between numbers.

The following axiom specifies that lotteries over lotteries only depend the outcomes and probabilities:

Axiom 9.4. *(Decomposability) ("no fun in gambling") An agent is indifferent between lotteries that have the same probabilities over the same outcomes, even if one or both is a lottery over lotteries. For example:*

$$[p : o_1, (1 - p) : [q : o_2, (1 - q) : o_3]]$$
$$\sim [p : o_1, (1 - p) * q : o_2, (1 - p) * (1 - q) : o_3].$$

Also $o_1 \sim [1 : o_1, 0 : o_2]$ for any outcomes o_1 and o_2.

This axiom specifies that it is only the outcomes and their probabilities that define a lottery. If an agent had a preference for gambling, that would be part of the outcome space.

These four axioms imply some structure on the preference between outcomes and lotteries. Suppose that $o_1 \succ o_2$ and $o_2 \succ o_3$. Consider whether the agent would prefer

- o_2 or
- the lottery $[p : o_1, (1 - p) : o_3]$

for different values of $p \in [0, 1]$. When $p = 1$, the agent prefers the lottery (because, by decomposability, the lottery is equivalent to o_1 and $o_1 \succ o_2$). When $p = 0$, the agent prefers o_2 (because the lottery is equivalent to o_3 and $o_2 \succ o_3$). At some stage, as p is varied, the agent's preferences flip between preferring o_2

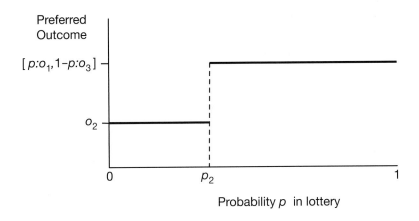

Figure 9.1: The preference between o_2 and the lottery, as a function of p

and preferring the lottery. Figure 9.1 shows how the preferences must flip as p is varied. On the X-axis is p and the Y-axis shows which of o_2 or the lottery is preferred. The following proposition formalizes this intuition.

Proposition 9.1. *If an agent's preferences are complete, transitive, and follow the monotonicity axiom, and if $o_1 \succ o_2$ and $o_2 \succ o_3$, there exists a number p_2 such that $0 \le p_2 \le 1$ and*

- *for all $p < p_2$, the agent prefers o_2 to the lottery (i.e., $o_2 \succ [p : o_1, (1-p) : o_3]$) and*
- *for all $p > p_2$, the agent prefers the lottery (i.e., $[p : o_1, (1-p) : o_3] \succ o_2$).*

Proof. By monotonicity and transitivity, if $o_2 \succeq [p : o_1, (1-p) : o_3]$ for any p then, for all $p' < p$, $o_2 \succ [p' : o_1, (1-p') : o_3]$. Similarly, if $[p : o_1, (1-p) : o_3] \succeq o_2$ for any p then, for all $p' > p$, $[p' : o_1, (1-p') : o_3] \succ o_2$. By completeness, for each value of p, either $o_2 \succ [p : o_1, (1-p) : o_3]$, $o_2 \sim [p : o_1, (1-p) : o_3]$ or $[p : o_1, (1-p) : o_3] \succ o_2$. If there is some p such that $o_2 \sim [p : o_1, (1-p) : o_3]$, then the theorem holds. Otherwise, a preference for either o_2 or the lottery with parameter p implies preferences for either all values greater than p or for all values less than p. By repeatedly subdividing the region that we do not know the preferences for, we will approach, in the limit, a value filling the criteria for p_2. $\square$

The preceding proposition does not specify what the preference of the agent is at the point p_2. The following axiom specifies that the agent is indifferent at this point.

Axiom 9.5. *(Continuity) Suppose $o_1 \succ o_2$ and $o_2 \succ o_3$, then there exists a $p_2 \in [0,1]$ such that*

$$o_2 \sim [p_2 : o_1, (1-p_2) : o_3].$$

The next axiom specifies that replacing an outcome in a lottery with an outcome that is not worse, cannot make the lottery worse.

Axiom 9.6. *(Substitutability) If $o_1 \succeq o_2$ then the agent weakly prefers lotteries that contain o_1 instead of o_2, everything else being equal. That is, for any number p and outcome o_3:*

$$[p : o_1, (1 - p) : o_3] \succeq [p : o_2, (1 - p) : o_3].$$

A direct corollary of this is that outcomes to which the agent is indifferent can be substituted for one another, without changing the preferences:

Proposition 9.2. *If an agent obeys the substitutability axiom and $o_1 \sim o_2$ then the agent is indifferent between lotteries that only differ by o_1 and o_2. That is, for any number p and outcome o_3 the following indifference relation holds:*

$$[p : o_1, (1 - p) : o_3] \sim [p : o_2, (1 - p) : o_3].$$

This follows because $o_1 \sim o_2$ is equivalent to $o_1 \succeq o_2$ and $o_2 \succeq o_1$, and we can use substitutability for both cases.

An agent is defined to be **rational** if it obeys the completeness, transitivity, monotonicity, decomposability, continuity, and substitutability axioms.

It is up to you to determine if this technical definition of rationality matches your intuitive notion of rationality. In the rest of this section, we show more consequences of this definition.

Although preferences may seem to be complicated, the following theorem shows that a rational agent's value for an outcome can be measured by a real number. Those value measurements can be combined with probabilities so that preferences with uncertainty can be compared using expectation. This is surprising for two reasons:

- It may seem that preferences are too multifaceted to be modeled by a single number. For example, although one may try to measure preferences in terms of dollars, not everything is for sale or easily converted into dollars and cents.

- One might not expect that values could be combined with probabilities. An agent that is indifferent between the money $\$(px + (1 - p)y)$ and the lottery $[p : \$x, (1 - p)\$y]$ for all monetary values x and y and for all $p \in [0, 1]$ is known as an **expected monetary value** (EMV) agent. Most people are not EMV agents, because they have, for example, a strict preference between \$1,000,000 and the lottery $[0.5 : \$0, 0.5 : \$2,000,000]$. (Think about whether you would prefer a million dollars or a coin toss where you would get nothing if the coin lands heads or two million if the coin lands tails.) Money cannot be simply combined with probabilities, so it may be surprising that there is a value that can be.

Proposition 9.3. *If an agent is rational, then for every outcome o_i there is a real number $u(o_i)$, called the **utility** of o_i, such that*

- $o_i \succ o_j$ *if and only if $u(o_i) > u(o_j)$ and*
- *utilities are linear with probabilities:*

$$u([p_1 : o_1, p_2 : o_2, \ldots, p_k : o_k]) = p_1 u(o_1) + p_2 u(o_2) + \cdots + p_k u(o_k).$$

Proof. If the agent has no strict preferences (i.e., the agent is indifferent between all outcomes) then define $u(o) = 0$ for all outcomes o.

Otherwise, choose the best outcome, o_{best}, and the worst outcome, o_{worst}, and define, for any outcome o, the utility of o to be the value p such that

$$o \sim [p : o_{best}, (1 - p) : o_{worst}].$$

The first part of the proposition follows from substitutability and monotonicity.

To prove the second part, any lottery can be reduced to a single lottery between o_{best} and o_{worst} by replacing each o_i by its equivalent lottery between o_{best} and o_{worst}, and using decomposability to put it in the form $[p : o_{best}, (1 - p) : o_{worst}]$, with p equal to $p_1 u(o_1) + p_2 u(o_2) + \cdots + p_k u(o_k)$. The details are left as an exercise. □

In this proof the utilities are all in the range $[0, 1]$, but any linear scaling gives the same result. Sometimes $[0, 100]$ is a good scale to distinguish it from probabilities, and sometimes negative numbers are useful to use when the outcomes have costs. In general, a program should accept any scale that is intuitive to the user.

A linear relationship does not usually exist between money and utility, even when the outcomes have a monetary value. People often are **risk averse** when it comes to money. They would rather have $\$n$ in their hand than some randomized setup where they expect to receive $\$n$ but could possibly receive more or less.

Example 9.1 Figure 9.2 (on the next page) shows a possible money–utility relationship for three agents. The topmost agent is risk averse, with a concave utility function. The agent with a straight-line plot is risk neutral. The lowest agent with a convex utility function is risk seeking.

The risk averse agent would rather have $\$300,000$ than a 50% chance of getting either nothing or $\$1,000,000$, but would prefer the gamble on the million dollars to $\$275,000$. They would also require more than a 73% chance of winning a million dollars to prefer this gamble to half a million dollars.

For the risk-averse agent, $u(\$999000) \approx 0.9997$. Thus, given this utility function, the risk-averse agent would be willing to pay $\$1000$ to eliminate a 0.03% chance of losing all of their money. This is why **insurance** companies exist. By paying the insurance company, say $\$600$, the risk-averse agent can change the lottery that is worth $\$999,000$ to them into one worth $\$1,000,000$

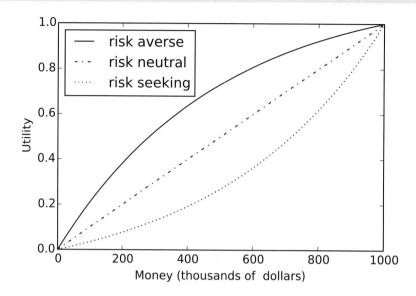

Figure 9.2: Money–utility relationships for agents with different risk profiles

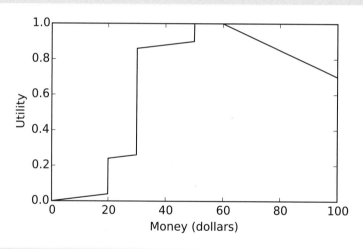

Figure 9.3: Possible money–utility relationship from Example 9.2

and the insurance companies expect to pay out, on average, about \$300, and so expect to make \$300. The insurance company can get its expected value by insuring enough houses. It is good for both parties.

Rationality does not impose any conditions on what the utility function looks like.

Example 9.2 Figure 9.3 shows a possible money–utility relationship for Chris who really wants a toy worth \$30, but would also like one worth \$20, and would like both even better. Apart from these, money does not matter much to Chris. Chris is prepared to take risks. For example, if Chris had $29, Chris would be very happy to bet $9 against a single dollar of another agent on a fair bet, such as a coin toss. This is reasonable because that $9 is not much use to Chris, but the extra dollar would enable Chris to buy the $30 toy. Chris does not want more than $60, because then Chris will worry about it being lost or stolen this will leave Chris open to extortion (e.g., by a sibling).

9.1.2 Factored Utility

Utility for an agent is a function of outcomes or states. Representing utilities in terms of features or variables typically results in more compact representations that are easier to reason with and more natural to acquire.

Suppose each outcome can be described in terms of features $X_1, \ldots, X_n$. An **additive utility** is one that can be decomposed into a sum of terms:

$$u(X_1, \ldots, X_n) = f_1(X_1) + \cdots + f_n(X_n).$$

Such a decomposition is making the assumption of **additive independence**.

When this can be done, it greatly simplifies **preference elicitation** – the problem of acquiring preferences from the user. This decomposition is not unique, because adding a constant to one of the terms and subtracting it from another gives the same utility. A **canonical form** for additive utility has a unique decomposition. Canonical forms are easier to acquire as each number can be acquired without considering the other numbers. To put additive utility into canonical form, for each feature X_i, define a local utility function $u_i(X_i)$ that has a value of 0 for the value of X_i in the worst outcome and 1 for the value of X_i in the best outcome, and a non-negative real weight, w_i. The weights should sum to 1. The utility as a function of the variables is:

$$u(X_1, \ldots, X_n) = w_1 * u_1(X_1) + \cdots + w_n * u_n(X_n).$$

To elicit such a utility function requires eliciting each local utility function and assessing the weights. Each feature, if it is relevant, must have a best value for an agent and a worst value for the agent. Assessing the local functions and weights can be done as follows. Consider just X_1; the other features then can be treated analogously. For feature X_1, values x_1 and x_1' for X_1, and fixed values $x_2, \ldots, x_n$ for $X_2, \ldots, X_n$:

$$u(x_1, x_2, \ldots, x_n) - u(x_1', x_2, \ldots, x_n) = w_1 * (u_1(x_1) - u_1(x_1')). \tag{9.1}$$

The weight w_1 can be derived when x_1 is the best outcome and x_1' is the worst outcome (because then $u_1(x_1) - u_1(x_1') = 1$). The values of u_1 for the other values in the domain of X_1 can be computed using Equation (9.1), making x_1' the worst outcome (as then $u_1(x_1') = 0$).

Challenges to Expected Utility

There have been a number of challenges to the theory of expected utility. The **Allais Paradox**, presented in 1953 [Allais and Hagen, 1979], is as follows. Which would you prefer of the following two alternatives?

A: $1m$ – one million dollars
B: lottery $[0.10 : \$2.5m, 0.89 : \$1m, 0.01 : \$0]$

Similarly, what would you choose between the following two alternatives?

C: lottery $[0.11 : \$1m, 0.89 : \$0]$
D: lottery $[0.10 : \$2.5m, 0.9 : \$0]$

It turns out that many people prefer A to B, and prefer D to C. This choice is inconsistent with the axioms of rationality. To see why, both choices can be put in the same form:

A,C: lottery $[0.11 : \$1m, 0.89 : X]$
B,D: lottery $[0.10 : \$2.5m, 0.01 : \$0, 0.89 : X]$

In A and B, X is a million dollars. In C and D, X is zero dollars. Concentrating just on the parts of the alternatives that are different seems intuitive, but people seem to have a preference for certainty.

Tversky and Kahneman [1974], in a series of human experiments, showed how people systematically deviate from utility theory. One such deviation is the **framing effect** of a problem's presentation. Consider the following.

- A disease is expected to kill 600 people. Two alternative programs have been proposed:

  Program A: 200 people will be saved
  Program B: with probability 1/3, 600 people will be saved, and with probability 2/3, no one will be saved

  Which program would you favor?

- A disease is expected to kill 600 people. Two alternative programs have been proposed:

  Program C: 400 people will die
  Program D: with probability 1/3 no one will die, and with probability 2/3 600 will die

  Which program would you favor?

Tversky and Kahneman showed that 72% of people in their experiments chose A over B, and 22% chose C over D. However, these are exactly the same choice, just described in a different way.

Prospect theory (on the next page), developed by Kahneman and Tversky, is an alternative to expected utility that better fits human behavior.

Assuming additive independence entails making a strong independence assumption. In particular, in Equation (9.1) (page 433), the difference in utilities must be the same for all values $x_2, \ldots, x_n$ for $X_2, \ldots, X_n$.

Additive independence is often not a good assumption. Consider binary features X and Y, with domains $\{x_0, x_1\}$ and $\{y_0, y_1\}$.

- Two values of X and Y are **complements** if having both is better than the sum of having the two separately. More formally, values x_1 and y_1 are complements if getting one when the agent has the other is more valuable than when the agent does not have the other:

$$u(x_1, y_1) - u(x_0, y_1) > u(x_1, y_0) - u(x_0, y_0).$$

- Two values are **substitutes** if having both is not worth as much as the sum of having each one. More formally, values x_1 and y_1 are substitutes if getting one when the agent has the other is less valuable than getting one when the agent does not have the other:

$$u(x_1, y_0) - u(x_0, y_0) > u(x_1, y_1) - u(x_0, y_1).$$

Example 9.3 For a purchasing agent in the travel domain, having a plane booking for a particular day and a hotel booking for the same day are complements: one without the other does not give a good outcome. Thus,

$$u(plane, hotel) - u(\neg plane, hotel) > u(plane, \neg hotel) - u(\neg plane, \neg hotel)$$

where the right side would be small or even negative.

Two different outings on the same day would be substitutes, assuming the person taking the holiday would enjoy one outing, but not two, on the same day. However, if the two outings are in close proximity to each other and require a long traveling time, they may be complements (the traveling time may be worth it if the person gets two outings).

Additive utility assumes there are no substitutes or complements. When there is interaction, we require a more sophisticated model, such as a **generalized additive independence** model, which represents utility as a sum of terms, where each term can be a factor over multiple variables. Elicitation of the generalized additive independence model is much more involved than eliciting an additive model, because a variable can appear in many factors.

9.1.3 Prospect Theory

Utility theory is a **normative theory** of rational agents that is justified by a set of axioms. **Prospect theory** is a **descriptive theory** of people that seeks to describe how humans make decisions. A descriptive theory is evaluated making

Figure 9.4: Human perception of length depends on the context

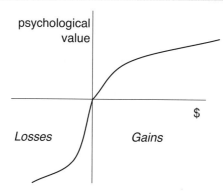

Figure 9.5: Money–value relationship for prospect theory

observations of human behavior and by carrying out controlled psychology experiments.

Rather than having preferences over outcomes, prospect theory considers the context of the preferences. The idea that humans do not perceive absolute values, but values in context is well established in psychology. Consider the Müller-Lyer illusion shown in Figure 9.4.   The horizontal lines are of equal length, but in the context of the other lines, they appear to be different. As another example, if you have one hand in cold water and one in hot water, and then put both into warm water, the warm water will feel very different to each hand. People's preferences also depend on context. Prospect theory is based on the observation that it is not the outcomes that people have preferences over; what matters is how much the choice differs from the current situation.

The relationship between money and value that is predicted by prospect theory is shown in Figure 9.5.   Rather than having the absolute wealth on the x-axis, this graph shows the difference from the current wealth. The origin of the x-axis corresponds to the current state of the person's wealth. This position is called the **reference point**. Prospect theory predicts:

- For gains, people are risk averse. This can be seen as the curve above the current wealth is concave.

- For losses, people are risk seeking. This can be seen as the curve below the current wealth is convex.

- Losses are approximately twice as bad as gains. The slope for losses is steeper than gains.

It is not just money that has such a relationship, but anything that has value. Prospect theory makes different predictions about how humans will act than does utility theory, as in the following examples from Kahneman [2011, pages 275, 291].

Example 9.4 Consider Anthony and Betty:

- Anthony's current wealth is $1 million.
- Betty's current wealth is $4 million.

They are both offered the choice between a gamble and a sure thing:

- Gamble: equal chance to end up owning $1 million or $4 million.
- Sure Thing: own $2 million

Utility theory predicts that, assuming they have the same utility curve, Anthony and Betty will make the same choice, as the outcomes are identical. Utility theory does not take into account the current wealth. Prospect theory makes different predictions for Anthony and Betty. Anthony is making a gain and so will be risk averse, and so will probably go with the sure thing. Betty is making a loss, and so will be risk seeking and go with the gamble. Anthony will be happy with the $2 million, and does not want to risk being unhappy. Betty will be unhappy with the $2 million, and has a chance to be happy if she takes the gamble.

Example 9.5 Twins Andy and Bobbie, have identical tastes and identical starting jobs. There are two jobs that are identical, except that

- job *A* gives a raise of $10000
- job *B* gives an extra day of vacation per month.

They are each indifferent to the outcomes and toss a coin. Andy takes job A, and Bobbie takes job B.

Now the company suggests they swap jobs with a $500 bonus.

Utility theory predicts that they will swap. They were indifferent and now can be $500 better off by swapping.

Prospect theory predicts they will not swap jobs. Given they have taken their jobs, they now have different reference points. Andy thinks about losing $10000. Bobbie thinks about losing 12 days of holiday. The loss is much worse than the gain of the $500 plus the vacation or salary. They each prefer their own job.

Empirical evidence supports the hypothesis that prospect theory is better than utility theory in predicting human decisions. However, just because it better matches a human's choices does not mean it is the best for an artificial agent. An artificial agent that must interact with humans should, however, take into account how humans reason. For the rest of this chapter we assume utility theory as the basis for an artificial agent's decision making and planning.

9.2   One-Off Decisions

Basic decision theory applied to intelligent agents relies on the following assumptions:

- Agents know what actions they can carry out.
- The effect of each action can be described as a probability distribution over outcomes.
- An agent's preferences are expressed by utilities of outcomes.

It is a consequence of Proposition 9.3 (page 431) that, if agents only act for one step, a rational agent should choose an action with the highest expected utility.

Dimensions (p. 31
flat
features
finite horizon
partially observab
stochastic
utility
non-learning
single agent
offline
perfect rationality

> **Example 9.6** Consider the problem of the delivery robot in which there is uncertainty in the outcome of its actions. In particular, consider the problem of going from position *o*109 in Figure 3.1 (page 80) to the *mail* position, where there is a chance that the robot will slip off course and fall down the stairs. Suppose the robot can get pads that will not change the probability of an accident but will make an accident less severe. Unfortunately, the pads add extra weight. The robot could also go the long way around, which would reduce the probability of an accident but make the trip much slower.
>
> Thus, the robot has to decide whether to wear the pads and which way to go (the long way or the short way). What is not under its direct control is whether there is an accident, although this probability can be reduced by going the long way around. For each combination of the agent's choices and whether there is an accident, there is an outcome ranging from severe damage to arriving quickly without the extra weight of the pads.

In one-off decision making, a **decision variable** is used to model an agent's choice. A decision variable is like a random variable, but it does not have an associated probability distribution. Instead, an agent gets to choose a value for a decision variable. A **possible world** specifies values for both random and decision variables. Each possible world has an associated utility. For each combination of values to decision variables, there is a probability distribution over the random variables. That is, for each assignment of a value to each decision variable, the measures of the worlds that satisfy that assignment sum to 1.

Figure 9.6 (page 440) shows a **decision tree** that depicts the different choices available to the agent and the outcomes of those choices. To read the decision

Whose Values?

Any computer program or person who acts or gives advice is using some value system to judge what is important and what is not.

> *Alice ... went on "Would you please tell me, please, which way I ought to go from here?"*
> *"That depends a good deal on where you want to get to," said the Cat.*
> *"I don't much care where –" said Alice.*
> *"Then it doesn't matter which way you go," said the Cat.*

> Lewis Carroll (1832–1898)
> *Alice's Adventures in Wonderland*, 1865

We all, of course, want computers to work on *our* value system, but they cannot act according to everyone's value system. When you build programs to work in a laboratory, this is not usually a problem. The program acts according to the goals and values of the program's designer, who is also the program's user. When there are multiple users of a system, you must be aware of whose value system is incorporated into a program. If a company sells a medical diagnostic program to a doctor, does the advice the program gives reflect the values of society, the company, the doctor, or the patient (all of whom may have very different value systems)? Does it determine the doctor's or the patient's values?

For autonomous cars, do the actions reflect the utility of the owner or the utility of society? Consider the choice between injuring n people walking across the road or injuring m family members by swerving to miss the pedestrians. How do the values of the lives trade off for different values of n and m, and different chances of being injured or killed? Drivers who most want to protect their family would have different trade-offs than the pedestrians. This situation has been studied using **trolley problems** where the tradeoffs are made explicit and people give their moral opinions.

If you want to build a system that gives advice to someone, you should find out what is true as well as what their values are. For example, in a medical diagnostic system, the appropriate procedure depends not only on patients' symptoms but also on their priorities. Are they prepared to put up with some pain in order to be more aware of their surroundings? Are they willing to put up with a lot of discomfort to live a bit longer? What risks are they prepared to take? Always be suspicious of a program or person that tells you what to do if it does not ask you what you want to do! As builders of programs that do things or give advice, you should be aware of whose value systems are incorporated into the actions or advice. If people are affected, their preferences should be taken into account, or at least they should be aware of whose preferences are being used as a basis for decisions.

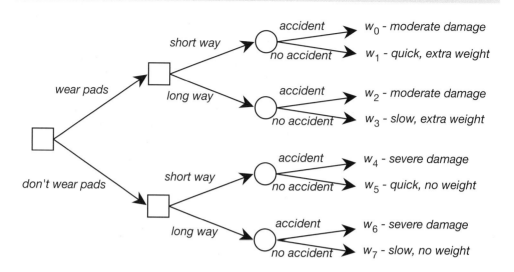

Figure 9.6: A decision tree for the delivery robot. Square boxes represent decisions that the robot can make. Circles represent random variables that the robot cannot observe before making its decision.

tree, start at the root (on the left in this figure). For the decision nodes, shown as squares, the agent gets to choose which branch to take. For each random node, shown as a circle, the agent does not get to choose which branch will be taken; rather there is a probability distribution over the branches from that node. Each leaf corresponds to a world, which is the **outcome** if the path to that leaf is followed.

Example 9.7 In Example 9.6 (page 438) there are two decision variables, one corresponding to the decision of whether the robot wears pads and one to the decision of which way to go. There is one random variable, whether there is an accident or not. Eight possible worlds correspond to the eight paths in the decision tree of Figure 9.6.

What the agent should do depends on how important it is to arrive quickly, how much the pads' weight matters, how much it is worth to reduce the damage from severe to moderate, and the likelihood of an accident.

The proof of Proposition 9.3 (page 431) specifies how to measure the desirability of the outcomes. Suppose we decide to have utilities in the range [0,100]. First, choose the best outcome, which would be w_5, and give it a utility of 100. The worst outcome is w_6, so assign it a utility of 0. For each of the other worlds, consider the lottery between w_6 and w_5. For example, w_0 may have a utility of 35, meaning the agent is indifferent between w_0 and $[0.35 : w_5, 0.65 : w_6]$, which is slightly better than w_2, which may have a utility of 30. w_1 may have a utility of 95, because it is only slightly worse than w_5.

Example 9.8 In medical **diagnosis**, decision variables correspond to various treatments and tests. The utility may depend on the costs of tests and treatment and whether the patient gets better, stays sick, or dies, and whether they have short-term or chronic pain. The outcomes for the patient depend on the treatment the patient receives, the patient's physiology, and the details of the disease, which may not be known with certainty.

The same approach holds for diagnosis of artifacts such as airplanes; engineers test components and fix them. In airplanes, you may hope that the utility function is to minimize accidents (maximize safety), but the utility incorporated into such decision making is often to maximize profit for a company and accidents are simply costs taken into account.

In a one-off decision, the agent chooses a value for each decision variable simultaneously. This can be modeled by treating all the decision variables as a single composite decision variable, D. The domain of this decision variable is the cross product of the domains of the individual decision variables.

Each world ω specifies an assignment of a value to the decision variable D and an assignment of a value to each random variable. Each world has a utility, given by the variable u.

A **single decision** is an assignment of a value to the decision variable. The **expected utility** of single decision $D = d_i$ is $\mathcal{E}(u \mid D = d_i)$, the expected value (page 355) of the utility conditioned on the value of the decision. This is the average utility of the worlds where the worlds are weighted according to their probability:

$$\mathcal{E}(u \mid D = d_i) = \sum_{\omega:D(\omega)=d_i} u(\omega) * P(\omega),$$

where $D(\omega)$ is the value of variable D in world ω, $u(\omega)$ is the value of utility in ω, and $P(\omega)$ is the probability of world ω.

An **optimal single decision** is the decision whose expected utility is maximal. That is, $D = d_{max}$ is an optimal decision if

$$\mathcal{E}(u \mid D = d_{max}) = \max_{d_i \in domain(D)} \mathcal{E}(u \mid D = d_i),$$

where $domain(D)$ is the domain of decision variable D. Thus,

$$d_{max} = \arg \max_{d_i \in domain(D)} \mathcal{E}(u \mid D = d_i).$$

Example 9.9 The delivery robot problem of Example 9.6 (page 438) is a single decision problem where the robot has to decide on the values for the variables *Wear_pads* and *Which_way*. The single decision is the complex decision variable $\langle Wear\_pads, Which\_way \rangle$. Each assignment of a value to each decision variable has an expected value. For example, the expected utility of *Wear_pads* = *true* $\wedge$ *Which_way* = *short* is given by

$$\mathcal{E}(u \mid wear\_pads \wedge Which\_way = short)$$

$$= P(accident \mid wear\_pads \wedge Which\_way = short) * u(w_0)$$
$$+ (1 - P(accident \mid wear\_pads \wedge Which\_way = short)) * u(w_1),$$

where $u(w_i)$ is the value of the utility in worlds w_i, the worlds w_0 and w_1 are as in Figure 9.6 (page 440), and *wear_pads* means *Wear_pads = true*.

9.2.1   Single-Stage Decision Networks

A decision tree is a state-based representation where each path from a root to a leaf corresponds to a state. It is, however, often more natural and more efficient to represent and reason directly in terms of features, represented as variables.

A **single-stage decision network** is an extension of a belief network with three kinds of nodes:

- **Decision nodes**, drawn as rectangles, represent decision variables. The agent gets to choose a value for each decision variable. Where there are multiple decision variables, we assume there is a total ordering of the decision nodes, and the decision nodes before a decision node D in the total ordering are the parents of D.

- **Chance nodes**, drawn as ovals, represent random variables. These are the same as the nodes in a belief network. Each chance node has an associated domain and a conditional probability of the variable, given its parents. As in a belief network, the parents of a chance node represent conditional dependence: a variable is independent of its non-descendants, given its parents. In a decision network, both chance nodes and decision nodes can be parents of a chance node.

- A **utility node**, drawn as a diamond, represents the utility. The parents of the utility node are the variables on which the utility depends. Both chance nodes and decision nodes can be parents of the utility node.

Each chance variable and each decision variable has a domain. There is no domain for the utility node. Whereas the chance nodes represent random variables and the decision nodes represent decision variables, there is no utility variable.

Associated with a decision network is a conditional probability for each chance node given its parents (as in a belief network) and a utility as a function of the utility node's parents. In the specification of the network, there are no functions associated with a decision (although the algorithm will construct a function).

Example 9.10 Figure 9.7 (on the next page) gives a decision network representation of Example 9.6 (page 438). There are two decisions to be made: which way to go and whether to wear padding. Whether the agent has an accident only depends on which way they go. The utility depends on all three variables.

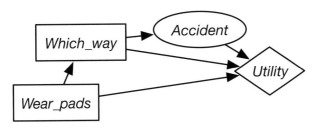

Which_way	Accident	Value
short	true	0.2
short	false	0.8
long	true	0.01
long	false	0.99

Wear_pads	Which_way	Accident	Utility
true	short	true	35
true	short	false	95
true	long	true	30
true	long	false	75
false	short	true	3
false	short	false	100
false	long	true	0
false	long	false	80

Figure 9.7: Single-stage decision network for the delivery robot

This network requires two factors: a factor representing the conditional probability, $P(Accident \mid Which\_way)$, and a factor representing the utility as a function of *Which_way*, *Accident*, and *Wear_pads*. Tables for these factors are shown in Figure 9.7.

A **policy** for a single-stage decision network is an assignment of a value to each decision variable. Each policy has an expected utility. An **optimal policy** is a policy whose expected utility is maximal. That is, it is a policy such that no other policy has a higher expected utility. The **value** of a decision network is the expected utility of an optimal policy for the network.

Figure 9.8 (on the next page) shows how **variable elimination** (page 372) is used to find an optimal policy in a single-stage decision network. After pruning irrelevant nodes and summing out all random variables, there will be a single factor that represents the expected utility for each combination of decision variables. This factor does not have to be a factor on *all* of the decision variables; however, those decision variables that are not included are not relevant to the decision.

Example 9.11 Consider running *VE_SSDN* on the decision network of Figure

1: **procedure** *VE_SSDN(DN)*
2:    **Inputs**
3:        *DN* a single stage decision network
4:    **Output**
5:        An optimal policy and the expected utility of that policy.
6:    Prune all nodes that are not ancestors of the utility node.
7:    Sum out all chance nodes.
8:    – at this stage there is a single factor F that was derived from utility
9:    Let v be the maximum value in F
10:    Let d be an assignment that gives the maximum value
11:    return d, v

Figure 9.8: Variable elimination for a single-stage decision network

9.7. No nodes are able to be pruned, so it sums out the only random variable, *Accident*. To do this, it multiplies both factors because they both contain *Accident*, and sums out *Accident*, giving the following factor:

Wear_pads	Which_way	Value
true	short	$0.2 * 35 + 0.8 * 95 = 83$
true	long	$0.01 * 30 + 0.99 * 75 = 74.55$
false	short	$0.2 * 3 + 0.8 * 100 = 80.6$
false	long	$0.01 * 0 + 0.99 * 80 = 79.2$

Thus, the policy with the maximum value – the optimal policy – is to take the short way and wear pads, with an expected utility of 83.

9.3   Sequential Decisions

Generally, agents do not make decisions in the dark without observing something about the world, nor do they make just a single decision. A more typical scenario is that the agent makes an observation, decides on an action, carries out that action, makes observations in the resulting world, then makes another decision conditioned on the observations, and so on. Subsequent actions can depend on what is observed, and what is observed can depend on previous actions. In this scenario, it is often the case that the sole reason for carrying out an action is to provide information for future actions. Actions that are carried out to just acquire information are called **information seeking actions**. Such actions are only ever needed in partially observable environments. The formalism does not need to distinguish information seeking actions from other actions. Typically actions will have both information outcomes as well as effects on the world.

Dimensions (p. 31)
flat
features
finite horizon
partially observabl
stochastic
utility
non-learning
single agent
offline
perfect rationality

A **sequential decision problem** models

- what actions are available to the agent at each stage

- what information is, or will be, available to the agent when it has to act

- the effects of the actions and

- the desirability of these effects.

Example 9.12 Consider a simple case of diagnosis where a doctor first chooses some tests and then treats a patient, taking into account the outcome of the tests. The reason the doctor may decide to do a test is so that some information (the test results) will be available at the next stage when treatment may be performed. The test results will be information that is available when the treatment is decided, but not when the test is decided. It is often a good idea to test, even if testing itself may harm the patient.

The actions available are the possible tests and the possible treatments. When the test decision is made, the information available will be the symptoms exhibited by the patient. When the treatment decision is made, the information available will be the patient's symptoms, what tests were performed, and the test results. The effect of the test is the test result, which depends on what test was performed and what is wrong with the patient. The effect of the treatment is some function of the treatment and what is wrong with the patient. The utility may include, for example, costs of tests and treatments, the pain and inconvenience to the patient in the short term, and the long-term prognosis.

9.3.1 Decision Networks

A **decision network** (also called an **influence diagram**) is a graphical representation of a finite sequential decision problem. Decision networks extend belief networks to include decision variables and utility. A decision network extends the single-stage decision network (page 442) to allow for sequential decisions, and allows both chance nodes and decision nodes to be parents of decision nodes.

In particular, a **decision network** is a directed acyclic graph (DAG) with chance nodes (drawn as ovals), decision nodes (drawn as rectangles), and a utility node (drawn as a diamond). The meaning of the arcs is:

- Arcs coming into decision nodes represent the information that will be available when the decision is made.

- Arcs coming into chance nodes represent probabilistic dependence.

- Arcs coming into the utility node represent what the utility depends on.

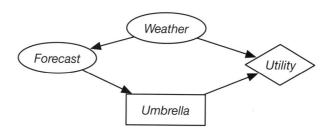

Example 9.13 Figure 9.9 shows a simple decision network for a decision of whether the agent should take an umbrella when it goes out. The agent's utility depends on the weather and whether it takes an umbrella. The agent does not get to observe the weather; it only observes the forecast. The forecast probabilistically depends on the weather.

As part of this network, the designer must specify the domain for each random variable and the domain for each decision variable. Suppose the random variable *Weather* has domain $\{norain, rain\}$, the random variable *Forecast* has domain $\{sunny, rainy, cloudy\}$, and the decision variable *Umbrella* has domain $\{take\_it, leave\_it\}$. There is no domain associated with the utility node. The designer also must specify the probability of the random variables given their parents. Suppose $P(Weather)$ is defined by

$$P(Weather=rain) = 0.3.$$

$P(Forecast \mid Weather)$ is given by

Weather	Forecast	Probability
norain	sunny	0.7
norain	cloudy	0.2
norain	rainy	0.1
rain	sunny	0.15
rain	cloudy	0.25
rain	rainy	0.6

Suppose the utility function, $u(Weather, Umbrella)$, is

Weather	Umbrella	Utility
norain	take_it	20
norain	leave_it	100
rain	take_it	70
rain	leave_it	0

There is no table specified for the *Umbrella* decision variable. It is the task of the planner to determine which value of *Umbrella* to select, as a function of the forecast.

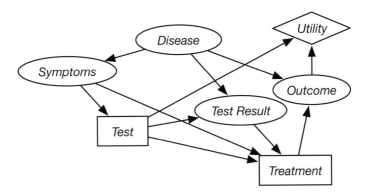

Figure 9.10: Decision network for idealized test-treat diagnosis scenario

Example 9.14 Figure 9.10 shows a decision network that represents the idealized diagnosis scenario of Example 9.12 (page 445). The symptoms depend on the disease. What test to perform is decided based on the symptoms. The test result depends on the disease and the test performed. The treatment decision is based on the symptoms, the test performed, and the test result. The outcome depends on the disease and the treatment. The utility depends on the costs of the test and on the outcome.

The outcome does not depend on the test, but only on the disease and the treatment, so the test presumably does not have side effects. The treatment does not directly affect the utility; any cost of the treatment can be incorporated into the outcome. The utility needs to depend on the test unless all tests cost the same amount.

The diagnostic assistant that is deciding on the tests and the treatments never actually finds out what disease the patient has, unless the test result is definitive, which it, typically, is not.

Example 9.15 Figure 9.11 (on the next page) gives a decision network that is an extension of the belief network of Figure 8.3 (page 365). The agent can receive a report of people leaving a building and has to decide whether or not to call the fire department. Before calling, the agent can check for smoke, but this has some cost associated with it. The utility depends on whether it calls, whether there is a fire, and the cost associated with checking for smoke.

In this sequential decision problem, there are two decisions to be made. First, the agent must decide whether to check for smoke. The information that will be available when it makes this decision is whether there is a report of people leaving the building. Second, the agent must decide whether or not to call the fire department. When making this decision, the agent will know whether there was a report, whether it checked for smoke, and whether it can see smoke. Assume that all of the variables are binary.

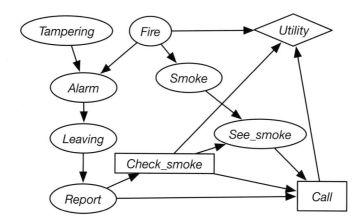

Figure 9.11: Decision network for the fire alarm decision problem

Check_smoke	Fire	Call	Utility
yes	true	yes	−220
yes	true	no	−5020
yes	false	yes	−220
yes	false	no	−20
no	true	yes	−200
no	true	no	−5000
no	false	yes	−200
no	false	no	0

Figure 9.12: Utility for fire alarm decision network

The information necessary for the decision network includes the conditional probabilities of the belief network and

- $P(See\_smoke \mid Smoke, Check\_smoke)$; how seeing smoke depends on whether the agent looks for smoke and whether there is smoke. Assume that the agent has a perfect sensor for smoke. It will see smoke if and only if it looks for smoke and there is smoke. See Exercise 9.9 (page 481).

- $u(Check\_smoke, Fire, Call)$; how the utility depends on whether the agent checks for smoke, whether there is a fire, and whether the fire department is called. Figure 9.12 provides this utility information. This utility function expresses the cost structure that calling has a cost of 200, checking has a cost of 20, but not calling when there is a fire has a cost of 5000. The utility is the negative of the cost.

A **no-forgetting agent** is an agent whose decisions are totally ordered in time, and the agent remembers its previous decisions and any information that was available to a previous decision.

A **no-forgetting decision network** is a decision network in which the decision nodes are totally ordered and, if decision node D_i is before D_j in the total ordering, then D_i is a parent of D_j, and any parent of D_i is also a parent of D_j.

Thus, any information available to D_i is available to any subsequent decision, and the action chosen for decision D_i is part of the information available for subsequent decisions. The no-forgetting condition is sufficient to make sure that the following definitions make sense and that the following algorithms work.

9.3.2 Policies

A **policy** specifies what the agent should do under all contingencies. A policy consists of a decision function for each decision variable. A **decision function** for a decision variable is a function that specifies a value for the decision variable for each assignment of values to its parents. Thus, a policy specifies, for each decision variable, what the agent will do for each of the possible observations.

Example 9.16 In Example 9.13 (page 446), some of the policies are:

- Always bring the umbrella.
- Bring the umbrella only if the forecast is "rainy."
- Bring the umbrella only if the forecast is "sunny."

There are eight different policies, because there are three possible forecasts and there are two choices for each forecast.

Example 9.17 In Example 9.15 (page 447), a policy specifies a decision function for *Check_smoke* and a decision function for *Call*. Some of the policies are:

- Never check for smoke, and call only if there is a report.
- Always check for smoke, and call only if it sees smoke.
- Check for smoke if there is a report, and call only if there is a report and it sees smoke.
- Check for smoke if there is no report, and call when it does not see smoke.
- Always check for smoke and never call.

There are four decision functions for *Check_smoke*. There are 2^8 decision functions for *Call*; for each of the eight assignments of values to the parents of *Call*, the agent can choose to call or not. Thus there are $4 * 2^8 = 1024$ different policies.

Expected Utility of a Policy

Each policy has an expected utility for an agent that follows the policy. A rational agent should adopt the policy that maximizes its expected utility.

A **possible world** specifies a value for each random variable and each decision variable. A possible world ω **satisfies** policy π if for every decision variable D, $D(\omega)$ has the value specified by the policy given the values of the parents of D in the possible world.

A possible world corresponds to a complete history and specifies the values of all random and decision variables, including all observed variables. Possible world ω satisfies policy π if ω is one possible unfolding of history given that the agent follows policy π.

The **expected utility of policy** π is

$$\mathcal{E}(u \mid \pi) = \sum_{\omega \text{ satisfies } \pi} u(\omega) * P(\omega),$$

where $P(\omega)$, the probability of world ω, is the product of the probabilities of the values of the chance nodes given their parents' values in ω, and $u(\omega)$ is the value of the utility u in world ω.

Example 9.18 Consider Example 9.13 (page 446), let π_1 be the policy to take the umbrella if the forecast is cloudy and to leave it at home otherwise. The worlds that satisfy this policy are:

Weather	Forecast	Umbrella
norain	sunny	leave_it
norain	cloudy	take_it
norain	rainy	leave_it
rain	sunny	leave_it
rain	cloudy	take_it
rain	rainy	leave_it

Notice how the value for the decision variable is the one chosen by the policy. It only depends on the forecast.

The expected utility of this policy is obtained by averaging the utility over the worlds that satisfy this policy:

$$
\begin{aligned}
\mathcal{E}(u \mid \pi_1) = {} & P(norain) * P(sunny \mid norain) * u(norain, leave\_it) \\
& + P(norain) * P(cloudy \mid norain) * u(norain, take\_it) \\
& + P(norain) * P(rainy \mid norain) * u(norain, leave\_it) \\
& + P(rain) * P(sunny \mid rain) * u(rain, leave\_it) \\
& + P(rain) * P(cloudy \mid rain) * u(rain, take\_it) \\
& + P(rain) * P(rainy \mid rain) * u(rain, leave\_it),
\end{aligned}
$$

where *norain* means *Weather* = *norain*, *sunny* means *Forecast* = *sunny*, and similarly for the other values.

1: **procedure** $VE\_DN(DN)$:
2:    **Inputs**
3:        DN a decision network
4:    **Output**
5:        An optimal policy and its expected utility
6:    **Local**
7:        DFs: a set of decision functions, initially empty
8:        Fs: a set of factors
9:    Remove all variables that are not ancestors of the utility node
10:    Create a factor in Fs for each conditional probability
11:    Create a factor in Fs for the utility
12:    **while** there are decision nodes remaining **do**
13:        Sum out each random variable that is not a parent of a decision node
14:        Let D be the last decision remaining
15:            $\triangleright$ D is only in a factor $F(D, V_1, \ldots V_k)$ where $V_1 \ldots V_k$ are parents of D
16:        Add $\max_D F$ to Fs.
17:        Add $\arg\max_D F$ to DFs.
18:    Sum out all remaining random variables
19:    Return DFs and the product of remaining factors

Figure 9.13: Variable elimination for decision networks

An **optimal policy** is a policy π^* such that $\mathcal{E}(u \mid \pi^*) \geq \mathcal{E}(u \mid \pi)$ for all policies π. That is, an optimal policy is a policy whose expected utility is maximal over all policies.

Suppose a binary decision node has n binary parents. There are 2^n different assignments of values to the parents and, consequently, there are 2^{2^n} different possible decision functions for this decision node. The number of policies is the product of the number of decision functions for each of the decision variables. Even small examples can have a huge number of policies. An algorithm that simply enumerates the policies looking for the best one will be very inefficient.

9.3.3 Variable Elimination for Decision Networks

Fortunately, an agent does not have to enumerate all of the policies; variable elimination (VE) can be adapted to find an optimal policy. The idea is first to consider the *last* decision, find an optimal decision for each value of its parents, and produce a factor of these maximum values. This results in a new decision network, with one less decision, that can be solved recursively.

Figure 9.13 shows how to use **variable elimination** for decision networks. Essentially, it computes the expected utility of an optimal decision. It eliminates the random variables that are not parents of a decision node by summing them out according to some elimination ordering. The ordering of the random variables being eliminated does not affect correctness and so it can be chosen for efficiency.

After eliminating all of the random variables that are not parents of a decision node, in a no-forgetting decision network, there must be one decision variable D that is in a factor F where all of the variables, other than D, in F are parents of D. This decision D the *last* decision in the ordering of decisions.

To eliminate that decision node, *VE_DN* chooses the values for the decision that result in the maximum utility. This maximization creates a new factor on the remaining variables and a decision function for the decision variable being eliminated. This decision function created by maximizing is one of decision functions in an optimal policy.

Example 9.19 In Example 9.13 (page 446), there are three initial factors representing $P(Weather)$, $P(Forecast \mid Weather)$, and $u(Weather, Umbrella)$. First, it eliminates *Weather* by multiplying all three factors and summing out *Weather*, giving a factor on *Forecast* and *Umbrella*,

Forecast	Umbrella	Value
sunny	take_it	12.95
sunny	leave_it	49.0
cloudy	take_it	8.05
cloudy	leave_it	14.0
rainy	take_it	14.0
rainy	leave_it	7.0

To maximize over *Umbrella*, for each value of *Forecast*, *VE_DN* selects the value of *Umbrella* that maximizes the value of the factor. For example, when the forecast is *sunny*, the agent should leave the umbrella at home for a value of 49.0.

VE_DN constructs an optimal decision function for *Umbrella* by selecting a value of *Umbrella* that results in the maximum value for each value of *Forecast*:

Forecast	Umbrella
sunny	leave_it
cloudy	leave_it
rainy	take_it

It also creates a new factor that contains the maximal value for each value of *Forecast*:

Forecast	Value
sunny	49.0
cloudy	14.0
rainy	14.0

It now sums out *Forecast* from this factor, which gives the value 77.0. This is the expected value of the optimal policy.

Example 9.20 Consider Example 9.15 (page 447). Before summing out any variables it has the following factors:

Meaning	Factor
$P(Tampering)$	$f_0(Tampering)$
$P(Fire)$	$f_1(Fire)$
$P(Alarm \mid Tampering, Fire)$	$f_2(Tampering, Fire, Alarm)$
$P(Smoke \mid Fire)$	$f_3(Fire, Smoke)$
$P(Leaving \mid Alarm)$	$f_4(Alarm, Leaving)$
$P(Report \mid Leaving)$	$f_5(Leaving, Report)$
$P(See\_smoke \mid Check\_smoke, Smoke)$	$f_6(Smoke, See\_smoke, Check\_smoke)$
$u(Fire, Check\_smoke, Call)$	$f_7(Fire, Check\_smoke, Call)$

The expected utility is the product of the probability and the utility, as long as the appropriate actions are chosen.

VE_DN sums out the random variables that are not parents of a decision node. Thus, it sums out *Tampering*, *Fire*, *Alarm*, *Smoke*, and *Leaving*. After these have been eliminated, there is a single factor, part of which (to two decimal places) is:

Report	See_smoke	Check_smoke	Call	Value
true	true	yes	yes	−1.33
true	true	yes	no	−29.30
true	true	no	yes	0
true	true	no	no	0
true	false	yes	yes	−4.86
true	false	yes	no	−3.68
...	...	...	...	...

From this factor, an optimal decision function can be created for *Call* by selecting a value for *Call* that maximizes *Value* for each assignment to *Report*, *See_smoke*, and *Check_smoke*.

Consider the case when *Report=true*, *See_smoke=true*, and *Check_smoke=yes*. The maximum of −1.33 and −29.3 is −1.33, so for this case, the optimal action is *Call=yes* with value −1.33. This maximization is repeated for the other values of *Report*, *See_smoke* and *Check_smoke*.

An optimal decision function for *Call* is

Report	See_smoke	Check_smoke	Call
true	true	yes	yes
true	true	no	yes
true	false	yes	no
...	...	...	...

The value for *Call* when *Report=true*, *See_smoke=true* and *Check_smoke=no* is arbitrary. It does not matter what the agent plans to do in this situation, because the situation never arises. The algorithm does not need to treat this as a special case.

The factor resulting from maximizing *Call* contains the maximum values for each combination of *Report*, *See_smoke*, and *Check_smoke*:

Report	See_smoke	Check_smoke	Value
true	true	yes	−1.33
true	true	no	0
true	false	yes	−3.68
. . .	. . .	. . .	. . .

Summing out *See_smoke* gives the factor

Report	Check_smoke	Value
true	yes	−5.01
true	no	−5.65
false	yes	−23.77
false	no	−17.58

Maximizing *Check_smoke* for each value of *Report* gives the decision function

Report	Check_smoke
true	yes
false	no

and the factor

Report	Value
true	−5.01
false	−17.58

Summing out *Report* gives the expected utility of −22.60 (taking into account rounding errors).

Thus, the policy returned can be seen as the rules

> *check_smoke* ← *report*.
>
> *call* ← *see_smoke*.
>
> *call* ← *report* ∧ ¬*check_smoke* ∧ ¬*see_smoke*.

The last of these rules is never used because the agent following the optimal policy does check for smoke if there is a report. It remains in the policy because *VE_DN* has not determined an optimal policy for *Check_smoke* when it is optimizing *Call*.

Note also that, in this case, even though checking for smoke has an immediate negative reward, checking for smoke is worthwhile because the information obtained is valuable.

The following example shows how the factor containing a decision variable can contain a subset of its parents when the VE algorithm optimizes the decision.

Example 9.21 Consider Example 9.13 (page 446), but with an extra arc from *Weather* to *Umbrella*. That is, the agent gets to observe both the weather and the forecast. In this case, there are no random variables to sum out, and the factor that contains the decision node and a subset of its parents is the original utility factor. It can then maximize *Umbrella*, giving the decision function and the factor:

Weather	Umbrella
norain	leave_it
rain	take_it

Weather	Value
norain	100
rain	70

Note that the forecast is irrelevant to the decision. Knowing the forecast does not give the agent any useful information. Summing out *Forecast* gives a factor where all of the values are 1.

Summing out *Weather*, where $P(Weather=norain) = 0.7$, gives the expected utility $0.7 * 100 + 0.3 * 70 = 91$.

9.4 The Value of Information and Control

Example 9.22 In Example 9.20 (page 453), the action *Check_smoke* provides information about fire. Checking for smoke costs 20 units and does not provide any direct reward; however, in an optimal policy, it is worthwhile to check for smoke when there is a report because the agent can condition its further actions on the information obtained. Thus, the information about smoke is valuable to the agent, even though smoke only provides imperfect information about whether there is fire.

One of the important lessons from this example is that an information-seeking action, such as *Check_smoke*, can be treated in the same way as any other action, such as *Call*. An optimal policy often includes actions whose only purpose is to find information, as long as subsequent actions can condition on some effect of the action. Most actions do not just provide information; they also have a more direct effect on the world.

Information is valuable to agents because it helps them make better decisions.

If X is a random variable and D is a decision variable, the **value of information** about X for decision D is how much extra utility can be obtained by knowing the value for X when decision D is made. This depends on what is controlled and what else is observed for each decision, which is the information provided in a decision network.

The value of information about X for decision D in no-forgetting decision network N is:

- the value of decision network N with an arc added from X to D, and with arcs added from X to the decisions after D to ensure that the network remains a no-forgetting decision network (page 449)

- minus the value of the decision network N where D does not have information about X, and the no-forgetting arcs are not added.

This is only defined when X is not a successor of D, because that would cause a cycle. (Something more sophisticated must be done when adding the arc from X to D causes a cycle.)

Example 9.23   In Example 9.13 (page 446), consider how much it could be worth to get a better forecast. The value of getting perfect information about the weather for the decision about whether to take an umbrella is the difference between the value of the network with an arc from *Weather* to *Umbrella* which, as calculated in Example 9.21, is 91 and the original network, which, as computed in Example 9.13 (page 446), is 77. Thus, the value of information about *Weather* for the *Umbrella* decision is $91 - 77 = 14$.

The value of information has some interesting properties:

- The value of information is never negative. The worst that can happen is that the agent can ignore the information.

- If an optimal decision is to do the same thing no matter which value of X is observed, the value of information X is zero. If the value of information X is zero, there is an optimal policy that does not depend on the value of X (i.e., the same action can be chosen no matter which value of X is observed).

The value of information is a bound on the amount the agent should be willing to pay (in terms of loss of utility) for information X for decision D. It is an upper bound on the amount that **imperfect information** about the value of X at decision D would be worth. Imperfect information is the information available from a noisy sensor of X. It is not worth paying more for a sensor of X than the value of information about X for the earliest decision that could use the information of X.

Example 9.24 In the fire alarm problem of Example 9.20 (page 453), the agent may be interested in knowing whether it is worthwhile try to detect tampering. To determine how much a tampering sensor could be worth, consider the value of information about tampering.

  The following are the values (the expected utility of the optimal policy, to one decimal point) for some variants of the network. Let N_0 be the original network.

- The network N_0 has a value of -22.6.

- Let N_1 be the same as N_0 but with an arc added from *Tampering* to *Call*. N_1 has a value of -21.3.

- Let N_2 be the same as N_1 except that it also has an arc from *Tampering* to *Check_smoke*. N_2 has a value of -20.9.

- Let N_3 be the same as N_2 but without the arc from *Report* to *Check_smoke*. N_3 has the same value as N_2.

The difference in the values of the optimal policies for the first two decision networks, namely 1.3, is the value of information about *Tampering* for the decision *Call* in network N_0. The value of information about *Tampering* for the decision *Check_smoke* in network N_0 is 1.7. Therefore installing a tampering sensor could at most give an increase of 1.7 in expected utility.

In the context N_3, the value of information about *Tampering* for *Check_smoke*, is 0. In the optimal policy for the network with both arcs, the information about *Alarm* is ignored in the optimal decision function for *Check_smoke*; the agent never checks for smoke when deciding whether to call in the optimal policy when *Alarm* is a parent of *Call*.

The **value of control** specifies how much it is worth to control a variable. In its simplest form, it is the change in value of a decision network where a random variable is replaced by a decision variable, and arcs are added to make it a no-forgetting network. If this is done, the change in utility is non-negative; the resulting network always has an equal or higher expected utility than the original network.

Example 9.25 In the fire alarm decision network of Figure 9.11 (page 448), you may be interested in the value of controlling tampering. This could, for example, be used to estimate how much it is worth to add security guards to prevent tampering. To compute this, compare the value of the decision network of Figure 9.11 (page 448) to the decision network where *Tampering* is a decision node and a parent of the other two decision nodes.

To determine the value of control, turn the *Tampering* node into a decision node and make it a parent of the other two decisions. The value of the resulting network is -20.7. This can be compared to the value of N_3 in Example 9.24 (which has the same arcs, and differs in whether *Tampering* is a decision or random node), which was -20.9. Notice that control is more valuable than information.

The previous description assumed the parents of the random variable that is being controlled become parents of the decision variable. In this case, the value of control is never negative. However, if the parents of the decision node do not include all of the parents of the random variable, it is possible that control is less valuable than information. In general, one must be explicit about what information will be available when controlling a variable.

Example 9.26 Consider controlling the variable *Smoke* in Figure 9.11 (page 448). If *Fire* is a parent of the decision variable *Smoke*, it has to be a parent of *Call* to make it a no-forgetting network. The expected utility of the resulting network with *Smoke* coming before *Check_smoke* is −2.0. The value of controlling *Smoke* in this situation is due to observing *Fire*. The resulting optimal decision is to call if there is a fire and not call otherwise.

Suppose the agent were to control *Smoke* without observing *Fire*. That is, the agent can decide to make smoke or prevent smoke, and *Fire* is not a parent of any decision. This situation can be modeled by making *Smoke* a decision variable with no parents. In this case, the expected utility is −23.20, which is worse than the initial decision network, because blindly controlling *Smoke* loses its ability to act as a sensor for *Fire*.

9.5 Decision Processes

The decision networks of the previous section were for finite-stage, partially observable domains. In this section, we consider indefinite horizon and infinite horizon problems.

Dimensions (p. 31)
flat
states
infinite horizon
fully observable
stochastic
utility
non-learning
single agent
offline
perfect rationality

Often an agent must reason about an ongoing process or it does not know how many actions it will be required to do. These are called **infinite horizon** problems when the process may go on forever or **indefinite horizon** problems when the agent will eventually stop, but it does not know when it will stop.

For ongoing processes, it may not make sense to consider only the utility at the end, because the agent may never get to the end. Instead, an agent can receive a sequence of **rewards**. These rewards incorporate the action costs in addition to any prizes or penalties that may be awarded. Negative rewards are called **punishments**. Indefinite horizon problems can be modeled using a stopping state. A **stopping state** or **absorbing state** is a state in which all actions have no effect; that is, when the agent is in that state, all actions immediately return to that state with a zero reward. Goal achievement can be modeled by having a reward for entering such a stopping state.

A Markov decision process can be seen as a Markov chain (page 384) augmented with actions and rewards or as a decision network extended in time. At each stage, the agent decides which action to perform; the reward and the resulting state depend on both the previous state and the action performed.

We only consider **stationary models** (page 385) where the state transitions and the rewards do not depend on the time.

A **Markov decision process** or an **MDP** consists of

- S, a set of states of the world

- A, a set of actions

- $P : S \times S \times A \to [0, 1]$, which specifies the **dynamics**. This is written as $P(s' \mid s, a)$, the probability of the agent transitioning into state s' given

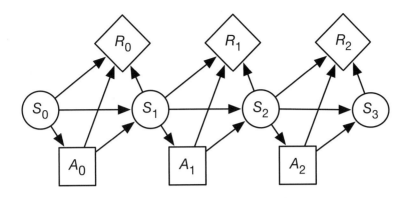

Figure 9.14: Decision network representing a finite part of an MDP

that the agent is in state s and does action a. Thus,

$$\forall s \in S \ \forall a \in A \ \sum_{s' \in S} P(s' \mid s, a) = 1.$$

- $R : S \times A \times S \to \Re$, where $R(s, a, s')$, the **reward function**, gives the expected immediate reward from doing action a and transitioning to state s' from state s. Sometimes it is convenient to use $R(s, a)$, the expected value of doing a in state s, which is $R(s, a) = \sum_{s'} R(s, a, s') * P(s' \mid s, a)$.

A finite part of a Markov decision process can be depicted using a decision network as in Figure 9.14.

Example 9.27 Suppose Sam wanted to make an informed decision about whether to party or relax over the weekend. Sam prefers to party, but is worried about getting sick. Such a problem can be modeled as an MDP with two states, *healthy* and *sick*, and two actions, *relax* and *party*. Thus

$$S = \{healthy, sick\}$$
$$A = \{relax, party\}$$

Based on experience, Sam estimate that the dynamics $P(s' \mid s, a)$ is given by

S	A	Probability of $s' = healthy$
healthy	*relax*	0.95
healthy	*party*	0.7
sick	*relax*	0.5
sick	*party*	0.1

So, if Sam is healthy and parties, there is a 30% chance of becoming sick. If Sam is healthy and relaxes, Sam will more likely remain healthy. If Sam is sick and relaxes, there is a 50% chance of getting better. If Sam is sick and parties, there is only a 10% chance of becoming healthy.

Sam estimates the (immediate) rewards to be:

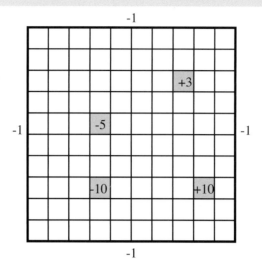

Figure 9.15: The grid world of Example 9.28

S	A	Reward
healthy	relax	7
healthy	party	10
sick	relax	0
sick	party	2

Thus, Sam always enjoys partying more than relaxing. However, Sam feels much better overall when healthy, and partying results in being sick more than relaxing does.

The problem is to determine what Sam should do each weekend.

Example 9.28 A grid world is an idealization of a robot in an environment. At each time, the robot is at some location and can move to neighboring locations, collecting rewards and punishments. Suppose that the actions are stochastic, so that there is a probability distribution over the resulting states given the action and the state.

Figure 9.15 shows a 10×10 grid world, where the robot can choose one of four actions: up, down, left, or right. If the agent carries out one of these actions, it has a 0.7 chance of going one step in the desired direction and a 0.1 chance of going one step in any of the other three directions. If it bumps into the outside wall (i.e., the location computed is outside the grid), there is a penalty of 1 (i.e., a reward of -1) and the agent does not actually move. There are four rewarding states (apart from the walls), one worth $+10$ (at position $(9, 8)$; 9 across and 8 down), one worth $+3$ (at position $(8, 3)$), one worth -5 (at position $(4, 5)$), and one worth -10 (at position $(4, 8)$). In each of these states, the agent gets the reward after it carries out an action in that state, not when it enters the state. When the agent reaches one of the states with positive reward (either $+3$ or $+10$), no matter what action it performs, at the next step it is flung, at random, to one of the four corners of the grid world.

Note that, in this example, the reward is a function of both the initial state and the final state. The agent bumped into the wall, and so received a reward of -1, if and only if the agent remains is the same state. Knowing just the initial state and the action, or just the final state and the action, does not provide enough information to infer the reward.

As with decision networks (page 445), the designer also has to consider what information is available to the agent when it decides what to do. There are two common variations:

- In a **fully observable Markov decision process (MDP)**, the agent gets to observe the current state when deciding what to do.

- A **partially observable Markov decision process (POMDP)** is a combination of an MDP and a **hidden Markov model** (page 387). At each time, the agent gets to make some (ambiguous and possibly noisy) observations that depend on the state. The agent only has access to the history of rewards, observations and previous actions when making a decision. It cannot directly observe the current state.

Rewards

To decide what to do, the agent compares different sequences of rewards. The most common way to do this is to convert a sequence of rewards into a number called the **value**, the **cumulative reward** or the **return**. To do this, the agent combines an immediate reward with other rewards in the future. Suppose the agent receives the sequence of rewards:

$$r_1, r_2, r_3, r_4, \ldots.$$

Three common reward criteria are used to combine rewards into a value V:

Total reward $V = \sum_{i=1}^{\infty} r_i$. In this case, the value is the sum of all of the rewards. This works when you can guarantee that the sum is finite; but if the sum is infinite, it does not give any opportunity to compare which sequence of rewards is preferable. For example, a sequence of \$1 rewards has the same total as a sequence of \$100 rewards (both are infinite). One case where the total reward is finite is when there are stopping states (page 458) and the agent always has a non-zero probability of eventually entering a stopping state.

Average reward $V = \lim_{n \to \infty} (r_1 + \cdots + r_n)/n$. In this case, the agent's value is the average of its rewards, averaged over for each time period. As long as the rewards are finite, this value will also be finite. However, whenever the total reward is finite, the average reward is zero, and so the average reward will fail to allow the agent to choose among different actions that each have a zero average reward. Under this criterion, the only thing that matters is where the agent ends up. Any finite sequence of bad actions does not affect the limit. For example, receiving \$1,000,000 followed by rewards of \$1 has the same average reward as receiving \$0 followed by rewards of \$1 (they both have an average reward of \$1).

Discounted reward $V = r_1 + \gamma r_2 + \gamma^2 r_3 + \cdots + \gamma^{i-1} r_i + \cdots$, where γ, the **discount factor**, is a number in the range $0 \leq \gamma < 1$. Under this criterion, future rewards are worth less than the current reward. If γ was 1, this would be the same as the total reward. When $\gamma = 0$, the agent ignores all future rewards. Having $0 \leq \gamma < 1$ guarantees that, whenever the rewards are finite, the total value will also be finite.

The discounted reward can be rewritten as

$$V = \sum_{i=1}^{\infty} \gamma^{i-1} r_i$$
$$= r_1 + \gamma r_2 + \gamma^2 r_3 + \cdots + \gamma^{i-1} r_i + \cdots$$
$$= r_1 + \gamma(r_2 + \gamma(r_3 + \cdots)).$$

Suppose V_k is the reward accumulated from time k:

$$V_k = r_k + \gamma(r_{k+1} + \gamma(r_{k+2} + \cdots))$$
$$= r_k + \gamma V_{k+1}.$$

To understand the properties of V_k, suppose $S = 1 + \gamma + \gamma^2 + \gamma^3 + \cdots$, then $S = 1 + \gamma S$. Solving for S gives $S = 1/(1 - \gamma)$. Thus, with the discounted reward, the value of all of the future is at most $1/(1 - \gamma)$ times as much as the maximum reward and at least $1/(1 - \gamma)$ times as much as the minimum reward. Therefore, the eternity of time from now only has a finite value compared with the immediate reward, unlike the average reward, in which the immediate reward is dominated by the cumulative reward for the eternity of time.

In economics, γ is related to the interest rate: getting \$1 now is equivalent to getting $\$(1 + i)$ in one year, where i is the interest rate. You could also see the discount rate as the probability that the agent survives; γ can be seen as the probability that the agent keeps going.

The rest of this chapter considers discounted rewards. The discounted reward is referred to as the **value**.

9.5.1   Policies

In a fully-observable Markov decision process, the agent gets to observe its current state before deciding which action to carry out. For now assume that the Markov decision process is fully observable. A **policy** specifies what the agent should do as a function of the state it is in. A **stationary policy** is a function $\pi : S \to A$. In a non-stationary policy the action is a function of the state and the time; we assume policies are stationary.

Given a reward criterion, a policy has an expected value for every state. Let $V^\pi(s)$ be the expected value of following π in state s. This specifies how much value the agent expects to receive from following the policy in that state. Policy π is an **optimal policy** if there is no policy π' and no state s such that $V^{\pi'}(s) > V^\pi(s)$. That is, it is a policy that has a greater or equal expected value at every state than any other policy.

Example 9.29 For Example 9.27 (page 459), with two states and two actions, there are $2^2 = 4$ policies:

- Always relax.
- Always party.
- Relax if healthy and party if sick.
- Party if healthy and relax if sick.

The total reward for all of these is infinite because the agent never stops, and can never continually get a reward of 0. To determine the average reward is left as an exercise (Exercise 9.14 (page 482)). How to compute the discounted reward is discussed in the next section.

Example 9.30 In the MDP of Example 9.28 (page 460) there are 100 states and 4 actions, therefore there are $4^{100} \approx 10^{60}$ stationary policies. Each policy specifies an action for each state.

For infinite horizon problems, a stationary MDP always has an optimal stationary policy. However for finite-stage problems, a non-stationary policy might be better than all stationary policies. For example, if the agent had to stop at time n, for the last decision in some state, the agent would act to get the largest immediate reward without considering the future actions, but for earlier decisions it may decide to get a lower reward immediately to obtain a larger reward later.

Value of a Policy

Consider how to compute the expected value, using the discounted reward of a policy, given a discount factor of γ. The value is defined in terms of two interrelated functions:

- $V^\pi(s)$ is the expected value of following policy π in state s.

- $Q^\pi(s, a)$, is the expected value, starting in state s of doing action a, then following policy π. This is called the **Q-value** of policy π.

Q^π and V^π are defined recursively in terms of each other. If the agent is in state s, performs action a, and arrives in state s', it gets the immediate reward of $R(s,a,s')$ plus the discounted future reward, $\gamma V^\pi(s')$. When the agent is planning it does not know the actual resulting state, so it uses the expected value, averaged over the possible resulting states:

$$Q^\pi(s,a) = \sum_{s'} P(s' \mid s,a)(R(s,a,s') + \gamma V^\pi(s'))$$
$$= R(s,a) + \gamma \sum_{s'} P(s' \mid s,a)V^\pi(s') \tag{9.2}$$

where $R(s,a) = \sum_{s'} P(s' \mid s,a)R(s,a,s')$.

$V^\pi(s)$ is obtained by doing the action specified by π and then following π:

$$V^\pi(s) = Q^\pi(s, \pi(s)).$$

Value of an Optimal Policy

Let $Q^*(s,a)$, where s is a state and a is an action, be the expected value of doing a in state s and then following the optimal policy. Let $V^*(s)$, where s is a state, be the expected value of following an optimal policy from state s.

Q^* can be defined analogously to Q^π:

$$Q^*(s,a) = \sum_{s'} P(s' \mid s,a)(R(s,a,s') + \gamma V^*(s'))$$
$$= R(s,a) + \gamma \sum_{s'} P(s' \mid s,a)\gamma V^*(s').$$

$V^*(s)$ is obtained by performing the action that gives the best value in each state:

$$V^*(s) = \max_a Q^*(s,a).$$

An optimal policy π^* is one of the policies that gives the best value for each state:

$$\pi^*(s) = \arg\max_a Q^*(s,a)$$

where $\arg\max_a Q^*(s,a)$ is a function of state s, and its value is an action a that results in the maximum value of $Q^*(s,a)$.

9.5.2   Value Iteration

Value iteration is a method of computing an optimal policy for an MDP and its value.

Value iteration starts at the "end" and then works backward, refining an estimate of either Q^* or V^*. There is really no end, so it uses an arbitrary end

1: **procedure** *Value_iteration*(S, A, P, R)
2:    **Inputs**
3:        S is the set of all states
4:        A is the set of all actions
5:        P is state transition function specifying $P(s' \mid s, a)$
6:        R is a reward function $R(s, a)$
7:    **Output**
8:        $\pi[S]$ approximately optimal policy
9:        $V[S]$ value function
10:    **Local**
11:        real array $V_k[S]$ is a sequence of value functions
12:        action array $\pi[S]$
13:    assign $V_0[S]$ arbitrarily
14:    $k := 0$
15:    **repeat**
16:        $k := k + 1$
17:        **for each** state s **do**
18:            $V_k[s] = \max_a R(s, a) + \gamma * \sum_{s'} P(s' \mid s, a) * V_{k-1}[s']$
19:    **until** termination
20:    **for each** state s **do**
21:        $\pi[s] = \arg\max_a R(s, a) + \gamma * \sum_{s'} P(s' \mid s, a) * V_k[s']$
22:    **return** π, V_k

Figure 9.16: Value iteration for MDPs, storing V

point. Let V_k be the value function assuming there are k stages to go, and let Q_k be the Q-function assuming there are k stages to go. These can be defined recursively. Value iteration starts with an arbitrary function V_0. For subsequent stages, it uses the following equations to get the functions for $k + 1$ stages to go from the functions for k stages to go

$$Q_{k+1}(s, a) = R(s, a) + \gamma * \sum_{s'} P(s' \mid s, a) * V_k(s')$$

$$V_k(s) = \max_a Q_k(s, a)$$

It can either save the $V[S]$ array or the $Q[S, A]$ array. Saving the V array results in less storage, but it is more difficult to determine an optimal action, and one more iteration is needed to determine which action results in the greatest value.

Figure 9.16 shows the value iteration algorithm when the V array is stored. This procedure converges no matter what the initial value function V_0 is. An initial value function that approximates V^* converges quicker than one that does not. The basis for many abstraction techniques for MDPs is to use some heuristic method to approximate V^* and to use this as an initial seed for value iteration.

Example 9.31 Consider the two-state MDP of Example 9.27 (page 459) with discount $\gamma = 0.8$. We write the value function as [*healthy_value, sick_value*], and the Q-function as [[*healthy_relax, healthy_party*], [*sick_relax, sick_party*]]. Suppose initially the value function is $[0, 0]$. The next Q-value is $[[7, 10], [0, 2]]$, so the next value function is $[10, 2]$ (obtained by Sam partying). The next Q-value is then

State	Action	Value		
healthy	*relax*	7+0.8*(0.95*10+0.05*2)	=	14.68
healthy	*party*	10+0.8*(0.7*10+0.3*2)	=	16.08
sick	*relax*	0+0.8*(0.5*10+0.5*2)	=	4.8
sick	*party*	2+0.8*(0.1*10+0.9*2)	=	4.24

So the next value function is $[16.08, 4.8]$. After 1000 iterations, the value function is $[35.71, 23.81]$. So the Q function is $[[35.10, 35.71], [23.81, 22.0]]$. Therefore, the optimal policy is to party when healthy and relax when sick.

Example 9.32 Consider the nine squares around the $+10$ reward of Example 9.28 (page 460). The discount is $\gamma = 0.9$. Suppose the algorithm starts with $V_0[s] = 0$ for all states s.

The values of V_1, V_2, and V_3 (to one decimal point) for these nine cells are

0	0	−0.1
0	10	−0.1
0	0	−0.1

V_1

0	6.3	−0.1
6.3	9.8	6.2
0	6.3	−0.1

V_2

4.5	6.2	4.4
6.2	9.7	6.6
4.5	6.1	4.4

V_3

After the first step of value iteration (in V_1) the nodes get their immediate expected reward. The center node in this figure is the $+10$ reward state. The right nodes have a value of -0.1, with the optimal actions being up, left, and down; each of these has a 0.1 chance of crashing into the wall for an immediate expected reward of -1.

V_2 are the values after the second step of value iteration. Consider the node that is immediately to the left of the $+10$ rewarding state. Its optimal value is to go to the right; it has a 0.7 chance of getting a reward of 10 in the following state, so that is worth 9 (10 times the discount of 0.9) to it now. The expected reward for the other possible resulting states is 0. Thus, the value of this state is $0.7 * 9 = 6.3$.

Consider the node immediately to the right of the $+10$ rewarding state after the second step of value iteration. The agent's optimal action in this state is to go left. The value of this state is

Prob	Reward		Future Value	
0.7 * (	0	+	0.9 * 10)	*Agent goes left*
+ 0.1 * (	0	+	0.9 * −0.1)	*Agent goes up*
+ 0.1 * (	−1	+	0.9 * −0.1)	*Agent goes right*
+ 0.1 * (	0	+	0.9 * −0.1)	*Agent goes down*

which evaluates to 6.173, which is approximated to 6.2 in V_2 above.

The +10 reward state has a value less than 10 in V_2 because the agent gets flung to one of the corners and these corners look bad at this stage.

After the next step of value iteration, shown on the right-hand side of the figure, the effect of the +10 reward has progressed one more step. In particular, the corners shown get values that indicate a reward in 3 steps.

An applet is available on the book website showing the details of value iteration for this example.

The value iteration algorithm of Figure 9.16 (page 465) has an array for each stage, but it really only needs to store the current and the previous arrays. It can update one array based on values from the other.

A common refinement of this algorithm is **asynchronous value iteration**. Rather than sweeping through the states to create a new value function, asynchronous value iteration updates the states one at a time, in any order, and stores the values in a single array. Asynchronous value iteration can store either the $Q[s, a]$ array or the $V[s]$ array. Figure 9.17 (on the next page) shows asynchronous value iteration when the Q array is stored. It converges faster than value iteration and is the basis of some of the algorithms for reinforcement learning (page 549). Termination can be difficult to determine if the agent must guarantee a particular error, unless it is careful about how the actions and states are selected. Often, this procedure is run indefinitely as an anytime algorithm (page 26) where it is always prepared to give its best estimate of the optimal action in a state when asked.

Asynchronous value iteration could also be implemented by storing just the $V[s]$ array. In that case, the algorithm selects a state s and carries out the update:

$$V[s] := R(s, a) + \gamma * \max_a \sum_{s'} P(s' \mid s, a) * V[s'].$$

Although this variant stores less information, it is more difficult to extract the policy. It requires one extra backup to determine which action a results in the maximum value. This can be done using

$$\pi[s] := R(s, a) + \gamma * \arg\max_a \sum_{s'} P(s' \mid s, a) * V[s'].$$

1: **procedure** *Asynchronous_value_iteration(S, A, P, R)*
2:     **Inputs**
3:         S is the set of all states
4:         A is the set of all actions
5:         P is state transition function specifying $P(s' \mid s, a)$
6:         R is a reward function $R(s, a)$
7:     **Output**
8:         $\pi[s]$ approximately optimal policy
9:         $Q[S, A]$ value function
10:    **Local**
11:        real array $Q[S, A]$
12:        action array $\pi[S]$
13:    assign $Q[S, A]$ arbitrarily
14:    **repeat**
15:        select a state s
16:        select an action a
17:        $Q[s, a] = R(s, a) + \gamma * \sum_{s'} P(s' \mid s, a) * \max_{a'} Q[s', a']$
18:    **until** termination
19:    **for each** state s **do**
20:        $\pi[s] = \arg\max_a Q[s, a]$
21:    **return** π, Q

Figure 9.17: Asynchronous value iteration for MDPs

Example 9.33 In Example 9.32 (page 466), the state one step up and one step to the left of the +10 reward state only had its value updated after three value iterations, in which each iteration involved a sweep through all of the states.

In asynchronous value iteration, the +10 reward state can be chosen first. Next, the node to its left can be chosen, and its value will be $0.7 * 0.9 * 10 = 6.3$. Next, the node above that node could be chosen, and its value would become $0.7 * 0.9 * 6.3 = 3.969$. Note that it has a value that reflects that it is close to a +10 reward after considering 3 states, not 300 states, as does value iteration.

9.5.3   Policy Iteration

Policy iteration starts with a policy and iteratively improves it. It starts with an arbitrary policy π_0 (an approximation to the optimal policy works best) and carries out the following steps starting from $i = 0$:

- Policy evaluation: determine $V^{\pi_i}(S)$. The definition of V^π is a set of $|S|$ linear equations in $|S|$ unknowns. The unknowns are the values of $V^{\pi_i}(S)$. There is an equation for each state. These equations can be solved

```
1: procedure Policy_iteration(S, A, P, R)
2:     Inputs
3:         S is the set of all states
4:         A is the set of all actions
5:         P is state transition function specifying P(s' | s, a)
6:         R is a reward function R(s, a)
7:     Output
8:         optimal policy π
9:     Local
10:        action array π[S]
11:        Boolean variable noChange
12:        real array V[S]
13:    set π arbitrarily
14:    repeat
15:        noChange := true
16:        Solve V[s] = R(s, a) + γ * Σ_{s'∈S} P(s' | s, π[s]) * V[s']
17:        for each s ∈ S do
18:            QBest := V[s]
19:            for each a ∈ A do
20:                Qsa := R(s, a) + γ * Σ_{s'∈S} P(s' | s, a) * V[s']
21:                if Qsa > QBest then
22:                    π[s] := a
23:                    QBest := Qsa
24:                    noChange := false
25:    until noChange
26:    return π
```

Figure 9.18: Policy iteration for MDPs

by a linear equation solution method (such as Gaussian elimination) or they can be solved iteratively.

- Policy improvement: choose $\pi_{i+1}(s) = \arg\max_a Q^{\pi_i}(s, a)$, where the Q-value can be obtained from V using Equation (9.2) (page 464). To detect when the algorithm has converged, it should only change the policy if the new action for some state improves the expected value; that is, it should set $\pi_{i+1}(s)$ to be $\pi_i(s)$ if $\pi_i(s)$ is one of the actions that maximizes $Q^{\pi_i}(s, a)$.

- Stop if there is no change in the policy, if $\pi_{i+1} = \pi_i$, otherwise increment i and repeat.

The algorithm is shown in Figure 9.18. Note that it only keeps the latest policy and notices if it has changed. This algorithm always halts, usually in a small number of iterations. Unfortunately, solving the set of linear equations is often time consuming.

A variant of policy iteration, called **modified policy iteration**, is obtained by noticing that the agent is not required to evaluate the policy to improve it; it can just carry out a number of backup steps using Equation (9.2) (page 464) and then do an improvement.

Policy iteration is useful for systems that are too big to be represented directly as MDPs. Suppose a controller has some parameters that can be varied. An estimate of the derivative of the cumulative discounted reward of a parameter a in some context s, which corresponds to the derivative of $Q(a, s)$, can be used to improve the parameter. Such an iteratively improving controller can get into a local maximum that is not a global maximum. Policy iteration for state-based MDPs does not result in non-optimal local maxima, because it is possible to improve an action for a state without affecting other states, whereas updating parameters can affect many states at once.

9.5.4   Dynamic Decision Networks

A Markov decision process is a state-based representation. Just as in classical planning (page 239), where reasoning in terms of features can allow for more straightforward representations and more efficient algorithms, planning under uncertainty can also take advantage of reasoning in term of features. This forms the basis for **decision-theoretic planning**.

Dimensions (p. 31)
flat
features
infinite horizon
fully observable
stochastic
utility
non-learning
single agent
offline
perfect rationality

A **dynamic decision network** (DDN) can be seen in a number of different ways:

- a factored representation of MDPs, where the states are described in terms of features

- an extension of decision networks to allow repeated structure for indefinite or infinite horizon problems

- an extension of dynamic belief networks (page 393) to include actions and rewards

- an extension of the feature-based representation of actions (page 244) or the CSP representation of planning (page 252) to allow for rewards and for uncertainty in the effect of actions.

A **dynamic decision network** consists of

- a set of state features

- a set of possible actions

- a two-stage decision network with chance nodes F_0 and F_1 for each feature F (for the features at time 0 and time 1, respectively) and decision node A_0, such that

- the domain of A_0 is the set of all actions

- the parents of A_0 are the set of time 0 features (these arcs are often not shown explicitly)

- the parents of time 0 features do not include A_0 or time 1 features, but can include other time 0 features as long as the resulting network is acyclic

- the parents of time 1 features can contain A_0 and other time 0 or time 1 features as long as the graph is acyclic

- there are probability distributions for $P(F_0 \mid parents(F_0))$ and $P(F_1 \mid parents(F_1))$ for each feature F

- the reward function depends on any subset of the action and the features at times 0 or 1.

As in a dynamic belief network, a dynamic decision network can be **unfolded** into a decision network by replicating the features and the action for each subsequent time. For a time horizon of n, there is a variable F_i for each feature F and for each time i for $0 \le i \le n$. For a time horizon of n, there is a variable A_i for each time i for $0 \le i < n$. The horizon, n, can be unbounded, which allows us to model processes that do not halt.

Thus, if there are k features for a time horizon of n there are $k * (n + 1)$ chance nodes (each representing a random variable) and k decision nodes in the unfolded network.

The parents of A_i are random variables F_i (so that the agent can observe the state). Each F_{i+1} depends on the action A_i and the features at time i and $i + 1$ in the same way, with the same conditional probabilities, as F_1 depends the action A_0 and the features at time 0 and 1. The F_0 variables modeled directly in the two-stage decision network.

Example 9.34   Example 6.1 (page 240) models a robot that can deliver coffee and mail in a simple environment with four locations. Consider representing a stochastic version of Example 6.1 as a dynamic decision network. We use the same features as in that example.

Feature $RLoc$ models the robot's location. The parents of variables $RLoc_1$ are $Rloc_0$ and A.

Feature RHC is true when the robot has coffee. The parents of RHC_1 are RHC_0, A_0, and $RLoc_0$; whether the robot has coffee depends on whether it had coffee before, what action it performed, and its location. The probabilities can encode the possibilities that the robot does not succeed in picking up or delivering the coffee, that it drops the coffee, or that someone gives it coffee in some other state (which we may not want to say is impossible).

Variable SWC is true when Sam wants coffee. The parents of SWC_1 include SWC_0, RHC_0, A_0, and $RLoc_0$. You would not expect RHC_1 and SWC_1 to be

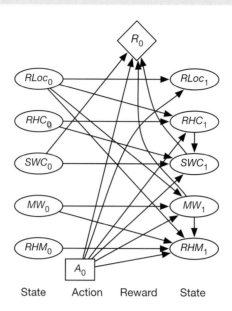

Figure 9.19: Two-stage dynamic decision network

independent because they both depend on whether or not the coffee was successfully delivered. This could be modeled by having one be a parent of the other.

The two-stage belief network representing how the state variables at time 1 depend on the action and the other state variables is shown in Figure 9.19. This figure also shows the reward as a function of the action, whether Sam stopped wanting coffee, and whether there is mail waiting.

Figure 9.20 (on the next page) shows the unfolded decision network for a horizon of 3.

Example 9.35 An alternate way to model the dependence between RHC_1 and SWC_1 is to introduce a new variable, CSD_1, which represents whether coffee was successfully delivered at time 1. This variable is a parent of both RHC_1 and SWC_1. Whether Sam wants coffee is a function of whether Sam wanted coffee before and whether coffee was successfully delivered. Whether the robot has coffee depends on the action and the location, to model the robot picking up coffee. Similarly, the dependence between MW_1 and RHM_1 can be modeled by introducing a variable MPU_1, which represents whether the mail was successfully picked up. The resulting DDN unfolded to a horizon of 2, but omitting the reward, is shown in Figure 9.21 (on the next page).

If the reward comes only at the end, variable elimination for decision networks, shown in Figure 9.13 (page 451), can be applied directly. Variable elimination for decision networks corresponds to value iteration. Note that in fully

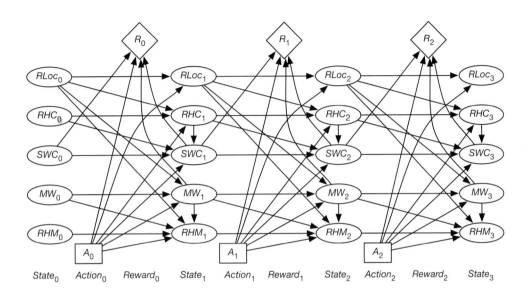

Figure 9.20: Dynamic decision network unfolded for a horizon of 3

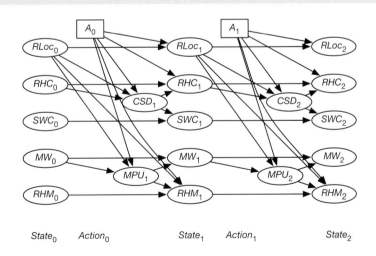

Figure 9.21: Dynamic decision network with intermediate variables for a horizon of 2, omitting the reward nodes

observable decision networks variable elimination does not require the no-forgetting condition. Once the agent knows the state, all previous decisions are irrelevant. If rewards are accrued at each time step, the algorithm must be augmented to allow for the addition (and discounting) of rewards. See Exercise 9.18 (page 485).

9.5.5   Partially Observable Decision Processes

A **partially observable Markov decision process (POMDP)** is a combination of an MDP (page 458) and a hidden Markov model (page 387). Instead of the state being observable, there are partial and/or noisy observations of the state that the agent gets to observe before it has to act.

Dimensions (p. 31)
flat
states
infinite horizon
partially observable
stochastic
utility
non-learning
single agent
offline
perfect rationality

A POMDP consists of

- S, a set of states of the world

- A, a set of actions

- O, a set of possible observations

- $P(S_0)$, which gives the probability distribution of the starting state

- $P(S' \mid S, A)$, which specifies the dynamics – the probability of getting to state S' by doing action A from state S

- $R(S, A, S')$, which gives the expected reward of starting in state S, doing action A, and transitioning to state S', and

- $P(O \mid S)$, which gives the probability of observing O given the state is S.

A finite part of a POMDP can be depicted using the decision diagram as in Figure 9.22 (on the next page).

There are three main ways to approach the problem of computing the optimal policy for a POMDP:

- Solve the associated dynamic decision network using variable elimination for decision networks (Figure 9.13 (page 451), extended to include discounted rewards). The policy created is a function of the history of the agent (page 54). The problem with this approach is that the history is unbounded, and the size of a policy is exponential in the length of the history. This only works when the history is short or is deliberately cut short.

- Make the policy a function of the belief state – a probability distribution over the states. Maintaining the belief state is the problem of filtering (page 388). The problem with this approach is that, with n states, the set of belief states is an $(n-1)$-dimensional real space. However, because the

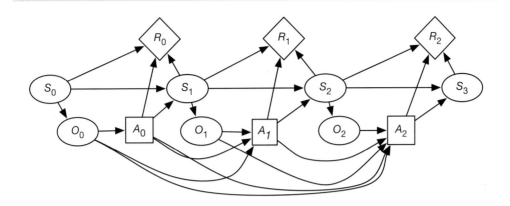

Figure 9.22: A POMDP as a dynamic decision network

value of a sequence of actions only depends on the states, the expected value is a linear function of the values of the states. Because plans can be conditional on observations, and we only consider optimal actions for any belief state, the optimal policy for any finite look-ahead, is piecewise linear and convex.

- Search over the space of controllers for the best controller (page 54). Thus, the agent searches over what to remember and what to do based on its belief state and observations. Note that the first two proposals are instances of this approach: the agent remembers all of its history or the agent has a belief state that is a probability distribution over possible states. In general, the agent may want to remember some parts of its history but have probabilities over some other features. Because it is unconstrained over what to remember, the search space is enormous.

9.6 Review

- Utility is a measure of preference that combines with probability.
- A decision network can represent a finite stage partially observable sequential decision problem in terms of features.
- An MDP can represent an infinite stage or indefinite stage sequential decision problem in terms of states.
- A fully observable MDP can be solved with value iteration or policy iteration.
- A dynamic decision network allows for the representation of an MDP in terms of features.

9.7   References and Further Reading

Utility theory, as presented here, was developed by Neumann and Morgenstern [1953] and was further developed by Savage [1972]. Keeney and Raiffa [1976] discuss utility theory, concentrating on multiattribute (feature-based) utility functions. For work on graphical models of utility and preferences, see Bacchus and Grove [1995] and Boutilier et al. [2004]. Walsh [2007] and Rossi et al. [2011] overview the use of preferences in AI.

Kahneman [2011] discusses the psychology behind how people make decisions under uncertainty and motivates prospect theory. Wakker [2010] provides a textbook overview of utility and prospect theories.

Decision networks or influence diagrams were invented by Howard and Matheson [1984]. A method using dynamic programming for solving influence diagrams can be found in Shachter and Peot [1992]. The value of information and control is discussed by Matheson [1990].

MDPs were invented by Bellman [1957] and are discussed by Puterman [1994] and Bertsekas [1995]. Mausam and Kolobov [2012] overview MDPs in AI. Boutilier et al. [1999] review lifting MDPs to features, known as decision-theoretic planning.

9.8   Exercises

Exercise 9.1   Prove that transitivity of $\succeq$ implies transitivity of $\succ$ (even when only one of the premises involves $\succeq$ and the other involves $\succ$). Does your proof rely on other axioms?

Exercise 9.2   Consider the following two alternatives

  i) In addition to what you currently own, you have been given $1000. You are now asked to choose one of these options:
       50% chance to win $1000 or get $500 for sure

  ii) In addition to what you currently own, you have been given $2000. You are now asked to choose one of these options:
       50% chance to lose $1000 or lose $500 for sure.

Explain how the predictions of utility theory and prospect theory differ for these alternatives.

Exercise 9.3   One of the decisions we must make in real life is whether to accept an invitation even though we are not sure we can or want to go to an event. Figure 9.23 (on the next page) gives a decision network for such a problem. Suppose that all of the decision and random variables are Boolean (i.e., have domain {*true, false*}). You can accept the invitation, but when the time comes, you still must decide whether or not to go. You might get sick in between accepting the invitation and having to decide to go. Even if you decide to go, if you have not accepted the invitation you may not be able to go. If you get sick, you have a good

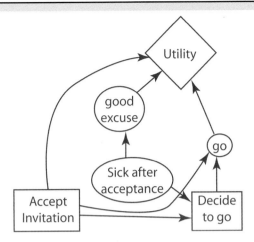

Figure 9.23: A decision network for an invitation decision

excuse not to go. Your utility depends on whether you accept, whether you have a good excuse, and whether you actually go.

(a) Give a table representing a possible utility function. Assume the unique best outcome is that you accept the invitation, you do not have a good excuse, but you do go. The unique worst outcome is that you accept the invitation, you do not have a good excuse, and you do not go. Make your other utility values reasonable.

(b) Suppose that you get to observe whether you are sick before accepting the invitation. Note that this is a different variable than if you are sick after accepting the invitation. Add to the network so that this situation can be modeled. You must not change the utility function, but the new observation must have a positive value of information. The resulting network must be no-forgetting.

(c) Suppose that, after you have decided whether to accept the original invitation and before you decide to go, you can find out if you get a better invitation (to an event that clashes with the original event, so you cannot go to both). Suppose you would prefer the later invitation than the original event you were invited to. (The difficult decision is whether to accept the first invitation or wait until you get a better invitation, which you may not get.) Unfortunately, having another invitation does not provide a good excuse. On the network, add the node "better invitation" and all relevant arcs to model this situation. [You do not have to include the node and arcs from part (b).]

(d) If you have an arc between "better invitation" and "accept invitation" in part (c), explain why (i.e., what must the world be like to make this arc appropriate). If you did not have such an arc, which way could it go to still fit the preceding story; explain what must happen in the world to make this arc appropriate.

Grade	Total Effort	Utility
A	Lot	
A	Little	
B	Lot	
B	Little	
C	Lot	
C	Little	
F	Lot	
F	Little	

Figure 9.24: Utility function for the study decision

(e) If there was not an arc between "better invitation" and "accept invitation" (whether or not you drew such an arc), what must be true in the world to make this lack of arc appropriate?

Exercise 9.4 Students have to make decisions about how much to study for each course. The aim of this question is to investigate how to use decision networks to help them make such decisions.

Suppose students first have to decide how much to study for the midterm. They can study a lot, study a little, or not study at all. Whether they pass the midterm depends on how much they study and on the difficulty of the course. As a rough approximation, they pass if they study hard or if the course is easy and they study a bit. After receiving their midterm grade, they have to decide how much to study for the final exam. The final exam result depends on how much they study and on the difficulty of the course. Their final grade (A, B, C or F) depends on which exams they pass; generally they get an A if they pass both exams, a B if they only pass the final, a C if they only pass the midterm, or an F if they fail both. Of course, there is a great deal of noise in these general estimates.

Suppose that their utility depends on their subjective total effort and their final grade. Suppose their subjective total effort (a lot or a little) depends on their effort in studying for the midterm and the final.

(a) Draw a decision network for a student decision based on the preceding story.

(b) What is the domain of each variable?

(c) Give appropriate conditional probability tables.

(d) What is the best outcome (give this a utility of 100) and what is the worst outcome (give this a utility of 0)?

(e) Give an appropriate utility function for a student who is lazy and just wants to pass (not get an F). The total effort here measures whether they (thought they) worked a lot or a little overall. Explain the best outcome and the worst outcome. Fill in copy of the table of Figure 9.24; use 100 for the best outcome and 0 for the worst outcome.

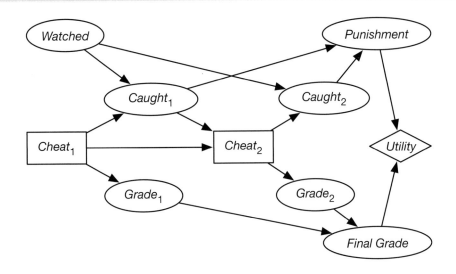

Figure 9.25: Decision about whether to cheat

(f) Given your utility function for the previous part, give values for the missing terms for one example that reflects the utility function you gave above :

Comparing outcome _____
and lottery $[p :$ _____, $1 - p :$ _____$]$
when $p =$ _____ the outcome is preferred to the lottery
when $p =$ _____ the lottery is preferred to the outcome.

(g) Give an appropriate utility function for a student who does not mind working hard and really wants to get an A, and would be very disappointed with a B or lower. Explain the best outcome and the worst outcome. Fill in copy of the table of Figure 9.24; use 100 for the best outcome and 0 for the worst outcome.

Exercise 9.5 Some students choose to cheat on exams, and instructors want to make sure that cheating does not pay. A rational model would specify that the decision of whether to cheat depends on the costs and the benefits. Here we will develop and critique such a model.

Consider the decision network of Figure 9.25. This diagram models a student's decisions about whether to cheat at two different times. If students cheat they may be caught cheating, but they could also get higher grades. The punishment (either suspension, cheating recorded on the transcript, or none) depends on whether they get caught at either or both opportunities. Whether they get caught depends on whether they are being watched and whether they cheat. The utility depends on their final grades and their punishment.

Use the probabilities from http://artint.info/code/aispace/cheat_decision.xml for the AISpace Belief network tool at http://www.aispace.org/bayes/. (Do a "Load from URL" in the "File" menu).

(a) What is an optimal policy? Give a description in English of an optimal policy. (The description should not use any jargon of AI or decision theory.) What is the value of an optimal policy?

(b) What happens to the optimal policy when the probability of being watched goes up? [Modify the probability of "Watched" in create mode.] Try a number of values. Explain what happens and why.

(c) What is an optimal policy when the rewards for cheating are reduced? Try a number of different parametrizations.

(d) Change the model so that once students have been caught cheating, they will be watched more carefully. [Hint: Whether they are watched at the first opportunity needs to be a different variable than whether they are watched at the second opportunity.] Show the resulting model (both the structure and any new parameters), and give the policies and expected utilities for various settings of the parameters.

(e) What does the current model imply about how cheating affects future grades? Change the model so that cheating affects subsequent grades. Explain how the new model achieves this.

(f) How could this model be changed to be more realistic (but still be simple)? [For example: Are the probabilities reasonable? Are the utilities reasonable? Is the structure reasonable?]

(g) Suppose the university decided to set up an honor system so that instructors do not actively check for cheating, but there is severe punishment for first offenses if cheating is discovered. How could this be modeled? Specify a model for this and explain what decision is optimal (for a few different parameter settings).

(h) Should students and instructors be encouraged to think of the cheating problem as a rational decision in a game? Explain why or why not in a single paragraph.

Exercise 9.6 Suppose that, in a decision network, the decision variable *Run* has parents *Look* and *See*. Suppose you are using VE to find an optimal policy and, after eliminating all of the other variables, you are left with a single factor:

Look	See	Run	Value
true	true	yes	23
true	true	no	8
true	false	yes	37
true	false	no	56
false	true	yes	28
false	true	no	12
false	false	yes	18
false	false	no	22

(a) What is the resulting factor after eliminating *Run*? [Hint: You do not sum out *Run* because it is a decision variable.]

(b) What is the optimal decision function for *Run*?

(c) What is the value of information about *Look* for the decision *Run* for the decision network where *See* is a parent of *Run*? That is, if the agent has the information about *See*, how much more is the information about *Look* worth?

Exercise 9.7 Suppose that, in a decision network, there were arcs from random variables "contaminated specimen" and "positive test" to the decision variable "discard sample." You solved the decision network and discovered that there was a unique optimal policy:

contaminated specimen	positive test	discard sample
true	*true*	*yes*
true	*false*	*no*
false	*true*	*yes*
false	*false*	*no*

What can you say about the value of information in this case?

Exercise 9.8 How sensitive are the answers from the decision network of Example 9.15 (page 447) to the probabilities? Test the program with different conditional probabilities and see what effect this has on the answers produced. Discuss the sensitivity both to the optimal policy and to the expected value of the optimal policy.

Exercise 9.9 In Example 9.15 (page 447), suppose that the fire sensor was noisy in that it had a 20% false positive rate,

$$P(see\_smoke|report \wedge \neg smoke) = 0.2,$$

and a 15% false negative rate,

$$P(see\_smoke|report \wedge smoke) = 0.85.$$

Is it still worthwhile to check for smoke?

Exercise 9.10 Consider the belief network of Exercise 8.12 (page 420). When an alarm is observed, a decision is made whether or not to shut down the reactor. Shutting down the reactor has a cost c_s associated with it (independent of whether the core was overheating), whereas not shutting down an overheated core incurs a cost c_m that is much higher than c_s.

(a) Draw the decision network to model this decision problem for the original system (i.e., with only one sensor).

(b) Specify the tables for all new factors that must be defined (you should use the parameters c_s and c_m where appropriate in the tables). Assume that the *utility* is the negative of *cost*.

(c) Show how variable elimination can be used to find the optimal decision. For each variable eliminated, show which variable is eliminated, how it is eliminated (through summing or maximization), which factors are removed, what factor is created, and what variables this factor is over. You are not required to give the tables.

Exercise 9.11 Consider the following decision network:

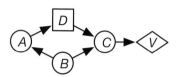

(a) What are the initial factors? (Give the variables in the scope of each factor, and specify any associated meaning of each factor.)

(b) Show what factors are created when optimizing the decision function and computing the expected value, for one of the legal elimination orderings. At each step explain which variable is being eliminated, whether it is being summed out or maximized, what factors are being combined, and what factors are created (give the variables they depend on, not the tables).

(c) If the value of information of A at decision D is zero, what does an optimal policy look like? (Give the most specific statement you can make about any optimal policy.)

Exercise 9.12 What is the main difference between asynchronous value iteration and standard value iteration? Why does asynchronous value iteration often work better than standard value iteration?

Exercise 9.13 Explain why we often use discounting of future rewards in MDPs. How would an agent act differently if the discount factor was 0.6 as opposed to 0.9?

Exercise 9.14 Consider the MDP of Example 9.29 (page 463).

(a) As the discount varies between 0 and 1, how does the optimal policy change? Give an example of a discount that produces each different policy that can be obtained by varying the discount.

(b) How can the MDP and/or discount be changed so that the optimal policy is to relax when healthy and to party when sick? Give an MDP that changes as few of the probabilities, rewards or discount as possible to have this as the optimal policy.

(c) The optimal policy computed in Example 9.31 (page 466) was to party when healthy and relax when sick. What is the distribution of states that the agent following this policy will visit? Hint: The policy induces a Markov chain (page 384), which has a stationary distribution. What is the average reward of this policy? Hint: The average reward can be obtained by computing the expected value of the immediate rewards with respect the stationary distribution.

Exercise 9.15 Consider a game world:

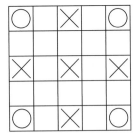

The robot can be at any one of the 25 locations on the grid. There can be a treasure on one of the circles at the corners. When the robot reaches the corner where the treasure is, it collects a reward of 10, and the treasure disappears. When there is no treasure, at each time step, there is a probability $P_1 = 0.2$ that a treasure appears, and it appears with equal probability at each corner. The robot knows its position and the location of the treasure.

There are monsters at the squares marked with an $\times$. Each monster randomly and independently, at each time step, checks whether the robot is on its square. If the robot is on the square when the monster checks, it has a reward of -10 (i.e., it loses 10 points). At the center point, the monster checks at each time step with probability $p_2 = 0.4$; at the other four squares marked with an $\times$, the monsters check at each time step with probability $p_3 = 0.2$.

Assume that the rewards are immediate upon entering a state: that is, if the robot enters a state with a monster, it gets the (negative) reward on entering the state, and if the robot enters the state with a treasure, it gets the reward upon entering the state, even if the treasure arrives at the same time.

The robot has eight actions corresponding to the eight neighboring squares. The diagonal moves are noisy; there is a $p_4 = 0.6$ probability of going in the direction chosen and an equal chance of going to each of the four neighboring squares closest to the desired direction. The vertical and horizontal moves are also noisy; there is a $p_5 = 0.8$ chance of going in the requested direction and an equal chance of going to one of the adjacent diagonal squares. For example, the actions up-left and up have the following results:

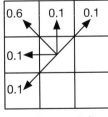

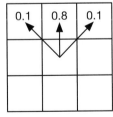

Action=up-left   Action=up

If the action results in crashing into a wall, the robot has a reward of -2 (i.e., loses 2) and does not move.

There is a discount factor of $p_6 = 0.9$.

(a) How many states are there? (Or how few states can you get away with?) What do they represent?

(b) What is an optimal policy?

(c) Suppose the game designer wants to design different instances of the game that have non-obvious optimal policies for a game player. Give three assignments to the parameters p_1 to p_6 with different optimal policies. If there are not that many different optimal policies, give as many as there are and explain why there are no more than that.

Exercise 9.16 Consider a 5×5 grid game similar to the game of the previous question. The agent can be at one of the 25 locations, and there can be a treasure at one of the corners or no treasure.

Assume the "up" action has same dynamics as in the previous question. That is, the agent goes up with probability 0.8 and goes up-left with probability 0.1 and up-right with probability 0.1.

If there is no treasure, a treasure can appear with probability 0.2. When it appears, it appears randomly at one of the corners, and each corner has an equal probability of treasure appearing. The treasure stays where it is until the agent lands on the square where the treasure is. When this occurs the agent gets an immediate reward of $+10$ and the treasure disappears in the next state transition. The agent and the treasure move simultaneously so that if the agent arrives at a square at the same time the treasure appears, it gets the reward.

Suppose we are doing asynchronous value iteration and have the value for each state as in the following grids. The number in a square represent the value of that state and empty squares have a value of zero. It is irrelevant to this question how these values got there.

The left grid shows the values for the states where there is no treasure and the right grid shows the values of the states when there is a treasure at the top-right corner. There are also states for the treasures at the other three corners, but assume that the current values for these states are all zero.

Consider the next step of asynchronous value iteration. For state s_{13}, which is marked by $*$ in the figure, and the action a_2, which is "up," what value is assigned to $Q[s_{13}, a_2]$ on the next value iteration? You must show all your work but do not have to do any arithmetic (i.e., leave it as an expression). Explain each term in your expression.

Exercise 9.17 In a decision network, suppose that there are multiple utility nodes, where the values must be added. This lets us represent a generalized additive utility function. How can the VE for decision networks algorithm, shown in Figure 9.13 (page 451), be altered to include such utilities?

Exercise 9.18 How can variable elimination for decision networks, shown in Figure 9.13 (page 451), be modified to include additive discounted rewards? That is, there can be multiple utility (reward) nodes, to be added and discounted. Assume that the variables to be eliminated are eliminated from the latest time step forward.

Chapter 10

Learning with Uncertainty

Learning without thought is labor lost; thought without learning is perilous.

Confucius (551 BC – 479 BC), The Confucian Analects

This chapter is about probabilistic models for supervised learning, unsupervised learning, learning belief networks and Bayesian learning, which treats learning as probabilistic inference.

10.1 Probabilistic Learning

One principled way to choose a model is choose a model that is most likely, given the data. That is, given a data set Es, choose a model m that maximizes the probability of the model given the data, $P(m \mid Es)$. The model that maximizes $P(m \mid Es)$ is called the **maximum a posteriori probability** model, or the **MAP** model.

The probability of model m given examples Es is obtained by using **Bayes' rule** (page 353):

$$P(m \mid Es) = \frac{P(Es \mid m) * P(m)}{P(Es)} . \tag{10.1}$$

The **likelihood**, $P(Es \mid m)$, is the probability that this model would have produced this data set. It is high when the model is a good fit to the data, and it is low when the model would have predicted different data. The **prior probability** $P(m)$ encodes the **learning bias** and specifies which models are a priori more likely. The prior probability of the model, $P(m)$, is used to bias the learning toward simpler models. Typically, simpler models have a higher prior probability. Using the prior is a form of regularization (page 304). The denominator $P(Es)$, called the **partition function**, is a normalizing constant to make sure that the probabilities sum to 1.

Because the denominator of Equation (10.1) is independent of the model, it may be ignored when choosing the most likely model. Thus, the MAP model is the model that maximizes

$$P(Es \mid m) * P(m) .\tag{10.2}$$

One alternative is to choose the **maximum likelihood model** – the model that maximizes $P(Es \mid m)$. The problem with choosing the maximum likelihood model is that, if the space of models is rich enough, a model exists that specifies that this particular data set will be produced, which has $P(Es \mid m) = 1$. Such a model may be a priori very unlikely. However, we may not want to exclude such a model, because it may be the true model, and, given enough data it might be the best model. Choosing the maximum likelihood model is equivalent to choosing the maximum a posteriori model with a uniform prior over hypotheses. Ockham's razor (page 272) suggests instead that we should prefer simpler hypotheses over more complex hypotheses.

10.1.1 Learning Probabilities

The above formulation of probabilities of models can be used to learn probabilities, as in the following example.

Example 10.1 Consider the problem of predicting the next toss of a thumbtack (drawing pin), where we define the outcomes *Tails* and *Heads* as follows:

Suppose you tossed a thumbtack a number of times and observed *Es*, a particular sequence of n_0 instances of *Tails* and n_1 instances of *Heads*. Assume the tosses are independent, and that *Heads* occurs with probability p. The likelihood is

$$P(Es \mid p) = p^{n_1} * (1 - p)^{n_0}.$$

This is a maximum when the log-likelihood

$$\log P(Es \mid p) = n_1 * \log p + n_0 * \log(1 - p)$$

is a maximum, which occurs when $p = \frac{n_1}{n_0 + n_1}$.

Note that if $n_0 = 0$ or $n_1 = 0$, this predicts a zero probability for an event that is possible.

The maximum likelihood estimator on the training data is not necessarily the best predictor on the test set.

A simple way both to solve the zero-probability problem and to take prior knowledge into account is to use a real-valued **pseudocount** (page 302) or **prior count** to which the training data are added.

Suppose an agent must predict a value for Y with domain $\{y_1, \ldots, y_k\}$, and there are no inputs. The agent starts with a pseudocount c_i for each y_i. These counts are chosen before the agent has seen any of the data. Suppose the agent observes some training examples, where n_i is the number of data points with $Y=y_i$. The probability of Y is estimated using

$$P(Y=y_i) = \frac{c_i + n_i}{\sum_{i'} c_{i'} + n_{i'}}.$$

This may be used to estimate probabilities even before any data have been seen, when the n_i are all 0.

If there is no prior knowledge, Laplace [1812] suggested that it is reasonable to set $c_i=1$. This method with a prior count of 1 is called **Laplace smoothing**. Laplace smoothing can be justified in terms of averaging over the probabilities (see Section 10.4, (page 512)).

Example 10.2 In Example 10.1, one possible prior for the model that says that heads occurs with probability p is

$$P(p) = p^{c_1} * (1 - p)^{c_0}$$

in which case the probability of the model given examples Es which consists of a particular sequence of n_0 tails and n_1 heads is

$$P(p \mid Es) \propto p^{c_1+n_1} * (1 - p)^{c_0+n_0}.$$

In this case, the MAP estimate for p, the probability of heads is:

$$p = \frac{c_1 \mid n_1}{c_0 + n_0 + c_1 + n_1}.$$

One reason for this prior is that you might not think that 0 or 1 is a reasonable estimate for the probability of heads (no matter how much data you have). It also reflects prior knowledge to be used when there are no data, and can be integrated with data. Moreover this prior has the same form as the posterior; both are described in terms of counts (a prior that has the same form as a posterior is called a **conjugate prior**).

To determine appropriate pseudocounts, consider the question, "How much more should an agent believe y_i if it had seen one example with y_i true than if it had seen no examples with y_i true?" If, with no examples of y_i true, the agent believes that y_i is impossible, c_i should be zero. If not, the ratio chosen in answer to that question should be equal to the ratio $(1 + c_i) : c_i$. If the pseudocount is 1, a value that has been seen once would be twice as likely as one that has been seen no times. If the pseudocount is 10, a value observed once would be 10% more likely than a value observed no times. If the pseudocount is 0.1, a value observed once would be 11 times more likely than a value observed no times. If there is no reason to choose one value in the domain of Y over another, all the values of c_i should be equal.

Typically, we do not have data without any prior knowledge. There is often a great deal of knowledge about a domain, either in the meaning of the symbols or in experience with similar examples, that can be used to improve predictions.

Probabilities from Experts

The use of pseudocounts also gives us a way to combine **expert opinion** and data. Often a single agent does not have good data but may have access to multiple experts who have varying levels of expertise and who give different probabilities.

There are a number of problems with obtaining probabilities from experts:

- experts' reluctance to give an exact probability value that cannot be refined,

- representing the uncertainty of a probability estimate,

- combining the numbers from multiple experts, and

- combining expert opinion with actual data.

Rather than expecting experts to give probabilities, the experts provide counts. Instead of giving a real number for the probability of A, an expert gives a pair of numbers as $\langle n, m \rangle$ that is interpreted as though the expert had observed n occurrences of A out of m trials. Essentially, the experts provide not only a probability but also an estimate of the size of the data set on which their opinion is based. Note that you should not necessarily believe an expert's sample size, as people are often overconfident in their abilities.

The counts from different experts can be combined together by adding the components to give the pseudocounts for the system. Whereas the ratio reflects the probability, different levels of confidence are reflected in the absolute values. Consider different ways to represent the probability 2/3. The pair $\langle 2, 3 \rangle$ reflects extremely low confidence that would quickly be dominated by data or other experts' estimates. The pair $\langle 20, 30 \rangle$ reflects more confidence – a few examples would not change it much, but tens of examples would. Even hundreds of examples would have little effect on the prior counts of the pair $\langle 2000, 3000 \rangle$. However, with millions of data points, even these prior counts would have little impact on the resulting probability estimate.

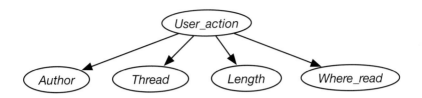

Figure 10.1: Belief network corresponding to a naive Bayes classifier

10.1.2 Probabilistic Classifiers

A **Bayes classifier** is a probabilistic model that is used for supervised learning. A Bayes classifier is based on the idea that the role of a **class** is to predict the values of features for members of that class. Examples are grouped in classes because they have common values for some of the features. Such classes are often called **natural kinds**. The learning agent learns how the features depend on the class and uses that model to predict the classification of a new example.

The simplest case is the **naive Bayes classifier**, which makes the independence assumption that the input features are conditionally independent of each other given the classification. The independence of the naive Bayes classifier is embodied in a belief network where the features are the nodes, the target feature (the classification) has no parents, and the target feature is the only parent of each input feature. This belief network requires the probability distributions $P(Y)$ for the target feature, or class, Y and $P(X_i \mid Y)$ for each input feature X_i. For each example, the prediction is computed by conditioning on observed values for the input features and querying the classification. Multiple target variables can be modeled and learned separately.

Example 10.3 Suppose an agent wants to predict the user action given the data of Figure 7.1 (page 273). For this example, the user action is the classification. The naive Bayes classifier for this example corresponds to the belief network of Figure 10.1. The input features form variables that are children of the classification.

Given an example with inputs $X_1 = v_1, \ldots, X_k = v_k$, Bayes' rule (page 353) is used to compute the posterior probability distribution of the example's classification, Y:

$$P(Y \mid X_1 = v_1, \ldots, X_k = v_k)$$
$$= \frac{P(X_1 = v_1, \ldots, X_k = v_k \mid Y) * P(Y)}{P(X_1 = v_1, \ldots, X_k = v_k)}$$
$$= \frac{P(X_1 = v_1 \mid Y) * \cdots * P(X_k = v_k \mid Y) * P(Y)}{\sum_Y P(X_1 = v_1 \mid Y) * \cdots * P(X_k = v_k \mid Y) * P(Y)}$$

$$= \frac{P(Y) * \prod_{i=1}^{k} P(X_i{=}v_i \mid Y)P(Y)}{\sum_Y P(Y) * \prod_{i=1}^{k} P(X_i{=}v_i \mid Y)P(Y)}$$

where the denominator is a normalizing constant to ensure the probabilities sum to 1.

Unlike many other models of supervised learning, the naive Bayes classifier can handle **missing data** where not all features are observed; the agent conditions on the features that are observed. Naive Bayes is optimal – it makes no independence assumptions – if only one of X_i is observed, and as more of the X_i are observed, the accuracy depends on how independent the X_i are given Y.

If every X_i is observed, this model is the same as a **logistic regression** (page 383) model, as the probability is proportional to a product, and so the logarithm is proportional to a sum. A naive Bayes model gives a direct way to assess the weights and allows for missing data. It however makes the assumption that the X_i are independent given Y, which may not hold. A linear regression model trained, for example, with gradient descent (page 295) can take into account dependencies, but does not work for missing data.

Learning a Bayes Classifier

To learn a classifier, the distributions of $P(Y)$ and $P(X_i \mid Y)$ for each input feature can be learned from the data, as described in Section 10.1.1 (page 488). Each conditional probability distribution $P(X_i \mid Y)$ may be treated as a separate learning problem for each value of Y.

The simplest case is to use the maximum likelihood estimate (the empirical proportion in the training data as the probability), where $P(X_i{=}x_i \mid Y{=}y)$ is the number of cases where $X_i{=}x_i \wedge Y{=}y$ divided by the number of cases where $Y{=}y$.

Example 10.4 Suppose an agent wants to predict the user action given the data of Figure 7.1 (page 273). For this example, the user action is the classification. The naive Bayes classifier for this example corresponds to the belief network of Figure 10.1. The training examples are used to determine the probabilities required for the belief network.

Suppose the agent uses the empirical frequencies as the probabilities for this example. The probabilities that can be derived from these data are

$P(User\_action{=}reads) = 9/18 = 0.5$

$P(Author{=}known \mid User\_action{=}reads) = 2/3$

$P(Author{=}known \mid User\_action{=}skips) = 2/3$

$P(Thread{=}new \mid User\_action{=}reads) = 7/9$

$P(Thread{=}new \mid User\_action{=}skips) = 1/3$

$P(Length{=}long \mid User\_action{=}reads) = 0$

$$P(Length=long \mid User\_action=skips) = 7/9$$
$$P(Where\_read=home \mid User\_action=reads) = 4/9$$
$$P(Where\_read=home \mid User\_action=skips) = 4/9 \, .$$

Based on these probabilities, the features *Author* and *Where_read* have no predictive power because knowing either does not change the probability that the user will read the article. The rest of this example ignores these features.

To classify a new case where the author is unknown, the thread is a followup, the length is short, and it is read at home,

$$P(User\_action=reads \mid Thread=followup \wedge Length=short)$$
$$= P(followup \mid reads) * P(short \mid reads) * P(reads) * c$$
$$= 2/9 * 1 * 1/2 * c$$
$$= 1/9 * c$$
$$P(User\_action=skips \mid Thread=followup \wedge Length=short)$$
$$= P(followup \mid skips) * P(short \mid skips) * P(skips) * c$$
$$= 2/3 * 2/9 * 1/2 * c$$
$$= 2/27 * c$$

where c is a normalizing constant. These must add up to 1, so c is $27/5$, thus

$$P(User\_action=reads \mid Thread=followup \wedge Length=short) = 0.6 \, .$$

This prediction does not work well on example e_{11}, which the agent skips, even though it is a *followup* and is *short*. The naive Bayes classifier summarizes the data into a few parameters. It predicts the article will be read because being short is a stronger indicator that the article will be read than being a follow-up is an indicator that the article will be skipped.

A new case where the length is long has a zero posterior probability that *User_action=reads*, no matter what the values of the other features. This is because $P(Length=long \mid User\_action=reads) = 0$.

The use of zero probabilities has some behaviors you may not want. First, some features become predictive: knowing just one feature value can rule out a category. A finite set of data might not be enough evidence to support such a conclusion. Second, if you use zero probabilities, it is possible that some combinations of observations are impossible, and the classifier will have a divide-by-zero error. See Exercise 10.1 (page 518). This is a problem not necessarily with using a Bayes classifier but rather in using empirical frequencies as probabilities. The alternative to using the empirical frequencies is to incorporate **pseudocounts** (page 302). A designer of the learner should carefully choose pseudocounts, as shown in the following example.

Example 10.5 Consider how to learn the probabilities for the **help system** of Example 8.35 (page 396), where a helping agent infers what help page a user is interested in based on the words in the user's query. The helping agent must learn the prior probability that each help page is wanted and the probability of each word given the help page wanted. These probabilities must be learned, because the system designer does not know a priori what words users will use in a query. The agent can learn from the words users actually use when looking for help. However, to be useful the system should also work before there are any data.

The learner must learn $P(H)$. It could start with a pseudocount (page 302) for each h_i. Pages that are a priori more likely should have a higher pseudocount. If the designer did not have any prior belief about which pages were more likely, the agent could use the same pseudocount for each page. To think about what count to use, the designer should consider how much more the agent would believe a page is the correct page after it has seen the page once; see Section 7.4.1 (page 301). It is possible to estimate this pseudocount if the designer has access to the data from another help system. Given the pseudocounts and some data, $P(h_i)$ is computed by dividing the count (the empirical count plus the pseudocount) associated with h_i by the sum of the counts for all the pages.

Similarly, the learner needs the probability $P(w_j \mid h_i)$, the probability that word w_j will be used given the help page is h_i. Because you may want the system to work even before it has received any data, the prior for these probabilities should be carefully designed, taking into account both the frequency of words in the language and the words in the help page itself.

Assume the following positive counts, which are observed counts plus suitable pseudocounts:

- c_i the number of times h_i was the correct help page
- $s = \sum_i c_i$ the total count
- u_{ij} the number of times h_i was the correct help page and word w_j was used in the query.

From these counts an agent can estimate the required probabilities:

$$P(h_i) = c_i/s$$
$$P(w_j \mid h_i) = u_{ij}/c_i$$

When a user claims to have found the appropriate help page, the counts for that page and the words in the query are updated. Thus, if the user indicates that h_i is the correct page, the counts s and c_i are incremented, and for each word w_j used in the query, u_{ij} is incremented.

This model does not use information about the wrong page. If the user claims that a page is not the correct page, this information is not used.

Given a set of words, Q, which the user issues as a query, the system can infer the probability of each help page:

$$P(h_i \mid Q) \propto P(h_i) * \prod_{w_j \in Q} P(w_j \mid h_i) * \prod_{w_j \notin Q} (1 - P(w_j \mid h_i))$$

$$= \frac{c_i}{s} * \prod_{w_j \in Q} \frac{u_{ij}}{c_i} * \prod_{w_j \notin Q} \frac{c_i - u_{ij}}{c_i}.$$

The system could present the help page with the highest probability given the query. Note that it is important to use the words not in the query as well as the words in the query. For example, if a help page is about printing, the work "print" may be very likely to be used. The fact that "print" is not in a query is strong evidence that this is not the appropriate help page.

The calculation above is very expensive. It requires a product for all possible words, not just those words used in the query. This is problematic as there may be many possible words, and users want fast responses. It is possible to rewrite the above equation so that one product is over all the words, and to readjust for the words in the query:

$$P(h_i \mid Q) \propto \frac{c_i}{s} * \prod_{w_j \in Q} \frac{u_{ij}}{c_i} * \prod_{w_j \in Q} \frac{c_i}{c_i - u_{ij}} * \prod_{w_j \in Q} \frac{c_i - u_{ij}}{c_i} * \prod_{w_j \notin Q} \frac{c_i - u_{ij}}{c_i}$$

$$= \frac{c_i}{s} * \prod_{w_j \in Q} \frac{u_{ij}}{c_i - u_{ij}} * \prod_{w_j} \frac{c_i - u_{ij}}{c_i}$$

$$= \Psi_i * \prod_{w_j \in Q} \frac{u_{ij}}{c_i - u_{ij}}$$

where $\Psi_i = \frac{c_i}{s} * \prod_{w_j} \frac{c_i - u_{ij}}{c_i}$ does not depend on Q and so can be computed offline. The fraction $u_{ij} / (c_i - u_{ij})$ corresponds to the odds (page 383) that word w_j appears in page h_i. The online calculation given a query only depends on the words in the query, which will be much faster than using all the words for reasonable queries.

The biggest challenge in building such a help system is not in the learning but in acquiring useful data. In particular, users may not know whether they have found the page they were looking for. Thus, users may not know when to stop and provide the feedback from which the system learns. Some users may never be satisfied with a page. Indeed, there may not exist a page they are satisfied with, but that information never gets fed back to the learner. Alternatively, some users may indicate they have found the page they were looking for, even though there may be another page that was more appropriate. In the latter case, the correct page may end up with its counts so low, it is never discovered. (See Exercise 10.2 (page 518).)

Although there are some cases where the naive Bayes classifier does not produce good results, it is extremely simple, it is easy to implement, and often it works very well. It is a good method to try for a new problem.

In general, the naive Bayes classifier works well when the independence assumption is appropriate, that is, when the class is a good predictor of the other features and the other features are independent given the class. This may be appropriate for **natural kinds**, where the classes have evolved because they are useful in distinguishing the objects that humans want to distinguish. Natural kinds are often associated with nouns, such as the class of dogs or the class of chairs.

The naive Bayes classifier can be expanded to allow some input features to be parents of the classification and to allow some to be children. The probability of the classification given its parents could be represented as a decision tree or a squashed linear function or a neural network. The children of the classification do not have to be independent. One representation of the children is as a **tree augmented naive Bayes (TAN) network**, where the children are allowed to have exactly one other parent other than the classification (as long as the resulting graph is acyclic). This allows for a simple model that accounts for interdependencies among the children. An alternative is to put structure in the class variable. A **latent tree model** decomposes the class variable into a number of latent variables that are connected together in a tree structure. Each observed variable is a child of one of the latent variables. The latent variables allow a model of the dependence between the observed variables.

10.1.3   MAP Learning of Decision Trees

The previous examples did not need the prior on the structure of models, as all the models were equally complex. However, for learning decision trees (page 285), you need a bias, typically in favor of smaller decision trees. The prior probability provides this bias.

If there are no examples with the same values for the input features but different values for the target feature, there are always multiple decision trees that fit the data perfectly. If the training examples do not cover every assignment to the input variables, multiple trees will fit the data perfectly. Moreover, for every assignment of values not observed, there are decision trees that perfectly fit the training set, and make opposite predictions on the unseen examples.

If there is a possibility of noise, none of the trees that perfectly fit the training set may be the best model. Not only do we want to compare the models that fit the data perfectly; we also want to compare those models with the models that do not necessarily fit the data perfectly. MAP learning provides a way to compare these models.

Suppose there are multiple decision trees that accurately fit the data. If m denotes one of those decision trees, $P(Es \mid m) = 1$. The preference for one decision tree over another depends on the prior probabilities of the decision trees; the prior probability encodes the learning bias (page 268). The preference for simpler decision trees over more complicated decision trees reflect the fact that simpler decision trees have a higher prior probability.

Bayes' rule gives a way to trade off simplicity and the ability to handle noise. Decision trees handle noisy data by having probabilities at the leaves. When there is noise, larger decision trees fit the training data better, because the tree can model random regularities (noise) in the training data. In decision tree learning, the likelihood favors bigger decision trees; the more complicated the tree, the better it can fit the data. The prior distribution typically favors smaller decision trees. When there is a prior distribution over decision trees, Bayes' rule specifies how to trade off model complexity and accuracy. The posterior probability of the model given the data is proportional to the product of the likelihood and the prior.

Example 10.6 Consider the data of Figure 7.1 (page 273), where the learner is required to predict the user's actions.

One possible decision tree is the one given on the left of Figure 7.6 (page 286). Call this decision tree d_2. The likelihood of the data is $P(Es \mid d_2) = 1$. That is, d_2 accurately fits the data.

Another possible decision tree is one with no internal nodes, and a single leaf that predicts *reads* with probability $\frac{1}{2}$. This is the most likely tree with no internal nodes, given the data. Call this decision tree d_0. The likelihood of the data given this model is

$$P(Es \mid d_0) = \left(\frac{1}{2}\right)^9 * \left(\frac{1}{2}\right)^9 \approx 0.00000149.$$

Another possible decision tree is one on the right of Figure 7.6 (page 286), with one split on *Length*, and with probabilities on the leaves given by $P(reads \mid Length=long) = 0$ and $P(reads \mid Length=short) = \frac{9}{11}$. Note that $\frac{9}{11}$ is the empirical frequency of *reads* among the training set with *Length=short*. Call this decision tree d_{1a}. The likelihood of the data given this model is

$$P(Es \mid d_{1a}) = 1^7 * \left(\frac{9}{11}\right)^9 * \left(\frac{2}{11}\right)^2 \approx 0.0543.$$

Another possible decision tree is one that just splits on *Thread*, and with probabilities on the leaves given by $P(reads \mid Thread=new) = \frac{7}{10}$ (as 7 out of the 10 examples with *Thread=new* have *User_action=reads*), and $P(reads \mid Thread=follow\_up) = \frac{2}{8}$. Call this decision tree d_{1t}. The likelihood of the data given d_{1t} is

$$P(Es \mid d_{1t}) = \left(\frac{7}{10}\right)^7 * \left(\frac{3}{10}\right)^3 * \left(\frac{6}{8}\right)^6 * \left(\frac{2}{8}\right)^2 \approx 0.000025.$$

These are just four of the possible decision trees. Which is best depends on the prior on trees. The likelihood of the data is multiplied by the prior probability of the decision trees to determine the posterior probability of the decision tree.

10.1.4   Description Length

The negative of the logarithm (base 2) of Formula (10.2) is

$$(-\log_2 P(Es \mid m)) + (-\log_2 P(m)).$$

This can be interpreted in terms of **information theory** (page 356). The first term is the number of bits it takes to describe the data given the model m, and the second term is the number of bits it takes to describe the model. A model that minimizes this sum is a **minimum description length (MDL)** model. The **MDL principle** is to choose the model that minimizes the number of bits it takes to describe both the model and the data given the model.

One way to think about the MDL principle is that the aim is to communicate the data as succinctly as possible. The model makes communication shorter. To communicate the data, first communicate the model, then communicate the data in terms of the model. The number of bits it takes to communicate the data using a model is the number of bits it takes to communicate the model plus the number of bits it takes to communicate the data in terms of the model.

As the logarithm function is monotonically increasing, the MAP model is the same the MDL model. Choosing a model with the highest posterior probability is the same as choosing a model with a minimum description length.

The description length gives us a way to have common units between probabilities and model complexity. They can both be described in terms of bits.

Example 10.7   In Example 10.6, the definition of the priors on decision trees was left unspecified. The notion of a description length provides a basis for assigning priors to decision trees; consider how many bits it takes to describe a decision tree (see Exercise 10.7 (page 520)). One must be careful defining the codes, because each code should describe a unique decision tree, and each decision tree should be described by a unique code.

Defining a code is difficult. It is often useful to approximate the description length of the model. One way to approximate the description length is to consider just representing the probabilistic parameters of the model. Let $|m|$ be the number of probabilistic parameters of the model. Suppose $|Es|$ is the number of training examples. There are at most $|Es| + 1$ different probabilities the model needs to distinguish. It takes $\log_2(|Es| + 1)$ bits to distinguish these probabilities. Thus, the problem of finding the MDL model can be approximated by minimizing

$$-\log_2 P(Es \mid m) + |m| * \log_2(|Es|)$$

This value is the **Bayesian information criteria (BIC)** score.

For a decision tree with probabilities at the leaves $|m|$ is the number of leaves. For a linear function or a neural network it is the number of numerical parameters.

10.2 Unsupervised Learning

This chapter has so far considered supervised learning, where target features are observed in the training data. In **unsupervised learning**, the target features are not given in the training examples. The aim is to construct a natural classification for the data.

One general method for unsupervised learning is **clustering**, which partitions the examples into **clusters** or **classes**. Each class predicts feature values for the examples in the class. Each clustering has a prediction error on the predictions. The best clustering is the one that minimizes the error.

Example 10.8   A diagnostic assistant may want to group treatments into groups that predict the desirable and undesirable effects of the treatment. The assistant may not want to give a patient a drug because similar drugs may have had disastrous effects on similar patients.

An intelligent tutoring system may want to cluster students' learning behavior so that strategies that work for one member of a class may work for other members.

In **hard clustering**, each example is placed definitively in a class. The class is then used to predict the feature values of the example. The alternative to hard clustering is **soft clustering**, in which each example has a probability distribution over its class. The prediction of the values for the features of an example is the weighted average of the predictions of the classes the example is in, weighted by the probability of the example being in the class. Soft clustering is described in Section 10.2.2 (page 503).

10.2.1 k-Means

The **k-means algorithm** is used for hard clustering. The training examples and the number of classes, k, are given as input. The algorithm assumes that the domain of each feature defining the examples is cardinal (so that differences in values make sense).

The algorithm constructs k classes, a prediction of a value for each feature for each class, and an assignment of examples to classes.

Suppose Es is the set of all training examples, and the input features are $X_1, \ldots, X_n$. Let $X_j(e)$ be the value of input feature X_j for example e. We assume that these are observed. We will associate a class with each integer $c \in \{1, \ldots, k\}$.

The k-means algorithm constructs:

- a function $class : Es \to \{1, \ldots, k\}$, which maps each example to a class. If $class(e) = c$, we say that e is in class c.

- for each feature X_j, a function $\widehat{X}_j$ from classes into the domain of X_j, where $\widehat{X}_j(c)$ gives the prediction for every member of class c of the value of feature X_j.

Example e is predicted to have value $\widehat{X}_j(class(e))$ for feature X_j.
The **sum-of-squares error** (page 276) is:

$$\sum_{e \in Es} \sum_{j=1}^{n} \left(\widehat{X}_j(class(e)) - X_j(e) \right)^2 .$$

The aim is to find the functions $class$ and $\widehat{X}_j$ that minimize the sum-of-squares error.

As shown in Proposition 7.1 (page 283), to minimize the sum-of-squares error, the prediction of a class should be the mean of the prediction of the examples in the class. When there are only a few examples, it is possible to search over assignments of examples to classes to minimize the error. Unfortunately, for more than a few examples, there are too many partitions of the examples into k classes for exhaustive search to be feasible.

The k-means algorithm iteratively improves the sum-of-squares error. Initially, it randomly assigns the examples to the classes. Then it carries out the two steps:

- For each class c and feature X_j, assign to $\widehat{X}_j(c)$ the mean value of $X_j(e)$ for each example e in class c:

$$\widehat{X}_j(c) \leftarrow \frac{\displaystyle\sum_{e:class(e)=c} X_j(e)}{|\{e : class(e) = c\}|}$$

where the denominator is the number of examples in class c.

- Reassign each example to a class: assign each example e to a class c that minimizes

$$\sum_{j=1}^{n} \left(\widehat{X}_j(c) - X_j(e) \right)^2 .$$

These two steps are repeated until the second step does not change the assignment of any example.

An algorithm that implements k-means is shown in Figure 10.2 (on the next page). It constructs the sufficient statistics to compute the mean of each class for each feature, namely $cc[c]$ is the number of examples in class c, and $fs[j, c]$ is the sum of the value for $X_j(e)$ for examples in class c. These are then used in the function $predn(j, c)$ which is the latest estimate of $\widehat{X}_j(c)$ and $class(e)$ the class of example e. It uses the current values of fs and cc to determine the next values (in fs_new and cc_new).

```
 1: procedure k-means(Xs, Es, k)
 2:     Inputs
 3:         Xs set of features, X = {X₁, ..., Xₙ}
 4:         Es set of training examples
 5:         k number of classes
 6:     Output
 7:         class: function from examples to classes
 8:         predn: function from feature and class to a value for that feature
 9:     Local
10:         integer cc[c], cc_new[c]              ▷ old and new class count for class c
11:         real fs[j, c], fs_new[j, c]           ▷ sum of feature Xⱼ for class c
12:         Boolean stable
13:     Initialize fs and cc randomly based on data
14:     define predn(j, c) = fs[j, c]/cc[c]       ▷ estimate of X̂ⱼ(c)
15:     define class(e) = arg minc ∑ⁿⱼ₌₁ (predn(j, c) − Xⱼ(e))²
16:     repeat
17:         fs_new and cc_new initialized to be all zero
18:         for each example e ∈ Es do
19:             c := class(e)
20:             cc_new[c]+ = 1
21:             for each feature Xⱼ ∈ Xs do
22:                 fs_new[j, c]+ = Xⱼ(e)
23:         stable := (fs_new = fs) and (cc_new = cc)
24:         fs := fs_new
25:         cc := cc_new
26:     until stable
27:     return class, predn
```

Figure 10.2: *k*-means for unsupervised learning

The random initialization could be assigning each example to a class at random, selecting k points at random to be representative of the classes, or assigning some, but not all, of the examples to construct the initial sufficient statistics. The latter two methods may be more useful if the data set is large, as they avoid a pass through the whole data set for initialization.

An assignment of examples to classes is **stable** if an iteration of k-means does not change the assignment. Stability requires that *arg min* in the definition of *class* gives a consistent value for each example in cases where more than one class is minimal. This algorithm has reached a stable assignment when each example is assigned to the same class in one iteration as in the previous iteration. When this happens, *fs* and *class_count* do not change, and so the Boolean variable *stable* becomes *true*.

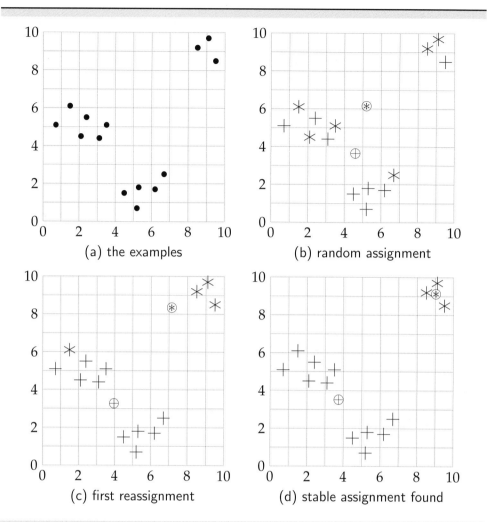

Figure 10.3: A trace of the k-means algorithm for $k = 2$ for Example 10.9

This algorithm will eventually converge to a stable local minimum. This is easy to see because the sum-of-squares error keeps reducing and there are only a finite number of reassignments. This algorithm often converges in a few iterations.

Example 10.9 Suppose an agent has observed the $\langle X, Y \rangle$ pairs:

$\langle 0.7, 5.1 \rangle$, $\langle 1.5, 6.1 \rangle$, $\langle 2.1, 4.5 \rangle$, $\langle 2.4, 5.5 \rangle$, $\langle 3.1, 4.4 \rangle$, $\langle 3.5, 5.1 \rangle$, $\langle 4.5, 1.5 \rangle$,
$\langle 5.2, 0.7 \rangle$, $\langle 5.3, 1.8 \rangle$, $\langle 6.2, 1.7 \rangle$, $\langle 6.7, 2.5 \rangle$, $\langle 8.5, 9.2 \rangle$, $\langle 9.1, 9.7 \rangle$, $\langle 9.5, 8.5 \rangle$.

These data points are plotted in Figure 10.3(a). The agent wants to cluster the data points into two classes ($k = 2$).

In Figure 10.3(b), the points are randomly assigned into the classes; one class is depicted as $+$ and the other as $*$. The mean of the points marked with $+$

is $\langle 4.6, 3.65 \rangle$, shown with $\oplus$. The mean of the points marked with $*$ is $\langle 5.2, 6.15 \rangle$, shown with $\circledast$.

In Figure 10.3(c), the points are reassigned according to the closer of the two means. After this reassignment, the mean of the points marked with $+$ is then $\langle 3.96, 3.27 \rangle$. The mean of the points marked with $*$ is $\langle 7.15, 8.34 \rangle$.

In Figure 10.3(d), the points are reassigned to the closest mean. This assignment is stable in that no further reassignment will change the assignment of the examples.

A different initial assignment to the points can give different clustering. One clustering that arises in this data set is for the lower points (those with a Y-value less than 3) to be in one class, and for the other points to be in another class.

Running the algorithm with three classes ($k = 3$) typically separates the data into the top-right cluster, the left-center cluster, and the lower cluster. However, there are other possible stable assignments that could be reached, such as, having the top three point in two different classes, and the other points in another class. It is even possible for a class to contain no examples.

Some stable assignments may be better, in terms of sum-of-squares error, than other stable assignments. To find the best assignment, it is often useful to try multiple starting configurations, using a **random restart** (page 145), and selecting a stable assignment with the lowest sum-of-squares error. Note that any permutation of the labels of a stable assignment is also a stable assignment, so there are invariable multiple local minima.

One problem with the k-means algorithm is that it is sensitive to the relative scale of the dimensions. For example, if one feature is *height*, another feature is *age*, and another is a binary feature, the different values need to be scaled so that they can be compared. How they are scaled relative to each other affects the classification.

To find an appropriate number of classes (the k), an agent could search over the number of classes. Note that $k + 1$ classes can always result in a lower error than k classes as long as more than k different values are involved. A *natural* number of classes would be a value k when there is a large reduction in error going from $k - 1$ classes to k classes, but there is only gradual reduction in error for larger values. While it is possible to construct $k + 1$ classes from k classes, the optimal division into three classes, for example, may be quite different from the optimal division into two classes.

10.2.2 Expectation Maximization for Soft Clustering

A **hidden variable** or **latent variable** is a probabilistic variable that is not observed in a data set. A Bayes classifier can be the basis for **unsupervised learning** by making the class a hidden variable.

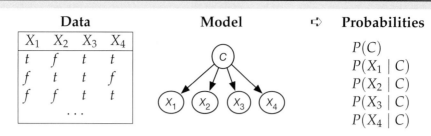

Figure 10.4: EM algorithm: Bayes classifier with hidden class

The **expectation maximization** or **EM algorithm** can be used to learn probabilistic models with hidden variables. Combined with a **naive Bayes classifier** (page 491), it does soft clustering, similar to the k-means algorithm, but where examples are probabilistically in classes.

As in the k-means algorithm, the training examples and the number of classes, k, are given as input.

Given the data, a naive Bayes model is constructed where there is a variable for each feature in the data and a hidden variable for the class. The class variable is the only parent of the other features. This is shown in Figure 10.4. The class variable has domain $\{1, 2, \ldots, k\}$ where k is the number of classes. The probabilities needed for this model are the probability of the class C and the probability of each feature given C. The aim of the EM algorithm is to learn probabilities that best fit the data.

The EM algorithm conceptually augments the data with a class feature, C, and a count column. Each original example gets mapped into k augmented examples, one for each class. The counts for these examples are assigned so that they sum to 1. For example, for four features and three classes, we could have

X_1	X_2	X_3	X_4
$\vdots$	$\vdots$	$\vdots$	$\vdots$
t	f	t	t
$\vdots$	$\vdots$	$\vdots$	$\vdots$

$\longrightarrow$

X_1	X_2	X_3	X_4	C	Count
$\vdots$	$\vdots$	$\vdots$	$\vdots$	$\vdots$	$\vdots$
t	f	t	t	1	0.4
t	f	t	t	2	0.1
t	f	t	t	3	0.5
$\vdots$	$\vdots$	$\vdots$	$\vdots$	$\vdots$	$\vdots$

The EM algorithm repeats the two steps:

- **E step**: Update the augmented counts based on the probability distribution. For each example $\langle X_1 = v_1, \ldots, X_n = v_n \rangle$ in the original data, the count associated with $\langle X_1 = v_1, \ldots, X_n = v_n, C = c \rangle$ in the augmented data is updated to

$$P(C = c \mid X_1 = v_1, \ldots, X_n = v_n).$$

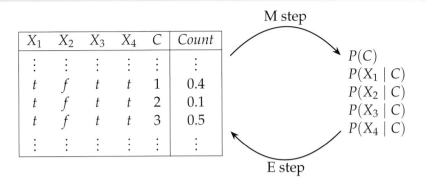

X_1	X_2	X_3	X_4	C	$Count$
$\vdots$	$\vdots$	$\vdots$	$\vdots$	$\vdots$	$\vdots$
t	f	t	t	1	0.4
t	f	t	t	2	0.1
t	f	t	t	3	0.5
$\vdots$	$\vdots$	$\vdots$	$\vdots$	$\vdots$	$\vdots$

M step

$P(C)$
$P(X_1 \mid C)$
$P(X_2 \mid C)$
$P(X_3 \mid C)$
$P(X_4 \mid C)$

E step

Figure 10.5: EM algorithm for unsupervised learning

Note that this step involves probabilistic inference. This is an **expectation** step because it computes the expected values.

- **M step**: Infer the probabilities for the model from the augmented data. Because the augmented data has values associated with all the variables, this is the same problem as learning probabilities from data in a naive Bayes classifier (page 492). This is a **maximization** step because it computes the maximum likelihood estimate or the maximum a posteriori probability (MAP) (page 487) estimate of the probability.

The EM algorithm starts with random probabilities or random counts. EM will converge to a local maximum of the likelihood of the data.

This algorithm returns a probabilistic model, which is used to classify an existing or new example. An example is classified using

$$P(C = c \mid X_1 = v_1, \ldots, X_n = v_n)$$
$$= \frac{P(C = c) * \prod_{i=1}^{n} P(X_i = v_i \mid C = c)}{\sum_{c'} P(C = c') * \prod_{i=1}^{n} P(X_i = v_i \mid C = c')} .$$

The algorithm does not need to store the augmented data, but maintains a set of **sufficient statistics**, which is enough information to compute the required probabilities. In each iteration, it sweeps through the data once to compute the sufficient statistics. The sufficient statistics for this algorithm are

- cc, the class count, a k-valued array such that $cc[c]$ is the sum of the counts of the examples in the augmented data with $class=c$

- fc, the feature count, a three-dimensional array such that $fc[i, v, c]$, for i from 1 to n, for each value v in $domain(X_i)$, and for each class c, is the sum of the counts of the augmented examples t with $X_i(t) = val$ and $class(t) = c$.

1: **procedure** *EM(Xs, Es, k)*
2:     **Inputs**
3:         *Xs* set of features, $Xs = \{X_1, \ldots, X_n\}$
4:         *Es* set of training examples
5:         *k* number of classes
6:     **Output**
7:         sufficient statistics for probabilistic model on X
8:     **Local**
9:         real $cc[c]$, $cc\_new[c]$ ▷ old and new class count
10:         real $fc[i, v, c]$, $fc\_new[i, v, c]$ ▷ old and new feature count
11:         real dc ▷ class probability for current example and class
12:         Boolean *stable*
13:     **repeat**
14:         $cc\_new[c]$ and $fc\_new[i, v, c]$ initialized to be all zero
15:         **for each** example $\langle v_1, \ldots, v_n \rangle \in Es$ **do**
16:             **for each** $c \in [1, k]$ **do**
17:                 $dc := P(C = c \mid X_1 = v_1, \ldots, X_n = v_n)$
18:                 $cc\_new[c] := cc\_new[c] + dc$
19:                 **for each** $i \in [1, n]$ **do**
20:                     $fc\_new[i, v_i, c] := fc\_new[i, v_i, c] + dc$
21:         $stable := (cc \approx cc\_new) \text{ and } (fc \approx fc\_new)$
22:         $cc := cc\_new$
23:         $fc := fc\_new$
24:     **until** *stable*
25:     **return** cc,fc

Figure 10.6: EM for unsupervised learning

The sufficient statistics from the previous iteration are used to infer the new sufficient statistics for the next iteration. Note that cc could be computed from fc, but it is easier to maintain cc directly.

The probabilities required of the model can be computed from cc and fc:

$$P(C{=}c) = \frac{cc[c]}{|Es|}$$

where $|Es|$ is the number of examples in the original data set (which is the same as the sum of the counts in the augmented data set).

$$P(X_i{=}v \mid C{=}c) = \frac{fc[i, v, c]}{cc[c]}.$$

Figure 10.6 gives the algorithm to compute the sufficient statistics, from which the probabilities are derived as above. Evaluating $P(C = c \mid X_1 = $

$v_1, \ldots, X_n = v_n)$ in line 17 relies on the counts in cc and fc. This algorithm has glossed over how to initialize the counts. One way is for $P(C \mid X_1 = v_1, \ldots, X_n = v_n)$ to return a random distribution for the first iteration, so the counts come from the data. Alternatively, the counts can be assigned randomly before seeing any data. See Exercise 10.6 (page 519).

The algoritm will eventually converge when cc and fc do not change much in an iteration. The threshold for the approximately equal in line 21 can be tuned to trade off learning time and accuracy. An alternative is to run the algorithms for a fixed number of iterations.

Notice the similarity with the k-means algorithm. The E step (probabilistically) assigns examples to classes, and the M step determines what the classes predict.

Example 10.10 Consider Figure 10.5 (page 505).

When example $\langle x_1, \neg x_2, x_3, x_4 \rangle$ is encountered in the data set, the algorithm computes

$$P(C{=}c \mid x_1 \wedge \neg x_2 \wedge x_3 \wedge x_4)$$
$$\propto P(X_1{=}1 \mid C{=}c) * P(X_2{=}0 \mid C{=}c) * P(X_3{=}1 \mid C{=}c)$$
$$\quad * P(X_4{=}1 \mid C{=}c) * P(C{=}c)$$
$$= \frac{fc[1,1,c]}{cc[c]} * \frac{fc[2,0,c]}{cc[c]} * \frac{fc[3,1,c]}{cc[c]} * \frac{fc[4,1,c]}{cc[c]} * \frac{cc[c]}{|Es|}$$
$$\propto \frac{fc[1,1,c] * fc[2,0,c] * fc[3,1,c] * fc[4,1,c]}{cc[c]^3}$$

for each class c and normalizes the results. Suppose the value computed for class 1 is 0.4, class 2 is 0.1 and for class 3 is 0.5 (as in the augmented data in Figure 10.5). Then $cc\_new[1]$ is incremented by 0.4, $cc\_new[2]$ is incremented by 0.1, etc. Values $fc\_new[1,1,1]$, $fc\_new[2,0,1]$, etc. are each incremented by 0.4. Next $fc\_new[1,1,2]$, $fc\_new[2,0,2]$ are each incremented by 0.1, etc.

Note that, as long as $k > 1$, EM virtually always has multiple local maxima. In particular, any permutation of the class labels of a local maximum will also be a local maximum. To try to find a global maximum, multiple restarts can be tried, and the model with the lowest log-likelihood returned.

10.3 Learning Belief Networks

A **belief network** (page 360) gives a probability distribution over a set of random variables. We cannot always expect an expert to be able to provide an accurate model; often we want to learn a network from data.

Learning a belief network from data has many variants depending on how much prior information is known and how complete the data set is. In the

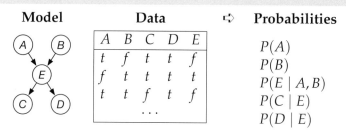

Figure 10.7: From the model and the data, learn the probabilities

simplest case, the structure is given, all the variables are observed in each example, and only the conditional probabilities of each variable given its parents must be learned. At the other extreme, the agent may not know the structure or even which variables exist, and there may be missing data, which cannot be assumed to be missing at random.

10.3.1 Learning the Probabilities

The simplest case occurs when a learning agent is given the structure of the model and all the variables have been observed. The agent must learn the conditional probabilities, $P(X_i \mid parents(X_i))$ for each variable X_i. Learning the conditional probabilities is an instance of **supervised learning** (page 268), where X_i is the target feature, and the parents of X_i are the input features.

For cases with few parents, each conditional probability can be learned separately using the training examples and prior knowledge, such as pseudocounts (page 302).

Example 10.11 Figure 10.7 shows a typical example. We are given the model and the data, and we must infer the probabilities.

For example, one of the elements of $P(E \mid AB)$ is

$$P(E{=}t \mid A{=}t \wedge B{=}f) = \frac{n_1 + c_1}{n_0 + n_1 + c_0 + c_1}$$

where n_1 is the number of cases where $E{=}t \wedge A{=}t \wedge B{=}f$, and $c_1 \geq 0$ is the corresponding pseudocount that is provided before any data is observed. Similarly, n_0 is the number of cases where $E{=}f \wedge A{=}t \wedge B{=}f$, and $c_0 \geq 0$ is the corresponding pseudocount.

If a variable has many parents, using counts and pseudocounts can suffer from overfitting (page 290). Overfitting is most severe when there are few examples for some of the combinations of the parent variables. In that case, the supervised learning techniques of Chapter 7 could be used. **Decision trees** (page 285) can be used for arbitrary discrete variables. **Logistic regression**

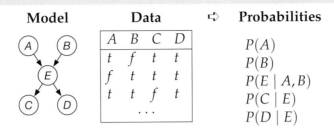

| Model | Data | | | | ⇨ | Probabilities |

A	B	C	D
t	f	t	t
f	t	t	t
t	t	f	t
. . .			

$P(A)$
$P(B)$
$P(E \mid A, B)$
$P(C \mid E)$
$P(D \mid E)$

Figure 10.8: Deriving probabilities with missing data

(page 383) and **neural networks** (page 308) can represent a conditional probability of a binary variable given its parents. For non-binary discrete variables, indicator variables (page 275) may be used.

10.3.2 Hidden Variables

The next simplest case is where the model is given, but not all variables are observed. A **hidden variable** or a **latent variable** is a variable in a belief network whose value is not observed for any of the examples. That is, there is no column in the data corresponding to that variable.

Example 10.12 Figure 10.8 shows a typical case. Assume that all the variables are binary. The model contains a hidden variable E that is in the model but not the data set. The aim is to learn the parameters of the model that includes the hidden variable E. There are 10 parameters to learn.

Note that, if E was not part of the model, the algorithm would have to learn $P(A)$, $P(B)$, $P(C \mid AB)$, $P(D \mid ABC)$, which has 14 parameters. The reason for introducing hidden variables is, paradoxically, to make the model simpler and, therefore, less prone to overfitting.

The **expectation maximization** or **EM** algorithm for learning belief networks with hidden variables is essentially the same as the EM algorithm for clustering (page 503). The E step, shown in Figure 10.9 (on the next page), involves probabilistic inference for each example to infer the probability distribution of the hidden variable(s) given the observed variables for that example. The M step of inferring the probabilities of the model from the augmented data is the same as in the fully observable case discussed in the previous section, but, in the augmented data, the counts are not necessarily integers.

10.3.3 Missing Data

Data can be incomplete in ways other than having an unobserved variable. A data set could simply be missing the values of some variables for some of the tuples. When some of the values of the variables are missing, one must be very

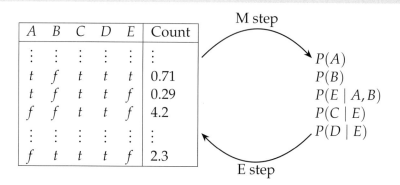

A	B	C	D	E	Count
⋮	⋮	⋮	⋮	⋮	⋮
t	f	t	t	t	0.71
t	f	t	t	f	0.29
f	f	t	t	f	4.2
⋮	⋮	⋮	⋮	⋮	⋮
f	t	t	t	f	2.3

M step

$P(A)$
$P(B)$
$P(E \mid A, B)$
$P(C \mid E)$
$P(D \mid E)$

E step

Figure 10.9: EM algorithm for belief networks with hidden variables

careful in using the data set because the missing data may be correlated with the phenomenon of interest.

> **Example 10.13** Suppose there is a (claimed) treatment for a disease that does not actually affect the disease or its symptoms. All it does is make sick people sicker. If patients were randomly assign to the treatment, the sickest people would drop out of the study, because they become too sick to participate. The sick people who took the treatment would drop out at a faster rate than the sick people who did not take the treatment. Thus, if the patients with missing data are ignored, it looks like the treatment works; there are fewer sick people among the people who took the treatment and remained in the study!

Data are **missing at random** when the reason the data is missing is not correlated with any of the variables being modeled. Data missing at random could be ignored or filled in using EM. However, "missing at random" is a strong assumption. In general, an agent should construct a model of why the data are missing or, preferably, it should go out into the world and find out why the data are missing.

10.3.4 Structure Learning

Suppose a learning agent has complete data and no hidden variables, but is not given the structure of the belief network. This is the setting for **structure learning** of belief networks.

There are two main approaches to structure learning:

- The first is to use the definition of a belief network in terms of conditional independence (page 360). Given a total ordering of variables, the parents of a variable X are defined to be a subset of the predecessors of X in the total ordering that render the other predecessors independent of X. Using the definition directly has two main challenges: the first is to determine the best total ordering; the second is to find a way to measure independence. It is difficult to determine conditional independence when there is limited data.

- The second method is to have a score for networks, for example, using the MAP model (page 487), which takes into account fit to the data and model complexity. Given such a measure, it is feasible to search for the structure that minimizes this error.

This section presents the second method, often called a **search and score** method.

Assume that the data is a set *Es* of examples, where each example has a value for each variable. The aim of the search and score method is to choose a model *m* that maximizes

$$P(m \mid Es) \propto P(Es \mid m) * P(m).$$

The likelihood, $P(Es \mid m)$, is the product of the probability of each example. Using the product decomposition, the product of each example given the model is the product of the probability of each variable given its parents in the model. Thus,

$$P(Es \mid m) * P(m) = \left(\prod_{e \in Es} P(e \mid m) \right) * P(m)$$

$$= \left(\prod_{e \in Es} \prod_{X_i} P_m^e(X_i \mid par(X_i, m)) \right) * P(m)$$

where $par(X_i, m)$ denotes the parents of X_i in the model *m*, and $P_m^e(\cdot)$ denotes the probability of example *e* as specified in the model *m*.

This is maximized when its logarithm is maximized. When taking logarithms, products become sums:

$$\log P(Es \mid m) + \log P(m) = \left(\sum_{e \in Es} \sum_{X_i} \log P_m^e(X_i \mid par(X_i, m)) \right) + \log P(m).$$

To make this approach feasible, assume that the prior probability of the model decomposes into components for each variable. That is, we assume the probability of the model decomposes into a product of probabilities of local models for each variable. Let $m(X_i)$ be the local model for variable X_i.

Thus, we want to maximize

$$\left(\sum_{e \in Es} \sum_{X_i} \log P_m^e(X_i \mid par(X_i, m)) \right) + \sum_{X_i} \log P(m(X_i))$$

$$= \sum_{X_i} \left(\sum_{e \in Es} \log P_m^e(X_i \mid par(X_i, m)) \right) + \sum_{X_i} \log P(m(X_i))$$

$$= \sum_{X_i} \left(\sum_{e \in Es} \log P_m^e(X_i \mid par(X_i, m)) + \log P(m(X_i)) \right).$$

Each variable could be optimized separately, except for the requirement that a belief network is acyclic. However, if you had a total ordering of the variables, there is an independent supervised learning problem to predict the probability of each variable given the predecessors in the total ordering. To approximate $\log P(m(X_i))$, the BIC score (page 498) is suitable. To find a good total ordering of the variables, a learning agent could search over total orderings, using search techniques such as local search (page 144) or branch-and-bound search (page 110).

10.3.5   General Case of Belief Network Learning

The general case is with unknown structure, hidden variables, and missing data; we may not even know which variables should be part of the model. Two main problems arise. The first is the problem of missing data discussed earlier. The second problem is computational; although there may be a well-defined search space, it is prohibitively large to try all combinations of variable ordering and hidden variables. If one only considers hidden variables that simplify the model (as seems reasonable), the search space is finite, but enormous.

One can either select the best model (e.g, the model with the highest posterior probability) or average over all models. Averaging over all models gives better predictions, but it is difficult to explain to a person who may have to understand or justify the model.

10.4   Bayesian Learning

Rather than choosing the most likely model or delineating the set of all models that are consistent with the training data, another approach is to compute the posterior probability of each model given the training examples.

The idea of **Bayesian learning** is to compute the posterior probability distribution of the target features of a new example conditioned on its input features and all the training examples.

Suppose a new case has inputs $X=x$ (which we write simply as x) and target features Y. The aim is to compute $P(Y \mid x \wedge Es)$, where Es is the set of training examples. This is the probability distribution of the target variables given the particular inputs and the examples. The role of a model is to be the assumed generator of the examples. If we let M be a set of disjoint and covering models, then reasoning by cases (page 349) and the chain rule give

$$P(Y \mid x \wedge Es) = \sum_{m \in M} P(Y \wedge m \mid x \wedge Es)$$

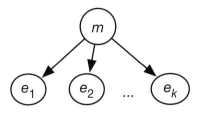

Figure 10.10: The i.i.d. assumption as a belief network

$$= \sum_{m \in M} P(Y \mid m \wedge x \wedge Es) * P(m \mid x \wedge Es)$$

$$= \sum_{m \in M} P(Y \mid m \wedge x) * P(m \mid Es) .$$

The first two equalities follow from the definition of conditional probability (page 350). The last equality relies on two assumptions: the model includes all the information about the examples that is necessary for a particular prediction, $P(Y \mid m \wedge x \wedge Es) = P(Y \mid m \wedge x)$, and the model does not change depending on the inputs of the new example, $P(m \mid x \wedge Es) = P(m \mid Es)$. Instead of choosing the best model, Bayesian learning relies on **model averaging**, averaging over the predictions of all the models, where each model is weighted by its posterior probability given the training examples.

$P(m \mid Es)$ can be computed using Bayes' rule:

$$P(m \mid Es) = \frac{P(Es \mid m) * P(m)}{P(Es)} .$$

Thus, the weight of each model depends on how well it predicts the data (the likelihood) and its prior probability. The denominator, $P(Es)$, is a normalizing constant to make sure the posterior probabilities of the models sum to 1. $P(Es)$ is called the **partition function**. Computing $P(Es)$ may be very difficult when there are many models.

A set $\{e_1, \ldots, e_k\}$ of examples are **independent and identically distributed (i.i.d.)**, given model m if examples e_i and e_j, for $i \neq j$, are independent given m. If the set of training examples Es is $\{e_1, \ldots, e_k\}$, the assumption that the examples are i.i.d. implies

$$P(Es \mid m) = \prod_{i=1}^{k} P(e_i \mid m) .$$

The i.i.d. assumption can be represented as a belief network, shown in Figure 10.10, where each of the e_i are independent given model m. If m is made into a discrete variable, any of the inference methods of the previous chapter could be used for inference in this network. A standard reasoning technique in such a network is to condition on every observed e_i and to query the model variable or an unobserved e_i variable.

The set of models may include structurally different models in addition to models that differ in the values of the parameters. One of the techniques of Bayesian learning is to make the parameters of the model explicit and to determine the distribution over the parameters.

Example 10.14 Consider the simplest learning task of learning a single Boolean random variable, Y, with no input features. (This is the case covered in Section 7.2.3 (page 283).) Each example specifies $Y = true$ or $Y = false$. The aim is to learn the probability distribution of Y given the set of training examples.

There is a single parameter, ϕ, that determines the set of all models. Suppose that ϕ represents the probability of $Y = true$. We treat ϕ as a real-valued random variable on the interval $[0, 1]$. Thus, by definition of ϕ, $P(Y = true \mid \phi) = \phi$ and $P(Y = false \mid \phi) = 1 - \phi$.

Suppose, first, an agent has no prior information about the probability of Boolean variable Y and no knowledge beyond the training examples. This ignorance can be modeled by having the prior probability distribution of the variable ϕ as a uniform distribution over the interval $[0, 1]$. This is the probability density function labeled $n_0=0, n_1=0$ in Figure 10.11 (on the next page).

We can update the probability distribution of ϕ given some examples. Assume that the examples, obtained by running a number of independent experiments, are a particular sequence of outcomes that consists of n_0 cases where Y is false and n_1 cases where Y is true.

The posterior distribution for ϕ given the training examples can be derived by Bayes' rule. Let the examples Es be the particular sequence of observations that resulted in n_1 occurrences of $Y=true$ and n_0 occurrences of $Y=false$. Bayes' rule gives us

$$P(\phi \mid Es) = \frac{P(Es \mid \phi) * P(\phi)}{P(Es)} .$$

The denominator is a normalizing constant to make sure the area under the curve is 1.

Given that the examples are i.i.d.,

$$P(Es \mid \phi) = \phi^{n_1} * (1 - \phi)^{n_0}$$

because there are n_0 cases where $Y=false$, each with a probability of $1 - \phi$, and n_1 cases where $Y=true$, each with a probability of ϕ.

Note that Es is the particular sequence of observations made. If the observation was just that there were a total of n_0 occurrences of $Y = false$ and n_1 occurrences of $Y = true$, we would get an different answer, because we would have to take into account all the possible sequences that could have given this count. The latter is known as the **binomial distribution**.

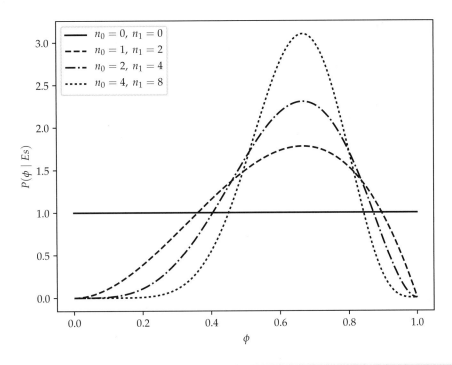

Figure 10.11: Beta distribution based on different samples

One possible prior probability, $P(\phi)$, is a uniform distribution on the interval $[0,1]$. This would be reasonable when the agent has no prior information about the probability.

Figure 10.11 gives some posterior distributions of the variable ϕ based on different sample sizes, and given a uniform prior. The cases are $(n_0 = 1, n_1 = 2)$, $(n_0 = 2, n_1 = 4)$, and $(n_0 = 4, n_1 = 8)$. Each of these peak at the same place, namely at $\frac{2}{3}$. More training examples make the curve sharper.

The distribution of this example is known as the **beta distribution**; it is parameterized by two counts, α_0 and α_1, and a probability p. Traditionally, the α_i parameters for the beta distribution are one more than the counts; thus, $\alpha_i = n_i + 1$. The beta distribution is

$$Beta^{\alpha_0, \alpha_1}(p) = \frac{1}{Z}p^{\alpha_1 - 1} * (1 - p)^{\alpha_0 - 1}$$

where Z is a normalizing constant that ensures the integral over all values is 1. Thus, the uniform distribution on $[0,1]$ is the beta distribution $Beta^{1,1}$.

Suppose instead that Y is a discrete variable with k different values. The generalization of the beta distribution to cover this case is known as the Dirichlet distribution. The **Dirichlet distribution** with two sorts of parameters, the "counts" $\alpha_1, \dots, \alpha_k$, and the probability parameters $p_1, \dots, p_k$, is

$$Dirichlet^{\alpha_1, \dots, \alpha_k}(p_1, \dots, p_k) = \frac{1}{Z} \prod_{j=1}^{k} p_j^{\alpha_j - 1}$$

where p_i is the probability of the ith outcome (and so $0 \leq p_i \leq 1$) and α_i is a non-negative real and Z is a normalizing constant that ensures the integral over all the probability values is 1. We can think of a_i as one more than the count of the ith outcome, $\alpha_i = n_i + 1$. The Dirichlet distribution looks like Figure 10.11 along each dimension (i.e., as each p_j varies between 0 and 1).

For many cases, averaging over all models weighted by their posterior distribution is difficult, because the models may be complicated (e.g., if they are decision trees or even belief networks). For the Dirichlet distribution, the expected value for outcome i (averaging over all p_j) is

$$\frac{\alpha_i}{\sum_j \alpha_j} .$$

The reason that the α_i parameters are one more than the counts in the definitions of the beta and Dirichlet distributions is to make this formula simple. This fraction is well defined only when the α_j are all non-negative and not all are zero.

Example 10.15   Consider Example 10.14 (page 514), which determines the value of ϕ based on a sequence of observations made up of n_0 cases where Y is false and n_1 cases where Y is true. Consider the posterior distribution as shown in Figure 10.11. What is interesting about this is that, whereas the most likely posterior value of ϕ is $\frac{n_1}{n_0 + n_1}$, the expected value (page 355) of this distribution is $\frac{n_1 + 1}{n_0 + n_1 + 2}$.

Thus, the expected value of the $n_0 = 1, n_1 = 2$ curve is $\frac{3}{5}$, for the $n_0 = 2, n_1 = 4$ case the expected value is $\frac{5}{8}$, and for the $n_0 = 4, n_1 = 8$ case it is $\frac{9}{14}$. As the learner gets more training examples, this value approaches $\frac{n}{m}$.

This estimate is better than $\frac{n}{m}$ for a number of reasons. First, it tells us what to do if the learning agent has no examples: use the uniform prior of $\frac{1}{2}$. This is the expected value of the $n = 0, m = 0$ case. Second, consider the case where $n = 0$ and $m = 3$. The agent should not use $P(y) = 0$, because this says that Y is impossible, and it certainly does not have evidence for this! The expected value of this curve with a uniform prior is $\frac{1}{5}$.

An agent does not have to start with a uniform prior; it could start with any prior distribution. If the agent starts with a prior that is a Dirichlet distribution, its posterior will be a Dirichlet distribution. The posterior distribution can be obtained by adding the observed counts to the α_i parameters of the prior distribution.

Thus, the beta and Dirichlet distributions provide a justification for using **pseudocounts** (page 301) for estimating probabilities. The pseudocount represents the prior knowledge. A flat prior gives a pseudocount of 1. Thus, **Laplace smoothing** (page 489) can be justified in terms of making predictions from initial ignorance.

In addition to using the posterior distribution of ϕ to derive the expected value, we can use it to answer other questions such as: What is the probability that the posterior probability, ϕ, is in the range $[a, b]$? In other words, derive $P((\phi \geq a \wedge \phi \leq b) \mid e)$. This is the problem that the Reverend Thomas Bayes solved more than 250 years ago [Bayes, 1763]. The solution he gave – although in much more cumbersome notation – was

$$\frac{\int_a^b p^n * (1-p)^{m-n}}{\int_0^1 p^n * (1-p)^{m-n}} .$$

This kind of knowledge is used in surveys when it may be reported that a survey is correct with an error of at most 5%, 19 times out of 20. It is also the same type of information that is used by probably approximately correct (PAC) learning (page 328), which guarantees an error at most ϵ at least $1 - \delta$ of the time. If an agent chooses the midpoint of the range $[a, b]$, namely $\frac{a+b}{2}$, as its hypothesis, it will have error less than or equal to $\frac{b-a}{2}$, just when the hypothesis is in $[a, b]$. The value $1 - \delta$ corresponds to $P(\phi \geq a \wedge \phi \leq b \mid e)$. If $\epsilon = \frac{b-a}{2}$ and $\delta = 1 - P(\phi \geq a \wedge \phi \leq b \mid e)$, choosing the midpoint will result in an error at most ϵ in $1 - \delta$ of the time. PAC learning gives worst-case results, whereas Bayesian learning gives the expected number. Typically, the Bayesian estimate is more accurate, but the PAC results give a guarantee of a bound on the error. The **sample complexity** (page 330), the number of samples required to obtain some given accuracy, for Bayesian learning is typically much less than that of PAC learning – many fewer examples are required to *expect to achieve* the desired accuracy than are needed to *guarantee* the desired accuracy.

10.5   Review

The main points you should have learned from this chapter are:

- Bayes' rule provides a way to incorporate prior knowledge into learning and a way to trade off fit-to-data and model complexity.

- EM and k-means are iterative methods to learn the parameters of models with hidden variables (including the case in which the classification is hidden).

- The probabilities and the structure of belief networks can be learned from complete data. The probabilities can be derived from counts. The structure can be learned by searching for the best model given the data.

- Missing values in examples are often not missing at random. Why they are missing is often important to determine.

- Bayesian learning replaces making a prediction from the best model with finding a prediction by averaging over all of the models conditioned on the data.

10.6   References and Further Reading

Bayes classifiers are discussed by Duda et al. [2001] and Langley et al. [1992]. Friedman and Goldszmidt [1996a] discuss how the naive Bayes classifier can be generalized to allow for more appropriate independence assumptions. TAN networks are described by Friedman et al. [1997]. Latent tree models are described by Zhang [2004].

EM is due to Dempster et al. [1977]. Unsupervised learning is discussed by Cheeseman et al. [1988].

Bayesian learning is overviewed by Loredo [1990], Jaynes [2003], [MacKay, 2003], and Howson and Urbach [2006]. See also books on Bayesian statistics such as Gelman et al. [2004] and Bernardo and Smith [1994]. Bayesian learning of decision trees is described in Buntine [1992]. Grünwald [2007] discusses the MDL principle. Ghahramani [2015] reviews how Bayesian probability is used in AI.

For an overview of learning belief networks, see Heckerman [1999], Darwiche [2009], and Koller and Friedman [2009]. Structure learning using decision trees is based on Friedman and Goldszmidt [1996b]. The Bayesian information criteria is due to Schwarz [1978]. Note that our definition (page 498) is slightly different; the definition of Schwarz is justified by a more complex Bayesian argument. Modeling missing data is discussed by Marlin et al. [2011] and Mohan and Pearl [2014].

10.7   Exercises

Exercise 10.1 Try to construct an artificial example where a naive Bayes classifier can give divide-by-zero error in test cases when using empirical frequencies as probabilities. Specify the network and the (non-empty) training examples. [Hint: You can do it with two features, say A and B, and a binary classification, say C, that has domain $\{0, 1\}$. Construct a data set where the empirical probabilities give $P(a|C = 0) = 0$ and $P(b|C = 1) = 0$.] What observation is inconsistent with the model?

Exercise 10.2 Consider designing a help system based on Example 10.5 (page 493). Discuss how your implementation can handle the following issues, and if it cannot whether it is a major problem.

(a) What should be the initial u_{ij} counts? Where might this information be obtained?

(b) What if the most likely page is not the correct page?

(c) What if users cannot find the correct page?

(d) What if users mistakenly think they have the correct page?

(e) Can some pages never be found?

(f) What should it do with common words that are independent of the help page?

(g) What about words that affect the meaning, such as "not"?

(h) How should it handle words it has never seen before?

(i) How can new help pages be incorporated?

Exercise 10.3 Suppose you have designed a help system based on Example 10.5 (page 493) and much of the underlying system which the help pages are about has changed. You are now very unsure about which help pages will be requested, but you may have a good model of which words will be used given the help page. How can the help system be changed to take this into account? [Hint: You may need different counts for $P(h_i)$ and $P(w_j \mid h_i)$.]

Exercise 10.4 Consider the unsupervised data of Figure 10.3 (page 502).

(a) How many different stable assignments of examples to classes does the k-means algorithm find when $k = 2$? [Hint: Try running the algorithm on the data with a number of different starting points, but also think about what assignments of examples to classes are stable.] Do not count permutations of the labels as different assignments.

(b) Estimate how many different stable assignments there are when $k = 3$.

(c) Estimate many different stable assignments are there when $k = 4$.

(d) Why might someone suggest that three is the natural number of classes in this example? Give a definition for "natural" number of classes, and use this data to justify the definition.

Exercise 10.5 Suppose the k-means algorithm is run for an increasing sequence of values for k, and that it is run for a number of times for each k to find the assignment with a global minimum error. Is it possible that a number of values of k exist for which the error plateaus and then has a large improvement (e.g., when the error for $k = 3$, $k = 4$, and $k = 5$ are about the same, but the error for $k = 6$ is much lower)? If so, give an example. If not, explain why.

Exercise 10.6 To initialize the EM algorithm in Figure 10.6 (page 506) consider two alternatives:

(a) allow P to return a random distribution the first time through the loop

(b) initialize cc and fc to random values

By running the algorithm on some data sets, determine which, if any, of these alternatives is better in terms of log loss (page 278) of the training data, as a function of the number of loops through the data set. Does it matter if cc and fc are not consistent with the semantics (counts that should be equal are not)?

Exercise 10.7 As outlined in Example 10.7 (page 498), define a code for describing decision trees. Make sure that each code corresponds to a decision tree (for every sufficiently long sequence of bits, the initial segment of the sequence will describe a unique decision tree), and each decision tree has a code. How does this code translate into a prior distribution on trees? In particular, how much does the likelihood of introducing a new split have to increase to offset the reduction in prior probability of the split (assuming that smaller trees are easier to describe than large trees in your code)?

Chapter 11

Multiagent Systems

Imagine a personal software agent engaging in electronic commerce on your behalf. Say the task of this agent is to track goods available for sale in various online venues over time, and to purchase some of them on your behalf for an attractive price. In order to be successful, your agent will need to embody your preferences for products, your budget, and in general your knowledge about the environment in which it will operate. Moreover, the agent will need to embody your knowledge of other similar agents with which it will interact (e.g., agents who might compete with it in an auction, or agents representing store owners) – including their own preferences and knowledge. A collection of such agents forms a multiagent system.

– Yoav Shoham and Kevin Leyton-Brown [2008, page xvii]

What should an agent do when there are other agents, with their own goals and preferences, who are also reasoning about what to do? An intelligent agent should not ignore other agents or treat them as noise in the environment. This chapter considers the problems of determining what an agent should do in an environment that includes other agents who have their own values.

11.1 Multiagent Framework

This chapter considers environments that contain multiple agents, with the following assumptions:

- The agents can act autonomously, each with its own information about the world and the other agents.

521

- The outcome depends on the actions of all of the agents.

- Each agent has its own utility that depends on the outcome. Agents act to maximize their own utility.

A **mechanism** specifies what actions are available to each agent and how the actions of the agents lead to outcomes. An agent acts **strategically** when it decides what to do based on its goals or utilities.

Sometimes we treat **nature** as an agent. Nature is defined as being a special agent that does not have preferences and does not act strategically. It just acts, perhaps stochastically. In terms of the agent architecture shown in Figure 1.3 (page 12), nature and the other agents form the environment for an agent. Agents that are not acting strategically are treated as part of nature. A strategic agent should not treat other strategic agents as part of nature, but rather it should be open to coordination, cooperation and perhaps negotiation with other strategic agents.

There are two extremes in the study of multiagent systems:

- fully **cooperative**, where the agents share the same utility function, and

- fully **competitive**, when one agent can only win when another loses; in **zero-sum games**, for every outcome, the sum of the utilities for the agents is zero.

Most interactions are between these two extremes, where the agents' utilities are synergistic in some aspects, competing in some, and other aspects are independent. For example, two commercial agents with stores next door to each other may both share the goal of having the street area clean and inviting; they may compete for customers, but may have no preferences about the details of the other agent's store. Sometimes their actions do not interfere with each other, and sometimes they do. Often agents are better off if they coordinate their actions through cooperation and negotiation.

Multiagent interactions have mostly been studied using the terminology of games following the seminal work of Neumann and Morgenstern [1953]. Many issues of interaction between agents can be studied in terms of games. Even quite small games highlight deep issues. However, the study of games is meant to be about general multiagent interactions, not just artificial games.

Multiagent systems are ubiquitous in artificial intelligence. From parlor games such as checkers, chess, backgammon, and Go, to robot soccer, to interactive computer games, to agents acting in complex economic systems, games are integral to AI. Games were one of the first applications of AI. The first operating checkers program dates back to 1952. A program by Samuel [1959] beat the Connecticut state checker champion in 1961. There was great fanfare when Deep Blue [Campbell et al., 2002] beat the world chess champion in 1997 and when AlphaGo [Silver et al., 2016] beat one of the world's top Go players in 2016. Although large, these games are conceptually simple because the agents observe the state of the world perfectly (they are fully observable). In most real-world interactions, the state of the world is only partially observable. There is now much interest in partially observable games like poker, where the environment is predictable (as the proportion of cards is known, even if the particular cards dealt is unknown), and robot soccer, where the environment is much less predictable. But all of these games are much simpler than the multi-agent interactions people perform in their daily lives, let alone the strategizing needed for bartering in marketplaces or on the Internet, where the rules are less well defined and the utilities are much more multifaceted.

11.2 Representations of Games

A mechanism represents the actions available to each agent and the (distribution over) outcomes for their joint actions. There are many representations for mechanisms in games, and multiagent interactions in general, that have been proposed in economics and AI. In AI, these representation typically allow the designer to model aspects of games that can be exploited for computational gain.

We present three representations; two of these are classic representations from economics. The first abstracts away all structure of the policies of the agents. The second models the sequential structure of games and is the foundation for much work on representing board games. The third representation moves away from the state-based representation to allow the representation of games in terms of features.

11.2.1 Normal Form Games

The most basic representation of games is the **normal form game** also known as the **strategic form game**. A normal form game consists of

- a finite set I of agents, typically identified with the integers $I = \{1, \ldots, n\}$
- a set of actions A_i for each agent $i \in I$. An **action profile** is a tuple $\langle a_1, \ldots, a_n \rangle$, which specifies that agent $i \in I$ carries out action a_i, where $a_i \in A_i$
- a utility function u_i for each agent $i \in I$ that, given an action profile, returns the expected utility for agent i given the action profile.

The joint action of all the agents (an action profile) produces an **outcome**. Each agent has a utility over each outcome. Each agent is trying to maximize its own utility. The utility for an agent is meant to encompass everything that the agent is interested in, including fairness, altruism and societal well-being.

Example 11.1 The game rock-paper-scissors is a common game played by children, and there is even a world championship. Suppose there are two

		Bob		
		rock	*paper*	*scissors*
	rock	0,0	−1,1	1,−1
Alice	*paper*	1,−1	0,0	−1,1
	scissors	−1,1	1,−1	0,0

Figure 11.1: Normal form for the rock-paper-scissors game

agents (players), Alice and Bob. There are three actions for each agent, so that

$$A_{Alice} = A_{Bob} = \{rock, paper, scissors\}.$$

For each combination of an action for Alice and an action for Bob there is a utility for Alice and a utility for Bob. This is often drawn in a table as in Figure 11.1. This is called a **payoff matrix**. Alice chooses a row and Bob chooses a column, simultaneously. This gives a pair of numbers: the first number is the payoff to the row player (Alice) and the second gives the payoff to the column player (Bob). Note that the utility for each of them depends on what both players do. An example of an action profile is $\langle scissors_{Alice}, rock_{Bob}\rangle$, where Alice chooses scissors and Bob chooses rock. In this action profile, Alice receives the utility of −1 and Bob receives the utility of 1. This game is a zero-sum game because one person wins only when the other loses.

This representation of a game may seem very restricted, because it only gives a one-off payoff for each agent based on single actions, chosen simultaneously, for each agent. However, the interpretation of an action in the definition is very general.

Typically, an "action" is not just a simple choice, but a **strategy**: a specification of what the agent will do under the various contingencies. The normal form, essentially, is a specification of the utilities given the possible strategies of the agents. This is why it is called the strategic form of a game.

More generally, the "action" in the definition of a normal-form game can be a **controller** (page 54) for the agent. Thus, each agent chooses a controller and the utility gives the expected outcome of the controllers run for each agent in an environment. Although the examples that follow are for simple actions, the general case has an enormous number of possible actions (possible controllers) for each agent.

11.2.2   Extensive Form of a Game

Whereas the normal form of a game represents controllers as single units, it is often more natural to specify the unfolding of a game through time. The extensive form of a game is an extension of a single-agent **decision tree** (page 438).

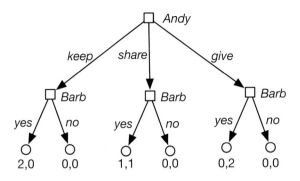

Figure 11.2: Extensive form of the sharing game

We first give a definition that assumes the game is fully observable (called *perfect information* in game theory).

A **perfect-information game** in **extensive form** or a **game tree** is a finite tree where the nodes are states and the arcs correspond to actions by the agents. In particular:

- Each internal node is labeled with an agent (or with *nature*). The agent is said to control the node.

- Each arc out of a node labeled with agent *i* corresponds to an action for agent *i*.

- Each internal node labeled with *nature* has a probability distribution over its children.

- The leaves represent final outcomes and are labeled with a utility for each agent.

The extensive form of a game specifies a particular unfolding of the game. Each path to a leaf, called a **run**, specifies one particular way that the game could proceed depending on the choices of the agents and nature.

A **strategy** for agent *i* is a function from nodes controlled by agent *i* into actions. That is, a strategy selects a child for each node that agent *i* controls. A **strategy profile** consists of a strategy for each agent.

Example 11.2 Consider a sharing game where there are two agents, Andy and Barb, and there are two identical items to be divided between them. Andy first selects how they will be divided: Andy keeps both items, they share and each person gets one item, or he gives both items to Barb. Then Barb gets to either reject the allocation and they both get nothing, or accept the allocation and they both get the allocated amount.

The extensive form of the sharing game is shown in Figure 11.2. Andy has 3 strategies. Barb has $2^3 = 8$ strategies; one for each combination of assignments to the nodes she controls. As a result, there are 24 strategy profiles.

Given a strategy profile, each node has a utility for each agent. The utility for an agent at a node is defined recursively from the bottom up:

- The utility for each agent at a leaf is given as part of the leaf.

- The utility for agent of a node controlled by that agent is the utility for the agent of the child node that is selected by agent's strategy.

- The utility for agent j of a node controlled by another agent i is the utility for agent j of the child node that is selected by agent i's strategy.

- The utility for agent i for a node controlled by nature is the expected value of the utility for agent i of the children. That is, $u_i(n) = \sum_c P(c)u_i(c)$, where the sum is over the children c of node n, and $P(c)$ is the probability that nature will choose child c.

Example 11.3 In the sharing game, suppose we have the following strategy profile: Andy chooses *keep* and Barb chooses *no, yes, yes* for each of the nodes she gets to choose for. Under this strategy profile, the utility for Andy at the leftmost internal node is 0, the utility for Andy at the center internal node is 1, and the utility for Andy at the rightmost internal node is 0. The utility for Andy at the root is 0.

The preceding definition of the extensive form of a game assumes that the agents can observe the state of the world (i.e., at each stage they know which node they are at). This means that the state of the game must be fully observable. In a **partially observable game** or an **imperfect-information game**, the agents do not necessarily know the state of the world when they have to decide what to do. This includes **simultaneous action games** where more than one agent needs to decide what to do at the same time. In such cases, the agents do not know which node they are at in the game tree. To model these games the extensive form of a game is extended to include information sets. An **information set** is a set of nodes, all controlled by the same agent and all with the same set of available actions. The idea is that the agent cannot distinguish the elements of the information set. The agent only knows the game state is at one of the nodes in the information set, not which node. In a strategy, the agent chooses one action for each information set; the same action is carried out at each node in the information set. Thus, in the extensive form, a strategy specifies a function from information sets to actions.

Example 11.4 Figure 11.3 (on the next page) gives the extensive form for the rock-paper-scissors game of Example 11.1 (page 523). The elements of the information set are in a rounded rectangle. In a strategy, Bob must treat each

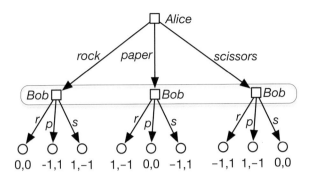

Figure 11.3: Extensive form of the rock-paper-scissors game

node in the information set the same. When Bob gets to choose his action, he does not know which action Alice has chosen.

11.2.3 Multiagent Decision Networks

The extensive form of a game is a state-based representation of the game. It is often more concise to describe states in terms of features. A **multiagent decision network** is a factored representation of a multiagent decision problem. It is like a **decision network** (page 445), except that each decision node is labeled with an agent that gets to choose a value for the node. There is a utility node for each agent specifying the utility for that agent. The parents of a decision node specify the information that will be available to the agent when it has to act.

Example 11.5 Figure 11.4 (on the next page) gives a multiagent decision network for a fire alarm example. In this scenario, there are two agents, Agent 1 and Agent 2. Each has its own noisy sensor of whether there is a fire. However, if they both call, it is possible that their calls will interfere with each other and neither call will work. Agent 1 gets to choose a value for decision variable $Call_1$ and only observes the value for the variable $Alarm_1$. Agent 2 gets to choose a value for decision variable $Call_2$ and only observes the value for the variable $Alarm_2$. Whether the call works depends on the values of $Call_1$ and $Call_2$. Whether the fire department comes depends on whether the call works. Agent 1's utility depends on whether there was a fire, whether the fire department comes, and whether they called – similarly for Agent 2.

A multiagent decision network can be converted into a normal-form game; however, the number of strategies may be enormous. If a decision variable has d states and n binary parents, there are 2^n assignments of values to parents and so d^{2^n} strategies. That is just for a single decision node; more complicated

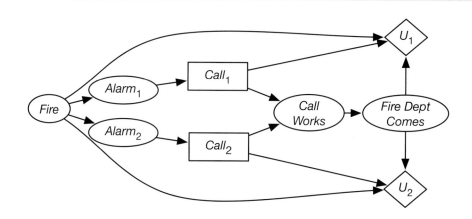

Figure 11.4: Multiagent decision network for Example 11.5

networks are even bigger when converted to normal form. Thus, algorithms that depend on enumerating strategies are impractical for anything but the smallest multiagent decision networks.

Other representations exploit other structures in multiagent settings. For example, the utility of an agent may depend on the number of other agents who do some action, but not on their identities. An agent's utility may depend on what a few other agents do, not directly on the actions of all other agents. An agent's utility may only depend on what the agents at neighboring locations do, and not on the identity of these agents or on what other agents do.

11.3   Computing Strategies with Perfect Information

The equivalent to full observability with multiple agents is called **perfect information**. In perfect-information games, agents act sequentially and, when an agent has to act, it gets to observe the state of the world before deciding what to do. Each agent acts to maximize its own utility.

A perfect-information game can be represented as an extensive form game where the information sets all contain a single node. They can also be represented as a multiagent decision network where the decision nodes are totally ordered and, for each decision node, the parents of that decision node include the preceding decision node and all of their parents (so they are multiagent counterpart of no-forgetting decision networks (page 449)).

Perfect-information games are solvable in a manner similar to fully observ-

Dimensions (p. 31)
flat
states
indefinite horizon
fully observable
deterministic
utility
non-learning
multiple agents
offline
perfect rationality

able single-agent systems. The can be solved backward, from the last decisions to the first, using dynamic programming or forward using search. The difference from the single-agent case is that the multiagent algorithm maintains a utility for each agent and, for each move, it selects an action that maximizes the utility of the agent making the move. The dynamic programming variant, called **backward induction**, starts from the end of the game, computing and caching the values and the plan of each node for each agent. It essentially follows the definition of the utility of a node for each agent, where the agent who controls the node gets to choose the action that maximizes its utility.

> **Example 11.6** Consider the sharing game of Figure 11.2 (page 525). For each of the nodes labeled with Barb, she gets to choose the value that maximizes her utility. Thus, she will choose "yes" for the right two nodes she controls, and would choose either for the leftmost node she controls. Suppose she chooses "no" for this node; then Andy gets to choose one of his actions: *keep* has utility 0 for him, *share* has utility 1, and *give* has utility 0, so he chooses to share.

In the case where two agents are competing so that a positive reward for one is a negative reward for the other agent, we have a two-agent **zero-sum game**. The value of such a game can be characterized by a single number that one agent is trying to maximize and the other agent is trying to minimize. Having a single value for a two-agent zero-sum game leads to a **minimax** strategy. Each node is either a MAX node, if it is controlled by the agent trying to maximize, or is a MIN node if it is controlled by the agent trying to minimize.

Backward induction could be used to find the optimal minimax strategy. From the bottom up, backward induction maximizes at MAX nodes and minimizes at MIN nodes. However, backward induction requires a traversal of the whole game tree. It is possible to prune part of the search tree by showing that some part of the tree will never be part of an optimal play.

> **Example 11.7** Consider searching in the game tree of Figure 11.5 (on the next page). In this figure, the square MAX nodes are controlled by the maximizing agent, and the round MIN nodes are controlled by the minimizing agent.
>
> Suppose the values of the leaf nodes are given or are computed given the definition of the game. The numbers at the bottom show some of these values. The other values are irrelevant, as we show here. Suppose we are doing a left-first depth-first traversal of this tree. The value of node h is 7, because it is the minimum of 7 and 9. Just by considering the leftmost child of i with a value of 6, we know that the value of i is less than or equal to 6. Therefore, at node d, the maximizing agent will go left. We do not have to evaluate the other child of i. Similarly, the value of j is 11, so the value of e is at least 11, and so the minimizing agent at node b will choose to go left.
>
> The value of l is less than or equal to 5, and the value of m is less than or equal to 4; thus, the value of f is less than or equal to 5, so the value of c will be less than or equal to 5. So, at a, the maximizing agent will choose to go left.

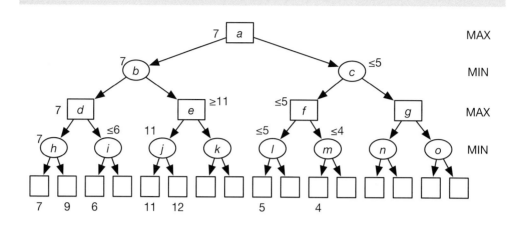

Figure 11.5: A zero-sum game tree showing which nodes can be pruned

> Notice that this argument did not depend on the values of the unnumbered leaves. Moreover, it did not depend on the size of the subtrees that were not explored.

The previous example analyzed what can be pruned. Minimax with **alpha-beta (α-β) pruning** is a depth-first **search** algorithm that prunes by passing pruning information down in terms of parameters α and β. In this depth-first search, a node has a score, which has been obtained from (some of) its descendants.

The parameter α is used to prune MIN nodes. Initially, it is the highest current value for all MAX ancestors of the current node. Any MIN node whose current value is less than or equal to its α value does not have to be explored further. This cutoff was used to prune the other descendants of nodes l, m, and c in the previous example.

The dual β parameter is used to prune MAX nodes.

The minimax algorithm with α-β pruning is given in Figure 11.6 (on the next page). It is called, initially, with

$MinimaxAlphaBeta(R, -\infty, \infty),$

where R is the root node. It returns a pair of the value for the node n and a path of choices that is best for each agent the results in this path. (Note that this path does not include n.) Line 13 performs β pruning; at this stage the algorithm knows that the current path will never be chosen, and so return a current score. Similarly, line 22 performs α-pruning. Line 17 and line 26 concatenate c to the path, as it has found a best path for the agent. In this algorithm, the path "*None*" is sometimes returned for non-leaf nodes; this only occurs when the algorithm has determined this path will not be used.

```
1: procedure Minimax_alpha_beta(n, α, β)
2:     Inputs
3:         n a node in a game tree
4:         α, β real numbers
5:     Output
6:         A pair of a value for node n, path that gives this value
7:     best := None
8:     if n is a leaf node then
9:         return evaluate(n), None
10:    else if n is a MAX node then
11:        for each child c of n do
12:            score, path := MinimaxAlphaBeta(c, α, β)
13:            if score ≥ β then
14:                return score, None
15:            else if score > α then
16:                α := score
17:                best := c : path
18:        return α, best
19:    else
20:        for each child c of n do
21:            score, path := MinimaxAlphaBeta(c, α, β)
22:            if score ≤ α then
23:                return score, None
24:            else if score < β then
25:                β := score
26:                best := c : path
27:        return β, best
```

Figure 11.6: Minimax with α-β pruning

Example 11.8 Consider running *MinimaxAlphaBeta* on the tree of Figure 11.5. We will show the recursive calls (and the values returned but not the paths.) Initially, it calls

$$MinimaxAlphaBeta(a, -\infty, \infty),$$

which then calls, in turn,

$$MinimaxAlphaBeta(b, -\infty, \infty)$$

$$MinimaxAlphaBeta(d, -\infty, \infty)$$

$$MinimaxAlphaBeta(h, -\infty, \infty).$$

This last call finds the minimum of both of its children and returns 7. Next the procedure calls

$MinimaxAlphaBeta(i, 7, \infty),$

which then gets the value for the first of i's children, which has value 6. Because $\alpha \geq \beta$, it returns 6. The call to d then returns 7, and it calls

$MinimaxAlphaBeta(e, -\infty, 7).$

Node e's first child returns 11 and, because $\alpha \geq \beta$, it returns 11. Then b returns 7, and the call to a calls

$MinimaxAlphaBeta(c, 7, \infty),$

which in turn calls

$MinimaxAlphaBeta(f, 7, \infty),$

which eventually returns 5, and so the call to c returns 5, and the whole procedure returns 7.

By keeping track of the values, the maximizing agent knows to go left at a, then the minimizing agent will go left at b, and so on.

The amount of pruning provided by this algorithm depends on the ordering of the children of each node. It works best if a highest-valued child of a MAX node is selected first and if a lowest-valued child of a MIN node is returned first. In implementations of real games, much of the effort is made to try to ensure this ordering.

Most real games are too big to carry out minimax search, even with α-β pruning. For these games, instead of only stopping at leaf nodes, it is possible to stop at any node. The value returned at the node where the algorithm stops is an estimate of the value for this node. The function used to estimate the value is an **evaluation function**. Much work goes into finding good evaluation functions. There is a trade-off between the amount of computation required to compute the evaluation function and the size of the search space that can be explored in any given time. It is an empirical question as to the best compromise between a complex evaluation function and a large search space.

11.4   Reasoning with Imperfect Information

In an **imperfect-information game**, or a **partially observable game**, an agent does not fully know the state of the world or the agents act simultaneously.

Partial observability for the multiagent case is more complicated than the fully observable multiagent case or the partially observable single-agent case. The following simple examples show some important issues that arise even in the case of two agents, each with a few choices.

		goalkeeper	
		left	right
kicker	left	0.6	0.2
	right	0.3	0.9

Probability of a goal

Figure 11.7: Soccer penalty kick. The kicker can kick to his left or right. The goalkeeper can jump to her left or right.

Example 11.9 Consider the case of a penalty kick in soccer as depicted in Figure 11.7. If the kicker kicks to his right and the goalkeeper jumps to her right, the probability of a goal is 0.9, and similarly for the other combinations of actions, as given in the figure.

What should the kicker do, given that he wants to maximize the probability of a goal and that the goalkeeper wants to minimize the probability of a goal? The kicker could think that it is better kicking to his right, because the pair of numbers for his right kick is higher than the pair for the left. The goalkeeper could then think that if the kicker will kick right, then she should jump left. However, if the kicker thinks that the goalkeeper will jump left, he should then kick left. But then, the goalkeeper should jump right. Then the kicker should kick right...

Each agent is potentially faced with an infinite regression of reasoning about what the other agent will do. At each stage in their reasoning, the agents reverse their decision. One could imagine cutting this off at some depth; however, the actions then are purely a function of the arbitrary depth. Even worse, if the goalkeeper knew the depth limit of reasoning for the kicker, she could exploit this knowledge to determine what the kicker will do and choose her action appropriately.

An alternative is for the agents to choose actions stochastically. Imagine that the kicker and the goalkeeper each secretly toss a coin to decide what to do. Consider whether the coins should be biased. Suppose that the kicker decides to kick to his right with probability p_k and that the goalkeeper decides to jump to her right with probability p_g. The probability of a goal is then

$$P(goal) = 0.9 p_k p_g + 0.3 p_k (1 - p_g) + 0.2 (1 - p_k) p_g + 0.6 (1 - p_k)(1 - p_g)$$

where the numbers (0.9, 0.3, etc.) come from Figure 11.7.

Figure 11.8 (on the next page) shows the probability of a goal as a function of p_k. The different lines correspond to different values of p_g.

There is something special about the value $p_k = 0.4$. At this value, the probability of a goal is 0.48, independent of the value of p_g. That is, no matter what the goalkeeper does, the kicker expects to get a goal with probability 0.48.

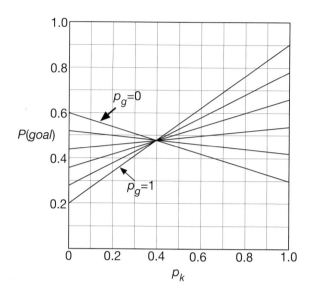

Figure 11.8: Probability of a goal as a function of action probabilities

If the kicker deviates from $p_k = 0.4$, he could do better or he could do worse, depending on what the goalkeeper does.

The plot for p_g is similar, with all of the lines meeting at $p_g = 0.3$. Again, when $p_g = 0.3$, the probability of a goal is 0.48.

The strategy with $p_k = 0.4$ and $p_g = 0.3$ is special in the sense that neither agent can do better by unilaterally deviating from the strategy. However, this does not mean that they cannot do better; if one of the agents deviates from this equilibrium, the other agent could do better by also deviating from the equilibrium. However, this equilibrium is safe for an agent in the sense that, even if the other agent knew the agent's strategy, the other agent cannot force a worse outcome for the agent. Playing this strategy means that an agent does not have to worry about double-guessing the other agent. In this game, each agent will get the best payoff it could guarantee to obtain.

So let us now extend the definition of a strategy to include randomized strategies.

Consider the normal form of a game where each agent chooses an action simultaneously. Each agent chooses an action without knowing what the other agents choose.

A **strategy** for an agent is a probability distribution over the actions for this agent. In a **pure strategy** one of the probabilities will be 1 and the rest will be 0. Thus an agent following a pure strategy is acting deterministically. The alternative to a pure strategy is a **stochastic strategy** where none of the probabilities will be 1, and so

Dimensions (p. 31)

flat

states

finite horizon

partially observable

stochastic

utility

non-learning

multiple agents

offline

perfect rationality

more than one action will have a non-zero probability. The set of actions with a non-zero probability in a strategy is called the **support set** of the strategy.

A **strategy profile** is an assignment of a strategy to each agent. If σ is a strategy profile, let σ_i be the strategy of agent i in σ, and let σ_{-i} be the strategies of the other agents. Then σ is $\sigma_i\sigma_{-i}$. If the strategy profile is made up of pure strategies, it is often called an **action profile**, because each agent is playing a particular action.

A strategy profile σ has an expected utility for each agent. Let $utility(\sigma, i)$ be the expected utility of strategy profile σ for agent i. The utility of a stochastic strategy profile can be computed by averaging the utilities of the basic actions that make up the profile given the probabilities of the actions.

A **best response** for an agent i to the strategies σ_{-i} of the other agents is a strategy that has maximal utility for that agent. That is, σ_i is a best response to σ_{-i} if, for all other strategies σ_i' for agent i,

$$utility(\sigma_i\sigma_{-i}, i) \geq utility(\sigma_i'\sigma_{-i}, i).$$

A strategy profile σ is a **Nash equilibrium** if, for each agent i, strategy σ_i is a best response to σ_{-i}. That is, a Nash equilibrium is a strategy profile such that no agent can do better by unilaterally deviating from that profile.

One of the great results of game theory, proved by Nash [1950], is that every finite game has at least one Nash equilibrium.

Example 11.10 In Example 11.9 (page 533), there is a unique Nash equilibrium where $p_k = 0.4$ and $p_g = 0.3$. This has the property that, if the kicker is playing $p_k = 0.4$, it does not matter what the goalkeeper does; the goalkeeper will have the same payoff, and so $p_g = 0.3$ is a best response (as is any other strategy). Similarly, if the goalkeeper is playing $p_g = 0.3$, it does not matter what the kicker does; and so every strategy, including $p_k = 0.4$, is a best response.

The only reason an agent would consider randomizing between two actions is if the actions have the same expected utility. All probabilistic mixtures of the two actions have the same utility. The reason to choose a particular value for the probability of the mixture is to prevent the other agent from exploiting a deviation.

Games can have multiple Nash equilibria. Consider the following two-agent, two-action game.

Example 11.11 Suppose there is a resource that two agents may want to fight over. Each agent chooses to act as a hawk or as a dove. Suppose the resource is worth R units, where $R > 0$. If both agents act as doves, they share the resource. If one agent acts as a hawk and the other as a dove, the hawk agent gets the resource and the dove agent gets nothing. If they both act like hawks, there is destruction of the resource and the reward to both is $-D$, where $D > 0$. This is depicted by the following payoff matrix:

Agent 2

		dove	hawk
Agent 1	dove	$R/2, R/2$	$0, R$
	hawk	$R, 0$	$-D, -D$

In this matrix, Agent 1 gets to choose the row, Agent 2 gets to choose the column, and the payoff in the cell is a pair consisting of the reward to Agent 1 and the reward to Agent 2. Each agent is trying to maximize its own reward.

In this game there are three Nash equilibria:

- In one equilibrium, Agent 1 acts as a hawk and Agent 2 as a dove. Agent 1 does not want to deviate because then they have to share the resource. Agent 2 does not want to deviate because then there is destruction.

- In the second equilibrium, Agent 1 acts as a dove and Agent 2 as a hawk.

- In the third equilibrium, both agents act stochastically. In this equilibrium, there is some chance of destruction. The probability of acting like a hawk goes up with the value R of the resource and goes down as the value D of destruction increases. See Exercise 11.2 (page 546).

In this example, you could imagine each agent doing some posturing to try to indicate what it will do to try to force an equilibrium that is advantageous to it.

Having multiple Nash equilibria does not come from being adversaries, as the following example shows.

Example 11.12 Suppose there are two people who want to be together. Agent 1 prefers they both go to the football game and Agent 2 prefers they both go shopping. They both would be unhappy if they are not together. Suppose they both have to choose simultaneously what activity to do. This is depicted by the following payoff matrix:

Agent 2

		football	shopping
Agent 1	football	2, 1	0, 0
	shopping	0, 0	1, 2

In this matrix, Agent 1 chooses the row, and Agent 2 chooses the column.

In this game, there are three Nash equilibria. One equilibrium is where they both go shopping, one is where they both go to the football game, and one is a randomized strategy.

This is a **coordination** problem. Knowing the set of equilibria does not actually tell either agent what to do, because what an agent should do depends on what the other agent will do. In this example, you could imagine conversations to determine which equilibrium they would choose.

Even when there is a unique Nash equilibrium, that Nash equilibrium does not guarantee the maximum payoff to each agent. The following example is a variant of what is known as the **prisoner's dilemma**.

Example 11.13 Imagine you are on a game show with a stranger who you will never see again. You each have the choice of

- taking $100 for yourself or
- giving $1000 to the other person.

This is depicted as the following payoff matrix:

		Player 2	
		take	give
Player 1	take	100, 100	1100, 0
	give	0, 1100	1000, 1000

No matter what the other agent does, each agent is better off if it takes rather than gives. However, both agents are better off if they both give rather than if they both take.

Thus, there is a unique Nash equilibrium, where both agents take. This strategy profile results in each player receiving $100. The strategy profile where both players give results in each player receiving $1000. However, in this strategy profile, each agent is rewarded for deviating.

There is a large body of research on the prisoner's dilemma, because it does not seem to be so rational to be greedy, where each agent tries to do the best for itself, resulting in everyone being worse off. One case where giving becomes preferred is when the game is played a number of times. This is known as the **sequential prisoner's dilemma**. One strategy for the sequential prisoner's dilemma is **tit-for-tat**: each player gives initially, then does the other agent's previous action at each step. This strategy is a Nash equilibrium as long as there is no last action that both players know about. See Exercise 11.7 (page 547).

Having multiple Nash equilibria arises not just from partial observability. It is possible to have multiple equilibria with a perfect-information game, and it is even possible to have infinitely many Nash equilibria, as the following example shows.

Example 11.14 Consider the sharing game of Example 11.2 (page 525). In this game there are infinitely many Nash equilibria. There is a set of equilibria where Andy shares, and Barb says *yes* to sharing for the center choice and can randomize between the other choices, as long as the probability of saying *yes* in the left-hand choice is less than or equal to 0.5. In these Nash equilibria, they both get 1. There is another set of Nash equilibria where Andy keeps, and Barb randomizes among her choices so that the probability of saying *yes* in the left branch is greater than or equal to 0.5. In these equilibria, Barb gets 0, and Andy gets some value in range [1, 2] depending on Barb's probability. There is a third set of Nash equilibria where Barb has a 0.5 probability of selecting *yes* at the leftmost node, selects *yes* at the center node, and Andy randomizes between *keep* and *share* with any probability.

Suppose the sharing game were modified slightly so that Andy offered a small bribe for Barb to say *yes*. This could be done by changing the 2, 0 payoff to be 1.9, 0.1. Andy may think, "Given the choice between getting 0.1 or 0, Barb will choose to get 0.1, so then I should *keep*." But Barb could think, "I should say *no* to 0.1, so that Andy shares and I get 1." In this example (even ignoring the rightmost branch), there are multiple pure Nash equilibria, one where Andy keeps, and Barb says *yes* at the leftmost branch. In this equilibrium, Andy gets 1.9 and Barb gets 0.1. There is another Nash equilibrium where Barb says *no* at the leftmost choice node and *yes* at the center branch and Andy chooses *share*. In this equilibrium, they both get 1. It would seem that this is the one preferred by Barb. However, Andy could think that Barb is making an empty **threat**. If he actually decided to *keep*, Barb, acting to maximize her utility, would not actually say *no*.

The backward induction algorithm only finds one of the equilibria in the modified sharing game of the previous example. It computes a **subgame-perfect equilibrium**, where it is assumed that the agents choose the action with greatest utility for them at every node where they get to choose. It assumes that agents do not carry out threats that it is not in their interest to carry out at the time. In the modified sharing game of the previous example, it assumes that Barb will say *yes* to the small bribe. However, when dealing with real opponents, we must be aware that they may follow through with threats that we may not think rational. Indeed, it might be better for an agent not to (appear to) be rational!

11.4.1 Computing Nash Equilibria

To compute a Nash equilibrium for a game in normal form, there are three steps:

1. Eliminate dominated strategies.

2. Determine **support set**, the set of actions which have non-zero probabilities.

3. Determine the probability for the actions in the support set.

It turns out that the second of these is the most difficult.

Eliminating Dominated Strategies

A strategy s_1 for a agent A **dominates** strategy s_2 for A if, for every action of the other agents, the utility of s_1 for agent A is higher than the utility of s_2 for agent A. This is formalized below. Any pure strategy dominated by another strategy can be eliminated from consideration. The dominating strategy could be a randomized strategy. Removing dominated strategies can be done repeatedly.

Example 11.15 Consider the following payoff matrix, where the first agent chooses the row and the second agent chooses the column. In each cell is a pair of payoffs: the payoff for Agent 1 and the payoff for Agent 2. Agent 1 has actions $\{a_1, b_1, c_1\}$. Agent 2 has actions $\{d_2, e_2, f_2\}$.

		Agent 2		
		d_2	e_2	f_2
	a_1	3,5	5,1	1,2
Agent 1	b_1	1,1	2,9	6,4
	c_1	2,6	4,7	0,8

(Before looking at the solution try to work out what each agent should do.)

Action c_1 can be removed because it is dominated by action a_1: Agent 1 will never do c_1 if action a_1 is available to it. Notice how the payoff for Agent 1 is greater doing a_1 than doing c_1, no matter what the other agent does.

Once action c_1 is eliminated, action f_2 can be eliminated because it is dominated for Agent 2 by the randomized strategy $0.5 * d_2 + 0.5 * e_2$.

Once c_1 and f_2 have been eliminated, b_1 is dominated by a_1, and so Agent 1 will do action a_1. Given that Agent 1 will do a_1, Agent 2 will do d_2. Thus, the payoff in this game will be 3 for Agent 1 and 5 for Agent 2.

Strategy s_1 **strictly dominates** strategy s_2 for Agent i if, for all action profiles σ_{-i} of the other agents,

$$utility(s_1\sigma_{-i}, i) > utility(s_2\sigma_{-i}, i)$$

in which case s_2 is **strictly dominated** by s_1. If s_2 is a pure strategy that is strictly dominated by some strategy s_1, then s_2 can never be in the support set of any Nash equilibrium. This holds even if s_1 is a stochastic strategy. Repeated elimination of strictly dominated strategies gives the same result, regardless of the order in which the strictly dominated strategies are removed.

There are also weaker notions of domination, where the greater than symbol in the preceding formula is replaced by greater than or equal. If the weaker notion of domination is used, there is always a Nash equilibrium with support of the non-dominated strategies. However, some Nash equilibria may be lost. Moreover, which equilibria are lost can depend on the order in which the dominated strategies are removed.

Computing Randomized Strategies

An agent will only randomize between actions if the actions all have the same utility to the agent, given the strategies of the other agents. This idea leads to a set of constraints that can be solved to compute a Nash equilibrium. If these constraints can be solved with numbers in the range $(0, 1)$, and the mixed strategies computed for each agent are not dominated by another strategy for the agent, then this strategy profile is a Nash equilibrium.

Recall that a support set (page 535) is a set of pure strategies that each have non-zero probability in a Nash equilibrium.

Once dominated strategies have been eliminated, an agent can search over support sets to determine whether the support sets form a Nash equilibrium. Note that, if there are n actions available to an agent, there are $2^n - 1$ non-empty subsets, and we have to search over combinations of support sets for the various agents. This is not feasible unless there are only a few non-dominated actions or there are Nash equilibria with small support sets. To find simple (in terms of the number of actions in the support set) equilibria, an agent can search from smaller support sets to larger sets.

Suppose agent i is randomizing between actions $a_i^1, \ldots, a_i^{k_i}$ in a Nash equilibrium. Let p_i^j be the probability that agent i does action a_i^j. Let σ_{-i} be the strategies for the other agents, which is a function of their probabilities. The fact that this is a Nash equilibrium gives the following constraints: $p_i^j > 0$, $\sum_{j=1}^{k_i} p_i^j = 1$, and, for all j, j'

$$utility(a_i^j \sigma_{-i}, i) = utility(a_i^{j'} \sigma_{-i}, i).$$

We also require that the utility of doing a_i^j is not less than the utility of doing an action outside of the support set. Thus, for all $a' \notin \{a_i^1, \ldots, a_i^{k_i}\}$,

$$utility(a_i^j \sigma_{-i}, i) \geq utility(a' \sigma_{-i}, i).$$

Example 11.16 In Example 11.9 (page 533), suppose the goalkeeper jumps right with probability p_g and the kicker kicks right with probability p_k.

If the goalkeeper jumps right, the probability of a goal is

$$0.9 p_k + 0.2(1 - p_k).$$

If the goalkeeper jumps left, the probability of a goal is

$$0.3 p_k + 0.6(1 - p_k).$$

The only time the goalkeeper would randomize is if these are equal; that is, if

$$0.9 p_k + 0.2(1 - p_k) = 0.3 p_k + 0.6(1 - p_k).$$

Solving for p_k gives $p_k = 0.4$.

Similarly, for the kicker to randomize, the probability of a goal must be the same whether the kicker kicks left or right:

$$0.2 p_g + 0.6(1 - p_g) = 0.9 p_g + 0.3(1 - p_g).$$

Solving for p_g gives $p_g = 0.3$.

Thus, the only Nash equilibrium has $p_k = 0.4$ and $p_g = 0.3$.

11.5 Group Decision Making

Often groups of people have to make decisions about what the group will do. It may seem that voting is a good way to determine what a group wants, and when there is a clear most-preferred choice, it is. However, there are major problems with voting when there is not a clear preferred choice, as shown in the following example.

Example 11.17 Consider a purchasing agent that has to decide on a holiday destination for a group of people, based on their preference. Suppose there are three people, Alice, Bob and Cory, and three destinations, X, Y, and Z. Suppose the agents have the following preferences, where $\succ$ means strictly prefers (page 427):

- Alice: $X \succ Y \succ Z$
- Bob: $Y \succ Z \succ X$
- Cory: $Z \succ X \succ Y$

Given these preferences, in a pairwise vote, $X \succ Y$ because two out of the three prefer X to Y. Similarly, in the voting, $Y \succ Z$ and $Z \succ X$. Thus, the preferences obtained by voting are not transitive. This example is known as the **Condorcet paradox**. Indeed, it is not clear what a group outcome should be in this case, because it is symmetric between the outcomes.

A **social preference function** gives a preference relation for a group. We would like a social preference function to depend on the preferences of the individuals in the group. It may seem that the Condorcet paradox is a problem unique to pairwise voting; however, the following result due to Arrow [1963] shows that such paradoxes occur with any social preference function.

Proposition 11.1 (Arrow's impossibility theorem). *If there are three or more outcomes, the following properties cannot simultaneously hold for any social preference function:*

- *The social preference function is complete and transitive (page 427).*
- *Every individual preference that is complete and transitive is allowed.*
- *If every individual prefers outcome o_1 to o_2, the group prefers o_1 to o_2.*
- *The group preference between outcomes o_1 and o_2 depends only on the individual preferences on o_1 and o_2 and not on the individual preferences on other outcomes.*
- *No individual gets to unilaterally decide the outcome (nondictatorship).*

When building an agent that takes the individual preferences and gives a social preference, you should be aware that you cannot have all of these intuitive and desirable properties. Rather than giving a group preference that has undesirable properties, it may be better to point out to the individuals how their preferences cannot be reconciled.

11.6   Mechanism Design

The earlier discussion on agents choosing their actions assumed that each agent gets to play in a predefined game. The problem of **mechanism design** is to design a game with desirable properties for various agents to play.

A **mechanism** specifies the actions available to each agent and the outcomes of each action profile. We assume that agents have utilities over outcomes.

There are two common properties that are desirable for a mechanism:

- A mechanism should be easy for agents to use. Given an agent's utility, it should be easy for the agent to determine what to do. A **dominant strategy** is a strategy for an agent that is best for the agent, no matter what the other agents do. If an agent has a dominant strategy, it can do its best action without the complicated strategic reasoning described in the previous sections. A mechanism is dominant-strategy **truthful** if it has a dominant strategy for each agent and, in the dominant strategy, an agent's best strategy is to declare its true preferences. In a mechanism that is dominant-strategy truthful, an agent simply declares its true preferences; the agent cannot do better by trying to manipulate the mechanism for its own gain.

- A mechanism should give the best outcome aggregated over all of the agents. For example, a mechanism is **economically efficient** if the outcome chosen is one that maximizes the sum of the utilities of the agents.

Example 11.18 Suppose you want to design a meeting scheduler, where users input the times they are available and the scheduler chooses a time for the meeting. One mechanism is for the users to specify when they are available or not, and for the scheduler to select the time that has the most people available. A second mechanism is for the users to specify their utility for the various times, and the scheduler chooses the time that maximizes the sum of the utilities. Neither of these mechanisms is dominant-strategy truthful.

For the first mechanism, users may declare that they are unavailable at some time to force a time they prefer. It is not clear that being available at a certain time is well defined; at some stage, users must decide whether it is easier to reschedule what they would have otherwise done at some particular time, rather than say they are unavailable at this time. Different people may have different thresholds as to what other activities can be moved.

For the second mechanism, suppose there are three people, Alice, Bob, and Cory, and they have to decide whether to meet on Monday, Tuesday, or Wednesday. Suppose they have the following utilities for the meeting days:

	Monday	Tuesday	Wednesday
Alice	0	8	10
Bob	3	4	0
Cory	11	7	6

The economically efficient outcome is to meet on Tuesday. However, if Alice were to change her evaluation of Tuesday to be 2, the mechanism would choose Wednesday. Thus, Alice has an incentive to misrepresent her values. It is not in Alice's interest to be honest.

Note that, if there is a mechanism that has dominant strategies, there is a mechanism that is dominant-strategy truthful. This is known as the **revelation principle**. To implement a dominant-strategy truthful mechanism, we could, in principle, write a program that accepts from an agent its actual preferences and provides to the original mechanism the optimal input for that agent. This program would optimally lie for the agent.

It turns out that it is essentially impossible to design a reasonable mechanism that is dominant-strategy truthful. Gibbard [1973] and Satterthwaite [1975] proved that, as long as there are three or more outcomes that are possible to be chosen, the only mechanisms with dominant strategies have a **dictator**: there is one agent whose preferences determine the outcome. This is known as the **Gibbard–Satterthwaite theorem**.

One way to obtain dominant-strategy truthful mechanisms is to introduce money. Assume that money can be added to utility so that, for any two outcomes o_1 and o_2, for each agent there is some (possibly negative) amount d such that the agent is indifferent between the outcomes o_1 and $o_2 + d$. By allowing agents to be paid to accept an outcome they would not otherwise prefer, or to pay for an outcome they want, we can ensure an agent does not gain by lying.

In a **VCG mechanism**, or a Vickrey–Clarke–Groves mechanism, the agents declare their values for each of the outcomes. The outcome that maximizes the sum of the declared values is chosen. Agents pay according to how much their participation affects the outcome. Agent i pays the sum of the value for the other agents for the chosen outcome minus the sum of the values for the other agents if i had not participated. The VCG mechanism is both economically efficient and dominant-strategy truthful, assuming that agents only care about their utility and not about other agents' utilities or other agents' payments.

Example 11.19 Consider the values of Example 11.18. Suppose the values given can be interpreted as equivalent to dollars; for example, Alice is indifferent between meeting on Monday or meeting on Tuesday and paying $8.00 (she is prepared to pay $7.99 to move the meeting from Monday to Tuesday, but not $8.01). Given these declared values, Tuesday is chosen as the meeting day. If Alice had not participated, Monday would have been chosen, and so the other agents have a net loss of 3, so Alice has to pay $3.00. The net value to her is then 5; the utility of 8 for the Tuesday minus the payment of 3. The declarations, payments, and net values are given in the following table:

	Monday	Tuesday	Wednesday	Payment	Net Value
Alice	0	8	10	3	5
Bob	3	4	0	1	3
Cory	11	7	6	0	7
Total	14	19	16		

Consider what would happen if Alice had changed her evaluation of Tuesday to 2. In this case, Wednesday would be the chosen day, but Alice would have had to pay $8.00, with a net value of 2, and so would be worse off. Alice cannot gain an advantage by lying to the mechanism. One way to think about the payment is that Alice needs to bribe the mechanism to go along with her favourite choice.

One common mechanism for selling an item, or a set of items, is an **auction**. A common auction type for selling a single item is an ascending auction, where there is a current offering price for the item that increases by a predetermined increment when the previous offering price has been met. Offering to buy the item at the current price is called a bid. Only one person may put in a bid for a particular price. The item goes to the person who put in the highest bid, and the person pays the amount of that bid.

Consider a VCG mechanism for selling a single item. Suppose there are a number of people who each put in a bid for how much they value an item. The outcome that maximizes the payoffs is to give the item to the person who had the highest bid. If they had not participated, the item would have gone to the second-highest bidder. Therefore, according to the VCG mechanism, the top bidder should get the item and pay the value of the second-highest bid. This is known as a **second-price auction**. The second price auction is equivalent (up to bidding increments) to having an ascending auction, where people specify how much they want to pay as a proxy bid, and there is an agent to convert the proxy bids into real bids. Bidding in a second-price auction is straightforward because the agents do not have to do complex strategic reasoning. It is also easy to determine a winner and the appropriate payment.

11.7 Review

This chapter has touched on some of the issues that arise with multiple agents. The following are the main points to remember:

- A multiagent system consists of multiple agents who act autonomously and have their own utility over outcomes. The outcomes depend on the actions of all the agents. Agents can compete, cooperate, coordinate, communicate, and negotiate.

- The strategic form or normal form of a game specifies the expected outcome given controllers for each agent.

- The extensive form of a game models agents' actions and information through time in terms of game trees.

- A multiagent decision network models probabilistic dependency and information availability.

- Perfect-information games can be solved by backing up values in game trees or searching the game tree using minimax with α-β pruning.

- In partially observable domains, sometimes it is optimal to act stochastically.

- A Nash equilibrium is a strategy profile for each agent such that no agent can increase its utility by unilaterally deviating from the strategy profile.

- By introducing payments, it is possible to design a mechanism that is dominant-strategy truthful and economically efficient.

11.8   References and Further Reading

For overviews of multiagent systems see Shoham and Leyton-Brown [2008], Vlassis [2007], Stone and Veloso [2000], Wooldridge [2002], and Weiss [1999]. Nisan et al. [2007] overview research frontiers in algorithmic game theory.

Multiagent decision networks are based on the MAIDs of Koller and Milch [2003]. Genesereth and Thielscher [2014] describe **general game playing** which uses logical representations for games.

Minimax with α-β pruning was first published by Hart and Edwards [1961]. Knuth and Moore [1975] and Pearl [1984] analyze α-β pruning and other methods for searching game trees. Ballard [1983] discusses how minimax can be combined with chance nodes. The Deep Blue chess computer, which beat Garry Kasparov, the world Chess champion in May 1997 is described by Campbell et al. [2002]. Silver et al. [2016] describe AlphaGo, the program that beat a top-ranked Go player in 2016.

Mechanism design is described by Shoham and Leyton-Brown [2008], Nisan [2007] and in microeconomics textbooks such as Mas-Colell et al. [1995]. Ordeshook [1986] describes group decision making and game theory.

11.9   Exercises

Exercise 11.1 Consider the game of Tic-Tac-Toe (also called Noughts and Crosses), which is played by two players, an "X" player and an "O" player who alternate putting their symbol in a blank space on a 3×3 game-board. A player's goal is to win by placing three symbols in a row, column, or diagonal; the game ends when a player wins or the board is filled. In the game shown below, player O has just made its third turn. It is Xs turn to make its fourth move. The playing agent needs to decide intelligently which of the available 3 moves X should choose next:

X1, X2, or X3. We have started the search tree, with three branches for the three possible moves for X:

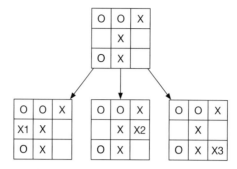

Draw the rest of the game tree. Assume the value of the tree is +1 for an X win, −1 for an O win, and 0 for a draw. Show how the values are backed up to give a value for each of the nodes. What should X do? Is it likely to win, lose or draw?

Could α-β pruning prune any of the tree?

Exercise 11.2 For the hawk–dove game of Example 11.11 (page 535), where $D > 0$ and $R > 0$, each agent is trying to maximize its utility. Is there a Nash equilibrium with a randomized strategy? What are the probabilities? What is the expected payoff to each agent? (These should be expressed as functions of R and D). Show your calculations.

Exercise 11.3 Which of the following games in normal form have a Nash equilibrium made up of pure strategies? For those that do, specify the pure strategy Nash equilibria. For those that do not, explain how you know there is no pure strategy Nash equilibrium.

(a)

		Player 2	
		a2	b2
Player 1	a1	10,10	110,0
	b1	0,110	100,100

(b)

		Player 2	
		a2	b2
Player 1	a1	10,10	11,20
	b1	0,11	20,1

(c)

		Player 2	
		a2	b2
Player 1	a1	10,20	5,10
	b1	7,11	20,12

Exercise 11.4 In Example 11.12 (page 536), what is the Nash equilibrium with randomized strategies? What is the expected value for each agent in this equilibrium?

Exercise 11.5 Consider the following normal-form game where the row player can choose action A, B or C and the column player could choose action D, E, or F:

	D	E	F
A	40, 40	120, 10	60, 30
B	30, 60	110, 60	90, 90
C	30, 110	100, 100	70, 120

where the pairs give the value of the outcome for the row player followed by the value for the column player.

(a) When eliminating dominant strategies, what strategies (if any) can be eliminated? Explain what is eliminated, and what cannot be eliminated.

(b) Specify a Nash equilibrium for this game. (For a randomized strategy, give just the actions that are randomized; you do not need to give the probabilities). Explain why it is a Nash equilibrium.

(c) Is there more than one Nash equilibrium? If so, give another one. If not explain why there is no other one.

(d) If the agents could coordinate, could they get a better outcome than in a Nash equilibrium? Explain why or why not.

Exercise 11.6 Answer the same questions as in the previous exercise for the following games:

i)

	D	E	F
A	2, 11	10, 10	3, 12
B	5, 7	12, 1	6, 5
C	6, 5	13, 2	4, 6

ii)

	D	E	F
A	80, 130	20, 10	130, 80
B	130, 80	30, 20	80, 130
C	20, 10	100, 100	30, 20

Exercise 11.7 Consider the sequential prisoner's dilemma (page 537).

(a) Suppose the agents play for a fixed number of times (say three times). Give two equilibria if there are two or more, otherwise give the unique equilibrium and explain why there is only one. Hint: Consider the last time first.

(b) Suppose there is a discount factor (page 462) of γ, which means there is a probability γ of stopping at each stage. Is tit-for-tat a Nash equilibrium for all values of γ? If so, prove it. If not, for which values of γ is it a Nash equilibrium?

Chapter 12

Learning to Act

Since in action it frequently happens that no delay is permissible, it is very certain that, when it is not in our power to determine what is true, we ought to act according to what is most probable.

Descartes [1637], Part III

12.1 Reinforcement Learning Problem

A **reinforcement learning (RL)** agent acts in an environment, observing its state and receiving rewards. From its perceptual and reward information, it must determine what to do. This chapter mainly considers fully observable, single-agent reinforcement learning. Section 12.10.2 (page 569) describes a simple form of multiagent reinforcement learning.

A reinforcement learning agent is characterized as follows:

- The learning agent is given the possible states and the set of actions it can carry out.

- At each time the agent observes the state of the environment and the reward received. We are assuming the environment is fully observable (page 28).

- At each time, after observing the state and reward, the agent carries out an action.

- The goal of the agent is to maximize its discounted reward (page 462), for some discount factor γ.

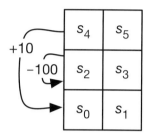

Figure 12.1: The environment of a tiny reinforcement learning problem

Reinforcement learning can be formalized in terms of **Markov decision processes** (page 458), in which the agent initially only knows the set of possible states and the set of possible actions. The dynamics, $P(s' \mid a, s)$, and the reward function, $R(s, a)$, are not given to the agent. As in an MDP, after each action, the agent observes the state it is in and receives a reward.

Example 12.1 Consider the domain shown in Figure 12.1. There are six states the agent could be in, labeled $s_0, \ldots, s_5$. The agent can observe what state it is in at any time. The agent has four actions: *upR, upC, left, right*. That is all the agent knows before it starts. It does not know how the states are configured, what the actions do, or how rewards are earned.

Figure 12.1 shows the configuration of the six states. Suppose the actions work as follows:

right The agent moves to the right in states s_0, s_2, s_4 with a reward of 0 and stays still in the other states, with a reward of -1.

left The agent moves one state to the left in states s_1, s_3, s_5, with a reward of 0. In state s_0, it stays in state s_0 and has a reward of -1. In state s_2, it has a reward of -100 and stays in state s_2. In state s_4, it receives a reward of 10 and moves to state s_0.

upC (for "up carefully") The agent goes up, except in states s_4 and s_5, where the agent crashes and stays still. It receives a reward of -1, except when it crashes, in which cases there is a reward of -2.

upR (for "up risky") With a probability of 0.8 it acts like *upC*, except the reward is -1 when it crashes, and is 0 otherwise. With probability 0.1 it acts as a *left*, and with probability 0.1 it acts as a *right*.

There is a discounted reward (page 462) with a discount of $\gamma = 0.9$. This can be translated as having a 0.1 chance of the agent leaving the game at any step, or as a way to encode that the agent prefers immediate rewards over future rewards.

The agent should try to go left from s_4 as often as possible to collect the reward of $+10$. Getting from s_0 to s_4, it can go past a dangerous cliff at s_2 where

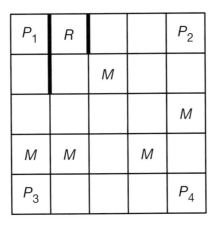

Figure 12.2: The environment of a grid game

there is a risk of falling off the cliff and getting a large negative reward, or going the longer and safer way around. Initially, it does not know this, but this is what it needs to learn.

Example 12.2 Figure 12.2 shows the domain of a more complex game. There are 25 grid locations the agent could be in. A prize could be on one of the corners, or there could be no prize. When the agent lands on a prize, it receives a reward of 10 and the prize disappears. When there is no prize, for each time step there is a probability that a prize appears on any one of the corners. Monsters can appear at any time on one of the locations marked M. The agent gets damaged if a monster appears on the square the agent is on. If the agent is already damaged, it receives a reward of -10. The agent can get repaired (so it is no longer damaged) by visiting the repair station marked R.

In this example, the state consists of four components: $\langle X, Y, D, P \rangle$, where X is the X-coordinate of the agent, Y is the Y-coordinate of the agent, D is Boolean and is true when the agent is damaged, and P is the position of the prize ($P = 0$ if there is no prize, $P = i$ if there is a prize at position P_i). Because the monsters are transient – knowing whether a monster appeared at a time does not provide any information about the future – it is not necessary to include them as part of the state. There are therefore $5 * 5 * 2 * 5 = 250$ states. The environment is fully observable, so the agent knows what state it is in. The agent does not know the meaning of the states; it doesn't know about the four components and it has no idea initially about being damaged or what a prize is.

The agent has four actions: *up*, *down*, *left*, and *right*. These move the agent one step – usually one step in the direction indicated by the name, but sometimes in one of the other directions. If the agent crashes into an outside wall or one of the interior walls (the thick lines near the location R), it remains where is was and receives a reward of -1.

The agent does not know any of the story given here. It just knows there are 250 states and 4 actions, which state it is in at each time, and what reward was received each time.

This game is simple, but it is surprisingly difficult to write a good controller for it. There are implementations available on the book website that you can play with and modify. Try to write a controller by hand for it; it is possible to write a controller that accumulates a reward of about 500 for each 1000 steps. This game is also difficult to learn, because visiting R is seemingly useless until the agent eventually learns that being damaged is bad, and that visiting R makes it not damaged. It must stumble on this while trying to collect the prizes. The states where there is no prize available do not last very long. Moreover, it has to learn this without being given the concept of *damaged*; all it knows, initially, is that there are 250 states and 4 actions.

Reinforcement learning is difficult for a number of reasons:

- The **credit assignment problem** or the **blame attribution problem** is the problem of determining which action was responsible for a reward or punishment. The action responsible may have occurred a long time before the reward was received. Moreover, not just a single action but rather a combination of actions carried out in the appropriate circumstances may be responsible for a reward. For example, you could teach an agent to play a game by rewarding it when it wins or loses; it must determine the brilliant moves, which usually occur long before the end, that were needed to win. As another example, you may try to train a dog by saying "bad dog" when you come home and find a mess. The dog has to determine, out of all of the actions it did, which of them were the actions that were responsible for the reprimand.

- Even if the dynamics of the world does not change, the effect of an action of the agent depends on what the agent will do in the future. What may initially seem like a bad thing for the agent to do may end up being an optimal action because of what the agent does in the future. This is common among planning problems, but it is complicated in the reinforcement learning context because the agent does not know, a priori, the effects of its actions.

- The **explore–exploit dilemma**: if an agent has worked out a good course of actions, should it continue to follow these actions (exploiting what it has determined) or should it explore to find better actions? An agent that never explores may act forever in a way that could have been much better if it had explored earlier. An agent that always explores will never use what it has learned. This dilemma is discussed further in Section 12.5 (page 557).

12.2 Evolutionary Algorithms

One way to solve reinforcement algorithms is to treat this as an optimization problem (page 160), with the aim of selecting a policy that maximizes the expected reward collected. This can be done with a **policy search** through the space of policies to find the best policy. A policy is a controller (page 54) that can be evaluated by running it in the agent acting in the environment.

> Dimensions (p. 31)
>
> flat
> states
> indefinite horizon
> fully observable
> stochastic
> utility
> learning
> single agent
> online
> bounded rationality

Policy search is often solved as a stochastic local search algorithm (page 148) by searching in the space of policies. A policy can be evaluated by running it in the environment a number of times.

Starting from an initial policy, the policy can be repeatedly evaluated in the environment and iteratively improved. This process is called an **evolutionary algorithm** because the agent, as a whole, is evaluated on how well it survives. This is often combined with genetic algorithms (page 157), which take us one step closer to the biological analogy of competing agents mutating genes.

Evolutionary algorithms have a number of issues. The first is the size of the state space. If there are n states and m actions, there are m^n policies. For example, for the game described in Example 12.1 (page 550), there are $4^6 = 4096$ different policies. For the game of Example 12.2 (page 551), there are 250 states, and so $4^{250} \approx 10^{150}$ policies. This is a very small game, but it has more policies than there are particles in the universe.

Second, evolutionary algorithms use experiences very wastefully. If an agent was in state s_2 of Example 12.1 (page 550) and it moved left, you would like it to learn that it is bad to go left from state s_2. But evolutionary algorithms wait until the agent has finished and judge the policy as a whole. Stochastic local search will randomly try doing something else in state s_2 and so may eventually determine that that action was not good, but it is very indirect. Genetic algorithms are slightly better in that the policies that have the agent going left in state s_2 will die off, but again this is very indirect.

Third, the performance of evolutionary algorithms can be very sensitive to the representation of the policy. The representation for a genetic algorithm should be such that crossover preserves the good parts of the policy. The representations are often tuned for the particular domain.

An alternative pursued in the rest of this chapter is to learn after every action. The components of the policy are learned, rather than the policy as a whole. By learning what do in each state, learning can have linear or polynomial time and space complexity in the number of states, rather than exponential in the number of states.

12.3   Temporal Differences

To understand how reinforcement learning works, consider how to average values that arrive to an agent sequentially.

Suppose there is a sequence of numerical values, $v_1, v_2, v_3, \ldots$, and the goal is to predict the next value, given the previous values. One way to do this is to have a running approximation of the expected value of v_i. For example, given a sequence of students' grades and the aim of predicting the next grade, a reasonable prediction may be to predict the average grade. This can be implemented by maintaining a **running average** (page 303), as follows:

Let A_k be an estimate of the expected value based on the first k data points $v_1, \ldots, v_k$. A reasonable estimate is the sample average:

$$A_k = \frac{v_1 + \cdots + v_k}{k} .$$

Thus,

$$k * A_k = v_1 + \cdots + v_{k-1} + v_k$$
$$= (k-1)A_{k-1} + v_k.$$

Dividing by k gives

$$A_k = \left(1 - \frac{1}{k}\right) * A_{k-1} + \frac{v_k}{k} .$$

Let $\alpha_k = \frac{1}{k}$; then

$$A_k = (1 - \alpha_k) * A_{k-1} + \alpha_k * v_k$$
$$= A_{k-1} + \alpha_k * (v_k - A_{k-1}). \tag{12.1}$$

The difference, $v_k - A_{k-1}$, is called the **temporal difference error** or **TD error**; it specifies how different the new value, v_k, is from the old prediction, A_{k-1}. The old estimate, A_{k-1}, is updated by α_k times the TD error to get the new estimate, A_k. The qualitative interpretation of the temporal difference formula is that if the new value is higher than the old prediction, increase the predicted value; if the new value is less than the old prediction, decrease the predicted value. The change is proportional to the difference between the new value and the old prediction. Note that this equation is still valid for the first value, $k = 1$, in which case $A_1 = v_1$.

This analysis assumes that all of the values have an equal weight. However, suppose you are keeping an estimate of the expected price of some item in the grocery store. Prices go up and down in the short term, but tend to increase slowly; the newer prices are more useful for the estimate of the current price than older prices, and so they should be weighted more in predicting new prices.

In reinforcement learning, the values are estimates of the effects of actions; more recent values are more accurate than earlier values because the agent is learning, and so they should be weighted more. One way to weight later examples more is to use Equation (12.1), but with α as a constant ($0 < \alpha \leq 1$) that does not depend on k. Unfortunately, this does not converge to the average value when there is variability in the values in the sequence, but it can track changes when the underlying process generating the values changes.

You could reduce α more slowly and potentially have the benefits of both approaches: weighting recent observations more and still converging to the average. You can guarantee convergence if

$$\sum_{k=1}^{\infty} \alpha_k = \infty \quad \text{and} \quad \sum_{k=1}^{\infty} \alpha_k^2 < \infty.$$

The first condition is to ensure that random fluctuations and initial conditions get averaged out, and the second condition guarantees convergence.

One way to give more weight to more recent experiences, but also converge to the average, is to set $\alpha_k = (r+1)/(r+k)$ for some $r > 0$. For the first experience $\alpha_1 = 1$, so it ignores the prior A_0. If $r = 9$, after 11 experiences, $\alpha_{11} = 0.5$ so it weights that experience as equal to all of its prior experiences. The parameter r should be set to be appropriate for the domain.

Note that guaranteeing convergence to the average is not compatible with being able to adapt to make better predictions when the underlying process generating the values keeps changing.

For the rest of this chapter, α without a subscript is assumed to be a constant. With a subscript it is a function of the number of cases used for the particular estimate.

12.4   Q-learning

In Q-learning and related RL algorithms, an agent tries to learn the optimal policy from its history of interaction with the environment. A **history** of an agent is a sequence of state–action–rewards:

$$\langle s_0, a_0, r_1, s_1, a_1, r_2, s_2, a_2, r_3, s_3, a_3, r_4, s_4 \ldots \rangle$$

which means that the agent was in state s_0 and did action a_0, which resulted in it receiving reward r_1 and being in state s_1; then it did action a_1, received reward r_2, and ended up in state s_2; then it did action a_2, received reward r_3, and ended up in state s_3; and so on.

Dimensions (p. 31)
flat
states
infinite horizon
fully observable
stochastic
utility
learning
single agent
online
bounded rationality

We treat this history of interaction as a sequence of experiences, where an **experience** is a tuple

$$\langle s, a, r, s' \rangle$$

which means that the agent was in state s, it did action a, it received reward r, and it went into state s'. These experiences will be the data from which the agent can learn what to do. As in decision-theoretic planning, the aim is for the agent to maximize its value, which is usually the discounted reward (page 462).

Recall (page 464) that $Q^*(s, a)$, where a is an action and s is a state, is the expected value (cumulative discounted reward) of doing a in state s and then following the optimal policy.

Q-learning uses temporal differences to estimate the value of $Q^*(s, a)$. In Q-learning, the agent maintains a table of $Q[S, A]$, where S is the set of states and A is the set of actions. $Q[s, a]$ represents its current estimate of $Q^*(s, a)$.

An experience $\langle s, a, r, s' \rangle$ provides one data point for the value of $Q(s, a)$. The data point is that the agent received the future value of $r + \gamma V(s')$, where $V(s') = \max_{a'} Q(s', a')$; this is the actual current reward plus the discounted estimated future value. This new data point is called a **return**. The agent can use the temporal difference equation (12.1) to update its estimate for $Q(s, a)$:

$$Q[s, a] := Q[s, a] + \alpha * \left(r + \gamma \max_{a'} Q[s', a'] - Q[s, a] \right)$$

or, equivalently,

$$Q[s, a] := (1 - \alpha) * Q[s, a] + \alpha * \left(r + \gamma \max_{a'} Q[s', a'] \right).$$

Figure 12.3 shows a Q-learning controller, where the agent is acting and learning at the same time. The $do(a)$ on line 15 specifies that the action a is the **command** (page 51) the controller sends to the body. The reward and the resulting state are the **percepts** (page 51) the controller receives from the body.

The Q-learner learns (an approximation of) the optimal Q-function as long as the agent explores enough, and there is no bound on the number of times it tries an action in any state (i.e., it does not always do the same subset of actions in a state).

Example 12.3 Consider the two-state MDP of Example 9.27 (page 459). The agent knows there are two states $\{healthy, sick\}$ and two actions $\{relax, party\}$. It does not know the model and it learns from the s, a, r, s' experiences. With a discount, $\gamma = 0.8$, $\alpha = 0.3$, and Q initially 0, the following is a possible trace (to a few significant digits and with the states and actions abbreviated):

s	a	r	s'	$Update = (1 - \alpha) * Q[s, a] + \alpha(r + \gamma max_{a'} Q[s', a'])$
he	re	7	he	$Q[he, re] = 0.7 * 0 + 0.3 * (7 + 0.8 * 0) = 2.1$
he	re	7	he	$Q[he, re] = 0.7 * 2.1 + 0.3 * (7 + 0.8 * 2.1) = 4.07$
he	pa	10	he	$Q[he, pa] = 0.7 * 0 + 0.3 * (10 + 0.8 * 4.07) = 3.98$
he	pa	10	si	$Q[he, pa] = 0.7 * 3.98 + 0.3 * (10 + 0.8 * 0) = 5.79$
si	pa	2	si	$Q[si, pa] = 0.7 * 0 + 0.3 * (2 + 0.8 * 0) = 0.06$
si	re	0	si	$Q[si, re] = 0.7 * 0 + 0.3 * (0 + 0.8 * 0.06) = 0.014$
si	re	0	he	$Q[si, re] = 0.7 * 0.014 + 0.3 * (0 + 0.8 * 5.79) = 1.40$

```
1: controller Q-learning(S, A, γ, α)
2:     Inputs
3:         S is a set of states
4:         A is a set of actions
5:         γ the discount
6:         α is the step size
7:     Local
8:         real array Q[S, A]
9:         states s, s'
10:        action a
11:    initialize Q[S, A] arbitrarily
12:    observe current state s
13:    repeat
14:        select an action a
15:        do(a)
16:        observe reward r and state s'
17:        Q[s, a] := Q[s, a] + α ∗ (r + γ ∗ max_{a'} Q[s', a'] − Q[s, a])
18:        s := s'
19:    until termination
```

Figure 12.3: Q-learning controller

> With α fixed, the Q-values will approximate, but not converge to, the values obtained with value iteration in Example 9.31 (page 466). The smaller α is, the closer it will converge to the actual Q-values, but the slower it will converge.

The controller of Figure 12.3 has α fixed. If α_k were decreasing appropriately it would converge to the actual Q-values. To implement this, there needs to be a separate α_k for each state–action pair, which can be implemented using an array, $visits[S, A]$, which counts the number of times action A was carried out in state S. Before line 17 of Figure 12.3, $visits[s, a]$ can be incremented, and α set to, say, $10/(9 + visits[s, a])$; see Exercise 12.5 (page 576).

12.5 Exploration and Exploitation

The Q-learner controller does not specify what the agent should actually do. The agent learns a Q-function that can be used to determine an optimal action. There are two things that are useful for the agent to do:

- **exploit** the knowledge that it has found for the current state s by doing one of the actions a that maximizes $Q[s, a]$

- **explore** in order to build a better estimate of the optimal Q-function; it
  should sometimes select a different action from the one that it currently
  thinks is best.

There have been a number of suggested ways to trade off exploration and
exploitation:

- The ϵ-**greedy exploration strategy**, where $0 \leq \epsilon \leq 1$, is the **explore probability**, is to select the greedy action (one that maximizes $Q[s,a]$) all but
  ϵ of the time and to select a random action ϵ of the time. It is possible
  to change ϵ through time. Intuitively, early in the life of the agent, it
  should act more randomly to encourage initial exploration and, as time
  progresses, it should act more greedily (reducing ϵ).

- One problem with an ϵ-greedy strategy is that it treats all of the actions,
  apart from the best action, equivalently. If there are a few seemingly good
  actions and other actions that look much less promising, it may be more
  sensible to select among the good actions: putting more effort toward
  determining which of the promising actions is best, and less effort to explore the actions that look worse. One way to do that is to select action a
  with a probability depending on the value of $Q[s,a]$. This is known as a
  soft-max action selection. A common method is to use a **Gibbs** or **Boltzmann distribution**, where the probability of selecting action a in state s
  is proportional to $e^{Q[s,a]/\tau}$. Thus in state s, the agent selects action a with
  probability

$$\frac{e^{Q[s,a]/\tau}}{\sum_a e^{Q[s,a]/\tau}}$$

  where $\tau > 0$ is the **temperature** specifying how randomly values should
  be chosen. When τ is high, the actions are chosen in almost equal amounts.
  As the temperature is reduced, the higher-valued actions are more likely
  to be chosen and, in the limit as $\tau \to 0$, the best action is always chosen.

- An alternative is **optimism in the face of uncertainty**: initialize the Q-
  function to values that encourage exploration. If the Q-values are initialized to high values, the unexplored areas will look good, so that a greedy
  search will tend to explore. This does encourage exploration; however,
  the agent can hallucinate that some state–action pairs are good for a long
  time, even though there is no real evidence for them being good. A state
  only gets to look bad when all its actions look bad; but when all of these
  actions lead to states that look good, it takes a long time to get a realistic view of the actual values. This is a case where old estimates of the
  Q-values can be quite bad estimates of the actual Q-value, and these can
  remain bad estimates for a long time. To get fast convergence, the initial
  values should be as close as possible to the final values; trying to make

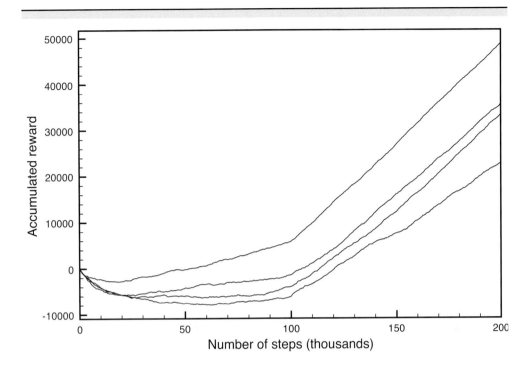

Figure 12.4: Cumulative reward as a function of the number of steps

them an overestimate will make convergence slower. In noisy environments, optimism in the face of uncertainty with no other mechanism for exploration, can mean that a good action never gets explored more because, by random chance, it gets a low Q-value from which it cannot recover.

It is interesting to compare the interaction of the exploration strategies with different choices for how α is updated. See Exercise 12.3 (page 575).

12.6 Evaluating Reinforcement Learning Algorithms

We can judge a reinforcement learning algorithm either by how good a policy it finds or by how much reward it receives while acting and learning. Which is more important depends on how the agent will be deployed. If there is sufficient time for the agent to learn safely before it is deployed, the final policy may be the most important. If the agent has to learn while being deployed, it may never get to the stage where it no longer need to explore, and the agent needs to maximize the reward it receives while learning.

One way to show the performance of a reinforcement learning algorithm is to plot the cumulative reward (the sum of all rewards received so far) as a function of the number of steps. One algorithm dominates another if its plot is consistently above the other.

Example 12.4   Figure 12.4 compares four runs of the Q-learner on the game of Example 12.2 (page 551).

The plots are for different runs that varied according to whether α was fixed, according to the initial values of the Q-function, and according to the randomness in the action selection. They all used greedy exploit of 80% (i.e., $\epsilon = 0.2$) for the first 100,000 steps, and 100% (i.e., $\epsilon = 0.0$) for the next 100,000 steps. The top plot dominated the others.

There can be a great deal of variability of each algorithm on different runs, so to actually compare these algorithms the same algorithm must be run multiple times.

There are three statistics of this plot that are important:

- The asymptotic slope shows how good the policy is after the algorithm has stabilized.

- The minimum of the curve shows how much reward must be sacrificed before it starts to improve.

- The zero crossing shows how long it takes until the algorithm has recouped its cost of learning.

The last two statistics are applicable when both positive and negative rewards are available and having these balanced is reasonable behavior. For other cases, the cumulative reward should be compared with reasonable behavior that is appropriate for the domain; see Exercise 12.2 (page 575).

It is also possible to plot the average reward (the accumulated reward per time step). This more clearly shows the value of policy eventually learned and whether the algorithm has stopped learning (when it is flat), but often has large variations for early times.

One thing that should be noted about the cumulative reward plot is that it measures total reward, yet the algorithms optimize discounted reward at each step. In general, you should optimize for, and evaluate your algorithm using, the optimality criterion that is most appropriate for the domain.

12.7   On-Policy Learning

Q-learning is an off-policy learner. An **off-policy learner** learns the value of an optimal policy independently of the agent's actions, as long as it explores enough. An off-policy learner can learn the optimal policy even if it is acting randomly. A learning agent should, however, try to exploit what it has learned

```
1:  controller SARSA(S, A, γ, α)
2:     Inputs
3:        S is a set of states
4:        A is a set of actions
5:        γ the discount
6:        α is the step size
7:     Local
8:        real array Q[S, A]
9:        state s, s'
10:       action a, a'
11:    initialize Q[S, A] arbitrarily
12:    observe current state s
13:    select an action a using a policy based on Q
14:    repeat
15:       do(a)
16:       observe reward r and state s'
17:       select an action a' using a policy based on Q
18:       Q[s, a] := Q[s, a] + α * (r + γ * Q[s', a'] − Q[s, a])
19:       s := s'
20:       a := a'
21:    until termination
```

Figure 12.5: SARSA: on-policy reinforcement learning

by choosing the best action, but it cannot just exploit because then it will not explore enough to find the best action. An off-policy learner does not learn the value of the policy it is following, because the policy it is following includes exploration steps.

There may be cases where ignoring what the agent actually does is dangerous: where there are large negative rewards. An alternative is to learn the value of the policy the agent is actually carrying out, which includes exploration steps, so that it can be iteratively improved. As a result, the learner can take into account the costs associated with exploration. An **on-policy learner** learns the value of the policy being carried out by the agent, including the exploration steps.

Dimensions (p. 31)
flat
states
infinite horizon
fully observable
stochastic
utility
learning
single agent
online
bounded rationality

SARSA (so called because it uses state–action–reward–state–action experiences to update the Q-values) is an *on-policy* reinforcement learning algorithm that estimates the value of the policy being followed. An experience in SARSA is of the form $\langle s, a, r, s', a' \rangle$, which means that the agent was in state s, did action a, received reward r, and ended up in state s', from which it decided to do action a'. This provides a new experience to update $Q(s, a)$. The new value that this experience provides is $r + \gamma Q(s', a')$.

Figure 12.5 gives the SARSA algorithm.

The Q-values that SARSA computes depend on the current exploration policy which, for example, may be greedy with random steps. It can find a different policy than Q-learning in situations when exploring may incur large penalties. For example, when a robot goes near the top of stairs, even if this is an optimal policy, it may be dangerous for exploration steps. SARSA will discover this and adopt a policy that keeps the robot away from the stairs. It will find a policy that is optimal, taking into account the exploration inherent in the policy.

Example 12.5 In Example 12.1 (page 550), the optimal policy is to go up from state s_0 in Figure 12.1 (page 550). However, if the agent is exploring, this action may be bad because exploring from state s_2 is very dangerous.

If the agent is carrying out the policy that includes exploration, "when in state s, 80% of the time select the action a that maximizes $Q[s, a]$, and 20% of the time select an action at random," going up from s_0 is not optimal. An on-policy learner will try to optimize the policy the agent is following, not the optimal policy that does not include exploration.

The Q-values of the optimal policy are less in SARSA than in Q-learning. The values for Q-learning and for SARSA (the exploration rate in parentheses) for the domain of Example 12.1, for a few state–action pairs are:

Algorithm	$Q[s_0, right]$	$Q[s_0, up]$	$Q[s_2, upC]$	$Q[s_2, up]$	$Q[s_4, left]$
Q-learning	19.48	23.28	26.86	16.9	30.95
SARSA (20%)	9.27	7.9	14.8	4.43	18.09
SARSA (10%)	13.04	13.95	18.9	8.93	22.47

The optimal policy using SARSA with 20% exploration is to go right in state s_0, but with 10% exploration the optimal policy is to go up in state s_0. With 20% exploration, this is the optimal policy because exploration is dangerous. With 10% exploration, going into state s_2 is less dangerous. Thus, if the rate of exploration is reduced, the optimal policy changes. However, with less exploration, it would take longer to find an optimal policy. The value Q-learning converges to does not depend on the exploration rate.

SARSA is useful when deploying an agent that is exploring in the world. If you want to do offline learning, and then use that policy in an agent that does not explore, Q-learning may be more appropriate.

12.8   Model-Based Reinforcement Learning

In many applications of reinforcement learning, plenty of time is available for computation between each action. For example, a physical robot may have many seconds between each action. Q-learning, which only does one backup per action, will not make full use of the available computation time.

An alternative to doing one Q-value update after each action is to use the experiences to learn a model. An agent can explicitly learn $P(s' \mid s,a)$ and $R(s,a)$. For each action that the agent carries out in the environment, the agent can do a number of steps of asynchronous value iteration (page 467) to give a better estimate of the Q-function.

Dimensions (p. 31)
flat
states
infinite horizon
fully observable
stochastic
utility
learning
single agent
online
bounded rationality

Figure 12.6 (on the next page) shows a generic model-based reinforcement learner. As with other reinforcement learning programs, it keeps track of $Q[S,A]$, but it also maintains a model of the dynamics, represented here as T, where $T[s,a,s']$ is the count of the number of times that the agent has done a in state s and ended up in state s'. This also maintains $C[s,a]$, which is the count of the number of times action a was carried out in state s. Note that $C[s,a] = \sum_{s'} T[s,a,s']$, and so we could save space but increase runtime by not storing C, but computing it when needed. The $R[s,a]$ array maintains the average reward obtained when doing action a in state s.

After each action, the agent observes the reward r and the resulting state s'. It then updates the transition-count matrices T and C as well as the average reward R. It then does a number of steps of asynchronous value iteration, using the updated probability model derived from T and the updated reward model.

There are three main undefined parts to this algorithm:

- Which Q-values should be updated? It seems reasonable that the algorithm should at least update $Q[s,a]$, because more data have been received on the transition probability and reward. From there it can either do random updates or determine which Q-values would change the most. The elements that potentially have their values changed the most are the $Q[s_1,a_1]$ with the highest probability of ending up at a Q-value that has changed the most (i.e., where $Q[s_2,a_2]$ has changed the most). This can be implemented by keeping a priority queue of Q-values to consider. To ensure these is no divide-by-zero error, it should only choose s_1,a_1 state–action pair for which $C[s_1,a_1] \neq 0$, or include pseudocounts for the transitions.

- How many steps of asynchronous value iteration should be done between actions? An agent could continue doing Q-updates until it has to act or until it gets new information. Figure 12.6 (on the next page) assumes that the agent acts and then does Q-updates until an observation arrives. When an observation arrives, the agent acts as soon as possible. There are may variants, including doing a fixed number of updates, which may be appropriate in games where it can act at any time. It is also possible to run the update in parallel with observing and acting.

- What should be the initial values for $Q[S,A]$? It requires some value for the transitions it has never experienced when updating Q. If it is using the exploration strategy of optimism in the face of uncertainty, it can use

---

1: **controller** *Model_based_reinforcement_learner*(S, A, γ)
2:     **Inputs**
3:         S is a set of states
4:         A is a set of actions
5:         γ the discount
6:     **Local**
7:         real array $Q[S, A]$
8:         real array $R[S, A]$
9:         integer array $T[S, A, S]$
10:         integer array $C[S, A]$
11:     initialize $Q[S, A]$ arbitrarily
12:     initialize $R[S, A]$ arbitrarily
13:     initialize $T[S, A, S]$ to zero
14:     initialize $C[S, A]$ to zero
15:     observe current state s
16:     select action a
17:     $do(a)$
18:     **repeat**
19:         observe reward r and state s'
20:         $T[s, a, s'] := T[s, a, s'] + 1$
21:         $C[s, a] := C[s, a] + 1$
22:         $R[s, a] := R[s, a] + \dfrac{r - R[s, a]}{C[s, a]}$
23:         $s := s'$
24:         select action a
25:         $do(a)$
26:         **repeat**
27:             select state s_1, action a_1 such that $C[s_1, a_1] \neq 0$
28:             $Q[s_1, a_1] := R[s_1, a_1] + \gamma * \sum\limits_{s_2} \dfrac{T[s_1, a_1, s_2]}{C[s_1, a_1]} * \max\limits_{a_2} Q[s_2, a_2]$
29:         **until** an observation arrives
30:     **until** termination

Figure 12.6: Model-based reinforcement learner

Rmax, the maximum reward possible, as the initial value for *R*, to encourage exploration. However, as in value iteration (page 464), the algorithm converges faster if it initializes *Q* to be as close as possible to the final *Q*-value.

This algorithm assumes that the rewards depend on the initial state and the action. If there are separate action costs and rewards for being in a state, and the agent can separately observe the costs and rewards, the reward function can be decomposed into $C[A]$ and $R[S]$, leading to more efficient learning.

It is difficult to directly compare the model-based and model-free reinforcement learners. Typically, model-based learners are much more efficient in terms of experience; many fewer experiences are needed to learn well. However, the model-free methods use less memory and often use less computation time. If experience was cheap, such as in a computer game, a different comparison would be needed than if experience was expensive, such as for a robot.

12.9   Reinforcement Learning with Features

Usually, there are too many states to reason about explicitly. The alternative to reasoning explicitly in terms of states is to reason in terms of features. In this section, we consider reinforcement learning that uses an approximation of the *Q*-function using a linear combination of features of the state and the action. There are more complicated alternatives such as using a decision tree or neural network, but the linear function often works well.

Dimensions (p. 31)
flat
features
infinite horizon
fully observable
stochastic
utility
learning
single agent
online
bounded rationality

The feature-based learners require more information about the domain than the reinforcement-learning methods considered so far. Whereas the previous reinforcement learners were provided only with the states and the possible actions, the feature-based learners require extra domain knowledge in terms of features. This approach requires careful selection of the features; the designer should find features adequate to represent the *Q*-function. This is often a difficult problem in **feature engineering**.

12.9.1   SARSA with Linear Function Approximation

SARSA with Linear Function Approximation, SARSA_LFA, uses a linear function of features to approximate the *Q*-function. This algorithm uses the on-policy method SARSA, because the agent's experiences sample the reward from the policy the agent is actually following, rather than sampling from an optimum policy.

SARSA_LFA uses features of both the state and the action. Suppose $F_1, \ldots, F_n$ are numerical features of the state and the action. Thus, $F_i(s, a)$ provides the value for the *i*th feature for state *s* and action *a*. These features can be binary, with domain $\{0, 1\}$, or other numerical features. These features will be used to represent the linear Q-function:

$$Q_{\overline{w}}(s, a) = w_0 + w_1 F_1(s, a) + \cdots + w_n F_n(s, a)$$

for some tuple of weights, $\overline{w} = \langle w_0, w_1, \ldots, w_n \rangle$ that have to be learned. Assume that there is an extra feature $F_0(s, a)$ whose value is always 1, so that w_0 is not a special case.

Example 12.6 Consider the grid game of Example 12.2 (page 551). From understanding the domain, and not just treating it as a black box, some possible features that can be computed and might be useful are:

- $F_1(s, a)$ has value 1 if action a would most likely take the agent from state s into a location where a monster could appear and has value 0 otherwise.

- $F_2(s, a)$ has value 1 if action a would most likely take the agent into a wall and has value 0 otherwise.

- $F_3(s, a)$ has value 1 if step a would most likely take the agent toward a prize.

- $F_4(s, a)$ has value 1 if the agent is damaged in state s and action a takes it toward the repair station.

- $F_5(s, a)$ has value 1 if the agent is damaged and action a would most likely take the agent into a location where a monster could appear and has value 0 otherwise. That is, it is the same as $F_1(s, a)$ but is only applicable when the agent is damaged.

- $F_6(s, a)$ has value 1 if the agent is damaged in state s and has value 0 otherwise.

- $F_7(s, a)$ has value 1 if the agent is not damaged in state s and has value 0 otherwise.

- $F_8(s, a)$ has value 1 if the agent is damaged and there is a prize ahead in direction a.

- $F_9(s, a)$ has value 1 if the agent is not damaged and there is a prize ahead in direction a.

- $F_{10}(s, a)$ has the value of the x-value in state s if there is a prize at location P_0 in state s. That is, it is the distance from the left wall if there is a prize at location P_0.

- $F_{11}(s, a)$ has the value $4 - x$, where x is the horizontal position in state s if there is a prize at location P_0 in state s. That is, it is the distance from the right wall if there is a prize at location P_0.

- $F_{12}(s, a)$ to $F_{29}(s, a)$ are like F_{10} and F_{11} for different combinations of the prize location and the distance from each of the four walls. For the case where the prize is at location P_0, the y-distance could take into account the wall.

1: **controller** $SARSA\_LFA(\overline{F}, \gamma, \eta)$
2:     **Inputs**
3:         $\overline{F} = \langle F_1, \ldots, F_n \rangle$: a set of features. Define $F_0(s, a) = 1$.
4:         $\gamma \in [0, 1]$: discount factor
5:         $\eta > 0$: step size for gradient descent
6:     **Local**
7:         weights $\overline{w} = \langle w_0, \ldots, w_n \rangle$, initialized arbitrarily
8:     observe current state s
9:     select action a
10:    **repeat**
11:       $do(a)$
12:       observe reward r and state s'
13:       select action a' (using a policy based on $Q_{\overline{w}}$)
14:       $\delta := r + \gamma * Q_{\overline{w}}(s', a') - Q_{\overline{w}}(s, a)$
15:       **for** $i = 0$ to n **do**
16:          $w_i := w_i + \eta * \delta * F_i(s, a)$
17:       $s := s'$
18:       $a := a'$
19:   **until** termination

Figure 12.7: SARSA with linear function approximation

An example linear function is

$$
\begin{aligned}
Q(s, a) \\
= 2.0 - 1.0 * F_1(s, a) - 0.4 * F_2(s, a) - 1.3 * F_3(s, a) \\
- 0.5 * F_4(s, a) - 1.2 * F_5(s, a) - 1.6 * F_6(s, a) + 3.5 * F_7(s, a) \\
+ 0.6 * F_8(s, a) + 0.6 * F_9(s, a) - 0.0 * F_{10}(s, a) + 1.0 * F_{11}(s, a) + \cdots.
\end{aligned}
$$

These are the learned values (to one decimal place) for one run of $SARSA\_LFA$ algorithm in Figure 12.7.

An experience in SARSA of the form $\langle s, a, r, s', a' \rangle$ (the agent was in state s, did action a, and received reward r and ended up in state s', in which it decided to do action a') provides the new estimate of $r + \gamma Q(s', a')$ to update $Q(s, a)$. This experience can be used as a data point for **linear regression** (page 291). Let $\delta = r + \gamma Q(s', a') - Q(s, a)$. Using Equation (7.3) (page 292), weight w_i is updated by

$$ w_i := w_i + \eta * \delta * F_i(s, a). $$

This update can then be incorporated into SARSA, giving the algorithm shown in Figure 12.7.

Although this program is simple to implement, **feature engineering** – choosing what features to include – is non-trivial. The linear function must not only convey the best action to carry out, it must also convey the information about what future states are useful.

Example 12.7   On the AIspace website, there is an open-source implementation of this algorithm for the game of Example 12.2 (page 551) with the features of Example 12.6 (page 566). Try stepping through the algorithm for individual steps, trying to understand how each step updates each parameter. Now run it for a number of steps. Consider the performance using the evaluation measures of Section 12.6 (page 559). Try to make sense of the values of the parameters learned.

Many variations of this algorithm exist:

- This algorithm tends to overfit to current experiences, and to forget about old experiences, so that when it goes back to a part of the state-space it has not visited recently, it will have to relearn. One modification is to remember old experiences ($\langle s, a, r, s \rangle$ tuples) and to carry out some steps of **action replay**, by doing some weight updates based on random previous experiences. Updating the weights requires the use of the next action a', which should be chosen according to the current policy, not the policy that was under effect when the experience occurred. If memory becomes an issue, some of the old experiences can be discarded.

- Different function approximations, such as a decision tree with a linear function at the leaves, could be used.

- A common variant is to have a separate function for each action. This is equivalent to the Q-function approximated by a decision tree that splits on actions and then has a linear function. It is also possible to split on other features.

- A linear function approximation can also be combined with other methods such as Q-learning, or model-based methods.

- In **deep reinforcement learning**, a deep learner (page 308) is used instead of the linear function approximation. This means that the features do not need to be engineered, but can be learned. Deep learning requires a large amount of data, and many iterations to learn, and can be sensitive to the architecture provided. A way to handle overfitting, such a regularization (page 304), is also required.

12.10   Multiagent Reinforcement Learning

12.10.1   Perfect-Information Games

For a **perfect-information game** (page 524), where agents take turns and observe the state of the world before acting, and each agent acts to maximize its own utility, the above reinforcement learning algorithms can work unchanged. An agent can assume that the other agents are part of the environment. This works whether the opponent is playing its optimal strategy or is also learning. The reason this works is that there is a unique Nash equilibrium which is the value for the agent of the current node in the game tree (page 524). This strategy is the best response to the other agents.

If the opponent is not playing its optimal strategy or converging to an optimal strategy, a learning agent could converge to a non-optimal strategy. It is possible for an opponent to train a learning agent to carry out a non-optimal strategy by playing badly, and then for the opponent to change to another strategy in order to exploit the agent's sub-optimal strategy. However, the learning agent could then learn from the (now) better opponent.

It is possible to use reinforcement learning to simulate both players in a game, and to learn for both. For two-player, zero-sum, perfect-information games, as in **minimax** (page 529), the game can be characterized by a single value that one agent is trying to minimize and the other is trying to maximize. In that case, an agent would learn $Q(s, a)$, an estimate of this value for being in state s and carrying out action a. The algorithms can remain essentially the same, but need to know which player's turn it is, and the Q-value would then be updated by maximizing or minimizing depending on which player's turn it is.

12.10.2   Learning to Coordinate

For multiple agents with imperfect information (page 532), including simultaneous action games, it is possible that there are multiple Nash equilibria, and that no deterministic strategy is optimal. Due to the existence of multiple equilibria, in many cases it is not clear what an agent should actually do, even if it knows all of the outcomes for the game and the utilities of the agents. However, most real strategic encounters are much more difficult, because the agents do not know the outcomes or the utilities of the other agents.

For games where the only Nash equilibria consist of randomized strategies, such as in the soccer penalty kick (Figure 11.7 (page 533)), learning any deterministic policy is not a good idea because any deterministic strategy can be exploited by the other agent. For other games with multiple Nash equilibria, such as those explored in Section 11.4

Dimensions (p. 31)
flat
states
finite horizon
partially observable
stochastic
utility
learning
multiple agents
online
perfect rationality

1: **controller** *Policy_hill_climbing*(A, α, δ)
2:     **Inputs**
3:         A a set of actions
4:         α step size for action estimate
5:         δ step size for probability change
6:     **Local**
7:         n the number of elements of A
8:         $P[A]$ a probability distribution over A
9:         $Q[A]$ an estimate of the value of doing A
10:        *a_best* the current best action
11:    $n := |A|$
12:    $P[A]$ assigned randomly such that $P[a] > 0$ and $\sum_{a \in A} P[a] = 1$
13:    Assign $Q[a]$ for each $a \in A$ arbitrarily
14:    **repeat**
15:        **select** action a based on P
16:        $do(a)$
17:        **observe** *payoff*
18:        $Q[a] := Q[a] + \alpha * (payoff - Q[a])$
19:        $a\_best := \arg\max(Q)$
20:        $P\_rest := 0$
21:        **for each** $a' \in A$ **do**
22:            **if** $a' \neq a\_best$ **then**
23:                $P[a'] := P[a'] - \delta$
24:                **if** $P[a'] < 0$ **then**
25:                    $P[a'] := 0$
26:                $P\_rest := P\_rest + P[a']$
27:            $P[a\_best] := 1 - P\_rest$
28:    **until** termination

Figure 12.8: Learning to coordinate

(page 532), agents may need to play multiple games to coordinate on a strategy profile where neither want to deviate.

Reinforcement learning can be extended to such situations by explicitly representing **stochastic policies**, which are policies that specify a probability distribution over actions. This automatically allows for a form of exploration, because any action with a non-zero probability will be tried repeatedly.

This section presents a simple algorithm to iteratively improve an agent's policy. The agents repeatedly play the same game. Each agent plays a stochastic strategy; the agent updates the probabilities of its actions based on the payoffs received. For simplicity, it only has a single state; the only thing that changes between times is the randomized policies of the other agents.

The **policy hill-climbing** controller of Figure 12.8 keeps updating its probability of the best action based on experience. The inputs are the set of actions, a step size α for changing the estimate of Q, a step size δ for changing the randomness of the policy. n is the number of actions (the number of elements of A).

A **stochastic policy** is a probability distribution over actions. The algorithm maintains its current stochastic policy in the P array and an estimate of the payoff for each action in the Q array. The agent carries out an action based on its current policy and observes the action's payoff. It then updates its estimate of the value of that action and modifies its current strategy by increasing the probability of its best action.

The algorithm initializes P randomly so that it is a probability distribution; Q is initialized arbitrarily.

At each stage, the agent selects an action a according to the current distribution P. It carries out the action a and observes the payoff it receives. It then updates its estimate of Q, using the temporal difference equation (12.1) (page 554).

It then computes a_best, which is the current best action according to its estimated Q-values. (Assume that, if there is more than one best action, one is chosen at random to be a_best.) It reduces the probability of the other actions by δ, ensuring that the probabilities never become negative. The probability of a_best is made to ensure all probabilities sum to 1. Note that if none of the probabilities of the other actions became negative (and needed to be adjusted back to 0), the probability of a_best is increased by $(n - 1) * \delta$.

This algorithm needs to trade off exploration and exploitation. One way to do this is to use an ϵ-greedy exploration strategy (page 558), which the following examples use with the explore probability of 0.05. An alternative is to make sure that the probability of any action never gets less than some threshold.

Open-source implementations of this learning controller are available from the book's website.

Example 12.8 Figure 12.9 (on the next page) shows a plot of the learning algorithm for the football–shopping game of Example 11.12 (page 536). This figure plots the probabilities for Agent 1 choosing shopping and Agent 2 choosing shopping for eight runs of the learning algorithm. Each line is one run. Each of the runs ends at the top-right corner or the bottom-left corner, where the agents have learned to coordinate. In these runs, the policies are initialized randomly, $\alpha = 0.1$, and $\delta = 0.01$.

If the other agents are playing a fixed strategy (even if it is a stochastic strategy), this algorithm converges to a best response (page 535) to that strategy (as long as α and δ are small enough, and as long as the agent randomly tries all of the actions occasionally).

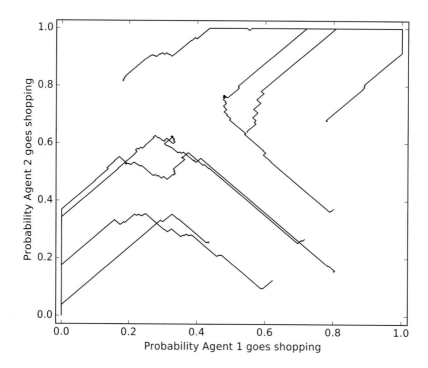

Figure 12.9: Learning for the football–shopping coordination example. The agents end up at the top-right corner or bottom-left corner, irrespective of where they start.

The following discussion assumes that all agents are using this learning controller.

If there is a unique Nash equilibrium in pure strategies, and all of the agents use this algorithm, they will converge to this equilibrium. Dominated strategies will have their probability set to zero. In Example 11.15 (page 539), it will find the Nash equilibrium. Similarly for the prisoner's dilemma in Example 11.13 (page 537), it will converge to the unique equilibrium where both agents take. Thus, this algorithm does *not* learn to **cooperate**, where cooperating agents will both *give* in the prisoner's dilemma to maximize their payoffs.

If there are multiple pure equilibria, this algorithm will converge to one of them. The agents thus learn to **coordinate**. For example, in the football–shopping game of Example 11.12 (page 536), it will converge to one of the equilibria of both shopping or both going to the football game, as shown in Figure 12.9. Which one it converges to depends on the initial strategies.

If there is only a randomized equilibrium, as in the penalty kick game of Example 11.9 (page 533), this algorithm tends to cycle around the equilibrium.

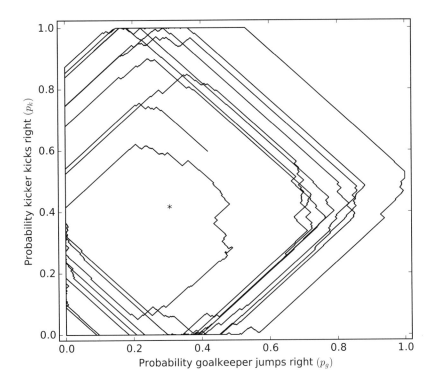

Figure 12.10: Learning for the soccer penalty kick example

Example 12.9 Figure 12.10 shows a plot of two players using the learning algorithm for Example 11.9 (page 533). This figure plots the probabilities for the goalkeeper jumping right and the kicker kicking right for one run of the learning algorithm. In this run, $\alpha = 0.1$ and $\delta = 0.001$. The learning algorithm cycles around the equilibrium never actually reaching the equilibrium. At equilibrium, marked with * in the figure, the kicker kicks right with probability 0.4 and the goalkeeper jumps right with probability 0.3 (see Example 11.16 (page 540)).

Consider a two-agent competitive game where there is only a randomized Nash equilibrium. If agent A is playing agent B and agent B is playing a Nash equilibrium, it does not matter which action in its support set is performed by agent A; they all have the same value to A. Thus, agent A will tend to wander off the equilibrium. Note that, when A deviates from the equilibrium strategy, the best response for agent B is to play deterministically. This algorithm, when used by agent B, eventually notices that A has deviated from the equilibrium and agent B changes its policy. Agent B will also deviate from the equilibrium. Then agent A can try to exploit this deviation. When they are both using this controller, each agents's deviation can be exploited, and they tend to cycle.

There is nothing in this algorithm to keep the agents on a randomized equilibrium. One way to try to make agents not wander too far from an equilibrium is to adopt a **win or learn fast (WoLF)** strategy: when the agent is winning it takes small steps (δ is small), and when the agent is losing it takes larger steps (δ is increased). While it is winning, it tends to stay with the same policy, and while it is losing, it tries to move quickly to a better policy. To define winning, a simple strategy is for an agent to see whether it is doing better than the average payoff it has received so far.

Note that there is no perfect learning strategy. If an opposing agent knew the exact strategy (whether learning or not) agent A was using, and could predict what agent A would do, it could exploit that knowledge.

12.11   Review

The following are the main points you should have learned from this chapter:

- A Markov decision process is an appropriate formalism for reinforcement learning. A common method is to learn an estimate of the value of doing each action in a state, as represented by the $Q(S, A)$ function.

- In reinforcement learning, an agent should trade off exploiting its knowledge and exploring to improve its knowledge.

- Off-policy learning, such as Q-learning, learns the value of the optimal policy. On-policy learning, such as SARSA, learns the value of the policy the agent is actually carrying out (which includes the exploration).

- Model-based reinforcement learning separates learning the dynamics and reward models from the decision-theoretic planning of what to do given the models.

12.12   References and Further Reading

For an introduction to reinforcement learning, see Szepesvári [2010], Sutton and Barto [1998], and Kaelbling et al. [1996]. Bertsekas and Tsitsiklis [1996] investigate function approximation and its interaction with reinforcement learning. Powell [2014] describes various applications of reinforcement learning to energy systems.

Mnih et al. [2015] describe how reinforcement learning combined with neural networks was used to solve classic Atari computer games, and Silver et al. [2016] show how learning can be used for the game of Go.

The learning of games and the WoLF strategy is based on PHC of Bowling and Veloso [2002]. Busoniu et al. [2008] survey multiagent reinforcement learning.

12.13   Exercises

Exercise 12.1   Explain how Q-learning fits in with the agent architecture of Section 2.2.1 (page 51). Suppose that the Q-learning agent has discount factor γ, a step size of α, and is carrying out an ϵ-greedy exploration strategy.

(a) What are the components of the belief state of the Q-learning agent?

(b) What are the percepts?

(c) What is the command function of the Q-learning agent?

(d) What is the belief-state transition function of the Q-learning agent?

Exercise 12.2   For the plot of the total reward as a function of time as in Figure 12.4 (page 559), the minimum and zero crossing are only meaningful statistics when balancing positive and negative rewards is reasonable behavior. Suggest what should replace these statistics when zero reward is not an appropriate definition of reasonable behavior. [Hint: Think about the cases that have only positive reward or only negative reward.]

Exercise 12.3   Compare the different parameter settings for the game of Example 12.2 (page 551). In particular compare the following situations

i) α varies, and the Q-values are initialized to 0.0

ii) α varies, and the Q-values are initialized to 5.0

iii) α is fixed to 0.1, and the Q-values are initialized to 0.0

iv) α is fixed to 0.1, and the Q-values are initialized to 5.0

v) Some other parameter settings.

For each of these, carry out multiple runs and compare

(a) the distributions of minimum values

(b) the zero crossing

(c) the asymptotic slope for the policy that includes exploration

(d) the asymptotic slope for the policy that does not include exploration. To test this, after the algorithm has explored, set the exploitation parameter to 100% and run additional steps.

Which of these settings would you recommend? Why?

Exercise 12.4   For the following reinforcement learning algorithms:

i) Q-learning with fixed α and 80% exploitation.

ii) Q-learning with fixed $\alpha_k = 1/k$ and 80% exploitation.

iii) Q-learning with $\alpha_k = 1/k$ and 100% exploitation.

iv) SARSA learning with $\alpha_k = 1/k$ and 80% exploitation.

v) SARSA learning with $\alpha_k = 1/k$ and 100% exploitation.

vi) Feature-based SARSA learning with soft-max action selection.

vii) A model-based reinforcement learner with 50% exploitation.

(a) Which of the reinforcement learning algorithms will find the optimal policy, given enough time?

(b) Which ones will actually follow the optimal policy?

Exercise 12.5 Consider four different ways to derive the value of α_k from k in Q-learning (note that for Q-learning with varying α_k, there must be a different count k for each state–action pair).

i) Let $\alpha_k = 1/k$.

ii) Let $\alpha_k = 10/(9+k)$.

iii) Let $\alpha_k = 0.1$.

iv) Let $\alpha_k = 0.1$ for the first 10,000 steps, $\alpha_k = 0.01$ for the next 10,000 steps, $\alpha_k = 0.001$ for the next 10,000 steps, $\alpha_k = 0.0001$ for the next 10,000 steps, and so on.

(a) Which of these will converge to the true Q-value in theory?

(b) Which converges to the true Q-value in practice (i.e., in a reasonable number of steps)? Try it for more than one domain.

(c) Which are able to adapt if the environment changes slowly?

Exercise 12.6 The model-based reinforcement learner allows for a different form of optimism in the face of uncertainty. The algorithm can be started with each state having a transition to a "nirvana" state, which has very high Q-value (but which will never be reached in practice, and so the probability will shrink to zero).

(a) Does this perform differently than initialing all Q-values to a high value? Does it work better, worse or the same?

(b) How high does the Q-value for the nirvana state need to be to work most effectively? Suggest a reason why one value might be good, and test it.

(c) Could this method be used for the other RL algorithms? Explain how or why not.

Exercise 12.7 Included the features for the grid game of Example 12.6 (page 566), are features that are the x-distance to the current treasure and features that are the y-distance to the current treasure. Chris thought that these were not useful as they do not depend on the action. Do these features make a difference? Explain why they might or might not. Do they make a difference in practice?

Exercise 12.8 In SARSA with linear function approximation, using linear regression to minimize $r + \gamma Q_{\overline{w}}(s', a') - Q_{\overline{w}}(s, a)$, gives a different algorithm than Figure 12.7 (page 567). Explain what you get and why what is described in the text may be preferable (or not).

Exercise 12.9 In Example 12.6 (page 566), some of the features are perfectly correlated (e.g., F_6 and F_7). Does having such correlated features affect what functions are able to be represented? Does it help or hurt the speed at which learning occurs? Test this empirically on some examples.

Exercise 12.10 Consider the policy improvement algorithm. At equilibrium the values of the most-preferred actions should be equal. Propose, implement and evaluate an algorithm where the policy does not change very much when the values of the most-preferred actions are close. [Hint: Consider having the probability of all actions change in proportion to the distance from the best action and use a temperature parameter in the definition of distance.]

Part IV

Reasoning, Learning and Acting with Individuals and Relations

Chapter 13

Individuals and Relations

> *There is a real world with real structure. The program of mind has been trained on vast interaction with this world and so contains code that reflects the structure of the world and knows how to exploit it. This code contains representations of real objects in the world and represents the interactions of real objects. The code is mostly modular..., with modules for dealing with different kinds of objects and modules generalizing across many kinds of objects.... The modules interact in ways that mirror the real world and make accurate predictions of how the world evolves....*
>
> *You exploit the structure of the world to make decisions and take actions. Where you draw the line on categories, what constitutes a single object or a single class of objects for you, is determined by the program of your mind, which does the classification. This classification is not random but reflects a compact description of the world, and in particular a description useful for exploiting the structure of the world.*
>
> – Eric B. Baum [2004, pages 169–170]

This chapter is about how to represent individuals (things, objects) and relationships among them. As Baum suggests in the quote above, the real world contains objects and we want compact representations of those objects. Such representations can be much more compact than representations in terms of features alone. This chapter considers logical representations and gives detailed examples of how to use such representations for natural language interfaces to databases. Later chapters address ontologies and the meaning of symbols, implementing knowledge-based systems, relational planning, relational learning, and probabilistic relational models.

13.1   Exploiting Relational Structure

One of the main lessons of AI is that successful agents exploit the structure of
the world. Previous chapters showed how states can be represented in terms
of features. Representing domains using features can be much more compact
than representing them using states explicitly, and algorithms can exploit this
compactness. There is, however, usually much more structure that can be exploited for representation and inference. In particular, this chapter considers
reasoning in terms of individuals and relations:

- **Individuals** are things in the world, whether they are concrete individuals such as people and buildings, imaginary individuals such as unicorns
  and programs that can reliably pass the Turing test, processes such a reading a book or going on a holiday, or abstract concepts such as money,
  courses and times. These are also called **entities**, **objects** or **things**.

- **Relations** specify what is true about these individuals. This is meant to
  be as general as possible and includes **properties**, which are that are true
  or false of single individuals, **propositions** (page 174), which are true or
  false independently of any individuals, as well as relationships among
  multiple individuals.

Example 13.1   In the representation of the electrical domain in Example 5.7
(page 183), the propositions up_s_2, up_s_3, and ok_s_2 have no internal structure.
There is no notion that the propositions up_s_2 and up_s_3 are about the same
relation, but with different individuals, or that up_s_2 and ok_s_2 are about the
same switch. There is no notion of individuals and relations.

   An alternative is to represent explicitly the individual switches s_1, s_2, s_3,
and the properties or relations, up and ok. Using this representation, "switch s_2
is up" is represented as $up(s_2)$. By knowing what up and s_1 represent, we do
not require a separate definition of $up(s_1)$. A binary relation, like $connected\_to$,
can be used to relate two individuals, such as $connected\_to(w_1, s_1)$.

Modeling in terms of individuals and relations has a number of advantages
over just using features:

- It is often the natural representation. Often features are properties of individuals, and this internal structure is lost in converting to features.

- An agent may have to model a domain without knowing what the individuals are, or how many there will be, and, thus, without knowing
  what the features are. When interacting with the environment, the agent
  can construct the features when it finds out which individuals are in the
  particular environment.

- An agent can do some reasoning without caring about the particular individuals. For example, it may be able to derive that something holds for

all individuals without knowing what the individuals are. Or, an agent may be able to derive that some individual exists that has some properties, without caring about other individuals. There may be some queries an agent can answer for which it does not have to distinguish the individuals.

- The existence of individuals could depend on actions or could be uncertain. For example, in planning in a manufacturing context, whether there is a working component may depend on many other subcomponents working and being put together correctly; some of these may depend on the agent's actions, and some may not be under the agent's control. Thus, an agent may have to act without knowing what features there are or what features there will be.

- Often there are infinitely many individuals an agent is reasoning about, and so infinitely many features. For example, if the individuals are sentences, the agent may only have to reason about a very limited set of sentences (e.g., those that could be meant by a person speaking, or those that may be sensible to generate), even though there may be infinitely many possible sentences, and so infinitely many features.

13.2   Symbols and Semantics

The basic idea behind the use of logic (see Chapter 5) is that, when knowledge base designers have a particular world they want to characterize, they can select that world as an **intended interpretation**, select meanings for the symbols with respect to that interpretation, and write, as clauses, what is true in that world. When a system computes a logical consequence of a knowledge base, a user that knows the meanings of the symbols can interpret this answer with respect to the intended interpretation. Because the intended interpretation is a model, and a logical consequence is true in all models, a logical consequence must be true in the intended interpretation. This chapter expands the language of propositional definite clauses to allow reasoning about individuals and relations. Atomic propositions now have internal structure in terms of relations and individuals.

Example 13.2   Figure 13.1 (on the next page) illustrates the general idea of semantics with individuals and relations. The person who is designing the knowledge base has a meaning for the symbols. The person knows what the symbols *kim*, *r123*, and *in* refer to in the domain and supplies a knowledge base of sentences in the representation language to the computer. These sentences have meaning to that person. She can ask queries using these symbols and with the particular meaning she has for them. The computer takes these sentences and queries, and it computes answers. The computer does not know what the

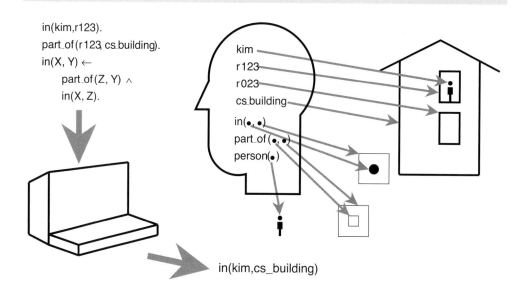

in(kim,r123).
part_of(r123, cs_building).
in(X, Y) ←
    part_of(Z, Y) ∧
    in(X, Z).

in(kim,cs_building)

Figure 13.1: The role of semantics. The meaning of the symbols are in the user's head. The computer takes in symbols and outputs symbols. The output can be interpreted by the user according to the meaning the user places on the symbols.

symbols mean. However, the person who supplied the information can use the meaning associated with the symbols to interpret the answer with respect to the world.

The mapping between the symbols in the mind and the individuals and relations denoted by these symbols is called a **conceptualization**. In this chapter, we assume that the conceptualization is in the user's head, or written informally, in comments. Making conceptualizations explicit is the role of a formal ontology (page 655).

What is the correct answer is defined independently of how it is computed. The correctness of a knowledge base is defined by the semantics, not by a particular algorithm for proving queries. As long as an inference algorithm is faithful to the semantics, it can be optimized for efficiency. This separation of meaning from computation lets an agent optimize performance while maintaining correctness.

13.3 Datalog: A Relational Rule Language

This section expands the syntax for the propositional definite clause language (page 182). The syntax is based on normal mathematical notation for predicate symbols but follows **Prolog**'s convention for variables.

Relationships to Traditional Programming Languages

The notion of logical semantics presented in this chapter should be contrasted with the procedural semantics of traditional programming languages like Fortran, C++, Lisp, Java or Python. The semantics for these languages specify the meaning of the language constructs in terms of what the computer will compute based on the program. This corresponds more closely to the proof theory presented here. Logical semantics gives a way to specify the relationships of the symbols to the world, and a way to specify the result of a program independently of how it is computed.

The definitions of semantics and reasoning theory correspond to the notions of a Tarskian semantics and proof in mathematical **logic**. Logic allows us to define knowledge independently of how it is used. Knowledge base designers or users can verify the correctness of knowledge if they know its meaning. People can debate the truth of sentences in the language. The same semantics can be used to establish the correctness of an implementation. One of the advances of logic programming was showing that logic could be given a procedural semantics, to hopefully give us the best of both worlds.

The notion of an individual is similar to the definition of an object in **object-oriented languages** such as Smalltalk, C++, or Java. The main difference is that the objects in object-oriented languages are computational objects rather than real physical objects. In an object-oriented language, a "person" object is a representation of a person; it is not the actual person. However, in the representation and reasoning systems considered in AI, the name "Chris" can denote an actual person.

In object-oriented languages, objects send each other messages. In the logical view, not only do we want to interact with objects, but we also want to reason about them. We may want to be able to predict what an object will do without getting the object to do it. We may want to predict the internal state from the observed behavior, for example, in a diagnostic task. We even want to reason about, and predict the behavior of, individuals who may be deliberately concealing information and may not want us to know what they are doing. For example, consider a "person" object: although there can be some interaction with the person, there is often much information about a person that you do not know. Because you cannot keep asking them for the information (which they may not know or may not want to tell you), you require some external representation of the information about that individual. It is even harder to interact with a chair or a disease, but we still may want to reason about them.

Programming language facilities often make assumptions about designed objects that are not appropriate for real objects. For example, in Java, objects have to fit into a single class hierarchy, whereas real-world individuals may have many roles and be in many classes; it is the complex interaction of these classes that specifies the behavior.

The **syntax** of **Datalog** is given by the following, where a **word** is a sequence of letters, digits, or an underscore ("_"):

- A logical **variable** is a word starting with an upper-case letter or with "_". For example *X*, *Room*, *B4*, *Raths*, and *The_big_guy* are all variables.

- A **constant** is a word that starts with a lower-case letter, or is a number constant or a string.

- A **predicate symbol** is a word that starts with a lower-case letter. Constants and predicate symbols are distinguishable by their context in a knowledge base.

  For example, *kim*, *r123*, *f*, *grandfather*, and *borogroves* can be constants or predicate symbols, depending on the context; *725* is a constant.

- A **term** is either a variable or a constant.

  For example *X*, *kim*, *cs422*, *mome*, or *Raths* can be terms.

- An **atomic symbol**, or simply an **atom**, is of the form p or $p(t_1, \ldots, t_n)$, where p is a predicate symbol and each t_i is a term. Each t_i is called an **argument** to the predicate.

  For example, *teaches*(*sue*, *cs422*), *in*(*kim*, *r123*), *father*(*bill*, *Y*), *happy*(*C*), *outgrabe*(*mome*, *Raths*), and *sunny* can all be atoms. From context in the atom *outgrabe*(*mome*, *Raths*), the symbol *outgrabe* is a predicate symbol and *mome* is a constant.

The notions of **definite clause**, **rule**, **query**, and **knowledge base** are the same as for propositional definite clauses (page 182) but with the expanded definition of atom. The definitions are repeated here.

- A **definite clause** is of the form

  $$h \leftarrow a_1 \wedge \ldots \wedge a_m.$$

  where h is an atom, the **head** of the clause, and each a_i is an atom. It can be read "h if a_1 and ... and a_m".

  If $m > 0$, the clause is called a **rule**. $a_1 \wedge \ldots \wedge a_m$ is the **body** of the clause.

  If $m = 0$ the arrow can be omitted and the clause is called **atomic clause** or **fact**. An atomic clause has an **empty body**.

- A **knowledge base** is a set of definite clauses.

- A **query** is of the form

  $$\text{ask } a_1 \wedge \ldots \wedge a_m.$$

- An **expression** is either a term, an atom, a definite clause, or a query.

In our examples, we will follow the Prolog convention that comments, which are ignored by the system, extend from a "%" to the end of the line.

Example 13.3 The following is a knowledge base:

$$grandfather(sam, X) \leftarrow father(sam, Y) \wedge parent(Y, X).$$
$$in(kim, R) \leftarrow teaches(kim, cs422) \wedge in(cs422, R).$$
$$slithy(toves) \leftarrow mimsy \wedge borogroves \wedge outgrabe(mome, Raths).$$

From context, *sam, kim, cs422, toves,* and *mome* are constants; *grandfather, father, parent, in, teaches, slithy, mimsy, borogroves,* and *outgrabe* are predicate symbols; and X, Y, R and *Raths* are variables.

The first two clauses about Kim and Sam may make some intuitive sense, even though we have not explicitly provided any formal specification for the meaning of sentences of the definite clause language. However, regardless of the mnemonic names' suggestiveness, as far as the computer is concerned, the first two clauses have no more meaning than the third. Meaning is provided only by virtue of a semantics.

An expression is **ground** if it does not contain any variables. For example, *teaches(chris, cs322)* is ground, but *teaches(Prof, Course)* is not ground.

The next section defines the semantics. We first consider ground expressions and then extend the semantics to include variables.

13.3.1 Semantics of Ground Datalog

The first step in giving the semantics of Datalog is to give the semantics for the ground (variable-free) case.

An **interpretation** is a triple $I = \langle D, \phi, \pi \rangle$

- D is a non-empty set called the **domain**. Elements of D are **individuals**.
- ϕ is a mapping that assigns to each constant an element of D.
- π is a mapping that assigns to each n-ary predicate symbol a function from D^n into $\{true, false\}$.

ϕ is a function from names into individuals in the world. The constant c is said to **denote** the individual $\phi(c)$. Here c is a symbol but $\phi(c)$ can be anything: a real physical individual such as a person or a virus, an abstract concept such as a course, love, the number 2, or a symbol.

$\pi(p)$ specifies whether the relation denoted by the n-ary predicate symbol p is true or false for each n-tuple of individuals. If predicate symbol p has no arguments, then $\pi(p)$ is either *true* or *false*. Thus, for predicate symbols with no arguments, this semantics reduces to the semantics of propositional definite clauses (page 175).

Example 13.4 Consider the world consisting of three individuals on a table:

These are drawn in this way because they are things in the world, not symbols. ✂ is a pair of scissors, ☎ is a telephone, and ✎ is a pencil.

Suppose the constants in our language are *phone*, *pencil*, and *telephone*. We have the predicate symbols *noisy* and *left_of*. Assume *noisy* is a unary predicate (it takes a single argument) and that *left_of* is a binary predicate (it takes two arguments).

An example interpretation that represents the individuals on the table is

- $D = \{$✂, ☎, ✎$\}$.
- $\phi(phone) =$ ☎, $\phi(pencil) =$ ✎, $\phi(telephone) =$ ☎.
- $\pi(noisy)$:

$\langle$✂$\rangle$	*false*	$\langle$☎$\rangle$	*true*	$\langle$✎$\rangle$	*false*

  $\pi(left\_of)$:

$\langle$✂,✂$\rangle$	*false*	$\langle$✂,☎$\rangle$	*true*	$\langle$✂,✎$\rangle$	*true*
$\langle$☎,✂$\rangle$	*false*	$\langle$☎,☎$\rangle$	*false*	$\langle$☎,✎$\rangle$	*true*
$\langle$✎,✂$\rangle$	*false*	$\langle$✎,☎$\rangle$	*false*	$\langle$✎,✎$\rangle$	*false*

Because *noisy* is unary, it takes a singleton individual and has a truth value for each individual.

Because *left_of* is a binary predicate, it takes a pair of individuals and is true when the first element of the pair is left of the second element. Thus, for example, $\pi(left\_of)(\langle$✂, ☎$\rangle) = true$, because the scissors are to the left of the telephone; $\pi(left\_of)(\langle$✎,✎$\rangle) = false$, because the pencil is not to the left of itself.

Note how the D is a set of things in the world. The relations are among the individuals in the world, not among the names. As ϕ specifies that *phone* and *telephone* refer to the same individual, exactly the same statements are true about them in this interpretation.

Example 13.5 Consider the interpretation of Figure 13.1 (page 584).

D is the set with four elements: the person Kim, room 123, room 023, and the CS building. This is not a set of four symbols, but it is the set containing the actual person, the actual rooms, and the actual building. It is difficult to write down this set and, fortunately, you never really have to. To remember the meaning and to convey the meaning to another person, knowledge base designers typically describe D, ϕ, and π by pointing to the physical individuals or a depiction of them (as is done in Figure 13.1) and describe the meaning in natural language.

The constants are *kim*, *r123*, *r023*, and *cs_building*. The mapping ϕ is defined by the gray arcs from each of these constants to an individual in the world in Figure 13.1.

The predicate symbols are *person*, *in*, and *part_of*. The meaning of these are meant to be conveyed in the figure by the arcs from the predicate symbols.

Thus, the person called Kim is in the room *r123* and is also in the CS building, and these are the only instances of the *in* relation that are true. Similarly, room *r123* and room *r023* are part of the CS building, and there are no other *part_of* relationships that are true in this interpretation.

Each ground term denotes an individual in an interpretation. A constant c denotes in I the individual $\phi(c)$.

A ground atom is either true or false in an interpretation. Atom $p(t_1, \ldots, t_n)$ is **true** in I if $\pi(p)(\langle t'_1, \ldots, t'_n \rangle) = \mathit{true}$, where t'_i is the individual denoted by term t_i, and is **false** in I otherwise.

Example 13.6   The atom $\mathit{in}(\mathit{kim}, \mathit{r123})$ is true in the interpretation of Example 13.5, because the person denoted by kim is indeed in the room denoted by $\mathit{r123}$. Similarly, $\mathit{person}(\mathit{kim})$ is true, as is $\mathit{part\_of}(\mathit{r123}, \mathit{cs\_building})$. The atoms $\mathit{in}(\mathit{cs\_building}, \mathit{r123})$ and $\mathit{person}(\mathit{r123})$ are false in this interpretation.

Logical connectives, models and logical consequences have the same meaning as in the propositional calculus (page 175):

- A ground clause is false in an interpretation if the head is false and the body is true (or is empty); otherwise, the clause is true in the interpretation.

- A **model** of a knowledge base KB is an interpretation in which all the clauses in KB are true.

- If KB is a knowledge base and g is a proposition, g is a **logical consequence** of KB, written $KB \models g$, if g is true in every model of KB. Thus $KB \not\models g$, meaning g is not a logical consequence of KB, when there is a model of KB in which g is false.

13.3.2   Interpreting Variables

When a variable appears in a clause, the clause is true in an interpretation only if the clause is true for all possible values of that variable.

To formally define semantics of variables, a **variable assignment**, ρ, is a function from the set of variables into the domain D. Thus, a variable assignment assigns an element of the domain to each variable. Given interpretation $\langle D, \phi, \pi \rangle$ and variable assignment ρ, each term denotes an individual in the domain. If the term is a constant, the individual is given by ϕ. If the term is a variable, the individual is given by ρ. Given an interpretation and a variable assignment, each atom is either true or false, using the same definition as earlier. Thus, given an interpretation and a variable assignment, each clause is either true or false.

A clause is true in an interpretation if it is true for all variable assignments. The variables are said to be **universally quantified** in the scope of the clause. Thus, a clause is false in an interpretation means there is a variable assignment under which the clause is false.

Example 13.7   The clause

$$part\_of(X, Y) \leftarrow in(X, Y).$$

is false in the interpretation of Example 13.5 (page 588), because under the variable assignment with X denoting Kim and Y denoting Room 123, the clause's body is true and the clause's head is false.

The clause

$$in(X, Y) \leftarrow part\_of(Z, Y) \wedge in(X, Z).$$

is true, because in all variable assignments where the body is true, the head is also true.

Logical consequence is defined in the same way as it was for propositional definite clauses in Section 5.1.2 (page 176): ground body g is a **logical consequence** of KB, written $KB \models g$, if g is true in every model of KB.

Example 13.8   Suppose the knowledge base KB is

$in(kim, r123).$

$part\_of(r123, cs\_building).$

$in(X, Y) \leftarrow$

   $part\_of(Z, Y) \wedge$

   $in(X, Z).$

The interpretation defined in Example 13.5 (page 588) is a model of KB, because each clause is true in that interpretation.

   $KB \models in(kim, r123)$, because this is stated explicitly in the knowledge base. If every clause of KB is true in an interpretation, then $in(kim, r123)$ must be true in that interpretation.

   $KB \not\models in(kim, r023)$. The interpretation defined in Example 13.5 is a model of KB, in which $in(kim, r023)$ is false.

   $KB \not\models part\_of(r023, cs\_building)$. Although $part\_of(r023, cs\_building)$ is true in the interpretation of Example 13.5, there is another model of KB in which $part\_of(r023, cs\_building)$ is false. In particular, the interpretation which is like the interpretation of Example 13.5, but where

$$\pi(part\_of)(\langle\langle\phi(r023), \phi(cs\_building)\rangle\rangle) = false$$

is a model of KB in which $part\_of(r023, cs\_building)$ is false.

   $KB \models in(kim, cs\_building)$. If the clauses in KB are true in interpretation I, it must be the case that $in(kim, cs\_building)$ is true in I, otherwise, there is an instance of the third clause of KB that is false in I – a contradiction to I being a model of KB.

The following example shows how the semantics treats variables appearing in a clause's body but not in its head.

Example 13.9   In Example 13.8, the variable Y in the clause defining *in* is universally quantified at the level of the clause; thus, the clause is true for all variable assignments. Consider particular values c_1 for X and c_2 for Y. The clause

$$in(c_1, c_2) \leftarrow$$
$$part\_of(Z, c_2) \land$$
$$in(c_1, Z).$$

is true for all variable assignments to Z. If there exists a variable assignment c_3 for Z such that $part\_of(Z, c_2) \land in(c_1, Z)$ is true in an interpretation, then $in(c_1, c_2)$ must be true in that interpretation. Therefore, you can read the last clause of Example 13.8 as "for all X and for all Y, $in(X, Y)$ is true if there exists a Z such that $part\_of(Z, Y) \land in(X, Z)$ is true."

The definite clause language makes universal quantification implicit. Sometimes it is useful to make quantification explicit. There are two quantifiers that are used in logic:

- $\forall X\ p(X)$, read "**for all** X, $p(X)$" means $p(X)$ is true for every variable assignment for X. X is said to be a **universally quantified**.

- $\exists X\ p(X)$, read "**there exists** an X such that $p(X)$" means $p(X)$ is true for some variable assignment for X. X is said to be **existentially quantified**.

The clause $P(X) \leftarrow Q(X, Y)$ means

$$\forall X\ \forall Y\ (P(X) \leftarrow Q(X, Y))$$

which is equivalent to

$$\forall X\ (P(X) \leftarrow \exists Y\ Q(X, Y)).$$

Thus, free variables that only appear in the body are existentially quantified in the scope of the body.

It may seem as though there is something peculiar about talking about a clause being true for cases where it does not make sense, as in the following example.

Example 13.10   Consider the clause

$$in(cs422, love) \leftarrow$$
$$part\_of(cs422, sky) \land$$
$$in(sky, love).$$

where *cs422* denotes a course, *love* denotes an abstract concept, and *sky* denotes the sky. Here, the clause is vacuously true in the intended interpretation according to the truth table for $\leftarrow$, because the clause's right-hand side is false in the intended interpretation.

As long as whenever the head is nonsensical, the body is also, the rule can never be used to prove anything nonsensical. When checking for the truth of a clause, you must only be concerned with those cases in which the clause's body is true. The convention that a clause is true whenever the body is false, even if it strictly does not make sense, makes the semantics simpler and does not cause any problems.

The Human's View of Semantics

The formal description of semantics does not tell us why semantics is interesting or how it can be used as a basis to build intelligent systems. The methodology for using semantics for propositional logic programs (page 177) can be extended to Datalog:

Step 1   Select the task domain or world to represent. This could be some aspect of the real world, for example, the structure of courses and students at a university or a laboratory environment at a particular point in time, some imaginary world, such as the world of Alice in Wonderland, or the state of the electrical environment if a switch breaks, or an abstract world, for example, the world of money, numbers and sets. Within this world, let the domain D be the set of all individuals or things that you want to be able to refer to and reason about. Also, select which relations to represent.

Step 2   Associate constants in the language with individuals in the world that you want to name. For each element of D you want to refer to by name, assign a constant in the language. For example, you may select the name *"kim"* to denote a particular professor, the name *"cs322"* for a particular introductory AI course, the name *"two"* for the number that is the successor of the number one, and the name *"red"* for the color of stoplights. Each of these names denotes the corresponding individual in the world.

Step 3   For each relation that you may want to represent, associate a predicate symbol in the language. Each n-ary predicate symbol denotes a function from D^n into $\{true, false\}$, which specifies the subset of D^n for which the relation is true. For example, the predicate symbol *"teaches"* of two arguments (a teacher and a course) may correspond to the binary relation that is true when the individual denoted by the first argument teaches the course denoted by the second argument. These relations need not be binary. They could have any number of arguments (zero or more). For example, *"is_red"* may be a predicate that has one argument.

These associations of symbols with their meanings form an **intended interpretation**.

Step 4   Write clauses that are true in the intended interpretation. This is often called **axiomatizing the domain**, where the given clauses are the **axioms** of the domain. If the person who is denoted by the symbol *kim* actually teaches the course denoted by the symbol *cs*322, you can assert the clause *teaches*(*kim*, *cs*322) as being true in the intended interpretation.

Step 5 Ask queries about the intended interpretation. The system gives answers that you can interpret using the meaning assigned to the symbols.

Following this methodology, the knowledge base designer does not actually tell the computer anything until step 4. The first three steps are carried out in the head of the designer. Of course, the designer should document the denotations to make their knowledge base understandable to other people, so that they remember each symbol's denotation, and so that they can check the truth of the clauses.

The world itself does not prescribe what the individuals are.

Example 13.11 In one conceptualization of a domain, *pink* may be a predicate symbol of one argument that is true when the individual denoted by that argument is pink. In another conceptualization, *pink* may be an individual that is the color pink, and it may be used as the second argument to a binary predicate *color*, which says that the individual denoted by the first argument has the color denoted by the second argument. Alternatively, someone may want to describe the world at a level of detail where various shades of *red* are not distinguished, and so the color *pink* would not be included. Someone else may describe the world in more detail, and decide that *pink* is too general a term, and use the terms *coral* and *salmon*.

When the individuals in the domain are real physical things, it is usually difficult to give the denotation without physically pointing at the individual. When the individual is an abstract individual – for example, a university course or the concept of love – it is virtually impossible to write the denotation. However, this does not prevent the system from representing and reasoning about such concepts.

Example 13.12 Example 5.7 (page 183) represented the electrical environment of Figure 5.2 (page 183) using propositions. Using individuals and relations can make the representation more intuitive, because the general knowledge about how switches work can be clearly separated from the knowledge about a specific house.

To represent this domain, the first step is to decide what individuals exist in the domain. In what follows, assume that each switch, each light, and each power outlet is an individual. Each wire between two switches and between a switch and a light is also an individual. Someone may claim that, in fact, there are pairs of wires joined by connectors and that the electricity flow must obey Kirchhoff's laws. Someone else may decide that even that level of abstraction is inappropriate because we should model the flow of electrons. However, an appropriate level of abstraction is one that is useful for the task at hand. A resident of the house may not know the whereabouts of the connections between the individual strands of wire or even the voltage. Therefore, we assume a flow model of electricity, where power flows from the outside of the house through wires to lights. This model is appropriate for the task of determining whether a light should be lit or not, but it may not be appropriate for other tasks.

Next, give names to each individual to which we want to refer. This is done in Figure 5.2 (page 183). For example, the individual w_0 is the wire between light l_1 and switch s_2.

Next, choose which relationships to represent. Assume the following predicates with their associated intended interpretations:

- $light(L)$ is true if the individual denoted by L is a light.
- $lit(L)$ is true if the light L is lit and emitting light.
- $live(W)$ is true if there is power coming into W; that is, W is live.
- $up(S)$ is true if switch S is up.
- $down(S)$ is true if switch S is down.
- $ok(E)$ is true if E is not faulty; E can be either a circuit breaker or a light.
- $connected\_to(X, Y)$ is true if component X is connected to Y such that current would flow from Y to X.

At this stage, the computer has not been told anything. It does not know what the predicates are, let alone what they mean. It does not know which individuals exist or their names.

Before anything about the particular house is known, the system can be told general rules such as

$$lit(L) \leftarrow light(L) \wedge live(L) \wedge ok(L).$$

Recursive rules let you state what is live from what is connected to what:

$$live(X) \leftarrow connected\_to(X, Y) \wedge live(Y).$$
$$live(outside).$$

For the particular house and configuration of components and their connections, the following facts about the world can be told to the computer:

$$light(l_1).$$
$$light(l_2).$$
$$down(s_1).$$
$$up(s_2).$$
$$ok(cb_1).$$
$$connected\_to(w_0, w_1) \leftarrow up(s_2).$$
$$connected\_to(w_0, w_2) \leftarrow down(s_2).$$
$$connected\_to(w_1, w_3) \leftarrow up(s_1).$$
$$connected\_to(w_3, outside) \leftarrow ok(cb_1).$$

These rules and atomic clauses are all that the computer is told. It does not know the meaning of these symbols. However, it can now answer queries about this particular house.

13.3.3 Queries with Variables

Queries are used to ask whether some statement is a logical consequence of a knowledge base. With propositional queries (page 185), a user can ask yes-or-no queries. Queries with variables allow the users to ask for the individuals that make the query true.

An **instance** of a query is obtained by substituting terms for the variables in the query. Each occurrence of a variable in a query must be replaced by the same term. Given a query with free variables, an **answer** is either an instance of the query that is a logical consequence of the knowledge base, or "*no*", meaning that no instances of the query logically follow from the knowledge base. Instances of the query are specified by providing values for the variables in the query. Determining which instances of a query follow from a knowledge base is known as **answer extraction**.

An answer of "no" does *not* mean that the query is false in the intended interpretation; it simply means that there is no instance of the query that is a logical consequence.

Example 13.13   Consider the clauses of Figure 13.2 (on the next page). The person who wrote these clauses presumably has some meaning associated with the symbols, and has written the clauses because they are true in some, perhaps imaginary, world. The computer knows nothing about rooms or directions. All it knows are the clauses it is given; and it can compute their logical consequences.

The user can ask the following query:

  ask $imm\_west(r105, r107)$.

and the answer is *yes*. The user can ask the query

  ask $imm\_east(r107, r105)$.

and the answer is, again, *yes*. The user can ask the query

  ask $imm\_west(r205, r207)$.

and the answer is *no*. This means it is not a logical consequence, not that it is false. There is not enough information in the database to determine whether or not $r205$ is immediately west of $r207$.

The query

  ask $next\_door(R, r105)$.

has two answers. One answer, with $R = r107$, means $next\_door(r107, r105)$ is a logical consequence of the clauses. The other answer is for $R = r103$. The query

  ask $west(R, r105)$.

% *imm_west*(*W*, *E*) is true if room *W* is immediately west of room *E*.

    imm_west(*r101*, *r103*).
    imm_west(*r103*, *r105*).
    imm_west(*r105*, *r107*).
    imm_west(*r107*, *r109*).
    imm_west(*r109*, *r111*).
    imm_west(*r131*, *r129*).
    imm_west(*r129*, *r127*).
    imm_west(*r127*, *r125*).

% *imm_east*(*E*, *W*) is true if room *E* is immediately east of room *W*.

    imm_east(*E*, *W*) ←
        imm_west(*W*, *E*).

% *next_door*(*R1*, *R2*) is true if room *R1* is next door to room *R2*.

    next_door(*E*, *W*) ←
        imm_east(*E*, *W*).
    next_door(*W*, *E*) ←
        imm_west(*W*, *E*).

% *two_doors_east*(*E*, *W*) is true if room *E* is two doors east of room *W*.

    two_doors_east(*E*, *W*) ←
        imm_east(*E*, *M*) ∧
        imm_east(*M*, *W*).

% *west*(*W*, *E*) is true if room *W* is west of room *E*.

    west(*W*, *E*) ←
        imm_west(*W*, *E*).
    west(*W*, *E*) ←
        imm_west(*W*, *M*) ∧
        west(*M*, *E*).

Figure 13.2: A knowledge base about rooms

has two answers: one for $R = r103$ and one for $R = r101$. The query

   ask $west(r105, R)$.

has three answers: one for $R = r107$, one for $R = r109$, and one for $R = r111$. The query

   ask $next\_door(X, Y)$.

has 16 answers, including

   $X = r103, Y = r101$
   $X = r105, Y = r103$
   $X = r101, Y = r103$

   $\cdots$.

13.4 Proofs and Substitutions

Both the bottom-up and top-down propositional proof procedures of Section 5.3.2 (page 186) can be extended to Datalog. A proof procedure extended for variables must account for the fact that a free variable in a clause means that all instances of the clause are true. A proof may have to use different instances of the same clause in a single proof.

13.4.1 Instances and Substitutions

An **instance** of a clause is obtained by uniformly substituting terms for variables in the clause. All occurrences of a particular variable are replaced by the same term.

The specification of which value is assigned to each variable is called a substitution. A **substitution** is a set of the form $\{V_1/t_1, \dots, V_n/t_n\}$, where each V_i is a distinct variable and each t_i is a term. The element V_i/t_i is a **binding** for variable V_i. A substitution is in **normal form** if no V_i appears in any t_j.

> **Example 13.14** For example, $\{X/Y, Z/a\}$ is a substitution in normal form that binds X to Y and binds Z to a. The substitution $\{X/Y, Z/X\}$ is not in normal form, because the variable X occurs both on the left and on the right of a binding.

The **application** of a substitution $\sigma = \{V_1/t_1, \dots, V_n/t_n\}$ to expression e, written $e\sigma$, is an expression that is the same as the original expression e except that each occurrence of V_i in e is replaced by the corresponding t_i. The expression $e\sigma$ is called an **instance** of e. If $e\sigma$ does not contain any variables, it is called a **ground instance** of e.

> **Example 13.15** Some applications of substitutions are
>
> $$p(a,X)\{X/c\} = p(a,c).$$
> $$p(Y,c)\{Y/a\} = p(a,c).$$
> $$p(a,X)\{Y/a,Z/X\} = p(a,X).$$
> $$p(X,X,Y,Y,Z)\{X/Z,Y/t\} = p(Z,Z,t,t,Z).$$
>
> Substitutions can apply to clauses, atoms, and terms. For example, the result of applying the substitution $\{X/Y,Z/a\}$ to the clause
>
> $$p(X,Y) \leftarrow q(a,Z,X,Y,Z)$$
>
> is the clause
>
> $$p(Y,Y) \leftarrow q(a,a,Y,Y,a).$$

A substitution σ is a **unifier** of expressions e_1 and e_2 if $e_1\sigma$ is identical to $e_2\sigma$. That is, a unifier of two expressions is a substitution that when applied to each expression results in the same expression.

> **Example 13.16** $\{X/a,Y/b\}$ is a unifier of $t(a,Y,c)$ and $t(X,b,c)$ as
>
> $$t(a,Y,c)\{X/a,Y/b\} = t(X,b,c)\{X/a,Y/b\} = t(a,b,c).$$

Expressions can have many unifiers.

> **Example 13.17** Atoms $p(X,Y)$ and $p(Z,Z)$ have many unifiers, including $\{X/b,Y/b,Z/b\}$, $\{X/c,Y/c,Z/c\}$, $\{X/Z,Y/Z\}$ and $\{Y/X,Z/X\}$. The last two unifiers are more general than the first two, because the first two both have X the same as Z and Y the same as Z but make more commitments to what these values are.

Substitution σ is a **most general unifier (MGU)** of expressions e_1 and e_2 if

- σ is a unifier of the two expressions, and
- if substitution σ' is also a unifier of e_1 and e_2, then $e\sigma'$ must be an instance of $e\sigma$ for all expressions e.

Expression e_1 is a **renaming** of e_2 if they differ only in the names of variables. In this case, they are both instances of each other.

If two expressions have a unifier, they have at least one MGU. The expressions resulting from applying the MGUs to the expressions are all renamings of each other. That is, if σ and σ' are both MGUs of expressions e_1 and e_2, then $e_1\sigma$ is a renaming of $e_1\sigma'$.

> **Example 13.18** $\{X/Z,Y/Z\}$ and $\{Z/X,Y/X\}$ are both MGUs of $p(X,Y)$ and $p(Z,Z)$. The resulting applications
>
> $$p(X,Y)\{X/Z,Y/Z\} = p(Z,Z)$$
> $$p(X,Y)\{Z/X,Y/X\} = p(X,X)$$
>
> are renamings of each other.

13.4.2 Bottom-up Procedure with Variables

The propositional bottom-up proof procedure (page 187) can be extended to Datalog by using ground instances of the clauses. A **ground instance** of a clause is obtained by uniformly substituting constants for the variables in the clause. The constants required are those appearing in the knowledge base or in the query. If there are no constants in the knowledge base or the query, one must be invented.

Example 13.19 Suppose the knowledge base is

$q(a)$.
$q(b)$.
$r(a)$.
$s(W) \leftarrow r(W)$.
$p(X, Y) \leftarrow q(X) \wedge s(Y)$.

The set of all ground instances is

$q(a)$.
$q(b)$.
$r(a)$.
$s(a) \leftarrow r(a)$.
$s(b) \leftarrow r(b)$.
$p(a, a) \leftarrow q(a) \wedge s(a)$.
$p(a, b) \leftarrow q(a) \wedge s(b)$.
$p(b, a) \leftarrow q(b) \wedge s(a)$.
$p(b, b) \leftarrow q(b) \wedge s(b)$.

The propositional bottom-up proof procedure of Section 5.3.2 (page 187) can be applied to the grounding to derive $q(a), q(b), r(a), s(a), p(a, a)$, and $p(b, a)$ as the ground instances that are logical consequences.

Example 13.20 Suppose the knowledge base is

$p(X, Y)$.
$g \leftarrow p(W, W)$.

The bottom-up proof procedure for query "ask g" must invent a new constant symbol, say c. The set of all ground instances is then

$p(c, c)$.
$g \leftarrow p(c, c)$.

The propositional bottom-up proof procedure will derive $p(c, c)$ and g.

If the query were "ask $p(b, d)$" the set of ground instances would change to reflect the constants b and d.

The bottom-up proof procedure applied to the grounding of the knowledge base is sound, because each instance of each rule is true in every model. This procedure is essentially the same as the variable-free case, but it uses the set of ground instances of the clauses, all of which are true because the variables in a clause are universally quantified.

This bottom-up procedure will eventually halt for Datalog because there are only finitely many grounded atoms, and one ground atom is added to the consequence set each time through the loop.

This procedure is also complete for ground atoms. That is, if a ground atom is a consequence of the knowledge base, it will be derived. To prove this, as in the propositional case (page 189), we construct a particular generic model. Recall that a model specifies the domain, what the constants denote, and what is true. A **Herbrand interpretation** is an interpretation where the domain is symbolic and consists of all constants of the language. A constant is invented if there are no constants in the knowledge base or the query. In a Herbrand interpretation, each constant denotes itself. Thus, in the definition of an interpretation (page 587), D and ϕ are fixed for a given program, and all that needs to be specified is π, which defines the predicate symbols.

Consider the Herbrand interpretation where the true atoms are the ground instances of the relations that are eventually derived by the bottom-up procedure. It is easy to see that this Herbrand interpretation is a model of the rules given. As in the variable-free case (page 187), it is a **minimal model** in that it has the fewest true atoms of any model. If $KB \models g$ for ground atom g, then g is true in the minimal model and, thus, is eventually derived.

Example 13.21 Consider the clauses of Figure 13.2 (page 596). The bottom-up proof procedure can immediately derive each instance of *imm_west* given as a fact. The algorithm can then add the *imm_east* atoms to the consequence set:

$imm\_east(r103, r101)$

$imm\_east(r105, r103)$

$imm\_east(r107, r105)$

$imm\_east(r109, r107)$

$imm\_east(r111, r109)$

$imm\_east(r129, r131)$

$imm\_east(r127, r129)$

$imm\_east(r125, r127)$

Next, the *next_door* relations that follow can be added to the set of consequences, including

$next\_door(r101, r103)$

$next\_door(r103, r101)$

```
1: procedure Unify(t₁, t₂)
2:     Inputs
3:         t₁, t₂: atoms or terms
4:     Output
5:         most general unifier of t₁ and t₂ if it exists or ⊥ otherwise
6:     Local
7:         E: a set of equality statements
8:         S: substitution
9:     E ← {t₁ = t₂}
10:    S = {}
11:    while E ≠ {} do
12:        select and remove α = β from E
13:        if β is not identical to α then
14:            if α is a variable then
15:                replace α with β everywhere in E and S
16:                S ← {α/β} ∪ S
17:            else if β is a variable then
18:                replace β with α everywhere in E and S
19:                S ← {β/α} ∪ S
20:            else if α is p(α₁, ..., αₙ) and β is p(β₁, ..., βₙ) then
21:                E ← E ∪ {α₁ = β₁, ..., αₙ = βₙ}
22:            else
23:                return ⊥
24:    return S
```

Figure 13.3: Unification algorithm for Datalog

The *two_door_east* relations can be added to the set of consequences, including

$$two\_door\_east(r105, r101)$$
$$two\_door\_east(r107, r103)$$

Finally, the *west* relations that follow can be added to the set of consequences.

13.4.3 Unification

The problem of **unification** is the following: given two atoms or terms, determine whether they unify, and, if they do, return a unifier of them. The unification algorithm finds a **most general unifier** (MGU) of two atoms or returns $\bot$ if they do not unify.

The unification algorithm is given in Figure 13.3. E is a set of equality statements implying the unification, and S is a set of equalities of the correct form of a substitution. In this algorithm, if α/β is in the substitution S, then, by construction, α is a variable that does not appear elsewhere in S or in E. In line

20, α and β must have the same predicate and the same number of arguments; otherwise the unification fails.

Example 13.22 Suppose you want to unify $p(X, Y, Y)$ with $p(a, Z, b)$. Initially E is $\{p(X, Y, Y) = p(a, Z, b)\}$. The first time through the while loop, E becomes $\{X = a, Y = Z, Y = b\}$. Suppose $X = a$ is selected next. Then S becomes $\{X/a\}$ and E becomes $\{Y = Z, Y = b\}$. Suppose $Y = Z$ is selected. Then Y is replaced by Z in S and E. S becomes $\{X/a, Y/Z\}$ and E becomes $\{Z = b\}$. Finally $Z = b$ is selected, Z is replaced by b, S becomes $\{X/a, Y/b, Z/b\}$, and E becomes empty. The substitution $\{X/a, Y/b, Z/b\}$ is returned as an MGU.

Consider unifying $p(a, Y, Y)$ with $p(Z, Z, b)$. E starts off as $\{p(a, Y, Y) = p(Z, Z, b)\}$. In the next step, E becomes $\{a = Z, Y = Z, Y = b\}$. Then Z is replaced by a in E, and E becomes $\{Y = a, Y = b\}$. Then Y is replaced by a in E, and E becomes $\{a = b\}$, and then $\perp$ is returned indicating that there is no unifier.

13.4.4   Definite Resolution with Variables

The top-down proof procedure (page 189) can be extended to handle variables by allowing instances of rules to be used in the derivation.

A **generalized answer clause** is of the form

$$yes(t_1, \ldots, t_k) \leftarrow a_1 \wedge a_2 \wedge \ldots \wedge a_m$$

where $t_1, \ldots, t_k$ are terms and $a_1, \ldots, a_m$ are atoms. The use of yes enables **answer extraction**: determining which instances of the query variables are a logical consequence of the knowledge base.

Initially, the generalized answer clause for query q is

$$yes(V_1, \ldots, V_k) \leftarrow q$$

where $V_1, \ldots, V_k$ are the variables that appear in q. Intuitively this means that an instance of $yes(V_1, \ldots, V_k)$ is true if the corresponding instance of the query is true.

The proof procedure maintains a current generalized answer clause.

At each stage, the algorithm selects an atom in the body of the generalized answer clause. It then chooses a clause in the knowledge base whose head unifies with the atom.

The **SLD resolution** of the generalized answer clause

$$yes(t_1, \ldots, t_k) \leftarrow a_1 \wedge a_2 \wedge \ldots \wedge a_m$$

on a_1 with the chosen clause

$$a \leftarrow b_1 \wedge \ldots \wedge b_p$$

where a_1 and a have most general unifier σ, is the answer clause

$$(yes(t_1, \ldots, t_k) \leftarrow b_1 \wedge \ldots \wedge b_p \wedge a_2 \wedge \ldots \wedge a_m)\sigma$$

where the body of the chosen clause has replaced a_1 in the answer clause, and the MGU σ is applied to the whole answer clause.

An **SLD derivation** is a sequence of generalized answer clauses $\gamma_0, \gamma_1, \ldots,$ γ_n such that

- γ_0 is the answer clause corresponding to the original query. If the query is q, with free variables $V_1, \ldots, V_k$, the initial generalized answer clause γ_0 is

$$yes(V_1, \ldots, V_k) \leftarrow q.$$

- γ_i is obtained by selecting an atom a_1 in the body of γ_{i-1}; choosing a *copy* of a clause $a \leftarrow b_1 \wedge \ldots \wedge b_p$ in the knowledge base whose head, a, unifies with a_i; replacing a_1 with the body, $b_1 \wedge \ldots \wedge b_p$; and applying the unifier to the whole resulting answer clause.

  The main difference between this and the propositional top-down proof procedure (page 189) is that, for clauses with variables, the proof procedure must take *copies* of clauses from the knowledge base. The copying renames the variables in the clause with new names. This is both to remove name clashes between variables and because a single proof may use different instances of a clause.

- γ_n is an answer. That is, it is of the form

$$yes(t_1, \ldots, t_k) \leftarrow .$$

  When this occurs, the algorithm returns the answer

$$V_1 = t_1, \ldots, V_k = t_k.$$

Notice how the answer is extracted; the arguments to *yes* keep track of the instances of the variables in the initial query that lead to a successful proof.

Figure 13.4 (on the next page) gives a non-deterministic algorithm that answer queries by searching for SLD derivations. This is non-deterministic (page 88) in the sense that all derivations can be found by making appropriate choices that do not fail. If all choices fail, the algorithm fails, and there are no derivations. The "choose" on line 13 is implemented using search. Recall that $Unify(a_i, a)$ returns an MGU of a_i and a, if there is one, and $\perp$ if they do not unify. The algorithm for *Unify* is given in Figure 13.3 (page 601).

Example 13.23 Consider the database of Figure 13.2 (page 596) and the query

  ask $two\_doors\_east(R, r107)$.

Figure 13.5 (page 605) shows a successful derivation with answer $R = r111$.

```
1:  non-deterministic procedure Prove_datalog_TD(KB, q)
2:      Inputs
3:          KB: a set of definite clauses
4:          Query q: a set of atoms to prove, with variables V₁, ..., Vₖ
5:      Output
6:          substitution θ if KB ⊨ qθ and fail otherwise
7:      Local
8:          G is a generalized answer clause
9:      Set G to generalized answer clause yes(V₁, ..., Vₖ) ← q
10:     while G is not an answer do
11:         Suppose G is yes(t₁, ..., tₖ) ← a₁ ∧ a₂ ∧ ... ∧ aₘ
12:         select atom a₁ in the body of G
13:         choose clause a ← b₁ ∧ ... ∧ bₚ in KB
14:         Rename all variables in a ← b₁ ∧ ... ∧ bₚ to have new names
15:         Let σ be Unify(a₁, a). Fail if Unify returns ⊥.
16:         G := (yes(t₁, ..., tₖ) ← b₁ ∧ ... ∧ bₚ ∧ a₂ ∧ ... ∧ aₘ)σ
17:     return {V₁ = t₁, ..., Vₖ = tₖ} where G is yes(t₁, ..., tₖ) ←
```

Figure 13.4: Top-down definite clause proof procedure for Datalog

---

Note that this derivation used two instances of the rule

$$imm\_east(E, W) \leftarrow imm\_west(W, E).$$

One instance eventually substituted $r111$ for E, and one instance substituted $r109$ for E.

When the atom $imm\_west(M_1, R)$ was selected, other choices of the clause to resolve with would have resulted in a partial derivation that could not be completed.

13.5   Function Symbols

Datalog requires a name, using a constant, for every individual about which the system reasons. Often it is simpler to identify an individual in terms of its components, rather than requiring a separate constant for each individual.

Example 13.24 In many domains, you want to be able to refer to a time as an individual. You may want to say that some course is held at 11:30 a.m. You do not want a separate constant for each possible time, although this is possible. It is better to define times in terms of, say, the number of hours past midnight and the number of minutes past the hour. Similarly, you may want to reason with facts about particular dates. You cannot give a constant for each date, as

$yes(R) \leftarrow two\_doors\_east(R, r107)$
    resolve with $two\_doors\_east(E_1, W_1) \leftarrow$
                $imm\_east(E_1, M_1) \wedge imm\_east(M_1, W_1).$
    substitution: $\{E_1/R, W_1/r107\}$
$yes(R) \leftarrow imm\_east(R, M_1) \wedge imm\_east(M_1, r107)$
    select leftmost conjunct
    resolve with $imm\_east(E_2, W_2) \leftarrow imm\_west(W_2, E_2)$
    substitution: $\{E_2/R, W_2/M_1\}$
$yes(R) \leftarrow imm\_west(M_1, R) \wedge imm\_east(M_1, r107)$
    select leftmost conjunct
    resolve with $imm\_west(r109, r111)$
    substitution: $\{M_1/r109, R/r111\}$
$yes(r111) \leftarrow imm\_east(r109, r107)$
    resolve with $imm\_east(E_3, W_3) \leftarrow imm\_west(W_3, E_3)$
    substitution: $\{E_3/r109, W_3/r107\}$
$yes(r111) \leftarrow imm\_west(r107, r109)$
    resolve with $imm\_west(r107, r109)$
    substitution: $\{\}$
$yes(r111) \leftarrow$

Figure 13.5: A derivation for query $two\_doors\_east(R, r107)$

there are infinitely many possible dates. It is easier to define a date in terms of the year, the month, and the day.

Using a constant to name each individual means that the knowledge base can only represent a finite number of individuals, and the number of individuals is fixed when the knowledge base is built. However, you may want to reason about a potentially infinite set of individuals.

Example 13.25 Suppose you want to build a system that takes questions in English and answers them by consulting an online database. In this case, each sentence is an individual. You do not want to have to give each sentence its own name, because there are too many English sentences to name them all. It may be better to name the words and then to specify a sentence in terms of the sequence of words in the sentence. This approach may be more practical because there are far fewer words to name than sentences, and each word has its own natural name. You may also want to specify the words in terms of the letters in the word or in terms of their constituent parts.

Example 13.26 You may want to reason about lists of students. For example, you may be required to derive the average mark of a class of students. A list of students is an individual that has properties, such as its length and its seventh element. Although it may be possible to name each list, it is very inconvenient to do so. It is much better to have a way to describe lists in terms of their elements.

Function symbols allow you to describe individuals indirectly. Rather than using a constant to describe an individual, an individual is described in terms of other individuals.

Syntactically a **function symbol** is a word starting with a lower-case letter. We extend the definition of a term (page 586) so that a **term** is either a variable, a constant, or of the form $f(t_1, \ldots, t_n)$, where f is a function symbol and each t_i is a term. Apart from extending the definition of terms, the language stays the same.

Terms only appear within predicate symbols. You do not write clauses that imply terms. You may, however, write clauses that include atoms that use function symbols.

The semantics of Datalog (page 587) must be expanded to reflect the new syntax. The definition of ϕ (page 587) is extended so that ϕ also assigns to each n-ary function symbol a function from D^n into D. A constant can be seen as a 0-ary function symbol (i.e., one with no arguments). Thus, ϕ specifies which individual is denoted by each ground term.

Example 13.27 Suppose you want to define dates, such as 20 July 1969, which is the date the first time a human was on the moon. You can use the function symbol ce (common era) so that $ce(Y, M, D)$ denotes a date with year Y, month M and day D. For example, $ce(1969, jul, 20)$ may denote 20 July 1969. Similarly, you can define the symbol bce to denote the date before the common era.

The only way to use the function symbol is to write clauses that define relations using the function symbol. There is no notion of *defining* the ce function; dates are not in a computer any more than people are.

To use function symbols, you can write clauses that are quantified over the arguments of the function symbol. For example, Figure 13.6 (on the next page) defines the $before(D_1, D_2)$ relation that is true if date D_1 is before date D_2 in a day.

This assumes the predicate "$<$" represents the relation "less than" between integers. This could be represented in terms of clauses, but is often predefined, as it is in Prolog. The months are represented by constants that consist of the first three letters of the month.

% *before*(D_1, D_2) is true if date D_1 is before date D_2

> *before*$(ce(Y1, M1, D1), ce(Y2, M2, D2)) \leftarrow$
>> $Y1 < Y2.$
> *before*$(ce(Y, M1, D1), ce(Y, M2, D2)) \leftarrow$
>> *month*$(M1, N1) \wedge$
>> *month*$(M2, N2) \wedge$
>> $N1 < N2.$
> *before*$(ce(Y, M, D1), ce(Y, M, D2)) \leftarrow$
>> $D1 < D2.$

% *month*(M, N) is true if month M is the Nth month of the year.

> *month*$(jan, 1).$
> *month*$(feb, 2).$
> *month*$(mar, 3).$
> *month*$(apr, 4).$
> *month*$(may, 5).$
> *month*$(jun, 6).$
> *month*$(jul, 7).$
> *month*$(aug, 8).$
> *month*$(sep, 9).$
> *month*$(oct, 10).$
> *month*$(nov, 11).$
> *month*$(dec, 12).$

Figure 13.6: Axiomatizing a "before" relation for dates in the common era

A knowledge base consisting of clauses with function symbols can compute any computable function. Thus, a knowledge base can be interpreted as a program, called a **logic program**. Logic programs are Turing complete; they can compute any function computable on a digital computer.

This expansion of the language has a major impact. With just one function symbol and one constant, the language contains infinitely many ground terms and infinitely many ground atoms. The infinite number of terms can be used to describe an infinite number of individuals.

Function symbols are used to build data structures, as in the following example.

Example 13.28 A tree is a useful data structure. You could use a tree to build a syntactic representation of a sentence for a natural language processing system.

You could decide that a labeled tree is either of the form $node(N, LT, RT)$ or of the form $leaf(L)$. Thus, $node$ is a function from a name, a left tree, and a right tree into a tree. The function symbol $leaf$ denotes a function from the label of a leaf node into a tree.

The relation $at\_leaf(L, T)$ is true if label L is the label of a leaf in tree T. It can be defined by

> $at\_leaf(L, leaf(L))$.
> $at\_leaf(L, node(N, LT, RT)) \leftarrow$
> > $at\_leaf(L, LT)$.
> $at\_leaf(L, node(N, LT, RT)) \leftarrow$
> > $at\_leaf(L, RT)$.

This is an example of a structural recursive program. The rules cover all of the cases for each of the structures representing trees.

The relation $in\_tree(L, T)$, which is true if label L is the label of an interior node of tree T, can be defined by

> $in\_tree(L, node(L, LT, RT))$.
> $in\_tree(L, node(N, LT, RT)) \leftarrow$
> > $in\_tree(L, LT)$.
> $in\_tree(L, node(N, LT, RT)) \leftarrow$
> > $in\_tree(L, RT)$.

Example 13.29 A **list** is an ordered sequence of elements. You can reason about lists using just function symbols and constants, without the notion of a list being predefined in the language. A list is either the empty list or an element followed by a list. You can invent a constant to denote the empty list. Suppose you use the constant nil to denote the empty list. You can choose a function symbol, say $cons(Hd, Tl)$, with the intended interpretation that it denotes a list with first element Hd and rest of the list Tl. The list containing the elements a, b, c would then be represented as

> $cons(a, cons(b, cons(c, nil)))$.

To use lists, one must write predicates that do something with them. For example, the relation $append(X, Y, Z)$ that is true when X, Y, and Z are lists, such that Z contains the elements of X followed by the elements of Z, can be defined recursively by

> $append(nil, L, L)$.
> $append(cons(Hd, X), Y, cons(Hd, Z)) \leftarrow$
> > $append(X, Y, Z)$.

There is nothing special about $cons$ or nil; we could have just as well used *foo* and *bar*.

| First-Order and Second-Order Logic |

First-order predicate calculus is a logic that extends propositional calculus (page 173) to include atoms with function symbols and logical variables. All logical variables must have explicit quantification in terms of "for all" ($\forall$) and "there exists" ($\exists$) (page 591). The semantics of first-order predicate calculus is like the semantics of logic programs presented in this chapter, but with a richer set of operators.

The language of logic programs forms a pragmatic subset of first-order predicate calculus, which has been developed because it is useful for many tasks. First-order predicate calculus can be seen as a language that adds disjunction and explicit quantification to logic programs.

First-order logic is *first order* because it allows quantification over individuals in the domain. First-order logic allows neither predicates as variables nor quantification over predicates.

Second-order logic allows for quantification over first-order relations and predicates whose arguments are first-order relations. These are second-order relations. For example, the second-order logic formula

$$\forall R\ symmetric(R) \leftrightarrow (\forall X \forall Y\ R(X, Y) \to R(Y, X))$$

defines the second-order relation *symmetric*, which is true if its argument is a symmetric relation.

Second-order logic seems necessary for many applications because transitive closure is not first-order definable. For example, suppose you want *before* to be the transitive closure of *next*, where $next(X, s(X))$ is true. Think of *next* meaning the "next millisecond" and *before* denoting "before." The natural first-order definition would be the definition

$$\forall X \forall Y\ before(X, Y) \leftrightarrow (Y = s(X) \vee before(s(X), Y)).\qquad(13.1)$$

This expression does not accurately capture the definition, because, for example,

$$\forall X \forall Y\ before(X, Y) \to \exists W\ Y = s(W)$$

does not logically follow from Formula (13.1), because there are nonstandard models of Formula (13.1) with Y denoting *infinity*. To capture the transitive closure, you require a formula stating that *before* is the minimal predicate that satisfies the definition. This can be stated using second-order logic.

First-order logic is **semi-decidable**, which means that a sound and complete proof procedure exists in which every true statement can be proved, but it may not halt. Second-order logic is undecidable; no sound and complete proof procedure can be implemented on a Turing machine.

13.5.1 Proof Procedures with Function Symbols

The proof procedures with variables carry over for the case with function symbols. The main difference is that the class of terms is expanded to include function symbols.

The use of function symbols involves infinitely many terms. This means that, when forward chaining on the clauses, we have to ensure that the selection criterion for selecting clauses is fair (page 88).

Example 13.30 To see why fairness is important, consider the following clauses:

$num(0)$.

$num(s(N)) \leftarrow num(N)$.

$a \leftarrow b$.

b.

An unfair strategy could initially select the first of these clauses to forward chain on and, for every subsequent selection, select the second clause. The second clause can always be used to derive a new consequence. This strategy never selects either of the last two clauses and thus never derives a or b.

This problem of ignoring some clauses forever is known as **starvation**. A **fair** selection criterion is one such that any clause available to be selected will eventually be selected. The bottom-up proof procedure can generate an infinite sequence of consequences and if the selection is fair, each consequence will eventually be generated and so the proof procedure is complete.

The top-down proof procedure is the same as for Datalog (see Figure 13.4 (page 604)). Unification becomes more complicated, because it must recursively descend into the structure of terms. There is one change to the unification algorithm (page 601): a variable X does not unify with a term t in which X occurs and is not X itself. Checking for this condition is known as the **occurs check**. If the occurs check is not used and a variable is allowed to unify with a term in which it appears, the proof procedure becomes unsound, as shown in the following example.

Example 13.31 Consider the knowledge base with only one clause:

$lt(X, s(X))$.

Suppose the intended interpretation is the domain of integers in which lt means "less than" and $s(X)$ denotes the integer after X. The query ask $lt(Y, Y)$ should fail because it is false in the intended interpretation; there is no number less than itself. However, if X and $s(X)$ could unify, this query would succeed. In this case, the proof procedure would be unsound because something could be derived that is false in a model of the axioms.

The unification algorithm of Figure 13.3 (page 601) requires one change to find the most general unifier of two terms with function symbols. The algorithm should return $\perp$ if it selects an equality $\alpha = \beta$, where α is a variable and β is a term that is not α, but contains α (or the other way around). This step is the **occurs check**. The occurs check is sometimes omitted (e.g., in Prolog), because removing it makes the proof procedure more efficient, even though removing it does make the proof procedure unsound.

The following example shows the details of SLD resolution with function symbols.

Example 13.32 Consider the clauses

$append(c(A, X), Y, c(A, Z)) \leftarrow$
   $append(X, Y, Z).$
$append(nil, Z, Z).$

For now, ignore what this may mean. Like the computer, treat this as a problem of symbol manipulation. Consider the following query:

ask $append(F, c(L, nil), c(l, c(i, c(s, c(t, nil))))).$

The following is a derivation:

$yes(F, L) \leftarrow append(F, c(L, nil), c(l, c(i, c(s, c(t, nil)))))$
   resolve with $append(c(A_1, X_1), Y_1, c(A_1, Z_1)) \leftarrow append(X_1, Y_1, Z_1)$
   substitution: $\{F/c(l, X_1), Y_1/c(L, nil), A_1/l, Z_1/c(i, c(s, c(t, nil)))\}$
$yes(c(l, X_1), L) \leftarrow append(X_1, c(L, nil), c(i, c(s, c(t, nil))))$
   resolve with $append(c(A_2, X_2), Y_2, c(A_2, Z_2)) \leftarrow append(X_2, Y_2, Z_2)$
   substitution: $\{X_1/c(i, X_2), Y_2/c(L, nil), A_2/i, Z_2/c(s, c(t, nil))\}$
$yes(c(l, c(i, X_2)), L) \leftarrow append(X_2, c(L, nil), c(s, c(t, nil)))$
   resolve with $append(c(A_3, X_3), Y_3, c(A_3, Z_3)) \leftarrow append(X_3, Y_3, Z_3)$
   substitution: $\{X_2/c(s, X_3), Y_3/c(L, nil), A_3/s, Z_3/c(t, nil)\}$
$yes(c(l, c(i, c(s, X_3))), L) \leftarrow append(X_3, c(L, nil), c(t, nil))$

At this stage both clauses are applicable. Choosing the first clause gives

   resolve with $append(c(A_4, X_4), Y_4, c(A_4, Z_4)) \leftarrow append(X_4, Y_4, Z_4)$
   substitution: $\{X_3/c(t, X_4), Y_4/c(L, nil), A_4/t, Z_4/nil\}$
$yes(c(l, c(i, c(s, X_3))), L) \leftarrow append(X_4, c(L, nil), nil)$

At this point, there are no clauses whose head unifies with the atom in the generalized answer clause's body. The proof fails.

Choosing the second clause instead of the first gives

   resolve with $append(nil, Z_5, Z_5)$
   substitution: $\{Z_5/c(t, nil), X_3/nil, L/t\}$

$$yes(c(l,c(i,c(s,nil))),t) \leftarrow$$

At this point, the proof succeeds, with answer $F = c(l,c(i,c(s,nil)))$, $L = t$.

For the rest of this chapter, we use the "syntactic sugar" notation of Prolog for representing lists. The empty list, *nil*, is written as [ ]. The list with first element E and the rest of the list R, which was $cons(E,R)$ in Example 13.29 (page 608) is now written as $[E \mid R]$. There is one other notational simplification: $[X \mid [Y]]$ is written as $[X,Y]$, where Y can be a sequence of values. For example, $[a \mid [\,]]$ is written as $[a]$, and $[b \mid [a \mid [\,]]]$ is written as $[b,a]$. The term $[a \mid [b \mid C]]$ is written as $[a,b \mid C]$.

Example 13.33 Using the list notation, *append* from the previous example can be written as

$$append([A \mid X], Y, [A \mid Z]) \leftarrow$$
$$\quad append(X,Y,Z).$$
$$append([\,], Z, Z).$$

The query

$$ask \; append(F, [L], [l,i,s,t])$$

has an answer $F = [l,i,s]$, $L = t$. The proof is exactly as in the previous example. As far as the proof procedure is concerned, nothing has changed; there is just a renamed function symbol and constant.

13.6   Applications in Natural Language

Natural language processing is an interesting and difficult domain in which to develop and evaluate representation and reasoning theories. All of the problems of AI arise in this domain; solving "the natural language problem" is as difficult as solving "the AI problem" because any domain can be expressed in natural language. The field of **computational linguistics** has a wealth of techniques and knowledge. In this book, we only give an overview.

There are at least three reasons for studying natural language processing:

- Users want to communicate on their terms and many prefer natural language to some artificial language or a graphical user interface. This is particularly important for casual users and those users, such as managers and children, who have neither the time nor the inclination to learn new interaction skills.

- There is a vast store of information recorded in natural language that could be accessible using computers. Information is constantly generated in the form of books, news, business and government reports, and scientific papers, many of which are available online. A system requiring a great deal of information must be able to process natural language to retrieve much of the information available on computers.

- Many of the problems of AI arise in a very clear and explicit form in natural language processing and, thus, it is a good domain in which to experiment with general theories.

The development of natural language processing provides the possibility of natural language interfaces to knowledge bases and natural language translation.

There are at least three major aspects of natural language:

Syntax The syntax describes the form of the language. It is usually specified by a grammar. Natural language is much more complicated than the formal languages used for logics and computer programs.

Semantics The semantics provides the meaning of the utterances or sentences of the language. Although general semantic theories exist, when we build a natural language understanding system for a particular application, we try to use the simplest representation we can. For example, in the development that follows, there is a fixed mapping between words and concepts in the knowledge base, which is inappropriate for many domains but simplifies development.

Pragmatics The pragmatic component explains how the utterances relate to the world. To understand language, an agent should consider more than the sentence; it has to take into account the context of the sentence, the state of the world, the goals of the speaker and the listener, special conventions, and the like.

To understand the difference among these aspects, consider the following sentences, which might appear at the start of an AI textbook

- *This book is about artificial intelligence.*
- *The green frogs sleep soundly.*
- *Colorless green ideas sleep furiously.*
- *Furiously sleep ideas green colorless.*

The first sentence would be quite appropriate at the start of such a book; it is syntactically, semantically, and pragmatically well formed. The second sentence is syntactically and semantically well formed, but it would appear very strange at the start of an AI book; it is not pragmatically well formed for that context. The last two sentences are attributed to linguist Noam Chomsky [1957]. The third sentence is syntactically well formed, but it is semantically nonsensical. The fourth sentence is syntactically ill formed; it does not make any sense – syntactically, semantically, or pragmatically.

We show in the next section how to write a natural language query answering system that is applicable to very narrow domains for which stylized natural language is adequate and in which little, if any, ambiguity exists. At the other extreme are shallow but broad systems, such as the help system presented in Example 8.35 (page 396) and Example 10.5 (page 493). Developing useful systems that are both deep and broad is difficult.

13.6.1 Using Definite Clauses for Context-Free Grammars

This section shows how to use definite clauses to represent aspects of the syntax and semantics of natural language.

Languages are defined by their legal sentences. Sentences are sequences of symbols. Here we assume that a **sentence** is represented as a list of atoms, where there is an atom for each **word** in the language. More sophisticated models often represent words in terms of their parts, for example removing the ending such as "ing" and "er".

The legal sentences are specified by a grammar.

Our first approximation of natural language is a context-free grammar. A **context-free grammar** is a set of **rewrite rules**, with **non-terminal** symbols transforming into a sequence of terminal and non-terminal symbols. A sentence of the language is a sequence of **terminal symbols** generated by such rewriting rules. For example, the grammar rule

$$sentence \longmapsto noun\_phrase, verb\_phrase$$

means that a non-terminal symbol *sentence* can be a *noun_phrase* followed by a *verb_phrase*. The symbol "$\longmapsto$" means "can be rewritten as."

For natural languages, the terminal symbols are typically the words of the language. If a sentence of natural language is represented as a list of words, the following definite clause means that a list of words is a sentence if it is a noun phrase followed by a verb phrase:

$$sentence(S) \leftarrow noun\_phrase(N) \wedge verb\_phrase(V) \wedge append(N, V, S).$$

To say that the word "computer" is a noun, you could write

$$noun([computer]).$$

There is an alternative, simpler representation of context-free grammar rules using definite clauses that does not require an explicit *append*, known as a **definite clause grammar (DCG)**. Each non-terminal symbol *s* becomes a predicate with two arguments, $s(L_1, L_2)$, which is true when list L_2 is an ending of list L_1 such that all of the words in L_1 before L_2 form a sequence of words of the category *s*. Lists L_1 and L_2 together form a **difference list** of words that make the class given by the non-terminal symbol, because it is the difference of these that forms the syntactic category.

Example 13.34 Under this representation, *noun_phrase*(L_1, L_2) is true if list L_2 is an ending of list L_1 such that all of the words in L_1 before L_2 form a noun phrase. L_2 is the rest of the sentence. You can think of L_2 as representing a position in a list after position L_1. The difference list represents the words between these positions.

The atomic symbol

$$noun\_phrase([the, student, passed, the, course, with, a, computer],$$
$$[passed, the, course, with, a, computer])$$

is true in the intended interpretation because "the student" forms a noun phrase.

The grammar rule

$$sentence \longmapsto noun\_phrase, verb\_phrase$$

means that there is a sentence between some L_0 and L_2 if there exists a noun phrase between L_0 and L_1 and a verb phrase between L_1 and L_2:

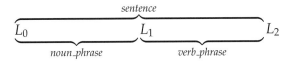

This grammar rule can be specified as the clause:

$$sentence(L_0, L_2) \leftarrow$$
$$\qquad noun\_phrase(L_0, L_1) \land$$
$$\qquad verb\_phrase(L_1, L_2).$$

In general, the rule

$$h \longmapsto b_1, b_2, \ldots, b_n$$

says that h is composed of a b_1 followed by a b_2, ..., followed by a b_n, and is written as the definite clause

$$h(L_0, L_n) \leftarrow$$
$$\qquad b_1(L_0, L_1) \land$$
$$\qquad b_2(L_1, L_2) \land$$
$$\qquad \vdots$$
$$\qquad b_n(L_{n-1}, L_n).$$

using the interpretation

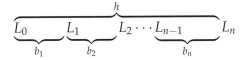

where the L_i are new variables.

To say that non-terminal h gets mapped to the terminal symbols, $t_1, ..., t_n$, one would write

$$h([t_1, \cdots, t_n \mid T], T)$$

using the interpretation

$$\overbrace{t_1, \cdots, t_n}^{h} T$$

Thus, $h(L_1, L_2)$ is true if $L_1 = [t_1, ..., t_n \mid L_2]$.

Example 13.35 The rule that specifies that the non-terminal h can be rewritten to the non-terminal a followed by the non-terminal b followed by the terminal symbols c and d, followed by the non-terminal symbol e followed by the terminal symbol f and the non-terminal symbol g, can be written as

$$h \longmapsto a, b, [c, d], e, [f], g$$

and can be represented as

$$
\begin{aligned}
h(L_0, L_6) \leftarrow \\
\quad a(L_0, L_1) \wedge \\
\quad b(L_1, [c, d \mid L_3]) \wedge \\
\quad e(L_3, [f \mid L_5]) \wedge \\
\quad g(L_5, L_6).
\end{aligned}
$$

Note that the translations $L_2 = [c, d \mid L_3]$ and $L_4 = [f \mid L_5]$ were done manually.

Figure 13.7 (on the next page) axiomatizes a simple grammar of English. Figure 13.8 (page 618) gives a simple dictionary of words and their parts of speech, which can be used with this grammar.

Example 13.36 Consider the sentence "The student passed the course with a computer." This is represented as a list of atoms, one for each word.

For the grammar of Figure 13.7 (on the next page) and the dictionary of Figure 13.8 (page 618), the query

ask *noun_phrase*([*the, student, passed, the, course, with, a, computer*], R).

will return

$$R = [\textit{passed, the, course, with, a, computer}].$$

For the query,

ask *sentence*([*the, student, passed, the, course, with, a, computer*], [ ]).

% A sentence is a noun phrase followed by a verb phrase.

$$sentence(L_0, L_2) \leftarrow$$
$$noun\_phrase(L_0, L_1) \wedge$$
$$verb\_phrase(L_1, L_2).$$

% A noun phrase is a determiner followed by adjectives followed by a noun
% followed by an optional prepositional phrase.

$$noun\_phrase(L_0, L_4) \leftarrow$$
$$det(L_0, L_1) \wedge$$
$$adjectives(L_1, L_2) \wedge$$
$$noun(L_2, L_3) \wedge$$
$$pp(L_3, L_4).$$

% Adjectives consist of a (possibly empty) sequence of adjectives.

$$adjectives(L, L).$$
$$adjectives(L_0, L_2) \leftarrow$$
$$adj(L_0, L_1) \wedge$$
$$adjectives(L_1, L_2).$$

% An optional prepositional phrase is either nothing or a preposition followed
% by a noun phrase.

$$pp(L, L).$$
$$pp(L_0, L_2) \leftarrow$$
$$preposition(L_0, L_1) \wedge$$
$$noun\_phrase(L_1, L_2).$$

% A verb phrase is a verb followed by a noun phrase and an optional
% prepositional phrase.

$$verb\_phrase(L_0, L_3) \leftarrow$$
$$verb(L_0, L_1) \wedge$$
$$noun\_phrase(L_1, L_2) \wedge$$
$$pp(L_2, L_3).$$

Figure 13.7: A context-free grammar for a restricted subset of English

$det(L, L)$.

$det([a \mid T], T)$.

$det([the \mid T], T)$.

$noun([student \mid T], T)$.

$noun([course \mid T], T)$.

$noun([computer \mid T], T)$.

$adj([practical \mid T], T)$.

$verb([passed \mid T], T)$.

$preposition([with \mid T], T)$.

Figure 13.8: A simple dictionary

the computer first proves *noun_phrase*, which has a unique answer, as above. It then tries to prove *verb_phrase*.

This sentence has two different parses, one using the clause instance

$verb\_phrase([passed, the, course, with, a, computer], [\,]) \leftarrow$
$\qquad verb([passed, the, course, with, a, computer],$
$\qquad\qquad [the, course, with, a, computer]) \wedge$
$\qquad noun\_phrase([the, course, with, a, computer], [\,]) \wedge$
$\qquad pp([\,], [\,])$

and one using the instance

$verb\_phrase([passed, the, course, with, a, computer], [\,]) \leftarrow$
$\qquad verb([passed, the, course, with, a, computer],$
$\qquad\qquad [the, course, with, a, computer]) \wedge$
$\qquad noun\_phrase([the, course, with, a, computer], [with, a, computer]) \wedge$
$\qquad pp([with, a, computer], [\,])$.

In the first of these, the prepositional phrase modifies the noun phrase (i.e., the course is with a computer); and in the second, the prepositional phrase modifies the verb phrase (i.e., the course was passed with a computer).

13.6.2 Augmenting the Grammar

A context-free grammar does not adequately express the complexity of the grammar of natural languages, such as English. Two mechanisms can be added to this grammar to make it more expressive:

- extra arguments to the non-terminal symbols and

- arbitrary constraints on the rules.

The extra arguments enable us to do several things: to construct a parse tree, to represent the semantic structure of a sentence, to incrementally build a query that represents a question to a database, and to accumulate information about phrase agreement (such as number, tense, gender, and person).

13.6.3   Building Structures for Non-terminals

You can add an extra argument to the predicates to represent a parse tree, forming a rule such as

$$sentence(L_0, L_2, s(NP, VP)) \leftarrow$$
$$noun\_phrase(L_0, L_1, NP) \wedge$$
$$verb\_phrase(L_1, L_2, VP).$$

which means that the parse tree for a sentence is of the form $s(NP, VP)$, where NP is the parse tree for the noun phrase and VP is the parse tree for the verb phrase.

This is important if you want some result from the syntactic analysis, not just to know whether the sentence is syntactically valid. The notion of a parse tree is a simplistic form of what is required because it does not adequately represent the meaning or the *deep structure* of a sentence. For example, you would really like to recognize that "Sam taught the AI course" and "the AI course was taught by Sam" have the same meaning, only differing in the active or passive voice.

13.6.4   Canned Text Output

There is nothing in the definition of the grammar that requires English input and the parse tree as output. A query of the grammar rules with the meaning of the sentence bound and a free variable representing the sentence can produce a sentence that matches the meaning.

One such use of grammar rules is to provide canned text output from logic terms; the output is a sentence in English that matches the logic term. This is useful for producing English versions of atoms, rules, and questions that a user – who may not know the intended interpretation of the symbols, or even the syntax of the formal language – can more easily understand.

Example 13.37   Figure 13.9 (on the next page) shows a grammar for producing canned text on schedule information. The query

ask $trans(scheduled(w21, cs422, clock(15, 30), above(csci333)), T, [\ ])$.

% $trans(Term, L_0, L_1)$ is true if $Term$ translates into the words contained in the
% difference list $L_0 - L_1$.

$trans(scheduled(S, C, L, R), L_1, L_8) \leftarrow$
  $trans(session(S), L_1, [of \mid L_3]) \land$
  $trans(course(C), L_3, [is, scheduled, at \mid L_5]) \land$
  $trans(time(L), L_5, [in \mid L_7]) \land$
  $trans(room(R), L_7, L_8)$.
$trans(session(w21), [the, winter, 2021, session \mid T], T)$.
$trans(course(cs422), [the, advanced, artificial, intelligence, course \mid T], T)$.
$trans(time(clock(0, M)), [12, :, M, am \mid T], T)$.
$trans(time(clock(H, M)), [H, :, M, am \mid T], T) \leftarrow$
  $H > 0 \land H < 12$.
$trans(time(clock(12, M)), [12, :, M, pm \mid T], T)$.
$trans(time(clock(H, M)), [H_1, :, M, pm \mid T], T) \leftarrow$
  $H > 12 \land$
  H_1 is $H - 12$.
$trans(room(above(R)), [the, room, above \mid L_1], L_2) \leftarrow$
  $trans(room(R), L_1, L_2)$.
$trans(room(csci333), [the, computer, science, department, office \mid T], T)$.

Figure 13.9: Grammar for output of canned English

produces the answer $T = [the, winter, 2021, session, of, the, advanced, artificial,$
$intelligence, course, is, scheduled, at, 3, :, 30, pm, in, the, room, above, the, computer,$
$science, department, office]$. This list could be rewritten as a sentence to the user.

This code used the Prolog infix predicate "**is**", where "V is E" is true when
expression E evaluates to number V, and the binary relations $>$ and $<$.

This grammar would probably not be useful for understanding natural language, because it requires a very stylized form of English; the user would have to use the exact translation of a term to get a legal parse.

13.6.5 Enforcing Constraints

Natural language imposes constraints which, for example, disallow sentences such as "A students eat." Words in a sentence must satisfy some agreement criteria. "A students eat." fails to satisfy the criterion of number agreement, which specifies whether the nouns and verbs are singular or plural.

Number agreement can be enforced in the grammar by parametrizing the non-terminals by the number and making sure that the numbers of the different parts of speech agree. You only need to add an extra argument to the relevant non-terminals.

Example 13.38 The grammar of Figure 13.10 (on the next page) does not allow "a students," "the student eat," or "the students eats," because all have number disagreement, but it allows "a green student eats," "the students," or "the student," because "the" can be either singular or plural.

To parse the sentence "the student eats," you issue the query

$$\text{ask } sentence([the, student, eats], [\,], Num, T)$$

and the answer returned is

$Num = singular,$
$T = s(np(definite, [\,], student, nopp), vp(eat, nonp, nopp)).$

To parse the sentence "the students eat," you issue the query

$$\text{ask } sentence([the, students, eat], [\,], Num, T)$$

and the answer returned is

$Num = plural,$
$T = s(np(definite, [\,], student, nopp), vp(eat, nonp, nopp)).$

To parse the sentence "a student eats," you issue the query

$$\text{ask } sentence([a, student, eats], [\,], Num, T)$$

and the answer returned is

$Num = singular,$
$T = s(np(indefinite, [\,], student, nopp), vp(eat, nonp, nopp)).$

Note that the only difference between the answers is whether the subject is singular and whether the determiner is definite.

13.6.6 Building a Natural Language Interface to a Database

You can augment the preceding grammar to implement a simple natural language interface to a database. The idea is that, instead of transforming subphrases into parse trees, you transform them directly into queries on a knowledge base. To do this, make the following simplifying assumptions, which are not always true, but form a useful first approximation:

- **nouns** and **adjectives** correspond to properties

% A sentence is a noun phrase followed by a verb phrase.

$sentence(L_0, L_2, Num, s(NP, VP)) \leftarrow$
  $noun\_phrase(L_0, L_1, Num, NP) \land$
  $verb\_phrase(L_1, L_2, Num, VP).$

% A noun phrase is empty or a determiner followed by adjectives followed by
% a noun followed by an optional prepositional phrase.

$noun\_phrase(L, L, Num, nonp).$
$noun\_phrase(L_0, L_4, Num, np(Det, Mods, Noun, PP)) \leftarrow$
  $det(L_0, L_1, Num, Det) \land$
  $adjectives(L_1, L_2, Mods) \land$
  $noun(L_2, L_3, Num, Noun) \land$
  $pp(L_3, L_4, PP).$

% A verb phrase is a verb, followed by a noun phrase, followed by an optional
% prepositional phrase.

$verb\_phrase(L_0, L_3, Num, vp(V, NP, PP)) \leftarrow$
  $verb(L_0, L_1, Num, V) \land$
  $noun\_phrase(L_1, L_2, N2, NP) \land$
  $pp(L_2, L_3, PP).$

% An optional prepositional phrase is either nothing or a preposition followed
% by a noun phrase. Only the null case is given here.

$pp(L, L, nopp).$

% Adjectives is a sequence of adjectives. Only the null case is given here.

$adjectives(L, L, [\,]).$

% The dictionary.

$det([a \mid L], L, singular, indefinite).$
$det([the \mid L], L, Num, definite).$
$noun([student \mid L], L, singular, student).$
$noun([students \mid L], L, plural, student).$
$verb([eats \mid L], L, singular, eat).$
$verb([eat \mid L], L, plural, eat).$

Figure 13.10: Grammar to enforce number agreement and build a parse tree

- **verbs** and **prepositions** correspond to a binary relation between two individuals, the **subject** and the **object**.

In this case, a noun phrase becomes an individual with a set of properties defining it. To answer a question, the system can find an individual that has these properties. A noun phrase followed by a verb phrase describes two individuals constrained by the verb.

Example 13.39 In the sentence, "a tall student passed a math course", the phrase "a tall student" is the subject of the verb "passed" and the phrase "a math course" is the object of the verb. For the individual S that is the subject, $tall(S)$ and $student(S)$ are true. For the individual O that is the object, $course(O)$ and $dept(O, math)$. The verb specifies that $passed(S, O)$. Thus the question "Who is a tall student that passed a math course?" can be converted into the query:

ask $tall(S) \wedge student(S) \wedge passed(S, O) \wedge course(O) \wedge dept(O, math)$.

The phrase "a tall student enrolled in cs312 that passed a math course" could be translated into

ask $tall(X) \wedge student(X) \wedge enrolled\_in(X, cs312) \wedge passed(X, O)$
$\wedge course(O) \wedge dept(O, math)$.

Figure 13.11 (on the next page) shows a simple grammar that parses an English question and answers it at the same time. This ignores most of the grammar of English, such as the differences between prepositions and verbs or between determiners and adjectives, and makes a guess at the meaning, even if the question is not grammatical. Adjectives, nouns and noun phrases refer to an individual. The extra argument to the predicates is an individual which satisfies the adjectives and nouns. Here an *mp* is a modifying phrase, which could be a prepositional phrase or a relative clause. A *reln*, either a verb or a preposition, is a relation between two individuals, the subject and the object, so these are extra arguments to the *reln* predicate.

Example 13.40 Suppose $question(Q, A)$ means A is an answer to question Q, where a question is a list of words. The following provides some ways questions can be asked from the clauses of Figure 13.11 (on the next page), even given the very limited vocabulary used there.

The following clause allows it to answer questions, such as "Is a tall student enrolled in a computer science course?" and returns the student:

$question([is \mid L_0], Ind) \leftarrow$
$\quad noun\_phrase(L_0, L_1, Ind) \wedge$
$\quad mp(L_1, [\,], Ind)$.

% A noun phrase is a determiner followed by adjectives followed by a noun
% followed by an optional modifying phrase:

$\quad$ *noun_phrase*$(L_1, L_4, Ind) \leftarrow$
$\qquad$ *adjectives*$(L_1, L_2, Ind) \land$
$\qquad$ *noun*$(L_2, L_3, Ind) \land$
$\qquad$ *mp*(L_3, L_4, Ind).

% Adjectives consist of a sequence of adjectives.

$\quad$ *adjectives*$(L_0, L_2, Ind) \leftarrow$
$\qquad$ *adj*$(L_0, L_1, Ind) \land$
$\qquad$ *adjectives*(L_1, L_2, Ind).
$\quad$ *adjectives*(L, L, Ind).

% An optional modifying phrase / relative clause is either a relation (verb or
% preposition) followed by a noun-phrase or nothing

$\quad$ *mp*$(L_0, L_2, Subject) \leftarrow$
$\qquad$ *reln*$(L_0, L_1, Subject, Object) \land$
$\qquad$ *noun_phrase*$(L_1, L_2, Object)$.
$\quad$ *mp*(L, L, Ind).

% *adj*(L_0, L_1, Ind) is true if $L_0 - L_1$ is an adjective that is true of *Ind*

$\quad$ *adj*$([computer, science \mid L], L, Ind) \leftarrow dept(Ind, comp\_sci)$.
$\quad$ *adj*$([tall \mid L], L, Ind) \leftarrow tall(Ind)$.
$\quad$ *adj*$([a \mid L], L, Ind)$. $\quad$ % *a* is treated as an adjective

% *noun*(L_0, L_1, Ind) is true if $L_0 - L_1$ is a noun that is true of *Ind*

$\quad$ *noun*$([course \mid L], L, Ind) \leftarrow course(Ind)$.
$\quad$ *noun*$([student \mid L], L, Ind) \leftarrow student(Ind)$.

% The following are for proper nouns:

$\quad$ *noun*$([Ind \mid L], L, Ind) \leftarrow course(Ind)$.
$\quad$ *noun*$([Ind \mid L], L, Ind) \leftarrow student(Ind)$.

% *reln*(L_0, L_1, Sub, Obj) is true if $L_0 - L_1$ is a relation on individuals *Sub* and *Obj*

$\quad$ *reln*$([enrolled, in \mid L], L, Subject, Object) \leftarrow enrolled\_in(Subject, Object)$.
$\quad$ *reln*$([passed \mid L], L, Subject, Object) \leftarrow passed(Subject, Object)$.

Figure 13.11: A grammar that directly answers a question

The following rule is used to answer questions, such as "Who is enrolled in a computer science course?", or "Who is enrolled in cs312" (assuming that $course(cs312)$ is true):

$question([who, is \mid L_0], Ind) \leftarrow$
$\qquad mp(L_0, [\,], Ind).$

The following rule is used to answer questions, such as "Who is a tall student?":

$question([who, is \mid L], Ind) \leftarrow$
$\qquad noun\_phrase(L, [\,], Ind).$

The following rule allows it to answer questions, such as "Who is tall?":

$question([who, is \mid L], Ind) \leftarrow$
$\qquad adjectives(L, [\,], Ind).$

The following rule can be used to answer questions, such as "Which tall student passed a computer science course?" or even "Which tall student enrolled in a math course passed a computer science course?":

$question([which \mid L_0], Ind) \leftarrow$
$\qquad noun\_phrase(L_0, L_1, Ind) \wedge$
$\qquad mp(L_1, [\,], Ind).$

The following rule allows it to answer questions that have "is" between the noun phrase and the modifying phrase, such as "Which tall student is enrolled in a computer science course?" or "Which student enrolled in a math course is enrolled in a computer science course?":

$question([which \mid L_0], Ind) \leftarrow$
$\qquad noun\_phrase(L_0, [is \mid L_1], Ind) \wedge$
$\qquad mp(L_1, [\,], Ind).$

The preceding grammar directly found an answer to the natural language question. One problem with this way of answering questions is that it is difficult to separate the cases where the program could not parse the language from the case where there were no answers; in both cases the answer is "no". This makes it difficult to debug such a program. An alternative is instead of directly querying the knowledge base while parsing, to build a **logical form** of the natural language – a logical proposition that conveys the meaning of the utterance – before asking it of the knowledge base. The semantic form can be used for other tasks such as telling the system knowledge, paraphrasing natural language, or even translating it into a different language.

You can construct a query by allowing noun phrases to return an individual and a list of constraints imposed by the noun phrase on the individual. Appropriate grammar rules are specified in Figure 13.12 (on the next page), and they are used with the dictionary of Figure 13.13 (page 627).

% A noun phrase is a determiner followed by adjectives followed by a noun
% followed by an optional prepositional phrase.

$noun\_phrase(L_0, L_4, Ind, C_0, C_4) \leftarrow$
$\quad det(L_0, L_1, Ind, C_0, C_1) \wedge$
$\quad adjectives(L_1, L_2, Ind, C_1, C_2) \wedge$
$\quad noun(L_2, L_3, Ind, C_2, C_3) \wedge$
$\quad pp(L_3, L_4, Ind, C_3, C_4).$

% Adjectives consist of a sequence of adjectives.

$adjectives(L, L, Ind, C, C).$
$adjectives(L_0, L_2, Ind, C_0, C_2) \leftarrow$
$\quad adj(L_0, L_1, Ind, C_0, C_1) \wedge$
$\quad adjectives(L_1, L_2, Ind, C_1, C_2).$

% An optional prepositional phrase is either nothing or a preposition followed
% by a noun phrase.

$pp(L, L, Ind, C, C).$
$pp(L_0, L_2, Sub, C_0, C_2) \leftarrow$
$\quad preposition(L_0, L_1, Sub, Obj, C_0, C_1) \wedge$
$\quad noun\_phrase(L_1, L_2, Obj, C_1, C_2).$

Figure 13.12: A grammar that constructs a query

In this grammar,

$noun\_phrase(L_0, L_1, O, C_0, C_1)$

means that list L_1 is an ending of list L_0, and the words in L_0 before L_1 form a
noun phrase. This noun phrase refers to the individual O. C_0 is an ending of
C_1, and the formulas in C_1, but not in C_0, are the constraints on the individual
O imposed by the noun phrase.

Procedurally, L_0 is the list of words to be parsed, and L_1 is the list of remaining words after the noun phrase. C_0 is the list of conditions coming into
the noun-phrase, and C_1 is C_0 with the extra conditions imposed by the noun-
phrase added.

Example 13.41 The query

ask $noun\_phrase([a, computer, science, course], [\,], Ind, [\,], C).$

will return

$C = [course(Ind), dept(Ind, comp\_science)].$

$det(L, L, O, C, C)$.

$det([a \mid T], T, O, C, C)$.

$det([the \mid T], T, O, C, C)$.

$noun([course \mid T], T, O, C, [course(O) \mid C])$.

$noun([student \mid T], T, O, C, [student(O) \mid C])$.

$noun([john \mid T], T, john, C, C)$.

$noun([cs312 \mid T], T, 312, C, C)$.

$adj([computer, science \mid T], T, O, C, [dept(O, comp\_science) \mid C])$.

$adj([tall \mid T], T, O, C, [tall(O) \mid C])$.

$preposition([enrolled, in \mid T], T, O_1, O_2, C, [enrolled(O_1, O_2) \mid C])$.

Figure 13.13: A dictionary for constructing a query

The query

> ask $noun\_phrase([a, tall, student, enrolled, in, a, computer,$
> $science, course], [\,], P, [\,], C)$.

returns

> $C = [course(X), dept(X, comp\_science), enrolled(P, X), student(P),$
> $tall(P)]$.

If the elements of list C are queried against a database that uses these relations and constants, precisely the tall students enrolled in a computer science course could be found.

13.6.7 Limitations

So far, we have assumed a very simple form of natural language. Our aim was to show what could be easily accomplished with simple tools rather than with a comprehensive study of natural language. Useful front ends to databases can be built with the tools presented by, for example, constraining the domain sufficiently and asking the user, if necessary, which of multiple competing interpretations are intended.

This discussion of natural language processing assumes that natural language is compositional; the meaning of the whole can be derived from the meaning of the parts. Compositionality is, in general, a false assumption. You usually must know the context and the situation in the world to discern what is meant by an utterance. Many types of ambiguity exist that can only be resolved by understanding the context of the words.

For example, one cannot always determine the correct reference of a description without knowledge of the context and the situation. A description does not always refer to a uniquely determined individual.

Example 13.42 Consider the following paragraph:

> The student took many courses. Two computer science courses and one mathematics course were particularly difficult. *The mathematics course...*

The referent is defined by the context and not just the description "*The mathematics course.*" There could be more mathematics courses, but we know from context that the phrase is referring to the particularly difficult one taken by the student.

Many problems of reference arise in database applications if the use of *"the"* or *"it"* is allowed or if words that have more than one meaning are permitted. Context is used to disambiguate references in natural language. Consider:

> *Who is the head of the mathematics department?*
> *Who is her secretary?*

It is clear from the previous sentence who "her" refers to, as long as the reader understands that heads are people who have a gender, but departments do not.

These examples and Winograd Schemas (page 5) demonstrate the importance of **pragmatics** (page 613), including context and background knowledge, in understanding natural language.

13.7 Equality

Sometimes it is useful to use more than one term to name a single individual. For example, the terms $4 * 4$, 2^4, $273 - 257$, and 16 may denote the same number. Sometimes, you want to have each name refer to a different individual. For example, you may want unique names for different courses in a university. Sometimes you do not know whether or not two names denote the same individual – for example, whether the 8 a.m. delivery person is the same as the 1 p.m. delivery person.

This section considers the role of equality, which allows us to represent whether or not two terms denote the same individual in the world. Note that, in the definite clause language presented earlier in the chapter, all of the answers were valid whether or not terms denoted the same individuals.

Equality is a special predicate symbol with a standard domain-independent intended interpretation.

Term t_1 **equals** term t_2, written $t_1 = t_2$, is true in interpretation I if t_1 and t_2 denote the same individual in I.

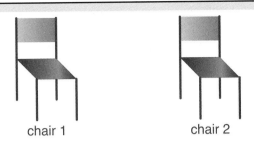

chair 1   chair 2

Figure 13.14: Two chairs

Equality does *not* mean similarity. If *a* and *b* are constants and $a = b$, it is not the case that there are two things that are similar or even identical. Rather, it means there is one thing with two names.

Example 13.43 Consider the world of two chairs given in Figure 13.14. In this world it is *not* true that $chair1 = chair2$, even though the two chairs may be identical in all respects; without representing the exact position of the chairs, they cannot be distinguished. It may be the case that $chairOnRight = chair2$. It is not the case that the chair on the right is *similar* to chair2. It *is* chair2.

13.7.1 Allowing Equality Assertions

Without allowing equality in the head of clauses, the only thing that is equal to a term in all interpretations is itself.

It is often useful to be able to assert or infer that two terms denote the same individual, such as $chairOnRight = chair2$. To allow this, the representation and reasoning system must be able to derive what follows from a knowledge base that includes clauses with equality in the head of clauses. There are two ways of doing this. The first is to axiomatize equality like any other predicate. The other is to build special-purpose inference machinery for equality.

Axiomatizing Equality

Equality can be axiomatized as follows. The first three axioms state that equality is reflexive, symmetric, and transitive:

$$X = X.$$
$$X = Y \leftarrow Y = X.$$
$$X = Z \leftarrow X = Y \wedge Y = Z.$$

The other axioms depend on the set of function and relation symbols in the language; thus, they form what is called an **axiom schema**.

The first schema specifies substituting term with an equal term does not affect the value of the function. The axiom schema is that for every *n*-ary function symbol f, there is a rule

$$f(X_1, \ldots, X_n) = f(Y_1, \ldots, Y_n) \leftarrow X_1 = Y_1 \wedge \cdots \wedge X_n = Y_n.$$

Similarly, for each n-ary predicate symbol p, there is a rule of the form

$$p(X_1, \ldots, X_n) \leftarrow p(Y_1, \ldots, Y_n) \wedge X_1 = Y_1 \wedge \cdots \wedge X_n = Y_n.$$

Example 13.44 The binary function $cons(X, Y)$ requires the axiom

$$cons(X_1, X_2) = cons(Y_1, Y_2) \leftarrow X_1 = Y_1 \wedge X_2 = Y_2.$$

The ternary relationship $prop(I, P, V)$ requires the axiom

$$prop(I_1, P_1, V_1) \leftarrow prop(I_2, P_2, V_2) \wedge I_1 = I_2 \wedge P_1 = P_2 \wedge V_1 = V_2.$$

Having these axioms explicit as part of the knowledge base turns out to be very inefficient. Moreover, the use of these rules is not guaranteed to halt using a top-down depth-first interpreter. For example, the symmetric axiom will cause an infinite loop unless identical subgoals are noticed.

Special-Purpose Equality Reasoning

Paramodulation is a way to augment a proof procedure to implement equality. The general idea is that, if $t_1 = t_2$, any occurrence of t_1 can be replaced by t_2. Equality can thus be treated as a **rewrite rule**, substituting equals for equals. This approach works best if you can select a **canonical representation** for each individual, which is a term that other representations for that individual can be mapped into.

One classic example is the representation of numbers. There are many terms that represent the same number (e.g., $4 * 4$, $13 + 3$, $273 - 257$, 2^4, 4^2, 16), but typically we treat the sequence of digits (in base ten) as the canonical representation of the number.

Universities invented student numbers to provide a canonical representation for each student. Different students with the same name are distinguishable and different names for the same person can be mapped to the person's student number.

13.7.2 Unique Names Assumption

Instead of being agnostic about the equality of each term and expecting the user to axiomatize which names denote the same individual and which denote different individuals, it is often easier to have the convention that different ground terms denote different individuals.

Example 13.45 Consider a student database example where a student must have two courses as science electives. Suppose a student has passed *math302* and *psyc303*; then you only know whether they have passed two courses if you know *math302* $\neq$ *psyc303*. That is, the constants *math302* and *psyc303* denote different courses. Thus, you must know which course numbers denote different courses. Rather than writing $n * (n - 1)/2$ inequality axioms for n individuals, it may be better to have the convention that every course number denotes a different course and thus the use of inequality axioms is avoided.

Under the **unique names assumption (UNA)** distinct ground terms denote different individuals. That is, for every pair of distinct ground terms t_1 and t_2, it assumes $t_1 \neq t_2$, where "$\neq$" means "not equal to."

The unique names assumption does *not* follow from the semantics for the definite clause language (page 587). As far as that semantics was concerned, distinct ground terms t_1 and t_2 could denote the same individual or could denote different individuals.

With the unique names assumption, inequality ($\neq$) can be in the bodies of clauses. If you want to use equality in the body of clauses, you can define equality by adding the clause $X = X$.

The unique names assumption can be axiomatized with the following axiom schema for inequality, which consists of the axiom schema for equality (page 629) together with the axiom schema:

- $c \neq c'$ for any distinct constants c and c'.
- $f(X_1, \ldots, X_n) \neq g(Y_1, \ldots, Y_m)$ for any distinct function symbols f and g.
- $f(X_1, \ldots, X_n) \neq f(Y_1, \ldots, Y_n) \leftarrow X_i \neq Y_i$, for any function symbol f. There are n instances of this schema for every n-ary function symbol f (one for each i such that $1 \leq i \leq n$).
- $f(X_1, \ldots, X_n) \neq c$ for any function symbol f and constant c.

With this axiomatization, ground terms are identical if and only if they unify. This is not the case for non-ground terms. For example, $a \neq X$ has some instances that are true – for example, when X has value b – and an instance which is false, namely, when X has value a.

The unique names assumption is very useful for database applications, in which you do not want, for example, to have to state that *kim* $\neq$ *sam* and *kim* $\neq$ *chris* and *chris* $\neq$ *sam*.

Sometimes the unique names assumption is inappropriate – for example, $2 + 2 \neq 4$ is wrong, and it may not be the case that *clark_kent* $\neq$ *superman*.

Top-Down Proof Procedure for the Unique Names Assumption

The top-down proof procedure incorporating the unique names assumption should not treat inequality as just another predicate, mainly because too many different individuals exist for any given individual.

If there is a subgoal $t_1 \neq t_2$, for terms t_1 and t_2 there are three cases:

1. t_1 and t_2 do not unify. In this case, $t_1 \neq t_2$ succeeds.

   For example, the inequality $f(X, a, g(X)) \neq f(t(X), X, b)$ succeeds because the two terms do not unify.

2. t_1 and t_2 are identical, including having the same variables in the same positions. In this case, $t_1 \neq t_2$ fails.

   For example, $f(X, a, g(X)) \neq f(X, a, g(X))$ fails.

   Note that, for any pair of ground terms, one of these first two cases must occur.

3. Otherwise, there are instances of $t_1 \neq t_2$ that succeed and instances of $t_1 \neq t_2$ that fail.

   For example, consider the subgoal $f(W, a, g(Z)) \neq f(t(X), X, Y)$. The MGU of $f(W, a, g(Z))$ and $f(t(X), X, Y)$ is $\{X/a, W/t(a), Y/g(Z)\}$. Some instances of the inequality, such as the ground instances consistent with the unifier, should fail. Any instance that is not consistent with the unifier should succeed. Unlike other goals, you do not want to enumerate every instance that succeeds because that would mean unifying X with every function and constant different than a, as well as enumerating every pair of values for Y and Z where Y is different than $g(Z)$.

The top-down proof procedure can be extended to incorporate the unique names assumption. Inequalities of the first type can succeed and those of the second type can fail. Inequalities of the third type can be **delayed**, waiting for subsequent goals to unify variables so that one of the first two cases occur. To delay a goal in the proof procedure of Figure 13.4 (page 604), when selecting an atom in the body of ac, the algorithm should select one of the atoms that is not being delayed. If there are no other atoms to select, and neither of the first two cases is applicable, the query should succeed. There is always an instance of the inequality that succeeds, namely, the instance where every variable gets a different constant that does not appear anywhere else. When this occurs, the user has to be careful when interpreting the free variables in the answer. The answer does not mean that it is true for every instance of the free variables, but rather that it is true for some instance.

Example 13.46 Consider the rules that specify whether a student has passed at least two courses:

$$passed\_two\_courses(S) \leftarrow$$
$$\quad C_1 \neq C_2 \wedge$$
$$\quad passed(S, C_1) \wedge$$
$$\quad passed(S, C_2).$$

$$passed(S,C) \leftarrow$$
$$grade(S,C,M) \wedge$$
$$M \geq 50.$$
$$grade(sam, engl101, 87).$$
$$grade(sam, phys101, 89).$$

For the query

ask $passed\_two\_courses(sam)$,

the subgoal $C_1 \neq C_2$ cannot be determined and so must be delayed. The top-down proof procedure can, instead, select $passed(sam, C_1)$, which binds $engl101$ to C_1. It can then call $passed(sam, C_2)$, which in turn calls $grade(sam, C_2, M)$, which can succeed with substitution $\{C_2/engl101, M/87\}$. At this stage, the variables for the delayed inequality are bound enough to determine that the inequality should fail.

Another clause can be chosen for $grade(sam, C_2, M)$, returning substitution $\{C_2/phys101, M/89\}$. The variables in the delayed inequality are bound enough to test the inequality and, this time, the inequality succeeds. It can then go on to prove that $89 > 50$, and the goal succeeds.

One question that may arise from this example is "why not simply make the inequality the last call, because then it does not need to be delayed?" There are two reasons. First, it may be more efficient to delay. In this example, the delayed inequality can be tested before checking whether $87 > 50$. Although this particular inequality test may be fast, in many cases substantial computation can be avoided by noticing violated inequalities as soon as possible. Second, if a subproof were to return one of the values before it is bound, the proof procedure should still remember the inequality constraint, so that any future unification that violates the constraint can fail.

13.8 Complete Knowledge Assumption

The complete knowledge assumption, as discussed in Section 5.6 (page 212), is the assumption that any statement that does not follow from a knowledge base is false. It also allows for proof by negation as failure.

To extend the complete knowledge assumption to logic programs with variables and functions symbols, we require axioms for equality, and the domain closure, and a more sophisticated notion of the completion. Again, this defines a form of **negation as failure**.

Example 13.47 Suppose a *student* relation is defined by

$$student(mary).$$
$$student(john).$$
$$student(ying).$$

The complete knowledge assumption would say that these three are the only students:

$$student(X) \leftrightarrow X = mary \lor X = john \lor X = ying.$$

That is, if X is *mary, john,* or *ying,* then X is a student, and if X is a student, X must be one of these three. In particular, *kim* is not a student.

Concluding $\neg student(kim)$ requires proving prove $kim \neq mary \land kim \neq john \land kim \neq ying$. To derive the inequalities, the unique names assumption (page 630) is required.

The complete knowledge assumption includes the unique names assumption. As a result, we assume the axioms for equality (page 629) and inequality (page 630) for the rest of this section.

The **Clark normal form** of the clause

$$p(t_1, \ldots, t_k) \leftarrow B.$$

is the clause

$$p(V_1, \ldots, V_k) \leftarrow \exists W_1 \ldots \exists W_m \, V_1 = t_1 \land \ldots \land V_k = t_k \land B.$$

where $V_1, \ldots, V_k$ are k variables that did not appear in the original clause, and $W_1, \ldots, W_m$ are the original variables in the clause. "$\exists$" means "there exists" (page 591). When the clause is an atomic clause (page 182), B is *true*.

Suppose all of the clauses for p are put into Clark normal form, with the same set of introduced variables, giving

$$p(V_1, \ldots, V_k) \leftarrow B_1.$$
$$\vdots$$
$$p(V_1, \ldots, V_k) \leftarrow B_n.$$

which is equivalent to

$$p(V_1, \ldots, V_k) \leftarrow B_1 \lor \ldots \lor B_n.$$

This implication is logically equivalent to the set of original clauses.

Clark's completion of predicate p is the equivalence

$$\forall V_1 \ldots \forall V_k \, p(V_1, \ldots, V_k) \leftrightarrow B_1 \lor \ldots \lor B_n$$

where **negation as failure** ($\sim$) in bodies is replaced by standard logical negation ($\neg$). The completion means that $p(V_1, \ldots, V_k)$ is true if and only if at least one body B_i is true.

Clark's completion of a knowledge base consists of the completion of every predicate symbol along with the axioms for equality (page 629) and inequality (page 630).

Example 13.48 For the clauses

> *student*(*mary*).
> *student*(*john*).
> *student*(*ying*).

the Clark normal form is

> *student*(*V*) ← *V* = *mary*.
> *student*(*V*) ← *V* = *john*.
> *student*(*V*) ← *V* = *ying*.

which is equivalent to

> *student*(*V*) ← *V* = *mary* ∨ *V* = *john* ∨ *V* = *ying*.

The completion of the *student* predicate is

> ∀*V student*(*V*) ↔ *V* = *mary* ∨ *V* = *john* ∨ *V* = *ying*.

Example 13.49 Consider the following recursive definition:

> *passed_each*([ ], *St*, *MinPass*).
> *passed_each*([*C* | *R*], *St*, *MinPass*) ←
>   *passed*(*St*, *C*, *MinPass*) ∧
>   *passed_each*(*R*, *St*, *MinPass*).

In Clark normal form, this can be written as

> *passed_each*(*L*, *S*, *M*) ← *L* = [ ].
> *passed_each*(*L*, *S*, *M*) ←
>   ∃*C* ∃*R L* = [*C* | *R*] ∧
>   *passed*(*S*, *C*, *M*) ∧
>   *passed_each*(*R*, *S*, *M*).

Here, we have removed the equalities that specify renaming of variables and have renamed the variables as appropriate. Thus, Clark's completion of *passed_each* is

> ∀*L* ∀*S* ∀*M passed_each*(*L*, *S*, *M*) ↔ *L* = [ ] ∨
>   ∃*C* ∃*R* (*L* = [*C* | *R*] ∧
>   *passed*(*S*, *C*, *M*) ∧
>   *passed_each*(*R*, *S*, *M*)).

Under the complete knowledge assumption, relations that cannot be defined using only definite clauses can now be defined.

Example 13.50 Suppose you are given a database of *course*(C) that is true if C is a course, and *enrolled*(S, C), which means that student S is enrolled in course C. Without the complete knowledge assumption, you cannot define *empty_course*(C) which is true if there are no students enrolled in course C. This is because there is always a model of the knowledge base where every course has someone enrolled.

Using negation as failure, *empty_course*(C) can be defined by

$$empty\_course(C) \leftarrow course(C) \wedge \sim has\_enrollment(C).$$
$$has\_enrollment(C) \leftarrow enrolled(S, C).$$

The completion of this is

$$\forall C \; empty\_course(C) \leftrightarrow course(C) \wedge \neg has\_enrollment(C).$$
$$\forall C \; has\_enrollment(C) \leftrightarrow \exists S \; enrolled(S, C).$$

Here we offer a word of caution. You should be very careful when you include free variables within negation as failure. They usually do not mean what you think they might. We introduced the predicate *has_enrollment* in the previous example to avoid having a free variable within a negation as failure. Consider what would have happened if you had not done this:

Example 13.51 One may be tempted to define *empty_course* in the following manner:

$$empty\_course(C) \leftarrow course(C) \wedge \sim enrolled(S, C).$$

which has the completion

$$\forall C \; empty\_course(C) \leftrightarrow \exists S \; course(C) \wedge \neg enrolled(S, C).$$

This is not correct. Given the clauses

$$course(cs422).$$
$$course(cs486).$$
$$enrolled(mary, cs422).$$
$$enrolled(sally, cs486).$$

the clause

$$empty\_course(cs422) \leftarrow course(cs422) \wedge \sim enrolled(sally, cs422)$$

is an instance of the preceding clause for which the body is true, and the head is false, because *cs422* is not an empty course. This is a contradiction to the truth of the preceding clause.

Note that the completion of the definition in Example 13.50 is equivalent to

$$\forall C \; empty\_course(C) \leftrightarrow course(C) \wedge \neg \exists S \; enrolled(S, C).$$

The existence is in the scope of the negation, so this is equivalent to

$$\forall C \; empty\_course(C) \leftrightarrow course(C) \wedge \forall S \; \neg enrolled(S, C).$$

13.8.1   Complete Knowledge Assumption Proof Procedures

The top-down proof procedure for negation as failure with the variables and functions is much like the top-down procedure for propositional negation as failure (page 219). As with the unique names assumption, a problem arises when there are free variables in negated goals.

Example 13.52   Consider the clauses

$$p(X) \leftarrow \sim q(X) \wedge r(X).$$
$$q(a).$$
$$q(b).$$
$$r(d).$$

According to the semantics, there is only one answer to the query ask $p(X)$, which is $X = d$. As $r(d)$ follows, so does $\sim q(d)$ and so $p(d)$ logically follows from the knowledge base.

When the top-down proof procedure encounters $\sim q(X)$, it should not try to prove $q(X)$, which succeeds (with substitution $\{X/a\}$). This would make the goal $p(X)$ fail, when it should succeed with $X = d$. Thus, the proof procedure would be incomplete. Note that, if the knowledge base contained $s(X) \leftarrow \sim q(X)$, the failure of $q(X)$ would mean $s(X)$ succeeding. Thus, with negation as failure, incompleteness leads to unsoundness.

As with the unique names assumption (Section 13.7.2 (page 630)), a sound proof procedure should delay the negated subgoal until the free variable is bound.

We require a more complicated top-down procedure when there are calls to negation as failure with free variables:

- Negation as failure goals that contain free variables must be delayed (page 682) until the variables become bound.

- If the variables never become bound, the goal **flounders**. In this case, you cannot conclude anything about the goal. The following example shows that you should do something more sophisticated for the case of floundering goals.

Example 13.53   Consider the clauses:

$$p(X) \leftarrow \sim q(X)$$
$$q(X) \leftarrow \sim r(X)$$
$$r(a)$$

and the query

$$\text{ask } p(X).$$

The completion of the knowledge base is

$$p(X) \leftrightarrow \neg q(X),$$

$$q(X) \leftrightarrow \neg r(X),$$
$$r(X) \leftrightarrow X = a.$$

Substituting $X = a$ for r gives $q(X) \leftrightarrow \neg X = a$, and so $p(X) \leftrightarrow X = a$. Thus, there is one answer, namely $X = a$, but delaying the goal will not help find it. A proof procedure should analyze the cases for which the goal failed to derive this answer. However, such a procedure is beyond the scope of this book.

13.9   Review

The following are the main points you should have learned from this chapter:

- In domains characterized by individuals and relations, constants denoting individuals and predicate symbols denoting relations can be reasoned with to determine what is true in the domain.

- Datalog is a logical language with constants, universally quantified variables, relations, and rules.

- Substitutions are used to make instances of atoms and rules. Unification makes atoms identical for use in proofs.

- Function symbols are used to denote a possibly infinite set of individuals described in terms of other individuals. Function symbols can be used to build data structures.

- It is possible to use definite clauses to represent natural language grammars.

- Equality between terms means that the terms denote the same individual.

- Clark's completion can be used to define the semantics of negation as failure under the complete knowledge assumption.

13.10   References and Further Reading

Datalog and logic programs are described by Kowalski [2014], Sterling and Shapiro [1994], and Garcia-Molina et al. [2009]. The history of logic programming is described by Kowalski [1988] and Colmerauer and Roussel [1996].

The work on negation as failure (page 212), as well as the unique names assumption (page 630), is based on the work of Clark [1978]. See the book by Lloyd [1987] for a formal treatment of logic programming in general and negation as failure in particular. Apt and Bol [1994] provide a survey of different techniques for handling negation as failure.

Jurafsky and Martin [2008] and Manning and Schütze [1999] provide excellent introductions to computational linguistics. The use of definite clauses for describing natural language is described by Pereira and Shieber [2002] and

Dahl [1994]. Lally et al. [2012] discuss how the use of natural language and logic programming was used in the IBM **Watson** system which beat the human world champion in Jeopardy!

13.11 Exercises

Exercise 13.1 Consider a domain with two individuals ($\prec$ and $\mathbf{☎}$), two predicate symbols (p and q), and three constants (a, b, and c). The knowledge base KB is defined by

$$p(X) \leftarrow q(X).$$
$$q(a).$$

(a) Give one interpretation that is a model of KB.

(b) Give one interpretation that is not a model of KB.

(c) How many interpretations are there? Give a brief justification for your answer.

(d) How many of these interpretations are models of KB? Give a brief justification for your answer.

Exercise 13.2 Consider the language that contains the constant symbols a, b, and c; the predicate symbols p and q; and no function symbols. We have the following knowledge bases built from this language:

$$KB_1 = \{\, p(a) \,\}$$
$$KB_2 = \{\, p(X) \leftarrow q(X) \,\}$$
$$KB_3 = \{\, p(X) \leftarrow q(X),$$
$$\qquad p(a),$$
$$\qquad q(b) \,\}.$$

Now consider possible interpretations for this language of the form $I = \langle D, \pi, \phi \rangle$, where $D = \{\prec, \mathbf{☎}, \textbf{+}, \textbf{✎}\}$.

(a) How many interpretations with the four domain elements exist for our simple language? Give a brief justification for your answer. [Hint: Consider how many possible assignments ϕ exist for the constant symbols, and consider how many extensions predicates p and q can have to determine how many assignments π exist.] Do not try to enumerate all possible interpretations.

(b) Of the interpretations outlined above, how many are models of KB_1? Give a brief justification for your answer.

(c) Of the interpretations outlined above, how many are models of KB_2? Give a brief justification for your answer.

(d) Of the interpretations outlined above, how many are models of KB_3? Give a brief justification for your answer.

Exercise 13.3 Consider the following knowledge base:

$r(a)$.

$r(e)$.

$p(c)$.

$q(b)$.

$s(a, b)$.

$s(d, b)$.

$s(e, d)$.

$p(X) \leftarrow q(X) \wedge r(X)$.

$q(X) \leftarrow s(X, Y) \wedge q(Y)$.

Show the set of ground atomic consequences derivable from this knowledge base. Assume that a bottom-up proof procedure is used and that at each iteration the first applicable clause is selected in the order shown. Furthermore, applicable constant substitutions are chosen in "alphabetic order" if more than one applies to a given clause; for example, if X/a and X/b are both applicable for a clause at some iteration, derive $q(a)$ first. In what order are consequences derived?

Exercise 13.4 In Example 13.23 (page 603), the algorithm fortuitously chose $imm\_west(r109, r111)$ as the clause to resolve against. What would have happened if another clause had been chosen? Show the sequence of resolutions that arise, and either show a different answer or give a generalized answer clause that cannot resolve with any clause in the knowledge base.

Exercise 13.5 In Example 13.23, we always selected the leftmost conjunct to resolve on. Is there a selection rule (a selection of which conjunct in the query to resolve against) that would have resulted in only one choice for this example? Give a general rule that – for this example, at least – results in fewer failing branches being made. Give an example where your rule does not work.

Exercise 13.6 In a manner similar to Example 13.23 (page 603), show derivations of the following queries:

(a) ask $two\_doors\_east(r107, R)$.

(b) ask $next\_door(R, r107)$.

(c) ask $west(R, r107)$.

(d) ask $west(r107, R)$.

Give all answers for each query.

Exercise 13.7 Consider the following knowledge base:

$has\_access(X, library) \leftarrow student(X)$.

$has\_access(X, library) \leftarrow faculty(X)$.

$has\_access(X, library) \leftarrow has\_access(Y, library) \land parent(Y, X).$

$has\_access(X, office) \leftarrow has\_keys(X).$

$faculty(diane).$

$faculty(ming).$

$student(william).$

$student(mary).$

$parent(diane, karen).$

$parent(diane, robyn).$

$parent(susan, sarah).$

$parent(sarah, ariel).$

$parent(karen, mary).$

$parent(karen, todd).$

(a) Provide an SLD derivation of the query $has\_access(todd, library)$.

(b) The query $has\_access(mary, library)$ has two SLD derivations. Give both of them.

(c) Does there exist an SLD derivation for $has\_access(ariel, library)$? Explain why or why not.

(d) Explain why the set of answers to the query $has\_access(X, office)$ is empty.

(e) Suppose the following clause is added to the knowledge base:

$has\_keys(X) \leftarrow faculty(X).$

What are the answers to the query $has\_access(X, office)$?

Exercise 13.8 What is the result of the following applications of substitutions?

(a) $f(A, X, Y, X, Y)\{A/X, Z/b, Y/c\}.$

(b) $yes(F, L) \leftarrow append(F, c(L, nil), c(l, c(i, c(s, c(t, nil)))))$
$\{F/c(l, X_1), Y_1/c(L, nil), A_1/l, Z_1/c(i, c(s, c(t, nil)))\}.$

(c) $append(c(A_1, X_1), Y_1, c(A_1, Z_1)) \leftarrow append(X_1, Y_1, Z_1)$
$\{F/c(l, X_1), Y_1/c(L, nil), A_1/l, Z_1/c(i, c(s, c(t, nil)))\}.$

Exercise 13.9 Give a most general unifier of the following pairs of expressions:

(a) $p(f(X), g(g(b)))$ and $p(Z, g(Y))$

(b) $g(f(X), r(X), t)$ and $g(W, r(Q), Q)$

(c) $bar(val(X, bb), Z)$ and $bar(P, P)$

Exercise 13.10 For each of the following pairs of atoms, either give a most general unifier or explain why one does not exist:

(a) $p(X, Y, a, b, W)$
$p(E, c, F, G, F)$

(b) $p(X, Y, Y)$
     $p(E, E, F)$

(c) $p(Y, a, b, Y)$
     $p(c, F, G, F)$

(d) $ap(F0, c(b, c(B0, L0)), c(a, c(b, c(b, c(a, emp))))))$
     $ap(c(H1, T1), L1, c(H1, R1))$

Exercise 13.11 List all of the ground atomic logical consequences of the following knowledge base:

$$q(Y) \leftarrow s(Y, Z) \wedge r(Z).$$
$$p(X) \leftarrow q(f(X)).$$
$$s(f(a), b).$$
$$s(f(b), b).$$
$$s(c, b).$$
$$r(b).$$

Exercise 13.12 Consider the following logic program:

$$f(empty, X, X).$$
$$f(cons(X, Y), W, Z) \leftarrow$$
$$\qquad f(Y, W, cons(X, Z)).$$

Give each top-down derivation, showing substitutions (as in Example 13.32) for the query

> ask $f(cons(a, cons(b, cons(c, empty))), L, empty)$.

What are all of the answers?

Exercise 13.13 Consider the following logic program:

$$rd(cons(H, cons(H, T)), T).$$
$$rd(cons(H, T), cons(H, R)) \leftarrow$$
$$\qquad rd(T, R).$$

Give a top-down derivation, showing all substitutions for the query

> ask $rd(cons(a, cons(cons(a, X), cons(B, cons(c, Z)))), W)$.

What is the answer corresponding to this derivation?
   Is there a second answer? If yes, show the derivation; if not, explain why.

Exercise 13.14 Consider the following logic program:

$$ap(emp, L, L).$$
$$ap(c(H, T), L, c(H, R)) \leftarrow$$
$$\qquad ap(T, L, R).$$
$$adj(A, B, L) \leftarrow$$
$$\qquad ap(F, c(A, c(B, E)), L).$$

(a) Give a top-down derivation (including all substitutions) for one answer to the query

$$ask \; adj(b, Y, c(a, c(b, c(b, c(a, emp))))).$$

(b) Are there any other answers? If so, explain where a different choice could be made in the derivation in the previous answer, and continue the derivation, showing another answer. If there are no other answers, explain why not.

[You are meant to do this exercise as if you were a computer, without knowing what the symbols mean. If you want to give a meaning to this program, you could read *ap* as *append*, *c* as *cons*, *emp* as *empty*, and *adj* as *adjacent*.]

Exercise 13.15 The aim of this question is to get practice writing simple logic programs.

(a) Write a relation *remove*(E, L, R) that is true if R is the list resulting from removing one instance of E from list L. The relation is false if E is not a member of L.

(b) Give all of the answers to the following queries:

$$ask \; remove(a, [b, a, d, a], R).$$
$$ask \; remove(E, [b, a, d, a], R).$$
$$ask \; remove(E, L, [b, a, d]).$$
$$ask \; remove(p(X), [a, p(a), p(p(a)), p(p(p(a)))], R).$$

(c) Write a relation *subsequence*(L1, L2) that is true if list L1 contains a subset of the elements of L2 in the same order.

(d) How many different proofs are there for each of the following queries:

$$ask \; subsequence([a, d], [b, a, d, a]).$$
$$ask \; subsequence([b, a], [b, a, d, a]).$$
$$ask \; subsequence([X, Y], [b, a, d, a]).$$
$$ask \; subsequence(S, [b, a, d, a]).$$

Explain why there are that many.

Exercise 13.16 In this question, you are to write a definite clause knowledge base for the design of custom video presentations.

Assume that the video is annotated using the relation

$$segment(SegId, Duration, Covers),$$

where *SegId* is an identifier for the segment. (In a real application this will be enough information to extract the video segment.) *Duration* is the running time of the segment (in seconds). *Covers* is a list of topics covered by the video segment. An example of a video annotation is the database

$$segment(seg0, 10, [welcome]).$$
$$segment(seg1, 30, [skiing, views]).$$

$segment(seg2, 50, [welcome, artificial\_intelligence, robots])$.

$segment(seg3, 40, [graphics, dragons])$.

$segment(seg4, 50, [skiing, robots])$.

A presentation is a sequence of segments. Represent a presentation by a list of segment identifiers.

(a) Axiomatize a predicate

$$presentation(MustCover, Maxtime, Segments)$$

that is true if $Segments$ is a presentation whose total running time is less than or equal to $Maxtime$ seconds, such that all of the topics in the list $MustCover$ are covered by a segment in the presentation. The aim of this predicate is to design presentations that cover a certain number of topics within a time limit.

For example, the query

ask $presentation([welcome, skiing, robots], 90, Segs)$.

should return at least the following two answers (perhaps with the segments in some other order):

$presentation([welcome, skiing, robots], 90, [seg0, seg4])$

$presentation([welcome, skiing, robots], 90, [seg2, seg1])$.

Give the intended interpretation of all symbols used and demonstrate that you have tested your axiomatization (including finding all answers to your query) in AILog or Prolog. Explain briefly why each answer is an answer.

(b) Assuming you have a good user interface and a way to actually view the presentations, list *three* things that the preceding program does not do that you may want in such a presentation system. (There is no correct answer for this part. You must be creative to get full marks.)

Exercise 13.17 Construct a knowledge base and a dictionary based on Figure 13.13 (page 627) to answer geographical questions such as that given in Figure 1.2 (page 10). For each query, either show how it can be answered or explain why it is difficult to answer given the tools presented in this chapter.

Chapter 14

Ontologies and Knowledge-Based Systems

The most serious problems standing in the way of developing an adequate theory of computation are as much ontological as they are semantical. It is not that the semantic problems go away; they remain as challenging as ever. It is just that they are joined – on center stage, as it were – by even more demanding problems of ontology.

– Smith [1996, p. 14]

How do you represent knowledge about a world to make it easy to acquire, debug, maintain, communicate, share, and reason with that knowledge? This chapter explores how to specify the meaning of symbols in intelligent agents, how to use the meaning for knowledge-based debugging and explanation, and, finally, how an agent can represent its own reasoning and how this may be used to build knowledge-based systems. As Smith points out in the quote above, the problems of ontology are central for building intelligent computational agents.

14.1 Knowledge Sharing

Having an appropriate representation is only part of the story of building a knowledge-based agent. We also should ensure that the knowledge can be acquired from people and from data. The knowledge for any non-trivial domain comes from diverse sources and at multiple points in time. Multiple sources need to **interoperate**, to work together, at both a syntactic level and a semantic level.

Recall (page 67) that an **ontology** is a specification of the meanings of the symbols in an information system. Here an information system can be a knowledge base, a sensor such as a thermometer, or some other source of information. The meaning of the symbols is sometimes just in the mind of the knowledge base designer, in a user manual, or in comments with the knowledge base. Increasingly, the specification of the meaning is in machine-interpretable form. This formal specification of the meaning is important for **semantic interoperability** – the ability of different knowledge bases to work together at a semantic level so that the meanings of symbols are respected.

Example 14.1 A purchasing agent has to know, when a website claims it has a good price on "chips," whether these are potato chips, computer chips, wood chips, or poker chips. An ontology would specify the meaning of the terminology used by the web site. Instead of using the symbol "chip", a website that adheres to ontologies may use the symbol "WoodChipMixed" as defined by some particular organization that has published an ontology. By using this symbol and declaring which ontology it is from, it should be unambiguous as to which use of the word *chip* is meant. A formal representation of the web page would use "WoodChipMixed". If another information source uses the symbol "ChipOfWood", some third party may declare that the use of the term "ChipOfWood" in that information source corresponds to a type of "WoodChipMixed" and therefore enable the information sources to be combined.

The specification does not need to define terminology precisely; it only needs to define terms well enough so they can be used consistently. Specifying that a thermometer measures the temperature in Celsius would be adequate for many applications, without needing to define what temperature is or the accuracy of the thermometer.

Before discussing how ontologies are specified, we first discuss how the logic of the previous chapter (with variables, terms, and relations) can be used to build flexible representations. These flexible representations allow for the modular addition of knowledge, including adding arguments to relations.

Given a specification of the meaning of the symbols, an agent can use that meaning for knowledge acquisition, explanation, and debugging at the knowledge level.

14.2 Flexible Representations

The first part of this chapter considers a way to build flexible representations using the tools of logic. These flexible representations are the basis of modern ontologies.

14.2.1   Choosing Individuals and Relations

Given a logical representation language, such as the one developed in the previous chapter, and a world to reason about, the people designing knowledge bases have to choose which individuals and relations to represent. It may seem that they can just refer to the individuals and relations that exist in the world. However, the world does not determine which individuals there are. How the world is divided into individuals is invented by whomever is modeling the world. The modeler divides up the world up into things so that the agent can refer to parts of the world that make sense for the task at hand.

Example 14.2   It may seem as though *"red"* is a reasonable property to ascribe to things in the world. You may do this because you want to tell the delivery robot to go and get the red parcel. In the world, there are surfaces absorbing some frequencies and reflecting other frequencies of light. Some user may have decided that, for some application, some particular set of reflectance properties should be called *red*. Some other modeler of the domain might decide on another mapping of the spectrum and use the terms *pink, scarlet, ruby,* and *crimson*, and yet another modeler may divide the spectrum into regions that do not correspond to words in any language but are those regions most useful to distinguish different categories of individuals.

Just as modelers choose which individuals to represent, they also choose which relations to use. There are, however, some guiding principles that are useful for choosing relations and individuals. These will be demonstrated through a sequence of examples.

Example 14.3 Suppose you decide that *"red"* is an appropriate category for classifying individuals. You could treat the name *red* as a unary relation and write that parcel *a* is red:

$red(a).$

If you represent the color information in this way, then you can easily ask what is red:

ask $red(X).$

The *X* returned are the red individuals.

With this representation, it is hard to ask the question, "What color is parcel *a*?" In the syntax of definite clauses, you cannot ask

ask $X(a).$

because, in languages based on first-order logic (page 609), predicate names cannot be variables. In second-order or higher-order logic, this would return any property of *a*, not just its color.

There are alternative representations that allow you to ask about the color of parcel a. There is nothing in the world that forces you to make *red* a predicate. You could just as easily say that colors are individuals too, and you could use the constant *red* to denote the color red. Given that *red* is a constant, you can use the predicate *color* where *color(Ind, Val)* means that physical individual *Ind* has color *Val*. "Parcel a is red" can now be written as

$color(a, red).$

What you have done is reconceive the world: the world now consists of colors as individuals that you can name, as well as parcels. There is now a new binary relation *color* between physical individuals and colors. Under this new representation you can ask, "What color red?" with the query

ask $color(X, red).$

and ask "What color is block a?" with the query

ask $color(a, C).$

To make an abstract concept into an object is to **reify** it. In the preceding example, we reified the color *red*.

Example 14.4   It seems as though there is no disadvantage to the new representation of colors in the previous example. Everything that could be done before can be done now. It is not much more difficult to write $color(X, red)$ than $red(X)$, but you can now ask about the color of things. So the question arises of whether you can do this to every relation, and what do you end up with?

You can do a similar analysis for the *color* predicate as for the *red* predicate in Example 14.3. The representation with *color* as a predicate does not allow you to ask the question, "Which property of parcel a has value *red*?" where the appropriate answer is "color." Carrying out a similar transformation to that of Example 14.3, you can view properties such as *color* as individuals, and you can invent a relation *prop* and write "individual a has the *color* of *red*" as

$prop(a, color, red).$

This representation allows for all of the queries of this and the previous example. You do not have to do this again, because you can write all relations in terms of the *prop* relation.

The **individual–property–value** representation is in terms of a single relation *prop* where

$prop(Ind, Prop, Val)$

means that individual *Ind* has value *Val* for property *Prop*. This is also called the **triple representation** because all of the relations are represented as **triples**.

The first element of the triple is called the **subject**, the second is the **verb**, and the third is the **object**, using the analogy that a triple is a simple three word sentence.

Sometimes we will write a triple as a simple three word sentence:

subject verb object.

meaning the atom

prop(*subject, verb, object*)

or in functional notation as

verb(*subject, object*)

The verb of a triple is a **property**. The **domain** of property p is the set of individuals that can appear as the subject of a triple when p is the verb. The **range** of a property p is the set of values that can appear as the object of a triple that has p as the verb.

An **attribute** is a property–value pair. For example, an attribute of a parcel may be that its color is red.

There are some predicates that may seem to be too simple for the triple representation:

Example 14.5   To transform *parcel*(*a*), which means that *a* is a parcel, there do not seem to be appropriate properties or values. There are two ways to transform this into the triple representation.

The first is to reify the concept parcel and to say that *a* is a parcel:

prop(*a, type, parcel*).

Here *type* is a special property that relates an individual to a class. The constant *parcel* denotes the class that is the set of all, real or potential, things that are parcels. This triple specifies that the individual *a* is in the class *parcel*, or more simply as the triple "a is_a parcel". Type is often written as **is_a**.

The second is to make parcel a property and write "*a* is a parcel" as

prop(*a, parcel, true*).

In this representation, *parcel* is a Boolean property which is true of things that are parcels.

A **Boolean property** is a property whose range is $\{true, false\}$, where *true* and *false* are constant symbols in the language.

On the other hand, some predicates may seem to be too complicated for the triple representation:

Example 14.6 Suppose you want to represent the relation

$$scheduled(C, S, T, R),$$

which is to mean that section S of course C is scheduled to start at time T in room R. For example, "section 2 of course $cs422$ is scheduled to start at 10:30 in room $cc208$" is written as

$$scheduled(cs422, 2, 1030, cc208).$$

To represent this in the triple representation, you can invent a new individual, a *booking*. Thus, the *scheduled* relationship is reified into a booking individual.

A booking has a number of properties, namely a course, a section, a start time, and a room. To represent "section 2 of course $cs422$ is scheduled at 10:30 in room $cc208$," you name the booking, say, the constant $b123$, and write

$$prop(b123, course, cs422).$$
$$prop(b123, section, 2).$$
$$prop(b123, start\_time, 1030).$$
$$prop(b123, room, cc208).$$

This new representation has a number of advantages. The most important is that it is modular; which values go with which properties can easily be seen. It is easy to add new properties such as the instructor or the duration. With the new representation, it is easy to add that "Fran is teaching section 2 of course $cs422$, scheduled at 10:30 in room $cc208$" or that the duration is 50 minutes:

$$prop(b123, instructor, fran).$$
$$prop(b123, duration, 50).$$

With *scheduled* as a predicate, it was very difficult to add the instructor or duration because it required adding extra arguments to every instance of the predicate.

14.2.2 Graphical Representations

You can interpret the *prop* relation in terms of a directed graph, where the relation

$$prop(Ind, Prop, Val)$$

is depicted with Ind and Val as nodes with an arc labeled with $Prop$ between them. Such a graph is called a **semantic network** or **knowledge graph**. There is a straightforward mapping form a knowledge graph into a knowledge base using the *prop* relation, as in the following example.

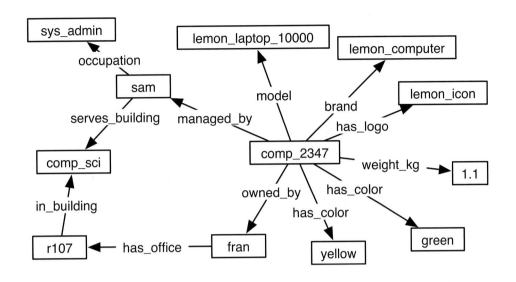

Figure 14.1: A semantic network

Example 14.7 Figure 14.1 shows a semantic network for the delivery robot showing the sort of knowledge that the robot might have about a particular computer in a university department. Some of the knowledge represented in the network is

> *prop*(*comp_2347, owned_by, fran*).
> *prop*(*comp_2347, managed_by, sam*).
> *prop*(*comp_2347, model, lemon_laptop_10000*).
> *prop*(*comp_2347, brand, lemon_computer*).
> *prop*(*comp_2347, has_logo, lemon_icon*).
> *prop*(*comp_2347, color, green*).
> *prop*(*comp_2347, color, yellow*).
> *prop*(*comp_2347, weight, light*).
> *prop*(*fran, has_office, r107*).
> *prop*(*r107, in_building, comp_sci*).

The network also shows how the knowledge is structured. For example, it is easy to see that computer number 2347 is owned by someone (Fran) whose office (r107) is in the *comp_sci* building. The direct indexing evident in the graph can be used by humans and machines.

This graphical notation has a number of advantages:

- It is easy for a human to see the relationships without being required to learn the syntax of a particular logic. The graphical notation helps the builders of knowledge bases to organize their knowledge.

- You can ignore the labels of nodes that just have meaningless names – for example, the name $b123$ in Example 14.6 (page 650), or $comp\_2347$ in Figure 14.1. You can just leave these nodes blank and make up an arbitrary name if you must map to the logical form.

14.2.3   Classes

Typically, you know more about a domain than a database of facts; you know general rules from which other facts can be derived. Which facts are explicitly given and which are derived is a choice to be made when designing and building a knowledge base.

Primitive knowledge is knowledge that is specifies explicitly in terms of facts. **Derived knowledge** is knowledge that can be inferred from other knowledge. Derived knowledge is typically specified using rules.

The use of rules allows for a more compact representation of knowledge. Derived relations allow for conclusions to be drawn from observations of the domain. This is important because you do not directly observe everything about a domain. Much of what is known about a domain is inferred from the observations and more general knowledge.

A standard way to use derived knowledge is to put individuals into classes, and then give general properties to classes so that individuals inherit the properties of classes. Grouping individuals into classes enables a more concise representation because the members of a class can share the attributes they have in common (see the box on page 656). This is the same issue that was discussed in the context of probabilistic classifiers (page 491).

A **class** is the set of those actual and potential individuals that would be members of the class. This is typically an **intensional set**, defined by a **characteristic function** that is true of members of the set and false of other individuals. The alternative to an intensional set is an **extensional set**, which is defined by listing its elements.

For example, the class *chair* is the set of all things that would be chairs. We do not want the definition to be the set of things that *are* chairs, because chairs that have not yet been built also fall into the class of chairs. We do not want two classes to be equivalent just because they have the same members. For example, the class of green unicorns and the class of chairs that are exactly 124 meters high are different classes, even though they may contain the same elements; they are both empty. A 124 meter high chair would not be a green unicorn.

The definition of class allows any set that can be described to be a class. For example, the set consisting of the number 17, the Tower of London, and the Prime Minister of Canada's left foot may be a class, but it is not very useful. A **natural kind** is a class such that describing individuals using the class is more succinct than describing individuals without the class. For example, "mammal" is a natural kind, because describing the common attributes of mammals makes a knowledge base that uses "mammal" more succinct than one that does not use "mammal" and instead repeats the attributes for every individual.

Class S is a subclass of class C means that S is a subset of C. That is, every individual of type S is of type C.

Example 14.8   Example 14.7 explicitly specified that the logo for computer *comp_2347* was a lemon icon. You may, however, know that all Lemon brand computers have this logo. An alternative representation is to associate the logo with *lemon_computer* and derive the logo of *comp_2347*. The advantage of this representation is that if you find another Lemon brand computer, you can infer its logo. Similarly each Lemon Laptop 10000 may weigh 1.1 kg.

An extended example is shown in Figure 14.2 (on the next page), where the shaded rectangles are classes, and arcs from classes are not the properties of the class but properties of the members of the class. The class of Lemon laptop 10000s would weigh much more than 1.1 kg.

The relationship between types and subclasses can be written as a definite clause:

$prop(X, type, C) \leftarrow$
$\qquad prop(S, subClassOf, C) \land$
$\qquad prop(X, type, S).$

You can treat *type* and *subClassOf* as special properties that allow **property inheritance**. Property inheritance occurs when a value for a property is specified at the class level and inherited by the members of the class. If all members of class c have value v for property p, this can be written in Datalog as

$prop(Ind, p, v) \leftarrow$
$\qquad prop(Ind, type, c).$

which, together with the aforementioned rule that relates types and subclasses, can be used for property inheritance.

Example 14.9   All Lemon computers have a lemon icon as a logo and have color yellow and color green (see the *logo* and *color* arcs in Figure 14.2 (on the next page)). All Lemon laptops 10000 have a weight of 1.1 kg. Lemon laptop 10000 is a subclass of Lemon computers. Computer *comp_2347* is a Lemon

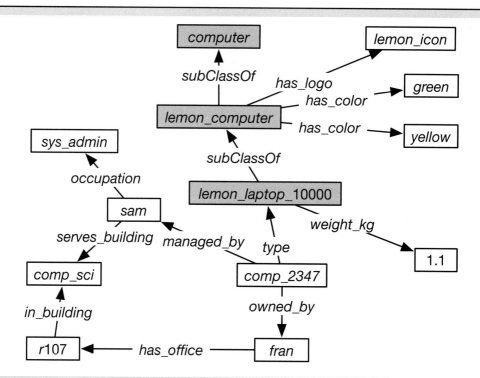

Figure 14.2: A semantic network allowing inheritance. Shaded nodes are classes.

laptop 10000. This knowledge can be represented by the following Datalog program:

$$prop(X, has\_logo, lemon\_icon) \leftarrow$$
$$\quad prop(X, type, lemon\_computer).$$
$$prop(X, has\_color, green) \leftarrow$$
$$\quad prop(X, type, lemon\_computer).$$
$$prop(X, has\_color, yellow) \leftarrow$$
$$\quad prop(X, type, lemon\_computer).$$
$$prop(X, weight\_kg, 1.1) \leftarrow$$
$$\quad prop(X, type, lemon\_laptop\_10000).$$
$$prop(lemon\_laptop\_10000, subClassOf, lemon\_computer).$$
$$prop(comp\_2347, type, lemon\_laptop\_10000).$$

From this Datalog program, and the clause involving *subClassOf* above, the logo, colors and weight of *comp_2347* can be derived. With the structured representation, to incorporate a new Lemon Laptop 10000, you only declare that it is a Lemon laptop 10000 and the colors, logo and weight can be derived through inheritance.

Some general guidelines are useful for deciding what should be primitive and what should be derived:

- When associating an attribute with an individual, select the most general class C that the individual is in, where all members of C have that attribute, and associate the attribute with class C. Inheritance can be used to derive the attribute for the individual and all other members of class C. This representation methodology tends to make knowledge bases more concise, and it means that it is easier to incorporate new individuals because members of C automatically inherit the attribute.

- Do not associate a contingent attribute of a class with the class. A **contingent attribute** is one whose value changes when circumstances change. For example, it may be true of the current computer environment that all of the computers come in cardboard boxes. However, it may not be a good idea to put that as an attribute of the *computer* class, because it would not be expected to be true as other computers are bought.

- Axiomatize in the causal direction (page 225). If a choice exists between making the cause primitive or the effect primitive, make the cause primitive. The information is then more likely to be stable when the domain changes. See Example 5.36 (page 225).

14.3 Ontologies and Knowledge Sharing

Building large knowledge-based systems is complex:

- Knowledge often comes from multiple sources and must be integrated. Moreover, these sources may not have the same division of the world. Often knowledge comes from different fields that have their own distinctive terminology and divide the world according to their own needs.

- Systems evolve over time and it is difficult to anticipate all future distinctions that should be made.

- The people involved in designing a knowledge base must choose what individuals and relationships to represent. The world is not divided into individuals; that is something done by intelligent agents to understand the world. Different people involved in a knowledge-based system should agree on this division of the world.

- It is often difficult to remember what your own notation means, let alone to discover what someone else's notation means. This has two aspects:

    - given a symbol used in the computer, determining what it means

---

Classes in Knowledge Bases and Object-Oriented Programming

The use of "individuals" and "classes" in knowledge-based systems is very similar to the use of "objects" and "classes" in **object-oriented programming (OOP) languages** such as **Smalltalk**, **Python** or **Java**. This should not be too surprising because they have an interrelated history. But there are important differences that tend to make the direct analogy often more confusing than helpful:

- Objects in OOP are computational objects; they are data structures and associated programs. A "person" object in Java is not a person. However, individuals in a knowledge base (KB) are (typically) things in the real world. A "person" individual in a KB can be a real person. A "chair" individual can be a real chair you can actually sit in; it can hurt you if you bump into it. You can send a message to, and get answers from, a "chair" object in Java, whereas a chair in the real world tends to ignore what you tell it. A KB is not typically used to interact with a chair, but to reason *about* a chair. A real chair stays where it is unless it is moved by a physical agent.

- In a KB, a representation of an object is only an approximation at one (or a few) levels of abstraction. Real objects tend to be much more complicated than what is represented. You typically do not represent the individual fibers in the fabric of a chair. In an OOP system, there are only the represented properties of an object. The system can know everything about a Java object, but not about a real individual.

- The class structure of Java is intended to represent designed objects. A systems analyst or a programmer gets to create a design. For example, in Java, an object is only a member of one lowest-level class. There is no multiple inheritance. Real objects are not so well behaved. The same person could be a football coach, a mathematician, and a mother.

- A computer program cannot be uncertain about its data structures; it has to select particular data structures to use. However, you can be uncertain about the types of things in the world.

- The representations in a KB do not actually do anything. In an OOP system, objects do computational work. In a KB, they just represent – that is, they just refer to objects in the world.

- While an object-oriented modeling language, like **UML**, may be used for representing KBs, it may not be the best choice. A good OO modeling tool has facilities to help build good designs. However, the world being modeled may not have a good design at all. Trying to force a good design paradigm on a messy world may not be productive.

– given a concept in someone's mind, determining what symbol to use. This has three aspects:

* determining whether the concept has already been defined

* if it has been defined, discovering what symbol has been used for it

* if it is not already defined, finding related concepts that it can be defined in terms of.

To share and communicate knowledge, it is important to be able to develop a common vocabulary and an agreed-on meaning for that vocabulary.

A **conceptualization** is a mapping between symbols used in the computer, the vocabulary, and the individuals and relations in the world. It provides a particular abstraction of the world and notation for that abstraction. A conceptualization for small knowledge bases can be in the head of the designer or specified in natural language in the documentation. This informal specification of a conceptualization does not scale to larger systems where the conceptualization must be shared.

In philosophy, **ontology** is the study of what exists. In AI, an **ontology** is a specification of the meanings of the symbols in an information system. That is, it is a specification of a conceptualization. It is a specification of what individuals and relationships are assumed to exist and what terminology is used for them. Typically, it specifies what types of individuals will be modeled, specifies what properties will be used, and gives some axioms that restrict the use of that vocabulary.

Example 14.10 An ontology of individuals that could appear on a map could specify that the symbol "ApartmentBuilding" will represent apartment buildings. The ontology will not define an apartment building, but it will describe it well enough so that others can understand the definition. We want other people, who who may call such buildings "Condos", "Flats" or "Apartment Complex" to be able to find the appropriate symbol in the ontology (see Figure 14.3 (page 659)). That is, given a concept, people want to be able to find the symbol, and, given the symbol, they want to be able to determine what it means.

An ontology may give axioms to restrict the use of some symbols. For example, it may specify that apartment buildings are buildings, which are human-constructed artifacts. It may give some restriction on the size of buildings so that shoeboxes cannot be buildings or that cities cannot be buildings. It may state that a building cannot be at two geographically dispersed locations at the same time (so if you take off some part of the building and move it to a different location, it is no longer a single building). Because apartment buildings are buildings, these restrictions also apply to apartment buildings.

The Semantic Web

The **semantic web** is a way to allow machine-interpretable knowledge to be distributed on the World Wide Web. Instead of just serving HTML pages that are meant to be read by humans, websites will also provide information that can be used by computers.

At the most basic level, **XML** (the Extensible Markup Language) provides a syntax designed to be machine readable, but which is also possible for humans to read. It is a text–based language, where items are tagged in a hierarchical manner. The syntax for XML can be quite complicated, but at the simplest level, the scope of a tag is either in the form $\langle tag \ldots / \rangle$, or in the form $\langle tag \ldots \rangle \ldots \langle / tag \rangle$.

A **URI** (a **Uniform Resource Identifier**) is used to uniquely identify a resource. A **resource** is anything that can be uniquely identified, including individuals, classes and properties. Often URIs use the syntax of web addresses.

RDF (the **Resource Description Framework**) is a language built on XML, for individual–property–value triples.

RDF–S (RDF Schema) lets you define resources (and so also properties) in terms of other resources (e.g., using *subClassOf*, and *subPropertyOf*). RDF–S also lets you restrict the domain and range of properties and provides containers: sets, sequences, and alternatives.

RDF allows sentences in its own language to be reified. This means that it can represent arbitrary logical formulas and so is not decidable in general. Undecidability is not necessarily a bad thing; it just means that you cannot put a bound on the time a computation may take. Logic programs with function symbols and programs in virtually all programming languages are undecidable.

OWL (the **Web Ontology Language**) is an ontology language for the World Wide Web. It defines some classes and properties with a fixed interpretation that can be used for describing classes, properties, and individuals. It has built-in mechanisms for equality of individuals, classes, and properties, in addition to restricting domains and ranges of properties and other restrictions on properties (e.g., transitivity, cardinality).

There have been some efforts to build large universal ontologies, such as **Cyc** (www.cyc.com), but the idea of the semantic web is to allow communities to converge on ontologies. Anyone can build an ontology. People who want to develop a knowledge base can use an existing ontology or develop their own ontology, usually building on existing ontologies. Because it is in their interest to have semantic interoperability, companies and individuals should tend to converge on standard ontologies for their domain or to develop mappings from their ontologies to others' ontologies.

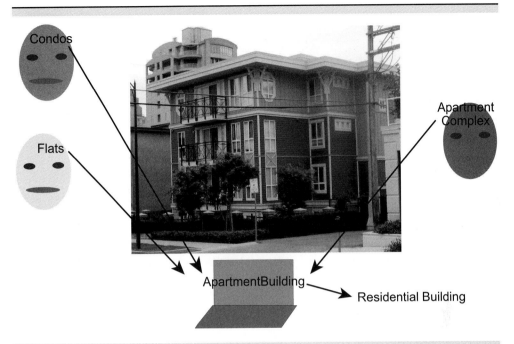

Figure 14.3: Mapping from a conceptualization to a symbol

Ontologies are usually written independently of a particular application and often involve a community agreeing on the meanings of symbols. An ontology consists of

- a vocabulary of the categories of the things (both classes and properties) that a knowledge base may want to represent

- an organization of the categories, for example into an inheritance hierarchy using *subClassOf* or *subPropertyOf*, or using Aristotelian definitions (on the next page), and

- a set of axioms restricting the definition of some of the symbols to better reflect their intended meaning – for example, that some property is transitive, or that the domain and range are restricted, or restrictions on the number of values a property can take for each individual. Sometimes relationships are defined in terms of more primitive relationships but, ultimately, the relationships are grounded out into **primitive relationships** that are not actually defined.

An ontology does not specify the individuals not known at design time. For example, an ontology of buildings would typically not include actual buildings. An ontology would specify those individuals that are fixed and should be shared, such as the days of the week, or colors.

Example 14.11 Consider a trading agent that is designed to find accommodations. Users could use such an agent to describe what accommodation they

Aristotelian Definitions

Categorizing objects, the basis for modern ontologies, has a long history. Aristotle [350 B.C.E.] suggested the definition of a class C in terms of

- **Genus**: a superclass of C. The plural of genus is genera.
- **Differentia**: the attributes that make members of the class C different from other members of the superclass of C.

He anticipated many of the issues that arise in definitions:

> If genera are different and co-ordinate, their differentiae are themselves different in kind. Take as an instance the genus "animal" and the genus "knowledge". "With feet", "two-footed", "winged", "aquatic", are differentiae of "animal"; the species of knowledge are not distinguished by the same differentiae. One species of knowledge does not differ from another in being "two-footed". [Aristotle, 350 B.C.E.]

Note that "co-ordinate" here means neither is subordinate to the other.

In the style of modern ontologies, we would say that "animal" is a class, and "knowledge" is a class. The property "two-footed" has domain "animal". If something is an instance of knowledge, it does not have a value for the property "two-footed".

To build an ontology based on **Aristotelian definitions**:

- For each class you may want to define, determine a relevant superclass, and then select those attributes that distinguish the class from other subclasses. Each attribute gives a property and a value.
- For each property, define the most general class for which it makes sense, and define the domain of the property to be this class. Make the range another class that makes sense (perhaps requiring this range class to be defined, either by enumerating its values or by defining it using an Aristotelian definition).

This can get quite complicated. For example, to define "luxury furniture", the superclass could be "furniture" and the distinguishing characteristics are cost is high and it feels soft. The softness of furniture is different than the softness of rocks. You also probably want to distinguish the squishiness from the texture (both of which may be regarded as soft).

The class hierarchy is an acyclic directed graph (DAG), forming a lattice. This methodology does not, in general, give a tree hierarchy of classes. Objects can be in many classes. Each class does not have a single most-specific superclass. However, it is still straightforward to check whether one class is a subclass of another, to check the meaning of a class, and to determine the class that corresponds to a concept in a person's head.

In rare cases, the natural class hierarchy forms a strict tree, most famously in the **Linnaean taxonomy** of living things. The reason this is a tree is because of evolution. Trying to force a tree structure in other domains has been much less successful.

want. The trading agent could search multiple knowledge bases to find suitable accommodations or to notify users when some appropriate accommodation becomes available. An ontology is required to specify the meaning of the symbols for the user and to allow the knowledge bases to interoperate. It provides the semantic glue to tie together the users' needs with the knowledge bases.

In such a domain, houses and apartment buildings may both be residential buildings. Although it may be sensible to suggest renting a house or an apartment in an apartment building, it may not be sensible to suggest renting an apartment building to someone who does not actually specify that they want to rent the whole building. A "living unit" could be defined to be the collection of rooms that some people, who are living together, live in. A living unit may be what a rental agency offers to rent. At some stage, the designer may have to decide whether a room for rent in a house is a living unit, or even whether part of a shared room that is rented separately is a living unit. Often the boundary cases – cases that may not be initially anticipated – are not clearly delineated but become better defined as the ontology evolves.

The ontology would not contain descriptions of actual houses or apartments because, at the time the ontology is defined, the designers will not know what houses will be described by the ontology. The ontology will change much slower than actual available accommodation.

The primary purpose of an ontology is to document what the symbols mean – the mapping between symbols (in a computer) and concepts (in someone's head). Given a symbol, a person is able to use the ontology to determine what it means. When someone has a concept to be represented, the ontology is used to find the appropriate symbol or to determine that the concept does not exist in the ontology. The secondary purpose, achieved by the use of axioms, is to allow inference or to determine that some combination of values is inconsistent. The main challenge in building an ontology is the organization of the concepts to allow a human to map concepts into symbols in the computer, and for the computer to infer useful new knowledge from stated facts.

14.3.1 Uniform Resource Identifiers

A **Uniform Resource Identifier** (**URI**) is a unique identifier for individuals or properties, or what is called resources. In the semantic web languages URIs are typically of the form ⟨url#name⟩, where url is of the form of a web page. This is often abbreviated to abbr:name, where abbr is an abbreviation that is locally declared to be an abbreviation for the full URI.

A URI has meaning because people use it with that meaning.

Example 14.12 The friend-of-a-friend (**foaf**) project is a simple ontology for publishing personal information about people.

The URI ⟨http://xmlns.com/foaf/0.1/#name⟩ is a property that relates a person and a string representation of the person's name. If someone intends to use this particular property, using this URI will enable others who also adopt this ontology (or map to it) to know which property is meant. As long as everyone who use the URI ⟨http://xmlns.com/foaf/0.1/#name⟩ means the same property, it does not matter what is at the URL http://xmlns.com/foaf/0.1/. That URL, at the time of writing, just redirects to a web page. However, the "friend-of-a-friend" project uses that name space to mean something. This works simply because people use it that way.

14.3.2 Description Logic

Modern ontology languages such as **OWL** (page 658) are based on **description logics**. A description logic is used to describe classes, properties, and individuals. One of the main ideas behind a description logic is to separate

- a **terminological knowledge base** (or **TBox**) describes the terminology; it defines what the symbols mean

- an **assertional knowledge base** (or **ABox**) specifies what is true at some point in time.

Usually, the terminological knowledge base is defined at the design time of the system and defines the ontology, and it only changes as the meaning of the vocabulary changes, which should be relatively rarely. The assertional knowledge base usually contains the knowledge that is situation specific and is only known at run time.

It is typical to use triples (page 648) to define the assertional knowledge base and a language such as OWL to define the terminological knowledge base.

The web ontology language (OWL) describes domains in terms of

- **Individuals** are things in the world that is being described (e.g., a particular house or a particular booking may be individuals).

- **Classes** are sets of individuals. A class is the set of all real or potential things that would be in that class. For example, the class "House" may be the set of all things that would be classified as a house, not just those houses that exist in the domain of interest.

- **Properties** are used to describe individuals. A **datatype property** has values that are primitive data types, such as integers or strings. For example, "streetName" may be a datatype property between a street and string. An **object property** has values that are other individuals. For example, "nextTo" may be a property between two houses, and "onStreet" may be a property between a house and a street.

OWL comes in a few variants that differ in restrictions imposed on the classes and properties, and how efficiently they can be implemented. For example, in OWL-DL a class cannot be an individual or a property, and a property is not an

C_k are classes, P_k are properties, I_k are individuals, and n is an integer. $\#S$ is the number of elements in set S.

Class	Class Contains
owl:Thing	all individuals
owl:Nothing	no individuals (empty set)
owl:ObjectIntersectionOf$(C_1, \ldots, C_k)$	individuals in $C_1 \cap \cdots \cap C_k$
owl:ObjectUnionOf$(C_1, \ldots, C_k)$	individuals in $C_1 \cup \cdots \cup C_k$
owl:ObjectComplementOf(C)	the individuals not in C
owl:ObjectOneOf$(I_1, \ldots, I_k)$	$I_1, \ldots, I_k$
owl:ObjectHasValue(P, I)	individuals with value I on property P, i.e., $\{x : x\,P\,I\}$
owl:ObjectAllValuesFrom(P, C)	individuals with all values in C on property P; i.e., $\{x : x\,P\,y \rightarrow y \in C\}$
owl:ObjectSomeValuesFrom(P, C)	individuals with some values in C on property P; i.e., $\{x : \exists y \in C$ such that $x\,P\,y\}$
owl:ObjectMinCardinality(n, P, C)	individuals x with at least n individuals of class C related to x by P, i.e., $\{x : \#\{y : xPy$ and $y \in C\} \geq n\}$
owl:ObjectMaxCardinality(n, P, C)	individuals x with at most n individuals of class C related to x by P, i.e., $\{x : \#\{y : xPy$ and $y \in C\} \leq n\}$
owl:ObjectHasSelf(P)	individuals x such that xPx.

Figure 14.4: Some OWL built-in classes and class constructors

individual. In OWL-Full, the categories of individuals, properties, and classes are not necessarily disjoint. OWL-DL comes in three profiles that are targeted towards particular applications, and do not allow constructs they do not need that would make inference slower. OWL 2 EL is designed for large biohealth ontologies, allowing rich structural descriptions. OWL 2 QL is designed to be the front end of database query languages. OWL 2 RL is a language that is designed for cases where rules are important.

OWL does not make the unique names assumption (page 630); two names do not necessarily denote different individuals or different classes. It also does not make the complete knowledge assumption (page 212); it does not assume that all the relevant facts have been stated.

Figure 14.4 gives some primitive classes and some class constructors. This figure uses set notation to define the set of individuals in a class. Figure 14.5 (on the next page) gives primitive predicates of OWL. The owl: prefixes are from OWL.

In these figures, xPy is a triple. Note that this is meant to define the mean-

OWL has the following predicates with a fixed interpretation, where C_k are classes, P_k are properties, and I_k are individuals; x and y are universally quantified variables.

Statement	Meaning
rdf:type(I, C)	$I \in C$
owl:ClassAssertion(C, I)	$I \in C$
rdfs:subClassOf(C_1, C_2)	$C_1 \subseteq C_2$
owl:SubClassOf(C_1, C_2)	$C_1 \subseteq C_2$
rdfs:domain(P, C)	if xPy then $x \in C$
owl:ObjectPropertyDomain(P, C)	if xPy then $x \in C$
rdfs:range(P, C)	if xPy then $y \in C$
owl:ObjectPropertyRange(P, C)	if xPy then $y \in C$
owl:EquivalentClasses$(C_1, C_2, \ldots, C_k)$	$C_i \equiv C_j$ for all i, j
owl:DisjointClasses$(C_1, C_2, \ldots, C_k)$	$C_i \cap C_j = \{\}$ for all $i \neq j$
rdfs:subPropertyOf(P_1, P_2)	xP_1y implies xP_2y
owl:EquivalentObjectProperties(P_1, P_2)	xP_1y if and only if xP_2y
owl:DisjointObjectProperties(P_1, P_2)	xP_1y implies not xP_2y
owl:InverseObjectProperties(P_1, P_2)	xP_1y if and only if yP_2x
owl:SameIndividual$(I_1, \ldots, I_n)$	$\forall j \forall k \; I_j = I_k$
owl:DifferentIndividuals$(I_1, \ldots, I_n)$	$\forall j \forall k \; j \neq k$ implies $I_j \neq I_k$
owl:FunctionalObjectProperty(P)	if xPy_1 and xPy_2 then $y_1 = y_2$
owl:InverseFunctionalObjectProperty(P)	if x_1Py and x_2Py then $x_1 = x_2$
owl:TransitiveObjectProperty(P)	if xPy and yPz then xPz
owl:SymmetricObjectProperty	if xPy then yPx
owl:AsymmetricObjectProperty(P)	xPy implies not yPx
owl:ReflexiveObjectProperty(P)	xPx for all x
owl:IrreflexiveObjectProperty(P)	not xPx for all x

Figure 14.5: Some RDF, RDF-S, and OWL built-in predicates

ing of the predicates, rather than any syntax. The predicates can be used with different syntaxes, such as XML, Turtle (a simple language of triples), or functional notation. Here we use the **OWL functional-style syntax** where the arguments of the constructors are written in parentheses, separated with spaces.

Example 14.13   As an example of a class constructor in OWL functional syntax:

ObjectHasValue(lc:has_logo lc:lemon_icon)

is the class of objects for which the individual lc:lemon_icon is a value for the property lc:has_logo.

ObjectSomeValuesFrom(lc:has_color lc:green)

is the class of all objects that have some green. That is the objects for which some of the colors of the object are green. Here lc:green is assumed to be a class of more specific colors such as emerald or forest-green.

MinCardinality(2 :owns :building)

is the class of all individuals who own two or more buildings. That is, the set $\{x : \exists i_1 \exists i_2 \, building(i_1) \wedge building(i_2) \wedge x :owns\ i_1 \wedge x :owns\ i_2 \wedge i_1 \neq i_2\}$.

The class constructors must be used in a statement, for example, to say that some individual is a member of this class or to say that one class is equivalent to some other class.

OWL does not have definite clauses. To say that all of the elements of a set S have value v for a predicate p, we say that S is a subset of the set of all things with value v for predicate p.

Example 14.14 Figure 14.6 (on the next page) shows a representation of (part of) Figure 14.2 (page 654).

The first line defines "lc:" to be an abbreviation. Thus lc:computer is an abbreviation for the URI

⟨http://artint.info/ontologies/lemon_computers.owl#computer⟩

The second line defines which ontology this is (the parenthesis ends at the last line).

lc:computer and lc:logo are both classes. lc:lemon_icon is a member of the class lc:logo. lc:has_logo is a property, with domain lc:computer and range lc:logo.

To state that all Lemon computers have a lemon icon as a logo, you say that the set of Lemon computers is a subset of the set of all things for which the property *has_logo* has value *lemon_icon*. The ontology specifies lc:lemon_computer is a subclass of lc:computer and a subclass of the set of individuals that have value lc:lemon_icon for the property lc:has_logo. That is, all Lemon computers have a lemon icon as a logo.

Green and yellow are subclasses of color. The property *has_color* applies to material entities, which are physical objects. Some of the colors of a Lemon computer are yellow and some are green.

Some of OWL and RDF or RDFS statementshave the same meaning. For example, rdf:type(I, C) means the same as owl:ClassAssertion(C, I), and rdfs:domain means the same as owl:ObjectPropertyDomain for object properties. Some ontologies use both definitions, because the ontologies were developed over long periods of time, with contributors who adopted different conventions.

There is one property constructor in OWL, owl:ObjectInverseOf(P), which is the inverse property of P; that is, it is the property P^{-1} such that $yP^{-1}x$ if

```
Prefix(lc:=<http://artint.info/ontologies/lemon_computers.owl#>)
Ontology(<http://artint.info/ontologies/lemon_computers.owl>

Declaration(Class(lc:computer))
Declaration(Class(lc:logo))
ClassAssertion(lc:logo lc:lemon_icon)
Declaration(ObjectProperty(lc:has_logo))
ObjectPropertyDomain(lc:has_logo lc:computer)
ObjectPropertyRange(lc:has_logo lc:logo)

Declaration(Class(lc:lemon_computer))
SubClassOf(lc:lemon_computer lc:computer)
SubClassOf(lc:lemon_computer
           ObjectHasValue(lc:has_logo lc:lemon_icon))

Declaration(Class(lc:color))
Declaration(Class(lc:green))
Declaration(Class(lc:yellow))
SubClassOf(lc:green lc:color)
SubClassOf(lc:yellow lc:color)
Declaration(Class(lc:material_entity))
SubClassOf(lc:computer lc:material_entity)
ObjectPropertyDomain(lc:has_color lc:material_entity)
ObjectPropertyRange(lc:has_color lc:color)
SubClassOf(lc:lemon_computer
           ObjectSomeValuesFrom(lc:has_color lc:green))
SubClassOf(lc:lemon_computer
           ObjectSomeValuesFrom(lc:has_color lc:yellow))
)
```

Figure 14.6: OWL functional syntax representation of Example 14.14

and only if *xPy*. Note that it is only applicable to object properties; datatype properties do not have inverses, because data types cannot be the subject of a triple.

The list of classes and statements in these figures is not complete. There are corresponding datatype classes for datatype properties, where appropriate. For example, owl:DataSomeValuesFrom and owl:EquivalentDataProperties have the same definitions as the corresponding object symbols, but are for datatype properties. There are also other constructs in OWL to define properties, comments, annotations, versioning, and importing other ontologies.

Example 14.15 Consider an Aristotelian definition (page 660) of an apartment building. We can say that an apartment building is a residential building with multiple units and the units are rented. (This is in contrast to a condominium building, where the units are individually sold, or a house, where there is only one unit.) Suppose we have the class *ResidentialBuilding* that is a subclass of *Building*.

The following defines the functional object property *numberOfUnits*, with domain *ResidentialBuilding* and range {*one, two, moreThanTwo*}.

```
Declaration(ObjectProperty(:numberOfunits))
FunctionalObjectProperty(:numberOfunits)
ObjectPropertyDomain(:numberOfunits :ResidentialBuilding)
ObjectPropertyRange(:numberOfunits
                    ObjectOneOf(:two :one :moreThanTwo))
```

The functional object property *ownership* with domain *ResidentialBuilding*, and range {*rental, ownerOccupied, coop*} can be defined similarly.

An apartment building is a *ResidentialBuilding* where the *numberOfUnits* property has the value *moreThanTwo* and the *ownership* property has the value *rental*. To specify this in OWL, we define the class of things that have value *moreThanTwo* for the property *numberOfUnits*, the class of things that have value *rental* for the property *ownership*, and say that *ApartmentBuilding* is equivalent to the intersection of these classes. In OWL functional syntax, this is

```
Declaration(Class(:ApartmentBuilding))
EquivalentClasses(:ApartmentBuilding
    ObjectIntersectionOf(
        :ResidentialBuilding
        ObjectHasValue(:numberOfunits :moreThanTwo)
        ObjectHasValue(:ownership :rental)))
```

This definition can be used to answer questions about apartment buildings, such as the ownership and the number of units. Apartment buildings inherit all of the properties of residential buildings.

The previous example did not really define *ownership*. The system has no idea what ownership actually means. Hopefully, a user will know what it means. Everyone who wants to adopt an ontology should ensure that their use of a property and a class is consistent with other users of the ontology.

A **domain ontology** is an ontology about a particular domain of interest. Most existing ontologies are in a narrow domain that people write for specific applications. There are some guidelines that have evolved for writing domain ontologies to enable knowledge sharing:

- If possible, use an existing ontology. This means that your knowledge base will be able to interact with others who use the same ontology.

- If an existing ontology does not exactly match your needs, import it and add to it. Do not start from scratch, because people who have used the existing ontology will have a difficult time also using yours, and others who want to select an ontology will have to choose one or the other. If your ontology includes and improves the other, others who want to adopt an ontology will choose yours, because their application will be able to interact with adopters of either ontology.

- Make sure that your ontology integrates with neighboring ontologies. For example, an ontology about resorts will have to interact with ontologies about food, beaches, recreation activities, and so on. Try to make sure that it uses the same terminology for the same things.

- Try to fit in with higher-level ontologies (see below). This will make it much easier for others to integrate their knowledge with yours.

- If you must design a new ontology, consult widely with other potential users. This will make it most useful and most likely to be adopted.

- Follow naming conventions. For example, call a class by the singular name of its members. For example, call a class "Resort" not "Resorts". Resist the temptation to call it "ResortConcept" (thinking it is only the concept of a resort, not a resort; see the box on page 669). When naming classes and properties, think about how they will be used. It sounds better to say that "$r1$ is of type Resort" than "$r1$ is of type Resorts", which is better than "$r1$ is of type ResortConcept".

- As a last option, specify the matching between ontologies. Sometimes ontology matching has to be done when ontologies are developed independently. It is best if matching can be avoided; it makes knowledge using the ontologies much more complicated because there are multiple ways to say the same thing.

OWL, when written in the OWL functional syntax, is much easier to read than when using XML. However, OWL is at a lower level than most people will want to specify or read. It is designed to be a machine-readable specification. There are many editors that let you edit OWL representation. One example is **Protégé** (http://protege.stanford.edu/). An ontology editor should support the following:

- It should provide a way for people to input ontologies at the level of abstraction that makes the most sense.

- Given a concept a user wants to use, an ontology editor should facilitate finding the terminology for that concept or determining that there is no corresponding term.

- It should be straightforward for someone to determine the meaning of a term.

- It should be as easy as possible to check that the ontology is correct (i.e., matches the user's intended interpretation for the terms).

- It should create an ontology that others can use. This means that it should use a standardized language as much as possible.

Classes and Concepts

When defining an ontology, it is tempting to name the classes **concepts**, because symbols represent concepts: mappings from the internal representation into the object or relations that the symbols represent.

For example, it may be tempting to call the class of unicorns "unicornConcept" because there are no unicorns, only the concept of a unicorn. However, unicorns and the concept of unicorns are very different; one is an animal and one is a subclass of knowledge. A unicorn has four legs and a horn coming out of its head. The concept of a unicorn does not have legs or horns. You would be very surprised if a unicorn appeared in a university lecture about ontologies, but you should not be surprised if the concept of a unicorn appeared. There are no instances of unicorns, but there are many instances of the concept of a unicorn. If you mean a unicorn, you should use the term "unicorn". If you mean the concept of a unicorn, you should use "concept of a unicorn". You should not say that a unicorn concept has four legs, because instances of knowledge do not have legs; animals, furniture and some robots have legs.

As another example, consider a tectonic plate, which is part of the Earth's crust. The plates are millions of years old. The concept of a plate is less than a hundred years old. Someone can have the concept of a tectonic plate in their head, but they cannot have a tectonic plate in their head. It should be clear that a tectonic plate and the concept of a tectonic plate are very different things, with very different properties. You should not use "concept of a tectonic plate" when you mean "tectonic plate" and vice versa.

Calling objects concepts is a common error in building ontologies. Although you are free to call things by whatever name you want, it is only useful for knowledge sharing if other people adopt your ontology. They will not adopt it if it does not make sense to them.

14.3.3 Top-Level Ontologies

Example 14.15 (page 667) defined a domain ontology for apartment building that could be used by people who want to write a knowledge base that refers to things that can appear on maps. Each domain ontology implicitly or explicitly assumes a higher-level ontology that it can fit into. The apartment building ontology assumes buildings are defined.

A **top-level ontology** provides a definition of *everything* at a very abstract level.

The goal of a top-level ontology is to provide a useful categorization on which to base other ontologies. Making it explicit how domain ontologies fit into an upper-level ontology promises to facilitate the integration of these ontologies. The integration of ontologies is necessary to allow applications to refer to multiple knowledge bases, each of which may use different ontologies.

Here we present a top-level ontology based on **BFO**, the **Basic Formal Ontology**. Figure 14.7 (on the next page) provides a decision tree which can be used to categorize anything into a number of high-level categories.

At the top is **entity**. OWL calls the top of the hierarchy **thing**. Essentially, everything is an entity.

Entities are divided into the disjoint classes of **continuants** and **occurrents**. A **continuant** is something that exists at an instant in time and continues to exist through time. Examples include a person, a finger, a country, a smile, the smell of a flower, and an email. When a continuant exists at any time, so do its parts. Continuants maintain their identity through time. An **occurrent** is something that has temporal parts, for example, a life, infancy, smiling, the opening of a flower, and sending an email. One way to think about the difference is to consider the entity's parts: a finger is part of a person, but is not part of a life; infancy is part of a life, but is not part of a person. Continuants participate in occurrents. Processes that last through time and events that occur at an instant in time are both occurrents.

A continuant is an **independent continuant**, or a **dependent continuant**. An **independent continuant** is an entity that can exist by itself or is part of another entity. For example, a person, a face, a pen, a flower, a country, and the atmosphere are independent continuants. A dependent continuant only exists by virtue of another entity and is not a part of that entity. For example, a smile, the ability to laugh, or the inside of your mouth, or the ownership relation between a person and a phone, can only exist in relation to another object or objects. Note that something that is a part of another object is an independent continuant; for example, while a heart cannot exist without a body, it can be detached from the body and still exist. This is different from a smile; you cannot detach a smile from a cat.

An independent continuant is either a **material entity** or an **immaterial entity**. A material entity has some matter as a part. Material entities are localized

1: **if** entity continues to exist through time **then**
2:     it is a **continuant**
3:     **if** it does not depend on another entity for its existence **then**
4:       it is an **independent continuant**
5:       **if** it has matter as a part **then**
6:         it is a **material entity**
7:         **if** it is a single coherent whole **then**
8:           it is an **object**
9:         **else**
10:           it is an **immaterial entity**
11:     **else**
12:       it is a **dependent continuant**
13:       **if** it is a property **then**
14:         **if** it is a property that all objects have **then**
15:           it is a **quality**
16:         **else if** it is a something that can be carried out **then**
17:           it is a **role**
18:         **else if** it is a something that can happen to an object **then**
19:           it is a **disposition**
20:         **if** it is a purpose of an object **then**
21:           it is a **function**
22: **else**
23:     it is an **occurrent**
24:     **if** it depends on a continuant **then**
25:       **if** it happens over time **then**
26:         it is a **process**
27:       **else**
28:         it is a **process boundary**
29:     **else if** it involves both space and time **then**
30:       it is a **spatio-temporal region**
31:     **else**
32:       it is a **temporal region**

Figure 14.7: Categorizing an entity in a top-level ontology

in space and can move in space. Examples of material entities are a person, a football team, Mount Everest, and Hurricane Katrina. Immaterial entities are abstract. Examples of immaterial entities are the first email you sent last Monday, a plan, and an experimental protocol. Note that you need a physical embodiment of an email to receive it (e.g., as text on your smartphone or spoken by a speech synthesizer), but the email is not that physical embodiment; a different physical embodiment could still be the same email.

A material entity that is a single coherent whole is an **object**. An object maintains its identity through time even if it gains or loses parts (e.g., a person who loses some hair, a belief, or even a leg, is still the same person). A person, a chair, a cake or a computer are all objects. The left leg of a person (if it is still attached to the person), a football team or the equator are not objects. If a robot were asked to find three objects, it would not be expected to bring a chair and claim the back, the seat and the left-front leg are three objects.

A **dependent continuant** depends on other objects. One type if dependent continuent is a **property**. The following are subtypes of **properties**:

- A **quality** is something that all objects of a particular type have for all of the time they exist – for example, the mass of a bag of sugar, the shape of a hand, the fragility of a cup, the beauty of a view, the brightness of a light, and the smell of the ocean. Although these can change, the bag of sugar always has a mass and the hand always has a shape.

- A **role** specifies a goal that is not essential to the object's design but can be carried out. Examples of roles include the role of being a judge, the role of delivering coffee, and the role of a desk to support a computer monitor.

- A **disposition** is something that may happen to an object, for example, the disposition of a cup to break if dropped, the disposition of vegetables to rot if not refrigerated, and the disposition of matches to light if they are struck when not wet.

- A **function** is a disposition that is a purpose of an object. For example, the function of a cup may be to hold coffee; the function of the heart is to pump blood.

The other major category of entities is the occurrent. An **occurrent** is any of the following:

- A **temporal region** is a region of time. A temporal region is either connected (if two points are in the region, so is every point in between) or scattered. Connected temporal regions are either intervals or instants (time points). Sunday, March 1, 2026, is a temporal interval; 3:31 p.m. EST on that day is a temporal point. Tuesdays from 3:00 to 4:00 GMT is a scattered temporal region.

- A **spatio-temporal region** is a region of multidimensional space-time. Spatio-temporal regions are either scattered or connected. Some examples of spatio-temporal regions are the space occupied by a human life, the border between Canada and the United States in 1812, and the region occupied by the development of a cancer tumor.

- A **process** is something that happens over time, has temporal parts, and depends on a continuant. For example, Joe's life has parts such as infancy, childhood, adolescence, and adulthood and involves a continuant, Joe. A holiday, writing an email, and a robot cleaning the lab are all processes.

- A **boundary of a process** is the instantaneous temporal boundary of a process, such as when a robot starts to clean up the lab, or a birth.

Designing a top-level ontology is difficult. It probably will not satisfy everyone. There always seem to be some problematic cases. In particular, boundary cases are often not well specified. However, using a standard top-level ontology should help in connecting ontologies together.

14.4 Implementing Knowledge-Based Systems

It is often useful for an agent to be able to represent and reason about its own reasoning in what is called **reflection**. Explicitly reasoning about its own representations and reasoning enables an agent to modify these for its own particular circumstances.

This section considers one use of reflection, namely, implementing lightweight tools for building new languages with features that are required for particular applications. By making it easy to implement new languages and tools, the best language for each application can be used. The language and tools can evolve as the application evolves.

A **meta-interpreter** for a language is an interpreter for the language written in the same language. Such an interpreter is useful because modifications allow for quick prototyping of new languages with useful features. Once the language has proven its utility, a compiler for the language may be developed to improve efficiency.

When implementing one language inside another, the language being implemented is called the **base language**, or sometimes the **object language**, and the language in which it is implemented is called the **metalanguage**. Expressions in the base language are said to be at the **base level**, and expressions in the metalanguage are at the **meta-level**. We first define a meta-interpreter for the definite clause language presented in Chapter 13. We then show how the base language can be modified or extended, and tools such as explanation and debugging facilities can be provided by modifying the meta-interpreter.

14.4.1 Base Languages and Metalanguages

We require a representation of the base-level expressions that can be manipulated by the interpreter to produce answers. Initially, the base language will also be the language of definite clauses. Recall (page 182) that the definite clause language is made up of terms, atoms, bodies, and clauses.

The metalanguage refers to these syntactic elements of the base language. Meta-level symbols will denote base-level terms, atoms, and clauses. Base-level terms will denote objects in the domain being modeled, and base-level predicates will denote relations in the domain.

When writing a logic programming meta-interpreter, there is a choice of how to represent variables. In the **non-ground representation**, base-level terms are represented as the same term in the metalanguage, so in particular, base-level variables are represented as meta-level variables. This is in contrast to the **ground representation**, where base language variables are represented as constants in the metalanguage. The non-ground representation means that meta-level unification is available to be used for unifying base-level terms. The ground representation allows the implementation of more sophisticated models of unification.

Example 14.16 The base-level term $foo(X, f(b), X)$, in a non-ground representation, will be represented as the meta-level term $foo(X, f(b), X)$.

In a ground representation, the base-level term $foo(X, f(b), X)$ may be represented as $foo(x, f(b), x)$, along with a declaration that x is a base-level variable.

We will develop a non-ground representation for definite clauses. The metalanguage must be able to represent all of the base-level constructs.

The base-level variables, constants, and function symbols are represented as the corresponding meta-level variables, constants, and function symbols. Thus, all terms in the base level are represented by the same term in the meta-level. A base-level predicate symbol p is represented by the corresponding meta-level function symbol p. Thus, the base-level atom $p(t_1, \ldots, t_k)$ is represented as the meta-level term $p(t_1, \ldots, t_k)$.

Base-level bodies are also represented as meta-level terms. If e_1 and e_2 are meta-level terms that denote base-level atoms or bodies, let the meta-level term $oand(e_1, e_2)$ denote the base-level conjunction of e_1 and e_2. Thus, $oand$ is a meta-level function symbol that denotes base-level conjunction.

Base-level definite clauses are represented as meta-level atoms. Base-level rule "$h \leftarrow b$" is represented as the meta-level atom $clause(h, b')$, where b' is the representation of body b. A base-level fact a is represented as the meta-level atom $clause(a, true)$, where the meta-level constant $true$ represents the base-level empty body.

Example 14.17 The base-level clauses from Example 13.12 (page 593),

$connected\_to(l_1, w_0)$.

Syntactic construct		Meta-level representation of the syntactic construct	
variable	X	variable	X
constant	c	constant	c
function symbol	f	function symbol	f
predicate symbol	p	function symbol	p
"and" operator	$\wedge$	function symbol	$\&$
"if" operator	$\leftarrow$	predicate symbol	$\Leftarrow$
clause	$h \leftarrow a_1 \wedge \cdots \wedge a_n.$	atom	$h \Leftarrow a_1 \ \& \ \cdots \ \& \ a_n$
clause	$h.$	atom	$h \Leftarrow true$

Figure 14.8: The non-ground representation for the base language

$connected\_to(w_0, w_1) \leftarrow up(s_2).$
$lit(L) \leftarrow light(L) \wedge ok(L) \wedge live(L).$

can be represented as the meta-level facts

$clause(connected\_to(l_1, w_0), true).$
$clause(connected\_to(w_0, w_1), up(s_2)).$
$clause(lit(L), oand(light(L), oand(ok(L), live(L)))).$

To make the base level more readable, we use the infix function symbol "&" rather than *oand*. Instead of writing $oand(e_1, e_2)$, we write $e_1 \ \& \ e_2$. The conjunction symbol "&" is an infix function symbol of the metalanguage that denotes an operator, between atoms, of the base language. This is just a syntactic variant of the "*oand*" representation. This use of infix operators makes it easier to read base-level formulas.

Instead of writing $clause(h, b)$, we write $h \Leftarrow b$, where $\Leftarrow$ is an infix meta-level predicate symbol. Thus, the base-level clause "$h \leftarrow a_1 \wedge \cdots \wedge a_n$" is represented as the meta-level atom

$h \Leftarrow a_1 \ \& \ \cdots \ \& \ a_n.$

This meta-level atom is true if the corresponding base-level clause is part of the base-level knowledge base. In the meta-level, this atom can be used like any other atom.

Figure 14.8 summarizes how the base language is represented in the meta-level.

Example 14.18 Using the infix notation, the base-level clauses of Example 14.17 are represented as the meta-level facts

$connected\_to(l_1, w_0) \Leftarrow true.$

% *prove*(*G*) is true if base-level body *G* is a logical consequence of the base-level
% clauses that are defined using the predicate symbol " $\Leftarrow$ ".

> *prove*(*true*).
> *prove*((*A* & *B*)) $\leftarrow$
>> *prove*(*A*) $\land$
>> *prove*(*B*).
>
> *prove*(*H*) $\leftarrow$
>> (*H* $\Leftarrow$ *B*) $\land$
>> *prove*(*B*).

Figure 14.9: The vanilla definite clause meta-interpreter

> *connected_to*(w_0, w_1) $\Leftarrow$ *up*(s_2).
> *lit*(*L*) $\Leftarrow$ *light*(*L*) & *ok*(*L*) & *live*(*L*).

This notation is easier for humans to read than the meta-level facts of Example 14.17, but as far as the computer is concerned, it is essentially the same.

The meta-level function symbol "&" and the meta-level predicate symbol " $\Leftarrow$ " are not predefined symbols of the meta-level. You could have used any other symbols. They are written in infix notation for readability.

14.4.2 A Vanilla Meta-Interpreter

This section presents a very simple **vanilla meta-interpreter** for the definite clause language written in the definite clause language. Subsequent sections augment this meta-interpreter to provide extra language constructs and knowledge engineering tools. It is important to first understand the simple case before considering the more sophisticated meta-interpreters presented later.

Figure 14.9 defines a meta-interpreter for the definite clause language. This is an axiomatization of the relation *prove*, where *prove*(*G*) is true when base-level body *G* is a logical consequence of the base-level clauses.

As with axiomatizing any other relation, we write the clauses that are true in the intended interpretation, ensuring that they cover all of the cases and that there is some simplification through recursion. This meta-interpreter essentially covers each of the cases allowed in the body of a clause or in a query, and it specifies how to solve each case. A body is either empty, a conjunction, or an atom. The empty base-level body *true* is trivially proved. To prove the base-level conjunction *A* & *B*, prove *A* and prove *B*. To prove atom *H*, find a base-level clause with *H* as the head, and prove the body of the clause.

$lit(L) \Leftarrow$
    $light(L) \, \&$
    $ok(L) \, \&$
    $live(L)$.
$live(W) \Leftarrow$
    $connected\_to(W, W_1) \, \&$
    $live(W_1)$.
$live(outside) \Leftarrow true$.
$light(l_1) \Leftarrow true$.
$light(l_2) \Leftarrow true$.
$down(s_1) \Leftarrow true$.
$up(s_2) \Leftarrow true$.
$up(s_3) \Leftarrow true$.
$connected\_to(l_1, w_0) \Leftarrow true$.
$connected\_to(w_0, w_1) \Leftarrow up(s_2) \, \& \, ok(s_2)$.
$connected\_to(w_0, w_2) \Leftarrow down(s_2) \, \& \, ok(s_2)$.
$connected\_to(w_1, w_3) \Leftarrow up(s_1) \, \& \, ok(s_1)$.
$connected\_to(w_2, w_3) \Leftarrow down(s_1) \, \& \, ok(s_1)$.
$connected\_to(l_2, w_4) \Leftarrow true$.
$connected\_to(w_4, w_3) \Leftarrow up(s_3) \, \& \, ok(s_3)$.
$connected\_to(p_1, w_3) \Leftarrow true$.
$connected\_to(w_3, w_5) \Leftarrow ok(cb_1)$.
$connected\_to(p_2, w_6) \Leftarrow true$.
$connected\_to(w_6, w_5) \Leftarrow ok(cb_2)$.
$connected\_to(w_5, outside) \Leftarrow true$.
$ok(X) \Leftarrow true$.

Figure 14.10: A knowledge base for house wiring

Example 14.19 Consider Figure 14.10 adapted from Example 13.12 (page 593). This can be seen from meta-level as a knowledge base of atoms, all with the same predicate symbol $\Leftarrow$. It can also be viewed as base-level knowledge base consisting of multiple rules. The vanilla meta-interpreter sees it as a collection of atoms.

The base-level goal $live(w_5)$ is asked with the following query to the meta-interpreter:

   ask $prove(live(w_5))$.

The third clause of $prove$ is the only clause matching this query. It then looks for a clause of the form $live(w_5) \Leftarrow B$ and finds

   $live(W) \Leftarrow connected\_to(W, W_1)\ \&\ live(W_1)$.

W unifies with w_5, and B unifies with $connected\_to(w_5, W_1)\ \&\ live(W_1)$. It then tries to prove

   $prove((connected\_to(w_5, W_1)\ \&\ live(W_1)))$.

The second clause for $prove$ is applicable. It then tries to prove

   $prove(connected\_to(w_5, W_1))$.

Using the third clause for $prove$, it looks for a clause with a head to unify with

   $connected\_to(w_5, W_1) \Leftarrow B$,

and find $connected\_to(w_5, outside) \Leftarrow true$, binding W_1 to $outside$. It then tries to prove $prove(true)$, which succeeds using the first clause for $prove$.

The second half of the conjunction, $prove(live(W_1))$ with $W_1 = outside$, reduces to $prove(true)$ which is, again, immediately solved.

14.4.3 Expanding the Base Language

The base language can be changed by modifying the meta-interpreter. The set of provable consequences can be enlarged by adding clauses to the meta-interpreter. The set of provable consequences can be reduced by adding conditions to the meta-interpreter clauses.

In all practical systems, not every predicate is defined by clauses. For example, it would be impractical to axiomatize arithmetic on current machines that can do arithmetic quickly. Instead of axiomatizing such predicates, it is better to call the underlying system directly. Assume the predicate $call(G)$ evaluates G directly. Writing $call(p(X))$ is the same as writing $p(X)$. The predicate $call$ is required because the definite clause language does not allow free variables as atoms.

Built-in procedures can be evaluated at the base level by defining the meta-level relation $built\_in(X)$ that is true if all instances of X are to be evaluated directly; X is a meta-level variable that must denote a base-level atom. Do not

% *prove*(*G*) is true if base-level body *G* is a logical consequence of the base-level
% knowledge base.

> *prove*(*true*).
> *prove*((*A* & *B*)) ←
> > *prove*(*A*) ∧
> > *prove*(*B*).
>
> *prove*((*A* ∨ *B*)) ←
> > *prove*(*A*).
>
> *prove*((*A* ∨ *B*)) ←
> > *prove*(*B*).
>
> *prove*(*H*) ←
> > *built_in*(*H*) ∧
> > *call*(*H*).
>
> *prove*(*H*) ←
> > (*H* ⇐ *B*) ∧
> > *prove*(*B*).

Figure 14.11: A meta-interpreter that uses built-in calls and disjunction

assume that *"built_in"* is provided as a built-in relation. It can be axiomatized
like any other relation.

The base language can be expanded to allow for disjunction in the body of
a clause, where the **disjunction**, *A* ∨ *B*, is true in an interpretation *I* when either
A is true in *I* or *B* is true in *I* (or both are true in *I*). Allowing disjunction in the
body of base-level clauses does not require disjunction in the metalanguage.

Figure 14.11 shows a meta-interpreter that allows built-in procedures to be
evaluated directly and allows disjunction in the bodies of rules. This requires
a database of built-in assertions and assumes that *call*(*G*) is a way to prove *G*
in the meta-level.

Example 14.20 An example of the kind of base-level rule the meta-interpreter
of Figure 14.11 can now interpret is

> *can_see* ⇐ *eyes_open* & (*lit*(l_1) ∨ *lit*(l_2)).

which says that *can_see* is true if *eyes_open* is true and either *lit*(l_1) or *lit*(l_2) is
true (or both).

Given such an interpreter, the meta-level and the base level are different
languages. The base level allows disjunction in the body. The meta-level does

% *bprove*(G, D) is true if G can be proved with a proof tree of depth less than or
% equal to number D.

> $bprove(true, D).$
> $bprove((A \mathbin{\&} B), D) \leftarrow$
> > $bprove(A, D) \land$
> > $bprove(B, D).$
>
> $bprove(H, D) \leftarrow$
> > $D \geq 0 \land$
> > D_1 is $D - 1 \land$
> > $(H \Leftarrow B) \land$
> > $bprove(B, D_1).$

Figure 14.12: A meta-interpreter for depth-bounded search

not require disjunction to provide it for the base language. The meta-level requires a way to interpret *call*(G), which the base level cannot handle. The base
level, however, can be made to interpret the command *call*(G) by adding the
following meta-level clause:

> $prove(call(G)) \leftarrow$
> > $prove(G).$

14.4.4   Depth-Bounded Search

The previous section showed how extra meta-level clauses can expand the
base language. This section shows how adding extra conditions to meta-level
clauses can restrict what can be proved.

A useful meta-interpreter is one that implements depth-bounded search.
This can be used to look for short proofs or as part of an iterative deepening searcher (page 94), which carries out repeated depth-bounded, depth-first
searches, increasing the bound at each stage.

Figure 14.12 gives an axiomatization of the relation *bprove*(G, D), which is
true if G can be proved with a proof tree of depth less than or equal to non-
negative integer D. This figure uses Prolog's infix predicate symbol "**is**", where
"V is E" is true if V is the numerical value of expression E. Within the expression, "$-$" is the infix subtraction function symbol. Thus, "D_1 is $D - 1$" is true
if D_1 is one less than the number D.

One aspect of this meta-interpreter is that, if D is bound to a number in
the query, this meta-interpreter will never go into an infinite loop. It will miss
proofs whose depth is greater than D. As a result, this interpreter is incomplete

% *hprove*(G, T) is true if base-level body G is a logical consequence of the base-
% level knowledge base, and T is a representation of the proof tree for the cor-
% responding proof.

> *hprove*(*true*, *true*).
> *hprove*$((A \,\&\, B), (L \,\&\, R)) \leftarrow$
> > *hprove*$(A, L) \land$
> > *hprove*(B, R).
> *hprove*$(H, if(H, built\_in)) \leftarrow$
> > *built_in*$(H) \land$
> > *call*(H).
> *hprove*$(H, if(H, T)) \leftarrow$
> > $(H \Leftarrow B) \land$
> > *hprove*(B, T).

Figure 14.13: A meta-interpreter that builds a proof tree

---

when D is set to a fixed number. However, every proof that can be found for the *prove* meta-interpreter can be found for this meta-interpreter if the value D is set large enough. The idea behind an iterative-deepening (page 94) searcher is to exploit this fact by carrying out repeated depth-bounded searches, each time increasing the depth bound. Sometimes the depth-bounded meta-interpreter can find proofs that *prove* cannot. This occurs when the *prove* meta-interpreter goes into an infinite loop before exploring all proofs.

This is not the only way to build a bounded meta-interpreter. An alternative measure of the size of proof trees could also be used. For example, you could use the number of nodes in the tree instead of the maximum depth of the proof tree. You could also make conjunction incur a cost by changing the second rule. (See Exercise 14.8.)

14.4.5 Meta-Interpreter to Build Proof Trees

To implement the how question of Section 5.4.3 (page 196), the interpreter can build a proof tree for a derived answer. Figure 14.13 gives a meta-interpreter that implements built-in predicates and builds a representation of a proof tree. This proof tree can be traversed to implement **how questions**. In this algorithm, a **proof tree** is either *true*, *built_in*, of the form $if(G, T)$ where G is an atom and T is a proof tree, or of the form $(L \,\&\, R)$ where L and R are proof trees.

Example 14.21 Consider the base-level clauses for the wiring domain (page 593) and the base-level query ask *lit*(L). There is one answer, namely $L = l_2$. The meta-level query ask $hprove(lit(L), T)$ returns the answer $L = l_2$ and the tree

$T = if(lit(l_2),$
$\qquad if(light(l_2), true) \&$
$\qquad if(ok(l_2), true) \&$
$\qquad if(live(l_2),$
$\qquad\qquad if(connected\_to(l_2, w_4), true) \&$
$\qquad\qquad if(live(w_4),$
$\qquad\qquad\qquad if(connected\_to(w_4, w_3),$
$\qquad\qquad\qquad\qquad if(up(s_3), true)) \&$
$\qquad\qquad\qquad if(live(w_3),$
$\qquad\qquad\qquad\qquad if(connected\_to(w_3, w_5),$
$\qquad\qquad\qquad\qquad\qquad if(ok(cb_1), true)) \&$
$\qquad\qquad\qquad\qquad if(live(w_5),$
$\qquad\qquad\qquad\qquad\qquad if(connected\_to(w_5, outside), true) \&$
$\qquad\qquad\qquad\qquad\qquad if(live(outside), true)))))).$

Although this tree can be understood if properly formatted, it requires a skilled user to understand it. The how questions of Section 5.4.3 (page 196) traverse this tree. The user only has to see clauses, not this tree. See Exercise 14.13 (page 687).

14.4.6 Delaying Goals

One of the most useful abilities of a meta-interpreter is to **delay** goals. Some goals, rather than being proved, can be collected in a list. At the end of the proof, the system derives the implication that, if the delayed goals were all true, the computed answer would be true.

Providing a facility for collecting goals that should be delayed is useful for a number of reasons:

- to implement proof by contradiction as used in consistency-based diagnosis (page 207) or to implement abduction (page 220), the assumables are delayed

- to delay (page 632) subgoals with variables, in the hope that subsequent calls will ground the variables (page 633), and

- to create new rules that leave out intermediate steps – for example, if the delayed goals are to be asked of a user or queried from a database.

Figure 14.14 gives a meta-interpreter that provides delaying. A base-level atom G can be made delayable using the meta-level fact $delay(G)$. The delayable atoms can be collected into a list without being proved.

If you can prove $dprove(G, [\,], D)$, you know that the implication $G \Leftarrow D$ is a logical consequence of the clauses, and $delay(d)$ is true for all $d \in D$. This idea

% $dprove(G, D_0, D_1)$ is true if D_0 is an ending of D_1 and G logically follows from
% the conjunction of the delayable atoms in D_1.

> $dprove(true, D, D)$.
> $dprove((A \& B), D_1, D_3) \leftarrow$
> > $dprove(A, D_1, D_2) \wedge$
> > $dprove(B, D_2, D_3)$.
> $dprove(G, D, [G|D]) \leftarrow$
> > $delay(G)$.
> $dprove(H, D_1, D_2) \leftarrow$
> > $(H \Leftarrow B) \wedge$
> > $dprove(B, D_1, D_2)$.

Figure 14.14: A meta-interpreter that collects delayed goals

of deriving a new clause from a knowledge base is an instance of **partial evaluation**. It is the basis for **explanation-based learning** which treats the derived clauses as learned clauses that can replace the original clauses.

Example 14.22   As an example of delaying for consistency-based diagnosis, consider the base-level knowledge base of Figure 14.10 (page 677), but without the rules for *ok*. Suppose, instead, that $ok(G)$ is delayable. This is represented as the meta-level fact

   $delay(ok(G))$.

The query

   ask $dprove(live(p_1), [\,], D)$.

has one answer, namely, $D = [ok(cb_1)]$. If $ok(cb_1)$ were true, then $live(p_1)$ would be true.

   The query

   ask $dprove((lit(l_2) \& live(p_1)), [\,], D)$.

has the answer $D = [ok(cb_1), ok(cb_1), ok(s_3)]$. If cb_1 and s_3 are *ok*, then l_2 will be lit and p_1 will be live.

   Note that $ok(cb_1)$ appears as an element of this list twice. *dprove* does not check for multiple instances of delayables in the list. A less naive version of *dprove* would not add duplicate delayables. See Exercise 14.9 (page 687).

14.5   Review

The following are the main points you should have learned from this chapter:

- Individual–property–value triples form a flexible, universal representation for relations.

- Ontologies allow for semantic interoperability and knowledge sharing.

- OWL ontologies are built from individuals, classes, and properties. A class is a set of real and potential individuals.

- A meta-interpreter can be used to build a lightweight implementation of a knowledge-based system that can be customized to fit the requirements of the representation language.

14.6   References and Further Reading

Sowa [2000] and Brachman and Levesque [2004] give an overview of knowledge representation. Davis [1990] is an accessible introduction to a wealth of knowledge representation issues in commonsense reasoning. Brachman and Levesque [1985] present many classic knowledge representation papers. See Woods [2007] for an overview of semantic networks.

For an overview of the philosophical and computational aspects of ontologies, see Smith [2003] and Sowa [2011]. For an overview of the semantic web see Antoniou and van Harmelen [2008], Berners-Lee et al. [2001], and Hendler et al. [2002]. Janowicz et al. [2015] explain the role of semantics in big data. The ontology summit (http://ontologforum.org/index.php/OntologySummit) produces an annual communique that provides a good summary of many issues in using ontologies.

The description of OWL in this chapter is based on OWL-2; see W3C OWL Working Group [2012], Hitzler et al. [2012], and Motik et al. [2012]. Krötzsch [2012] describes the OWL 2 profiles.

DBpedia [Auer et al., 2007], and **YAGO** [Suchanek et al., 2007; Hoffart et al., 2013; Mahdisoltani et al., 2015], **Wikidata** [Vrandečić and Krötzsch, 2014], (http://www.wikidata.org/) and Knowledge Vault [Gabrilovich et al., 2014] are large knowledge bases that use triples and ontologies to represent facts about millions of entities.

The top-level ontology is based on **BFO**, the **Basic Formal Ontology**, described in Grenon and Smith [2004], Smith [2015], Arp et al. [2015] and the ontology of Sowa [2000]. Other top-level ontologies include DOLCE [Gangemi et al., 2003], Cyc [Panton et al., 2006] and SUMO [Niles and Pease, 2001; Pease, 2011]. A more lightweight and widely used ontology is at http://schema.org.

SNOMED Clinical Terms (SNOMED CT) [IHTSDO, 2016] is a large medical ontology that is used in clinical practice. You can explore it at http://browser. ihtsdotools.org/.

Meta-interpreters for logic are discussed by Bowen [1985] and Kowalski [2014]. See the collection by Abramson and Rogers [1989].

14.7 Exercises

Exercise 14.1 There are many possible kinship relationships you could imagine like mother, father, great-aunt, second-cousin-twice-removed, and natural-paternal-uncle. Some of these can be defined in terms of the others, for example:

$$brother(X, Y) \leftarrow father(X, Z) \wedge natural\_paternal\_uncle(Y, Z).$$
$$sister(X, Y) \leftarrow parent(Z, X) \wedge parent(Z, Y) \wedge$$
$$female(X) \wedge different(X, Y).$$

Give two quite different representations for kinship relationships based on different relations being primitive.

Consider representing the primitive kinship relationship using relation

$$children(Mother, Father, List\_of\_children)$$

What advantages or disadvantages may this representation have compared to the two you designed above?

Exercise 14.2 A travel site has a database that represents information about hotels and feedback from users that uses the relations:

$$hotel(Id, Name, City, Province, Country, Address)$$
$$reported\_clean(Hotel, RoomNumber, Cleanliness, day(Year, Month, Day))$$

Show how the following facts can be represented using triple notation, using vocabulary that make sense:

```
hotel(h345,"The Beach Hotel",victoria,bc,
      canada,"300 Beach St").
reported_clean(h345,127,clean,day(2013,01,25)).
```

Is it reasonable to represent the hotel name and address as strings? Explain.

Exercise 14.3 Sam has proposed that any n-ary relation $P(X_1, X_2, X_3, ..., X_n)$ can be reexpressed as $n - 1$ binary relations, namely,

$$P_1(X_1, X_2).$$
$$P_2(X_2, X_3).$$
$$P_3(X_3, X_4).$$
$$\vdots$$

$$P_{n-1}(X_{n-1}, X_n).$$

Explain to Sam why this may not be such a good idea. What problems would arise if Sam tried to do this? Use an example to demonstrate where the problem arises.

Exercise 14.4 Write an ontology for the objects that often appear on your desk that may be useful for a robot that is meant to tidy your desk. Think of the categories that (a) the robot can perceive and (b) should be distinguished for the task.

Exercise 14.5 Suppose a "beach resort" is a resort near a beach that the resort guests can use. The beach has to be near the sea or a lake, where swimming is permitted. A resort must have places to sleep and places to eat. Write a definition of beach resort in OWL.

Exercise 14.6 A luxury hotel has multiple rooms to rent, each of which is comfortable and has a view. The hotel must also have more than one restaurant. There must be menu items for vegetarians and for meat eaters to eat in the restaurants.

(a) Define a luxury hotel in OWL, based on this description. Make reasonable assumptions where the specification is ambiguous.

(b) Suggest three other properties you would expect of a luxury hotel. For each, give the natural language definition and the OWL specification.

Exercise 14.7 For the following, explain how each is categorized by the top-level ontology of Section 14.3.3 (page 670):

(a) your skin

(b) the period at the end of the first sentence of this chapter

(c) the excitement a child has before a vacation

(d) the trip home from a vacation

(e) a computer program

(f) summer holidays

(g) the ring of a telephone

(h) the dust on your desk

(i) the task of cleaning your office

(j) the diagnosis of flu in a person

(k) France

Based on this experience, suggest and justify a modification of the top-level ontology. Think about categories that are not exclusive or other distinctions seem to be fundamental.

Exercise 14.8 Consider two ways to modify the depth-bound meta-interpreter of Figure 14.12 (page 680):

(a) The bound is on number of instances of base-level atoms that appear in the proof. Why might this be better or worse than using the depth of the tree?

(b) Allow different base-level atoms to incur different costs on the bound. For example, some atoms could have zero cost, and some atoms could incur a high cost. Give an example of where this might be useful. What conditions on the atom costs would guarantee that, when a positive bound is given, the proof procedure does not go into an infinite loop?

Exercise 14.9 The program of Figure 14.14 (page 683) allows duplicate delayed goals. Write a version of *dprove* that returns minimal sets of delayed goals, in their simplest form.

Exercise 14.10 Write a meta-interpreter that can ask multiple sources for information. Suppose that each source is identified by a universal resource identifier (URI). Suppose you have the predicates

- *can_answer*(Q, URI) is true if the source given by *URI* can answer questions that unify with Q.

- *reliability*(URI, R) is true if R is some numerical measure of reliability of URI. You can assume that R is in the range $[-100, 100]$, in which the higher number means that it is more reliable.

- *askSite*$(URI, Q, Answer)$ is true when you ask the source *URI* a question Q, it gives the *Answer* that is one of $\{yes, no, unknown\}$. Note that although *can_answer* and *reliability* can be simple databases, *askSite* is a sophisticated program that accesses the web or asks a human a question.

Write a meta-interpreter that can utilize multiple information sources and returns a reliability of the answer, where the reliability of an answer is the minimum of the reliabilities of the information sources used. You must have some convention for when no external sources were used (e.g., a reliability of 200). You can only ask an information source a question that you have recorded that it can answer.

Exercise 14.11 Write a meta-interpreter that allows for asking the users yes-or-no questions. Make sure it does not ask questions to which it already knows the answer.

Exercise 14.12 Extend the ask-the-user meta-interpreter from the previous question to allow for questions that ask for instances. The system could ask the user questions like "for which X is $P(X)$ true?", where the user can give an instance or tell the system there are no more instances. One feature that is useful is to be able to interpret declarations that a predicate is functional and respond accordingly. For example, it might be better to ask for the height of a person than ask many yes-no questions about their height.

Exercise 14.13 Write a program that takes in a tree produced from the meta-interpreter that builds proof trees as shown in Figure 14.13 (page 681) and lets someone traverse the tree using how questions.

Exercise 14.14 Write a meta-interpreter that allows both how and why questions. In particular, it should allow the user to ask how questions about a goal that has been proved after a why question. Explain how such a program may be useful.

Exercise 14.15 Write a meta-interpreter for definite clauses that does iterative deepening search. Make sure that it only returns one answer for each proof and that the system says *no* whenever the depth-first searcher says *no*. This should be based on the depth-bounded meta-interpreter (page 680) and the iterative deepening search algorithm (page 96).

Exercise 14.16 Build an iterative deepening abductive reasoning system to find minimal consistent sets of assumables to imply a goal. This can be based on the depth-bounded meta-interpreter of Figure 14.12 (page 680), and the delaying meta-interpreter of Figure 14.14 (page 683) to collect assumptions. The depth bound should be based on the number of assumables used in the proof. Assume that the assumables are all ground.

This should be done in two parts:

(a) Find the minimal sets of assumables that imply some g using iterative deepening on the number of assumables. When g is *false*, this program finds the minimal conflicts.

(b) Based on part (a), find the minimal explanations of g by interleaving finding conflicts and finding minimal sets of assumables that imply g.

Exercise 14.17 In this question, you will write a meta-interpreter for parametrized logic programs. These are logic programs that can use constants in arithmetic expressions. The values for the constants are given as part of the input to the meta-interpreter.

Assume that an environment is a list of terms of the form $val(Parm, Val)$, where Val is the value associated with parameter $Parm$. Assume that each parameter only appears once in an environment. An example environment is $[val(a, 7), val(b, 5)]$.

In AILog, you can use <= as the base-level implication and & as the base-level conjunction. AILog has <= defined as an infix operator and *number* is a built-in predicate.

(a) Write a predicate $lookup(Parm, Val, Env)$ that is true if parameter $Parm$ has value Val in environment Env.

(b) Write a predicate $eval(Exp, Val, Env)$ that is true if parametrized arithmetic expression Exp evaluates to number Val in environment Env. An expression is either

- of the form $(E_1 + E_2)$, $(E_1 * E_2)$, (E_1/E_2), $(E_1 - E_2)$, where E_1 and E_2 are parameterized arithmetic expressions;

- a number; or

- a parameter.

Assume that the operators have their usual meaning, that numbers evaluate to themselves, and that parameters evaluate to their value in the environment. You can use the AILog predicates *is*, use infix as N is E, which is true if (unparametrized) expression E evaluates to number N, and *number(E)*, which is true if E is a number.

(c) Write a predicate *pprove*(*G*, *Env*) that is true if goal *G* is a logical consequence of the base-level KB, where parameters are interpreted in environment *Env*. An example interaction with AILog is

```
ailog: tell f(X,Y) <= Y is 2*a+b*X.
ailog: ask pprove(f(3,Z),[val(a,7),val(b,5)]).
Answer: pprove(f(3,29),[val(a,7),val(b,5)]).
  [ok,more,how,help]: ok.
ailog:  ask pprove(f(3,Z),[val(a,5),val(b,7)]).
Answer: pprove(f(3,31),[val(a,5),val(b,7)]).
  [ok,more,how,help]: ok.
ailog: tell dsp(X,Y) <= Z is X*X*a & Y is Z*Z*b.
ailog: ask pprove(dsp(3,Z),[val(a,7),val(b,5)]).
Answer: pprove(dsp(3,19845),[val(a,7),val(b,5)]).
  [ok,more,how,help]: ok.
ailog: ask pprove(dsp(3,Z),[val(a,5),val(b,7)]).
Answer: pprove(dsp(3,14175),[val(a,5),val(b,7)]).
  [ok,more,how,help]: ok.
```

Chapter 15

Relational Planning, Learning, and Probabilistic Reasoning

What is now required is to give the greatest possible development to mathematical logic, to allow to the full the importance of relations, and then to found upon this secure basis a new philosophical logic, which may hope to borrow some of the exactitude and certainty of its mathematical foundation. If this can be successfully accomplished, there is every reason to hope that the near future will be as great an epoch in pure philosophy as the immediate past has been in the principles of mathematics. Great triumphs inspire great hopes; and pure thought may achieve, within our generation, such results as will place our time, in this respect, on a level with the greatest age of Greece.

– Bertrand Russell [1917]

The representation dimension (page 23) has, as its top level, reasoning in terms of individuals and relations. Reasoning in terms of relations allows for compact representations that can be built before the agent encounters particular individuals. When an agent finds out about an individual, it can make inferences about that individual. This chapter outlines how, in planning, learning and probabilistic reasoning, feature-based representations can be expanded to deal also with individuals and relations. In each of these areas, the relational representation benefits from being able to be built before the individuals are known and, therefore, before the features are known. As Russell points out in the quote above, relational reasoning brings great advantages over propositional and feature-based representations.

15.1   Planning with Individuals and Relations

A robot that can deliver parcels to people needs a model of the world before it knows which parcels exist and which people may need deliveries. It might need to be programmed before it knows the environment which it will inhabit. A tutoring system needs to work for multiple students and multiple problems, and needs to be programmed before it knows about the students and all of the problems. A purchasing agent, when it is being designed and built, will not know about all of the hotels and rooms it can book, and will not know about the people and their goals or preferences. In all of these cases, the agent's goals and its environment are described in

Dimensions (p. 31)
flat
relational
infinite horizon
fully observable
deterministic
goal directed
non-learning
single agent
offline
perfect rationality

terms of individuals and relations. When the agent's knowledge base is built, and before the agent knows the objects it should reason about, it requires a representation that is independent of the individuals. Thus, it must go beyond feature-based representations. When the individuals become known, the agent may be able to ground the representations by substituting the known individuals for the logical variables, and just use features. Often, it is useful to reason in terms of the non-grounded representations.

With a relational representation, time can be **reified** (page 648), or made into an individual. **Time** can be represented in terms of individual points in time or temporal intervals. This section presents two relational representations that differ in how time is represented.

15.1.1   Situation Calculus

The **situation calculus** represents states in terms of the actions required to reach them. The situation calculus can be seen as a relational version of the feature-based representation of actions (page 244).

Here we consider only a single agent, a fully observable environment, and deterministic actions.

The situation calculus is defined in terms of situations. A **situation** is either

- *init*, the initial situation, or

- $do(A, S)$, the situation resulting from doing action A in situation S, if it is possible to do action A in situation S.

Example 15.1   Consider the domain of Figure 3.1 (page 80). Suppose in the initial situation, *init*, the robot, Rob, is at location $o109$ and there is a key $k1$ at the mail room and a package at *storage*. Suppose $move(Ag, L_0, L_1)$ is the action of agent Ag moving from location L_0 to location L_1.

$do(move(rob, o109, o103), init)$

is the situation resulting from Rob moving from position *o109* in situation *init* to position *o103*. In this situation, Rob is at *o103*, the key *k1* is still at *mail*, and the package is at *storage*.

The situation

> *do*(*move*(*rob*, *o103*, *mail*),
> *do*(*move*(*rob*, *o109*, *o103*),
> *init*))

is one in which the robot has moved from position *o109* to *o103* to *mail* and is currently at mail. Suppose Rob then carries out the action *pickup*(*rob*, *k1*), which is to pick up the key *k1*. The resulting situation is

> *do*(*pickup*(*rob*, *k1*),
> *do*(*move*(*rob*, *o103*, *mail*),
> *do*(*move*(*rob*, *o109*, *o103*),
> *init*))).

In this situation, Rob is at position *mail* carrying the key *k1*.

A situation may be associated with a state. There are two main differences between situations and states:

- Multiple situations may refer to the same state if multiple sequences of actions lead to the same state. That is, equality between situations is not the same as equality between states.

- Not all states have corresponding situations. A state is **reachable** if a sequence of actions can reach that state from the initial state. States that are not reachable do not have a corresponding situation.

Some *do*(*A*, *S*) terms do not correspond to any state. Sometimes an agent must reason about such a (potential) situation without knowing whether *A* is possible in state *S*, or whether *S* is possible.

Example 15.2   The term *do*(*unlock*(*rob*, *door1*), *init*) does not denote a state at all, because it is not possible for Rob to unlock the door when Rob is not at the door and does not have the key.

The situations:

> *init*
>
> *do*(*move*(*rob*, *o103*, *o109*), *do*(*move*(*rob*, *o103*, *o109*), *init*))
>
> *do*(*move*(*rob*, *o103*, *ts*), *do*(*move*(*rob*, *o103*, *ts*), *init*))

all represent the same state, with the robot at location *o103*, and everything else that is true in the initial state. In the last two situations, the robot has moved away from *o103* and back again. This assumes that the resources used by the robot are not being modeled; if the resources were modeled, the last two situations may represent different states from *init* as the battery level may be less.

A **static relation** is a relation for which the truth value does not depend on the situation; that is, its truth value is unchanging through time. A **dynamic relation** is a relation for which the truth value depends on the situation. To represent what is true in a situation, predicate symbols denoting dynamic relations have a situation argument so that the truth can depend on the situation. A predicate symbol with a situation argument is called a **fluent**.

Example 15.3 The relation $at(O, L, S)$ is true when object O is at location L in situation S. Thus, at is a fluent.

The atom

$at(rob, o109, init)$

is true if the robot rob is at position $o109$ in the initial situation. The atom

$at(rob, o103, do(move(rob, o109, o103), init))$

is true if robot rob is at position $o103$ in the situation resulting from rob moving from position $o109$ to position $o103$ from the initial situation. The atom

$at(k1, mail, do(move(rob, o109, o103), init))$

is true if $k1$ is at position $mail$ in the situation resulting from Rob moving from position $o109$ to position $o103$ from the initial situation.

A dynamic relation is axiomatized by specifying the situations in which it is true. This is done inductively in terms of the structure of situations, as follows:

- Axioms with *init* as the situation parameter are used to specify what is true in the initial situation.

- A **primitive relation** is defined by specifying when it is true in situations of the form $do(A, S)$ in terms of what is true in situation S. That is, primitive relations are defined in terms of what is true at the previous situation.

- A **derived relation** is defined using clauses with a variable in the situation argument. The truth of a derived relation in a situation depends on what else is true in the same situation.

- A **static relation** is defined without reference to the situation.

Example 15.4 Suppose the delivery robot, Rob, is in the domain depicted in Figure 3.1 (page 80). Rob is at location $o109$, the parcel is in the storage room, and the key is in the mail room. The following axioms describe this initial situation:

$at(rob, o109, init)$.
$at(parcel, storage, init)$.
$at(k1, mail, init)$.

The *adjacent* relation is a dynamic, derived relation defined as follows:

$$adjacent(o109, o103, S).$$
$$adjacent(o103, o109, S).$$
$$adjacent(o109, storage, S).$$
$$adjacent(storage, o109, S).$$
$$adjacent(o109, o111, S).$$
$$adjacent(o111, o109, S).$$
$$adjacent(o103, mail, S).$$
$$adjacent(mail, o103, S).$$
$$adjacent(lab2, o109, S).$$
$$adjacent(P_1, P_2, S) \leftarrow$$
$$between(Door, P_1, P_2) \wedge$$
$$unlocked(Door, S).$$

Notice the free S variable; these clauses are true for all situations. The situation term, S, cannot be omitted because which rooms are adjacent depends on which doors are unlocked. This can change from situation to situation.

The *between* relation is static and does not require a situation variable:

$$between(door1, o103, lab2).$$

We also model whether or not an object is being carried. If an object is not being carried, we say that the object is sitting at its location. A carried object moves with the object carrying it. An object is at a location if it is sitting at that location or is being carried by an object at that location. Thus, $at(Object, Location, Situation)$ is a derived relation:

$$at(Ob, P, S) \leftarrow$$
$$sitting\_at(Ob, P, S).$$
$$at(Ob, P, S) \leftarrow$$
$$carrying(Ob1, Ob, S) \wedge$$
$$at(Ob1, P, S).$$

Note that this definition allows for Rob to be carrying a bag, which, in turn, is carrying a book.

The **precondition** (page 240) of an action specifies when it is possible to carry out the action. The relation $poss(A, S)$ is true when action A is possible in situation S. This is typically a derived relation.

Example 15.5 An autonomous agent can put down an object it is carrying:

$$poss(putdown(Ag, Obj), S) \leftarrow$$
$$autonomous(Ag) \wedge$$
$$carrying(Ag, Obj, S).$$

For the *move* action, an autonomous agent can move from its current position to an adjacent position:

$poss(move(Ag, P_1, P_2), S) \leftarrow$
   $autonomous(Ag) \wedge$
   $adjacent(P_1, P_2, S) \wedge$
   $sitting\_at(Ag, P_1, S).$

The precondition for the unlock action is more complicated. The agent must be on the correct side of the door and carrying the appropriate key:

$poss(unlock(Ag, Door), S) \leftarrow$
   $autonomous(Ag) \wedge$
   $between(Door, P_1, P_2) \wedge$
   $at(Ag, P_1, S) \wedge$
   $opens(Key, Door) \wedge$
   $carrying(Ag, Key, S).$

The *between* relation is not symmetric; some doors can only be opened with a key from one side.

What is true in each situation is defined recursively in terms of the previous situation and what action occurred between the situations. As in the feature-based representation of actions (page 244), **causal rules** specify when a relation becomes true and **frame rules** specify when a relation remains true.

Example 15.6   The primitive relation *unlocked* can be defined by specifying how different actions can affect its being true. A door is unlocked in the situation resulting from an unlock action, as long as the unlock action was possible. This is represented using the causal rule:

$unlocked(Door, do(unlock(Ag, Door), S)) \leftarrow$
   $poss(unlock(Ag, Door), S).$

Suppose the only action to make the door locked is to lock the door. Thus, *unlocked* is true in a situation following an action if it was true before, if the action was not to lock the door, and if the action was possible:

$unlocked(Door, do(A, S)) \leftarrow$
   $unlocked(Door, S) \wedge$
   $A \neq lock(Door) \wedge$
   $poss(A, S).$

This is a frame rule.

Example 15.7   The *carrying* predicate can be defined as follows.

An agent is carrying an object after picking up the object:

$carrying(Ag, Obj, do(pickup(Ag, Obj), S)) \leftarrow$
$\quad poss(pickup(Ag, Obj), S).$

The only action that undoes the *carrying* predicate is the *putdown* action. Thus, *carrying* is true after an action if it was true before the action, and the action was not to put down the object. This is represented in the frame rule:

$carrying(Ag, Obj, do(A, S)) \leftarrow$
$\quad carrying(Ag, Obj, S) \wedge$
$\quad poss(A, S) \wedge$
$\quad A \neq putdown(Ag, Obj).$

Example 15.8 The atom $sitting\_at(Obj, Pos, S_1)$ is true in a situation S_1 resulting from object Obj moving to Pos, as long as the action was possible:

$sitting\_at(Obj, Pos, do(move(Obj, Pos_0, Pos), S)) \leftarrow$
$\quad poss(move(Obj, Pos_0, Pos), S).$

The other action that makes *sitting_at* true is the *putdown* action. An object is sitting at the location where the agent who put it down was located:

$sitting\_at(Obj, Pos, do(putdown(Ag, Obj), S)) \leftarrow$
$\quad poss(putdown(Ag, Obj), S) \wedge$
$\quad at(Ag, Pos, S).$

The only other time that *sitting_at* is true in a (non-initial) situation is when it was true in the previous situation and it was not undone by an action. The only actions that undo *sitting_at* are a *move* action or a *pickup* action. This can be specified by the following frame axiom:

$sitting\_at(Obj, Pos, do(A, S)) \leftarrow$
$\quad poss(A, S) \wedge$
$\quad sitting\_at(Obj, Pos, S) \wedge$
$\quad \forall Pos_1 \ A \neq move(Obj, Pos, Pos_1) \wedge$
$\quad \forall Ag \ A \neq pickup(Ag, Obj).$

Note that the quantification in the body is not the standard quantification for rules. This can be represented in a standard manner as:

$sitting\_at(Obj, Pos, do(A, S)) \leftarrow$
$\quad poss(A, S) \wedge$
$\quad sitting\_at(Obj, Pos, S) \wedge$
$\quad \sim move\_action(A, Obj, Pos) \wedge$
$\quad \sim pickup\_action(A, Obj).$
$move\_action(move(Obj, Pos, Pos_1), Obj, Pos).$

$pickup\_action(pickup(Ag, Obj), Obj).$

where $\sim$ is negation as failure (page 633). These clauses are designed not to have a free variable in the scope of the negation.

Example 15.9 The situation calculus can represent more complicated actions than can be represented with simple addition and deletion of propositions in the state description.

Consider the *drop_everything* action in which an agent drops everything it is carrying. In the situation calculus, the following axiom can be added to the definition of *sitting_at* to say that everything the agent was carrying is now on the ground:

$sitting\_at(Obj, Pos, do(drop\_everything(Ag), S)) \leftarrow$
  $poss(drop\_everything(Ag), S) \land$
  $at(Ag, Pos, S) \land$
  $carrying(Ag, Obj, S).$

A frame axiom for *carrying* specifies that an agent is not carrying an object after a *drop_everything* action.

$carrying(Ag, Obj, do(A, S)) \leftarrow$
  $poss(A, S) \land$
  $carrying(Ag, Obj, S) \land$
  $A \neq drop\_everything(Ag) \land$
  $A \neq putdown(Ag, Obj).$

The *drop_everything* action thus affects an unbounded number of objects.

The situation calculus is used for **planning** by asking for a situation in which a goal is true. Answer extraction (page 595) is used to find a situation in which the goal is true. This situation can be interpreted as a sequence of actions for the agent to perform.

Example 15.10 Suppose the goal is for the robot to have the key $k1$. The following query asks for a situation where this is true:

ask $carrying(rob, k1, S).$

This query has the following answer:

$S = do(pickup(rob, k1),$
      $do(move(rob, o103, mail),$
          $do(move(rob, o109, o103),$
              $init))).$

The preceding answer can be interpreted as a way for Rob to get the key: it moves from *o109* to *o103*, then to *mail*, where it picks up the key.

The goal of delivering the parcel (which is, initially, in the lounge, *lng*) to *o111* can be asked with the query

ask $at(parcel, o111, S)$.

This query has the following answer:

$$S = do(move(rob, o109, o111),$$
$$do(move(rob, lng, o109),$$
$$do(pickup(rob, parcel),$$
$$do(move(rob, o109, lng), init))))).$$

Therefore, Rob should go to the lounge, pick up the parcel, go back to *o109*, and then go to *o111*.

Using the top-down proof procedure (page 602) on the situation calculus definitions is very inefficient, because a frame axiom is almost always applicable. A complete proof procedure, such as iterative deepening, searches through all permutations of actions even if they are not relevant to the goal. The use of answer extraction does not negate the necessity for efficient planners, such as the ones in Chapter 6.

15.1.2 Event Calculus

The second relational representation for reasoning about actions and change, the **event calculus**, models how the truth value of relations changes because of events occurring at certain times. Time can be modeled as either continuous or discrete.

Events are modeled as occurring at particular times. Event E occurring at time T is written as $event(E, T)$.

Events make some relations true and some no longer true:

- $initiates(E, R, T)$ is true if event E makes primitive relation R true at time T

- $terminates(E, R, T)$ is true if event E makes primitive relation R no longer true at time T.

Time T is a parameter to *initiates* and *terminates* because the effect of an event can depend on what else is true at the time. For example, the effect of attempting to unlock a door depends on the position of the robot and whether it is carrying the appropriate key.

Relations are either true or false at any time. In the event calculus, relations are reified, where $holds(R, T)$ means that relation R is true at time T. This is analogous to having T as the last argument to R in the situation calculus.

The use of the meta-predicate *holds* allows general rules that are true for all relations.

Derived relations are defined in terms of primitive relations and other derived relations for the same time.

Primitive relation R holds at time T if an event occurred before T that made R true, and there was no intervening event that made R no longer true. This can be specified as follows:

$$holds(R, T) \leftarrow$$
$$\quad event(E, T_0) \land$$
$$\quad T_0 < T \land$$
$$\quad initiates(E, R, T_0) \land$$
$$\quad \sim clipped(R, T_0, T).$$
$$clipped(R, T_0, T) \leftarrow$$
$$\quad event(E_1, T_1) \land$$
$$\quad terminates(E_1, R, T_1) \land$$
$$\quad T_0 < T_1 \land$$
$$\quad T_1 < T.$$

The atom $clipped(R, T_0, T)$ means there is an event between times T_0 and T that makes R no longer true; $T_0 < T_1$ is true if time T_0 is before time T_1. Here $\sim$ is negation as failure (page 633), and so these clauses mean their completion.

Actions are represented in terms of what properties they initiate and terminate. As in the situation calculus, the preconditions of actions are specified using the *poss* relation.

Example 15.11 The *pickup* action initiates a *carrying* relation, and it terminates a *sitting_at* relation as long as the preconditions for *pickup* are true:

$$initiates(pickup(Ag, Obj), carrying(Ag, Obj), T) \leftarrow$$
$$\quad poss(pickup(Ag, Obj), T).$$
$$terminates(pickup(Ag, Obj), sitting\_at(Obj, Pos), T) \leftarrow$$
$$\quad poss(pickup(Ag, Obj), T).$$
$$poss(pickup(Ag, Obj), T) \leftarrow$$
$$\quad autonomous(Ag) \land$$
$$\quad Ag \neq Obj \land$$
$$\quad holds(at(Ag, Pos), T) \land$$
$$\quad holds(sitting\_at(Obj, Pos), T).$$

This implies that if a *pickup* is attempted when the preconditions do not hold, nothing happens. It is also possible to write clauses that specify what happens under different circumstances, such as when a pickup is attempted for an object that is being held by something else.

Given particular action occurrences, and making the complete knowledge assumption that all intervening events are specified, the top-down proof procedure with negation as failure can be used to prove what is true.

The event calculus is different from the situation calculus in that it is based on a temporal representation rather than a state-based representation; the T argument in the event calculus is a time and not a state or situation. This means that an agent can reason about discrete or continuous time. Multiple agents carrying out actions in time can be modeled by specifying when the various actions by the agents occurred. The situation calculus requires interleaving the actions by different agents. The event calculus also lends itself to the case where events have durations. Given the times that events occurred, the effect can depend on the duration between times. Planning in the situation calculus is done by constructing a proof of the existence of a situation. In the event calculus, planning is done by **abduction** (page 220), which is used to hypothesize the occurrence of events to make a goal true.

15.2   Relational Learning

The tasks involved with making predictions of a relation based on observed relations are covered under the umbrella of **relational learning**. This could encompass making predictions about what relations are true of individuals, making predictions about which terms denote the same individual, and making predictions about the existence of individuals with certain properties and relationships with other individuals.

This section considers two instances of learning relations. The first is learning a relation in terms of other relations. The second can be used for learning a relation even if there are no other relations defined.

15.2.1   Structure Learning: Inductive Logic Programming

The task of predicting which relations are true based on the truth of other relations has mainly been carried out in the framework of logic programming, and so is typically called **inductive logic programming**.

Example 15.12 Suppose a trading agent has a data set, in terms of individual–property–value **triples** (page 648), about which resorts a person likes, as in Figure 15.1 (on the next page).

The agent wants to learn what Joe likes. What is important is not the value of the *likes* property, which is just a meaningless name, but the properties of the individual denoted by the name. Feature-based representations cannot do anything with this data set beyond learning that Joe likes *resort_14*, but not *resort_35*.

Individual	Property	Value
joe	*likes*	*resort_14*
joe	*dislikes*	*resort_35*
...	...	...
resort_14	*type*	*resort*
resort_14	*near*	*beach_18*
beach_18	*type*	*beach*
beach_18	*covered_in*	*ws*
ws	*type*	*sand*
ws	*color*	*white*
...	...	...

Figure 15.1: Data about holiday preferences

The theory the agent should learn is that, for example, Joe likes resorts near sandy beaches. This theory can be expressed as a logic program:

$$prop(joe, likes, R) \leftarrow$$
$$prop(R, type, resort) \land$$
$$prop(R, near, B) \land$$
$$prop(B, type, beach) \land$$
$$prop(B, covered\_in, S) \land$$
$$prop(S, type, sand).$$

Logic programs provide the ability to be able to represent deterministic theories about individuals and relations. This rule can be applied to resorts and beaches that Joe has not yet visited.

The input to an inductive logic programming learner includes the following:

- A is a set of atoms whose definitions the agent is learning.
- E^+ is a set of ground instances of elements of A, called the **positive examples**, that are observed to be true.
- E^- is a set of ground instances of elements of A, called the **negative examples**, that are observed to be false.
- B, the **background knowledge**, is a set of clauses that define relations that can be used in the learned logic programs.
- H is a space of possible hypotheses. H is often represented implicitly as a set of operators that can generate the possible hypotheses. Each hypothesis is a logic program.

Example 15.13 In Example 15.12, suppose the agent wants to learn what Joe likes. In this case, the inputs are

- $A = \{prop(joe, likes, R)\}$
- $E^+ = \{prop(joe, likes, resort\_14), \dots\}$. For the example that follows, assume there are many such items that Joe likes.
- $E^- = \{prop(joe, likes, resort\_35), \dots\}$. These are written in the positive form; they have been observed to be false.
- $B = \{prop(resort\_14, type, resort), prop(resort\_14, near, beach\_18), \dots\}$. This set contains all of the background facts about the world that are not instances of A. The agent is not learning about these.
- H is a set of logic programs defining $prop(joe, likes, R)$. The heads of the clauses unify with $prop(joe, likes, R)$. H is too big to enumerate.

All of these, except for H, are given explicitly in the formulation of the problem.

The aim is to find a simplest hypothesis $h \in H$ such that

$B \wedge h \models E^+$ and

$B \wedge h \not\models E^-$.

That is, the hypothesis implies the positive evidence and does not imply the negative evidence. It must be **consistent** with the negative evidence being false.

The aim is to find an element of the version space (page 325), where the elements of the version space are logic programs. This is similar to the definition of abduction (page 220), in which the knowledge base in abduction corresponds to the background knowledge. The hypothesis space of inductive logic programming is the set of logic programs. The second condition corresponds to consistency.

Assume that there is a single target $A = \{t(X_1, \dots, X_n)\}$ The hypothesis space consists of possible definitions for this relation using a logic program.

There are two main strategies used in inductive logic programming:

- The first strategy is to start with the simplest hypotheses and make them more complicated to fit the data. Because the logic program only states positive facts, the simplest hypothesis is the empty program, which specifies that $t(X_1, \dots, X_n)$ is always false. This is is the most specific hypothesis (page 325), but is not correct unless E^+ is empty. The second simplest hypothesis is the most general hypothesis (page 325), which is simply that $t(X_1, \dots, X_n)$ is always true. This hypothesis implies the positive examples, but it also implies the negative examples, if any exist. One strategy involves a **general-to-specific search**. It tries to find the simplest hypothesis that fits the data by searching the hypothesis space from the most general hypothesis to more complex hypotheses, always implying the positive examples, until a hypothesis that does not imply the negative examples is found.

- The second strategy is to start with a hypothesis that fits the data and to make it simpler while still fitting the data. A hypothesis that fits the data is the set of positive examples. This strategy involves a **specific-to-general search**: start with the very specific hypothesis in which only the positive examples are true, and then generalize the clauses, avoiding the negative cases.

Here we expand on the general-to-specific search for definite clauses. The initial hypothesis contains a single clause:

$$\{t(X_1, \ldots, X_n) \leftarrow\}.$$

A **specialization operator** takes a set G of clauses and returns a set S of clauses that specializes G. To specialize means that $S \models G$.

The following are three primitive specialization operators:

- Split a clause in G on condition c. Clause $a \leftarrow b$ in G is replaced by two clauses: $a \leftarrow b \wedge c$ and $a \leftarrow b \wedge \neg c$.

- Split a clause $a \leftarrow b$ in G on a variable X that appears in a or b. Clause $a \leftarrow b$ is replaced by the clauses

$$a \leftarrow b \wedge X = t_1.$$

$$\ldots$$

$$a \leftarrow b \wedge X = t_k.$$

where the t_i are terms.

- Remove a clause that is not necessary to prove the positive examples.

The last operation changes the predictions of the clause set. Those cases no longer implied by the clauses are false.

These primitive specialization operators are used together to form the operators of H. The operators of H are combinations of primitive specialization operations designed so that progress can be evaluated using a **greedy lookahead**. That is, the operators are defined so that one step is adequate to evaluate progress.

The first two primitive specialization operations should be carried out judiciously to ensure that the simplest hypothesis is found. An agent should carry out the splitting operations only if they make progress. Splitting is only useful when combined with clause removal. For example, adding an atom to the body of a clause is equivalent to splitting on the atom and then removing the clause containing the negation of the atom. A higher-level specialization operator may be to split on the atom $prop(X, type, T)$ for some variable X that appears in the clause, split on the values of T, and remove the resulting clauses that are not required to imply the positive examples. This operator makes progress on determining which types are useful.

```
1:  non-deterministic procedure Inductive_logic_program_TD(t, B, E⁺, E⁻, Rs)
2:     Inputs
3:         t: an atom whose definition is to be learned
4:         B: background knowledge is a logic program
5:         E⁺: positive examples
6:         E⁻: negative examples
7:         Rs: set of specialization operators
8:     Output
9:         logic program that classifies E⁺ positively and E⁻ negatively or ⊥ if
    no program can be found
10:    Local
11:        H is a set of clauses
12:    H ← {t(X₁, ..., Xₙ) ←}
13:    while there is e ∈ E⁻ such that B ∪ H ⊨ e do
14:        if there is r ∈ Rs such that B ∪ r(H) ⊨ E⁺ then
15:            choose r ∈ Rs such that B ∪ r(H) ⊨ E⁺
16:            H ← r(H)
17:        else
18:            return ⊥
19:    return H
```

Figure 15.2: Top-down induction of a logic program

Figure 15.2 shows a nondeterministic algorithm for the top-down induction of a logic program. It maintains a single hypothesis that it iteratively improves until finding a hypothesis that fits the data or until it fails to find such a hypothesis. The "choose" of line 15 can be implemented by search.

At each time step it chooses an operator to apply with the constraint that every hypothesis entails the positive examples. This algorithm glosses over two important details:

- which operators to consider and
- which operator to select.

The operators should be at a level so that they can be evaluated according to which one is making progress toward a good hypothesis. In a manner similar to decision tree learning (page 289), the algorithm can perform a myopically optimal choice. That is, it chooses the operator that makes the most progress in minimizing the error. The error of a hypothesis can be the number of negative examples that are implied by the hypothesis.

Example 15.14 Consider Example 15.12 (page 701), in which the agent must learn about Joe's likes and dislikes.

The first hypothesis is that Joe likes everything:

$$\{prop(joe, likes, R) \leftarrow \},$$

which is inconsistent with the negative evidence.

It can split the clause on conditions or split on a variable. The only way for the specialization to make progress – to prove fewer negative examples while implying all positive examples – is for the created rules to contain the variable R in the body.

- It could consider splitting on the property *type*, splitting on the value of *type*, and keeping only those that are required to prove the positive examples. This results in the following clause (assuming the positive examples only include resorts):

$$\{prop(joe, likes, R) \leftarrow prop(R, type, resort)\}.$$

  There can be other clauses if the positive examples include things other than resorts that Joe likes. If the negative examples include non-resorts, this split would be useful in reducing the error.

- It could consider splitting on other properties that can be used in proofs of the positive examples, such as *near*, resulting in

$$\{prop(joe, likes, R) \leftarrow prop(R, near, B)\}$$

  if all of the positive examples are near something. If some of the negative examples are not near anything, this specialization could be useful in reducing the error.

- It could consider splitting on the variable R, considering different constants for R. This does not allow for generalization.

It could then choose whichever of these splits makes the most progress. In the next step it could add the other one, other properties of R, or properties of B.

15.2.2   Learning Hidden Properties: Collaborative Filtering

Consider the problem of, given some tuples of a relation, predicting whether other tuples are true. Here we provide an algorithm that does this, even if there are no other relations defined.

In a **recommender system** users are given personalized recommendations of items they may like, and may not be aware of. One technique for recommender systems is predict the rating of a user on an item from the ratings of similar users or similar items, by what is called **collaborative filtering**.

One of the tasks for recommender systems is the **top-n** task, where n is a positive integer, say 10, which is to present the user n items they have not rated, and to judge the recommendation by how much the user likes one of

User	Item	Rating	Timestamp
196	242	3	881250949
186	302	3	891717742
22	377	1	878887116
244	51	2	880606923
253	465	5	891628467
...	...	...	...

Figure 15.3: Part of the MovieLens data set

these items. One way to select the items is to estimate the rating of each item for a user and to present the n items with the highest predicted rating. An alternative is to take the diversity of the recommendations into account; it may be better to recommend very different items than to recommend similar items.

Example 15.15   MovieLens (https://movielens.org/) is a movie recommendation system that acquires movie ratings from users. The rating is from 1 to 5 stars, where 5 stars is better. A data set for such a problem is of the form of Figure 15.3, where each user is given a unique number, each item (movie) is given a unique number, and the timestamp is the Unix standard of seconds since 1970-01-01 UTC. These data can be used in a recommendation system to make predictions of other movies a user might like.

Consider the problem of predicting the rating for an item by a user. This prediction can be used to give **personalized recommendations**: recommend the items with the highest predicted ratings for a user on items they have not rated. The recommendations for each user may be different when they have provided different ratings. In the example above, the items were movies, but they could also be consumer goods, restaurants, holidays, or other items.

We develop an algorithm that does not take properties of the items or the users into account. It simply suggests items based on what other people have liked. It could potentially do better if it takes properties of the items and the users into account.

Suppose Es is a data set of $\langle u, i, r \rangle$ triples, where $\langle u, i, r \rangle$ means user u gave item i a rating of r. (We are ignoring the timestamp here.) Let $\hat{r}(u, i)$ be the predicted rating of user u on item i. The aim is to optimize the sum-of-squares error:

$$\sum_{\langle u,i,r \rangle \in Es} (\hat{r}(u, i) - r)^2.$$

which penalizes large errors much more than small errors. As with most machine learning, we want to optimize for the test examples (page 270), not for the training examples.

Here we give a sequence of more sophisticated predictions:

Make a single prediction In the simplest case, we could predict the same rating for all users and items: $\widehat{r}(u, i) = \mu$, where μ is the mean rating. Recall (page 283) that if we are predicting the same for every user, predicting the mean minimizes the sum-of-squares error.

Add user and item biases Some users might give, on average, higher ratings than other users, and some movies may have higher ratings than other movies. We can take this into account using

$$\widehat{r}(u, i) = \mu + ib[i] + ub[u]$$

where item i has an item-bias parameter $ib[i]$ and user u has a user-bias parameter $ub[u]$. The parameters $ib[i]$ and $ub[u]$ are chosen to minimize the sum-of-squares error. If there are n users and m items, there are $n + m$ parameters to tune (assuming μ is fixed). Finding the best parameters is an optimization problem that can be done with a method like gradient descent (page 165), as was used for the linear learner (page 293).

One might think that $ib[i]$ should be directly related to the average rating for item i and $ub[u]$ should be directly related to the average rating for user u. However, it is possible that $ub[u] < 0$ even if all of the ratings for

---

Netflix Prize

There was a considerable amount of research on collaborative filtering with the **Netflix Prize** to award $1,000,000 to the team that could improve the prediction accuracy of Netflix's proprietary system, measured in terms of sum-of-squares by 10%. Each rating gives a user, a movie, the rating from 1 to 5 stars, and a date and time the rating was made. The data set consisted of approximately 100 million ratings from 480,189 anonymized users on 17,770 movies that was collected over a 7 year period. The prize was won in 2009 by a team that averaged over a collection of hundreds of predictors, some of which were quite sophisticated. After 3 years of research the winning team beat out another team by just 20 minutes to win the prize. They both had solutions which had essentially the same error, which was just under the threshold to win. Interestingly, an average of the two solutions was better than either alone.

The algorithm presented here is the basic algorithm that gave the most improvement.

The Netflix data set is no longer available because of **privacy** concerns. Although users were only identified by a number, there was enough information, if combined with other information, to potentially identify some of the users.

user u were above the mean μ. This can occur if user u only rated very popular movies and rated them lower than other people.

Optimizing the $ib[i]$ and $ub[u]$ parameters can help get better estimates of the ratings, but it does not help in personalizing the recommendations, because the movies are still ordered the same for every user.

Add a hidden property We could hypothesize that there is an underlying property of users and movies that makes more accurate predictions. For example, we could have the age of users, and the age-appropriateness of movies. Instead of using observed properties, we can invent a hidden property and tune it to fit the data.

The hidden property has a value $ip[i]$ for item i and a value $up[u]$ for user u. The product of these is used to predict the rating of that item for that user:

$$\widehat{r}(u, i) = \mu + ib[i] + ub[u] + ip[i] * up[u]$$

If $ip[i]$ and $up[u]$ are both positive or both negative, the property will increase the prediction. If one $ip[i]$ or $up[u]$ is negative and the other is positive, the property will decrease the prediction.

Example 15.16 Figure 15.4 (on the next page) shows a plot of the ratings as a function of a single property. This was for a subset of the MovieLens data set, where we selected 20 movies that had the most ratings, then we selected 20 users who had the most ratings for these movies. It was then trained for 1000 iterations of gradient descent, with a single property.

On the x-axis are the users, ordered by their value, $up[u]$, on the property. On the y-axis are the movies, ordered by their value, $ip[i]$ on the property. Each rating is then plotted against the user and the movie, so that triple $\langle u, i, r \rangle$ is depicted by plotting r at the (x, y) position $(up[u], ip[i])$. Thus each vertical column of numbers corresponds to a user, and each horizontal row of numbers is a movie. The columns overlap if two users have very similar values on the property. The rows overlap for movies that have very similar values on the property. The users and the movies where the property values are close to zero are not affected by this property, as the prediction uses the product of values of the properties.

What we would expect is that generally high ratings are in the top-right and the bottom-left, as these are the ratings that are positive in the product, and low ratings in the top-left and bottom-right, as their product is negative. Note that what is high and low is relative to the user and movie biases; what is high for one movie may be different from what is high for another movie.

Add k hidden properties There might not be just one property that makes users like movies, but there may be many such properties. Here we introduce

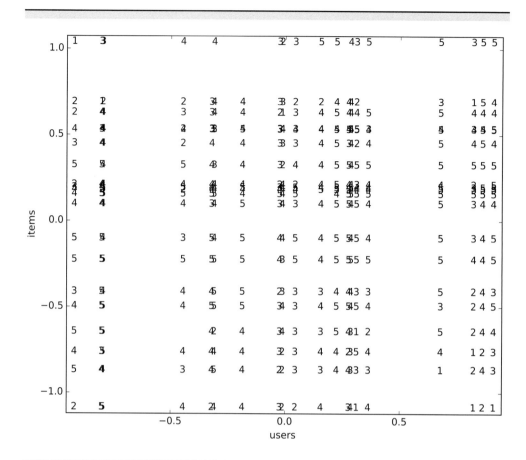

Figure 15.4: Movie ratings by users as a function of a single property

k such properties. There is a value $ip[i,p]$ for every item i and property $p \in \{1,\ldots,k\}$, and a value $up[u,p]$ for every user u and property p. The contributions of the properties are added. This gives the prediction:

$$\widehat{r}(u,i) = \mu + ib[i] + ub[u] + \sum_p ip[i,p] * up[u,p]$$

This is often called a **matrix factorization** method as the summation corresponds to matrix multiplication.

Regularize To avoid overfitting, a **regularization** (page 304) term can be added to prevent the parameters from growing too much and overfitting the given data. Here an L_2 regularizer (page 305) for each of the parameters is added to the optimization. The goal is to choose the parameters to

$$minimize \left(\sum_{\langle u,i,r \rangle \in Es} (\widehat{r}(u,i) - r)^2 \right.$$

$$+ \lambda \left(\sum_i (ib[i]^2 + \sum_p ip[i,p]^2) + \sum_u (ub[u]^2 + \sum_p up[u,p]^2) \right)$$
(15.1)

where λ is a regularization parameter, which can be tuned by cross validation (page 306).

We can optimize the *ib*, *ub*, *ip*, and *up* parameters using stochastic gradient descent (page 292). The algorithm is shown in Figure 15.5 (on the next page). Note that $ip[i,p]$, $up[u,p]$ need to be initialized randomly (and not to the same value) to force each property to be different.

This algorithm can be evaluated by how well it predicts future ratings. We can train it with the data up to a certain time, and test it on future data.

The algorithm can be improved in various ways including

- taking into account observed attributes of items and users. This is important for the **cold-start problem**, which is how to make recommendations about new items or for new users

- taking the timestamp into account, as users' preferences may change and items may come in and out of fashion.

15.3 Statistical Relational Artificial Intelligence

Statistical relational AI is about representations, inference and learning when there is uncertainty about properties of individuals, relations among individuals, the identity of individuals and even about the existence of individuals.

15.3.1 Relational Probabilistic Models

The belief network probability models of Chapter 8 were defined in terms of features. Many domains are best modeled in terms of individuals and relations. Agents must often build models before they know what individuals are in the domain and, therefore, before they know what random variables exist. When the probabilities are being learned, the probabilities often do not depend on the individuals. Although it is possible to learn about an individual, an agent must also learn general knowledge that it can apply when it finds out about a new individual.

Example 15.17 Consider the problem of predicting how well students will do in courses they have not taken. Figure 15.6 (page 713) shows some fictional data designed to show what can be done. Students s_3 and s_4 have the same averages, on courses with the same averages. However, we may be able to distinguish them as we know something about the courses they have taken.

```
 1:  procedure Collaborative_filter_learner(Es, η, λ)
 2:     Inputs
 3:         Es: set of ⟨user, item, rating⟩ triples
 4:         η: gradient descent step size
 5:         λ: regularization parameter
 6:     Output
 7:         function to predict rating for a ⟨user, item⟩ pair
 8:     μ :=  average rating
 9:     assign ip[i, p], up[u, p] randomly
10:     assign ib[i], ub[u] arbitrarily
11:     define r̂(u, i) = μ + ib[i] + ub[u] + Σₚ ip[i, p] * up[u, p]
12:     repeat
13:                                        ▷ Update parameters from training data
14:         for each ⟨u, i, r⟩ ∈ Es do
15:             error := r̂(u, i) − r
16:             ib[i] := ib[i] − η * error
17:             ub[u] := ub[u] − η * error
18:             for each property p do
19:                 ip[i, p] := ip[i, p] − η * error * up[u, p]
20:                 up[u, p] := up[u, p] − η * error * ip[i, p]
21:                                        ▷ Regularize the parameters
22:         for each item i do
23:             ib[i] := ib[i] − η * λ * ib[i]
24:             for each property p do
25:                 ip[i, p] := ip[i, p] − η * λ * ip[i, p]
26:         for each user u do
27:             ub[u] := ub[u] − η * λ * ub[u]
28:             for each property p do
29:                 up[u, p] := up[u, p] − η * λ * up[u, p]
30:     until termination
31:     return r̂
```

Figure 15.5: Gradient descent for collaborative filtering

Student	Course	Grade
s_1	c_1	a
s_2	c_1	c
s_1	c_2	b
s_2	c_3	b
s_3	c_2	b
s_4	c_3	b
s_3	c_4	?
s_4	c_4	?

Figure 15.6: Predict which student will do better in course c_4

This is a different problem than the cases consider in Chapter 7 because the values of properties *Student* and *Course* are individuals, and we want to make predictions based on the properties of the individuals. None of the methods in that chapter would work on such data.

Example 15.18 Consider the problem of an intelligent tutoring system diagnosing students' arithmetic errors. From observing a student's performance on a number of examples, the tutor should try to determine whether or not the student understands the task and, if not, work out what the student is doing wrong so that appropriate remedies can be applied.

Consider the case of diagnosing two-digit addition of the form

$$
\begin{array}{cccc}
 & x_1 & x_0 \\
+ & y_1 & y_0 \\
\hline
z_2 & z_1 & z_0
\end{array}
$$

The student is given the values for the xs and the ys and provides values for the zs.

Students' answers depend on the problem (the xs and ys) and whether they know basic addition and whether they know how to carry. A belief network for this example is shown in Figure 15.7 (on the next page). The carry into digit i, given by the variable C_i, depends on the X_i, Y_i, and C_{i-1}, the carry for the previous digit (except for the initial case), and on whether the student knows how to carry. The z-value for digit i, given by the variable Z_i, depends on the X_i, Y_i, C_i, and whether the student knows basic addition.

By observing the value of the xs and the ys in the problem and the value of zs given by the student, the posterior probability that the student knows addition and knows how to carry can be inferred. One feature of the belief network model is that it allows students to make random errors; even though they know how to perform two-digit arithmetic, they can still get the wrong answer occasionally.

The problem with this representation is that it is inflexible. A flexible representation would allow for the addition of multiple digits, multiple problems,

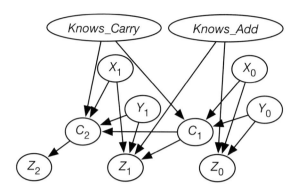

Figure 15.7: Belief network for two-digit addition

multiple students, and multiple times. Multiple digits require the replication of the network for the digits. Multiple times allow for modeling how students' knowledge and their answers change over time, even if the problems do not change over time.

If the conditional probabilities were stored as tables, the size of those tables would be enormous. For example, if the X_i, Y_i, and Z_i variables each have a domain size of 11 (the digits 0 to 9 or the blank), and the C_i and *Knows_Add* variables are binary, a tabular representation of

$$P(Z_1|X_1, Y_1, C_1, Knows\_Add)$$

would have a size greater than 4000. There is much more structure in the conditional probability than is expressed in the tabular representation. Tabular representations are not the only representation of conditional probabilities (page 381). We present a probabilistic extension of logic programs below that allows for both relational probabilistic models and compact descriptions of conditional probabilities.

A **relational probability model (RPM)** or **probabilistic relational model** is a model in which the probabilities are specified on the relations, independently of the actual individuals. Different individuals share the probability parameters.

A **parameterized random variable** is of the form $R(t_1, \ldots, t_n)$, where each t_i is a term (a logical variable or a constant). Thus it corresponds to either an atomic symbol or a term (page 586). The parameterized random variable is said to be parameterized by the logical variables that appear in it. A ground instance of a parameterized random variable is obtained by substituting constants for the logical variables in the parameterized random variable. The ground instances of a parameterized random variable correspond to random variables. The domain of the random variable is the range of R. A Boolean parameterized random variable R corresponds to a predicate symbol.

We use the Datalog convention (page 584) that logical variables start with an upper-case letter and constants start with a lower-case letter. Random variables and functions are written starting with an upper-case letter, with the corresponding proposition in lower case (e.g., $Diff(c_1)=true$ is written as $diff(c_1)$, and $Diff(c_1)=false$ is written as $\neg diff(c_1)$).

Example 15.19 For a relational probability model of the multidigit arithmetic problem outlined above, there is a separate x-variable for each digit D and for each problem P, represented by the parameterized random variable $X(D,P)$. Thus, for example, $X(1,prob17)$ may be a random variable representing the x-value of the first digit of problem 17. Similarly there is a parameterized random variable, $Y(D,P)$, which represents a random variable for each digit D and problem P.

There is a variable for each student S and time T that represents whether S knows how to add properly at time T. The parameterized random variable $Knows\_add(S,T)$ represents whether student S knows addition at time T. The random variable $Knows\_add(fred,mar23)$ is true if Fred knows addition on March 23. Similarly, there is a parameterized random variable $Knows\_carry(S,T)$.

There is a different z-value and a different carry for each digit, problem, student, and time. These values are represented by the parameterized random variables $Z(D,P,S,T)$ and $Carry(D,P,S,T)$. So, $Z(1,prob17,fred,mar23)$ is a random variable representing the answer Fred gave on March 23 for digit 1 of problem 17. Function Z has range $\{0,\ldots,9,blank\}$, so this set is the domain of the random variables that are the ground instances of $Z(D,P,S,T)$.

A **plate model** consists of

- a directed graph in which the nodes are parameterized random variables,
- a population of individuals for each logical variable, and
- a conditional probability of each node given its parents.

We draw a rectangle – a **plate** – around the parameterized random variables that share a logical variable. There is a plate for each logical variable. A plate model means its grounding – the belief network in which nodes are all ground instances of the parameterized random variables (each logical variable replaced by an individual in its population). That is, the variables in each plate are replicated for each individual. The conditional probabilities of the grounded belief network are the same as the corresponding instances of the plate model. This notation is redundant, as the logical variables are specified in both the plates and the arguments. Sometimes one of these is omitted; often the arguments are omitted when they can be inferred from the plates.

Example 15.20 Figure 15.8 (on the next page) gives a plate model for predicting student grades. There is a plate C for the courses and a plate S for the students. The parameterized random variables are

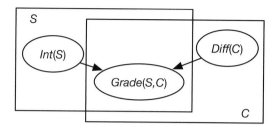

Figure 15.8: A plate model to predict the grades of students

- $Int(S)$ which represents whether student S is intelligent
- $Diff C)$, which represents whether course C is difficult,
- $Grade(S,C)$ which represents the grade of student S in course C.

The probabilities for $P(Int(S))$, $P(Diff C))$, and $P(Grade(S,C) \mid Int(S), Diff C))$ need to be specified. If I and D are Boolean (with range *true* and *false*) and Gr has range $\{a,b,c\}$ then there are 10 parameters that define the probability distribution. Suppose $P(Int(S)) = 0.5$ and $P(Diff C)) = 0.5$ and $P(Grade(S,C) \mid Int(S), Diff C))$ is defined by the following table:

$Int(S)$	$Diff C)$	$Grade(S,C)$		
		a	b	c
true	*true*	0.5	0.4	0.1
true	*false*	0.9	0.09	0.01
false	*true*	0.01	0.1	0.9
false	*false*	0.1	0.4	0.5

Eight parameters are required to define $P(Grade(S,C) \mid Int(S), Diff C))$ because there are four cases, and each case requires two numbers to be specified; the third can be inferred to ensure the probabilities sum to one.

Figure 15.9 (on the next page) shows a grounding for 3 students *sam*, *chris* and *kim*, and 2 courses, c_1 and c_2. If there were n students and m courses, in the grounding there would be n instances of $Int(S)$, m instances of $Diff C)$ and $n*m$ instances of $Grade(S,C)$. So there would be $n+m+n*m$ random variables in the grounding.

Consider conditioning on the data given in Figure 15.6 (page 713), and querying the variables corresponding to the last two rows. There are 4 courses and 4 students, and so there would be 24 variables in the grounding. All of the instances of $Grade(S,C)$ that are not observed or queried can be pruned (page 379) or never constructed in the first place, resulting in the belief network of Figure 15.10 (page 718). From this network, conditioned on the *obs*, the observed grades of Figure 15.6 (page 713), and using the probabilities above,

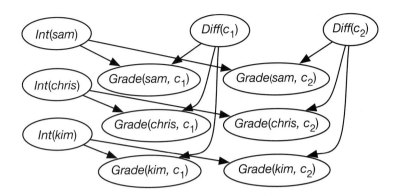

Figure 15.9: A grounding for 3 students and 2 courses

the following posterior probabilities can be derived:

	a	b	c
$P(Grade(s_3, c_4) \mid obs)$	0.491	0.245	0.264
$P(Grade(s_4, c_4) \mid obs)$	0.264	0.245	0.491

Thus, this model predicts that s_3 is likely to do better than s_4 in course c_4.

Example 15.21 A plate model for the multidigit addition problem of Example 15.19 (page 715) is shown in Figure 15.11 (on the next page). The rectangles correspond to plates. For the plate labeled with D, P, an instance of each variable exists for each digit D and problem P. One way to view this is that the instances come out of the page, like a stack of plates. Similarly, for the plate labeled S, T, there is a copy of the variables for each student S and each time T. For the variables in the intersection of the plates, there is a random variable for each digit D, problem P, student S, and time T.

The plate representation denotes the same independence as a belief network (page 362); each node is independent of its non-descendants given its parents. This dependence is inherited by a corresponding ground belief network. Thus, for particular values $d \in dom(D)$, $p \in dom(P)$, $s \in dom(S)$, and $t \in dom(T)$, $Z(d, p, s, t)$ is a random variable, with parents $X(d, p)$, $Y(d, p)$, $Carry(d, p, s, t)$ and $Knows\_add(s, t)$. There is a loop in the plate model on the $Carry(D, P, S, T)$ parameterized random variable because the carry for one digit depends on the carry for the previous digit for the same problem, student, and time. Similarly, whether students know how to carry at some time depends on whether they knew how to carry at the previous time. The ground network needs to be acyclic.

There is a conditional probability of each parameterized random variable, given its parents. This conditional probability is shared among its ground instances.

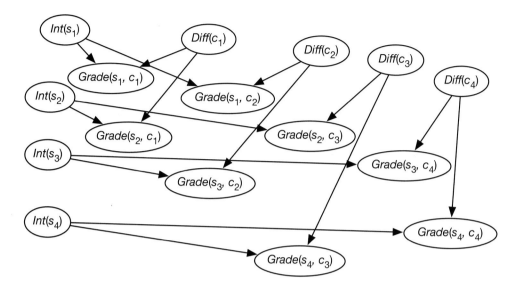

Figure 15.10: A grounding that is sufficient to predict from the data in Figure 15.6 (page 713)

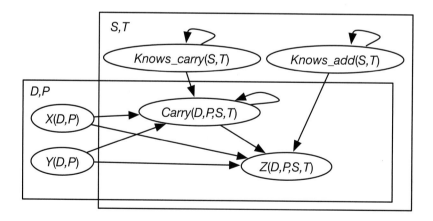

Figure 15.11: Belief network with plates for multidigit addition

Unfortunately, the plate representation is not adequate when the dependency occurs among different instances of the same relation. In the preceding example, $Carry(D, P, S, T)$ depends, in part, on $Carry(D - 1, P, S, T)$, that is, on the carry from the previous digit (and there is some other case for the first digit). To represent such examples, it is useful to be able to specify how the logical variables interact, as is done in logic programs.

One representation that combines the ideas of belief networks, plates, and logic programs is the **independent choice logic (ICL)**. The ICL consists of a set of independent choices, a logic program that gives the consequences of the choices, and probability distributions over the choices. In more detail, the ICL is defined as follows:

An **alternative** is a set of atoms (page 586) all sharing the same logical variables. A **choice space** is a set of alternatives such that none of the atoms in the alternatives unify with each other. An ICL theory contains

- a choice space C. Let C' be the set of ground instances of the alternatives. Thus, C' is a set of sets of ground atoms.
- an acyclic (page 204) logic program (that can include negation as failure), in which the head of the clauses does not unify with an element of an alternative in the choice space.
- a probability distribution over each alternative. All instances of an alternative have the same probability.

The atoms in the logic program and the choice space can contain constants, variables, and function symbols.

A **selector function** selects a single element from each alternative in C'. There is a **possible world** for each selector function. The logic program specifies what is true in each possible world. Atom g is true in a possible world if it follows from the atoms selected by the selector function added to the logic program. The probability of proposition g is given by a measure over sets of possible worlds, where the atoms in different ground instances of the alternatives are probabilistically independent. The instances of an alternative share the same probabilities, and the probabilities of different instances are multiplied.

Example 15.22 Consider the choice space $C = \{\{a_1, a_2\}, \{b_1, b_2, b_3\}\}$, the logic program L:

$$c \leftarrow a_1 \wedge b_1$$
$$c \leftarrow a_2 \wedge b_3$$
$$d \leftarrow c$$
$$d \leftarrow b_2$$

and the distribution over the first alternative, $P(a_1) = 0.7, P(a_2) = 0.3$ and over the second alternative $P(b_1) = 0.5, P(b_2) = 0.4, P(b_3) = 0.1$.

There are 6 possible worlds:

World	Selection		Implied by L		probability
w_0	a_1	b_1	c	d	0.35
w_1	a_1	b_2	$\neg c$	d	0.28
w_2	a_1	b_3	$\neg c$	$\neg d$	0.07
w_3	a_2	b_1	$\neg c$	$\neg d$	0.15
w_4	a_2	b_2	$\neg c$	d	0.12
w_5	a_2	b_3	c	d	0.03

so, under this model, $P(c) = 0.35 + 0.03 = 0.38$, and $P(d) = 0.35 + 0.28 + 0.12 + 0.03 = 0.78$.

You do not need to enumerate all possible worlds to compute probabilities. Abduction (page 220) can be used to find descriptions of the sets of worlds in which g is true. The atoms in the alternatives are made assumable (page 206), with different atoms in the same alternative declared to be inconsistent. If the explanations are pairwise inconsistent, the probability of g can be computed by adding the probabilities of the explanations. If they are not pairwise inconsistent they can be made pairwise consistent.

An ICL theory can be seen as a causal model (page 371) in which the causal mechanism is specified as a logic program and the background variables, corresponding to the alternatives, have independent probability distributions over them. It may seem that this logic, with only unconditionally independent atoms and a deterministic logic program, is too weak to represent the sort of knowledge required. However, even without logical variables, the independent choice logic can represent anything that can be represented in a belief network, as in the following example:

Example 15.23 Consider representing the belief network of Example 8.15 (page 364) in the ICL. The same technique works for any belief network.

Fire and tampering have no parents, so they can be represented directly as alternatives:

$\{fire, nofire\}$,

$\{tampering, notampering\}$.

The probability distribution over the first alternative is $P(fire) = 0.01$, $P(nofire) = 0.99$. Similarly, $P(tampering) = 0.02$, $P(notampering) = 0.89$.

The dependence of *Smoke* on *Fire* can be represented using two alternatives:

$\{smokeWhenFire, nosmokeWhenFire\}$,

$\{smokeWhenNoFire, nosmokeWhenNoFire\}$,

with $P(smokeWhenFire) = 0.9$ and $P(smokeWhenNoFire) = 0.01$. Two rules can be used to specify when there is smoke:

$smoke \leftarrow fire \wedge smokeWhenFire.$

$smoke \leftarrow {\sim}fire \wedge smokeWhenNoFire.$

where $\sim$ is negation as failure (page 633), and so these clauses mean their completion.

To represent how *Alarm* depends on *Fire* and *Tampering*, there are four alternatives:

$$\{alarmWhenTamperingFire, noalarmWhenTamperingFire\},$$
$$\{alarmWhenNoTamperingFire, noalarmWhenNoTamperingFire\},$$
$$\{alarmWhenTamperingNoFire, noalarmWhenTamperingNoFire\},$$
$$\{alarmWhenNoTamperingNoFire, noalarmWhenNoTamperingNoFire\},$$

where $P(alarmWhenTamperingFire) = 0.5$, $P(alarmWhenNoTamperingFire) = 0.99$, and similarly for the other atoms using the probabilities from Example 8.15 (page 364). There are also rules specifying when *alarm* is true, depending on tampering and fire:

$$alarm \leftarrow tampering \wedge fire \wedge alarmWhenTamperingFire.$$
$$alarm \leftarrow \sim tampering \wedge fire \wedge alarmWhenNoTamperingFire.$$
$$alarm \leftarrow tampering \wedge \sim fire \wedge alarmWhenTamperingNoFire.$$
$$alarm \leftarrow \sim tampering \wedge \sim fire \wedge alarmWhenNoTamperingNoFire.$$

Other random variables are represented analogously, using the same number of alternatives as there are assignments of values to the parents of a node.

An ICL representation of a conditional probability can be seen as a rule form of a decision tree (page 285) with probabilities at the leaves. There is a rule and an alternative for each branch. Non-binary alternatives are useful when non-binary variables are involved.

The independent choice logic may not seem very intuitive for representing standard belief networks, but it can make complicated relational models much simpler, as in the following example.

Example 15.24 Consider the parameterized version of the multidigit addition of Example 15.19 (page 715). The plates correspond to logical variables.

There are three cases for the value of $Z(D, P, S, T)$. The first is when the student knows addition at this time, and the student did not make a mistake. In this case, they get the correct answer:

$$z(D, P, S, T, V) \leftarrow$$
$$x(D, P, Vx) \wedge$$
$$y(D, P, Vy) \wedge$$
$$carry(D, P, S, T, Vc) \wedge$$
$$knowsAddition(S, T) \wedge$$
$$\sim mistake(D, P, S, T) \wedge$$
$$V \text{ is } (Vx + Vy + Vc) \text{ div } 10.$$

We use the convention that the last variable in the atom corresponds to the value. Thus the atom $z(D, P, S, T, V)$ is true when the parameterized random variable $Z(D, P, S, T)$ has value V, and similarly for the other atoms.

There is an alternative for whether or not the student happened to make a mistake in this instance:

$$\forall D \forall P \forall S \forall T \{noMistake(D, P, S, T), mistake(D, P, S, T)\},$$

where the probability of $mistake(D, P, S, T)$ is 0.05, assuming students make an error in 5% of the cases even when they know how to do arithmetic.

The second case is when the student knows addition at this time but makes a mistake. In this case, we assume that the students are equally likely to pick each of the digits:

$$z(D, P, S, T, V) \leftarrow$$
$$\quad knowsAddition(S, T) \wedge$$
$$\quad mistake(D, P, S, T) \wedge$$
$$\quad selectDig(D, P, S, T, V).$$

There is an alternative that specifies which digit the student chose:

$$\forall D \forall P \forall S \forall T \{selectDig(D, P, S, T, V) \mid V \in \{0, \ldots, 9\}\}.$$

Suppose that, for each v, the probability of $selectDig(D, P, S, T, v)$ is 0.1.

The final case is when the student does not know addition. In this case, the student selects a digit at random:

$$z(D, P, S, T, V) \leftarrow$$
$$\quad \sim knowsAddition(S, T) \wedge$$
$$\quad selectDig(D, P, S, T, V).$$

These three rules cover all of the rules for z; it is much simpler than the table of size greater than 4000 that was required for the tabular representation and it also allows for arbitrary digits, problems, students, and times. Different digits and problems give different values for $X(D, P)$, and different students and times have different values for whether they know addition.

The rules for *carry* are similar. The main difference is that the carry in the body of the rule depends on the previous digit.

Whether a student knows addition at any time depends on whether they knew addition at the previous time. Presumably, the student's knowledge also depends on what actions occur (what the student and the teacher do). Because the ICL allows standard logic programs (with "noise"), either of the representations for modeling change introduced at the start of this chapter can be used.

AILog, as used in the previous chapters, also implements ICL.

Relational, Identity, and Existence Uncertainties

The models of Section 15.3 are concerned with **relational uncertainty**; uncertainty about whether a relation is true of some individuals. For example, a probabilistic model of $likes(X, Y)$ for $X \neq Y$, whether different people like each other, could depend on properties of X and Y and other relations they are involved in. A probabilistic model for $likes(X, X)$ is about whether people like themselves. Models about who likes whom may be useful, for example, for a tutoring system to determine whether two people should work together.

Given constants *sam* and *chris*, we can use the first of these models for $likes(sam, chris)$ only if we know that *sam* and *chris* are different people. The problem of **identity uncertainty** concerns uncertainty of whether, or not, two terms denote the same individual. This is a problem for medical systems, where it is important to determine whether the person who is interacting with the system now is the same person as one who visited yesterday. This problem is particularly difficult if the patient is non-communicative or wants to deceive the system, for example, to get drugs. This problem is also referred to as **record linkage**, as the problem is to determine which (medical) records are for the same person.

In all of the above cases, the individuals are known to exist; to give names to Chris and Sam presupposes that they exist. Given a description, the problem of determining whether there exists an individual that fits the description is the problem of **existence uncertainty**. Existence uncertainty is problematic because there may be no individuals who fit a description or there may be multiple individuals. We cannot give properties to non-existent individuals, because individuals that do not exist do not have properties. If we want to give a name to an individual that exists, we need to be concerned about which individual we are referring to if there are multiple individuals that exist. One particular case of existence uncertainty is **number uncertainty**, about the number of individuals that exist. For example, a purchasing agent may be uncertain about the number of people who would be interested in a package tour, and whether to offer the tour depends on the number of people who may be interested.

Reasoning about existence uncertainty can be very tricky if there are complex roles involved, and the problem is to determine whether there are individuals to fill the roles. Consider a purchasing agent who must find an apartment for Sam and her son Chris. Whether Sam wants an apartment probabilistically depends, in part, on the size of her room and the color of Chris' room. However, individual apartments do not come labeled with Sam's room and Chris' room, and there may not exist a room for each of them. Given a model of an apartment Sam would want, it is not obvious how to condition on the observations.

15.4   Review

The following are the main points you should have learned from this chapter:

- Relational representations are used when an agent requires models to be given or learned before it which individuals it will encounter.

- Many of the representations in earlier chapters can be made relational.

- The situation calculus represents time in terms of the action of an agent, using the *init* constant and the *do* function.

- Event calculus allows for continuous and discrete time and axiomatizes what follows from the occurrence of events.

- Inductive logic programming can be used to learn relational models, even when the values of features are meaningless names.

- Collaborative filtering can be used to make predictions about instances of relations from other instances by inventing hidden properties.

- Plate models and the independent choice logic allow for the specification of probabilistic models before the individuals are known.

15.5   References and Further Reading

The situation calculus was proposed by McCarthy and Hayes [1969]. The form of the frame axioms presented here can be traced back to Kowalski [2014], Schubert [1990], and Reiter [1991]. Reiter [2001] presents a comprehensive overview of the situation calculus; see also Brachman and Levesque [2004]. The event calculus was proposed by Kowalski and Sergot [1986]. There have been many other suggestions about how to solve the **frame problem**, which is the problem of concisely specifying what does not change during an action. Shanahan [1997] provides an excellent introduction to the issues involved in representing change and to the frame problem in particular.

For overviews of inductive logic programming see Muggleton and De Raedt [1994], Muggleton [1995], and Quinlan and Cameron-Jones [1995].

The Netflix prize, and the winning algorithms are described at http://www.netflixprize.com/. The collaborative filtering algorithm is based on Koren et al. [2009]. The MovieLens data sets are described by Harper and Konstan [2015] and available from http://grouplens.org/datasets/movielens/.

Statistical relational AI is described by De Raedt et al. [2016]. Plate models are due to Buntine [1994], who used them to characterize learning. Independent choice logic was proposed by Poole [1993, 1997] and implemented in Problog [De Raedt et al., 2007]. De Raedt et al. [2008] and Getoor and Taskar [2007] provide collections of papers that provide overviews on probabilistic relational models and how they can be learned. Domingos and Lowd [2009] discuss how (undirected) relational models can provide a common target representation for AI.

15.6   Exercises

Some of these exercises can use AILog, a simple logical reasoning system that implements much the reasoning discussed in this chapter. It is available from the book website (http://artint.info). Some of these can also be done in Prolog or Problog.

Exercise 15.1 Add to the situation calculus example (also available from the book web page) the ability to paint an object. In particular, add the predicate

   $color(Obj, Col, Sit)$

that is true if object Obj has color Col in situation Sit.
   The parcel starts off blue. Thus, we have an axiom:

   $color(parcel, blue, init)$.

There is an action $paint(Obj, Col)$ to paint object Obj with color Col. For this exercise, assume objects can only be painted red, and they can only be painted when the object and the robot are both at position $o109$. Colors accumulate on the robot. There is nothing that undoes an object being a color; if you paint the parcel red, it is both red and blue – of course this is unrealistic, but it makes the problem simpler.
   Axiomatize the predicate $color$ and the action $paint$ using situation calculus.
   You can do this without using more than three clauses (apart from the clause defining the color in the initial situation), where none of the clauses has more than two atomic symbols in the body. You do not require equality, inequality, or negation as failure. Test it in AILog.
   Your output should look something like the following:

```
ailog: bound 12.
ailog: ask color(parcel,red,S).
Answer:  color(parcel,red, do(paint(parcel,red),
                    do(move(rob,storage,o109),
                      do(pickup(rob,parcel),
                        do(move(rob,o109,storage),
                          init)))))).
```

Exercise 15.2 In this exercise, you will add a more complicated paint action than in the previous exercise.
   Suppose the object $paint\_can(Color)$ denotes a can of paint of color $Color$.
   Add the action $paint(Obj, Color)$ that results in the object changing its color to $Color$. (Unlike in the previous question, the object only has one color at a time.) The painting can only be carried out if the object is sitting at $o109$ and an autonomous agent is at position $o109$ carrying the can of paint of the appropriate color.

Exercise 15.3 AILog performs depth-bounded search. You will notice that the processing time for the previous questions was slow, and you required a depth bound that was close to the actual depth bound to make it work in a reasonable amount of time.

In this exercise, estimate how long an iterative deepening search will take to find a solution to the following query:

```
ask sitting_at(parcel,lab2,S).
```

(Do not bother to try it – it will take too long to run.)

(a) Estimate the smallest bound necessary to find a plan. [Hint: How many steps are needed to solve this problem? How does the number of steps relate to the required depth bound?] Justify your estimate.

(b) Estimate the branching factor of the search tree. To do this you should look at the time for a complete search at level $k + 1$ versus a complete search at level k. You should justify your answer both experimentally (by running the program) and theoretically (by considering what is the branching factor). You do not have to run cases with a large run time to do this problem.

(c) Based on your answers to parts (a) and (b), and the time you found for some run of the program for a small bound, estimate the time for a complete search of the search tree at a depth one less than that required to find a solution. Justify your solution.

Exercise 15.4 In this exercise, you will investigate using event calculus for the robot delivery domain.

(a) Represent the *move* action in the event calculus.

(b) Represent each of the sequences of actions in Example 15.10 (page 698) in the event calculus.

(c) Show that event calculus can derive the appropriate goals from the sequence of actions given in part (b).

Exercise 15.5 Suppose that, in event calculus, there are two actions, *Open* and *Close*, and a relation *opened* that is initially, at time 0, false. Action *Open* makes *opened* true, and action *Close* makes *opened* false. Suppose that action *Open* occurs at time 5, and action *Close* occurs at time 10.

(a) Represent this in event calculus.

(b) Is *opened* true at time 3? Show the derivation.

(c) Is *opened* true at time 7? Show the derivation.

(d) Is *opened* true at time 13? Show the derivation.

(e) Is *opened* true at time 5? Explain.

(f) Is *opened* true at time 10? Explain.

(g) Suggest an alternative axiomatization for *holds* that has different behavior at times 5 and 10.

(h) Argue for one axiomatization as being more sensible than the other.

Exercise 15.6 Give some concrete specialization operators that can be used for top-down inductive logic programming. They should be defined so that making progress can be evaluated myopically. Explain under what circumstances the operators will make progress.

Exercise 15.7 Change the stochastic gradient descent algorithm of Figure 15.5 (page 712) so it minimizes Formula (15.1), but regularizes after each example. Hint: You need to consider how many times each parameter is updated for one iteration through the data set and adjust the regularization parameter accordingly.

Exercise 15.8 An alternative regularization for collaborative filtering is to minimize

$$\sum_{\langle u,i,r \rangle \in D} \left((\hat{r}(u,i) - r)^2 + \lambda (ib[i]^2 + ub[u]^2 + \sum_p (ip[i,p]^2 + up[u,p]^2)) \right)$$

(a) How this differ from the regularization of Formula (15.1) (page 711)? [Hint: Compare the regularization for the items or users with few ratings with those with many ratings.]

(b) How does the code of Figure 15.5 (page 712) need to be modified to implement this regularization?

(c) Which works better in on test data? [Hint: You will need to set λ to be different for each method; for each method, choose the value of λ by cross validation.]

Exercise 15.9 A simple modification for the gradient descent for collaborative filtering can be used to predict $P(rating > threshold)$ for various values of threshold in $\{1, 2, 3, 4\}$. Modify the code so that it learns such a probability. [Hint: Make the prediction the sigmoid of the linear function as in logistic regression.] Does this modification work better for the task of recommending the top-n movies, for, say $n = 10$, where the aim is to have the maximum number of movies rated 5 in the top-n list? Which threshold work best? What if the top-n is judged by the number of movies rated 4 or 5?

Exercise 15.10 Suppose Boolean parameterized random variables $young(Person)$ and $cool(Item)$ are parents of Boolean $buys(Person, Item)$. Suppose there are 3000 people and 200 items.

(a) Draw this in plate notation.

(b) How many random variables are in the grounding of this model?

(c) How many numbers need to be specified for a tabular representation of this model. (Do not include any numbers that are functions of other specified numbers.)

(d) Draw the grounding belief network assuming the population of *Person* is $\{sam, chris\}$ and the population of *Item* is $\{iwatch, mortgage, spinach\}$.

(e) What could be observed to make $cool(iwatch)$ and $cool(mortgage)$ probabilistically dependent on each other given the observations?

Exercise 15.11 For the representation of addition in Example 15.24 (page 721), it was assumed that the observed Z-values would all be digits. Change the representation so that the observed values can be digits, a blank, or *other*. Give appropriate probabilities.

Exercise 15.12 Suppose you have a relational probabilistic model for movie prediction, which represents

$$P(likes(P, M) \mid age(P), genre(M))$$

where $age(P)$ and $genre(M)$ are a priori independent.

(a) What is the treewidth (page 380) of the ground belief network (after pruning irrelevant variables) for querying $age(Sam)$ given the following observations?

Person	Movie	likes
Sam	Hugo	yes
Chris	Hugo	no
Sam	The Help	no
Sam	Harry Potter 6	yes
Chris	Harry Potter 6	yes
Chris	AI	no
Chris	The Help	no
David	AI	yes
David	The Help	yes

(b) For the same probabilistic model, for m movies, n people and r ratings, what is the worst-case treewidth of the corresponding graph (after pruning irrelevant variables), where only ratings are observed? [Hint: The treewidth depends on the structure of the observations; think about how the observations can be structured to maximize the treewidth.]

(c) For the same probabilistic model, for m movies, n people, and r ratings, what is the worst-case treewidth of the corresponding graph, where only some of the ratings but all of the genres are observed?

Exercise 15.13 Represent the electrical domain of previous chapters in ICL, so that it will run in AILog. The representation should include the probabilistic dependencies of Example 8.17 (page 367) and the relations of Example 13.12 (page 593).

Part V

Retrospect and Prospect

Chapter 16

Retrospect and Prospect

Computation is the fire in our modern-day caves. By 2056, the computational revolution will be recognised as a transformation as significant as the industrial revolution. The evolution and widespread diffusion of computation and its analytical fruits will have major impacts on socioeconomics, science and culture.

– Eric Horvitz [2006]

In this chapter, we stand back and give a big-picture view of artificial intelligence in terms of the agent design space (page 21), and the future of AI. By placing many of the representation schemes in the agent design space, the relationships among the representations become more apparent. This allows us to see where the frontier of AI research now lies and to get a sense of the evolution of the field. We also consider some of the many social and ethical consequences that have arisen from the development and application of intelligent computational agents. As Horvitz points out in the quote above, computation is changing the world; we must be aware of its positive and negative impacts.

16.1 Dimensions of Complexity Revisited

What has AI research achieved? Where do the current frontier issues lie? To get a systematic sense of the big picture, the agent design space (page 21) for AI systems was described in terms of ten dimensions. It is instructive to see how representations presented in the book can be positioned in that space.

Figure 16.1 (on the next page) reviews the dimensions of complexity and classifies, in terms of the values for each dimension, some of the representations we have covered.

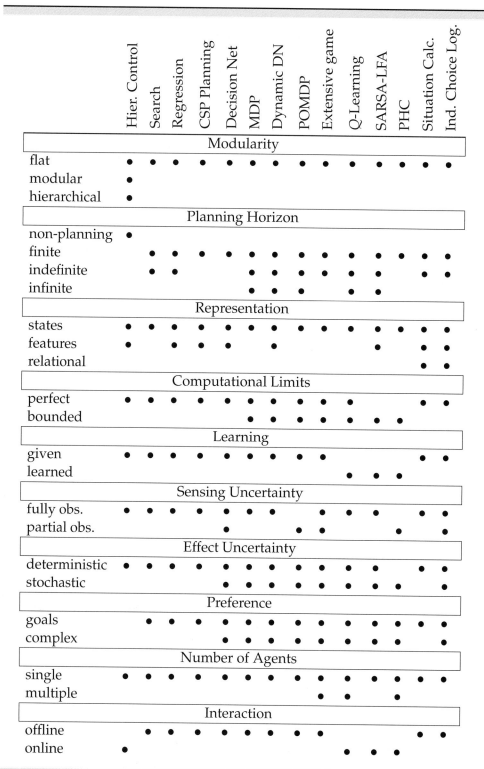

Figure 16.1: Some representations rated by dimensions of complexity

Agent Models

Hierarchical control (page 56) allows for hierarchical reasoning. As presented, it did not involve planning or goals, but it can be combined with other techniques. For example, it is possible to do reinforcement learning at multiple levels of a hierarchy, or even to learn the hierarchy.

State-space search, as presented in Chapter 3, allows for an indefinite horizon but otherwise gives the simplest value in all the other dimensions. Regression planning (page 249), using either the STRIPS representation or the feature-based representation extends state-space search to reason in terms of features. Constraint satisfaction problem (CSP) planning (page 252) allows for pruning the search space based on both the initial situation and the goal, but at the cost of planning for only a finite stage.

Decision networks (page 445) represent features, stochastic effects, partial observability, and complex preferences in terms of utilities. However, as with CSP planning, these networks only reason for a finite stage planning horizon.

Markov decision processes (MDPs) (page 458) allow for indefinite and infinite stage problems with stochastic actions and complex preferences; however, they are state-based representations that assume the state is fully observable. Dynamic decision networks (dynamic DN) (page 470) extend MDPs to allow feature-based representation of states. They extend decision networks to allow for indefinite or infinite horizons, but they do not model sensing uncertainty. Partially observable MDPs (POMDPs) (page 474) allow for a partially observable state but are much more difficult to solve.

The extensive form of a game (page 524) extends state-space search to include multiple agents. It can handle partially observable domains through the use of information sets (page 526). Multiagent decision networks (page 527) extend decision networks to allow for multiple agents.

Q-learning (page 555) extends MDPs to allow for learning, but only deals with states. SARSA-LFA, SARSA with linear function approximation of the Q-function (page 565), does reinforcement learning with features.

The policy hill climbing (PHC) algorithm (page 570) allows for learning with multiple agents, but it only allows a single state and a planning horizon of 1 (it plays a repeated single-step game); the only uncertainty is in the actions of the other agents. It can be seen as a reinforcement learning algorithm with a single state but with multiple agents.

The situation calculus (page 692) and the event calculus (page 699) allow for the representation of individuals and relations and an indefinite planning horizon, but do not represent uncertainty.

The independent choice logic (page 719) is a relational representation that allows for the representation of uncertainty in the effect of actions, sensing uncertainty, and utilities; however, in this most general framework, reasoning is more general and so possibly less efficient than POMDPs.

Dimensions Revisited

None of planning representations presented in the table handle hierarchical decomposition. However, large bodies of work exist on hierarchical planning and hierarchical reinforcement learning that are not presented in this book.

All of the representations can handle finite stage planning, for example by treating the features at different times as different variables. The planning systems based on (discounted or average) rewards can handle infinite stage planning, where the agents go on forever collecting rewards. It does not make sense for goal-oriented systems to go on forever.

All of the representations can handle states as the degenerate case. Reasoning in terms of features is the main design choice for many of the representations. Only the last two representations in Figure 16.1 allow for relational models, although many of the algorithms could potentially be made relational.

Bounded rationality underlies many of the approximation methods used for applications; however, making the explicit trade-off between thinking and acting, in which the agent reasons about whether it should act immediately or think more, is still relatively rare.

Figure 16.1 only shows three learning algorithms, although it is possible to learn the models for the others, for example, learning the conditional probabilities (page 488) or the structure (page 510) of probabilistic models (as model-based reinforcement learning (page 562) learns probabilities for an MDP), or learning the structure of relational models (page 701).

The dimension that adds the most difficulty to the task of building an agent is sensing uncertainty. There are many ways to represent the function from the history of the agent to its actions. Ways to extend planning with sensing uncertainty and indefinite and infinite horizon problems are discussed in the context of POMDPs (page 474). How to handle sensing in all of its forms is one of the most active areas of current AI research.

The models that can use stochastic actions can also handle deterministic actions (as deterministic is a special case of stochastic). Some of them, such as MDPs and the reinforcement learning algorithms work very well in deterministic domains. Policy hill climbing (PHC) is not listed as working with deterministic actions, as it models the other agents as stochastic, even if they eventually converge to deterministic policies.

The models that can handle complex cardinal preferences can also handle goals by giving a reward to goal achievement (and perhaps a negative reward to not achieving a reward at each step, although a preference for not wasting time is also handled by discounting).

Dealing with multiple agents is much more difficult than planning for a single agent. Multiple agents can be cooperative or competitive, or more often somewhere in between, where they can compete in some aspects and cooperate in others. Sometimes, not being (or not appearing to be) rational is advantageous to an agent (see Example 11.14 (page 537)).

We have considered interaction as a single dimension, whereas real agents have to make quick online decisions as well as make more long-term decisions. Agents need to reason about multiple time-scales, and what can appear as offline in relation to a decision that has to be made in a second, could be seen as an online decision at the scale of days. No agent has the luxury of unlimited offline computation without risking never getting started.

As can be seen, this book has presented a small part of the design space of AI. The current frontier of research goes well beyond what is covered in this textbook. There is much active research in all areas of AI. There have been and continue to be impressive advances in planning, learning, perception, natural language understanding, robotics, and other subareas of AI. Most of this work considers multiple dimensions and how they interact. The is a growing interest for considering all of the dimensions and multiple tasks simultaneously (for example, under the rubric of **artificial general intelligence**), but doing everything well is difficult.

The decomposition of AI into subareas is not surprising. The design space is too big to explore all at once. Once a researcher has decided to handle, say, relational domains and reasoning about the existence of objects, it is difficult to add sensor uncertainty. If a researcher starts with learning with infinite horizons, it is difficult to add hierarchical reasoning, let alone learning with infinite horizons and relations together with hierarchies.

Some particular points in design space that have been at the frontier of research over the past few years include the following:

- hierarchical reinforcement learning, where the agent learns at multiple levels of abstraction at once
- multiagent reinforcement learning
- relational probabilistic learning
- natural understanding that takes into account ambiguity, context, and pragmatics to give appropriate answers
- robot cars that can drive through uncertain environments
- intelligent tutoring systems that take into account noisy sensors of students' emotions
- supervised deep learning for perception, where deep learning is used to learn low-level and higher-level features (and ones in-between) which work together to make predictions.

As AI practitioners, we still do not know how to build an agent that acts rationally in infinite-stage, partially observable domains consisting of individuals and relations in which there are multiple agents acting autonomously. Arguably humans do this, perhaps by reasoning hierarchically and approximately. Although we may not yet be able to build an intelligent artificial agent with human-level performance, we may have the building blocks to develop one. The main challenge is handling the complexity of the real world. However, so far there seem to be no intrinsic obstacles to building computational embodied agents capable of human-level performance.

16.2   Social and Ethical Consequences

As the science and technology of AI matures, smart artifacts are being deployed at an accelerating rate. Their widespread deployment is having, and will have, profound ethical, psychological, social, economic, and legal consequences for human society and for our planet. Here we can only raise, and skim the surface of, some of these issues. Artificial autonomous agents are, in one sense, simply the next stage in the development of technology. In that sense, the normal concerns about the impact of technological development apply, but in another sense the new technologies represent a profound discontinuity.

Autonomous agents perceive, decide, and act on their own. This is a radical, qualitative change in technology and in our image of technology. This development raises the possibility that these agents could take unanticipated actions beyond human control. As with any disruptive technology, there will be substantial positive and negative consequences – many that will be difficult to judge and many that humans simply will not, or cannot, foresee.

As an example, **autonomous vehicles** are being developed and deployed. Thrun [2006] presents an optimistic view of autonomous vehicles. The positive impact of having intelligent cars and trucks will be enormous. There is the **safety** aspect of reducing the annual carnage on the roads; it is estimated that 1.2 million people are killed, and more than 50 million are injured, in traffic accidents each year worldwide. Vehicles could communicate and negotiate at intersections. Besides the consequent reduction in accidents, there could be up to three times the traffic throughput. The improvements in road usage efficiency come both from smarter intersection management and from platooning effects, whereby automated, communicating vehicles can safely follow each other very closely because they can communicate their intentions before acting and they react much quicker than people. This increase in road utilization has potential positive side effects. It not only decreases the capital and maintenance cost of highways, but has potential ecological savings of using highways so much more efficiently instead of paving over farmland. Elderly and disabled people would be able to get around on their own. People could dispatch their vehicles to the parking warehouse autonomously and then recall them later. Individual car ownership could become mostly obsolete. People could simply order up the most suitable vehicle for the trip. Automated warehouses could store vehicles more efficiently than using surface land for parking. Much of the current paved space in urban areas could be used for playgrounds, housing or even urban farms. The rigid distinction between private vehicles and public transit could dissolve.

On the other hand, experimental autonomous vehicles are seen by many as precursors to robot tanks, military cargo movers, and automated warfare. Although there may be, in some sense, significant benefits to robotic warfare, there are also very real dangers. In the past, these were only the nightmares of science fiction. Now, as automated warfare becomes a reality, we have to confront those dangers.

So there are two radically different, but not inconsistent, optimistic and pessimistic scenarios for the outcomes of the development of autonomous vehicles. This suggests the need for wise ethical consideration of their use. The stuff of science fiction is rapidly becoming science fact.

AI is now mature, both as a science and, in its technologies and applications, as an engineering discipline. Many opportunities exist for AI to have a positive impact upon our planet's environment. **Computational sustainability** is an emerging discipline studying how computational techniques, including AI, can be used to improve planetary sustainability in the ecological, economic and social realms. AI researchers and development engineers potentially have part of the skills required to address aspects of concerns of global warming, poverty, food production, arms control, health, education, the aging population, and demographic issues. They will have to work with domain experts, and be able to convince domain experts that the AI solutions are not just new snake oil. We can, as a simple example, provide access to tools for learning about AI, such as **AIspace**, so that people are empowered to understand and try AI techniques on their own problems, rather than relying upon opaque blackbox commercial systems. Games and competitions based upon AI systems can be very effective learning, teaching, and research environments, as shown by the success of **RoboCup** for robot soccer.

We have already considered some of the environmental impacts of intelligent cars and smart traffic control. A **combinatorial auction** is an auction in which agents bid on packages, consisting of combinations of discrete items. This is difficult because preferences are usually not additive (page 433), but items are typically complements or substitutes (page 435). Work on combinatorial auctions, already applied to spectrum allocation (allocation of radio frequencies to companies for television or cell phones) and logistics (planning for transporting goods), could further be applied to support carbon markets, to optimize energy supply and demand, and to mitigate climate change. There is much work on smart energy controllers using distributed sensors and actuators which improve energy use in buildings. We could use qualitative modeling techniques for climate scenario modeling. The ideas behind constraint-based systems can be applied to analyze sustainable systems. A **sustainable system** is in balance with its environment, satisfying short-term and long-term constraints on the resources it consumes and the outputs it produces.

Assistive technology for disabled and aging populations is being pioneered by many researchers. Assisted cognition is one application but also assisted perception and assisted action in the form of, for example, smart wheelchairs and companions for older people and nurses' assistants in long-term care facilities. However, Sharkey [2008] warns of some of the dangers of relying on robotic assistants as companions for the elderly and the very young. As with autonomous vehicles, researchers must ask cogent questions about the use of their creations.

This reliance on autonomous intelligent agents, raises the question: Can we **trust** robots? There are some real reasons why we cannot yet rely upon robots to do the right thing. They are not fully trustworthy and reliable, given the way they are built now. So, can they do the right thing? Will they do the right thing? What *is* the right thing? As evidenced by popular movies and books, in our collective subconscious, the fear exists that eventually robots may become completely autonomous, with free will, intelligence, and consciousness; they may rebel against us as Frankenstein-like monsters.

This raises questions about ethics: What are the ethics at the robot–human interface? Should there be ethical codes, for humans and for robots? It is clear that there should. There are already robot liability and insurance issues. There will have to be legislation that targets robot issues. Many countries and states are now developing robot regulations and laws. There will have to be professional codes of ethics for robot designers and engineers just as there are for engineers in all other disciplines. We will have to factor the issues around what we should do ethically in designing, building, and deploying robots. How should robots make decisions as they develop more autonomy? What should we humans do ethically and what ethical issues arise for us as we interact with robots? Should we give them any rights? There are human rights codes; will there be robot rights codes, as well?

To factor these issues, let us break them down into three fundamental questions that must be addressed:

- What should we humans do ethically in designing, building, and deploying robots?

- How should robots ethically decide, as they develop autonomy and free will, what to do?

- What ethical issues arise for us as we interact with robots?

In considering these questions we shall consider some interesting, if perhaps naive, proposals put forward by the science fiction novelist Isaac Asimov Asimov [1950], one of the earliest thinkers about these issues. Asimov's **Laws of Robotics** are a good basis from which to start because, at first glance, they seem logical and succinct. His original three Laws are:

I. A robot may not harm a human being, or, through inaction, allow a human being to come to harm.

II. A robot must obey the orders given to it by human beings except where such orders would conflict with the First Law.

III. A robot must protect its own existence, as long as such protection does not conflict with the First or Second Laws.

Asimov's answers to the three questions posed above are as follows. First, you must put those laws into every robot and, by law, manufacturers would have to do that. Second, robots should always have to follow the prioritized laws. But he did not say much about the third question. Asimov's plots arise mainly from the conflict between what the humans intend the robot to do and what it actually does, or between literal and sensible interpretations of the laws, because they are not codified in any formal language. Asimov's fiction explored many hidden implicit contradictions in the laws and their consequences.

There are ongoing discussions of robot ethics, but the discussions usually presuppose technical abilities that we just do not yet have. Joy [2000] was so concerned about our inability to control the dangers of new technologies that he called, unsuccessfully, for a moratorium on the development of robotics (and AI), nanotechnology, and genetic engineering. In this book, we have presented a coherent view of the agent design space and clarified the design principles for intelligent agents, including robots. This could provide a more technically informed framework for the development of social, ethical and legal codes for intelligent agents.

Many of the concerns about AI **safety** come down to issues of **trust**. Can one trust a deep learning system that has been trained on a vast array of images to classify human faces reliably? What if the (secret) training images have implicit bias? That bias would then be reflected in the classification process. The internal weights in the deep learning network may not be open to user inspection. Even if they are inspectable, they are opaque; they do not inform us about the bias or how to rectify it. Moreover, in the systems that are continually learning, the weights keep changing.

What are the factors that lead to us to trust agents? Formal verifiability, transparency, explanatory capacity, and reliable performance are some such factors. Having systems which are only semi-autonomous initially until they are trusted based on experience is one approach. Another is to use inverse reinforcement learning to learn a human user's values and then align the agent with those values. In **inverse reinforcement learning** an agent learns the dynamics of the world and a reward function from the traces of other agents' observed behavior. The development of techniques for designing and building safe, trustworthy and transparent agents is now being urgently pursued in the AI research community.

Many of the issues require attention beyond the AI community. Economic and regulatory concerns will require policy decisions at all levels of governance, from municipal to global. Issues of social and economic equity will, almost certainly, require some regulation of corporate activity, given the winner-take-all dynamics and the network effects of many markets for intelligent agents and their services. **Regulatory capture**, whereby the regulated companies exert influence on the regulators and the regulations, will be a key concern.

Some of these concerns are addressed in a report from *The One Hundred Year Artificial Intelligence Project* [Stone et al., 2016, p. 10]:

> A vigorous and informed debate about how to best steer AI in ways that enrich our lives and our society, while encouraging creativity in the field, is an urgent and vital need. AI technologies could widen existing inequalities of opportunity if access to them – along with the high-powered computation and large-scale data that fuel many of them – is unfairly distributed across society. These technologies will improve the abilities and efficiency of people who have access to them. Policies should be evaluated as to whether they foster democratic values and equitable sharing of AI's benefits, or concentrate power and benefits in the hands of a fortunate few.
>
> As this report documents, significant AI-related advances have already had an impact on North American cities over the past fifteen years, and even more substantial developments will occur over the next fifteen. Recent advances are largely due to the growth and analysis of large data sets enabled by the internet, advances in sensory technologies and, more recently, applications of "deep learning". In the coming years, as the public encounters new AI applications in domains such as transportation and healthcare, they must be introduced in ways that build trust and understanding, and respect human and civil rights. While encouraging innovation, policies and processes should address ethical, privacy, and security implications, and should work to ensure that the benefits of AI technologies will be spread broadly and fairly.

It is possible that computers and robots will become so intelligent that they will be able to create autonomously even more powerful computers and robots, in a bootstrapping spiral. The point at which computers will not need people to create even more powerful computers has been called the **singularity**. One of the fears is that after the singularity, computers may not need humans, or may even harm us, accidentally or deliberately. These concerns are prompting the development of research programs that promote beneficial AI and AI safety. The singularity is not implausible, as there are already factories that manufacture machines, where the manufacturing is carried out by robots, employing few people. As argued earlier, **organizations** (page 6) can be more intelligent than their individual members. It is clear that a corporation with computers is more intelligent than any individual computer, so the singularity may arise with corporations before individual computers, with corporations acting with no effective human oversight. Computers are already replacing humans for tasks that involve intelligence, and it is expected that this will continue.

By automating intellectual tasks as well as manual tasks, AI promises (or threatens) to trigger a fourth industrial revolution [Brynjolfsson and McAfee, 2014; Schwab and Forum, 2016], where it is not only manual tasks that are automated, but also jobs requiring intelligence and perhaps even creativity. Whereas in previous industrial revolutions, new jobs were created to keep most of the population employed, the result of the next revolution may be to require far fewer people to work for money in order fulfill the needs of people and the environment. This raises the related questions of how to share the wealth that will be created, and what the people who are otherwise not required to keep the paid economy functioning should do. One mechanism that has been suggested is to provide a **universal basic income** or **negative income tax**, where everyone receives an income, so that anyone has the option to do unpaid work, such as child-rearing or caregiving, to do more creative endeavors, to become more entrepreneurial, to get more education or just do nothing. This will leave the paid jobs to those who really want those jobs and the additional income. The basic income can increase as fewer people are required in the paid economy. It is also possible that the cumulative effect of automation is to further concentrate wealth in a small elite stratum of society, favoring capital over labor. Mitigating this inequality may also require a redistributive wealth tax of some form [Piketty, 2014]. Previous episodes of great change created social upheaval, scapegoating of minorities, and even wars. It is important to consider the global effects of the technologies and ways to mitigate such undesirable consequences.

Robotics may not be the AI technology with the greatest impact. Consider the embedded, ubiquitous, distributed intelligence in the World Wide Web and other global computational networks. This amalgam of human and artificial intelligence can be seen as evolving to become a **World Wide Mind**. The impact of this global net on the way we discover, and communicate, new knowledge is already comparable to the effects of the development of the printing press. As Marshall McLuhan [1964] argued, "We first shape the tools and thereafter our tools shape us". Although he was thinking more of books, advertising, and television, this concept applies even more to the global net and autonomous agents. The kinds of agents we build, and the kinds of agents we decide to build, will change us as much as they will change our society; we should make sure it is for the better. Margaret Somerville [2006] is an ethicist who argues that the species *Homo sapiens* is evolving into *Techno sapiens* as we project our abilities out into our technology at an accelerating rate. Many of our old social and ethical codes are broken; they do not work in this new world. As co-creators of the new science and technology of AI, it is our joint responsibility to pay attention and to act.

16.3   References and Further Reading

Hierarchical planning is discussed by Nau [2007]. Hierarchical reinforcement learning is covered by Dieterich [2000b]. Multiagent reinforcement learning is addressed by Stone [2007]. Inverse reinforcement learning is introduced in Ng et al. [2000]

Mackworth [2009] presents some of the dangers and potentials of AI. The *One Hundred Year Study on Artificial Intelligence* (https://ai100.stanford.edu) is a longitudinal study of AI. It has issued a report, "Artificial Intelligence and Life in 2030" [Stone et al., 2016] outlining recent progress in AI, forecasting developments up to 2030 and studying their impact on North American urban life and policy. The dangers of robotic warfare are outlined by Sharkey [2008] and Singer [2009a,b]. The estimate of traffic accidents is from Peden et al. [2004] and the estimate of the increase in traffic throughput is from Dresner and Stone [2008].

AIspace is described in Knoll et al. [2008].The development of RoboCup is sketched by Visser and Burkhard [2007].

Computational sustainability is introduced in Gomes [2009]. Assistive technology systems are described by Pollack [2005], Liu et al. [2006] and Yang and Mackworth [2007]. Smart wheelchairs are discussed by Mihailidis et al. [2007] and Viswanathan et al. [2007].

Shelley [1818] wrote about Dr. Frankenstein and his monster. Anderson and Leigh Anderson [2007] discuss robot ethics. Issues in robot regulation and robot law are covered in Calo [2014] and Calo et al. [2016]. The economic, social and employment impacts of AI and robotics are covered in Brynjolfsson and McAfee [2011, 2014] and Ford [2015]. Amodei et al. [2016] addresses issues in AI safety. The World Wide Mind is cited by Hillis [2008] and Kelly [2008].

16.4   Exercises

Exercise 16.1 Election Prediction Large corporations do not like unpredictability, so they want a better way to predict the outcome of upcoming elections so they can plan appropriately for future governments. Your company has been asked about the feasibility of building a tool for predicting the results of an upcoming election. You will have access to data about the outcome of previous elections, demographic data from the census about the people in the riding at the time of the election and polling data if it was available. The goal is to predict the probability of which party will win each riding if an election were held today. A rival company has proposed solving it by combining hidden Markov models and relational probabilistic models.

(a) Explain how this problem fits into the abstraction of an agent as studied in this course.

(b) Explain how the rival company's solution may work, and explain why they may have chosen the technologies they proposed.

(c) What is the most challenging part of solving this problem? What would you recommend as a way to solve this? Justify any recommendation made.

Exercise 16.2 Find some AI applications and classify the current state-of-the-art for that application in terms of the dimensions. Does the application automate what Kahneman [2011] calls System 1 or System 2 (page 57) or neither or both?

Exercise 16.3 There have been proposals made for a global ban on the use of Lethal Autonomous Weapon Systems (LAWS). Investigate and describe the current status of action on a ban on the use of LAWS. Present a brief argument in favor or against such a ban.

Exercise 16.4 Consider the use of robots and companions for the elderly (or for infants). Investigate and describe briefly the current state of the art for these companions. Present three reasons in favor of their use and three reasons against.

Exercise 16.5 Human rights and animal rights are well recognized. Outline a case for or against robot rights. Be specific about the robot rights you are discussing.

Mathematical Preliminaries and Notation

This appendix gives some definitions of fundamental mathematical concepts that are used in AI, but are traditionally taught in other courses. It also introduces some notation and data structures that are used in various parts of the book.

A.1   Discrete Mathematics

The mathematical concepts we build on include:

sets   A **set** has elements (members). We write $s \in S$ if s is an element of set S. The elements in a set define the set, so that two sets are equal if they have the same elements.

tuples   An n-tuple is an ordered grouping of n elements, written $\langle x_1, \ldots, x_n \rangle$. A 2-tuple is a **pair**, and a 3-tuple is a **triple**. Two n-tuples are equal if they have the same members in the corresponding positions. If S is a set, S^n is the set of n-tuples $\langle x_1, \ldots, x_n \rangle$ where x_i is a member of S. $S_1 \times S_2 \times \cdots \times S_n$ is the set of n-tuples $\langle x_1, \ldots, x_n \rangle$ where each x_i is in S_i.

relations   A **relation** is a set of n-tuples. The tuples in the relation are said to be *true* of the relation. An alternative definition is in terms of the relation's **characteristic function**, a function on tuples that is true for a tuple when the tuple is in the relation and false when it is not.

functions   A **function**, or **mapping**, f from set D, the **domain** of f, into set R, the **range** of f, written $f : D \rightarrow R$, is a subset of $D \times R$ such that for every

745

$d \in D$ there is a unique $r \in R$ such that $\langle d, r \rangle \in f$. We write $f(d) = r$ if $\langle d, r \rangle \in f$.

While these may seem like obscure definitions for common-sense concepts, you can now use the common-sense concepts comfortable in the knowledge that if you are unsure about something, you can check the definitions.

A.2 Functions, Factors and Arrays

Many of the algorithms in this book manipulate representations of functions. We extend the standard definition of function on sets to include functions on variables. A **factor** is a representation of a function. An **array** is an explicit representation of a function that can have its individual components modified.

If S is a set, we write $f(S)$ to be a function, with domain S. Thus, if $c \in S$, then $f(c)$ is a value in the range of f. $f[S]$ is like $f(S)$, but individual components can be updated. This notation is based on that of Python, C and Java (but C and Java only allow S to be the set of integers $\{0, \ldots, n-1\}$ for arrays of size n). Thus $f[c]$ is a value in the range of f. If $f[c]$ is assigned a new value, it will return that new value.

This notation can be extended to (algebraic) variables. If X is an algebraic variable with domain D, then $f(X)$ is a function that given a value $x \in D$, returns a value in the range of f. This value is often written as $f(X = x)$ or simply as $f(x)$. Similarly, $f[X]$ is an array indexed by X, that is, it is a function of X whose components can be modified.

This notation can also be extended to set of variables. $f(X_1, X_2, \ldots, X_n)$ is a function such that given a value v_1 for X_1, a value v_2 for X_2, ..., and a value v_n for X_n returns a value in the range of f. Note that it is the name of the variable that is important, not the position. This factor applied to the specific values is written as $f(X_1 = v_1, X_2 = v_2, \ldots, X_n = v_n)$. The set of variables, $X_1, X_2, \ldots, X_n$ is called the **scope** of f. The array $f[X_1, X_2, \ldots, X_n]$ is a function on $X_1, X_2, \ldots, X_n$ where the values can be updated.

Assigning just some of the variables gives a function on the remaining variables. Thus, for example, if f is a function with scope $X_1, X_2, \ldots, X_n$, then $f(X_1 = v_1)$ is a function of $X_2, \ldots, X_n$, such that

$$(f(X_1 = v_1))(X_2 = v_2, \ldots, X_n = v_n) = f(X_1 = v_1, X_2 = v_2, \ldots, X_n = v_n)$$

Factors can be added, multiplied or composed with any other operation level on the elements. If f_1 and f_2 are factors, then $f_1 + f_2$ is a factor with scope the union of the scopes of f_1 and f_2, defined pointwise:

$$(f_1 + f_2)(X_1 = v_1, X_2 = v_2, \ldots, X_n = v_n)$$
$$= f_1(X_1 = v_1, X_2 = v_2, \ldots, X_n = v_n) + f_2(X_1 = v_1, X_2 = v_2, \ldots, X_n = v_n)$$

where we assume that f_1 and f_2 ignore variables not in their scope. Multiplication and other binary operators work similarly.

Example 1.1 Suppose $f_1(X, Y) = X + Y$ and $f_2(Y, Z) = Y + Z$. Then $f_1 + f_2$ is $X + 2Y + Z$, which is a function of X, Y and Z. Similarly $f_1 \times f_2 = (X + Y) \times (Y + Z)$.

$f_1(X = 2)$ is a function of Y, defined by $2 + Y$.

Suppose that variable W has domain $\{0, 1\}$ and X has domain $\{1, 2\}$, the factor $f_3(W, X)$ can be defined by a table such as:

W	X	value
0	1	2
0	2	1
1	1	0
1	2	3

$f_3 + f_1$ is a function on W, X, Y, such that, for example,

$$(f_3 + f_1)(W = 1, X = 2, Y = 3) = 3 + 5 = 8$$

Similarly, $(f_3 \times f_1)(W = 1, X = 2, Y = 3) = 3 \times 5 = 15$.

Other operations on factors are defined in the book.

A.3 Relations and the Relational Algebra

Relations are common in AI and database systems. The **relational algebra** defines operations on relations and is the basis of relational databases.

A **scope** S is a set of variables. A **tuple** t on scope S, has a value on each variable in its scope. A variable can be seen as a function on tuples; one that returns the value for that variable for that tuple. We write $X(t)$ to be the value of tuple t on variable X. The value of $X(t)$ must be in $dom(X)$. This is like the mathematical notion of tuple, except the index is given by a variable, not by an integer.

A **relation** is a set of tuples, all with the same scope. A relation is often given a name. The scope of the tuples is often called the relation **scheme**. A **relational database** is a set of relations. A scheme of a relational database is the set of pairs of relation names and relation schemes.

A relation with scope $X_1, \ldots, X_n$ can be seen as a Boolean factor on $X_1, \ldots, X_n$, where the true elements are represented as tuples.

Often a relation is written as a table.

Example 1.2 The following is a tabular depiction of a relation, *enrolled*:

Course	Year	Student	Grade
cs322	2008	fran	77
cs111	2009	billie	88
cs111	2009	jess	78
cs444	2008	fran	83
cs322	2009	jordan	92

The heading gives the scheme, namely $\{Course, Year, Student, Grade\}$, and every other row is a tuple. The first tuple, call it t_1 is defined by $Course(t_1) = cs322$, $Year(t_1) = 2008$, $Student(t_1) = fran$, $Grade(t_1) = 77$.

The order of the columns and the order of the rows is not significant.

If r a relation with scheme S, and c is a condition on the variables in S, the **selection** of c in r, written $\sigma_c(r)$, is the set of tuples in r for which c holds. The selection has the same scheme as r.

If r is a relation with scheme S, and $S_0 \subseteq S$, the **projection** of r onto S_0, written $\pi_{S_0}(r)$, is the set of tuples of r where the scope is restricted to S_0.

Example 1.3 Suppose *enrolled* is the relation given in Example A.2.

The relation $\sigma_{Grade>79}(enrolled)$ selects those tuples in *enrolled* where the grade is over 79. This is the relation:

Course	Year	Student	Grade
cs111	2009	billie	88
cs444	2008	fran	83
cs322	2009	jordan	92

The relation $\pi_{\{Student, Year\}}(enrolled)$ specifies what years students were enrolled:

Student	Year
fran	2008
billie	2009
jess	2009
jordan	2009

Notice how the first and the fourth tuple of *enrolled* become the same tuple in the projection; they represent the same function on $\{Student, Year\}$.

If two relations on the same scheme, the **union, intersection** and **set difference** of these are defined as the corresponding operations on the set of tuples.

If r_1 and r_2 are two relations, the natural **join** of r_1 and r_2, written $r_1 \bowtie r_2$ is a relation where

- the scheme of the join is the union of the scheme of r_1 and the scheme of r_2,

- a tuple is in the join, if the tuple restricted to the scope of r_1 is in the relation r_1 and the tuple restricted to the scope of r_2 is in the relation r_2.

Example 1.4 Consider the relation *assisted*:

Course	Year	TA
cs322	2008	yuki
cs111	2009	sam
cs111	2009	chris
cs322	2009	yuki

The join of *enrolled* and *assisted*, written *enrolled* ⋈ *assisted* is the relation:

Course	Year	Student	Grade	TA
cs322	2008	fran	77	yuki
cs111	2009	billie	88	sam
cs111	2009	jess	78	sam
cs111	2009	billie	88	chris
cs111	2009	jess	78	chris
cs322	2009	jordan	92	yuki

Note how in the join, the information about *cs444* was lost, as there was no TA in that course.

References

Abelson, H. and DiSessa, A. (1981), *Turtle Geometry: The Computer as a Medium for Exploring Mathematics*. MIT Press. 71

Abramson, H. and Rogers, M. H. (Eds.) (1989), *Meta-Programming in Logic Programming*. MIT Press. 685

Agre, P. E. (1995), Computational research on interaction and agency. *Artificial Intelligence*, 72:1–52. 71

Albus, J. S. (1981), *Brains, Behavior and Robotics*. BYTE Publications. 71

Allais, M. and Hagen, O. (Eds.) (1979), *Expected Utility Hypothesis and the Allais Paradox*. Reidel. 434

Amodei, D., Olah, C., Steinhardt, J., Christiano, P., Schulman, J., and Mané, D. (2016), Concrete Problems in AI Safety. *ArXiv e-prints*, arXiv:1606.06565. 742

Anderson, M. and Leigh Anderson, S. L. (2007), Machine ethics: Creating an ethical intelligent agent. *AI Magazine*, 28(4):15–26. 742

Andrieu, C., de Freitas, N., Doucet, A., and Jordan, M. I. (2003), An introduction to MCMC for machine learning. *Machine Learning*, 50(1–2):5–43. 415

Antoniou, G. and van Harmelen, F. (2008), *A Semantic Web Primer*. MIT Pres, 2nd edition. 684

Apt, K. and Bol, R. (1994), Logic programming and negation: A survey. *Journal of Logic Programming*, 19,20:9–71. 227, 638

Aristotle (350 B.C.E.), *Categories*. Translated by E. M. Edghill, http://classics.mit.edu//Aristotle/categories.html. 660

Arp, R., Smith, B., and Spear, A. (2015), *Building Ontologies with Basic Formal Ontology*. MIT Press. 684

Arrow, K. (1963), *Social Choice and Individual Values*. Wiley, 2nd edition. 541

Asimov, I. (1950), *I, Robot*. Doubleday. 738

Auer, S., Bizer, C., Kobilarov, G., Lehmann, J., Cyganiak, R., and Ives, Z. G. (2007), DB-pedia: A nucleus for a web of open data. In *6th International Semantic Web Conference (ISWC)*. 684

Bacchus, F. and Grove, A. (1995), Graphical models for preference and utility. In *Uncertainty in Artificial Intelligence (UAI-95)*, pages 3–10. 476

Bacchus, F. and Kabanza, F. (1996), Using temporal logic to control search in a forward chaining planner. In Ghallab, M. and Milani, A. (Eds.), *New Directions in AI Planning*, pages 141–153, ISO Press. 261

Bäck, T. (1996), *Evolutionary Algorithms in Theory and Practice*. Oxford University Press. 168

Ballard, B. W. (1983), The ∗-minimax search procedure for trees containing chance nodes. *Artificial Intelligence*, 21(3):327–350. 545

Baum, E. B. (2004), *What is Thought?* MIT Press. 581

Bayes, T. (1763), An essay towards solving a problem in the doctrine of chances. *Philosophical Transactions of the Royal Society of London*, 53:370–418, http://rstl.royalsocietypublishing.org/content/53/370.short. 517

Bell, J. L. and Machover, M. (1977), *A Course in Mathematical Logic*. North-Holland. 227

Bellman, R. (1957), *Dynamic Programming*. Princeton University Press. 476

Bernardo, J. M. and Smith, A. F. M. (1994), *Bayesian Theory*. Wiley. 518

Berners-Lee, T., Hendler, J., and Lassila, O. (2001), The semantic web: A new form of web content that is meaningful to computers will unleash a revolution of new possibilities. *Scientific American*, May:28–37. 684

Bertelè, U. and Brioschi, F. (1972), *Nonserial Dynamic Programming*. Academic Press. 167

Bertsekas, D. P. (1995), *Dynamic Programming and Optimal Control*. Athena Scientific, two volumes. 476

Bertsekas, D. P. and Tsitsiklis, J. N. (1996), *Neuro-Dynamic Programming*. Athena Scientific. 574

Besnard, P. and Hunter, A. (2008), *Elements of Argumentation*. MIT Press. 228

Bickel, P. J., Hammel, E. A., and O'Connell, J. W. (1975), Sex bias in graduate admissions: Data from Berkeley. *Science*, 187(4175):398–404. 415

Bishop, C. M. (1995), *Neural Networks for Pattern Recognition*. Oxford University Press. 332

Bishop, C. M. (2008), *Pattern Recognition and Machine Learning*. Springer-Verlag. 331

Blum, A. and Furst, M. (1997), Fast planning through planning graph analysis. *Artificial Intelligence*, 90:281–300. 261

Bobrow, D. G. (1967), Natural language input for a computer problem solving system. In Minsky, M. (Ed.), *Semantic Information Processing*, pages 133–215, MIT Press. 9

Bobrow, D. G. (1993), Artificial intelligence in perspective: a retrospective on fifty volumes of Artificial Intelligence. *Artificial Intelligence*, 59:5–20. 46

Boddy, M. and Dean, T. L. (1994), Deliberation scheduling for problem solving in time-constrained environments. *Artificial Intelligence*, 67(2):245–285. 46

Bodlaender, H. L. (1993), A tourist guide through treewidth. *Acta Cybernetica*, 11(1–2):1–21. 415

Boutilier, C., Brafman, R. I., Domshlak, C., Hoos, H. H., and Poole, D. (2004), CP-nets: A tool for representing and reasoning with conditional ceteris paribus preference statements. *Journal of Artificial Intelligence Research*, 21:135–191. 476

Boutilier, C., Dean, T., and Hanks, S. (1999), Decision-theoretic planning: Structual assumptions and computational leverage. *Journal of Artificial Intelligence Research*, 11:1–94. 476

Bowen, K. A. (1985), Meta-level programming and knowledge representation. *New Generation Computing*, 3(4):359–383. 685

Bowling, M. and Veloso, M. (2002), Multiagent learning using a variable learning rate. *Artificial Intelligence*, 136(2):215–250. 574

Brachman, R. J. and Levesque, H. J. (Eds.) (1985), *Readings in Knowledge Representation*. Morgan Kaufmann. 684

Brachman, R. J. and Levesque, H. J. (2004), *Knowledge Representation and Reasoning*. Morgan Kaufmann. 46, 684, 724

Breiman, L. (2001), Random forests. *Machine Learning*, 45(1):5–32. 332

Breiman, L., Friedman, J. H., Olshen, R. A., and Stone, C. J. (1984), *Classification and Regression Trees*. Wadsworth and Brooks. 332

Brémaud, P. (1999), *Markov Chains: Gibbs Fields, Monte Carlo Simulation and Queues*. Springer. 415

Brin, S. and Page, L. (1998), The anatomy of a large-scale hypertextual web search engine. *Computer Networks and ISDN Systems (Proceedings of the Seventh International World Wide Web Conference)*, 30(1–7):107–117, http://www.sciencedirect.com/science/article/pii/S016975529800110X. 386

Briscoe, G. and Caelli, T. (1996), *A Compendium of Machine Learning*, Volume 1: *Symbolic Machine Learning*. Ablex. 331

Brooks, R. A. (1986), A robust layered control system for a mobile robot. *IEEE Journal of Robotics and Automation*, 2(1):14–23. 71

Brooks, R. A. (1990), Elephants don't play chess. *Robotics and Autonomous Systems*, 6:3–15. 46

Brooks, R. A. (1991), Intelligence without representation. *Artificial Intelligence*, 47:139–159. 71

Bryce, D. and Kambhampati, S. (2007), A tutorial on planning graph-based reachability heuristics. *AI Magazine*, 28(1):47–83. 261

Brynjolfsson, E. and McAfee, A. (2011), *Race against the Machine: How the Digital Revolution is Accelerating Innovation, Driving Productivity, and Irreversibly Transforming Employment and the Economy*. Digital Frontier, Lexington, MA. 742

Brynjolfsson, E. and McAfee, A. (2014), *The Second Machine Age: Work, Progress, and Prosperity in a Time of Brilliant Technologies*. W. W. Norton & Company. 741, 742

Buchanan, B. G. (2005), A (very) brief history of artificial intelligence. *AI Magazine*, 26(4):53–60. 3, 46

Buchanan, B. G. and Feigenbaum, E. A. (1978), Dendral and Meta-Dendral: Their applications dimension. *Artificial Intelligence*, 11:5–24. 9

Buchanan, B. G. and Shortliffe, E. (Eds.) (1984), *Rule-Based Expert Systems: The MYCIN Experiments of the Stanford Heuristic Programming Project*. Addison-Wesley. 9

Buntine, W. (1992), Learning classification trees. *Statistics and Computing*, 2:63–73. 518

Buntine, W. L. (1994), Operations for learning with graphical models. *Journal of Artificial Intelligence Research*, 2:159–225. 724

Burch, R. (2008), Charles Sanders Peirce. *The Stanford Encyclopedia of Philosophy*, http://plato.stanford.edu/archives/spr2008/entries/peirce/. 227

Busoniu, L., Babuska, R., and Schutter, B. D. (2008), A comprehensive survey of multi-agent reinforcement learning. *EEE Transactions on Systems, Man, and Cybernetics, Part C: Applications and Reviews*, 38(2):156–172. 574

Calo, R. (2014), The case for a federal robotics commission. *Brookings Institution Center for Technology Innovation*. 742

Calo, R., Froomkin, A. M., and Kerr, I. (2016), *Robot Law*. Edward Elgar Publishing. 742

Campbell, M., Hoane Jr., A. J., and Hse, F.-h. (2002), Deep Blue. *Artificial Intelligence*, 134(1–2):57–83. 522, 545

Castillo, E., Gutiérrez, J. M., and Hadi, A. S. (1996), *Expert Systems and Probabilistic Network Models*. Springer-Verlag. 414

Chapman, D. (1987), Planning for conjunctive goals. *Artificial Intelligence*, 32(3):333–377. 261

Cheeseman, P., Kelly, J., Self, M., Stutz, J., Taylor, W., and Freeman, D. (1988), Autoclass: A Bayesian classification system. In *Proc. Fifth International Conference on Machine Learning*, pages 54–64, reprinted in Shavlik and Dietterich [1990]. 518

Cheng, J. and Druzdzel, M. (2000), AIS-BN: An adaptive importance sampling algorithm for evidential reasoning in large Bayesian networks. *Journal of Artificial Intelligence Research*, 13:155–188, http://www.jair.org/papers/paper764.html. 415

Chesnevar, C., Maguitman, A., and Loui, R. (2000), Logical models of argument. *ACM Computer Surveys*, 32(4):337–383. 228

Chomsky, N. (1957), *Syntactic Structures*. Mouton and Co. 613

Chrisley, R. and Begeer, S. (2000), *Artificial intelligence: Critical Concepts in Cognitive Science*. Routledge. 46, 761

Clark, K. L. (1978), Negation as failure. In Gallaire, H. and Minker, J. (Eds.), *Logic and Databases*, pages 293–322, Plenum Press. 227, 638

Cohen, P. R. (2005), If not Turing's test, then what? *AI Magazine*, 26(4):61–67. 46

Colmerauer, A., Kanoui, H., Roussel, P., and Pasero, R. (1973), Un système de communication homme-machine en français. Technical report, Groupe de Researche en Intelligence Artificielle, Université d'Aix-Marseille. 227

Colmerauer, A. and Roussel, P. (1996), The birth of Prolog. In Bergin, T. J. and Gibson, R. G. (Eds.), *History of Programming Languages–II*, pages 331–367, ACM Press/Addison-Wesley. 9, 638

Copi, I. M., Cohen, C., and McMahon, K. (2016), *Introduction to Logic*. Macmillan, 14th edition. 227

Cormen, T. H., Leiserson, C. E., Rivest, R. L., and Stein, C. (2001), *Introduction to Algorithms*. MIT Press and McGraw-Hill, 2nd edition. 120

Cover, T. M. and Thomas, J. A. (1991), *Elements of Information Theory*. Wiley. 415

Culberson, J. and Schaeffer, J. (1998), Pattern databases. *Computational Intelligence*, 14(3):318–334. 120

Dahl, V. (1994), Natural language processing and logic programming. *Journal of Logic Programming*, 19,20:681–714. 639

Darwiche, A. (2009), *Modeling and Reasoning with Bayesian Networks*. Cambridge University Press. 414, 415, 518

Dasarathy, B. V. (1991), NN concepts and techniques. In Dasarathy, B. V. (Ed.), *Nearest Neighbour (NN) Norms: NN Pattern Classification Techniques*, pages 1–30, IEEE Computer Society Press. 332

Davis, E. (1990), *Representations of Commonsense Knowledge*. Morgan Kaufmann. 684

Davis, E. (2015), A collection of Winograd schemas. http://www.cs.nyu.edu/faculty/davise/papers/WinogradSchemas/WSCollection.html. 6, 48

Davis, J. and Goadrich, M. (2006), The relationship between precision-recall and ROC curves. In *Proceedings of the 23rd International Conference on Machine Learning (ICML)*, pages 233–240. 332

Davis, M., Logemann, G., and Loveland, D. (1962), A machine program for theorem proving. *Communications of the ACM*, 5(7):394–397. 227

Davis, M. and Putnam, H. (1960), A computing procedure for quantification theory. *Journal of the ACM*, 7(3):201–215. 167

de Kleer, J. (1986), An assumption-based TMS. *Artificial Intelligence*, 28(2):127–162. 227

de Kleer, J., Mackworth, A. K., and Reiter, R. (1992), Characterizing diagnoses and systems. *Artificial Intelligence*, 56:197–222. 227

De Raedt, L., Frasconi, P., Kersting, K., and Muggleton, S. H. (Eds.) (2008), *Probabilistic Inductive Logic Programming*. Springer. 724

De Raedt, L., Kersting, K., Natarajan, S., and Poole, D. (2016), *Statistical Relational Artificial Intelligence: Logic, Probability, and Computation*. Morgan & Claypool. 724

De Raedt, L., Kimmig, A., and Toivonen, H. (2007), ProbLog: A probabilistic Prolog and its application in link discovery. In *Proceedings of the 20th International Joint Conference on Artificial Intelligence (IJCAI)*, pages 2462–2467. 724

Dean, T. and Kanazawa, K. (1989), A model for reasoning about persistence and causation. *Computational Intelligence*, 5(3):142–150. 415

Dean, T. L. and Wellman, M. P. (1991), *Planning and Control*. Morgan Kaufmann. 46, 71

Dechter, R. (1996), Bucket elimination: A unifying framework for probabilistic inference. In Horvitz, E. and Jensen, F. (Eds.), *Proc. Twelfth Conference on Uncertainty in Artificial Intelligence (UAI-96)*, pages 211–219. 415

Dechter, R. (2003), *Constraint Processing*. Morgan Kaufmann. 167

Dechter, R. (2013), *Reasoning with Probabilistic and Deterministic Graphical Models: Exact Algorithms*. Synthesis Lectures on Artificial Intelligence and Machine Learning, Morgan & Claypool. 415

Dechter, R. and Pearl, J. (1985), Generalized best-first search strategies and the optimality of A*. *Journal of the Association for Computing Machinery*, 32(3):505–536. 118, 119

Dellaert, F., Fox, D., Burgard, W., and Thrun, S. (1999), Monte Carlo localization for mobile robots. In *IEEE International Conference on Robotics and Automation (ICRA)*. 415

Dempster, A., Laird, N., and Rubin, D. (1977), Maximum liklihood from incomplete data via the EM algorithm. *Journal of the Royal Statistical Society B*, 39:1–38, with discussion. 518

Denil, M., Matheson, D., and de Freitas, N. (2014), Narrowing the gap: Random forests in theory and in practice. In *International Conference on Machine Learning (ICML)*. 332

Descartes, R. (1637), *Discourse on the Method of Rightly Conducting One's Reason and of Seeking Truth in the Sciences*. http://www.gutenberg.org/ebooks/59. 549

Dietterich, T. G. (2000a), An experimental comparison of three methods for constructing ensembles of decision trees: Bagging, boosting, and randomization. *Machine Learning*, 40(2):139–158. 332

Dietterich, T. G. (2000b), Hierarchical reinforcement learning with the MAXQ value function decomposition. *Journal of Artificial Intelligence Research*, 13:227–303. 742

Dietterich, T. G. (2002), Ensemble learning. In Arbib, M. (Ed.), *The Handbook of Brain Theory and Neural Networks*, pages 405–408, MIT Press, 2nd edition. 332

Dijkstra, E. W. (1959), A note on two problems in connexion with graphs. *Numerische Mathematik*, 1:269–271, http://dl.acm.org/citation.cfm?id=2722945. 119

Dijkstra, E. W. (1976), *A Discipline of Programming*. Prentice-Hall. 261

Domingos, P. (2012), A few useful things to know about machine learning. *Communications of the ACM*, 55(10):78–87. 331

Domingos, P. and Lowd, D. (2009), *Markov Logic: An Interface Layer for Artificial Intelligence*. Synthesis Lectures on Artificial Intelligence and Machine Learning, Morgan & Claypool. 724

Doucet, A., de Freitas, N., and Gordon, N. (Eds.) (2001), *Sequential Monte Carlo in Practice*. Springer-Verlag. 415

Doyle, J. (1979), A truth maintenance system. AI Memo 521, MIT Artificial Intelligence Laboratory. 227

Dresner, K. and Stone, P. (2008), A multiagent approach to autonomous intersection management. *Journal of Artificial Intelligence Research*, 31:591–656. 742

Duda, R. O., Hart, P. E., and Stork, D. G. (2001), *Pattern Classification*. Wiley-Interscience, 2nd edition. 331, 332, 518

Dung, P. (1995), On the acceptability of arguments and its fundamental role in nonmonotonic reasoning, logic programming and n-person games. *Artificial Intelligence*, 77(2):321–357. 227

Enderton, H. B. (1972), *A Mathematical Introduction to Logic*. Academic Press. 227

Felner, A., Korf, R. E., and Hanan, S. (2004), Additive pattern database heuristics. *Journal of Artificial Intelligence Research*, 22:279–318. 120

Fikes, R. E. and Nilsson, N. J. (1971), STRIPS: A new approach to the application of theorem proving to problem solving. *Artificial Intelligence*, 2(3–4):189–208. 261

Forbus, K. D. (1996), Qualitative reasoning. In *CRC Hand-book of Computer Science and Engineering*, CRC Press, http://www.qrg.northwestern.edu/papers/Files/crc7.pdf. 71

Ford, M. (2015), *Rise of the Robots: Technology and the Threat of a Jobless Future*. Basic Books. 742

Freuder, E. C. and Mackworth, A. K. (2006), Constraint satisfaction: An emerging paradigm. In Rossi, F., Van Beek, P., and Walsh, T. (Eds.), *Handbook of Constraint Programming*, pages 13–28, Elsevier. 167

Friedman, N. and Goldszmidt, M. (1996a), Building classifiers using Bayesian networks. In *Proc. 13th National Conference on Artificial Intelligence*, pages 1277–1284. 518

Friedman, N. and Goldszmidt, M. (1996b), Learning Bayesian networks with local structure. In *Proc. Twelfth Conference on Uncertainty in Artificial Intelligence (UAI-96)*, pages 252–262. 518

Friedman, N., Greiger, D., and Goldszmidt, M. (1997), Bayesian network classifiers. *Machine Learning*, 29:103–130. 518

Gabbay, D. M., Hogger, C. J., and Robinson, J. A. (Eds.) (1993), *Handbook of Logic in Artificial Intelligence and Logic Programming*. Clarendon Press, 5 volumes. 227

Gabrilovich, E., Heitz, G., Horn, W., Lao, N., Murphy, K., Strohmann, T., Sun, S., and Zhang, W. (2014), Knowledge vault: A web-scale approach to probabilistic knowledge fusion. In *20th ACM SIGKDD Conference on Knowledge Discovery and Data Mining*. 684

Galton, F. (1886), Regression towards mediocrity in hereditary stature. *Journal of the Anthropological Institute*, 15:246–263, http://galton.org/essays/1880-1889/galton-1886-jaigi-regression-stature.pdf. 299

Gangemi, A., Guarino, N., Masolo, C., and Oltramari, A. (2003), Sweetening wordnet with dolce. *AI Magazine*, 24(3):13–24. 684

Garcia-Molina, H., Ullman, J. D., and Widom, J. (2009), *Database Systems: The Complete Book*. Prentice Hall, 2nd edition. 638

Gardner, H. (1985), *The Mind's New Science*. Basic Books. 46

Geffner, H. and Bonet, B. (2013), *A Concise Introduction to Models and Methods for Automated Planning*. Synthesis Lectures on Artificial Intelligence and Machine Learning, Morgan & Claypool. 261

Gelman, A., Carlin, J. B., Stern, H. S., and Rubin, D. B. (2004), *Bayesian Data Analysis*. Chapman and Hall/CRC, 2nd edition. 518

Genesereth, M. and Thielscher, M. (2014), *General Game Playing*. Morgan & Claypool. 545

Getoor, L. and Taskar, B. (Eds.) (2007), *Introduction to Statistical Relational Learning*. MIT Press. 724

Ghahramani, Z. (2015), Probabilistic machine learning and artificial intelligence. *Nature*, 521(7553):452–459, http://dx.doi.org/10.1038/nature14541. 518

Gibbard, A. (1973), Manipulation of voting schemes: a general result. *Econometrica*, 41:587–601. 543

Glorot, X., Bordes, A., and Bengio, Y. (2011), Deep sparse rectifier neural networks. In *Proc. 14th International Conference on Artificial Intelligence and Statistics*, pages 315–323. 332

Goldberg, D. E. (1989), *Genetic Algorithms in Search, Optimization and Machine Learning*. Addison-Wesley. 168

Goldberg, D. E. (2002), *The Design of Innovation: Lessons from and for Competent Genetic Algorithms*. Addison-Wesley. 168

Goldberg, Y. (2016), A primer on neural network models for natural language processing. *Journal of Artificial Intelligence Research*, 57:345–420. 332

Gomes, C. P. (2009), Computational sustainability: Computational methods for a sustainable environment, economy, and society. *The Bridge*, 39(4):5–13. 742

Goodfellow, I., Bengio, Y., and Courville, A. (2016), *Deep Learning*. MIT Press, http://www.deeplearningbook.org. 332

Green, C. (1969), Application of theorem proving to problem solving. In *Proc. 1st International Joint Conference on Artificial Intelligence*, pages 219–237. 227

Grenon, P. and Smith, B. (2004), Snap and span: Towards dynamic spatial ontology. *Spatial Cognition and Computation*, 4(1):69–103. 684

Grosz, B. (2012), What question would Turing pose today? *AI Magazine*, 33(4):73–81. 46

Grünwald, P. D. (2007), *The Minimum Description Length Principle*. MIT Press. 415, 518

Halevy, A., Norvig, P., and Pereira, F. (2009), The unreasonable effectiveness of data. *IEEE Intelligent Systems*, 24(2):8–12. 331

Halpern, J. Y. (2003), *Reasoning about Uncertainty*. MIT Press. 414

Harper, F. M. and Konstan, J. A. (2015), The MovieLens datasets: History and context. *ACM Transactions on Interactive Intelligent Systems*, 5(4). 724

Hart, P. E., Nilsson, N. J., and Raphael, B. (1968), A formal basis for the heuristic determination of minimum cost paths. *IEEE Transactions on Systems Science and Cybernetics*, 4(2):100–107. 119

Hart, T. P. and Edwards, D. J. (1961), The tree prune (TP) algorithm. Memo 30, MIT Artificial Intelligence Project. 545

Hastie, T., Tibshirani, R., and Friedman, J. (2009), *The Elements of Statistical Learning: Data Mining, Inference, and Prediction*. Springer, 2nd edition. 331

Haugeland, J. (1985), *Artificial Intelligence: The Very Idea*. MIT Press. 8, 46, 71

Haugeland, J. (Ed.) (1997), *Mind Design II: Philosophy, Psychology, Artificial Intelligence*. MIT Press, revised and enlarged edition. 46, 763, 764, 769

Haussler, D. (1988), Quantifying inductive bias: AI learning algorithms and Valiant's learning framework. *Artificial Intelligence*, 36(2):177–221, reprinted in Shavlik and Dietterich [1990]. 332

Hayes, P. J. (1973), Computation and deduction. In *Proc. 2nd Symposium on Mathematical Foundations of Computer Science*, pages 105–118, Czechoslovak Academy of Sciences. 227

Heckerman, D. (1999), A tutorial on learning with Bayesian networks. In Jordan, M. (Ed.), *Learning in Graphical Models*, MIT Press. 518

Hendler, J., Berners-Lee, T., and Miller, E. (2002), Integrating applications on the semantic web. *Journal of the Institute of Electrical Engineers of Japan*, 122(10):676–680, http://www.w3.org/2002/07/swint. 684

Henrion, M. (1988), Propagating uncertainty in Bayesian networks by probabilistic logic sampling. In Lemmer, J. F. and Kanal, L. N. (Eds.), *Uncertainty in Artificial Intelligence 2*, pages 149–163, Elsevier Science. 415

Hertz, J., Krogh, A., and Palmer, R. G. (1991), *Introduction to the Theory of Neural Computation*. Lecture Notes, Volume I, Santa Fe Institute Studies in the Sciences of Complexity, Addison-Wesley. 332

Hewitt, C. (1969), Planner: A language for proving theorems in robots. In *Proc. 1st International Joint Conference on Artificial Intelligence*, pages 295–301. 227

Hillis, W. D. (2008), A forebrain for the world mind. *Edge: World Question Center*, http://www.edge.org/q2009/q09_12.html#hillis. 742

Hinton, G., Deng, L., Yu, D., Dahl, G., et al. (2012), Deep neural networks for acoustic modeling in speech recognition: The shared views of four research groups. *Signal Processing Magazine, IEEE*, 29(6):82–97. 332

Hitzler, P., Krötzsch, M., Parsia, B., Patel-Schneider, P. F., and Rudolph, S. (Eds.) (2012), *OWL 2 Web Ontology Language Primer (Second Edition)*. W3C Recommendation 11 December 2012, http://www.w3.org/TR/owl2-primer/. 684

Hobbs, J. R., Stickel, M. E., Appelt, D. E., and Martin, P. (1993), Interpretation as abduction. *Artificial Intelligence*, 63(1–2):69–142. 227

Hoffart, J., Suchanek, F., Berberich, K., and Weikum, G. (2013), YAGO2: A spatially and temporally enhanced knowledge base from Wikipedia. *Artificial Intelligence*, 194:28–61. 684

Holland, J. H. (1975), *Adaption in Natural and Artificial Systems: an introductory analysis with applications to biology, control, and artificial intelligence*. University of Michigan Press. 168

Hoos, H. H. and Stützle, T. (2004), *Stochastic Local Search: Foundations and Applications*. Morgan Kaufmann. 168

Horvitz, E. J. (1989), Reasoning about beliefs and actions under computational resource constraints. In Kanal, L., Levitt, T., and Lemmer, J. (Eds.), *Uncertainty in Artificial Intelligence 3*, pages 301–324, Elsevier. 46

Horvitz, E. J. (2006), Eric Horvitz forecasts the future. *New Scientist*, 2578:72. 731

Howard, R. A. and Matheson, J. E. (1984), Influence diagrams. In Howard, R. A. and Matheson, J. E. (Eds.), *The Principles and Applications of Decision Analysis*, Strategic Decisions Group. 476

Howson, C. and Urbach, P. (2006), *Scientific Reasoning: the Bayesian Approach*. Open Court, 3rd edition. 518

IHTSDO (2016), *SNOMED CT Starter Guide*. International Health Terminology Standards Development Organisation, http://snomed.org. 685

Janowicz, K., van Harmelen, F., Hendler, J. A., and Hitzler, P. (2015), Why the data train needs semantic rails. *AI Magazine*, 36(1):5–14. 684

Jaynes, E. T. (2003), *Probability Theory: The Logic of Science*. Cambridge University Press, http://omega.albany.edu:8008/JaynesBook.html. 518

Jensen, F. V. (1996), *An Introduction to Bayesian Networks*. Springer-Verlag. 414

Joy, B. (2000), Why the future doesn't need us. *Wired*, http://www.wired.com/wired/archive/8.04/joy.html. 739

Jurafsky, D. and Martin, J. H. (2008), *Speech and Language Processing: An Introduction to Natural Language Processing, Computational Linguistics, and Speech Recognition*. Prentice Hall, 2nd edition. 415, 638

Kaelbling, L. P., Littman, M. L., and Moore, A. W. (1996), Reinforcement learning: A survey. *Journal of Artificial Intelligence Research*, 4:237–285. 574

Kahneman, D. (2011), *Thinking, Fast and Slow*. Allen Lane. 57, 71, 418, 437, 476, 743

Kakas, A. and Denecker, M. (2002), Abduction in logic programming. In Kakas, A. and Sadri, F. (Eds.), *Computational Logic: Logic Programming and Beyond*, pages 402–436, Springer-Verlag. 227

Kakas, A. C., Kowalski, R. A., and Toni, F. (1993), Abductive logic programming. *Journal of Logic and Computation*, 2(6):719–770. 227

Kambhampati, S., Knoblock, C. A., and Yang, Q. (1995), Planning as refinement search: a unified framework for evaluating design tradeoffs in partial order planning. *Artificial Intelligence*, 76:167–238, special issue on Planning and Scheduling. 261

Karimi, H., Nutini, J., and Schmidt, M. (2016), Linear convergence of gradient and proximal-gradient methods under the polyak-łojasiewicz condition. In *European Conference on Machine Learning (ECML)*. 332

Kautz, H. and Selman, B. (1996), Pushing the envelope: Planning, propositional logic and stochastic search. In *Proc. 13th National Conference on Artificial Intelligence*, pages 1194–1201. 261

Kearns, M. and Vazirani, U. (1994), *An Introduction to Computational Learning Theory*. MIT Press. 332

Keeney, R. L. and Raiffa, H. (1976), *Decisions with Multiple Objectives*. John Wiley and Sons. 476

Kelly, K. (2008), A new kind of mind. *Edge: World Question Center*, http://www.edge.org/q2009/q09_1.html#kelly. 742

Kirkpatrick, S., Gelatt, C. D., and Vecchi, M. P. (1983), Optimization by simulated annealing. *Science*, 220:671–680. 168

Kirsh, D. (1991a), Foundations of AI: the big issues. *Artificial Intelligence*, 47:3–30. 46

Kirsh, D. (1991b), Today the earwig, tomorrow man? *Artificial Intelligence*, 47:161–184. 71

Knoll, B., Kisynski, J., Carenini, G., Conati, C., Mackworth, A., and Poole, D. (2008), AIspace: Interactive tools for learning artificial intelligence. In *Proc. AAAI 2008 AI Education Workshop*, page 3. 742

Knuth, D. E. and Moore, R. W. (1975), An analysis of alpha-beta pruning. *Artificial Intelligence*, 6(4):293–326. 545

Koller, D. and Friedman, N. (2009), *Probabilisitic Graphical Models: Principles and Techniques*. MIT Press. 414, 518

Koller, D. and Milch, B. (2003), Multi-agent influence diagrams for representing and solving games. *Games and Economic Behavior*, 45(1):181–221, http://people.csail.mit.edu/milch/papers/geb-maid.pdf. 545

Kolodner, J. and Leake, D. (1996), A tutorial introduction to case-based reasoning. In Leake, D. (Ed.), *Case-Based Reasoning: Experiences, Lessons, and Future Directions*, pages 31–65, AAAI Press/MIT Press. 332

Koren, Y., Bell, R., and Volinsky, C. (2009), Matrix factorization techniques for recommender systems. *IEEE Computer*, 42(8):30–37. 724

Korf, K. E. (1985), Depth-first iterative deepening: An optimal admissible tree search. *Artificial Intelligence*, 27(1):97–109. 119

Kowalski, R. A. (1974), Predicate logic as a programming language. In *Information Processing 74*, pages 569–574, North-Holland. 227

Kowalski, R. A. (1988), The early history of logic programming. *Communications of the ACM*, 31(1):38–43. 9, 638

Kowalski, R. A. (2014), *Logic for Problem Solving, Revisited*. Books on Demand. 638, 685, 724

Kowalski, R. A. and Sergot, M. (1986), A logic-based calculus of events. *New Generation Computing*, 4(1):67–95. 724

Koza, J. R. (1992), *Genetic Programming: On the Programming of Computers by Means of Natural Selection*. MIT Press. 168

Krizhevsky, A., Sutskever, I., and Hinton, G. (2012), Imagenet classification with deep convolutional neural networks. In *Proc. Advances in Neural Information Processing Systems 25*, pages 1090–1098. 332

Krötzsch, M. (2012), OWL 2 Profiles: An introduction to lightweight ontology languages. In Eiter, T. and Krennwallner, T. (Eds.), *Proceedings of the 8th Reasoning Web Summer School, Vienna, Austria*, pages 112–183, Springer, http://korrekt.org/page/OWL_2_Profiles. 684

Kuipers, B. (2001), Qualitative simulation. In Meyers, R. A. (Ed.), *Encyclopedia of Physical Science and Technology*, pages 287–300, Academic Press, 3rd edition, http://www.cs.utexas.edu/users/qr/papers/Kuipers-epst-01.html. 71

Lakatos, I. (1976), *Proofs and Refutations: The Logic of Mathematical Discovery*. Cambridge University Press. 118

Lally, A., Prager, J. M., McCord, M. C., Boguraev, B. K., Patwardhan, S., Fan, J., Fodor, P., and Chu-Carroll, J. (2012), Question analysis: How Watson reads a clue. *IBM Journal of Research and Development*, 56(3/4). 9, 639

Langley, P., Iba, W., and Thompson, K. (1992), An analysis of Bayesian classifiers. In *Proc. 10th National Conference on Artificial Intelligence*, pages 223–228. 518

Laplace, P. (1812), *Théorie Analytique de Probabilités*. Courcier. 343, 489

Latombe, J.-C. (1991), *Robot Motion Planning*. Kluwer Academic Publishers. 71

Lawler, E. L. and Wood, D. E. (1966), Branch-and-bound methods: A survey. *Operations Research*, 14(4):699–719. 119

LeCun, Y., Bengio, Y., and Hinton, G. (2015), Deep learning. *Nature*, 521(7553):436–444. 332

LeCun, Y., Bottou, L., Orr, G., and Muller, K. (1998), Efficient backprop. In Orr, G. and K., M. (Eds.), *Neural Networks: Tricks of the Trade*, Springer, http://yann.lecun.com/exdb/publis/pdf/lecun-98b.pdf. 332

Leibniz, G. W. (1677), *The Method of Mathematics: Preface to the General Science*. Selections reprinted by Chrisley and Begeer [2000]. 173

Lenat, D. B. and Feigenbaum, E. A. (1991), On the thresholds of knowledge. *Artificial Intelligence*, 47:185–250. 46

Levesque, H. J. (1984), Foundations of a functional approach to knowledge representation. *Artificial Intelligence*, 23(2):155–212. 227

Levesque, H. J. (2012), *Thinking as Computation*. MIT Press. 46

Levesque, H. J. (2014), On our best behaviour. *Artificial Intelligence*, 212:27–35. 5, 46

Lichman, M. (2013), UCI machine learning repository. http://archive.ics.uci.edu/ml. 332

Liu, A. L., Hile, H., Kautz, H., Borriello, G., Brown, P. A., Harniss, M., and Johnson, K. (2006), Indoor wayfinding: Developing a functional interface for individuals with cognitive impairments. In *Proceedings of the 8th International ACM SIGACCESS Conference on Computers and Accessibility*, pages 95–102, Association for Computing Machinery. 742

Lloyd, J. W. (1987), *Foundations of Logic Programming*. Symbolic Computation Series, Springer-Verlag, 2nd edition. 227, 638

Lopez, A. and Bacchus, F. (2003), Generalizing GraphPlan by formulating planning as a CSP. In *Proc. 18th International Joint Conference Artificial Intelligence (IJCAI)*, pages 954–960. 261

López, B. (2013), *Case-Based Reasoning: A Concise Introduction*. Synthesis Lectures on Artificial Intelligence and Machine Learning, Morgan & Claypool. 332

Loredo, T. (1990), From Laplace to supernova SN 1987A: Bayesian inference in astrophysics. In Fougère, P. (Ed.), *Maximum Entropy and Bayesian Methods*, pages 81–142, Kluwer Academic Press, http://bayes.wustl.edu/gregory/articles.pdf. 518

Lowe, D. G. (1995), Similarity metric learning for a variable-kernel classifier. *Neural Computation*, 7:72–85. 332

Luenberger, D. G. (1979), *Introduction to Dynamic Systems: Theory, Models and Applications*. Wiley. 71

MacKay, D. (2003), *Information Theory, Inference, and Learning Algorithms*. Cambridge University Press. 415, 518

Mackworth, A. K. (1977), On reading sketch maps. In *Proc. Fifth International Joint Conference on Artificial Intelligence*, pages 598–606. 167

Mackworth, A. K. (1993), On seeing robots. In Basu, A. and Li, X. (Eds.), *Computer Vision: Systems, Theory, and Applications*, pages 1–13, World Scientific Press. 71

Mackworth, A. K. (2009), Agents, bodies, constraints, dynamics and evolution. *AI Magazine*. 742

Mahdisoltani, F., Biega, J., and Suchanek, F. M. (2015), YAGO3: A knowledge base from multilingual wikipedias. In *Conference on Innovative Data Systems Research (CIDR 2015)*, http://suchanek.name/work/publications/cidr2015.pdf. 684

Manning, C. and Schütze, H. (1999), *Foundations of Statistical Natural Language Processing*. MIT Press. 415, 638

Marlin, B. M., Zemel, R. S., Roweis, S. T., and Slaney, M. (2011), Recommender systems, missing data and statistical model estimation. In *Proceedings of the 22nd International Joint Conference on Artificial Intelligence (IJCAI)*, pages 2686–2691. 518

Mas-Colell, A., Whinston, M. D., and Green, J. R. (1995), *Microeconomic Theory*. Oxford University Press. 545

Matheson, J. E. (1990), Using influence diagrams to value information and control. In Oliver, R. M. and Smith, J. Q. (Eds.), *Influence Diagrams, Belief Nets and Decision Analysis*, chapter 1, pages 25–48, Wiley. 476

Mausam and Kolobov, A. (2012), *Planning with Markov Decision Processes: An AI Perspective*. Synthesis Lectures on Artificial Intelligence and Machine Learning, Morgan & Claypool. 476

McAllester, D. and Rosenblitt, D. (1991), Systematic nonlinear planning. In *Proc. 9th National Conference on Artificial Intelligence*, pages 634–639. 261

McCarthy, J. (1986), Applications of circumscription to formalizing common-sense knowledge. *Artificial Intelligence*, 28(1):89–116. 227

McCarthy, J. and Hayes, P. J. (1969), Some philosophical problems from the standpoint of artificial intelligence. In Meltzer, M. and Michie, D. (Eds.), *Machine Intelligence 4*, pages 463–502, Edinburgh University Press. 9, 724

McCulloch, W. and Pitts, W. (1943), A logical calculus of ideas immanent in nervous activity. *Bulletin of Mathematical Biophysics*, 5:115–133. 9, 332

McDermott, D. and Hendler, J. (1995), Planning: What it is, what it could be, an introduction to the special issue on planning and scheduling. *Artificial Intelligence*, 76:1–16. 261

McLuhan, M. (1964), *Understanding Media: The Extensions of Man*. New American Library. 741

Meir, R. and Rätsch, G. (2003), An introduction to boosting and leveraging. In *Advanced Lectures on Machine Learning*, pages 119–184, Springer., http://www.boosting.org/papers/MeiRae03.pdf. 332

Mendelson, E. (1987), *Introduction to Mathematical Logic*. Wadsworth and Brooks, 3rd edition. 227

Michie, D., Spiegelhalter, D. J., and Taylor, C. C. (Eds.) (1994), *Machine Learning, Neural and Statistical Classification*. Series in Artificial Intelligence, Ellis Horwood. 332

Mihailidis, A., Boger, J., Candido, M., and Hoey, J. (2007), The use of an intelligent prompting system for people with dementia. *ACM Interactions*, 14(4):34–37. 742

Minsky, M. L. (1952), A neural-analogue calculator based upon a probability model of reinforcement. Technical report, Harvard University Psychological Laboratories. 9, 332

Minsky, M. L. (1961), Steps towards artificial intelligence. *Proceedings of the IEEE*, 49:8–30, http://web.media.mit.edu/~minsky/papers/steps.html. 120

Minsky, M. L. (1975), A framework for representing knowledge. In Winston, P. (Ed.), *The Psychology of Computer Vision*, pages 211–277, McGraw-Hill, alternative version is in Haugeland [1997]. 9

Minsky, M. L. (1986), *The Society of Mind*. Simon and Schuster. 32

Minsky, M. L. and Papert, S. (1988), *Perceptrons: An Introduction to Computational Geometry*. MIT Press, expanded edition. 9, 332

Minton, S., Johnston, M. D., Philips, A. B., and Laird, P. (1992), Minimizing conflicts: a heuristic repair method for constraint satisfaction and scheduling problems. *Artificial Intelligence*, 58(1-3):161–205. 168

Mitchell, M. (1996), *An Introduction to Genetic Algorithms*. MIT Press. 168

Mitchell, T. (1997), *Machine Learning*. McGraw-Hill. 331, 332

Mitchell, T. M. (1977), Version spaces: A candidate elimination approach to rule learning. In *Proc. 5th International Joint Conference on Artificial Intelligence*, pages 305–310. 332

Mnih, V., Kavukcuoglu, K., Silver, D., et al. (2015), Human-level control through deep reinforcement learning. *Nature*, 518:529–533, http://www.nature.com/nature/journal/v518/n7540/abs/nature14236.html. 574

Mohan, K. and Pearl, J. (2014), Graphical models for recovering probabilistic and causal queries from missing data. In Welling, M., Ghahramani, Z., Cortes, C., and Lawrence, N. (Eds.), *Advances of Neural Information Processing 27 (NIPS Proceedings)*, pages 1520–1528, http://ftp.cs.ucla.edu/pub/stat_ser/r442.pdf. 518

Moore, E. F. (1959), The shortest path through a maze. In *Proceedings of the International Symposium on the Theory of Switching*, pages pp. 285–292, Harvard University Press. 119

Motik, B., Patel-Schneider, P. F., and Grau, B. C. (Eds.) (2012), *OWL 2 Web Ontology Language: Direct Semantics*. W3C Recommendation 11 December 2012, 2nd edition, http://www.w3.org/TR/owl2-direct-semantics/. 684

Muggleton, S. (1995), Inverse entailment and Progol. *New Generation Computing*, 13(3,4):245–286. 724

Muggleton, S. and De Raedt, L. (1994), Inductive logic programming: Theory and methods. *Journal of Logic Programming*, 19,20:629–679. 724

Murphy, K. P. (2012), *Machine Learning: A Probabilistic Perspective*. MIT Press. 331, 415

Muscettola, N., Nayak, P., Pell, B., and Williams, B. (1998), Remote agent: to boldly go where no AI system has gone before. *Artificial Intelligence*, 103:5–47. 232

Nash, J. F. (1950), Equilibrium points in N-person games. *Proceedings of the National Academy of Sciences of the United States of America*, 36:48–49. 535

Nau, D. S. (2007), Current trends in automated planning. *AI Magazine*, 28(4):43–58. 261, 742

Neumann, J. V. and Morgenstern, O. (1953), *Theory of Games and Economic Behavior*. Princeton University Press, 3rd edition. 476, 522

Newell, A. and Simon, H. A. (1956), The logic theory machine: A complex information processing system. Technical Report P-868, The Rand Corporation, http://shelf1.library.cmu.edu/IMLS/MindModels/logictheorymachine.pdf. 8

Newell, A. and Simon, H. A. (1976), Computer science as empirical enquiry: Symbols and search. *Communications of the ACM*, 19:113–126, reprinted in Haugeland [1997]. 19, 46

Ng, A. Y. (2004), Feature selection, L1 vs. L2 regularization, and rotational invariance. In *Proceedings of the Twenty-first International Conference on Machine Learning*. 332

Ng, A. Y., Russell, S. J., et al. (2000), Algorithms for inverse reinforcement learning. In *International Conference on Machine Learning (ICML)*, pages 663–670. 742

Niles, I. and Pease, A. (2001), Towards a standard upper ontology. In Welty, C. and Smith, B. (Eds.), *Proceedings of the 2nd International Conference on Formal Ontology in Information Systems (FOIS-2001)*, http://www.adampease.org/professional/FOIS.pdf. 684

Nilsson, N. J. (1971), *Problem-Solving Methods in Artificial Intelligence*. McGraw-Hill. 119

Nilsson, N. J. (2007), The physical symbol system hypothesis: Status and prospects. In Lungarella, M. et al. (Eds.), *50 Years of AI, Festschrift*, pages 9–17, Springer, http://ai.stanford.edu/~nilsson/OnlinePubs-Nils/PublishedPapers/pssh.pdf. 46

Nilsson, N. J. (2010), *The Quest for Artificial Intelligence: A History of Ideas and Achievements*. Cambridge University Press. 46

Nisan, N. (2007), Introduction to mechanisn design (for computer scientists). In Nisan, N. and other (Eds.), *Algorithmic Game Theory*, chapter 9, pages 209–242, Cambridge University Press. 545

Nisan, N., Roughgarden, T., Tardos, E., and Vazirani, V. V. (Eds.) (2007), *Algorithmic Game Theory*. Cambridge University Press. 545

Nocedal, J. and Wright, S. (2006), *Numerical Optimization*. Springer-Verlag. 332

Ordeshook, P. C. (1986), *Game Theory and Political Theory: An Introduction*. Cambridge University Press. 545

Page, L., Brin, S., Motwani, R., and Winograd, T. (1999), The pagerank citation ranking: Bringing order to the web. Technical Report SIDL-WP-1999-0120, Stanford InfoLab, http://dbpubs.stanford.edu/pub/1999-66. 386

Panton, K., Matuszek, C., Lenat, D., Schneider, D., Witbrock, M., Siegel, N., and Shepard, B. (2006), Common sense reasoning – from Cyc to intelligent assistant. In Cai, Y. and Abascal, J. (Eds.), *Ambient Intelligence in Everyday Life*, pages 1–31, Springer. 684

Pearl, J. (1984), *Heuristics*. Addison-Wesley. 119, 545

Pearl, J. (1988), *Probabilistic Reasoning in Intelligent Systems: Networks of Plausible Inference*. Morgan Kaufmann. 414

Pearl, J. (2009), *Causality: Models, Reasoning and Inference*. Cambridge University Press, 2nd edition. 228, 415

Pease, A. (2011), *Ontology: A Practical Guide*. Articulate Software Press. 684

Peden, M. et al. (Eds.) (2004), *World Report on Road Traffic Injury Prevention*. World Health Organization. 742

Peng, Y. and Reggia, J. A. (1990), *Abductive Inference Models for Diagnostic Problem-Solving*. Symbolic Computation – AI Series, Springer-Verlag. 227

Pereira, F. C. N. and Shieber, S. M. (2002), *Prolog and Natural-Language Analysis*. Microtome Publishing. 638

Piketty, T. (2014), *Capital in the Twenty-First Century*. Harvard University Press, https://books.google.ca/books?id=J222AgAAQBAJ. 741

Pollack, M. E. (2005), Intelligent technology for an aging population: The use of AI to assist elders with cognitive impairment. *AI Magazine*, 26(2):9–24. 742

Poole, D. (1993), Probabilistic Horn abduction and Bayesian networks. *Artificial Intelligence*, 64(1):81–129. 724

Poole, D. (1997), The independent choice logic for modelling multiple agents under uncertainty. *Artificial Intelligence*, 94:7–56, http://cs.ubc.ca/~poole/abstracts/icl.html, special issue on economic principles of multi-agent systems. 724

Poole, D., Goebel, R., and Aleliunas, R. (1987), Theorist: A logical reasoning system for defaults and diagnosis. In Cercone, N. and McCalla, G. (Eds.), *The Knowledge Frontier: Essays in the Representation of Knowledge*, pages 331–352, Springer-Verlag. 227

Poole, D., Mackworth, A., and Goebel, R. (1998), *Computational Intelligence: A Logical Approach*. Oxford University Press. xxv

Posner, M. I. (Ed.) (1989), *Foundations of Cognitive Science*. MIT Press. 46

Powell, W. (2014), Energy and uncertainty: Models and algorithms for complex energy systems. *AI Magazine*, 35(3):8–21. 574

Price, C. J. et al. (2006), Qualitative futures. *The Knowledge Engineering Review*, 21(04):317–334, http://journals.cambridge.org/article_S026988890600097X. 71

Puterman, M. (1994), *Markov Decision Processes: Discrete Stochastic Dynamic Programming*. John Wiley and Sons. 476

Quinlan, J. R. (1986), Induction of decision trees. *Machine Learning*, 1:81–106, reprinted in Shavlik and Dietterich [1990]. 332

Quinlan, J. R. (1993), *C4.5 Programs for Machine Learning*. Morgan Kaufmann. 332

Quinlan, J. R. and Cameron-Jones, R. M. (1995), Induction of logic programs: FOIL and related systems. *New Generation Computing*, 13(3,4):287–312. 724

Rabiner, L. (1989), A tutorial on hidden Markov models and selected applications in speech recognition. *Proceedings of the IEEE*, 77(2):257–286. 415

Reiter, R. (1991), The frame problem in the situation calculus: A simple solution (sometimes) and a completeness result for goal regression. In Lifschitz, V. (Ed.), *Artificial Intelligence and Mathematical Theory of Computation: Papers in Honor of John McCarthy*, pages 359–380, Academic Press. 724

Reiter, R. (2001), *Knowledge in Action: Logical Foundations for Specifying and Implementing Dynamical Systems*. MIT Press. 724

Robinson, J. A. (1965), A machine-oriented logic based on the resolution principle. *Journal ACM*, 12(1):23–41. 227

Rosenblatt, F. (1958), The perceptron: A probabilistic model for information storage and organization in the brain. *Psychological Review*, 65(6):386–408. 9, 294, 332

Rosenschein, S. J. and Kaelbling, L. P. (1995), A situated view of representation and control. *Artificial Intelligence*, 73:149–173. 71

Rossi, F., Venable, K. B., and Walsh, T. (2011), *A Short Introduction to Preferences: Between Artificial Intelligence and Social Choice*. Synthesis Lectures on Artificial Intelligence and Machine Learning, Morgan & Claypool. 476

Rubinstein, R. Y. (1981), *Simulation and the Monte Carlo Method*. John Wiley and Sons. 415

Rumelhart, D. E., Hinton, G. E., and Williams, R. J. (1986), Learning internal representations by error propagation. In Rumelhart, D. E. and McClelland, J. L. (Eds.), *Parallel Distributed Processing*, chapter 8, pages 318–362, MIT Press, reprinted in Shavlik and Dietterich [1990]. 332

Russell, B. (1917), *Mysticism and Logic and Other Essays*. Allen and Unwin. 691

Russell, S. (1997), Rationality and intelligence. *Artificial Intelligence*, 94:57–77. 46

Russell, S. and Norvig, P. (2010), *Artificial Intelligence: A Modern Approach*. Prentice Hall, 3rd edition, http://aima.cs.berkeley.edu/. 46

Sacerdoti, E. D. (1975), The nonlinear nature of plans. In *Proc. 4th International Joint Conference on Artificial Intelligence*, pages 206–214. 261

Samuel, A. L. (1959), Some studies in machine learning using the game of checkers. *IBM Journal on Research and Development*, 3(3):210–229. 8, 522

Sandholm, T. (2007), Expressive commerce and its application to sourcing: How we conducted \$35 billion of generalized combinatorial auctions. *AI Magazine*, 28(3):45–58. 46

Satterthwaite, M. (1975), Strategy-proofness and Arrow's conditions: existence and correspondence theorems for voting procedures and social welfare functions. *Journal of Economic Theory*, 10:187–217. 543

Savage, L. J. (1972), *The Foundation of Statistics*. Dover, 2nd edition. 476

Schank, R. C. (1990), What is AI, anyway? In Partridge, D. and Wilks, Y. (Eds.), *The Foundations of Artificial Intelligence*, pages 3–13, Cambridge University Press. 46

Schapire, R. E. (2002), The boosting approach to machine learning: An overview. In *MSRI Workshop on Nonlinear Estimation and Classification*, Springer-Verlag. 332

Schubert, L. K. (1990), Monotonic solutions to the frame problem in the situation calculus: An efficient method for worlds with fully specified actions. In Kyburg, H. E., Loui, R. P., and Carlson, G. N. (Eds.), *Knowledge Representation and Defeasible Reasoning*, pages 23–67, Kluwer Academic Press. 724

Schwab, K. and Forum, W. E. (2016), *The Fourth Industrial Revolution*. World Economic Forum, https://books.google.ca/books?id=mQQwjwEACAAJ. 741

Schwarz, G. (1978), Estimating the dimension of a model. *Annals of Statistics*, 6(2):461–464, https://projecteuclid.org/euclid.aos/1176344136. 518

Settles, B. (2012), *Active Learning*. Synthesis Lectures on Artificial Intelligence and Machine Learning, Morgan & Claypool. 332

Shachter, R. and Peot, M. A. (1992), Decision making using probabilistic inference methods. In *Proc. Eighth Conference on Uncertainty in Artificial Intelligence (UAI-92)*, pages 276–283. 476

Shanahan, M. (1989), Prediction is deduction, but explanation is abduction. In *Proc. 11th International Joint Conference on Artificial Intelligence (IJCAI-89)*, pages 1055–1060. 227

Shanahan, M. (1997), *Solving the Frame Problem: A Mathematical Investigation of the Common Sense Law of Inertia*. MIT Press. 724

Sharkey, N. (2008), The ethical frontiers of robotics. *Science*, 322(5909):1800 – 1801, DOI: 10.1126/science.1164582. 738, 742

Shavlik, J. W. and Dietterich, T. G. (Eds.) (1990), *Readings in Machine Learning*. Morgan Kaufmann. 332, 754, 758, 766, 769

Shelley, M. W. (1818), *Frankenstein; or, The Modern Prometheus*. Lackington, Hughes, Harding, Mavor and Jones. 742

Shoham, Y. (2016), Why knowledge representation matters. *Communications of the ACM*, 59(1):47–49. 46

Shoham, Y. and Leyton-Brown, K. (2008), *Multiagent Systems: Algorithmic, Game Theoretic, and Logical Foundations*. Cambridge University Press. 521, 545

Silver, D., Huang, A., Maddison, C. J., Guez, A., Sifre, L., van den Driessche, G., Schrittwieser, J., Antonoglou, I., Panneershelvam, V., Lanctot, M., Dieleman, S., Grewe, D., Nham, J., Kalchbrenner, N., Sutskever, I., Lillicrap, T., Leach, M., Kavukcuoglu, K., Graepel, T., and Hassabis, D. (2016), Mastering the game of Go with deep neural networks and tree search. *Nature*, 529(7587):484–489. 522, 545, 574

Simon, H. A. (1995), Artificial intelligence: an empirical science. *Artificial Intelligence*, 77(1):95–127. 46

Simon, H. A. (1996), *The Sciences of the Artificial*. MIT Press, 3rd edition. 46, 49, 71

Singer, P. W. (2009a), Robots at war: The new battlefield. *The Wilson Quarterly*, http://wilsonquarterly.com/stories/robots-at-war-the-new-battlefield/. 742

Singer, P. W. (2009b), *Wired for War: The Robotics Revolution and Conflict in the 21st Century*. Penguin. 742

Smith, B. (2003), Ontology. In Floridi, L. (Ed.), *Blackwell Guide to the Philosophy of Computing and Information*, pages 155–166, Blackwell, http://ontology.buffalo.edu/smith/articles/ontology_pic.pdf. 684

Smith, B. (2015), Basic formal ontology 2.0: Specification and user's guide. Technical report, Institute for Formal Ontology and Medical Information Science (IFOMIS), https://github.com/bfo-ontology/BFO/wiki. 684

Smith, B. C. (1991), The owl and the electric encyclopedia. *Artificial Intelligence*, 47:251–288. 46

Smith, B. C. (1996), *On the Origin of Objects*. MIT Press. 645

Somerville, M. (2006), *The Ethical Imagination: Journeys of the Human Spirit*. House of Anansi Press. 742

Sowa, J. F. (2000), *Knowledge Representation: Logical, Philosophical, and Computational Foundations*. Brooks Cole. 46, 684

Sowa, J. F. (2011), Future directions for semantic systems. In Tolk, A. and Jain, L. C. (Eds.), *Intelligence-based Software Engineering*, pages 23–47, Springer-Verlag, http://www.jfsowa.com/pubs/futures.pdf. 684

Spall, J. C. (2003), *Introduction to Stochastic Search and Optimization: Estimation, Simulation*. Wiley. 168

Spiegelhalter, D. J., Franklin, R. C. G., and Bull, K. (1990), Assessment, criticism and improvement of imprecise subjective probabilities for a medical expert system. In Henrion, M., Shachter, R. D., Kanal, L., and Lemmer, J. (Eds.), *Uncertainty in Artificial Intelligence 5*, pages 285–294, North-Holland. 332

Spirtes, P., Glymour, C., and Scheines, R. (2001), *Causation, Prediction, and Search*. MIT Press, 2nd edition. 228, 415

Sterling, L. S. and Shapiro, E. Y. (1994), *The Art of Prolog: Advanced Programming Techniques*. MIT Press, 2nd edition. 638

Stillings, N. A., Feinstein, M. H., Garfield, J. L., Rissland, E. L., Rosenbaum, D. A., Weisler, S. E., and Baker-Ward, L. (1987), *Cognitive Science: An Introduction*. MIT Press. 46

Stone, P. (2007), Learning and multiagent reasoning for autonomous agents. In *The 20th International Joint Conference on Artificial Intelligence (IJCAI-07)*, pages 13–30, http://www.cs.utexas.edu/~pstone/Papers/bib2html-links/IJCAI07-award.pdf. 742

Stone, P., Brooks, R., Brynjolfsson, E., Calo, R., Etzioni, O., Hager, G., Hirschberg, J., Kalyanakrishnan, S., Kamar, E., Kraus, S., Leyton-Brown, K., Parkes, D., Press, W., Saxenian, A., Shah, J., Tambe, M., and Teller, A. (2016), Artificial intelligence and life in 2030: One hundred year study on artificial intelligence: Report of the 2015-2016 study panel. Technical report, Stanford University, http://ai100.stanford.edu/2016-report. 740, 742

Stone, P. and Veloso, M. (2000), Multiagent systems: A survey from a machine learning perspective. *Autonomous Robots*, 8:345–383. 545

Suchanek, F. M., Kasneci, G., and Weikum, G. (2007), YAGO: A core of semantic knowledge – unifying WordNet and Wikipedia. In *16th international World Wide Web conference (WWW 2007)*. 684

Sutton, R. S. and Barto, A. G. (1998), *Reinforcement Learning: An Introduction*. MIT Press. 574

Szepesvári, C. (2010), *Algorithms for Reinforcement Learning*. Synthesis Lectures on Artificial Intelligence and Machine Learning, Morgan & Claypool. 574

Tarski, A. (1956), *Logic, Semantics, Metamathematics*. Clarendon Press, papers from 1923 to 1938 collected and translated by J. H. Woodger. 227

Tate, A. (1977), Generating project networks. In *Proc. 5th International Joint Conference on Artificial Intelligence*, pages 888–893. 261

Tharp, T. (2003), *The Creative Habit: Learn It and Use It for Life*. Simon and Schuster. 425

Thrun, S. (2006), Winning the DARPA grand challenge. In *Innovative Applications of Artificial Intelligence Conference, (IAAI-06)*, pages 16–20. 736

Thrun, S., Burgard, W., and Fox, D. (2005), *Probabilistic Robotics*. MIT Press. 415

Turing, A. (1950), Computing machinery and intelligence. *Mind*, 59:433–460, reprinted in Haugeland [1997]. 5, 46

Tversky, A. and Kahneman, D. (1974), Judgment under uncertainty: Heuristics and biases. *Science*, 185:1124–1131. 434

Valiant, L. G. (1984), A theory of the learnable. *Communications of the ACM*, 27:1134–1142, reprinted in Shavlik and Dietterich [1990]. 332

van Beek, P. and Chen, X. (1999), Cplan: A constraint programming approach to planning. In *AAAI-99*, pages 585–590. 261

van Emden, M. H. and Kowalski, R. A. (1976), The semantics of predicate logic as a programming language. *Journal ACM*, 23(4):733–742. 227

Visser, U. and Burkhard, H.-D. (2007), Robocup: 10 years of achievements and challenges. *AI Magazine*, 28(2):115–130. 742

Viswanathan, P., Mackworth, A. K., Little, J. J., and Mihailidis, A. (2007), Intelligent wheelchairs: Collision avoidance and navigation assistance for older adults with cognitive impairment. In *Proc. Workshop on Intelligent Systems for Assisted Cognition*. 742

Vlassis, N. (2007), *A Concise Introduction to Multiagent Systems and Distributed Artificial Intelligence*. Synthesis Lectures on Artificial Intelligence and Machine Learning, Morgan & Claypool. 545

Vrandečić, D. and Krötzsch, M. (2014), Wikidata: A free collaborative knowledgebase. *Communications of the ACM*, 57(10):78–85. 684

W3C OWL Working Group (Ed.) (2012), *OWL 2 Web Ontology Language Document Overview*. W3C Recommendation 11 December 2012, 2nd edition, http://www.w3.org/TR/owl2-overview/. 684

Wakker, P. P. (2010), *Prospect Theory: For Risk and Ambiguity*. Cambridge University Press. 476

Waldinger, R. (1977), Achieving several goals simultaneously. In Elcock, E. and Michie, D. (Eds.), *Machine Intelligence 8: Machine Representations of Knowledge*, pages 94–136, Ellis Horwood. 261

Walsh, T. (2007), Representing and reasoning with preferences. *AI Magazine*, 28(4):59–69. 476

Wang, H. (1960), Toward mechanical mathematics. *IBM Journal of Research and Development*, 4(1):2–22. 8

Warren, D. H. D. and Pereira, F. C. N. (1982), An efficient easily adaptable system for interpreting natural language queries. *Computational Linguistics*, 8(3–4):110–122, http://portal.acm.org/citation.cfm?id=972944. 9

Weiss, G. (Ed.) (1999), *Multiagent Systems: A Modern Approach to Distributed Artificial Intelligence*. MIT Press. 545

Weld, D. S. (1992), Qualitative physics: Albatross or eagle? *Computational Intelligence*, 8(2):175–186, introduction to special issue on the future of qualitative physics. 71

Weld, D. S. (1994), An introduction to least commitment planning. *AI Magazine*, 15(4):27–61. 261

Weld, D. S. (1999), Recent advances in AI planning. *AI Magazine*, 20(2). 261

Weld, D. S. and de Kleer, J. (Eds.) (1990), *Readings in Qualitative Reasoning about Physical Systems*. Morgan Kaufmann. 71

Wellman, M. P. (2011), *Trading Agents*. Synthesis Lectures on Artificial Intelligence and Machine Learning, Morgan & Claypool. 46

Whitehead, A. N. and Russell, B. (1910, 1912, 1913), *Principia Mathematica*. 2nd edn, 1925 (Vol. 1), 1927 (Vols 2, 3), Cambridge University Press. 8

Whitley, D. (2001), An overview of evolutionary algorithms. *Journal of Information and Software Technology*, 43:817–831, http://www.cs.colostate.edu/~genitor/2001/overview.pdf. 168

Wilkins, D. E. (1988), *Practical Planning: Extending the Classical AI Planning Paradigm*. Morgan Kaufmann. 261

Winograd, T. (1972), *Understanding Natural Language*. Academic Press. 5, 9

Winograd, T. (1990), Thinking machines: Can there be? Are we? In Partridge, D. and Wilks, Y. (Eds.), *The Foundations of Artificial Intelligence: A Sourcebook*, pages 167–189, Cambridge University Press. 46

Woods, W. A. (2007), Meaning and links. *AI Magazine*, 28(4):71–92. 684

Wooldridge, M. (2002), *An Introduction to Multiagent Systems*. John Wiley and Sons. 545

Yang, Q. (1997), *Intelligent Planning: A Decomposition and Abstraction-Based Approach*. Springer-Verlag. 261

Yang, S. and Mackworth, A. K. (2007), Hierarchical shortest pathfinding applied to route-planning for wheelchair users. In *Proc. Canadian Conference on Artificial Intelligence, AI-2007*. 742

Zhang, N. L. (2004), Hierarchical latent class models for cluster analysis. *Journal of Machine Learning Research*, 5(6):697–723. 518

Zhang, N. L. and Poole, D. (1994), A simple approach to Bayesian network computations. In *Proc. 10th Canadian Conference on Artificial Intelligence*, pages 171–178. 415

Zhang, Y. and Mackworth, A. K. (1995), Constraint nets: A semantic model for hybrid dynamic systems. *Theoretical Computer Science*, 138:211–239. 71

Zilberstein, S. (1996), Using anytime algorithms in intelligent systems. *AI Magazine*, 17(3):73–83. 46

Index